Advances in Intelligent Systems and Computing

Volume 919

The series "Advances in Intelligent Systems and Computing" contains publications on theory, applications, and design methods of Intelligent Systems and Intelligent Computing. Virtually all disciplines such as engineering, natural sciences, computer and information science, ICT, economics, business, e-commerce, environment, healthcare, life science are covered. The list of topics spans all the areas of modern intelligent systems and computing such as: computational intelligence, soft computing including neural networks, fuzzy systems, evolutionary computing and the fusion of these paradigms, social intelligence, ambient intelligence, computational neuroscience, artificial life, virtual worlds and society, cognitive science and systems, Perception and Vision, DNA and immune based systems, self-organizing and adaptive systems, e-Learning and teaching, human-centered and human-centric computing, recommender systems, intelligent control, robotics and mechatronics including human-machine teaming, knowledge-based paradigms, learning paradigms, machine ethics, intelligent data analysis, knowledge management, intelligent agents, intelligent decision making and support, intelligent network security, trust management, interactive entertainment, Web intelligence and multimedia.

The publications within "Advances in Intelligent Systems and Computing" are primarily proceedings of important conferences, symposia and congresses. They cover significant recent developments in the field, both of a foundational and applicable character. An important characteristic feature of the series is the short publication time and world-wide distribution. This permits a rapid and broad dissemination of research results.

** Indexing: The books of this series are submitted to ISI Proceedings, EI-Compendex, DBLP, SCOPUS, Google Scholar and Springerlink **

More information about this series at http://www.springer.com/series/11156

Alessandro Luigini
Editor

Proceedings of the 1st International and Interdisciplinary Conference on Digital Environments for Education, Arts and Heritage

EARTH 2018

 Springer

Editor
Alessandro Luigini
Free University of Bozen
Bressanone, Italy

ISSN 2194-5357   ISSN 2194-5365   (electronic)
Advances in Intelligent Systems and Computing
ISBN 978-3-030-12239-3   ISBN 978-3-030-12240-9   (eBook)
https://doi.org/10.1007/978-3-030-12240-9

Library of Congress Control Number: 2019932784

This Springer imprint is published by the registered company Springer Nature Switzerland AG
The registered company address is: Gewerbestrasse 11, 6330 Cham, Switzerland

Preface

The book presents the proceedings of the homonymous conference organized at the Free University of Bozen-Bolzano on 5 and 6 July 2018. A few months before, in October 2017 a conference entitled *Ambienti digitali per l'educazione all'arte e al patrimonio*[1], organized at the Faculty of Education of Bressanone of the Free University of Bozen-Bolzano, anticipated what is documented here, laying the foundations for a long-term scientific and cultural project that is symmetrical to the interdisciplinary research *VAR.HEE. Virtual and Augmented Reality for Heritage Education in school and museum Experience* which will end in 2021. The main aim of the project as a whole is the strengthening and structuring of interdisciplinary links between scholars interested in heritage education.

In fact, on the one hand the scholars of graphic representation, which have always been largely involved in the documentation, survey and enhancement of heritage, and on the other hand the scholars of the art education and museum didactics seem to forge two sides of the same coin: the safeguarding of the value of the arts and of the heritage for the formation of individuals and, therefore, of a society able to develop itself starting from the memory of its own expressive capacity in the history.

In particular, it is a technology that seems to be the "mirror" in which scholars of representation and pedagogists reflect, look at each other and look alike: digital technology applied to the arts and heritage. In fact, the environments described in the volume are digital, and the experiences that a prevalent part of Western society makes every day become digital. We draw information, we build relationships, we buy services or products, and we spend our free time and leave a trace of our existence in digital environments, whether they are contained in a mobile device or in the physical space in which we find ourselves. In this context, where the individual is formed, acts and relates to the world, a primacy of representation emerges, which from digital technologies has received a significant increase in possible declinations. We speak through the representation of our voice and our interlocutor

---

[1] Conference proceedings are available in open access here: http://ojs.francoangeli.it/_omp/index.php/oa/catalog/book/334.

on the phone, we watch entertainment contents via digital devices, we interact via social networks, we buy in online stores, and this list could be expanded to include a significant range, quantity and quality, of more or less daily activities.

The support for the interdisciplinary exchange has been favored not only by the meeting of scholars of representation and pedagogy of art, but also by the contribution, fundamental for us, of two other areas of research that greatly affect the good result of the practices that here propose: cognitive psychology, which shows us how our mind and our brain react and elaborate the experiences with art and heritage in digital environments, and the economy of culture, which shows us how the museum models have presented new paradigms able to fostering the flourishing of good practices in the art world.

Categorizing the contributions in this book is not simple due to the marked interdisciplinarity that most of the contributions pursue. However, as a result of the submission phase, we have been able to identify some sub-themes that would allow for the creation of environments for the discussion as homogeneous as possible. The ten sessions were: visual heritage, digital heritage 1 and 2, augmented reality, immersive, education, archaeology, territory and maps, museum ideas and museum life. All the contributions were selected through a double-blind peer review.

The International Scientific Committee followed and evaluated all parallel sessions, and awarded three prizes as Best Paper Award: one for senior section and two for junior section. The senior section consists of scholars from Italian and foreign universities or research centres. The junior section consists of grant researcher, Ph. D., Ph.D. students, and freelance researcher. Each member of the International Scientific Committee expressed a preference for each section.

For the senior section:

Fabrizio Gay, Irene Cazzaro, Università Iuav di Venezia
Venetian perspective boxes: when the images become environments. Low-tech, high-knowledge media for teaching the historical heritage of the interior/exterior environments.

For the junior section:

Silvia Calegari, Matteo Dominoni, Università di Milano-Bicocca
The Pollicina Project. A collaborative and educational social suite to build cultural itineraries.

Ramona Feriozzi e Alessandro Olivieri, Università di Camerino
Video game for learning the projective geometry. Analysis of virtual spaces through discipline of representation.

About 100 submissions, over 80 speeches, 10 keynote speakers in 2 plenary sessions, 34 members of the scientific committee, over 50 reviewers are the numbers that tell the conference. Thanks to all those who have allowed the proper development from preparation to the holding of the conference.

Alessandro Luigini
Demis Basso
Stefano Brusaporci
Massimiliano Lo Turco
Matteo Moretti
Chiara Panciroli
Monica Parricchi
Daniele Rossi
Federica Viganò
Franca Zuccoli

The original version of the book frontmatter was revised: Editor provided corrections has been incorporated. The correction to the book frontmatter is available at https://doi.org/10.1007/978-3-030-12240-9_77

Committees

Programme Committee

Alessandro Luigini	Libera Università di Bolzano [C]
Demis Basso	Libera Università di Bolzano
Stefano Brusaporci	Università de L'Aquila
Massimiliano Lo Turco	Politecnico di Torino
Matteo Moretti	Libera Università di Bolzano
Chiara Panciroli	Alma Mater Studiorum - Università di Bologna
Monica Parricchi	Libera Università di Bolzano
Daniele Rossi	Università di Camerino
Federica Viganò	Libera Università di Bolzano
Franca Zuccoli	Università di Milano-Bicocca

Scientific Committee

Coordination

Alessandro Luigini	Libera Università di Bolzano

Members

Giuseppe Amoruso	Politecnico di Milano
Demis Basso	Libera Università di Bolzano
Paolo Belardi	Università di Perugia
Stefano Brusaporci	Università de L'Aquila
Vito Cardone	Presidente UID
Eugene Ch'ng	University of Nottingham Ningbo China
Annalisa Cicerchia	ISTAT

Paolo Clini	Università Politecnica delle Marche
Alessandro Colombi	Libera Università di Bolzano
Francesco Gabellone	CNR
Andrea Giordano	Università di Padova
Nicole Goetschi Danesi	Haute Ecole Pédagogique, Lucerne, Switzerland
Susan Hazan	Curator of New Media of The Israel Museum, Jerusalem, Israel
Sorin Hermon	The Cyprus Institute
Mona Hess	UCL's Global University, UK
Richard Huerta	Universitat de València, Spain
Marinos Ioannides	Cyprus University of Technology, Cyprus
Elena Ippoliti	Sapienza Università di Roma
Massimiliano Lo Turco	Politecnico di Torino
Berta Martin	Università degli Studi di Urbino Carlo Bo
Stefano Mastandrea	Università degli Studi Roma tre
Victor Menchero	Sanchez University of Castilla-La Mancha, Spain
Matteo Moretti	Libera Università di Bolzano
Antonella Nuzzaci	Università degli Studi de L'Aquila
Chiara Panciroli	Alma Mater Studiorum - Università di Bologna
Monica Parricchi	Libera Università di Bolzano
Paola Puma	Università di Firenze
Daniele Rossi	Università di Camerino
Pier Luigi Sacco	IRVAPP, Fondazione Bruno Kessler
Pier Giuseppe Rossi	Università di Macerata
Alberto Sdegno	Università di Trieste
Roberta Spallone	Politecnico di Torino
Rosella Tomassoni	Università degli Studi di Cassino
Maurizio Unali	Università degli Studi G. d'Annunzio Chieti-Pescara
Federica Viganò	Libera Università di Bolzano
Ornella Zerlenga	Università della Campania
Franca Zuccoli	Università di Milano-Bicocca

Organizing Secretariat

Event Managers

Ilaria Buniolo	Libera Università di Bolzano
Massimo Eccli	Libera Università di Bolzano
Alexa Perbellini	Libera Università di Bolzano

Members

Ramona Feriozzi	Università di Camerino
Pamela Maiezza	Università de L'Aquila
Anita Macauda	Alma Mater Studiorum - Università di Bologna
Starlight Vattano	Libera Università di Bolzano

Organized by:

Freie Universität Bozen
Libera Università di Bolzano
Università Liedia de Bulsan

Under the patronage of:

With the support of:

FONDAZIONE
CASSA DI RISPARMIO DI BOLZANO

Foreword: Future Perspectives on Transdisciplinary Issues

I've come with a great pleasure at this conference which, as Alessandro Luigini remembered, the UID—(Italian Union for Drawing)—sponsored. As furthermore, the UID sponsored last year at the previous conference, *IMMAGINI?* held in Brixen in November.

We did this with conviction because of the interesting topic; it is one of that border issues that I like a lot, and a scientific society, like ours, has to deal with.

Like you can remember, last year the UID yearly conference was focused on the topic "Territories and frontiers of the Representation". It was a chance to strongly reflect, because if scientific communities have to move on the borders (admitting that borders could be traced relating to scientific knowledge), making constant efforts in moving them upwards, overcoming them and going over to produce something new.

A work like this is not easy in big structures, without a great inertia to the change. And we are an enough big community, with more than 200 structured in the scientific disciplinary sector ICAR/17[2] and with at least more than the half of other not structured scholars. Also, big associations have the same difficulties, due to several reasons about academic policy that you know or can imagine, on which I will not deal with, but that we have to keep in mind. Likewise, bigger more consolidated and ancient universities have the same. The new, younger, smaller realities have less inertness to change because they do not have consolidated pre-existences, which often take the form of difficult-to-move boulders or mountains that can not be climbed: in spite of the declared choices to pursue innovation, which they want to do and are often able to do, having tools and skills that offer great chances of success. Instead, the chance to engage with the new is almost intrinsic in

---

[2] The scientific disciplinary contents of the Scientific Disciplinary Sector ICAR/17 concern the representation of architecture and the environment, in its broad sense of cognitive means of the laws that govern the formal structure, of a tool for the analysis of existing values, of expressive act and of visual communication of the design idea with different scalar dimensions. D.M. 4 ottobre 2000 – Settori scienfitico-disciplinari Pubblicato su G.U. n. 249 del 24 ottobre 2000 – supplemento ordinario 175.

small groups and in those ones less historicized, which can operate as avant-garde because in them it is easier to find—and to give feasibility to—reckless people who, with few constraints, push themselves in exploration to see beyond the consolidated borders.

For conviction and personal experience, I believe in a lot on these dynamics, in great possibilities which offer less crystallized situations.

When from the historic Faculty of Engineering of Naples, the oldest in Italy and at the time still the only one in the city, I arrived at the University of Salerno, it was an obligatory passage waiting to be called to Naples, because Naples was able to announce competitions for professors in the ICAR sector17.

The Faculty of Engineering of Salerno was much smaller compared to that one of Naples and without history, since it could claim only 10 years as such and 20 ones as biennium of Engineering. I was convinced it had no reason to exist, like other small provincial universities. After some time, according to the allocations that were taking place, feasibility spaces available, I said to myself: «I'm fine here, I can build what I want, like I want, I don't have breaks and insurmountable obstacles that I would find elsewhere; I can stretch like I want, within fields and issues that I prefer. I will not go away from here». So, when the colleagues from Naples proposed me to come back home, I thanked them, but I refused.

This is the advantage, together with a lot of disadvantages, that offers situations like this, like that one now Luigini is living. He had to move not only about fifty kilometres but hundreds. In the origin place, already historically rooted, it would be more difficult, if not impossible, to have the same positive conditions.

We need things like these because, individually and like scientific community, we must open new ways, to make difficult and stimulating bets, which are a lot, as you can imagine. It is no longer just a matter of venturing into the field of infographics or digital representation, which we have been cultivating for many years; it is also a matter of meeting and dialogue, working together, with other scientific communities, including those outside architecture and engineering, which are our original and still privileged field of action.

We can not continue only (it may seem a contradiction but it is not, because we are a scientific community) with our specific and our well-known and well-established spaces for us, but outside, in the national and international academic context, they are most often completely unrecognizable from other scientific realities and communities; at best totally outdated.

We cannot cultivate transversal, multidisciplinary and interdisciplinary relationships, nor transdisciplinary ones, like I prefer to say: because we must not limit ourselves only to meet and dialogue with experts from other disciplinary sectors but also to make an individual effort to go beyond our borders. Without leading to the detrimental "all-purpose", we must be able to deeply understand the specifics and the reasons of others, to move with them with ease.

Therefore, I follow with great interest the work that Luigini is doing in this young university, meeting and dialoguing with other scientific and academic realities. It is a fundamental work, in the interest and for the growth of all of us; I am convinced about this, and I have practiced it for a long time. When I became Dean of the Faculty of Engineering in my university, relying on this power, I pushed myself to cultivate relationships and to conquer spaces in the other universities, different from ours, with which we could grow and mutually enrich ourselves. We started courses within the ICAR/17 sector at the faculties of Communication and Education. In the Faculty of Education we transferred a researcher, Carolina Carluccio, who later became an associate professor, who developed interesting initiatives for the growth of our entire local group and for our entire sector, at a national level.

It is therefore with great interest that I come here, as I am going elsewhere. Elena Ippoliti, highly efficient Secretary of our scientific society, told me that this year I went a lot more around, and I participated in conferences and seminars more than how many times I change. A little is because this year I'm pensioner, so there is more possibility to move. A little is because the initiatives that take place around Italy and abroad are now very many.

In recent years, especially with the management of the last Scientific Technical Committee, to be renewed in autumn, the UID has radically changed. We opened the windows, let in new air and brought young teachers to the government of the scientific society, by entrusting important assignments to many associate professors, carried out with commitment and excellent results. Because on certain innovative themes, to face and win new challenges, not only new energy is needed, but, as we Neapolitans say, "ci vuole la capa fresca", free from conditioning; we need young people who are curious, motivated and prepared, able to dialogue with determination with the experience and maturity of the elderly and who can reflect with coolness and detachment, renouncing if necessary to fascinating but naive and sudden falling in love.

It is evident that it was not enough to open the rooms, to let in new air and new people; it was also necessary to get out of those dark and asphyxiated rooms. This is why UID has sponsored many local scientific appointments, even abroad, and has progressively been transformed into a widespread scientific association, and not a vertical one; widespread in the academic environment and that also locally relates to other academic realities.

This path also favors the growth of the new all-round teaching class: made not only of exemplary professors from an educational point of view and exceptional researchers, often closed in their own restricted world and free from reality and academic dynamics, but of prepared and awared people, able to know and to intervene successfully in that complex reality. We absolutely need this.

I have been doing many jobs, in academia and outside; I prefer someone like teaching and researching than to others; I did someone better than others. For sure, I have been loving to be a talent scout: identifying talented people with strong motivations, seeing them grow in their own environment and, with discretion, helping them to mature, to give the best of themselves, even outside of that environment, in different, wider and more complex contexts.

For this reason, I willingly go around, even if with some difficulty, because I would prefer to do other things more, starting from the conclusion of many in progress studies, for which I believe that by now time is less and less. Also to see at work, in various contexts, the generation of young teachers and members of the UID that is growing. Sometimes, I reflect myself in them, and I see myself or other older teachers who managed to establish themselves and to achieve something useful for our scientific community. Always, these sorties outside home are an opportunity not only to go and see what moves around but also to assess and verify the level of growth, evolution and maturation of these new levers. And I must say that the picture is certainly positive and comforting, that we can be proud of helping to grow an excellent generation of professors and researchers - here widely and significantly represented - that bode well for the future of our scientific society and our scientific-disciplinary sector; ready to give us the change, as it should be, as soon as possible.

Vitale Cardone
President of Unione Italiana per il Disegno (UID)

Foreword: Developing New Reading Keys in Media Studies

The EARTH conference was an interesting example of exploring hybrid spaces in which various themes are intertwined, generating analogies that favor the investigation in sectors in which the old schemes seem to no longer provide useful interpretative tools. At EARTH18 research on multimodal languages, on IT resources, on new approaches to heritage and on new perspectives in education have found an integration space. As stated in the call, the concept of an ecosystem emerged that focuses not on the individual disciplinary territories but on the interactions between them and the dialogue between old and new languages, between the analogue and the digital world, between presence and distance. A third space is created that eliminates past dichotomies between virtual and real and, more generally, between dualisms that are no longer generative. In this context, a term assumes the role of pivot and at the same time is at the centre of a profound reconciliation: design. Once the separation and the diachrony between design time, action time, and documentation time have passed, the digital links the artefact producer and product artefact transforming the latter into an event never ripe, an eternal beta that keeps its umbilical cord with artefacts and realities that produce it. This is the case for texts produced with a word processor, for images produced with a photograph-editing programme, or, more generally, for the creations of the current digital production. The project is not just an initial idea or the guideline to develop the product: many applications to design are an action space where the project idea and the realization of the same evolve together and continually refer to each other. Today, new interests in the educational field emerge from multiple perspectives around the concept of design. Laurillard (2014), but not only, defines teaching as "design science" and the teacher as a designer who knows how to build paths suitable for the situation in which he/she operates. At the same time, teaching as implementation of rigid schemes no longer seems effective in the complex current context that requires the ability to think of paths in which they intertwine with different combinatorial and interrelated situations, inter- and intra-personal processes. If design becomes a space of action, which dialogues with the interactive processes typical of the action, many perplexities fall on the possibility of common reflections in different sectors and between hard and soft sectors while once the role that the event played in man science seemed to require a specific design model.

This scenario widens the possibility of dialogue between various research areas that impact with the same processes and with the same problems: the industrial design sector in which attention to creativity and to the relationship with innovation leads to watch with interest in training; the field of design that studies the impact and potential of new technologies on processing processes and productions; neurosciences that offer new interpretations on the processes connected to decision, creativity and emotions; the museology which, due to digital languages, on the one hand, and for new social needs linked to civil competences, on the other hand, revises both its role and its means of expression. This creates an intricate and intriguing plot that reifies the concept of ecosystem and places as central the relationships built between the practices generated by different disciplines and between the interpretative keys upstream of the same practices. SIREM, the Italian Society of Research on Medial Education, which has long been among its objectives to promote a dialogue and a common reflection among various subjects interested in the issues of media, training, and digital technologies, has found in EARTH2018 a fertile field to share practices and processes of interpretation with companies that, while moving in territories other than educational, can contribute to develop new keys to reading useful to operate in the worlds that the sociocultural context is unveiling.

Pier Giuseppe Rossi
President of Società Italiana per la Ricerca Educativa e Mediale (SIREM)

Welcome Speeches

Free University of Bozen Between Interdisciplinarity and Internationality

Paolo Lugli

Rektor of Free University of Bozen-Bolzano, Italy

We are a young University we just celebrated our 20th anniversary last year, a very small University of about 4,000 students the largest Faculty that we have is the Faculty of Education which is about 40–45% of our students. It is a trilingual university, we teach courses in English, in German and in Italian and we are the only Italian University which does that.

Recently, we got good news in a ranking that was the census ranking done together with Repubblica newspaper we have been classified the best between the small non-state Universities and actually we had valued that this is a very good evaluation also compared to larger mostly known university.

The topic of the Conference EARTH2018 actually fulfils very well what are the objective of our university. We are interdisciplinary, we are international, because of the language but also because of the percentage of students that come to study from abroad.

So, I hope you enjoy your time reading the proceedings of the EARTH 2018 conference in Bressanone.

Arrivederci, Alles gute, all the best for you.

EARTH: A Necessity Within the Realm of Liberty

Michael Gaidoschik

Vice-Dean of Faculty of Education, Free University of Bozen-Bolzano, Italy

In July 2018, the Faculty of Education within the Free University of Bozen – Bolzano was happy and proud to host EARTH 2018, the conference whose proceedings you now hold in your hands – or rather read on your screen. We as a Faculty of Education are, by definition, interested in education in all its aspects, and for all age groups. Arts, heritage, and digital tools to explore and conserve them, which have been the topics of EARTH 2018, are quite in the heart of education.

Nowadays it might be allowed again, and maybe important now and then, to quote Karl Marx, who wrote about the realm of liberty that starts only where the realm of necessity has its end.

Arts, in that distinction, would clearly form an important part of the realm of liberty. But of course that means nothing else than that art is a necessity for human beings; that to unfold our humanity we cannot do without art in all its forms.

Digital tools should help us to enhance our freedom – at least I would hope so; but of course, I myself, writing this as the Vice Dean of this Faculty, am just a mathematic educator and by far not an expert in digital tools. Therefore, my view and expectation may be deemed rather naïve by those who met for three days of intensive talks and lectures at EARTH 2018 that form the basis of what you can read in this volume.

I like to thank warmly Professor Luigini and his team for having organized this high ranked conference and now having edited these precious proceedings. Our Faculty is proud to be the only one in Italy to have in Alessandro Luigini a tenured professor in the field ICAR17. We do hope that this will serve as a model for other Italian universities, considering the fact that in the last years a new way of visual and graphic education has been developed here in Brixen – Bressanone, from the encounter of Italian and German-speaking tradition, a particular heritage of this splendid region we as a Faculty of Education feel obliged to make fruitful for the future.

The proceedings are, as the conference has been, an impressive collection of international expertise in the field. I am confident that the reader will find in these pages what a good conference, hence good proceedings are about: an inspiring mix of confirmation and provocation of thoughts. So let yourself be confirmed and provoked!

Towards a Future Still to Build

Peter Brunner

Major of Brixen-Bressanone, Italy

On behalf of the City of Brixen-Bressanone we thank the Free University of Bozen-Bolzano for this important work.

Over the centuries, the city has flourished as a cultural and educational centre of the region. Thanks to its geographical position, in the heart of Europe and on the hinge between the Latin and German-speaking worlds, Brixen-Bressanone has experienced a strong cultural and artistical vocation that is reflected in the streets of its old town, in its ancient buildings and the vibrant cultural scene. This aptitude must be preserved and encouraged.

With its ambitious project, the Free University of Bozen-Bolzano wants to put digital and visual technology at the service of cultural heritage in order to preserve and make it accessible to a wide audience. *Digital environment for education, arts and heritage*, projects us towards a future still to build. As administrators we are proud and grateful to be part of this initiative which opens new horizons for the profiling of Brixen-Bressanone as cultural city.

Therefore we extend our gratitude to the Free University of Bozen-Bolzano and to all those who have contributed to the project. We wish you all a good reading.

In the Circle of Art

Claudio Andolfo

Direttore Ripartizione Cultura Italiana - Provincia
Autonoma di Bolzano, Italy

In the Circle of Art is a multimedia exhibition held at the "Trevi" Cultural Centre of Bolzano, offering visitors the opportunity to take an innovative journey through the history of art and narrating its currents and tensions, styles and protagonists. A 360° projection and a variety of devices provide an insight into the visual content through the use of next generation technology (including 75" multitouch screens, virtual reality and a videogame for kids, free to download for smartphone and tablet), by means of which the approach can be adapted to suit age group of the visitor. The project was conceived by the *Ufficio Cultura italiana* (Office for Italian Culture) and developed in collaboration with the *Intendenza scolastica di lingua italiana* (Italian Language Educational Authority) of the Provincial Government of Bolzano and is aimed at a predominantly young target group. The educational aims of the exhibition are fostered by the resolve to draw students of all ages towards the languages of art, and focus on the relationships between art currents, styles and techniques from ancient to contemporary times. Advanced multimedia technology, in particular touch technology, offers a new approach and manner of interpreting the many and various languages of art.

Previous *Circle of Art* exhibitions addressed the following themes: the female figure in art (Donne D'arte, 2013), landscapes (Paesaggio a Nordest, 2014), wars of the 19th Century (Conflitto, 2015) and time and money (tempo & denaro, 2016/2017), the latter of which also saw the inauguration of a new virtual reality section.

During the exhibition, visitors had the exclusive opportunity to try out two VR visors, glasses or helmets designed to visualise and interact with virtual media. These visors are currently still in the development phase, and are the object of a great deal of curiosity amongst technology fans and in cultural and artistic circles. From graphic experience to archaeology, 3D reconstructions of places and works of art breathe life into a wide variety of paths, and "time & money" came up with an extremely effective means of tying in this new technology with the themes of the exhibition.

Visitors wearing the VR visors also had the opportunity to take a virtual tour of the exhibition *Dall'oggi al domani, 24 ore nell'arte contemporanea (From today to tomorrow, 24 hours in contemporary art)* organised by the Museo Macro in Rome.

The current *In the Circle of Art (2018/2019)* exhibition, the fifth, focuses on the theme of sports and athletic disciplines and offers a journey through the world of art, legend and prowess in athletics, games and sports, narrated in virtual imagery and material works of art.

Museums and Digital Environment

Antonio Lampis

Director-General of Museums at MIBACT

I am pleased to introduce this conference on the issue of digital technology in museums because it is the theme on which we are committed, as Director-General, in the creation of the national museum system. Networking museums today regardless of ownership - state, regional, municipal, diocesan, private, university, corporate museums - cannot happen without exactly as I said a "common digital home", a digital network that allows the exchange of best practices, the constant meeting of data and the exchange and verification of these data, social budgets, reporting and many other needs that museums have to confront.

The national museum system is emerging at this time and the accreditation and liaison procedures that are extremely important will have to go through the digital platform, where we try to make a system of accreditation of the many museums that will enter the system with zero bureaucracy, without paper instances. In this case, the very recent approval of the minimum quality levels of 4 April is immediately transformed into a self-assessment questionnaire which, compiled online, will allow museums to have a vote on achieving minimum quality levels and improvement levels, a self-reading through the digital tool that will allow in order to have a vote and will allow the commission that evaluates and supervises the accreditation process, to work quickly and work through the comparison of data in real time.

Recently, the book edited by Alessandro Luigini and Chiara Panciroli for FrancoAngeli under a common license[3], which deals with the educational potential of digital environments, deals with a subject that I have worked for twenty years in my previous work and which I use today in museums to stimulate them to think about the needs of young generations to approach museums through the use of digital tools in a story that is consistent with the changed minds, the minds completely changed the generations of millennials.

---

[3]Luigini A, Panciroli C (eds.) (2018) *Ambienti digitali per l'educazione all'arte e al patrimonio.* Milano: Franco Angeli. Available open access at: http://ojs.francoangeli.it/_omp/index.php/oa/catalog/book/334.

This is a fundamental challenge on which all the museums are called to discuss quickly, we are working within the General Directorate on the theme of 3D modeling as a tool for the temporary reconstruction of the evolution of the era for some great archaeological finds and in this I would like Italy to become among the world's leading countries in experimentation and research.

This is an extremely present theme in this 2018, European Year of Heritage, where the European Union in its decision underlined for the achievement of a better emergence of the role of heritage for the economy, for the employment of young people, for the people's well-being, more sustainable governance is needed and more sustainable governance is not achieved without a powerful digital link and more attention to younger generations. And even this second indication of the European Union is not obtained without extreme confidence with the potential of digital environments and their role in education.

Contents

Visual Heritage

Communication

Digital Heritage 1

Education

Immersive

Keynote Lectures

Four Dichotomies on Digital Environments Between Art, Heritage and Education: Opening Address

Alessandro Luigini[⊠]

Faculty of Education, Free University of Bozen-Bolzano,
Viale Ratisbona 16, 39042 Brixen-Bressanone, BZ, Italy
alessandro.luigini@unibz.it

1 Art, Heritage and Digital Environment

As already mentioned, information technologies are deeply pervasive, and for some decades have been enhancing and changing every field of life at an ever-faster rate. As recalled in the text with which the European Union in May 2017 set up the European Year of Heritage 2018, the need to promote the contact between heritage and the younger generations is one of the main challenges. Challenges that, probably, also pass for information technology.

In recent years, increasingly powerful IT devices have become available to increasingly extended audiences, amplifying, in fact, the effects of the information revolution until recently relegated to large socio-economic processes or restricted professional or research fields. Currently buy a smartphone more powerful than the computer that sent the first man on the moon is available to everyone, even users with limited availability of money. In the field of education experience in art and heritage, it seems that the acceleration of this process of basic technological availability has made easily accessible technologies such as 3D printing - currently printers of sufficient quality for most common uses cost as much as a smartphone mid-range - and virtual or augmented reality despite the applications of these technologies still remain quantitatively, and sometimes qualitatively, unsatisfactory. In the formative experience of art and heritage, both in education and in museum-exhibition, today we can include all the capacity for increasing reality that digital technologies have promised for decades: from immersive VR through stereoscopic viewers to the use of smartphone or tablet for the use of augmentative contents, the accessible technological devices actually make the application possibilities endless. Infinite not for a technophile or cyber-literary approach, but because these technologies directly affect our real experience of the space acted, both physical and digital, and for this reason all the contexts of human action are potentially affected. For different reasons, however, our interest is focused on the potential of such technologies of increased spatial experience in the pedagogical use of art and heritage, i.e. how VR and AR technologies can decisively enhance the training role that art and heritage have acquired over the past few decades.

A. Luigini (Ed.): EARTH 2018, AISC 919, pp. 3–12, 2019.
https://doi.org/10.1007/978-3-030-12240-9_1

2 Four Dichotomies: Starting from the Differences

The scientific proposal of the conference supports the construction of a transversal knowledge path, involving different sectors of research, aiming at the systematization of a participated dialogue and therefore shared on the themes around the digital heritage. To feed this path we try to deepen four dichotomies.

Let's start from the differences.

2.1 Authenticity/Reproducibility

The first dichotomy is on the relationship between authenticity and reproducibility of the work of art, starting from the reflection developed by Benjamin who in his famous essay *"Das Kunstwerk im Zeitalter seiner technischen Reproduzierbarkeit"* focuses on the possibility of reproducing technically the performing arts (musical incisions, films), as well as the figurative ones (photographs). But in the specific case, there are three concepts on which to focus, that is, the value of *uniqueness* that in some way every artworks had up to that moment and that with the reproducibility loses; *authenticity*, i.e. the difference between an authentic and a reproduced work; lastly, *hic et nunc,* the characteristic of an artwork realized or observed "here and now", not elsewhere and at any time.

2.1.1 Objectile

In the mid-nineties, an interesting experience on which we want to focus our attention, is Objectile, the project developed by the French architect Bernard Cache.

Objectile is first and foremost an exhibition organized in Paris in 1996, in which Cache poses with a pansytic attitude with respect to the relationship between architecture, design, philosophy and mathematics. He is concerned that digital technologies at some point give us the opportunity to move from a concept of object to that of objectil. The term is used by Gille Deleuze in "The Fold. Leibniz and the Baroque", a milestone of the philosophy "frequented" by the architects and designers of those years, and defines it in this way, citing Bernard Cache: «There exists thus a series of curves that not only imply constant parameters for each and every curve, but the reduction of variables to a 'single and unique variability' of the touching or tangent curve: the fold. The goal is no longer defined by an essential form, but reaches a pure functionality, as if declining a family of curves, framed by parameters, inseparable from a series of possible declensions or from a surface of variable curvature that it is itself describing. This new object we can call objectile. As Bernard Cache has demonstrated, this is a very modern conception of the technological object»[1] (Fig. 1).

To understand the applicative implications of this concept we refer to Cache's homonymous but subsequent experience, which founds a company through its website it was possible to buy objects, i.e. prototypes objects starting from mathematical algorithms with which the user-buyer could interact producing "Conformations"

[1] Deleuze, G. (1997). *THE FOLD. Leibniz adn the Baroque.* London-New York: Continuum. In several cases Deleuze cites a publication by Bernarde Cache, *L'ameublement du territoire*, actually published in 1997 with the title of *Terre Meuble*.

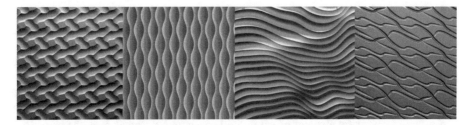

Fig. 1. Some patterns (objectiles) resulting from the modification of the Objectil algorithms.

completely personalized. Unique objects because they are the result of the user-buyer interaction with the basic algorithm. An authentic object, because it has been created for the user-purchaser who, therefore, receives the authentic prototype.

2.1.2 Human Part

To understand what today could mean reproducibility it would be too simple to remember the possibilities granted by the economic accessibility of 3D printing and its consequent diffusion. But in the experimental field, it is interesting to note a work conducted by the Bioengineer group Josè Luis Jorcano who used a mix of cells and nutrients in 2014 managed to print portions of skin to be used to repair tissues in the post-operative phase, as well as other applications. The point of contact with the above-mentioned experiences corresponds to that dimension which is proper to representation,

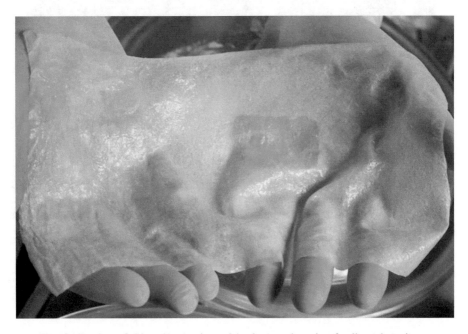

Fig. 2. Portion of skin printed using a 3d printer and a mix of cells and nutrients.

that is to make present what is not present, to make present something that is absent at a given moment which has to do with the experience of user. As it happens with the graphic representation, or with the three-dimensional printing of an object (Fig. 2).

But what happens when this prototyped, printed element is "installed" on the patient? Can we still speak of a representation of something that has now been assimilated as an integral part of the human body? Can we still refer to the representation of that object that until then was placed in the digital space, or does the "model" itself constitute the authentic element of the individual, though different from the others?

2.2   Authorship/Participation

The second dichotomy on which we want to reflect is authorship/participation. Consider the famous painting by Verrocchio "The baptism of Christ", painted while the young Leonardo da Vinci, "a bottega" from Verrocchio together with Sandro Botticelli, took his first steps, and on whose story Vasari dwells:

«[Per] Andrea del Verrocchio […che stava] faccendo una tavola dove San Giovanni battezzava Cristo, Leonardo lavorò un Angelo, che teneva alcune vesti; e benché fosse giovanetto, lo condusse di tal maniera che molto meglio de le figure d'Andrea stava l'Angelo di Leonardo. Il che fu cagione ch'Andrea mai più non volle toccar colori, sdegnatosi che un fanciullo ne sapesse più di lui»[2].

Fig. 3. Comparison between the angels painted by Leonardo da Vinci (and Sandro Botticelli) and the Christ of their master Andrea del Verrocchio. Andrea del Verrocchio, Leonardo da Vinci, "Baptism of Christ", 1475, Gallerie degli Uffizi, Florence. By permission of the Ministry of Heritage and Cultural Activities, Italy

---

[2] Giorgio Vasari, *Le vite de' più eccellenti pittori, scultori e architettori, Vita di Leonardo da Vinci pittore e scultore fiorentino*, 1568.

Vasari reminds us of the fact that Verrocchio refuses to continue to paint the pupil's advanced technique through envy, but the most interesting aspect concerns the paternity of the work, known for years as the "Baptism of Christ" of the Verrocchio; and it was precisely thanks to the presence of a young Leonardo, from a certain point in history, that the most recent historiography managed in some way to reconstruct the construction of this painting (Fig. 3).

The fundamental aspect is that any painting of the workshop of that period, or even later, may evidently be associated with the work of others and not only with the hand of the creator. Then, once again, the question of authorship is posed as something inseparable and rigid or participated and shared. It is clear that during the realization of the Angel, recently interpreted as the work of Botticelli, Leonardo had the master's indication on the elaboration of the subject, but the personal contribution of the student in the pictorial work is also clear, as Vasari also reports, achieves with a certain amount of autonomy the instructions received.

2.2.1 From Renaissance Workshop to Brian Eno: Autopoiesis

Maintaining a transdisciplinary approach, let us now reflect on the work of the famous musician, Brian Eno, who already in the sixties had extensively used electronic and then digital technologies to generate music. I do not intentionally use the concept of "composing" by borrowing the substantial differentiation that the musician puts into being between the notion of "composition" and that of "generation" of a piece. In 1975 Brian Eno published Discreet Music, an experimental album on whose cover he writes:

«I have gravitated towards situations and system that, once set into operation, could create music with little or no intervention on my part.

This is to say, I tend towards the role of planner and programmer, and then become an audience to the results».

Could it therefore be inferred that the musician is renouncing his own authorship? Evidently not, but most likely he is testing a different paradigm, in a relationship between authoriality and execution (Fig. 4).

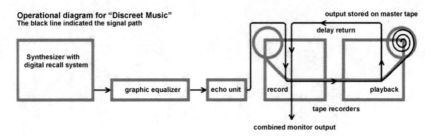

Fig. 4. Structure of the generative process used in Brian Eno's Discreet Music.

With a very similar approach, Fabio Bianchino, an Italian artist who deals with generative art, tells the conformation of his works[3]:

«In the evening I give instructions to the machine, which in the arc of the night processes the data and generates lines, shapes and colors independently. In the morning, when I wake up, I evaluate the results obtained. If I like the product I keep it, if it does not satisfy me I throw it».

In reality, on an international level, this type of approach, especially within generative art that directly concerns digital representation and digital heritage, is extremely widespread.

But continuing to think about the concept of authorship, think of the project by Oliver Auber, poietic generator, a poietic generator or more precisely a shared space in a digital environment with a 4 × 4 matrix containing four experiences of poietic generation. In this project a small digital space is provided to the user in which it is possible to choose and change the colors of the individual cells, interacting also with the previous user's work.

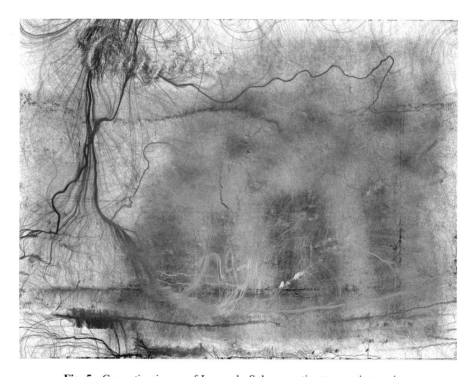

Fig. 5. Generative image of Leonardo Solaas reacting to user interaction.

---

[3] Cit. in MANCUSO, M. (2008). *Generative Nature. Estetica, ripetitività, selezione e adattamento.* Digicult. [30 January 2016]. Available at da: http://www.digicult.it/it/the-agency/lectures/generative-nature-fabrica-workshop.

What happens is that autopoiesis, that is, the automatism of constructing a figurative configuration, turns out to be a perfectly shared and participatory process, based in reality on the original idea of real authorship of the artist. A similar approach, of monitoring the user's action takes place, in a certain sense, also through the figurative works of the Argentinian artist Leonardo Solaas who records the behavior of the users within his websites (Fig. 5).

Recently, another Italian artist, Guido Segni, has proposed a work that has as a configurational moment a participatory process. The project entitled *Demand Full Laziness*, funded by a crowdfunding campaign with a five-year planning, time in which the artist claims the right to idleness. The possibility offered by the project is precisely that of reflecting on doing nothing, the subject in fact rests, reads a book, watches television: basically idleness. A webcam programmed inside the digital environment captures images, modifies them and deforms them using algorithms, continuously framing the artist, and the user participating in the crowdfunding will receive the work - the printed image elaborated by the algorithm - of the moment precise in which he adheres to the project. At this point the question concerning the paternity of the work arises spontaneously and specifically, if this is to be attributed entirely to the author or to those who participate in the project, which makes the project possible and determines its figurative structure.

2.3   Communication/Experience

The third dichotomy concerns the relationship between communication and experience. This is a dualism linked to the last fifty years of a system previously relegated to the dimension of "knowledge communication" but which slowly, following the passage from printed paper to interactive media, as well as the possibilities provided by the construction of hypertexts and digital spaces, has allowed us to achieve a clear and clear paradigm shift between communication and experience. A process of interchange also traceable in the project *Bloom: Open Space* by Brian Eno, which allows us to draw a line of continuity between the Sixties and today, just using an interactive virtual reality installation aimed not only at the realization of the performance but to its visual and sound configuration (Fig. 6).

It is therefore necessary to start making a distinction between communication and experience because the unquestionable development of digital heritage, favored by current technologies, has made available an extraordinary amount of material, so extraordinary that it becomes difficult to manage. Think of the *Europeana* platform, one of the main portals of documentation of the historical and artistic heritage through which it is possible to benefit from millions of works of art, which stimulates to reflect on the actual meaning of management this huge information patrimony. In fact, some questions arise: can we concretely state that we are benefiting from the works? Can an online generalist research be considered a cultural operation? Evidently not. In fact, the construction of this system is based on the narration, on the storytelling that relates works of art, often already linked to each other for historical, expressive, etc., but which is not sufficient compared to the large amount of material that instead it is contained in the portal. Accessibility is not enough: it is necessary to build meaningful experiences through narrative contents.

Fig. 6. Europeana home page: on 5th July 2018 there were 56,694,919 digitalized artwork.

2.4   Representation/Digital Environment: Conclusions

The last dichotomy on which I would like to focus on the concept of representation and that of the digital environment. A satellite photo taken from Google Earth already allows you to experience a digital environment that is complex enough to study, from a technical point of view, the effects on digital culture, on sociology, on technology, on the many disciplines that deal with the man towards life experiences and in the specific case of the digital environment (Fig. 7).

In any case, it must be emphasized that it is not a simple representation system, in fact, it is not turning our gaze towards a digital representation of the world that we can even superficially be aware of its form. Many, among philosophers, sociologists and geographers, have explained how from a certain moment of history the representations of the world no longer correspond to its image, but to the world itself that has become a representation of the models. Google Earth is one of those systems that has aimed to configure itself as a container of any content produced in the world to be able to contain any experience of any user.

A totality therefore that gives the possibility to reach the conclusion of our path to explain the proposal that we considered fundamental to propose with this conference. The idea of the acronym is developed starting from the clear reference to the English word earth, earth, which consists of the words Education, Art and Heritage, the topics specifically investigated through the study of digital environments. And it is precisely this kind of approach to knowledge and our life that we wanted to develop here, taking into account the pivotal role played by the authenticity of each experience that we conduct, in a participatory manner, within digital environments and that is to be configured in the effective quality of an individual authoriality of experience.

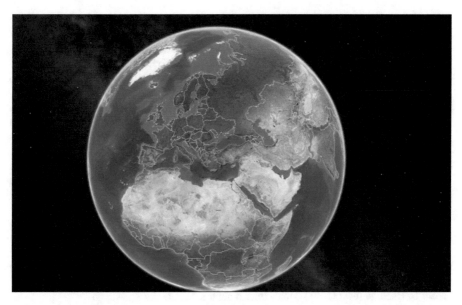

Fig. 7. The interface of Google Earth represents the World and (potentially) all its contents.

References

Abruzzese A (2006) L'innovazione tra post-democrazia e post-umanità. In: D.e Kerckhove D, Tursi A (eds) Dopo la democrazia? Il potere e la sfera pubblica nell'epoca di internet. Apogeo, Milano

Anceschi G (1992) L'oggetto della raffigurazione. Etas Libri, Milano

Benjamin W (1936–1991) L'opera d'arte nell'epoca della sua riproducibilità tecnica. Arte e società di massa (orig. Das Kunstwerk im Zeitalter seiner technischen Reproduzierbarkeit, 1936). Einaudi, Torino

Brusaporci A (2017) Digital innovations in architectural heritage conservation: emerging research and opportunities. IGI Global, Hershey

Bryan E (1975) Discreet music. EG records/virgin records

Cache B (2011) A plea for euclid. Projectiles, architectural words 6. Architectural Association Publications, London

Capucci PL (1993) L'influenza delle tecnologie sul corpo e sulle sue facoltà. Baskerville, Bologna

De Kerckhove D (2007) Dall'alfabeto a internet. L'homme «littéré»: alfabetizzazione, cultura, tecnologia. Mimesis, Milano

Deleuze G (1997) The Fold. Leibniz adn the Baroque. Continuum, London

Eco U (1992) Il secondo diario minimo. Bompiani, Milano

Farinelli F (2004) Geografia. Un'introduzione ai modelli del mondo. Einaudi, Torino

Gombrich E (1980) Lo specchio e la mappa: teoria della rappresentazione. In: Calabrese O (ed) Semiotica della pittura. Il Saggiatore, Milano

Levy P (1994) L'Intelligence collective. Pour une anthropologie du cyberespace, La Découverte, Paris. Tr. it. (1996). L'intelligenza collettiva. Per un'antropologia del cyberspazio. Feltrinelli, Milano

Levy P (1995) Qu'est-ce que le virtuel?, La Découverte. Paris. Tr. it. Il virtuale. (1997). Raffaello Cortina, Milano

Longo GO (1998) Il nuovo Golem. Laterza, Roma-Bari

Luigini A (2017) Tre ipotesi sugli sviluppi futuri della modellazione 3D/three hypotesis about future development of modeling 3D. In: Empler T (ed) 3DModeling&BIM. Progettazione, design, proposte per la ricostruzione, pp 440–453. DEI, Roma

Luigini A, Panciroli C (eds) (2018) Ambienti digitali per l'educazione all'arte e al patrimonio. Franco Angeli, Milano

Luigini A (2018) Geografie visuali e geografie numeriche. Paradigmi digitali nella rappresentazione del paesaggio. In: Bianconi F, Filippucci M (eds) Il paesaggio prossimo. Realtà, rappresentazione, progetto, pp 39–44. Gangemi Editore, Roma

Maldonado T (1993) Reale e Virtuale. Feltrinelli, Milano

Mancuso M (2008) Generative Nature. Estetica, ripetitività, selezione e adattamento. Digicult, 30 January 2016. http://www.digicult.it/it/the-agency/lectures/generative-nature-fabrica-workshop

Manovich L (2003) New media from Borges to HTML. In: Wardrip-Fruin N, Montfort N (eds) The new media reader. MIT Press, London, pp 13–25

Perra D (2007) Impatto digitale. Dall'immagine elaborata all'immagine partecipata: il computer nell'arte contemporanea. Baskerville, Bologna

Rheingold H (1993) La realtà virtuale. I mondi artificiali generati dal computer e il loro potere di trasformare la società. Baskerville, Bologna

Sacchi L, Unali M (eds) (2003) Architettura e cultura digitale. Skira, Milano

Vasari G (1568) Le vite de' più eccellenti pittori, scultori e architettori, Vita di Leonardo da Vinci pittore e scultore fiorentino

Virtual Reality: The Use of Images for the Interpretation and Experience of Culture and Heritage

Eugene Ch'ng[✉]

NVIDIA Joint-Lab on Mixed Reality, NVIDIA Technology Centre,
University of Nottingham Ningbo China, Ningbo, China
eugene.chng@nottingham.edu.cn

Abstract. Much of our understanding of our world is via images, images which we see with our eyes and those which are formed in our minds as a consequence, and all these occur through our bodily actions within the context and the spaces in which we move and act. In the present, we manipulate information via gestural actions, accessing objects through screens of various sizes pervading our lives, which contributes to our action on and the understanding of our worlds. In the academia too and increasingly within the data-science oriented industry, interactive visualisation used within research and corporations has become part of the process rather than the product. It seems that the greater part of our existence has been saturated with digital representations and that we have been herded into digital worlds, although incompletely. Now that Virtual Reality is ready, the means to a fuller immersion and experience in terms of spatial-temporal awareness, self-awareness, and embodied action has become accessible, we need to ask what the phenomenological implications in our interpretation and experience of culture and heritage are? And how will this transform the way we conduct our research? This communication explores our transition from the real into the virtual, and presents perspectives from various projects at the NVIDIA Joint-Lab on Mixed Reality.

Hello and welcome to the NVIDIA Joint-Lab on Mixed Reality.

My name is Eugene Ch'ng, I'm a professor of Cultural Computing here at the University of Nottingham's China campus. I am also director of the NVIDIA Joint-Lab on Mixed Reality, an NVIDIA Technology Center located here and supported by NVIDIA.

If you turn around and follow me, you can see that we have several tools available for VR research. We are a development center for VR and AR, Virtual Reality and Augmented Reality, and we deal with different areas of research, but in particular those related to cultural heritage: monuments, sites, objects, text and behaviors.

I will first introduce you to my laboratory. My speech focuses on the sharing of cultural heritage through VR technologies. I will therefore not only talk about VR, but also about the technologies that make it possible to create all sorts of VR and AR applications.

© Springer Nature Switzerland AG 2019
A. Luigini (Ed.): EARTH 2018, AISC 919, pp. 13–18, 2019.
https://doi.org/10.1007/978-3-030-12240-9_2

I am presently co-editor-in-chief of Presence: Teleoperators & Virtual Environments of the MIT Press Journal and for this Journal we accept articles related to the application, and art and science of VR and virtual environments. If you have original articles with good contents and that meet publication standards do send them in, they will be welcomed.

The vision of my laboratory concerns Virtual Reality and Augmented Reality, but within the spectrum between the two realities we focus on Mixed Reality, on the coexistence between the real and the virtual.

With a few exceptions, we build our machines so that they are suitable for the GPUs supported by NVIDIA. We have several professional tools that we use for processing big data, from social networks and VR applications. We have several funded projects, one of which is an "agent-based modeling" project modeling ancient ecosystems located in the North Sea submerged 10,000 years ago due to climate change. It is therefore an archaeological project which concerns cultural heritage. I also collaborate with the research group that has mapped the entire landscapes of Stonehenge in a digital format and with which we have discovered 17 new monuments. We also used the digital map, which we presented at the Royal Society Summer Science Exhibition 2015 to crowd-source people's behaviors and to understand how they would use their surroundings for burying their dead relatives. The study was published in "Virtual Systems and Multimedia" conference two years ago. For other projects, visit the "Curious Travelers: Visualising Heritage" website. In China I have a funded project for building a 3D objects database of the entire Silk Road from both the land and the sea.

What is important is a global platform that is capable of reproducing cultural heritage. When reproducing, documenting or recording cultural heritage, we are not talking only about images, videos or 360° videos, but we increasingly refer to high quality three-dimensional images. 3D scanning techniques are becoming more widespread, less expensive and more accessible. In the past, laser scanning was very expensive and were not accessible to many laboratories or even museums, but photogrammetric techniques can use almost any digital cameras, so you can simply use a high-definition camera from a smartphone and get high quality results.

ReACH (Reproduction of Art and Cultural Heritage) is an initiative supported by UNESCO, led by the Victoria & Albert Museum in collaboration with the Peri Charitable Foundation. This initiative has reviewed and redrafted Henry Cole's 1867 Convention on the Reproduction of Art. At the time, works of art were in fact reproduced through physical and analogue instruments. But now, 150 years have passed and a review was necessary. I was invited as one of their global consultant and an expert on digital heritage to contribute to the program which has taken me to Beijing for roundtable discussions, to London for the V&A ReACH declaration, to Abu Dhabi for the making of the technical policy. Just last week I gave a speech in Paris, at the UNESCO headquarters on the theme of sustainable digital heritage, on the challenges of storage and sharing. A book titled "Copy Culture" has been published containing several case studies and articles on the reproduction of art, of which a digital version is also available. The ReACH community, to which I belonged helps support individuals and organizations which do not have access to resources and knowledge for such works.

Why is cultural heritage so important? It is important because it allows us to preserve our identity, our social and national values. A plaque outside the Museum of Afghanistan states that: "A nation stays alive when its culture is alive". The historian Nancy Dupree said that "a nation maintains its integrity only when its members preserve the values of its history and its heritage."

Then there is also value and economic impact – Stonehenge visitors pay not only for the entrance fee, but also for the trip, the hotels, as well as various purchases. As you can see from the graph, the national cultural heritage contributes to a turnover of about 26.37 billion according to a 2008 study. In the past, about 10–20 years ago, digital technology has transformed documentation and analysis of cultural heritage, made significant progresses but focusing on sites that are very old. For example, Stonehenge has a history of thousands of years, or this other site at Geldeston, of which we have a video in which we see archaeologists pulling out an Iron Age stake which in the past lines the banks of a river which brings residences into the village. Apart from the physical labor there is also the need for laser scanning which accompanies the work. This is a video from 2011/2012 of which you are able see laser scans producing very high quality models. However, laser scanning is a very expensive activity which requires tools and expertise to process models. Things have changed with photogrammetry approaches.

After my visit to London, and as I was returning to China to participate in a TEDx talk, I downloaded data of the UNESCO World Heritage Sites and generated a chart demonstrating that the oldest site registered in the World Heritage list is millions of years old. There were several concentrated sites in the middle segment that are hundreds of thousands of years old and finally we have the youngest site at 29 years old – the Sydney Opera House. You can see that great world organizations and museums focus on that part of the heritage that is very dated and are ancient. But the problem of ancient sites is that the memories have disappeared, and there aren't written documents, and therefore analyzing and interpreting these monuments are very difficult. Looking at this chart you can see that sites that are less than a hundred years old have live memories and I think these sites are important. Our laboratory focuses on sites that are still alive.

It could happen to you in Rome, even if your hometown is, for example, Bressanone. Returning to your hometown for the Christmas holidays, you would begin to think about the feelings you will have as you return home and the sense of warmth which may arise. Even looking at old photos will trigger memories that could be sweet or bitter. I therefore think that it is important in capturing living memories. When I look at this picture when I was around 3–4 years old – I and my brother sitting on the Mercedes-Benz, I was immediately transported back to that moment. I know that there is a tree here which emits a fragrant smell and it is about 7.00 pm in the evening. Going home there is my grandfather who falls asleep in front of the TV and snores very loudly, and so on. These images are therefore able to bring us into the spaces of our memories. I call all these things, the images, videos and objects "Anchors of memory" or "memory anchors". Even physical structures are anchors of memory. When we access our past memories, we get a good feeling and this is important because they represent our roots and our identity. Yet all these memory anchors reside only in our mind. When we share stories, our friends and family can only imagine them. We could tell a good story to bring them into this memory, but to them they are only imagination, they will never be in the same memory space.

What virtual reality allows us to do is not only to share stories, but also to bring the audience, the members of our family into our memory spaces. Virtual Reality has been in development for a long time. It goes back to Ivan Sutherland who had a vision that one day we would have had a window into the virtual world and the images would have improved to such an extent as to seem real. Nowadays in the 21st century, we have achieved his VR prediction.

Virtual Reality is based on the "3 Is": Immersion, Interaction and Imagination. These three collectively simulate the sense of presence. As compared to 10–20 years ago, Virtual Reality has become accessible, inexpensive and powerful. We can not only record the movement of our head, but also our orientation and our position, including the position of our body if we use the controllers. We have controllers that allow us to interact with the surrounding virtual environment.

Virtual Reality has become a very powerful tool and it is how it is used for creating value. In our laboratory we do a lot of research, in particular studies on users. Several articles will be published soon in this regard. We essentially look at human behavior, the sense of presence, nostalgia, memory and imagination. Presence can be induced in different ways and we simulate virtual 'reality' using different techniques. From the point of view of VR devices, they are now very accessible – for £1,500 you can own a good workstation and probably some of the tools shown in my slides.

The video shows a rendering in real-time of a character that is real (in 3D), not just a 2D image. All the details such as the translucency of the skin are entirely simulated with extremely powerful graphics cards. Looking at this other scene, no one would ever imagine that it is a real-time simulation in which one can actually walk inside. If we can simulate something so real, can we also store our memories in that space? This is the question we ask. If we are able to walk through this scene, apart from the feeling of the dampness on the floor, we have the sensation of being actually inside it. This shows that reality can be simulated with Virtual Reality.

In the video, I was at a site in Japan and capturing a scene using only my iPhone and photogrammetry techniques that have become very common among the virtual environments community, or to Hawaii or in China using a drone for capturing landscapes. I found that I am able to reconstruct reality in virtual reality. It takes only a few minutes to capture a series of images for 3D reconstruction. This is the digitization of spaces, structures, monuments and objects of our memories. We also need to visualize them and this requires much more than simply acquiring data. Visualization allows us to add value to the data we have acquired.

I have begun acquiring several memory anchors. I was in a beach in Australia with my children a year ago and whilst they were playing with sand I decided that maybe I should capture that moment so that I can later share it with the other family members. With only photos one could only imagine the location, and one could not be at the same place we were at where we have taken the photos. At the NVIDIA Joint-Lab on Mixed Reality we have several tools that can allow us, through the networks to bring more people into the same place. Beyond the photos and videos that we were able to share with friends and relatives, we are now able to further access the spaces in which our memories reside with VR.

20 to 30 years from now, Virtual Reality will probably be the main technology for sharing memories. Today we share photos and videos through social media, but in the future we will be able to share our memories through 3D spaces.

We recently visited an old village in Ningbo, China where, with a drone we acquired 3D data of the entire village. Here, you can see a little house in which a couple lives, the woman who is blind walks around the house, cuts vegetables, cooks, brought condiments to the table, and etc. You can observe the quality of the data acquisition, which takes time to process. Once completed, the virtual environment allows you to interact with the objects. This is a scene outside the kitchen. We see an old tofu mold, with which the 80 years old couple has prepared tofu for us. In this other scene as you can see, one can also build 3D models and not only acquire them through 3D capture that which has ceased to exist. See also an old basket here.

Creating Virtual Reality from the reality around us is a simple process. We took several images and using photogrammetry that I have mentioned before, the 3D scene is created. This is followed by a processing phase. If it is not a particularly complex interactive environment, no VR programming will be necessary. After the simple process it will be possible to share the spaces created for the future.

This is the tofu maker scene with my PhD student Shengdan Cai exploring it. Both for her, myself and my other students, entering that scene brought the same sensation experienced when we were actually in that village. With the experience gained through this particular project, we think therefore that memories can be inserted and transmitted with Virtual Reality. All objects in the scene have been acquired in 3D, but the environment and some parts of the scene are rebuilt, with visual effects added. Thus a scene is reconstructed which can give particular sensations. Here, I took a plate with coins on it and here I dropped the coins. In this other scene we combined the Oculus Rift with the controllers, here are some museum workers supporting our work.

Here, we have a much more elaborate project concerning the creation of an entire ancient village. In our portfolio we currently have a project combining Virtual Reality with Augmented Reality.

This concludes and summarizes my speech. I think that in the future there will be a shorter distance between the real and the virtual thanks to the ability to share 3D contents and environments, within which it will be possible to enter virtual spaces rather than simple 2D photos and videos in social media. We have looked at the value of cultural heritage and how it contributed to the economy, but also to our identity, our roots, our history and our national values. I have also talked about the importance of acquiring memories, especially living ones contained within structures, architectures, monuments and objects before they are lost forever. These are living memories within a hundred years old, a range of time which are perhaps uninteresting for museums and global organizations.

Virtual Reality is accessible today, accompanied by technologies that can allow us to acquire and share our "anchors of memory", which can take us back to where we were many years ago. I think that sharing 3D objects and environments will become as common as photos and videos in the future. This is my prediction. The ReACH Initiative, led by the Victoria & Albert Museum, which I am involved in, is a global platform that contributes to this possibility through the expertise and technical documents that people can access and learn from.

With this I conclude my speech. My final sentence is: In the future, the past will be as accessible as the present, thanks to Virtual Reality.

The Digital Museum as a Third Space: Giving Shape to Conceptualization

P. G. Rossi[1] and C. Panciroli[2(✉)]

[1] Department of Education Sciences, Cultural Heritage and Tourism,
University of Macerata, P.le Luigi Bertelli, 62100 Macerata, Italy
`piergiuseppe.rossi@unimc.it`
[2] Department of Education Sciences "G.M. Bertin",
University of Bologna, via Filippo Re 6, 40126 Bologna, Italy
`chiara.panciroli@unibo.it`

Abstract. MOdE - Museo Officina dell'Educazione is a virtual and multimodal museum. It is multimodal not due to the presence of different languages, but also the presence of different action spaces. The museum has exhibition rooms, documentation but also "blank" rooms, where the visitor can assemble materials that are already in the museum or collected in their own informal contexts, to produce meanings. The museum therefore becomes a third space in that formal and informal contexts are hybridized and new artifacts are constructed - thus proving that it is generative. This work seeks to draw the attention to the function of the MOdE blank rooms as active spaces that contribute to the production of common threads that can be used to overcome the fragmentary nature of current contexts and the identities that they house, whilst also highlighting how hybrid spaces, third spaces, are the keys to education in a complex society.

Keywords: Virtual museum · Digital artefacts · Digital environments · Multimodality · Fragment · Layout

1 Introduction

The study analyses the meaning and sense of digital environments to understand if they can be third spaces. Some digital environments can be seen not as separate from the real, but as *third spaces* in which, according to Flessner (2014), the formal and the informal, presence and distance, the "real" and the digital are combined to build new meanings. In these third spaces it is possible to work to aggregate and re-process materials and experiences from the first and second spaces, to reflect on them, to understand the experiences encountered in the informal with the lenses of theory and to rethink theories based on experiences. In this sense, digital environments as a third space are virtual museums offering tools for the customization and construction of new artifacts.

In particular, the analysis focuses on the virtual museum, starting from the experience of the MOdE and its blank rooms, to understand if and how a specific digital experience can reify the third space.

A. Luigini (Ed.): EARTH 2018, AISC 919, pp. 19–26, 2019.
https://doi.org/10.1007/978-3-030-12240-9_3

The research question is the following: can a virtual museum in which the user can aggregate materials and process their own emergence of meaning, become a third space in which common threads are built connecting knowledge fragments building both the meaning of specific themes and individual pathways?

2 Theoretical Framework

Today's society is characterized by the fragment, that is, by the presence of many blocks that are difficult to reduce with the characteristic logics of both the Aristotelian syllogism and the Hegelian dialectic. The fragments can be aggregated, but the absence of meta-narratives militates against the possibility of hierarchies or reductions to the general and also against unique and unambiguous narratives. The fragments must therefore be connected with common threads that do not reduce differences, but connect them with weak ties often based on topological logics. In particular, the fragment is one of the elements that characterize current culture and communication. Today, the first page of a newspaper consists of fragments or multiple inputs, often over twenty, comprising squares in which there is a title, often an image and a brief text. The reader moves between these items and must construct an overall vision by tracing recursive trajectories across the page. A further example of fragments in the school environment is provided by the knowledge in a classroom in which each student has his/her own baggage constructed from a range of sources, including informal sources. In fact, the information and knowledge which a student brings to the classroom is different from those of his or her colleagues and while at one time it was possible to identify a certain number of narratives that were shared by all the students, today the narrated "stories", increasingly conveyed by the media, belong to an infinite, multicultural catalogue with no common background in the classroom, just as there is no single shared story. All of which produces the complexity of the classroom and the difficulties of teaching which today require the construction of meanings based on the fragments that are present.

The fragments are self-validating and non-reducible: it is impossible to place them on a single scale, based on a classification or using a Hegelian synthesis. The fragments are distant from one another, but not different, which would still provide comparability. Distance it is easier to address with topological methods than logic. The fragments in fact require the presence of a structure, a layout, which has its own autonomous logic. The layout connects and builds meanings, very often with a limited rationale or a context-linked rationale. Layouts function with a spatial logic through aggregation, proximity and position, often without starting from a unifying idea and proposing a bottom-up process. So the ability to produce meaningful, culturally and socially relevant aggregations is today an important civil competence. In this regard, Flessner proposes the third space as a locus for hybridizations between unresolvable dualisms.

In particular, for Gutiérrez et al. (1999) the third space becomes a place in which the availability of forms of mediation and resources and the organization of activities is reflected in the opportunity to learn and participate to support the development of new trajectories of meaning.

Digital can be seen within third space theory as a meeting point of worlds, where they are combined and produce understandings. Digital technologies contain fragments and at the same facilitate actions. They are repositories of different media - texts, images, videos, sounds, graphics - that offer many ways to manipulate individual fragments or build networks that aggregate them: creating outlines and maps, assigning keywords and tags, linking various objects and building complex patchworks. As Flessner suggests, in the third space, not only do physical and cognitive artifacts come from the other two spaces, but outputs emerge that add meaning and sense (Luigini and Panciroli 2018). Therefore, digital and multimodal environments are third spaces when they act as a bridge between different environments: formal and informal contexts, real and digital spaces, spaces of experience and working practices and spaces for reflection and learning. The role of digital and multimodal environments as third spaces is not only that of aggregating, connecting, inserting materials from different outputs, but also of bringing out new meanings, evidence, reflections and sense networks (Rossi 2010, Rivoltella 2014).

It is important to clarify the meaning of multimodality.

The first definition comes from *cultural studies*, in which multimodal depends not only on the presence of different languages, but also on modes that are simultaneously languages, actions, sociality (Kress 2009). In this sense, multimodal is an area of action.

The second definition comes from neuroscientific research. In particular, *Embodied Simulation* theory holds that sensory and motor systems are intrinsically multimodal because they respond to and process information associated with multiple sensory modalities and that multimodality can be seen as an intrinsic property of the vast majority of brain areas (Cuccio and Gallese 2018).

Both approaches to multimodality, while derived from different perspectives, focus on action and this centrality shifts the focus to the process. This shift is not irrelevant: if aggregation is considered to be a process that exalts the spatial position of concepts seen as objects, it can be assimilated into sensory-motor processes and is connected both to research in embodied cognition and to analogies identified in the neurosciences between sensory-motor processes and cognitive processes, in addition to affective and emotional ones.

3   Modes of Inquiry

The MOdE, Museo Officina dell'Educazione, created in 2008 by the Department of Educational Sciences of the University of Bologna, is a digital and multimodal space in which users can not only browse and view materials, but also build their own rooms: blank rooms (Panciroli and Pizzigoni 2013). The MOdE consists of two main areas - exhibition and documentation - supported by an additional area dedicated to education. The exhibition space involves setting up virtual rooms and workshops dedicated to specific thematic areas (art teaching, history of education, children's literature, special education, etc.) and is marked by significant relationships between galleries of images, video, audio and textual analyses. The documentation space seeks to disseminate and enhance good practices with cultural heritage (Panciroli 2010).

Inside the exhibition area there are blank rooms that offer visitors a space for reworking contents where they can aggregate artifacts internal to the museum or external materials, collected from their own experience. In fact, the itineraries offered by museums increasingly off the visitor the opportunity to participate in the same way as those who design and produce contents, in a shared writing. In this regard, the personal spaces offered to visitors by some important digital real museums, such as the Prado and the Rijksmuseum (*Mi Prado and Rijksstudio*) are significant. In these areas users can either collect images of works that stimulate their interest, or create galleries/albums within sequences that they consider to be particularly significant.

In terms of the architecture of virtual museums, in the blank rooms each new object inserted in addition to or replacing another involves a re-formulation of meaning, just as the blank rooms are not rigidly defined, but can be continuously transformed and implemented (Manovich 2013). In this sense, the blank rooms can be considered to be artefacts, part of an ecosystem that must be conceived and analysed as a complex system and not as an isolated entity.

The research intends to investigate what meanings and what methodologies are used in the creation of a blank room, in relation to two contexts: university teaching and school education.

There are 22 blank rooms, each of which has been designed and built by a university or school class. 1125 students have participated in the experimentation in the last two years.

The survey was carried out by 3 researchers who were present while the students created the blank rooms and interviewed them in groups at the end of the work. All students also completed a questionnaire to identify the skills acquired.

Research data	
Number of researchers involved in the research project	3
Number of students involved in the experimentation	1125
Number of blank rooms created	22

3.1   Experimentation

The visitors/students mainly used two room construction approaches, characterized by continuous recursiveness between the real and the virtual:

- Thematic/textual approach. The expert suggests a theme and, through interactive visits in challenging cultural environments (real and/or virtual museums), the students come to the definition of a project to set up a blank room through a specific profile. During the cultural pathways the students are led to look for images and information as "hooking and memorizing elements", necessary to convey the meanings that they wish to communicate through this environment.
- Object/visual approach. Students start by exploring tangible and/or intangible works in the rooms of the MOdE virtual museum and/or other museums and digital and/or physical places of cultural interest.

The objects act as iconic, symbolic mediators, giving form to conceptualizations.

From the analysis of the rooms, two types of output emerged:

- *the simple artifact* configured as a semantically self-validating unit, in the form of an image, video and/or text and which, therefore, represents a museum object that can be catalogued and described;
- *The complex artifact*, a set of objects related to a theme, linked together by a complex network of meanings, able to propose original narrative pathways.

An example of a simple artifact is a single photomontage *The first porticoes in the XI century* (Fig. 1), created by the students starting by reworking several images. This artifact has its own semantic autonomy and shows the historical reconstruction of the ancient porticoes of Bologna in a new and personal way.

The first porticoes in the XI century // Immagine 7 di 10

Fig. 1. Image re-worked by students for the preparation of the Blank Room *The Evolution of Bologna*

A second work, *The Evolution of Bologna* (Fig. 2) is a complex artifact created by the students starting from more simple artifacts (videos, images, audio, texts), also including *The first porticoes in the XI century*. It was interesting to see that the students did not juxtapose these products, but created a semantic and narrative network to reconstruct the heritage of the city by showing each characterizing element (building, monument, etc.) based on a double vision of past vs present.

In both cases the underlying processes are similar and recall many of the cognitive operations indicated above. First of all the artifacts produced can be seen as a *patchwork* i.e. an aggregation of different materials coming from multiple sources. Sometimes they are fragments taken from museums or the web; on other occasions they are independent productions of the students, their photographs or videos. And this perhaps better emphasizes how the museum can be seen as a third space: in the artifact, the elements derived from the cultural heritage connect with the elements that come from the students' everyday lives (Panciroli and Macauda 2017). Personal experience therefore becomes the instrument for re-reading and reinterpreting the works of museums, in the same way that the works of museums become the tool for observing their own experiences from another perspective, for assigning new senses and re-processing them emotionally and cognitively.

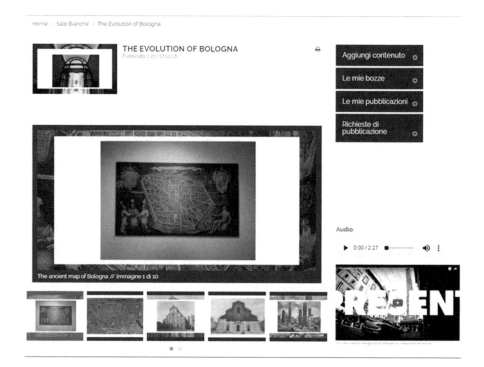

Fig. 2. Blank room *The Evolution of Bologna*

Data Analysis

The reading of the questionnaires and the interviews revealed the following outcomes. Many students stated that the proposed activity led to an active learning process, based on a constructivist and problematic approach, on exploration, research and planning in relation to the intellectual and socio-relational dimensions (collaborative learning). 65% of students said that the virtual visit required them to be creative and provided tools and guidelines for productive activity. Furthermore, 48% of students emphasized that the production made it possible for them to gain awareness of their experiences and encouraged the re-processing or collection of various materials in their personal experiences.

72% also highlighted how the immersion required by the work was an innovative educational experience that the students found stimulating for building and processing knowledge. To this end, multimodality had a strongly generative role capable of activating previously unforeseen relationships and connections (56%). Some students in fact underlined how some relationships and meanings emerged during the processing of materials and how, in particular, it was actually an extensive use of images and videos that promoted reflections on themes that were not present in the initial phase of the work.

During the preparation of the room which facilitated group activities, some students highlighted how working on the blank room facilitated a focus on individual and collective identity and the construction of shared pathways, resulting from the integration of different experiences.

Finally, the majority of students highlighted the importance of accessing a large number of systems of resources and tools to facilitate cognitive and identity processes and of making contact with different cultural agencies, real and virtual.

4 Conclusions

With the dissemination of digital environments enabling the user/visitor to design and produce content in a shared writing, based on new possibilities of interaction, the virtual museum becomes a third space in which formal and informal contexts, real and digital spaces meet, combine and produce new meanings and where instances of creativity and expression and of citizenship and identity development can be connected.

The blank rooms as artifacts act as iconic and symbolic mediators to give concrete form, based on a narrative approach, to the conceptualizations deriving from the experiences of visiting museums. This mediation activity requires that visitors edit content to write original narratives and the narrative process that develops from multiple fragments, processing meaningful aggregations, takes account of the way in which the user relates to, understands and internalizes the museum objects. Every object in fact needs a story, a point of view, an experience that gives it meaning and at the same time gives sense and meaning to the experiences of the students. The key element is precisely the interaction between personal experience and shared, culturally relevant objects that play the role of boundary objects between different identity trajectories and different processes within each subjectivity. The fragments that the blank rooms present for collection and development, by linking the assets to their own lives, are the fundamental prerequisite for the construction of an active and responsible citizenship by young people and of complex identities open to a plural future.

References

Cuccio V, Gallese V (2018) The neural exploitation hypothesis and its implications for an embodied approach to language and cognition: insights from the study of action verbs processing and motor disorders in Parkinson's disease. Cortex. https://doi.org/10.1016/j.cortex.2018.01.01

Flessner R (2014) Revisiting reflection: utilizing third spaces in teacher education. Educ Forum 78(3):231–247

Gutiérrez KD, Baquedano-López P, Tejeda C (1999) Rethinking diversity: hybridity and hybrid language practices in the third space. Mind Cult Act 6(4):286–303

Kress G (2009) Multimodality: a social semiotic approach to contemporary communication. Routledge, London

Luigini A, Panciroli C (2018) Ambienti digitali per l'educazione all'arte e al patrimonio. FrancoAngeli, Milano

Manovich L (2013) Software takes command. Bloomsbury Academic, New York

Arduini G (2012) La realtà aumentata e nuove prospettive educative. Educ Sci Soc 3:209–216

Panciroli C (2010) Il modello di Museo Virtuale dell'Educazione dell'Università di Bologna. Ricerche di pedagogia e didattica, vol 5

Panciroli C, Pizzigoni FD (2013) A cura di, Il museo come officina di esperienze con il patrimonio: l'esempio del MOdE. QuiEdit, Verona

Panciroli C (2017) Ecosistemi digitali. In: Corazza L (ed) Apprendere con i video digitali. Per una formazione online aperta a tutti, pp 13–32. FrancoAngeli, Milano

Panciroli C, Macauda A (2017) The space as an educational and a didactic tool of interpretation: the example of the atelier of "The child and the city". Ricerche di Pedagogia e Didattica 12:131–140

Rossi PG (2010) Tecnologia e costruzione di mondi: post-costruttivismo, linguaggi e ambienti di apprendimento. Armando, Roma

Rivoltella PC (2014) La previsione. Neuroscienze, apprendimento, didattica. Editrice La Scuola, Brescia

Visitor's Approaches, Personality Traits and Psycho-Physiological Well-Being in Different Art Style Museums

Stefano Mastandrea[✉]

Department of Education, Roma Tre University, Via del Castro Pretorio, 20, 00185 Rome, Italy
stefano.mastandrea@uniroma3.it

Abstract. The aim of this contribution is to address a line of research, conducted in the last ten years, on visitor's approaches to different art styles museums (ancient vs. modern), and the educational aspects regarding the young adult's museum visits experience.

Keywords: Art museum · Visitor's approach · Art styles · Art and well-being · Young adults museum's visits

1 Introduction

Museums are often described as informal contexts of learning, with the potential to offer different kinds of knowledge, from art to history, from science to technology (Bartels and Hein 2003; Nardi 2004). The museum is a place where the imagination is activated, and the curiosity and intellectual reflection facilitated. The museum visit is an opportunity to establish an interactive relationship with the exhibited objects (Antinucci 2004); in this way the process of the construction of knowledge relating to artistic, historical, scientific and technological events is implemented.

One of the museum's functions is also to contribute to the acquisition of the individual and social identity of a community. The works exhibited in a museum are the expression of the identity of a community at different levels: local, regional, national and international.

Museum, according to Nuzzacci (2002), can have three main functions (1) the conservation of art collections; (2) the exhibition of the works in order to make them accessible to the public; (3) the enhancement of the specific identity and the history of its collections through continuous research to increase their completeness and significance. These functions need to be considered altogether; no one of these can be ignored without compromising the role and the identity of the museum.

© Springer Nature Switzerland AG 2019
A. Luigini (Ed.): EARTH 2018, AISC 919, pp. 27–33, 2019.
https://doi.org/10.1007/978-3-030-12240-9_4

2 Visitor's Approach to Different Art Styles Museum

Two researches (Mastandrea et al. 2007; 2009) conducted in four different art museums according to the art styles of the collection hosted (the Borghese and the Braschi museums in Rome vs. the Guggenheim museum in Venice and the National Gallery of Modern Art in Rome, respectively ancient/figurative and modern/contemporary art), showed that visitors of ancient art museums put into action behaviors dictated by motivations, expectations, and interests intent on the acquisition of understanding and knowledge, that is, they took a kind of cognitive approach to the aesthetic experience. The visitors of the Guggenheim and National Gallery of Modern Art, on the other hand, seem to have preferred an emotional, pleasure-seeking approach. The answers provided to various questions (i.e., visitors' expectations, motivations, and satisfactions regarding the visit) describe the experience of Guggenheim visitors in terms of pleasure, of having seen fascinating works, of having been moved emotionally; indicators of a desire to learn about art were present but remained secondary. Concerning personality traits ("openness to the experience" and "sensation seeking"; Costa and McCrae 1992; Zuckerman 1979), no difference between the two groups on the "openness to experience" dimension was found (both groups reported high scores). It seems reasonable that people who go to museums do so with an open mind, an interest in culture, and the desire of acquiring new experiences, no matter the type of museum (Chirumbolo et al. 2014; Furnham and Walker 2001). The difference, on this topic, is probably more between people that go and that do not go to museums (DiMaggio 1996; Mastandrea and Crano 2019), instead of the difference between people who choose museums with different kinds of artistic expressions. Differences on the two typologies of visitors taken into consideration was rather on the "sensation seeking" characteristic and emotion aroused (Mastandrea et al. 2011). People who go to modern art museums are willing to go in search of sensation more than people who go to ancient art museums. This finding can be related to what Feist and Brady (2004) found between preference for abstract versus representative art; we can apply it also to visitors of art museums of the two types considered.

3 Art Museum Visit and Well Being

In another study we aimed to explore difference on visitors' health and well-being (Mastandrea et al. 2018). We confronted a laboratory study with a museum context study. In a first laboratory study, a sort of virtual museum visit was simulated (such as a virtual tour showed on museum websites). Two different slide shows of 15 pictures each, differentiated by the art styles (figurative art, abstract art) and a control slide show (urban-settings stimuli) were presented to 3 different groups of participants. Different measures, physiological (blood pressure and heart rate) and behavioural were used. Findings show that heart rate decrease for the figurative art group only; diastolic blood pressure decrease for figurative and control group. Participants felt more relaxed after viewing figurative art stimuli.

In the second study we wanted to address the topic of restoration during a real art experience in museum settings. The experience of the art in museum contexts should provide more clear evidence to these preliminary laboratory results (Mastandrea et al. 2018). The research aimed to assess, through physiological measurements such as blood pressure and heart rate, whether exposure to art museums and to different art styles (figurative vs. modern art) was able to enhance visitors' well-being in terms of relaxing and stress reduction (Clow and Freedhoi 2006). The research was conducted in the National Gallery of Modern Art in Rome, which hosts two collections, one of the nineteenths- and one of the twentieth-centuries, figurative and modern art, respectively. Seventy-seven undergraduate students with no training in the arts participated in the research. The effects of the two art styles on measures of stress were compared. Psycho-physiological characteristics such as blood pressure and heart rate and self-report liking preference were measured before and after the visit to the two different art styles collections (figurative and modern). Blood pressure comprises two measures: systolic and diastolic. Both depend on the activity of the heart muscle that contracts (systole) and relaxes (diastole) between each heartbeat. Systolic blood pressure can be used to discriminate a state of well-being from a disease (Mancia et al. 2013); at the age of the participants, the SBP may detect emotional changes. Results show that participants exposed to figurative art significantly decreased systolic blood pressure compared to those exposed to modern art while no differences were found in the heart rate before and after the visit. In conclusion it can be said that findings suggest that museum visits can have health benefits, and figurative art may decrease systolic blood pressure.

4   Young Adult Museum Visits in an International Context

The second part of this contribution deals with the young adult's museum experience (Mastandrea and Maricchiolo 2016). From an educational point of view, the museum is often described as an informal way of learning on several topics such as art, history, science, etc. We know, from several researches that museums very often are not very attractive for adolescents and young adults (Fleming 1999; Mason and McCarthy 2008; Mastandrea 2015; Prince and Schadla-Hall 1985). The literature on young adults' participation to cultural events is not very systematic. According to different surveys (in Australia and New Zealand, France, Germany, Italy, USA), the public between the age between 18 and 27 that visited at least one museum during the previous 12 months of the survey are not very numerous. These surveys suggest that in different parts of the world, museums do not look very attractive for many young people.

The aim of the present research was to conduct a survey on a large scale, in different countries (Austria, France, Hungary, Italy, New Zealand, Portugal, Taiwan, USA) to investigate several psychological and pedagogical features like personality traits, motivations, emotions, attitudes and learning processes regarding the museum visits experience.

Measure. An ad hoc questionnaire was created for the research aims to explore socio-demographic variables (including parents education level), personality traits, art education, past visits to museums in the past (with school, family, and autonomously), numbers and typology of museum visited in the last 12 months, the experience of museum visits with particular reference to motivation, attitudes, emotional experience, and learning processes. In this contribution the most important findings will be addressed.

Data Collection. The questionnaire was administered either as paper and pencil or online using the LimeSurvey platform. The paper and pencil questionnaires were administered to students after the end of the classes; completing the questionnaire took an average of about 20 min. Regarding the administration through the LimeSurvey platform, students were invited to participate via email including the link to the online questionnaire.

Participants. Participants were 2,352 undergraduate University students of different Faculties: Education, Psychology and Sociology. We decided to have a homogeneous sample concerning the interest towards that arts and museums, therefore the students from Art Faculties were not considered. Regarding the gender, female was 1,697 (72.3%) and male 650 (27.7%); the age range was 18–31, with a mean of 21.06 (SD 2.5). The numbers of participants were different among Countries.

Results and Discussion. One of the main questions was the visits to museums in the last 12 months. With this question we wanted to have information concerning participants real interest in museum attendance.

Results showed that 24.4% of all participants had not visited any museum in the previous 12 months. As a general data, about one fourth of the sample did not visit any museum in the previous year. But there were quite big differences among countries; participants from Taiwan and Austria reported the highest numbers of visits.

Concerning the typology of museums, modern art museums were visited more than other types of museums (39%), followed by demographic museum (30%), ancient art (27%), archeological sites (21%), house museum (20%), science museum (17%) and architecture (17%). These findings show that the museums of modern/contemporary art were the most preferred; probably because the art language of the artworks hosted in these museums are seen as more similar to the language of the young adult visitors (Mastandrea et al. 2007; 2009).

Participants reported a good level of satisfaction with their museum visits in the last year (M 3.7, SD 0.8, on a 5 points scale). They reported also a good level of learning from the museum visit (M 3.2; SD 0.9); moreover, the memories of these museum experiences were very positive and vivid (Curci et al. 2015; Lanciano et al. 2013).

Participants reported to have received more art training at school than out of school, even if the difference is not so big, respectively 2.86 (SD = .86) and 2.64 (SD = 1.2). The correlation between museum visit and art education was higher for art education received out of school ($r = .278$; $p = 0 .001$) than at school ($r = .181$; $p = 0.001$). The visit satisfaction was correlated both to art education received at school ($r = .158$; $p = 0.001$) and out of school ($r = .125$; $p = 0.001$).

Regarding the question whom the participants visited museums with, it is interesting to note that only 2.7% never visited museum with the school. It means that the education at school offers a good opportunity to visit museums of different typology. We have also to highlight that quite a big percentage of participants, exactly the 15.4% have never visited a single museum with their parents; their parents did not offer them this opportunity. The 21.9% never visit museums with friends, 48% never with the partner and 66.4% never alone.

Overall, the most prevalent emotions associated with museum visit were positive emotions (Mastandrea 2011; 2014). Answers on several emotions (positive: curiosity, interest, pleasure, aesthetic enjoyment, wonder, fun, well-being, and negative: melancholy, boredom, distress) were asked through a 5-point Likert scale (Mastandrea 2017; Mastandrea and Umiltà 2016). All these emotions were entered in a principal component factor analysis using a varimax rotation. All the items were loaded in 2 factors which explained the 54.26% of the variance. The first factor (eigenvalue of 4.48) included all positive emotions (*curiosity, interest, pleasure, aesthetic enjoyment, wonder, fun, well-being*). The second factor (eigenvalue of 1.56) explains the negative emotions (*melancholy, boredom, distress*). Moreover, the aggregation of positive emotions reached a quite high mean score 3.49 while negative emotions 1.68; this findings show that the museum visit experience is mainly an overall positive experience. However, emotions varied according to the kind of museum visited (Mastandrea and Maricchiolo 2014; 2016). Performing a linear regression analysis, with ancient, modern and science museums as the dependent variable and emotions as the independent variables, findings show that specific emotions were related to different kind of museum; for example, the aesthetic enjoyment was present in ancient and modern art museum while fun with the modern art and science museum and curiosity was concerned only with science museum.

A question was dedicated to those participants that did not visit any museum in the past 12 months; it was asked what were the reasons in a multiple choice question with the following answers: lack of interest, lack of opportunity, lack of time, lack of people to go with, lack of information, high price of the ticket, limited hours of opening. These motives were entered in a principal components factor analysis using a *varimax* rotation. The items loaded on 3 factors that explained 60.39% of the variance. The first factor (eigenvalue of 2.02; we call it "External reason") comprised the following items: *lack of time, lack of opportunity* and *lack of people to go with*. The second factor (eigenvalue 1.17; "Internal reason") included items such as *lack of information* and *lack of interest*. The third factor (eigenvalue 1.10; "Museum related reason") comprised the items *high price of the tickets* and *limited hours of opening*. Interesting to note is that participants show also a positive attitude towards museum, but they have no opportunity in terms of people to go with.

The last question we considered was the intention to visit a museum in the next 6 months. The answer was: not at all (9.0%), a little bit (18.7%), somewhat (34.6%), much (22.2%) and very much (15.5%). Compared to the question on the museum visit in the last 12 months the data are very different. In comparison to the about 25% of the sample who did not visit any museum, if the participants were asked about their willing to go to a museum in the next months, even if it is not the same question (in the first case was the real behavior while in the second was only the intention), there is a considerable decrease: only 9.0% do not want to visit museums in the future. Therefore, it is plausible that if participants would have more opportunities in terms of information and people to go with they will consider to go to museum.

Conclusion. In conclusion it can be said that about 75% of the total sample visited at least one museum in the last 12 months and about 40% visited between 2 and 5 museums in a year. Compared to the other data from the several surveys reported in the introduction, collected by other researchers in different countries in the past, the results obtained in our research show quite different and interesting results. Our findings show a sort of inverted direction regarding the museum visit per year compared to previous surveys: in those researches about the 75% of young adult never visited a museum in the last 12 months while from our data we can see that a 25% of participants of the total sample never visited a museum in the last 12 months. Our sample was composed by university students, therefore people that are more interested in cultural activities such as museum visits. On the contrary there is still a 25% of participants that never visited a museum in the last 12 months, therefore some work from an educational point of view has still to be done. What is also surprising is that about the 15% of the total sample never visited a museum in their life with their parents. On the contrary, only 2.4% never visited a museum with the school. Art training and museum visited received at school could be a good opportunity to improve the possibility to have a museum experience in the future. One of the aim of following studies will be to provide indications to school and other educational and social institution to incentivize young people museum visits.

References

Antinucci F (2004) Comunicare nel museo. Laterza, Roma

Bartels DM, Hein GE (2003) Learning in setting than schools. Educ Res 32(6):38–43

Chirumbolo A, Brizi A, Mastandrea S, Mannetti L (2014) Beauty is no quality in things themselves: epistemic motivation affects implicit preferences for art. PLoS ONE 9(10): e110323. https://doi.org/10.1371/journal.pone.0110323

Clow A, Fredhoi C (2006) Normalisation of salivary cortisol levels and self-report stress by a brief lunchtime visit to an art gallery by London City workers. J Holist Healthc 3(2):29–32

Costa PT, McCrae RR (1992) Revised NEO personality inventory and NEO five-factor inventory. Psychological Assessment Resources, Odessa

Curci A, Lanciano T, Maddalena C, Mastandrea S, Sartori G (2015) Flashbulb memories of the Pope's resignation: explicit and implicit measures across differing religious groups. Memory 23(4):529–544

DiMaggio P (1996) Are art-museum visitors different from other people? The relationship between attendance and social and political attitudes in the United States. Poetics 24:161–180

Feist GJ, Brady TR (2004) Openness to experience, nonconformity, and the preference for abstract art. Empirical Stud Arts 22:77–89

Fleming D (1999) A question of perception. Mus J 4:29–31

Furnham A, Walker J (2001) Personality and judgments of abstract, pop art, and representational paintings. Eur J Pers 15:57–72

Lanciano T, Curci A, Mastandrea S, Sartori G (2013) Do automatic mental associations detect a flashbulb memory? Memory 21(4):482–493

Mancia G, Fagard R, Narkiewicz K, Redón J, Zanchetti A, Böhm M, Christiaens T, Cifkova R, De Backer G, Dominiczak A, Galderisi M, Grobbee DE, Jaarsma T, Kirchhof P, Kjeldsen SE, Laurent S, Manolis AJ, Nilsson PM, Ruilope LM, Schmieder RE, Sirnes PA, Sleight P, Viigimaa M, Waeber B, Zannad F (2013) 2013 ESH/ESC guidelines for the management of arterial hypertension: the task force for the management of arterial hypertension of the European Society of Hypertension (ESH) and of the European Society of Cardiology (ESC) Blood pressure 22:193–278

Mason D, McCarthy C (2008) The feeling of exclusion: young people's perceptions of art galleries. Mus Manage Curatorship 21:20–31

Mastandrea S (2011) Il ruolo delle emozioni nell'esperienza estetica. Rivista di Estetica 48 (3):95–111

Mastandrea S (2014) How emotions shape aesthetic experiences. In: Tinio P, Smith J (eds) The Cambridge handbook of the psychology of aesthetics and the arts. Cambridge University Press, Cambridge, pp 500–518

Mastandrea S (2015) Psicologia dell'arte. Carocci, Roma

Mastandrea S (2017) Psicologia della percezione. Carocci, Roma

Mastandrea S, Maricchiolo F (2014) Implicit and explicit aesthetic evaluation of design objects. Art Percept 1–2(2):141–162

Mastandrea S, Umiltà MA (2016) Futurist art: motion and aesthetics as a function of title. Front Hum Neurosci 10:201. https://doi.org/10.3389/fnhum.2016.00201

Mastandrea S, Bartoli G, Bove G (2007) Learning through ancient art and experiencing emotions with contemporary art: comparing visits in two different museums. Empirical Stud Arts 25 (2):173–191

Mastandrea S, Bartoli G, Bove G (2009) Preferences for ancient and modern art museums: visitor experiences and personality characteristics. Psychol Aesthetic Creativity Arts 3(3):164–173

Mastandrea S, Bartoli G, Carrus G (2011) The automatic aesthetic evaluation of different art and architectural styles. Psychol Aesthetic Creativity Arts 5(2):126–134

Mastandrea S, Maricchiolo F (eds) (2016) The role of the museum in the education of young adults: motivation, emotion and learning. Roma Tre Press. ISBN 978-88-97524-83-0

Mastandrea S, Maricchiolo F, Carrus G, Giovannelli I, Giuliani V, Berardi D (2018) Visits to figurative art museums may lower blood pressure and stress. Arts Health 1–10. https://doi.org/10.1080/17533015.2018.1443953

Nardi E (2004) Museo e pubblico: Un rapporto educativo. Franco Angeli, Milan

Nuzzaci A (2002) I musei pedagogici. Kappa Edizioni, Roma

Prince D, Schadla-Hall RT (1985) The image of the museum: a case study of Kingston upon Hull. Mus J 85:39–45

Zuckerman M (1979) Sensation seeking: beyond the optimal level of arousal. Erlbaum, Hillsdale

Mastandrea S, Crano W (2019) Peripheral factors affecting the evaluation of artworks. Empir Stud Arts 37(1):82–91

New Interoperable Tools to Communicate Knowledge of Historic Cities and Their Preservation and Innovation

Andrea Giordano[✉]

Department of Civil, Environmental Engineering and Architecture (ICEA),
Università di Padova, Via Venezia 1, 35100 Padua, Italy
andrea.giordano@unipd.it

Abstract. This research underlines the close relationship between communication, representation and sharing data; it shows also how new media gather these three features linked to cultural sites. The scientific analysis can be improved by multimedia processes starting from a correct data acquisition (archival documents, laser scans and photogrammetric surveys) and passing through the organization of information in 3D models that can be implemented by interoperable BIM platforms. The new digital opportunities make the researcher able to communicate the data through the design of apps, interactive systems for multimedia devices, web platforms and immersive reality, another important goal is the integration of the 3D models as means of analysis in conservation processes of the architectural asset.

Keywords: Transformation visualization · HBIM · Interoperability · Multimedia devices

1 Introduction

We have been witnessing the progressive transformation of methods and strategies in the organization of an exhibition, in its design, in the options and in the modalities of communication. Indeed, these changes are affected by the ICT, Information Communication Technology, however, often finding - as we have had the opportunity to say elsewhere (Giordano 2015) - plus a 'spectacularization' of the event, to the detriment of a cultural-educational increase, which should instead aspire. Yet the 'spectacular' characteristics should not be demonized *tout court*, but only if we consider an event improperly transformed into a 'spectacle', with the consequence of looking for or making it trying to stand out mainly the astonishing and sensational aspects; in this regard, it seems fundamental to remember that the etymology of the word 'spectacle' - from lat. *spectacŭlu(m)*, derived from *spectāre* 'to look, to watch, to observe' - directly involves the gaze of an observer as an active part in an exhibition. Nonetheless, new technologies and ICTs have changed several of the factors that contribute to the organization of an exhibition strategy:

(1) the museum, which usually 'turn out to be' the place where collect most of the Cultural Heritage to be enjoyed in the 'spectacle';

© Springer Nature Switzerland AG 2019
A. Luigini (Ed.): EARTH 2018, AISC 919, pp. 34–43, 2019.
https://doi.org/10.1007/978-3-030-12240-9_5

(2) the sense of Cultural Heritage, which today has taken on new meanings;
(3) the cultural and technical skills that contribute to the preparation of an exhibition with tools, contents and outputs;
(4) finally, the role of the observer, who is no longer a mere spectator, in terms of perceptual mode and fruition sensitivity.

2 From *Visualizing Venice* to *Visualizing Cities*

In this *milieu*, therefore, the renewed interest in the disciplines of Representation is evident, not only in the educational-academic field; these disciplines are now involved in the design *tout-court*, both on architectural and urban scale, of a museum narrative, inducing us to reflect and rediscover how the procedures of representation forms are configured as a privileged tool not only for the design and/or measurement and management of what we identify with the terms 'architecture' and 'city' and with the relative protection, but also and above all for their fruition, of a communicative-cognitive nature. This, moreover, to emphasize the importance of visual communication than the verbal and written (or, as we shall see shortly, together with it). The most lucid and articulated modern position around this topic is that of Leonardo Da Vinci (1452–1519) who, in the *Trattato della Pittura*, reiterates the supremacy of sight on hearing, underlining the communicative readiness of an image in reference to a written document. Leonardo's acute considerations on the comparison between painting and poetry have full validity in today's scientific world, but on the other hand they appear outdated, because ICTs allow us to go beyond the limits of space and time. For this reason, even if the only appeal - today possible - to a hyper-textual organization of knowledge can subvert and renew the classical linearity of the text, it is not possible to prepare a digital visualization of the transformations of architecture and the city only through a hypertext. This is where the creation of new processes and codes of visualization, knowledge and communication come into play, making easy and immediate the rapid and accurate analysis of a vast amount of complex and variable data, all aimed at the simultaneous representation of complex problems, urban and architectural. In this perspective it was born *Visualizing Cities*, a research project emanating from *Visualizing Venice* (www.visualizingvenice.org), which involves the University of Padua, Duke University (NC, USA), and the IUAV University of Venice, finalized to the communication of knowledge for the conservation and innovation of historical places, also through 'museum-like' experiences (Huffman et al. 2017).

Visualizing Cities therefore can be considered as a moment of historical research about the city, configuring itself as a process of deepening, in a canonical sense, like the investigation about sources and documents that support a certain urban 'circumstance'. In this regard the disciplinary component related to architectural and urban history remains central, also if alone it is not able to study and analyze a portion of a city or an architecture included in it (Giordano 2017). This happens because it is important to have also an acute contribution that allows to 'decrypt' information and graphic-documentary sources, inserting and linking them in a context that, maybe, does not exist anymore. Indeed, it is possible to find a sort of 'vagueness' of historical sources in order to understand the different contents interpreting them philologically and, simultaneously, tracing their relationship with the present city. This is why everything found in archives, libraries or funds - archival, iconographic and textual documentation often of an exceptional value, not only from a historical point of view but above all for their meanings - has to be 'reworked' in a scientific-methodological path that incorporate all the basics of the disciplines of Representation with the contribution that ICT can give them today. This is the intent that led, therefore, to the creation of an inter-university and international project that, placing itself as initiative in *Digital Humanities*, involves more 'actors' of multidisciplinary origin, in order to generate not simple models or digital maps of the cities, but dynamic models - interactive and interoperable - able to show the process of change and transformation over time, and implementing a new way of communicating and sharing spatial-temporal knowledge, not only for a expert public. Relating in particular to public, using computerized platforms, websites and apps, *Visualizing Cities* 'illuminates' the consistency of urban environments as evolving processes that constantly respond and reflect the change not only in urban and architectural, but also in social-economic, religious, and political terms. Subsequently, the city itself becomes a virtual 'museum', if we consider all the meanings, mentioned above, that contribute to the organization of an exhibition strategy that new technologies and ICT radically transformed.

3   Methodology

From an operative point of view the research embraces a methodology extremely simple, set on three consequential phases:

- identification, gathering and organization of primary and secondary sources;
- data processing and managing;
- the outputs.

Primary sources are all those documents that scholars, intellectuals, theorists or observers produced at the time of the events: according to Storey (1999), "primary sources originate in the time period that historians are studying. They vary a great deal because these data may include personal memoirs, government documents, transcripts of legal proceedings, oral histories and traditions, archaeological and biological evidence, and visual sources like paintings and photographs". Then, in our case, it is fundamental to research archival documents - available in original format or in microfilm, in digital format, or even publishing -, maps, cadastral maps, atlases, drawings, old photos and aerial shots of the city. These sources, witnessing only a subject of investigation concerning the city, must be systematized, *in primis* temporally, in a visual time-line linking each date to the document that, previously digitized, is organized in an *ad hoc* database.

Secondary sources are on the one hand the bibliography relative to the case study, on the other hand the retrieval of all metric and geometric data through traditional, laser scanners, and photogrammetric survey operations: case by case, we will adopt the right strategy to obtain the greatest number of metric/geometric data which, once processed, contribute to the correct achievement of the virtual model of the considered portion of the city (Fig. 1).

Fig. 1. The Eremitani church in Padova (M.R. Cundari). The interactive 3D model of the Eremitani district (E. Fincato, A. Niero, C. Monteleone).

The second operational phase is focused on the data processing and managing. Starting from the geo-referencing of all maps and cartography, a GIS has been set up that manages spatial, quantitative and qualitative data, in order to relate spatial-temporal information to each other: in the specific case (Figs. 2 and 3) of *Visualizing Venice* it has been realized VISU, a HGIS, Historical GIS (Ferrighi 2015). In close relation with the it, we proceed with a 3D modeling, implemented on the basis of information coming from primary sources, to support the historical reconstruction of a specific 'fragment' of city - and secondary - to obtain a virtual model based on the current situation. In the first case, for example (Fig. 4a, b), using perspective restitution procedures, the conditions of sets in the city of Venice, portrayed in perspective, were virtually recreated: this is the case, for example, of the perspective restitution of paintings by Canaletto depicting Campo Santi Giovanni e Paolo (Giordano 2014).

In the second case H-BIM modeling was implemented for the city and for the historical buildings. With this acronym we indicate the Historic Building Information Modeling, which differs from BIM, exploiting it for historic buildings. The features of this mode of 3D modeling consist in the fact that is not pure 'generation of shapes' (metric/geometric/stylistic) but, above all, 'information': in this way, the 3D model loads of multiple data, becoming itself a repository that allows to understand not only the configuration but also the technological, constructive, estimative conformation, not

38   A. Giordano

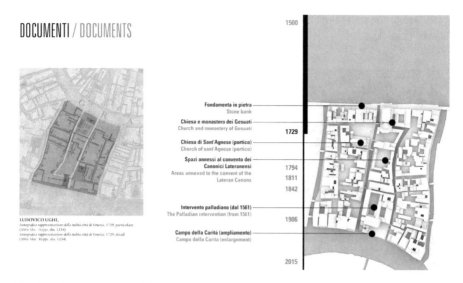

Fig. 2. Primary sources and data elaboration: GIS and timeline. The Accademia insula in Venice – 1700 ca. (L. Galeazzo, E. Svalduz, P. Borin, C. Monteleone, F. Panarotto, I. Friso, A. Ferrighi).

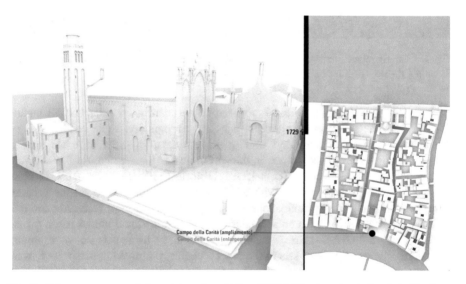

Fig. 3. Primary sources and data elaboration: GIS and BIM. The Accademia insula in Venice – 1700 ca. Visualization of the interactive and interoperable 3D model of Campo della Carità (L. Galeazzo, E. Svalduz, P. Borin, C. Monteleone, F. Panarotto, I. Friso, A. Ferrighi).

to mention the management set-up, of the modeled building. So for both, BIM and HBIM, the valid definition - according to ISO 29481-1:2010 + National BIM Standard - is: "A shared digital representation of physical and functional characteristics of any built object (including buildings, bridges, roads, etc.) which forms a reliable basis for

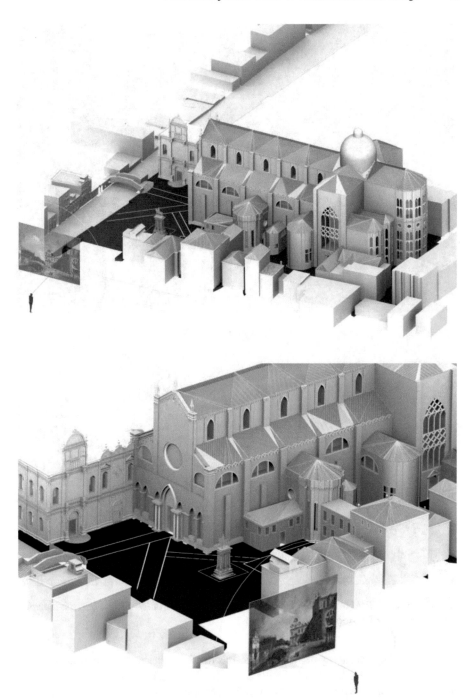

Fig. 4. a, b The scene and virtual reality: the observer standpoint.

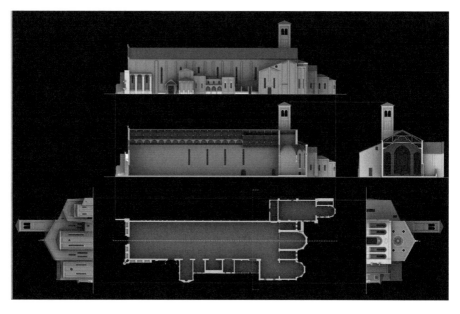

Fig. 5. a, b The HBIM of the Eremitani church and the creation of HBIM families: the monofora of the side facade (P. Borin, F. Panarotto).

decisions during its life-cycle; defined as existing from earliest conception to demo-lition". In both cases the aim is to create a so-called 'as built' model, that it can be considered as an object - although virtual - actually 'built' (Fig. 5a, b). And if the achievement of a 'double' of reality (whether existing or just designed) brings together the two modeling 'processes' - and not just 'programs' -, we wanted to experiment with the new procedure, proposed by Murphy already in 2009, considering H-BIM as: "…a new system of modeling historic structures. It begins with remote collection of survey data using terrestrial laser scanning combined with digital cameras". Through this so-called 'scan-to-BIM' procedure it is possible to process the data coming from the laser scanner or photogrammetric survey operations, translating each point-cloud into a BIM model (including recording, merging/stitching, cleaning) with automatic object recognition thanks to a so-called 'semantic labeling', in an attempt to integrate: according to Yang et al. (2016), "… both semantically rich models from Building Information Modeling (BIM) and Geographical Information Systems (GIS) to build the detailed 3D historic model". As we know this process of labeling passes through the previous creation of so-called 'families': it is basically the creation of a sort of library of objects (whether they are constructive, decorative or structural elements) to be automatically and semantically associated with what is being modeled, operating the data taken from the survey operations. Moreover, always in the context of a semantic modeling, it was possible to load the model of the information related to the changes occurred on the site or on the single considered architecture, being able to 'fill' the virtual clone also of all related information, for example the state of conservation and decay in which it occurs simultaneously for every architectural aspect and/or urban site (Borin et al. 2015). The last step was to make this 'hyper-computerized' model 'navigable', so that all the data, geo-localized, can be a solid basis for further developments related to: humanities (art, literature and music - paintings, images, photos, statues, music, novel); religion (charity, orders, hospitals); municipal administration (public buildings, political decisions, demography); daily life features (people, shops, crafts, entertainment, myths and legends); thematic examples (evolution of urbanization, popular myths and legends, wars, the history of buildings). In this way all the historical events related to the urban space can be organized in a flexible and scalable platform.

Fig. 6. Interactive sliders, to overlap virtually historic maps to the actual situation of the city (Campo Santi Giovanni e Paolo).

4 Outputs and Conclusions

The third and last phase, the one concerning the outputs, has therefore seen the realization of:

1. Interactive and interoperable models representing the 'time going by', using BIM models of buildings to obtain dynamic views of urban transformations as well as what can not be seen because inaccessible;
2. 3D prototypes to 'touch' a reality no longer existing;
3. Images and videos, these organized following precise story-telling;
4. Interactive sliders, to virtually superimpose historical maps on the current situation (Fig. 6);
5. Augmented reality/mixed reality, to 'increase' the perception of the current surrounding environment through sensors that also reproduce sounds, images, videos, 3D models or GPS data for tourism purposes (Fig. 7).

Fig. 7. Interactive models to augment the reality. (C. Monteleone, I. Friso)

All these outputs are then implemented to stimulate the implicit tendency of our cognitive system to perceive and easily remember the architectural and urban transformations of a city.

Acknowledgements. The research activity presented in the paper is coordinated by Paul Jaskot (Duke University), Andrea Giordano (University of Padova), Guido Zucconi (IUAV University), founded by Caroline Bruzelius (Duke University) and Donatella Calabi (IUAV University).

References

Huffman LK, Giordano A, Bruzelius C (eds) (2017) Visualizing Venice. Mapping and modeling time and change in a city. Routledge, London and New York

Giordano A (2017) Mapping Venice. From visualizing Venice to visualizing cities. In: Piga BEA, Salerno R (eds) Urban design and representation. A multidisciplinary and multisensory approach. Springer, Cham, pp 143–151

Yang X, Koehl M, Grussenmeyer P, Macher H (2016) Complementarity of historic building information modelling and geographic information systems. In: The international archives of the photogrammetry, remote sensing and spatial information sciences, vol. XLI-B5. 2016 XXIII ISPRS Congress, 12–19 July 2016, Prague, Czech Republic

Giordano A (2015) Guardare/Fruire una mostra: il ruolo delle nuove tecnologie di rappresentazione. In: Giordano A, Rossi M, Svalduz E (eds) Costruire il Tempio, Carpi 2015

Ferrighi A (2015) Cities over space and time. historical GIS for urban history. In: Brusaporci S (ed) Emerging digital tools for architectural surveying, modeling, and representation. IGI Global, Hershey

Borin P, Giordano A, Cundari MR (2015) Which survey for which digital model: critical analysis and interconnections. In: Le vie dei Mercanti XIII International Forum – Heritage and Technology, June 2015, p 28

Giordano A (2014) La città dipinta di Canaletto, tra espansione dello spazio e visioni dinamiche. In: Buccaro A, De Seta C (eds) Città mediterranee in trasformazione. Identità e immagine del paesaggio urbano tra Sette e Novecento. Collana: Polis, 6. Napoli: Edizioni Scientifiche Italiane

ISO 29481-1:2010 + National BIM Standard (2010)

Murphy M, McGovern E, Pavia S (2009) Historic Building Information Modelling (HBIM). Struct. Surv. 27(4):311–327

Storey WK (1999) Writing history: a guide for Students. Oxford University Press, New York

Leonardo da Vinci (1817) Trattato della Pittura, Differenza infra poesia e pittura. In: Manzi G (ed) Stamperia de Romanis

New Media Exhibit at the Musée des Civilisations de L'Europe et de la Méditerranée

Case Study: Virtual Journey Through the History of the FSJ, Marseille

Franz Fischnaller[(⊠)]

Accademia Albertina di Belle Arti di Torino, Turin, Italy
franz.fischnaller@albertina.academy

Abstract. This paper discusses the design of a digital heritage exhibit entitled: Virtual Journey through the history of Fort Saint Jean (VJ-FSJ) project, a multi-disciplinary technology-based exhibit, which combines mixed media display systems, holographic imaging, video mapping on 3D printed models, augmented audio-visual environments, digital heritage narrative and storytelling embedded within physical and virtual architecture. Based in Fort Saint-Jean (FSJ), a historical and architectural site of Marseille, the exhibit planned to open in 2018, at the Musée des Civilisations de L'Europe et de la Méditerranée (MuCEM) in Marseille, France.

Keywords: DH museum exhibitions · Cultural heritage ·
Digital narrative and storytelling · Education in museums · 3D printing ·
Video mapping · Holographic techniques · Mixed media installation ·
Cross-disciplinary research and design practice

1 Introduction

1.1 Project Research Framework and Background

VJ-FSJ project is one of the outcome of an ongoing interdisciplinary research project namely: New generation interaction in cultural heritage: immersive, interactive exhibitions within the field of art and architecture in museums (NGI-CH research).

Carried out by Fischnaller [1], as artist and researcher in residence at the Institut d'études avancées - Exploratoire Méditerranéen de l'interdisciplinarité of Aix-Marseille University (IMéRA) [2], in partnership with the MuCEM [3] and MAP Laboratoires [4]. The project outcomes were the result of a collaborative effort and support of institutions and experts from the fields of history, archaeology, architecture, design, social science, engineering, technology, storytelling, communications and management. The paper begins by presenting a general overview of the research, project background, goals, aims, historical framework, heritage context, and then moves on to address outcomes such as: case study (exhibit design), methodologies, technologies and design solutions, then closes with conclusions and lessons learned.

© Springer Nature Switzerland AG 2019
A. Luigini (Ed.): EARTH 2018, AISC 919, pp. 44–52, 2019.
https://doi.org/10.1007/978-3-030-12240-9_6

1.2   Research Context - Motivation – Goals

In the past two decades, museums have seen rapid changes in terms of the application of information technology, which has been used to represent their collections in new ways. Museums provide a public service and communicate through collections associated with information and applications which create new visions of museum issues for the visitors [5].

NGI-CH research focuses on the intersection of Art, humanities and social sciences (history, archaeology and cultural studies) combined with leading technologies and advanced new digital media tools with the aim of empowering engaging and creative design solutions for the fruition of content and cultural heritage experience [6]. A major motivation behind the research is to envision experimental approaches for exhibit design solutions that can provide context for enhancing the creation of high quality digital heritage experience [7]. Digital Heritage [DH] works that can strengthen the European capability for the creation of new forms of digital entertainment and engagement based on cultural heritage, and that can promote the use of new technologies such as new media and new modalities of access making DH more accessible to the global community [8]. NGI-CH responded to the challenge of how technology and digital media can be effectively used to support the museums practice for the growing need to create DH experiences with richer interpretations of the past and enhancing the audience's knowledge improving the communicability and the fruition of cultural contents for a new understanding of the past while attracting a wider audience and public engagement [9].

1.3   Trans-Disciplinary Approach and Multi-disciplinary Design Methodology

NGI-CH project principles are based upon connecting different forms of knowledge and shared practices across the field of art, design, cultural heritage, humanities, social sciences with emphasis on the use and intersection of leading technologies applied to the field of Cultural Heritage. The research embraces a interdisciplinary-based research methodology combined with cross-disciplinary fertilization, strategic collaboration and knowledge creation [10].

1.4   Audience Mission

VJ-FSJ stems from the criteria that audience development plays a crucial role for successful museum management strategies [11]. A major exhibit mission is to stimulate users' learning and curiosity and to go beyond the picture (cultural assets, artifacts, heritage buildings, etc.) related to FSJ and to explore the story in/behind and around this iconic cultural heritage site [12]. In this vein, this paper discusses the NGI-CH research and VJ-FSJ project (outcome).

2   Cultural Heritage, Context, Phases and Framework

2.1   Project Summary

The VJ-FSJ project consists in the design of a permanent exhibit representing the history and evolution of FSJ, a military complex and protagonist of the history of Marseille with a focus on five historical periods (49 BC, 1423, 1660, 1943, today). The design is articulated into two components:

A. Time&Space Media Exhibit: Exhibit design and scenography, design for tech solutions, mixed media installations, projection and display systems.

B. FSJ-Digital Animation: Script & Storyboard, concept and content design (3D digital narrative, storytelling, animation and video mapping on 3D printed models).

2.2   FSJ Historical Patrimony and Cultural Heritage Context

Considered a historical monument since 1964, the FSJ, built in 1660 by Louis XIV at the entrance to the Old Port is today one of the three sites that constitute the MuCEM [13]. A complete restoration carried out between 2009 and 2013 allows the public to visit the historic building, as well as the new building, named J4, designed by architects Rudy Ricciotti and Rolland Carta [14]. Since 2013 FSJ is linked by two thin bridges to the historical district Le Panier, and to the MuCEM [15]. Although the foundations of the FSJ date back to the end of the twelfth century. The construction of the fortification on the site of the former Commanderie of the Hospitallers of St. John of Jerusalem dates back to the sixteenth century, when Louis XIV decided to strengthen the city's defenses [16]. It has retained a military relevance for more than three centuries. During the Second World War, German troops stored there a munitions depot whose explosion at the liberation of Marseille caused the destruction of many old buildings [17]. Vestiges of the very first Greek occupied around 600 BC were discovered in the site of the FSJ [18]. FSJ owes its name to the commanderie des Hospitaliers de Saint-Jean de Jérusalem established the extension of the mound Saint-Laurent, towards the end of the 12th century [19].

2.3   Historical Periods of the Exhibit Content

The content of the exhibit is based on the exploration of five historical periods: 49 BC: the arrival of the Romans and the taking of the city to the Greeks by Jules Caesar; 1423: The sacking and looting of the city by the Aragonese; 1660: The recovery of the city by Louis XIV and construction of Fort St Jean; 1943: the German occupation; Today: contemporary period with the construction phases of the MuCEM (time lapse).

2.4   Project Phases, Accomplishment and Current Stage

VJ-FSJ Project was conceived in twelve phases; Phases 0 to 4 were completed during IméRA research residence, Phases 5 to 9 were completed by the author of this paper under the direction of the MuCEM. Phases 10 to 12 are currently ongoing and being carried out by and under the direction of the MuCEM.

3   The Exhibit: Concept and Design Solutions

3.1   Concept

VJ-FSJ project was conceived to deliver the design of a permanent exhibit representing the history and evolution of FSJ with focus on five historical periods, offering visitors a holistic audio visual multilayered journey through key historical moments that shaped the history of Marseilles [20]. The design combines digital content with mixed media installation, technology and tools embedded in real and virtual architecture [21].

3.2   Component A: Time&Space Media Exhibit

Exhibit Design and scenography, tech solutions, media installations, projection and display systems:

3.2.1   Exhibit Space: Gallérie des Officiers FSJ – MuCEM

The exhibit has been designed ad hoc for the Galerie des offices located in FSJ, a linear structure articulated by seven rooms, and an open walkway. The rooms are arranged one beside the other connected through a one way only front open corridor (entrance and exit) with a view to the Olt Port of Marseilles. Total area of the exhibit space: 155,76 m^2, public circulation area: 85,7 m^2, backstage area: 70,06 m^2. Each room has a useful area for the public ranging from 15 to 22 m^2 maximum. In room O.01 to O.04 is installed a fix showcase occupying half of the entire room; in Room O.05 are installed four columns in with historical artefacts are exposed and from this room the public can enter to Room O.06 and Room O.07.

3.2.2   Design, Scenography and Technology: Room O.01 to O.07

For each room has been designed specifically technological settings and installations, seamless integrated within the required architectonic framework (Table 1).

All rooms ROOM O.01 to O.06 are cached by boxes cladded with MDF painted in black at the top and bottom of the existing structures to frame the vision to each specific projection system to create a feeling of immersivity.

SOUND REINFORCEMENT SYSTEM: Audio Digital Matrix 8 IN – 8 OUT, Multichannel Power amplifier – 8 OUTput, Loudspeakers Wall Mount, Mediaplayer Audio 2 CH.

AUDIO/VIDEO CONTROL SYSTEM: All audio-visuals are connected to a server to be able to command the entire setup of the sequences of the different areas of the exhibit. Network Integrated Controller, RS-232 ports/IR/Lan/I-O7Web server, Power Supply, Tabletop Touch Panel 10″, Power Supply, Rack Mount Switch – 24 Ports, Customer Application Software Plus Graphic Mask, Steel Enclosure Rack.

Air conditioning: 2000 m^3/h, Power of 6.2 KW, exhaust duct passage in existing false floor.

Table 1. Tech setup for each room

ROOM O.01	Front projection 300 × 196 cm, plasterboard painted dark gray; Retroprojection video (280 × 40 cm) on polymer film stuck stiched on the vetrin from the insidein the height according to the glare of the children; 3D printed landscape model in the size of 320 × 170 × 10 cm, centered at the elevated groundfloor in front of the screen with vertical Video-mapping on the model; Framing vision and cache by boxes at the top and bottom of the window, cladded with black MDF. 3 Videoprojectors: HD PANASONIC PT-RZ670, lentille ultra wide angle - Panasonic 0.38–0.40:1 - ET-DLE030, 4 mm thin Transparent Polymer Glass for retroprojection (Size: 280 × 40 cm); Super player 4K Datapath x4, audio: Yamaha ma2030
ROOM O.02	Front video projection on the back wall (300 × 196 cm), plasterboard painted dark gray; Framing vision and cache by boxes at the top and bottom of the window, cladding with MDF in black; 1 Videoprojector – HD – PANASONIC PT-RZ670, Wideangle Lens 0,7; Super player 4K, audio: Yamaha ma2030
ROOM O.03	3D printed model of FSJ (280 × 157 cm) placed on a 50 cm high platform in the back of the preinserted showcase; Double video front-projection in panorama on screens (600 × 134 cm) arranged at 90° and inclined; Framing vision and cache by boxes at the top and bottom of the showcase; 2 Videoprojectors - HD PANASONIC PT-RZ670; lentille ultra wide angle - Panasonic 0.38–0.40:1 – ET-DLE030; Super player 4K Datapath x4, audio: Yamaha ma2030; Projection on 3D Model with special lighting system
ROOM O.04	Front video projection (300 × 196 cm) on inclined wall at the back of the room with HD PANASONIC PT-RZ670; LENTILLE ULTRA WIDE ANGLE - Panasonic 0.38–0.40:1 – ET-DLE030; Super player 4K Datapath x4, audio: Yamaha ma2030
ROOM O.05	4 Glass-vitrines distributed in the room that host the only 4 physical (originals) historic artefacts
ROOM O.06	3 video panoramas made of 12 vertically installed 12 "video monitors LCD 55" Seamless – 3.7 mm BEZEL, independent structure in front of the existing showcases; Total image resolution: 12960 × 1920 px; Super player 4K, Datapath DL8 and 3 Datapath x4, audio: Yamaha MT3 and 4 Yamaha VCX3 F
ROOM O.07 Tunnel 15 m	4 Holographic projection system (Pepper's Ghost) made of 4 self-supporting metallic modules (Element Z) integrating each 1 Monitor LCD 75″ - SAMSUNG ME75B mounted at the upper part and reflecting on the Beamsplitter (70/30) at 45° in the size of 115 × 200 cm; arranged in the tunnel at a distance of 250 cm each; the 4 layered projected "magic illusion" is visible by small openings in the door. The video sequences are distributed on the Super player and the 4K Datapath x4

3.3   Component B: FSJ-Digital Animation-Script & Storyboard

3.3.1   FSJ-Digital Animation Periods - Script & Storyboard, Sequences (SQ)

Room O.05 - Historical Objects (Selection by Myriame Morel) installed in 4 columns, NO ANIMATION (Table 2);
Room O.06 - Time: 2 min - 1 Sequence (SQ)
SQ.1: *TIMELAPS of J4,* Timelaps Construction of the MuCEM (J4);
Room O.07 | Tunnel - Time: 2 min - 4 Sequences (SQ)
SQ.1, 2, 3 and 4: Time laps Period I, II, III and IV- All 4 scenes are combined to one unique animation in 4K, distributed on 4 beam-splitters mounted in 45°.
TRANSITION Room O.01 – O.04 - 30 s each
[M] flying from left to right with blur effect in the background (flash-fwd to next Period/room); animation total time: 19:30 min.

Table 2. Concept and content design in periods and sequences for the Digital Narrative, storytelling, Video, 3D digital animation and video mapping on 3D printed models

PERIOD I: 49 BC	PERIOD III: 1660
Room O.01: Time: 3 min, 4 Sequences	Room O.03: Time: 3 min, 3 Sequences
SQ.1: The birth of the Avatar Massalia [M]	SQ.1: Marseille appropriation by Louis XIV
SQ.2: The Greek in Marseilles	SQ.2: Virtual Journey through time and space
SQ.3: The Siege of Marseilles (Massilia)	SQ.3: The Creation of FSJ
SQ.4: Marseilles before the 1423	
PERIOD II: 1423	**PERIOD IV: 1943**
Room O.02: Time: 3 min, 4 Sequences	Room O.04: Time: 3 min, 2 Sequences
SQ.1: The chains of the port of Marseille	SQ.1: The eighteen century-A glance to FSJ "End/middle of the 19th to the 20th century"
SQ.2: The conquest of Marseille by the Aragonese	SQ.2: The second world war: FSJ, Marseilles
SQ.3: Marseille rises from the ashes	
SQ.4: "Le prêche de Marie Madeleine"	

3.3.2   Content Distribution, Narrative Walk Through, Visitors Experience

In room 1, 2, 3 and 4 the content of 49 BC, 1423, 1660, 1943 is projected through video animation; Room 1 and 3 has additional video mapping on 3D printed models. In room 5, four glass-columns are installed containing each one physical, historical artifact; room 6 (contemporary period) displays the time lapse of the construction of the new Building of the MuCEM, J4 on a 360° set-up of vertically positioned screens, while 4 holographic displays are installed in room 7 (Tunnel) representing the journey through the four historical periods of the FSJ, namely "FSJ through time and space". The digital content is synchronized in sequences in and throughout the rooms. Each sequence lasting 3 min with a 30-s video transition with a countdown that provides the necessary time for the visitor to walk into the following room, experiencing a continuous flow through the narration of the content. Each room within the gallery presents a different technological setting and installation, however the design has been conceived as a continuous and interconnected holistic installation.

4   Conclusions and Challenges

This paper can be considered as input in this continuing process or research and design. It is not a blueprint of 'how to do it', but I hope that it offers some useful areas for reflection that this project research and case-study can deliver meaningful insights and to contribute to what is already a robust cross-disciplinary research and practice, already taking place within the field of cultural heritage. The nature and character of the Gallérie des officers in addition to other factors inherent to the exhibit space presented several challenges and problem to solve in order to obtain coherent, aesthetic and efficient design solutions. A major challenge in a research is usually time, this was also the case in this project. Regardless the short term provided to deliver the project, specifically, phases 5 to 9, the expected outcome was delivered on time and with the quality requested, fulfilling all the premises the objective demanded. Another challenge faced in this project was to build an efficient approach to work with the museum organizational structures, their method and model, the practice to develop their exhibitions. This had implied to add a considerable time investment that was needed to incorporated in the pre-existing project development time line (Fig. 1).

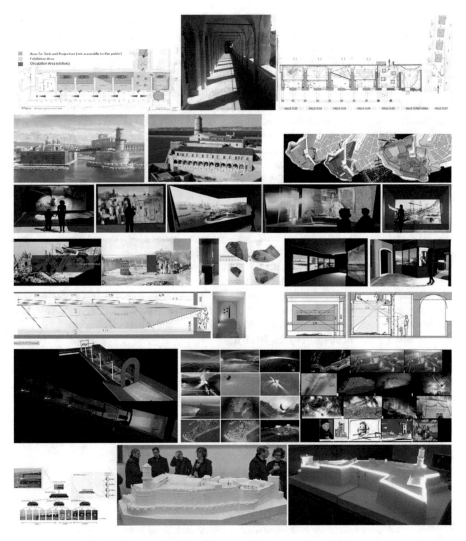

Fig. 1. Imges related to the setup and content in exhibit space

Acknowledgements. The authors wish to thank different institutions and people involved in the development of the research case and study presented in this paper.

References

1. Fischnaller F. IMéRA - Institute for Advanced Study. https://imera.univ-amu.fr/en/resident/franz-fischnaller
2. Fondation IMéRA - Institut d'études avancées - Aix Marseille Université. https://imera.univ-amu.fr/

3. Mucem—Musée des civilisations de l'Europe et de la Méditerranée. http://www.mucem.org/
4. The power of intersection across art, architecture, interactive design, science and technology. http://www.map.cnrs.fr/?p=3984
5. Fahy A (1995) New technologies for museum communication. In: Hooper-Greenhill E (ed) Museums Media, Message. Routledge Publisher, London, p 82
6. Imera.univ-amu.fr.   https://imera.univ-amu.fr/sites/imera.univ-amu.fr/files/agenda/files/colloquefranz_fischnaller_mucem_imera_20_mai_2015_0.pdf
7. Fischnaller F (2016) Immersive Museums … THE ARCHITECTURE OF THE SENSES - Technology in the Arts, Humanities and Cultural Heritage. (Sorbonne Universités - LAMS - VALE – POLYRE), giornale Kermes, Nardini Editore
8. H2020-REFLECTIVE-2014-2015. https://ec.europa.eu/research/participants/portal/desktop/en/opportunities/h2020/calls/h2020-reflective-2014-2015.html#c,topics=callIdentifier/t/H2020-REFLECTIVE-2014-2015/1/1/1/default-group&callStatus/t/Forthcoming/1/1/0/default-group&callStatus/t/Open/1/1/0/default-group&callStatus/t/Closed/1/1/0/default-group&+identifier/desc
9. Museums & Society 2034: trends and potential futures – PolicyArchive research. policyarchive.org/12355.pdf. Version 1.0 December 2008
10. Gamsau.map.archi.fr. http://www.gamsau.map.archi.fr/wp-content/uploads/ColloqueFranz-Fischnaller-MuCEM-IM%C3%A9RA-20-mai-20151.pdf
11. Museums for visitors: Audience development - A crucial role for successful museum management strategies Christian WALTL. http://intercom.museum/documents/1-4Waltl.pdf
12. https://imera.univ-amu.fr/sites/imera.univ-amu.fr/files/agenda/files/colloquefranz_fischnaller_mucem_imera_20_mai_2015_0.pdf
13. Fort Saint-Jean (Marseille). https://en.wikipedia.org/wiki/Fort_Saint-Jean_(Marseille)
14. From the J4 to the fort Saint-Jean. http://www.mucem.org/en/your-visit/j4-fort-saint-jean
15. Le Mucem. http://www.mucem.org/le-mucem
16. Are the Mucem and the Fort Saint-Jean the same thing? http://www.mucem.org/en/are-mucem-and-fort-saint-jean-same-thing
17. Marseille History 4: Under the Nazi occupation. http://www.theprovenceherald.com/marseille-history-4-under-the-nazi-occupation/
18. History of Marseille. https://en.wikipedia.org/wiki/History_of_Marseille
19. A Marseille, Bouches-du-Rhône, depuis plusieurs décennies, le fort Saint-Jean. https://www.inrap.fr/fort-saint-jean-commanderie-des-hospitaliers-4610
20. Les nouvelles technologies dans les domaines des arts et du patrimoine culturel. http://www.mmsh.univ-aix.fr/news/Pages/flash-013.aspx
21. Séminaire L'éclat, le geste et la société - Approches interdisciplinaires - Séminaire Sorbonne Universités

Digital Technologies in Heritage Conservation. Methods of Teaching and Learning This M.Sc. Degree, Unique in Germany

M. Hess[1(✉)], C. Schlieder[2], A. Troi[3], O. Huth[3], M. Jagfeld[3],
J. Hindmarch[1], and A. Henrich[2]

[1] Institute for Archaeology, Heritage Science and Art History, Humanities
Faculty, University of Bamberg, Am Zwinger, 96047 Bamberg, Germany
mona.hess@uni-bamberg.de
[2] Faculty of Information System and Applied Computer Sciences,
University of Bamberg, An der Spinnerei, 96047 Bamberg, Germany
[3] Faculty of Design, Coburg University of Applied Sciences and Arts,
Am Hofbrauhaus 1, 96450 Coburg, Germany

Abstract. A new master's degree commenced in 2017 at the University of
Bamberg. The purpose of the M.Sc. Digital Technologies in Heritage Conservation is to impart theoretical and practical knowledge and develop competence
in critical assessment and object-oriented solutions. The aims, curriculum and
methods of teaching will be discussed in this paper.

Keywords: Architecture · Engineering · Computer science ·
Heritage conservation · Digital technologies · Curriculum ·
Object-based learning (OBL)

1 Introduction

In his 'Ten books of architecture', Vitruvius Pollo requires that an engineer-architect
must be multi-talented with a diverse education with knowledge based on *fabrica*
(craftsmanship) and *ratiocinatio* (intellectual work), enabling him to judge all other
crafts. He specifies ten fields of knowledge in which an architect should be well versed:
writing, drawing, geometry, arithmetic, history, philosophy, music, medicine, law and
astronomy (Vitruvius 2001).

The new master's joint programme M.Sc. in 'Digital Technologies in Heritage
Conservation' aims to provide students with a similarly diverse set of skills, encompassing digital craftsmanship and intellectual skills along with many of Vitruvius'
original set, adapted to today's high-tech world. Its contents and mission will be
described in this paper.

A. Luigini (Ed.): EARTH 2018, AISC 919, pp. 53–63, 2019.
https://doi.org/10.1007/978-3-030-12240-9_7

2 Brief Introduction to Object Based Teaching and Learning (OBL) in Heritage Conservation

It has been observed that the use of object-based teaching and learning (OBL) as a form of 'student-centred' and 'activity-based learning' will be beneficial to students as a method of internalising and retaining theoretical and applied knowledge (Marie 2011). Object-based teaching and learning as a methodology, used in conjunction with university collections, can benefit teaching across many disciplines and departments (Hannan et al. 2013).

Furthermore, the combination of OBL with new technologies – such as those introduced in this Masters programme - contributes to active and experiential learning experiences and will help students to understand the issues involved in the digital and physical diagnosis and reproduction of an object. Kolb's research is strongly linked to pedagogies of active and experiential learning, which sees hands-on engagement with the object of study as key to personal meaning-making and the long-term retention of ideas (Kolb 1984).

Other research based at University College London uses a variety of methods to gauge relevant benefits for learners by using museum objects during OBL (Chatterjee et al. 2015). Object-based learning in connection with new digital technologies has also been discussed by (Loy 2014) which proposes using 3D printing in the classroom to create a new learning environment for students in design education, enhancing creative output.

Tiballi describes the use of OBL in higher education as a method for better cognitive and affective processing, and for learning through interaction with an authentic or even reproduced object. OBL increases observational skills, contextual knowledge, and empathetic imagination of the students, in particular, 'haptic engagement, which includes tactile, kinaesthetic, experiential and embodied knowledge, requires a student to become fully immersed in the learning environment' (Tiballi 2015).

The beneficial effect for learning can also be observed in the interaction with museum artefacts and on-site examination and digitisation of historic buildings, and are integrated into the new M.Sc. Programme which is outlined from Sect. 3 onwards. OBL for teaching digital technologies in heritage has already been successfully applied in the UCL Bachelor of Arts and Sciences (BASc) and its interdisciplinary elective 'Technologies in Arts and Cultural Heritage'. In the BASc module, OBL has been very effective in promoting the successful acquisition of subject-specific knowledge and technical skills in the domain of digital workflows for heritage conservation (Hess et al. 2017).

3 Development of the New M.Sc. Degree Program

A new Master of Science degree 'Digital Technologies in Heritage Conservation' commenced in October 2017 at the University of Bamberg, Germany. The aim is to expand the teaching expertise of the heritage science department alongside the well-established Master of Arts degree in Heritage Conservation. Over the last several decades, graduates of the M.A. Heritage Conservation program have gone on to fill many important positions in the heritage sector, and the same is hoped for the newly created M.Sc. The aim is to provide new students with an interdisciplinary skill set at the interface between heritage and technology.

The new degree course is taught and coordinated between the University of Bamberg and Coburg University of Applied Sciences and Arts, and is supported by The Free State of Bavaria and the Technology Alliance Upper Franconia (Technologie Allianz Oberfranken/TAO, https://www.tao-oberfranken.de/). It is also part of the 'Digital Campus Bavaria' campaign for the overall integration of digital competencies into the curriculum (https://www.km.bayern.de/studenten/digitalisierung/hochschule-digitaler-campus.html). Both the University of Bamberg and Coburg University of Applied Sciences and Arts enjoy an excellent reputation in the monument, object and engineering sciences as well as in application-oriented digital technologies (University of Bamberg 2017).

4   Profile of the Degree Program

The new Master's programme 'Digital Technologies in Heritage Conservation', unique in Germany, offers an overview of the abilities and limits of current and developing digital technologies and provides the opportunity for students to gain in-depth knowledge in the application of digital technologies. The aim of this programme is to impart theoretical and practical knowledge in four main areas: **computer science** (cultural informatics and media informatics), **digital technologies** (2D and 3D optical surface imaging, measurement and analysis, monitoring, simulation), **engineering principles** (building physics and structural analysis) and **sensor technology** for a great variety of measurements in heritage conservation, as well as developing competence in **critical assessment and object-oriented solutions**. While the focus is on the assessment of heritage buildings and collections, students will also develop an awareness of the importance of cultural assets considered as knowledge stores, historical sources and components of regional identities. Details of the modules are outlined in Sect. 5 below.

The programme was developed after observing the need for technology developments in the heritage and engineering sector. Therefore, the teaching objectives include attention to state-of-the art technology developments towards integration into heritage. Today, innovative digitisation and imaging technologies (often developed first in engineering and industrial quality-control) are being adopted in the fields of heritage conservation, monument preservation, museum studies and management as well as for the protection of cultural assets. The digital recording of buildings and objects is now as much a part of the preservation of historical monuments as the permanent monitoring of the condition of a building with intelligent sensor systems. Finite-element modelling (FEM) supports the assessment of structures and decision making for eventually needed repair, while numeric analysis in building physics can help avoid long-term degradation and increase the energy efficiency and usability of buildings.

The interdisciplinary team of teachers, the unique vocational profile and the modern technical equipment on this programme guarantee state-of-the-art training. The course is designed to accept a heterogeneous group of people with the aim to deliver a tailored-program for each student. Whilst in this degree course the topics and activities are naturally centred on historic materials, objects and buildings, the methodology of OBL also benefits joint projects involving students across multiple disciplines, departments and universities.

Admission to this program requires a German or equivalent University degree with a standard period of study of at least six semesters (three years) and 180 ECTS points in a related programme. These include architecture, civil engineering and courses in the fields of preservation of historical monuments and cultural property, restoration as well as building conservation and construction, computer science and applied computer science, digital humanities, archaeology, geography, surveying, archival studies, cultural management and communication design. Non-German native speakers require a B2 language qualification.

Completion of the two year M.Sc. (Master of Science) degree will give students a postgraduate qualification with high employability, equip them to take on highly technical tasks in heritage conservation and cultural management and allow them to fill professional roles where built heritage and museum issues interface with technological developments. The first graduates from this programme will be in the workforce in 2020.

5   Degree Structure

This M.Sc. course consists of core, advanced and specialist module groups, as well as a practice-based final master's thesis (Fig. 1). The core modules introduce the topics relevant to the application of digital technologies in heritage conservation while the advanced and specialist modules allow students to focus on specific areas:

- **Digital modelling in heritage conservation** (subjects include: Building Information Modelling, Support Structure Simulation)
- **Digital analysis and monitoring in heritage conservation** (subjects include: Preservation Sciences, Buildings Physics, Monitoring, Structural Analysis)
- **Digital networking and knowledge distribution in the preservation of monuments** (subjects include: Web Technologies, Computing in the Humanities)

The specialist modules expand on the content of the advanced courses. The degree culminates with a practice-based master thesis centred on questions in heritage conservation, working in conjunction with institutions and authorities.

5.1   Digital Technologies in Heritage Conservation, University of Bamberg

Introduction to Digital Technologies in Heritage Conservation: In this module, a general introduction to heritage conservation including the theoretical basis are taught as a prerequisite for working in the field. The digital technologies relevant for the preservation of historical monuments are presented, and placed in a scientific-historical context. Both the potentials and limits of their application are discussed (Fig. 2a).

Core modules (45 ECTS-points)
Digital cultural heritage technologies, informatics in monument preservation, digital object recording, digital archiving, signal analysis, building physics in cultural heritage, virtual modelling.

Advanced modules (15 ECTS-points)
Digital modelling, digital analysis/monitoring, information & network technologies, knowledge transfer & public engagement.

Specialist modules (30 ECTS-points)
Digital modelling, digital analysis/monitoring, information & network technologies, knowledge transfer & public engagement.

Master's thesis (30 ECTS-points)
Practice based project

Fig. 1. Degree structure of the M.Sc. Digital Technologies in Heritage Conservation – a Master's degree with 120 ECTS.

Object Recording: The students receive a theoretical and practical introduction to the potentials and methods of digital object recording. The objectives of fit-for-purpose data acquisition in heritage are explained, and different methods of recording compared. In addition to teaching the principles of optical imaging technologies (photography, photogrammetry and 3D scanning) and the practical demonstration of standard imaging techniques available on the market, digital heritage case studies and the use and workflows of these technologies in real-world scenarios are presented. Students are given the opportunity to develop their skills in a practical residential course, where the process of learning by doing is encouraged (Figs. 2b and 3a).

Fig. 2. Students receive theoretical classes in core modules, here digital reproduction and practical introductions to technical equipment in the classroom. **a:** Motivation for 3D printing and reproduction based on 3D imaging is explained in a lecture. **b:** A group of students are taught how to use a total station/theodolite for 3D point-based imaging. **c:** A student is observing a thin-section of mortar in the microscope at an exercise in conservation science.

Virtual Modelling/Processing of 3D Data: The data collected at the residential course of the object recording module forms the basis for this module in which the principles of data processing are introduced. Here, the students are introduced to a variety of techniques including modelling point clouds to CAD files, the photogrammetry workflow, automatic geometry extraction, metric inspection, and the creation of virtual reconstructions. Pathways to 3D printing and to the development of Virtual Reality apps are taught (Fig. 3b).

Digital Modelling: The students deepen their knowledge of digital and mathematical 3D modelling. The module is divided into two parts: In the first, an introduction to Building Information Modelling (BIM) and its connection to infrastructure planning are taught at Coburg University. The second part of the module takes place at the University of Bamberg and includes virtual and parametric modelling with a focus on Heritage BIM (HBIM).

Digital Archiving: One of the aims of the new master's program is to bridge the gap to the digital humanities. In this course, students are introduced to the potential of digitisation and the fundamentals of collecting, archiving and disseminating data, as well as digital and metadata standards used in cultural heritage and 'memory institutions' such as museums, archives and heritage authorities. The course is supplemented by an excursion to the nearby State Archives as well as lectures from guests active in digital heritage activities.

Conservation Science: This module relates in-depth knowledge of conservation and restoration sciences from an art technology and materials science perspective. The focus is on the analysis of available analytical technologies, the anamnesis and diagnosis of material changes of historical substance and their therapeutic options, as well as inventory and condition recording by cartographic documentation and stratigraphic analysis (see Fig. 2c).

Fig. 3. Students experience the full gamut of on-site work and lab-based processing. **a:** Students work hands-on in an 18th century church near Bayreuth, Bavaria, and are using 3D fringe-projection scanning on an epitaph. The target for 3D laser scanning of the complete church is also visible. The practical projects allow learning by doing, and students are faced with problems they have not encountered in the classroom. Errors are part of the learning process. **b:** Students working in the computer cluster on the creation of architectural plans and sections from 3D laser scans of the same church.

5.2   Digital Analysis and Monitoring in Heritage Conservation, Coburg

Signal Analysis and Measurement Technology: The students are familiarized with the possibilities of sensor technology and common measurement data acquisition systems and receive an introduction to the further treatment of measurement signals.

Building Physics for Heritage Buildings: The module aims at preparing students - with and without previous knowledge of building physics - for the special questions posed by heritage buildings. The focus is therefore on understanding phenomena, identifying the influencing factors, selecting the right models and recognising the degree of precision of results –always based on practical examples. Active discussion within the course is encouraged, preparing students for the interdisciplinary discussion they will encounter in their professional lives.

Historic Materials and Structural Engineering: Students are given an introduction to the history and development of structural engineering techniques, and obtain an overview of the construction and chemical properties of historic materials. Students learn to model, identify and calculate static determined load-bearing structures such as beams and arches and they are to be able to describe the principle load bearing behaviour of walls, slabs and domes. An introduction to the computer modelling of bearing structures is given and geotechnical aspects and the influence of subsoil on damage and durability are taught.

Structural Simulation: Digital Modelling and Structures: This module deals with simulation of structures. Teaching includes the examination of historical structures by state-of-the-art calculation methods i.e. framework simulation programs and the Finite-Element-Method, in order to clarify the load-bearing behaviour and determine the causes of existing damage. Planning of necessary repair measures in accordance with the special requirements of historic monuments is also taught, with a focus on historical roof constructions, arches and vaults (Fig. 4).

Building Physics – Evaluation and Refurbishment: The theory imparted and the simulation tools introduced are applied directly to a practical refurbishment example in Bamberg. Among other things, static and dynamic thermal simulations at building and component level are compared, hygrothermal phenomena are simulated with different software packages and results evaluated. Damage models (salts, humidity) are applied to both monitored and simulated data (Fig. 5).

Monitoring and System Analysis with Digital Data Acquisition Systems: Students acquire in-depth knowledge of the potentials of analysis and building monitoring using digital recording systems, non-destructive or low-destructive object and material analysis, the connection between damage mechanisms, damage progression and the preservation strategies at the monument, and the connection between building construction and object monitoring. These competences are applied to structures such as vaults, historical roof constructions and natural stone masonry buildings (Fig. 6).

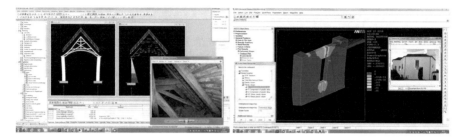

Fig. 4. Student exercises, Baroque church. **a:** Framework model of the collar beam roof without centering beam, horizontal thrust of the roof acts on the outside wall. **b:** Finite – Element – Model (FEM) of the wall; the horizontal thrust causes vertical cracks.

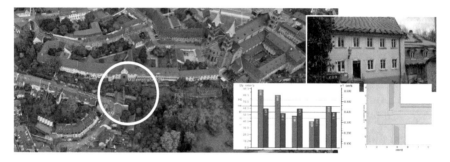

Fig. 5. This historic building in Bamberg the served as an application case for the students. The figure shows the building and its urban context, evaluation of different refurbishment options and an example for a hygrothermal evaluation of a building detail.

5.3   Computer Science, University of Bamberg

The part of the curriculum devoted to computer science has been designed by two co-authors of this article who teach in the fields of cultural informatics and media informatics. In the planning phase, they addressed a number of critical questions. Which competencies in computing should the graduates possess? What skill level should they achieve? Which topics from computer science are most relevant to the digital workflows of heritage conservation? Finally, and related to the first three questions: How many of the program's total course hours should be assigned to computing?

While there are established curricular recommendations for undergraduate courses in computer science, most notably the Body of Knowledge compiled by the professional organizations ACM and IEEE-CS (Computing Science Curricula 2013), there is much less material available for the design of interdisciplinary programs. To the best of our knowledge, no recommendations exist for a computer science curriculum that is integrated into a heritage conservation program, neither at the undergraduate nor the graduate level.

It was clear, however, that the computer science curriculum should prepare graduates for a rapidly changing professional world. The curriculum designers wanted the graduates to become expert users of digital technologies, who do not just master tools but who also have a thorough understanding of fundamental concepts and methods from computer science. This understanding enables them to design digital workflows in heritage conservation, to bridge small gaps in such workflows by writing code, and to participate as a knowledgeable partner in the requirement analysis process for software solutions addressing larger gaps. In essence, this is how the planning team answered the questions of competencies and skill levels.

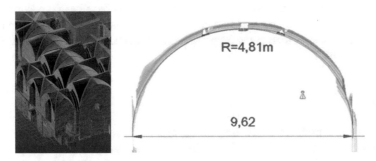

Fig. 6. The terrestrial 3D-scan of a gothic vault and the resultant derivation of their construction principles.

The selection of topics from computer science was guided by their importance for the field of heritage conservation. An obligatory general introduction to computing, which includes fundamental concepts such as relational data bases or operating systems serves as the base of the curriculum. All other courses are electives. With respect to the choice of teaching methods, it proved especially helpful that the curriculum designers could draw on extensive experience with an existing program, the M.Sc. Computing in the Humanities. Although the two programs have different objectives, they share the challenge of introducing students to computing who have not been trained in a natural science or an engineering discipline. For those students, the single most important form of teaching are the lab sessions, in which they work on practical problems such as data modelling or programming tasks.

For the **general introduction into computing** in the first semester, an existing introductory course for students from the humanities was revised specifically to serve the digital technologies in heritage conservation program. This concerns in particular the part dedicated to information systems (e.g. digital libraries, geoinformation systems). A new teaching concept was developed for the practical exercises in the lab sessions, which impart special competences, e.g. a Linux introduction in the context of treatment of operating system concepts.

In the second semester, the students choose one of two electives. Option 1 is a **programming course** that teaches a first object-oriented programming language using examples relevant to the domain of heritage conservations. Version management systems and build management tools are also covered. Direct feedback showed that GUI programming is particularly time-consuming for the students. In the next teaching cycle this content will be replaced by a deepening of the basic programming part.

Option 2 is a course on **web technologies**. The exercises were planned to suit the special requirements of digital technologies in heritage conservation. One unit was designed with concepts of Data-Driven-Documents (D3.js), which by default are only considered for simple 2D graphics, and are now combined with 3D visualizations based on the JavaScript library A-Frame. Furthermore, a stronger focus was placed on the use of Content Management Systems (CMS) for information portals.

The third semester provides a further set of electives: a course on **digital libraries and social computing**, a course on **computer graphics and animation**, and an **introduction to media informatics**. New teaching concepts have been developed for the lab sessions of all these courses. In summary, the students spend slightly more than 15% of their total work load in the program on computer science, that is, 19 ECTS from a total of 120 ECTS.

6   Conclusion

This paper has introduced a new degree program in 'Digital Technologies in Heritage Conservation' with direct connection to technological developments. The programme answers the needs of specialists at the interface of heritage conservation and technology.

It opens up opportunities to teach digital technology skills that are of use in the cultural sector and beyond. There is still, however, a challenge in selecting the appropriate methods for teaching and learning in the context of an ever-changing and fast moving technological environment, where existing technologies are constantly evolving whilst new techniques are being introduced from other fields such as engineering, computer science and medical imaging.

With an increasing demand in the cultural heritage sector for the use of innovative digital technologies to aid institutions in fulfilling their research, preservation and public engagement remits, it is vital that heritage professionals are educated in these new techniques. Similarly, it is also important that technology experts are made aware of the particular issues faced by the heritage sector. Graduates of 'Digital Technologies in Heritage conservation', the future stakeholders in the heritage field, will be aware of the potentials of new technologies and methodologies for cultural heritage and will be able to encourage and facilitate knowledge exchange in both directions.

Acknowledgements. The activity presented in the paper is part of the Digital Campus Bavaria and 'Bayern Digital' program by the Bavarian State Government, and Technology Alliance Upper Franconia. We would like to thank Prof. Dr. Holger Falter and Prof. Dr.-Ing. Stephan Breitling for the first concepts and grant application in the year 2015 that provided the opportunity to put this programme into practice under the co-authors joint development and under the lead of Prof. Dr. Mona Hess, University of Bamberg since October 2017. Photographs of students are reproduced with their kind permission.

References

Chatterjee HJ, Hannan L, Thomson L (2015) An Introduction to object-based learning and multisensory engagement. In: Engaging the senses: object-based learning in higher education, pp 1–18. Ashgate

Computing Science Curricula (2013) Final report of the Joint Task Force of the Association for Computing Machinery and the IEEE-Computer Society

Hannan L, Chatterjee HJ, Duhs R (2013) Object based learning: a powerful pedagogy for higher education. In: Boddington A, Boys J, Speight C (eds) Museums and higher education working together. Ashgate, Farnham, pp 159–168

Hess M, Garside D, Nelson T, Robson S, Weyrich T (2017) Object-based teaching and learning for a critical assessment of digital technologies in arts and cultural heritage. ISPRS Int Arch Photogrammetry Remote Sens Spat Inf Sci XLII-2-W5:349–354

Kolb DA (1984) Chapter 2: the process of experiential learning. In: Experiential learning: experience as the source of learning and development, 1 edn. Prentice Hall, Englewood Cliffs

Loy J (2014) eLearning and eMaking: 3D printing blurring the digital and the physical. Educ Sci 4:108–121. https://doi.org/10.3390/educsci4010108

Marie J (2011) The role of object-based learning in transferable skills development. UMAC Journa 3:187-190

Tiballi A (2015) Engaging the past: haptics and object-based learning in multiple dimensions. In: Hannan L, Chatterjee HJ (eds) Engaging the senses: object-based learning in higher education. Ashgate, Farnha, pp 57–75

University of Bamberg (2017) Master of Science "Digital Technologies in Heritage Conservation." https://www.uni-bamberg.de/ddt/ma-digitale-denkmaltechnologien/. Accessed 28 Jun 2018

Vitruvius (2001) Vitruvius: "Ten books on architecture." Cambridge University Press

Visual Heritage

Structure from Motion Systems: Application Possibilities in Education and Cultural Heritage. New Approach Methods to Education and Preservation

Marco Felli[✉]

DICEAA | Department of Civil, Construction-Architectural,
Environmental Engineering, University of L'Aquila,
Via Giovanni Gronchi 18, 67100 L'Aquila, Italy
marco.felli@graduate.univaq.it

Abstract. This paper aims to show the important role of Structure from Motion Systems in the fields of education and cultural heritage. Starting from an introduction about the Structure from Motion Systems and their development in the last years, there will be shown the modes of operation and some of the possible uses of this approach according some advantages.

In particular, the use of these systems is suggested by the quick resolution of knowledge, representation and surveying problems. The possibility to create 3d models from simple pictures gives the advantage of managing the models with semi-automatic methods and software, which require simple and, differently from other devices in the other representation approaching methodology, cheap and comfortable instruments, as smartphone, cameras, laptops. The development of applications for this kind of devices let a large use of this approach among a lot of people, in particular as an instrument for cultural and historic education for children.

Keywords: Education · Cultural heritage · Preservation · 3d models

1 Introduction. Structure from Motion Systems. Brief History and Development

Structure from Motion (hereinafter called "SfM") Systems represent one of the final steps of the development of technologies for survey activities; their important purpose is the restitution in the 3d-space of the focused objects' points and also the related positions of the shooting devices from a series of pictures.

SfM Systems use collinear equations, which create a correlation between the points of the support in which the image is created (slab/camera film/camera sensor) and the 3d-coordinates of the object's points; through the bipolar geometry, the software which use SfM systems are able to find in the 3d space the position of the photographic grip point. Using this method more times in both "directions" (from picture to 3d-model through collinear equation, so to grip points through bipolar geometry, and then the reverse way), the device is able to create the model of the pictured object.

© Springer Nature Switzerland AG 2019
A. Luigini (Ed.): EARTH 2018, AISC 919, pp. 67–75, 2019.
https://doi.org/10.1007/978-3-030-12240-9_8

The development of this kind of approach is mostly recent; indeed, the first experimentations were complicated and required expensive instruments. One of the first photographic systems was the Rolleimetric: this instrument comprised a desktop, printer and a graphics tablets, thanks to which all the analogic information of the picture were processed; the manual identification of homologues points among the pictures took a lot of time, so the use of this system wasn't so widespread. Thanks to the development of calculators, technologies in general (for example the improvement of instruments for acquiring images, the development of digital cameras and their distortion corrections) and, in particular, the creation of feature extraction algorithms, now we are able to use this kind of approach in a semi-automatic way. These algorithms are the same which are used for the elaboration of panoramic photos in smartphones and cameras (Fig. 1).

Fig. 1. Example of panoramic photos (Felli 2017)

The "more comfortable" approach and using of this technology represents the most important benefits and advantages of this kind of approach: thanks simple pictures (taken for example from cameras or smartphones or other devices) using automatic or semi-automatic software, we are able to recreate a 3d model of simple objects in the 3d space for different fields of application.

The most important thing to know in this kind of survey is the possibility of using simple object, as smartphones or cameras, for taking picture around an object and creating its virtual 3d-model with available software. This comfortable approach let us to analyze and depict complex objects, architectures, sculptures etc. and also to create smaller "copies" of the object we want to analyze thanks to 3d-prints. This aspect can be very important in lot of fields: in this paper, our target is to underline the importance in education and preservation of cultural heritage.

2   Application Possibilities in Preservation

Thanks to its comfortable and quick use, the SfM system can be used in lots of fields; one of these possibilities is the preservation and its facets as architecture, archaeology, geomatics and landscape in general.

In cultural heritage, the SfM approach in survey operations can improve in an easily way the preservation of important things, as sculptures, architectures and archaeology areas. In particular, the comfortable and easy-accessible method can give perfect restitutions of objects through an easier, cheaper and quicker way than the traditional ones.

As shown in Fig. 2, one of the possible purposes of this method is the creation of point clouds, which can be useful for the creation of surveys, with 3d texturized models, orthophotos, renderings; also, the point cloud could be exported in other software as a reference for different types of modeling, for example in the structural models. This method can be used for complex architectures (or in cases in which we don't have laser scanner), but also in other fields in which the photogrammetric and 3d-models are required, for example for sculptures and archaeology ruins.

Fig. 2. Mission San Jose y San Miguel Aguayo, San Antonio, Texas. Screenshot from the software (*Agisoft Photoscan*) (Felli 2017)

2.1 Case Study in Preservation

In this section, we are going to analyze SfM System's use for a restoration project thesis in architecture. The case study is the church of San Sebastiano in Rosciolo De' Marsi of the 15th century, province of L'Aquila, in central Italy. The church has several important historical architectural elements which preciously characterize the building in the contextual area. The main access is a portal with a decoration upon the architrave, with frescoes in the lunette and a single round window on the top. The interior of the church is half divided with a wall, which was realized during the fifties after the collapse of few parts of the building for reopening the church for religious purposes. In the counter-facade we can see a precious fresco, realized in 1564 (there is the date of the work) in decay conditions.

The church, in ruined conditions, caused by a series of destroying earthquakes in the 20th century, was hardly accessible: the roof is collapsed in some parts and the external walls are in ruined, with no resistance to eventual seismic actions (Fig. 3a).

a)   b)

Fig. 3. Church of Saint Sebastiano in Rosciolo De' Marsi (AQ, Italy), 15th cent. (a) pictures of the church, interior and exterior (b) the drone used for the survey, the screenshot of the application, the drone during the survey

The particular situation of the building, with collapsed parts, requires a detailed survey: the difficulty related to reach this target without laser scanner has been solved thanks to SfM System.

The chosen support is a drone, of X Quadricopter typology, with four Brushless electric engines and speed regulatory PWM 400 kHz of 30 A. The drone, remote controlled, had a photocamera; in this case, a smartphone Motorola Moto G with own camera of 15 MP has been used; with a hotspot connection generated by the phone itself, and with the application Mobizen, the phone has been controlled in remote from a laptop (Fig. 3b). The support of the camera is a Gimbal with two degrees of freedom to be regulated before the fly. After the calculation of the GSD (Ground Sample Distance, as the parameter which explains the resolution of a single restitution according the relation among the dimensions of the frame and the building, and also according the focal distance of the camera, the dimension of the pixels and also the distance from the building), which is 0.13 cm/pixel (so each pixel represents 1.3 mm of the true object), the fly has been designed according the best conditions of illumination during the day: generally, the used time for the survey consist in about seven hours, then the effective time about three ones.

After the realization of different pictures according the designed itinerary, and inserting other pictures took manually, there are used some software for the data elaboration.

With the software Agisoft Photoscan Professional, thanks the recognition of remarkable points, it has been possible individuating the realized pictures in the 3d space. Once the pictures were aligned, the software created the first *sparse* point cloud, with no details, but able to give a first and quick check to the result. In the following phase, the software realized a more detailed elaboration, and created a *dense* point cloud, whose points became the vertex of the surfaces of the mesh. After texturized the mesh, the software created the orthophotos with the restitutions of each façade of the building (Fig. 4). The texturized model, furthermore, is also exported as an object for 3d restitutions.

Fig. 4. Church of Saint Sebastiano in Rosciolo De' Marsi (AQ, Italy), 15th cent. Restitution of the main façade (Felli 2016)

Thanks to the photogrammetric survey, the restoration project starts from a detailed knowledge about the structure and the form, with lot of studies about the architectural elements (Fig. 5); also, from this survey it is possible analyze the decays of the surfaces at a deepened level.

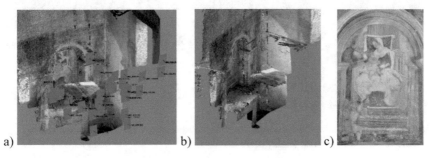

Fig. 5. Church of Saint Sebastiano in Rosciolo De' Marsi (AQ, Italy), 15th cent. (a) and (b) different views of the point cloud of the altar with frescos; the software identifies the provisional scaffolding (c) final restitution of the frescos

3 Application Possibilities in Education

The education in the last centuries improved also the relations between educational aspects and technologies. Nowadays, one aspect of the children's upbringing is related to the use of smart object, in particular mobile phones and tablets; also education, in the last years, is using these devices: technological objects, as smartphones, tablets, LIM (Italian acronym for multimedia interactive whiteboard) became important services of teaching in primary and secondary school education. Today, students start learning also thanks to these kinds of instruments in lot of fields, for example in drawing arts. Teaching to draw today is not only the operation of taking pencils and sketching something on papers, but it can consider also the printing of 3d-object from technological and common devices. According this introduction, we can approach to the use of SfM systems also in education, taking as a reference a case study performed to a group of university students.

3.1   Case Study in Education

In January 2017, in Figurative Drawing Laboratory class, at University of L'Aquila, Master Degree in Primary Education Sciences, a lecture about the importance of digital instruments in drawing arts in primary schools has been performed to the students: in particular, according the education of the students as future teachers, SfM System has been introduced as a possibility of education for children in drawing arts. After the introduction of the method and an explanation about the processes for creating virtual 3d-models, the class tried to apply for different example objects. In particular, a group of students tried to create the virtual 3d model of a person (Fig. 6), in front of the class, then the other students had been divided in different couples for each object to be reproduced in 3d model.

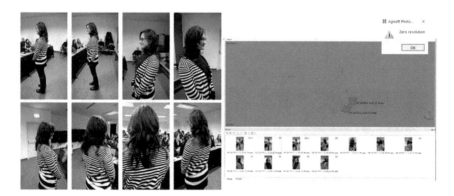

Fig. 6. Pictures around the person to be reproduced as a 3d model (left), then the attempt on the software (*Agisoft Photoscan*) (right) (Felli 2017)

After the explanation of the method, during the break between theory and application part, all the students downloaded a free-source software (recommended during the lesson) for their own smartphone, laptop or tablet.

The first group of students tried to create a virtual model of a colleague; as shown in Fig. 6, after the realization of pictures around the person, the students tried to create the model on a laptop, with the software *Agisoft Photoscan*. In this case, the software didn't create the point cloud (the software aligned only two pictures, but the minimum number of pictures for the points' placement in the 3d space is at least three), because, during taking the pictures, the students had made a series of mistakes: in particular, taking also in consideration the bad lighting conditions, the focus of the photos in some cases was not correct, and they didn't perform the minimum number of pictures which let the software to recognize the key points in the frames (in Fig. 6, on the right side, there is the screenshot of the software with the error "zero resolution" after the command of point cloud generation).

Differently from the previous case, a group of students succeeded to create a model. Taking as reference object a key ring with some small object (a puppet and a small Tour Eiffel, with a "coffee key", Fig. 7a), they realized more pictures around the objects (in this case 21), in a way that the software (also in this case *Agisoft Photoscan*) recognized the key points, so it was able to align the frames in the 3d space; after the aligning, it created first the point clouds (first the sparse and then the dense ones), then elaborated the texturized mesh. In this case, the resolution of the model was not high, because the available time of the exercitation didn't allow the students to perform more detailed processing (Fig. 7b).

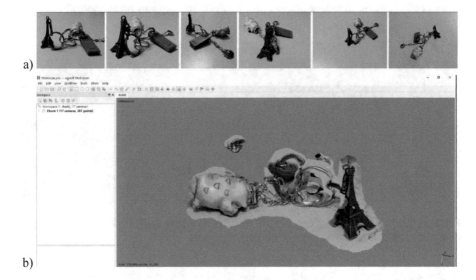

Fig. 7. One of the used objects during the exercitation (a) some of the used pictures (b) the 3d model of the object in the software *Agisoft Photoscan*

At the end of the exercitation, the students had a debate about the potential use of this approach in education applications. They learnt the importance and the easy access to this kind of resources, the comfortable "requirements" for using it; also they enjoyed, as children can enjoy with the application of this methodology in arts primary classes (of course in a training with the teachers or parents).

4   Approaching Both Preservation and Education: Possibilities

As seen in the previous paragraphs, the SfM systems could help the studies in preservation and improve the possibilities in education. In some cases, this kind of approach could interest both fields at the same time, taking advantage from the educational projects conducted in primary, secondary and high schools. In this case there are a lot of possibilities: students can do studies and final presentations about local historic and important "objects": SfM, and so virtual 3d models, for example could be used for represent and describe architectures, sculptures and historic objects in general; in this way, the students improve different aspects as their capacity of group coordination, creation of relations with local people and, also, to the local context, and interdisciplinary approaching to the study. The church shown in Fig. 8 has been proposed as case study in a project directed to two classes of secondary school: the students, divided in groups, aim to create an illustrative brochure with the history and the description of the church (which is one of the churches in the interested school town) and the precious interior elements, the frescoes: SfM in this case is useful for the representation of the frescoes also as 3d elements, not only in orthophotos.

Fig. 8. Church of Madonna di Loreto (15th century), Magliano De' Marsi (AQ, Italy): general view of the interior and a particular of the chapel frescoes.

Another example of field of application could be also the school-job-alternation in high schools, with the collaboration among schools and local authorities, as municipality, superintendence and cultural associations.

5   Conclusions

SfM systems are one of the possibilities for approaching to the representation of an object, but they also constitute one of the quickest, most comfortable and economic resources; their ease of use, with the technologic aspects and cheap costs, aim to develop an appropriate and smart use of devices, especially in children. Only in this way these systems can constitute a smart and different approach to the knowledge in preservation and education, otherwise they are simply used as games and hobbies.

Acknowledgements. The activity presented in the paper is part of the thesis work of M. Felli in Construction Engineering-Architecture at the University of L'Aquila, "Restoration project of the Church of San Sebastiano in Rosciolo De' Marsi, 15th cent. (AQ, Italy)" (July, 2016). The education case study is part of a lesson of Disegno Figurativo (prof. M. Centofanti with the collaboration of S. Brusaporci and M. Felli), Master Degree in Science of Primary Education, Department of Human Sciences, University of L'Aquila (January, 2017).

References

Bezoari G, Monti C, Selvini A (1992) La fotogrammetria per l'architettura. Liguori Editore, Napoli
Felli M (2016) Restauro della Chiesa di San Sebastiano in Rosciolo Dei Marsi, Master's degree thesis in Architectural Restoration, Master Degree in Construction-Architectural Engineering (Relator: prof. M. Centofanti; Correlators: prof. S. Brusaporci, F. Di Fabio), University of L'Aquila, DICEAA | Dept. Of Civil, Construction-Architectural, Environmental Engineering
Ippoliti E (2013) Valorizzare il patrimonio culturale: esperienze per Ascoli Piceno - Shedding light on the Cultural Heritage: the Ascoli Piceno experience. Roma: Aracne. https://www.int-arch-photogramm-remote-sens-spatial-inf-sci.net/
Ippoliti E, Meschini A, Sicuranza F (2015) Digital photogrammetry and structure from motion for architectural heritage: comparison and integration between procedures. In: Brusaporci S (ed) Handbook of research on emerging digital tools for architectural surveying, modeling and representation, advances in geospatial technologies (AGT) Book Series
Micheletti N, Chandler JH, Lane SN (2015) Structure from Motion (SfM) Photogrammetry, British Society for Geomorphology. http://geomorphology.org.uk/sites/default/files/geom_tech_chapters/2.2.2_sfm.pdf
Sicuranza F (2013) Sperimentazioni di sistemi di structure from motion per la restituzione di apparati decorative. Tesi di Dottorato di Ricerca in Scienze della Rappresentazione e del Rilievo, Università degli Studi di Roma "La Sapienza", Dipartimento di Storia, Disegno e Restauro dell'Architettura. http://hdl.handle.net/10805/2116

Video Games for Learning Projective Geometry: Analysis of Virtual Spaces Through the Disciplines of Representation

Ramona Feriozzi[(✉)] and Alessandro Olivieri

School of Architecture and Design (SAAD), University of Camerino,
Ascoli Piceno, Italy
{ramona.feriozzi,alessandro.olivieri}@unicam.it

Abstract. This work investigates the teaching possibilities of video games, analyzing in particular those video game products that might be of assistance when learning projective geometry. For this purpose, various video games were examined that make use of geometry to create visual riddles that can be solved by gamers only thanks to knowledge of the rules of projection.

Keywords: Video game · Projective geometry · Teaching ·
Descriptive geometry · Edutainment

1 Introduction

"Anyone who tries to make a distinction between education and entertainment doesn't know the first thing about either". These words by Marshall McLuhan are now more appropriate than ever: the idea that entertainment and education are irreconcilable has now been dispelled, and this has led to the increasing confirmation of video games as possible educational means. This re-evaluation took off with Paul Gee, who proposed them as implicit learning models: through experience, without prior study, gamers acquire the rules of the game. The contrast with classical teaching methods is clear. In this context, the present work analyses in particular those video game products that might be of assistance in learning descriptive geometry. In fact, while video gaming is a young sector, its existence is based on the rules of descriptive geometry, which were already set down in 1700.

A video game is an "electronic device that allows for play through interaction with images on a screen". This definition clarifies that the particular aspect of these video games—with respect to other games—resides precisely in the interaction with the two-dimensional images instead of with real objects. In fact, the process of reproducing images on a screen makes use of all the projective principles that allow plane images to be obtained from three-dimensional figures; it is therefore dependent on the rules of descriptive geometry.

This has been demonstrated in the history of this medium. Quickly summarizing the evolutionary path of the sector through some meaningful examples, the link with the discipline of representation becomes clear.

© Springer Nature Switzerland AG 2019
A. Luigini (Ed.): EARTH 2018, AISC 919, pp. 76–85, 2019.
https://doi.org/10.1007/978-3-030-12240-9_9

Pong, one of the first video games on the market, allowed ping pong to be played through a plan view of the gaming table. In fact, the first method of representation used was orthogonal projection, which we also find in later "platform games", that is, two-dimensional games in which one must solve various riddles by jumping on platforms suspended in the air at different levels. Super Mario is probably the most famous example of this type, in which the player has to use the world from a frontal perspective.

Over the years, the complexity of the games has increased together with the spatial dimensions involved. Games in axonometric projection then appeared on the market, an example of which is Q*bert, which presented a pyramid-shaped gaming field of cubes in isometric axonometric view.

Games in perspective were the last to be developed because they required a greater computing capacity. In fact, perspective was and is currently used to simulate an immersive view in first person. This represents a notable change, because it assumes a moving point of view, and not a static one, as in the preceding cases. Games such as Maze Wars were the first to reach the market, presenting essential graphics with halls drawn with black lines on a white background (Fig. 1).

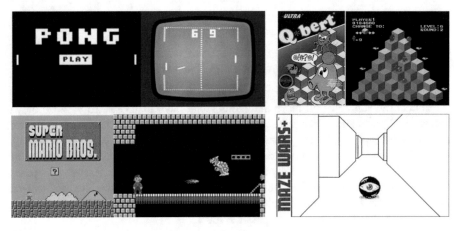

Fig. 1. Screenshots drawn during gameplay from Pong, Q*bert, Super Mario Bros. and Maze Wars.

Therefore, while it is true that descriptive geometry is at the basis of the video games, it is also true that these are not designed with a teaching aim and cannot substitute classical learning methods. The work presented therefore aims to critically analyze and frame a well-defined category of video games using the discipline of representation. Contrary to many others, this category can favor the understanding of rules of projection.

2   Object of Study

The object of the present research is those video games that use descriptive geometry and force the player to reflect on the underlying rules of projection.

The reality represented is never objective: "Reality is perception. Perception is subjective", says a character from the video game *Fez* (see Sect. 3.2). In fact, the process of projecting a three-dimensional object onto a two-dimensional plane depends strictly on the center of projection, that is, the center of view. This characteristic is used in this particular type of video game to create perceptual riddles and ambiguities: reading a two-dimensional representation moves through a critical process to interpret signs that allow the brain to rise to the correct spatial homologue. However, this is not a unique procedure, since a single projection may reflect infinite objects in space (Fig. 2).

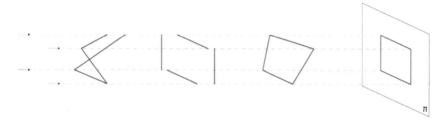

Fig. 2. Planar projection and corresponding spatial homologues.

This is the source of all those ambiguities that have given rise to various known impossible figures and which have inspired artists and mathematicians such as Escher. Learning descriptive geometry commonly occurs through the study of schematic simplification of projective processes. In some cases, the risk is that the student learns the rules of projection without fully understanding the implications. For these purposes, the interactive nature of video games instead is particularly useful since it forces the user to not reach the representation passively, but to make an experience of it, manipulating the scene in order to pass the level.

3   Research and Analysis

The research phase for the video games examined winds up being rather difficult because there is no specific body of literature on the topic. Today's video games are so different and diverse that categorizing them according to only one parameter is impossible. A game is commonly defined based on both the genre, that is, the mechanics of play, and the type of spatiality it involves. In other words, for example, considering the genre, one can distinguish action games, adventure games, strategy games, role-playing games, puzzle games, shooter games, and many others as well. If, instead, one considers the game space and the player's point of view, one can speak of first or third person, isometry or two-dimensions, top down (that is, with a view from above to below), or frontal view, etc.

Amid this variety of genres, puzzle games are the ones that commonly involve visual paradoxes. These are brainteasers in which logical or strategic riddles are proposed. It is not surprising that the titles examined all fall under this category, given that the impossible figures are already graphical enigmas that defy logical thought.

The selected titles were classified according to the projective method used, with a consequent division into two categories: those based on parallel projections, which were in turn divided into orthogonal and axonometric projections, and those based on central projections.

It is important to note that the videogame world is so vast that an analysis of all the titles on the market would be difficult, without considering that isolated instances of impossible figures can be found in every genre and type of game. For these reasons, the choice was made to list only the best-known games and those specifically dedicated to the topic. The most representative video games were examined and for each, a three-dimensional schematic of the types of recurring paradoxical environments was proposed. These reconstructions aim to clarify the visual expedients that create ambiguities on the plane of projection highlighting the projective rules involved.

3.1 Parallel Projection: Axonometric View

The impossible figures represented in axonometric view are probably the most well known as well as the most numerous, and indeed, there are many popular games in this category. These include Monument Valley, a puzzle game released by Ustwo Games in 2014 and the winner of many prizes as well as one of the best-known examples of video games based on projective gimmicks. The main character in the game, princess Ida, has to undertake a journey of penance through mazes with optical illusions and impossible objects. This game, which falls under the category of isometric games, requires modifying the spatial geometry in order to take advantage of the above-mentioned paradoxes.

The example in the figure (Fig. 3) shows one of the first levels of the game, in which a two-level structure is presented for Ida to climb. The main idea is to rotate an L-shaped element on the horizontal plane to connect the two levels with the use of a projective trick. The schematic of the structure shows how the two planes, α and β, situated respectively at heights h_0 and h_1, would seem to lie on the same plane after the central walkway is rotated. The rotation occurs around a vertical axis, so it is paradoxical that a horizontal gangway can create a bridge between platforms situated at different heights.

This can occur only in isometric projection where, using the same projective trick as the Penrose triangle, points separated in space seem to coincide on the plane of projection. At this point, α and β are visually found on the same plane, thereby creating a single surface that Ida can travel on to beat the level.

Before Monument Valley, Sony had already proposed a puzzle game of this type: Echochrome. The dynamics of the game are similar to the previous one, but this time the player rotates the view in order to identify the plane of projection on which the illusion is generated (Fig. 4).

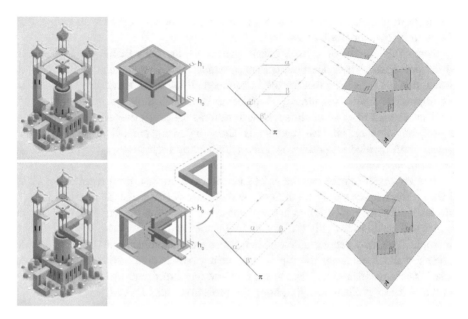

Fig. 3. Geometrical explanation of the visual paradox in the second level of Monument Valley. The graphical connection between the two planes (α and β) is possible because the representation refers to two spatial conditions.

perspective traveling: perspective traveling:

when two separate pathways appear to be touching.   when two separate pathways appear to be touching,
they are

Fig. 4. Echochrome: using the same projective trick as the Penrose stairs, the pathways in the screenshots appear to be touching.

Like orthographic projections, axonometric projections are also used in video games to bring together elements separated in space, thereby reconstructing on the screen the path of the game.

3.2 Parallel Projection: Orthographic View

Among the puzzle games that use orthographic projection, the most famous is certainly Fez. In this game, the player guides an amusing character named Gomez in search of lost fragments of a cube. At first glance, Fez may look like a common "platform game". In reality, the game is more complex. Everything starts when the main character is given a hat - a fez, to be precise - that makes him aware of the existence of a third dimension and allows him to see the other faces of his "flat" village. The world of Fez is, in fact, three-dimensional, but the player experiences it only through four orthographic projections that are none other than lateral elevations of three-dimensional structures. The player's skill consists not so much in jumping without falling from one platform to another, but in choosing which "face" of the world to travel through to get past certain obstacles.

The four views (Fig. 5) show the side elevations of a tower that Gomez has to climb. In the first elevation, the jump is impossible because the platform where the main character is located is too far from the top of the tower. By rotating the point of view by 90°, however, the two steps appear to be close together in the new plane of projection. The schematic of the images provides a reconstruction of the three-dimensional structure of the level. From the axonometric view, it is clear that point A, where the character is located, is rather far from point B; in the same way, the projections of the two points on planes π_2 and π_4 are also well separated. The projections A' and B' on π_1 are instead very close, such that the character can jump to the top of the tower and complete the quest.

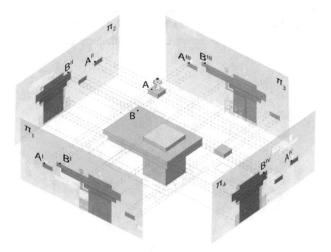

Fig. 5. Fez: schematic reconstruction of the three-dimensional geometry in the first level.

Crush is another video game worth mentioning. The main character, the insomniac Danny, has to jump from one platform to another to reach the final objective of the game, i.e., discover the cause of his insomnia. In contrast to Gomez's world, however, the world in which Danny moves is three-dimensional and appears in perspective view, but the character can only move on some steps by using projective tricks, that is, making the 3D world collapse onto a 2D plane.

For example, the screens (Fig. 6) show two views of the same environment, first in perspective and then in orthographic projection. In the second screen, the two steps, which were first far from each other, appear to touch thanks to a "crushing" of the space onto the plane of projection.

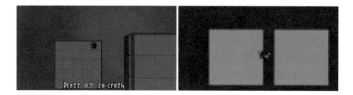

Fig. 6. Fez: Crush: the two screens show the "crush" of the space into the planar view.

In contrast to *Fez*, it is also possible to move to a plan view in *Crush*. This provides the solution to a new series of problems related to the difference in height of the platforms. The two cases analysed for the category of orthographic projections allows the general principles regulating this type of puzzle game to be systematized. These are essentially platform games that exploit parallel projection to bring elements that are otherwise well separated in space together on a single plane.

The schematic (Fig. 7) shows the general projective trick used in these games: the three suspended platforms appear to touch when projected onto precise planes. For example, block A is next to B in the plane horizontal view, while B is near C in the vertical view. Therefore, to move a character from A to C, the player should solve the riddle first on plane π_1 in order to move to B, and then on plane π_2 to reach C.

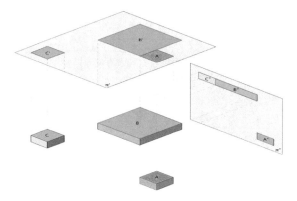

Fig. 7. Generic orthographic projective trick used to overcome horizontal and vertical gaps between platforms.

3.3   Central Projection: Perspective

Among the various titles selected, the decision was made to analyse *Museum of Simulation Technology* (MoST) developed by Pillow Castle. The game was presented for the first time at the Sense of Wonder Night at the Tokyo Game Show in September 2013, but today, despite several years of work, it is still in the developmental phase. MoST mainly uses two types of graphical paradoxes: one can be ascribed to anamorphosis; the other instead uses field depth to vary the perceived size of the objects.

In the first case, a series of planes situated in space do not reveal particular characteristics unless the player is positioned at the right observation point. This is a projection from the player's own point of view: an image projected on various surfaces at different distances will be recomposed in its entirely only when observed from the same centre of projection.

In the second case, instead, the basic principle of central projection is used, according to which monocular vision occurs through a band of projective rays that are centred on the eye of the observer. For this reason, two points pertaining to the same ray will be perceived as overlapping (Fig. 8).

Fig. 8. Museum of Simulation Technology: screenshots showing a pawn assuming different dimensions.

In the game, some interactive elements help the user to solve certain riddles. When the player grabs one of these objects, it is positioned at the centre of the view of the game and thereafter can assume numerous sizes.

When the picture plane is found at a distance d from the observer (Fig. 9), the pawn in the figure will have a height equal to h; moving the frame to distance d', the object will be scaled to height h', and so on. The player is free to modify the size of the pawn without perceiving the change until it rests on the ground and becomes part of the game environment again, scaled based on the choices made. This mechanism allows the objects to be sized as desired to overcome obstacles or height differences.

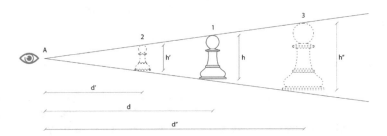

Fig. 9. Schematic reconstruction of the projective trick used to enlarge the pawn: the object is scaled accordingly to the movement of the projection plane but the observer doesn't perceive the changes.

The second case examined is *Perspective* – a free unique first-person platformer, an experimental puzzle that combines a 2D platform and first-person 3D in a single game.

When the game starts, the user is found in a three-dimensional environment allowing freedom of movement. To advance through the levels, however, the user should guide a second avatar that can move only on projections of the 3D environment.

Moving within the solid space, the user has to find and line up blue elements that constitute the plane on which the second avatar is situated. Since the elements are spread throughout the area of the game, only once an optimal point of view is found can the character move along the blue platforms using the apparent alignment of the blocks (Fig. 10). In this way, it is possible to circumvent obstacles that would otherwise be impossible to overcome. This case also uses plane projections and the trick of looking at unaligned objects from a given point of view to make the objects appear contiguous.

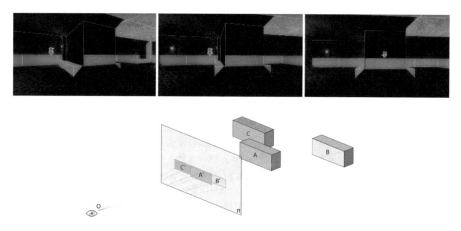

Fig. 10. Perspective. A free unique first-person platformer: above screens of the in-game mode; below the perspective trick used to overcome the gaps between the platforms. The platforms are contiguous on the projection plane.

4   Conclusions

The appeal of video games, especially for young people, derives from the involvement that playing entails. For this, it is not necessary to know how the game is played, because the rules are learned automatically during play and are only later reflected upon. The process of continual discovery stimulates gamers' curiosity while the challenge implied by the riddles helps to tolerate the frustration that inevitably accompanies learning through experience.

The use of virtual spaces and the possibility of manipulating them pushes the player to learn the rules, which, in this type of game, correspond to the rules of projective geometry. Expert players are not the ones who know or have deduced the rules of projection, but rather those who are capable of using them to their advantage.

This capacity is not developed easily with passive study, but rather is an immediate consequence of practice and experience.

With this research, therefore, the aim is not to confirm that is enough to play the above-mentioned titles to learn descriptive geometry. Theoretical study is anyway necessary, but without direct experience, it is likely less understandable and therefore difficult to apply.

References

Migliari R (2008) Geometria descrittiva, vol 1. Metodi e costruzioni. CittàStudi Editore, Turin

Ernst B (1996) Optical illusions. Taschen, Cologne

Penrose R (2002) The emperor's new mind. Oxford University Press, New York

Bittanti M (2004) Per una cultura dei videogames. Teorie prassi del videogiocatore. Unicopli, Milan

Gee JP (2003) What video games have to teach us about learning and literacy. Palgrave McMillian, New York

Pecchinenda G (2010) Videogiochi e cultura della simulazione. La nascita dell' "homo game". Editori Laterza, Bari

Luhan MC (1964) Gli strumenti del comunicare. Il saggiatore, Milan

Moates D, Schumacher G (1983) Psicologia dei processi cognitivi. Il Mulino, Bologna

Disciplines of Representation and Photographic Culture. The Strategic Plan for Photography Development in Italy 2018–2022

Antonella Salucci[✉]

Department of Architecture (Dd'A), Università degli Studi "G. d'Annunzio"
di Chieti e Pescara, Viale Pindaro 42, 62 Roma 9, 65127 Pescara, Italy
antonella.salucci@unich.it

Abstract. The field of application of the study concerns the interference between Photography and the disciplines of Representation in relation to the education to Image and Heritage. The research proposes some reflections on the "Strategic Plan for Photography Development in Italy 2018–2022", drawn up by MiBACT an recently published.

The Photography, in this contest, is regarded as an irreplaceable language, a widespread expressive medium, an agile exploration tool, a privileged digital environment for unreleased visual narration – especially in relation to the spread of social networks – as a matter of fact Photography offers new semantic spaces for both experiencing and educating to tangible and intangible heritage. The contribution will be developed according to two complementary areas: a theoretical-procedural and an applicative-methodological one. On the one end it consists in the analysis of the recent "Strategic Plan of Photography in Italy 2018–2022" of the MiBACT and its potential interactions with didactics and research in the academic field; on the other hand, it deals with the presentation of some case studies related to specific didactic and research experiments carried out within the Degree courses in Architecture and Design.

Keywords: Representation · Photography · Ephemeral heritage ·
Architectural photography · Cultural heritage

1 Introduction

The field of application of the study concerns the interference between Photography and the disciplines of Representation in relation to the education to Image and Heritage. The research proposes some reflections on the "Strategic Plan for Photography Development in Italy 2018–2022", drawn up by MiBACT an recently published.

The Photography, in this contest, is regarded as an irreplaceable language, a widespread expressive medium, an agile exploration tool, a privileged digital environment for unreleased visual narration – especially in relation to the spread of social networks – as a matter of fact Photography offers new semantic spaces for both experiencing and educating to tangible and intangible heritage.

© Springer Nature Switzerland AG 2019
A. Luigini (Ed.): EARTH 2018, AISC 919, pp. 86–94, 2019.
https://doi.org/10.1007/978-3-030-12240-9_10

The contribution will be developed according to two complementary areas: a theoretical-procedural and an applicative-methodological one: on the on end consist in the analysis of the recent "Strategic Plan of Photography in Italy 2018–2022" of the MiBACT and its potential interactions with didactics and research in the academic field; on the other hand, in the presentation of some case studies related to specific didactic and research experiments carried out within the Degree courses in Architecture and Design.

The Strategic Plan for the development of Italian Photography 2018–2022 is the result of a team work of the Ministry of Heritage, Culture and Tourism – MiBACT – in order to: "Protect, enhance and promote photography in Italy as historical heritage and a contemporary language, storage medium, means of expression and understanding of reality, useful for fostering inclusion and increasing individual critical awareness on the part of citizens. The aim is to define a development plan aimed at adapting public actions to the technical and economic changes in the industry and create new opportunities, nationally and internationally, for Italian photography" (MiBACT 2017).

Following the work of the General States, on September 28, 2017 the Joint Working Group of the National University Council of MIUR and of the Higher Cultural Heritage and Landscape Council of MiBACT took office, with the task off formulating "proposals to promote forms of systematic collaboration between the two ministries and to ensure both more effective research, better quality training and more consistent with the professional profiles being defined in the field of cultural heritage" (MiBACT 2017).

The work table set up on an "open and participated" method was launched in the spring of last year with the "General States of Photography" (Rome, 6 April 2017); it continued over several months with a series of public conferences in all the regions of Italy – "MiBACT for photography: new strategies and new views on the territory" – which have agreed to formulate a shared planning line between MiBACT and MIUR, which led to the "Strategic Development Plan for Photography in Italy 2018–2022". With the aim of amplifying the "dissemination and knowledge of photographic culture", the Plan concerns three areas: (1) Photographic Heritage: collections, archives; (2) Contemporary Creation (support for artistic production and enhancement internationalization processes) (3) Education and Training (image education from kindergartens to University and residencies).

In this direction the aim of the contribution is to analyze one of the varied identity of the Representation both in the research and the didactical experience through the exemplification of case studies oriented towards the integration of theoretical and practical multidisciplinary knowledge, including photography.

The photographic representation, the subject of this paper, is among the most effective documentary evidence of the Intangible Cultural Heritage; an irreplaceable medium for investigating the multiple ephemeral creativities of the architectural-cultural landscape, allowing the scholar to make subsequent critical evaluations.

The result is a path of reflection on methodologies of Representation to monitor, communicate, preserve each cultural heritage, both tangible and intangible. The last one in particular – expression of a modification of space, even if temporary – produces perceptual outcomes in time that are always different, connoting fragile and ephemeral originality that can only be surveyed by Photography.

2   The Strategic Development Plan for Photography in Italy

Photography is a cultural asset, a language, an opportunity for knowledge.

About education in the academic field the Strategic Plan proposes training modules with the aim of adapting the public intervention to the technical and economic changes of the photography system in Italy.

The plan – conceived as a programmatic outcome of some consultation tables distributed on the national territory – was launched on the introductory days of the General States of Photography that were held in Rome and Reggio Emilia on Spring 2017: Rome 06/06/2017, "Conservation and enhancement of heritage: Memory, Identity, Future"; "New horizons for professional photography"; Strategies and Governance for Photography"; Reggio Emilia 05/05/2017, "Photography, information, post truth: digital revolution and social media"; "Images, body and imaginary between real and virtual".

The general objective is to answer to some urgent questions that adapt the photographic culture system to contemporary times; among the various issues on the consultation table: "How to optimize the intervention of the public sector on the level of protection of the photographic image education?".

Public consultation tables were opened before the Plan was drawn up. The participatory debates – "MiBACT for photography: new strategies and new views on the territory" – disseminated throughout the territory were held in the operational headquarters of the various associations, foundations and institutions operating in the field of photographic culture, each conference is avaluable on the Web in the YouTube MiBACT channel: # 1 Palermo 27/05/2017, "Photography, Anthropology, Sicily: Heritage and Experiences"; # 2 Milan 8/06/2017, "Photography and society: document or artistic expression"; # 3 Senigallia 17/06/2017, "Land of photography: Marche's influence on photography in Italy after World War II"; # 4 Torino 22/06/2017, "Photographic papers: the census of collections and photographic archives in Italy"; # 5 Treviso 29/06/2017, "What are you looking at? The culture of images"; # 6 Cortona 15/07/2017, "A tribe that shoots Instagram as an alphabet of images", # 7 Savignano 9/09/2017 "Punctum. Photography and Festival System. Proposals and objectives"; # 8 Bibbiena 16/09/2017, "Redefining amateur photography"; # 9 Parma 06/10/2017 "Art and photography: the perspective of institutions and the market"; # 10 Matera 14/10/2017, "Material and immaterial landscape: photographic campaigns and new territories of the gaze"; # 11 Lodi 21/10/2017, "Photography as an instrument of change. communication through images, from photojournalism to NGOs"; # 12 Florence 23/10/2017, "Photography and museums: conservation, restoration and enhancement"; # 13 Bolzano 26/10/2017, "Profession: photography. An analysis of the evolution of professional photography"; # 14 Sarno 13/11/2017, " Local photographic archives: testimonies of commitment and protection"; # 15 Urbino 16/11/2017, "Rethinking the training. On Photography"; # 16 Crotone 11/23/2017, "Photographing territories: communicating identities and values to promote attractiveness"; # 17 Cagliari 01/12/2017, "Identità. Photography and Photographs"; # 18 Naples 04/12/2017, "Naples, photography and the arts"; # 19 Lucca 10/12/2017 "The word to photographers".

The Central Institute for Cataloguing and Documentation has established since 2015 a portal dedicated to the census of collections and photographic archives in Italy – www.censimento.fotografia.italia.it – it operates according to three objectives. The first, to create a cognitive map of photography in Italy: where it is disseminated?; which institutes preserve it?; what features does it have?. The second, to create a national meta-archive where photographic collections and founds can be sent in relation, both with the institutions that manage them, and with each other, aiming at determining a "network-of-networks" system in favor of collective knowledge.

Therefore, the Plan calls for actions to enhance the assets made up of the immense photographic deposits in the past, as well as actions aimed at nurturing the creativity for the future generations, as photography is a heritage and a potentiality – as some scholars argue – who will govern images in the future will control the transmission of knowledge, language, attitudes and, more generally, of culture.

The Plan also proposes specific actions in relation with the need to adapt the education system to the contemporaneity, as regards education to the photographic image. This becomes urgent precisely for the diffusion of photography as a language. However, there is no specific Disciplinary-Sector in which the world of photography – that is to say, photographic-culture – is included, it would allow to transmit the skills of widely diffused, extremely complex and above all constantly changing processes.

The themes of smart-photography and social sharing occupy a wide margin of the debate that led to the formulation of the Strategic Plan for Photography; for example Instagram, the most widespread social network that operate through images according to algorithms based on recognizable factors in three main types of interactions: 'interest', 'timeliness', 'relationship'. With regard to the present discussion, this aspect of the Plan gives us the opportunity to present some case studies between teaching and research (Fig. 3).

The context in which the Strategic Plan operates is part of a vision of contemporaneity that considers photography, in its relations with globalization and with the pervasive methods of digital acquisition and distribution of photographic contents made by the reciprocal connections of digital devices. On the one hand, these devices, have amplified the use of this expressive language, on the other they have re-defined the global map of the world of photography and of the related heritages, such as archives and collections. It is noted that "the photographic sector, in general negligence, was the first to undergo profound transformations, caused by the birth of multinational companies capable of raising waves of mergers and acquisitions without precedents" (MiBACT 2018, 9).

The Plan examines also the future of photographic 'memories': "The real risk is that the future photographic memories of current and future generations are held, in unquestionable monopoly regime, by external for-profit subjects whose ultimate purpose is certainly not philanthropic: the generation of Millennials is the first that has implicitly, more often unconsciously accepted, the privatization and outsourcing of their collective memories. A process not without deep implications." (MiBACT 2018, 13).

In line with the Italian photographic tradition, considering the recent "dynamics" of sharing contemporary photographic production, the Plan aspires to "bring the photographers' gaze on Italy" through the funding of photographic commissions and curatorial initiatives with the aim of: promoting the development of contemporary photographic culture through public procurement campaigns; increasing the photographic heritage preserved in public collections; reiterating the fundamental role of photography and art in reading and understanding the economic, social and cultural transformations taking place in the country. These are the launching of public procedures allowed to "public and private non-profit museums, public and private non-profit institutions, university institutes, foundations and non-profit cultural committees and cultural associations in Italy, which have carried out activities related to themes of photography and image on an ongoing basis over the last three years" (MiBACT 2018, 60).

A specific chapter concerns the "Educational and training policies" in which the placement of photographic practice – "photographic gesture" – in the contemporary socio-political system - understood both as an expressive language and as a powerful instrument of investigation is underlined. This awareness urgently requires a double intervention on the one hand a structured intervention of "education to the eye" in all schools of every order and degree; on the other hand, it is considered necessary to consider that "it is evident how the photographic culture can today claim to integrate the training paths, contaminating itself with other disciplines and becoming part of the educational proposal organically" (MiBACT 2018, 66).

3   The Contribution of Photography and Disciplines of Represenation. Didactic and Research Experiences

At the conclusion of these brief notes we present two case studies related to specific didactic and research experiences carried out within the Degree courses in Architecture and Design.

The first case study proposes a reading of the material and immaterial qualities of an Italian landscape presented in the Abruzzo Pavilion at the Milan Universal Exposition 2015 (Salucci 2016) (Figs. 1 and 2).

An image sequence illustrates the experience of a multimedia exhibition space, conceived and created by a team of the Department of Architecture of the 'G. d'Annunzio' University of Chieti and Pescara. The succession of frames proposed invites you to read a space that draws an inestimable cultural heritage in which biodiversity, micro-cities and Made-in-Italy tradition merge. The landscape peculiarities of Abruzzo narrated in the multimedia spaces of the exhibition, are observed, represented and fixed in time by a photographic apparatus that conforms both as a document, process, testimony, and as a memory of a collective event, of a climate, of an empathy. The image translation of some "visions" authorizes the perception of a performance that exhibits cultural landscapes and suggests emotional paths. It is an attempt to attribute the intelligible notation function to the photographic fragment, just like a visual note drawn on a travel notebook. In this direction the images, foreseen by the photographic project, operate. A sort of "unit-still-photographer" captures the instant visual impact of scenes, subjects and space. It proposes a story through images, through a limited number of "back-stages-photos", in which some subjects – three figures, reiterated in each scene – place the observer in a dimension of the anthropological experience of the investigated places. An aesthetic choice that intends to underline rituals, customs, popular expressions elsewhere dispersed and still so felt within this landscape that some authors have defined 'plural'.

Fig. 1. Abruzzi Pavilion EXPO Milano 2015. The "suspended mountain" model in resin of the Gran Sasso with the peak facing downwards at the entrance zone on the North-West Cardo. The experience of the ephemeral space of the Abruzzi Pavilion presented at the 2015 Universal Exhibition in Milan. An image sequence illustrates the experience of a multimedia space draws on a priceless cultural heritage, combining biodiversity, small towns and the Made-in-Italy tradition. Design by Susanna Ferrini, Department of Architecture of Pescara (Photography by Antonella Salucci 2015)

The selected frames are designed as a multiple view. This view is based on the anthropological value of the photographic image: both that related to the cultural landscape of Abruzzo itself, and that relating to the ephemeral space of the exhibition itinerary. The presence of the three figures, replicated in each frame, proposes suggestions of the popular tradition of Abruzzo: on the one hand, it triggers a dimensional and tactile relationship with the outfitting; on the other, it symbolizes the unmistakable identity and ritual traits that for centuries have reproduced a specific dimension of the past.

A second case that we present refers to the activities of the laboratory of the Surveying Architecture course of the "Gabriele d'Annunzio" University of Chieti and Pescara (Salucci 2017) (Figs. 3 and 4).

With the aim of detecting and representing some urban spaces through photography, the student is required to design and produce a work on which are placed some photographic images representative of the personal way of "living" the Viale Pindaro, the avenue that runs along the buildings of the university center of Pescara.

In order to portray some aspects related to the daily use of some spaces connecting the environments where the study activities are carried out: the space in-between. The aim is to creatively investigate a collective space by experimenting with the capture of a temporal fragment, the testimony of collective living, with an instrument of daily use

Fig. 2. Abruzzo Pavilion Expo 2015. Multimedia contents on the wall describe the qualities of the Abruzzo cultural landscape according to the main altimetry (Photography by Antonella Salucci)

Fig. 3. Photography as a Medium for Urban Regeneration. A Case Study on the University District of Pescara. Photographic survey project. Photography contest for Instagram #fotografarevialepindaro. Architecture Survey course A.A. 2015–18 (www.allievivialepindaro.wordpress. com).

Fig. 4. Elements of Architecture: Italian Entryways. Architecture Survey course A. A. 2017/18; prof. A. Salucci; Allievi: Barbacane, Ciavattella, De Carlo, Nasuti. (Photography by Riccardo Nasuti)

such as the smart-phone. The workshop in the form of the photographic contest has allowed an unprecedented and interesting reading of the urban landscape that characterizes the university district of the Polo Pindaro in Pescara which is composed of an architectural material that we could define varied and sometimes dissonant. The collective spaces of transit, parking, entertainment, meeting, socialization, waiting for rest, are fixed on the sensor by the same users of those spaces, as witnesses of a collective dwelling.

References

Fondazione Symbola (2017): Io sono cultura - 2017. L'Italia della qualità e della bellezza sfida la crisi. In: Io sono cultura. Quaderni di Symbola. http://www.symbola.net/assets/files/IoSonoCultura_2017_DEF_1498646352.pdf. Accessed May 2017

Koolhass R (2014) Fundamentals. Architettura non Architetti. Monditalia. La Biennale di Venezia, 14ª Mostra Internazionale di Architettura Venezia 2014. Venezia: Marsilio

MiBACT (2017) Stati Generali della Fotografia. Conservazione e Valorizzazione del Patrimonio. Memoria, Identità, Futuro. http://www.beniculturali.it/mibac/export/MiBAC/sito-MiBAC/Contenuti/MibacUnif/Comunicati/visualizza_asset.html_1766819048.html. Accessed 11 Sept 2017

MiBACT (2018) Piano Strategico di Sviluppo della Fotografia in Italia 2018–2022. http://www.beniculturali.it/mibac/multimedia/MiBAC/documents/1525355716796_Piano_Strategico_di_Sviluppo_della_Fotografia_in_Italia-1.pdf. Accessed May 2018

Reschke A (ed) (2017) Wim Wenders. I pixel di Cezanne. Contrasto, Roma

Rosselli P (2009) Sandwich Digitale. La vita Segreta dell'Immagine Fotografica, Macera Quodlibet, Macerata

Salucci A (2016) Exhibiting the Landscape. Images for the Abruzzi Pavilion at EXPO Milano 2015. In: Territori e frontiere della rappresentazione XXXIX Convegno Internazionale dei Docenti delle Discipline della Rappresentazione XIV Congresso UID, Napoli 14-15-16/09/2016. Gangemi Editore, Roma, pp 815–820

Salucci A (2017) Photography as a medium for urban regeneration. A case study on the University District of Pescara, Italy. In: IMMAGINI? image and imagination between representation, communication, education and psychology. Proceedings of the international and interdisciplinary conference, Brixen, Italy, 27-28/11/2017. MDPI AG. https://doi.org/10.3390/proceedings1090939

Salucci A, Marino G (2017) Photography and video for a representation of the intangible cultural heritage of Abruzzo. In: Putting tradition into practice: heritage, place and design. Proceedings of 5th INTBAU international annual event. Milano, Italy, 5–6 July 2017. Lecture Notes in Civil Engineering, vol 3. Springer International Publishing AG 2018, pp 727–736, ISBN 978-3-319-57936-8, ISSN 2366-2557. https://doi.org/10.1007/978-3-319-57937-5

Trione V (2014) Effetto città. Arte cinema modernità, Bompiani, Roma

Unali M (2010) Architettura effimera. In: Enciclopedia Italiana XXI Secolo. Gli spazi e le arti. Treccani, Roma, pp 345–354. http://www.treccani.it/enciclopedia/architettura-effimera_(XXI-Secolo)/. Accessed 14 Apr 2017

Unali M (2015) Representing the intangible Cultural Heritage and the Poetics of the Ephemeral. In: Giovannini M, Arena P, Raffa P (eds) Spazi e Culture del Mediterraneo Ricerca PRIN 2009-2011. Fabbrica della Conoscenza 52. Napoli: Edizioni La Scuola Di Pitagora, Napoli, pp 1027–1041

Venetian Perspective Boxes: When the Images Become Environments

Low-Tech High-Knowledge Media for Teaching the Historical Heritage of the (Interior/Exterior) Environments

Fabrizio Gay$^{(\boxtimes)}$ and Irene Cazzaro

Università IUAV di Venezia, Santa Croce 191, 30135 Venice, Italy
fabrizio@iuav.it

Abstract. The contribution focuses on the comparison of two types of case studies: (1) educational devices dedicated to the historical heritage of the Interior Design and (2) artistic (on-site) installations dedicated to the experience of the landscape. Both cases are characterised by low digital technology, high level of analogic experience, translation of images between different visual and haptic media in real environments that still function as *wunderkammern*. Our aim is to study the semiotic device shared by these different cases.

Keywords: Intermediality · Arts and sciences · Immersive visualization · Interior Design · Displaying · Optical boxes

1 Interiors and Exteriors in (Immersive) Translation

Let's imagine two cases. The first is that of a box that - placed in a room - reproduces another room in an immersive way. The second case is a room that reproduces, at the bottom of the spectator's eyeball, an average day of the horizon of the southern Venetian lagoon condensed in about ten minutes: it's *Your black horizon* (2005), the pavilion created by Olafur Eliasson on the southern shore of the island of San Lazzaro degli Armeni.

The first case concerns a series of traditional perspective boxes made in 2017 by first-year students of the IUAV Interior Design course, learning the techniques of analogical and digital representation dedicated to the specific object of their studies.

Both cases are part of the same secular tradition: that of optical boxes that exploit the analogy between eye and room.

The perspective boxes of the 17th century (Fig. 1) are representations of interiors inside a box; that is, they have walls painted inside with images of interiors in perspectives that are extended on multiple faces and that can be seen through one (sometimes two) peephole/s placed in the vertical faces that exhibit typically allegorical paintings on the outside in the form of personifications or still life (Leeman 1976). Thus, the eye of the viewer, placed outside, can observe through the pinhole and the

© Springer Nature Switzerland AG 2019
A. Luigini (Ed.): EARTH 2018, AISC 919, pp. 95–105, 2019.
https://doi.org/10.1007/978-3-030-12240-9_11

most interesting effect is that we can compare a completely illusive (deceptive) view and a non-illusive but anamorphic one.

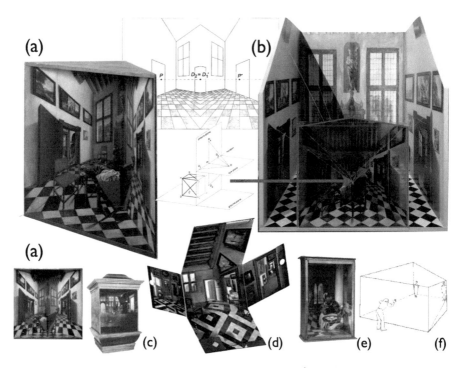

Fig. 1. Examples of perspective boxes dating back to the 17th century with a scheme of the perceptive illusion experiment known as "Ames room" (f). (a) Elinga's perspective box, located in the Bredius Museum, Den Haag, [Panel 84 × 82 × 42 cm] compared to the educational reconstruction of the interior that it represents (b) and to other examples of similar objects of the same period preserved at the Copenhagen Nationalmuseet (c) [45 × 58,5 × 49 cm], the London National Gallery (d) [58 × 88 × 60.5 cm], the Detroit Institute of Arts (e) [41.9 × 30.2 × 28.3 cm].

The deceptive effectiveness of the perspective box depends on a few factors (Palmer 1999):

- On the fact that the visual field of the spectator, obliged to perceive through the peephole, includes only that of the painted perspective whose point of view must exactly coincide with the position of the eye;
- On the fact that the main distance used in the tracing of the perspective image is proportional to the one between the retina and the optical centre of the pupil;
- On the fact that the painting is illuminated in such a way that the differences in illumination between the inner faces of the box are not perceived.

The variability in shapes and dimensions of the box, its material and the lighting device are aspects that qualify it as a curious object that participates in the furnishings of an actually inhabited interior (Pierantoni 2012; Stoichita 1998).

The comparison between two regimes of perception (deceptive and anamorphic) also occurs in the case of Eliasson's installation. Here the viewer is inside the pavilion and does not perceive anything but the variations in intensity and tint of a thin luminous line that he (deceptively) considers as the result of the actual external light. In this case as well, the device is based on the comparison between two perception regimes: outside and inside the environment image (Fig. 2).

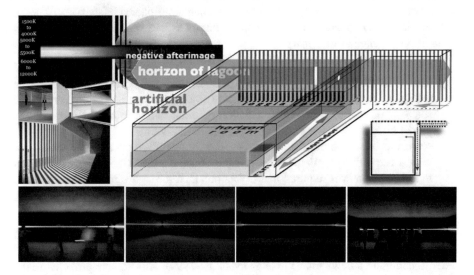

Fig. 2. Diagrams and photographs showing Olafur Eliasson's installation "*Your black horizon*" and explaining the mechanism on which it is based.

Both the perspective boxes and Eliasson's installation belong to the ancient genealogy of spectacular demonstration machines - conceived at the same time as a work of art and as experimental machines to magnify a small set of physical phenomena – which had the greatest success in the baroque encyclopedism, or the so-called "natural magic".

The perspective boxes, in particular, are one of the cases of "optical machines" that exploited, besides the perspective, the laws of dioptrics and catoptrics on flat and curved surfaces. This is another reason why we have provided examples of catoptric and dioptric boxes as indications addressed to the students invited to create "Venetian perspective boxes".

2   Translations: From Image to Environment, from Digital Image to Physical Object

Both cases function as "representations" concerning their installation site: Venice.

This is clear in the case of Eliasson's pavilion on the island of San Lazzaro, an installation that reproduces the daily variation of the chromatic temperature of the southern lagoon of Venice in a contracted time.

Even the creation of perspective boxes assigned as an exercise to Interior Design students was related to "Venetian themes". The request was to create a small object – a (perspective or catoptric) optical machine similar to those found in the baroque *wunderkammern* – capable of evoking an actual Venetian atmosphere (Griffero 2010) not in its "meteorological" phenomena, but through cultural aspects, that is, evoking elements of an actual "Venetian imaginary".

Specifically, the requirements were the following:

(1)   seen from the outside, the optical (perspective or catoptric) box, had to be recognisable as a precious and problematic object, likely to be sold in Venice as a souvenir or a small domestic installation, without falling into the stereotypes of tourist kitsch: the *gondola*, the *bricola*, the mask, etc....

(2)   seen in its interior show, the box had to actually reproduce the image of an interior with a recognisable "Venetian" character (Bachelard 2006). For this purpose a figured interior was required and it was obtained through a reconstruction made from cinematic sequences of some canonical films of the Venetian imaginary, especially from *Fellini's Casanova* (1975) (Fig. 3).

The required exercise was therefore configured as a translation of images between media - cinema, photography, geometric design - and between different objects, in order to configure a new "image object" (Malraux 1994). An example provided to the students was our project of a catoptric box capable of evoking a spatial and atmospheric effect similar to one of the initial scenes of Fellini's Casanova (Fig. 4): the house on the islet of San Bartolo where - under the hidden eyes of the French ambassador - the intricate embrace of Maddalena and Casanova is consumed.

It is a scene where space works explicitly as a modern peep-show for the French ambassador (unobserved observer), as well as for the spectator. It was therefore quite obvious, for various reasons, to interpret our optical box as a real "optical toy", that is, as a peep-box based on the device of the "infinity mirror" and the kaleidoscope, since this device was already manifested in "baroque" form in the scene of the film.

The project therefore tries to hybridise the different images coming from the genealogy of these "interiors" and of these optical machines. Therefore, the inside of the box\ does not reproduce exactly the set of the scene of the film, rather it recalls the main space: the octagonal baroque *"cabinet aux miroirs"* placed between the alcove and the gallery (covered with ceramics with erotic figurations) coming from a circular courtyard.

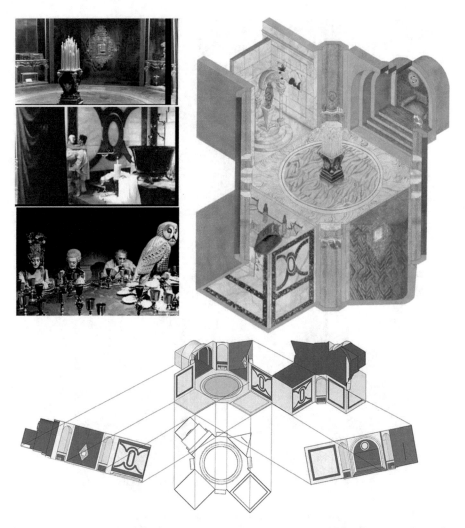

Fig. 3. Restitution of a room from *Fellini's Casanova* through unfolded axonometry. Diagrams by Alessia Cudicio and Beatrice Vio-Genova.

The box realises a single actual slice - a quarter - of a large octagonal room covered with a vault which appears as an image created by mutual reflection of two mirrors arranged on two orthogonal symmetry axes of the octagon. Finally, a third semi-transparent mirror wall, at an angle of 45° to the two mirrors, produces - by mutual reflection - the image of an unlimited extension of octagonal rooms separated by square vestibules (Fig. 4).

Fig. 4. Concept of the optical toy "San Bartolo", reminiscent of a scene from *Fellini's Casanova*. The "infinity mirror" device produces an endless repetition of bright octagonal rooms and dark square vestibules.

It is therefore a real box with five vertical walls - two of which are empty - which offers a kaleidoscopic spectacle for two different conditions of the spectator:

(1) When the spectator is placed behind the fifth semi-reflecting wall and observes from the outside, in the shade (like the French ambassador), the inside of the box illuminated by the ceiling, he sees an unlimited proliferation of octagonal rooms and empty vestibules;

(2) But if two observers look out at the two open thresholds of the room, they see their image iterated in the *mise en abyme*: the illusory and unlimited proliferation of dark vestibules and illuminated octagonal rooms.

Finally, the setting up of this perspective box can better define the relationship between the film scene and the optical spectacle it offers. Alongside the kaleidoscope box, other representations of the starting scene must appear.

In the development of the exercise, particular attention was paid to the reconstruction by means of parallel projection, adopting a form of unfolded axonometry.

These graphic restitutions of the scenes through unfolded axonometry are further objects to display next to the perspective boxes, so that, in the exhibition of the works, the opportunities for comparison between deceptive simulations and geometric representations of the same spaces are multiplied (Fig. 5).

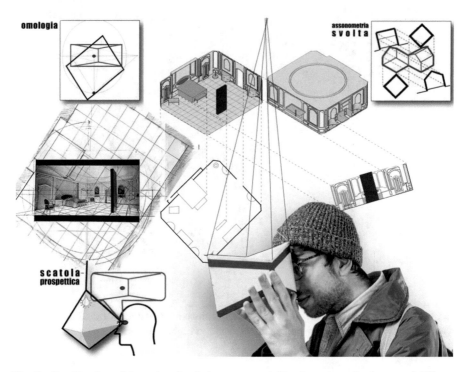

Fig. 5. Combination of deceptive simulations - generated by the perspective box - and different graphic restitutions of the room where the last scene of Kubrick's "*2001: A Space Odissey*" takes place.

3   Low-Tech Digital Bricolage

The construction of perspective boxes has been conceived as an educational exercise of fundamental importance for the acquisition of the geometric skills of an interior designer.

The restitution of the spaces portrayed in sequences of film frames was carried out using traditional photogrammetric methods and digital photomodelling techniques.

In addition to traditional knowledge of geometrical restitution of perspective, the exercise helps the student understand the potential of some software beyond the intention of their creators.

In this case some functions of the Sketchup software, although not planned for this purpose, have been used to determine the exact position of the point of view from which a photograph was taken or the perspective of an architectural painting was created (Fig. 6).

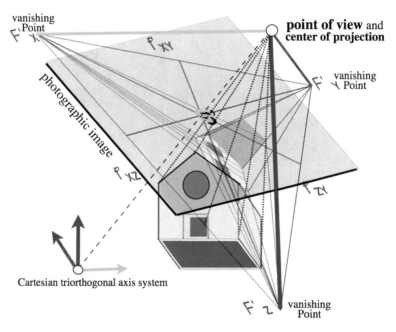

Fig. 6. Geometric scheme - used by the Sketchup software – that allows to find the projection centre (or point of view) of a photographic image on which the vanishing points of three objectively triortognal directions can be identified.

Sketchup is a modelling software that offers the possibility - through the Match Photo command - to adapt his spatial references - the three coordinated triorthogonal axes - to three triorthogonal directions testified in a perspective image: a photograph or a drawing that is constructed by means of a central projection. In general, this function is used to insert the model of a new object into photographed scenes - to turn them into realistic photomontages - or to make actual perspective restitutions from photographs, by directly drawing the faces of the model following the lines witnessed by the photograph.

However, we did not use the Match Photo function for these purposes. The most interesting thing for us is that this function calculates the exact position of the photographic point of view or perspective.

Precisely, by asking the user to specify three triorthogonal directions represented in the photograph by their three vanishing points, Sketchup exactly identifies the centre of projection of the image as the intersection of the three projecting lines - obviously triorthogonal as well - that start from those three vanishing points. However, the software does not explain to the user the position of the projection centre.

We can infer the finding of the projection centre of the photo only when we want to build a model from a photograph and use the command "Project Textures from Photo" that, in fact, projects photos on the model's faces. In that operation Sketchup uses the projection centre (the point of view) of the photograph as the centre of that projection.

The perspective box is precisely built with a heterodox use of that function: projecting the image on a surface of the box, or on a shell with a geometry that doesn't correspond to the one of the depicted interior (Fig. 7).

Fig. 7. Perspective box created using the Sketchup software. As seen in the picture of the open box, the device features two different views referred to the same interior.

4 Conclusions

In the case studies analysed here, the cognitive outcome depends on three main factors:

(1) the fact that the devices are used as "objects" with the function of "maps" of a (real or virtual) physical place in relation to the actually experienced space;

(2) that these objects are strongly evocative and recognisable in specific traditions of use: especially the artificial landscape in a natural place, the souvenir or the furnishing object;
(3) that the object-maps have different statutes and are comparable by combining a deceptive and a non-deceptive experience of the same phenomena.

In this sense the image becomes "immersive", not so much because it is obtained through digital tools, but because it is both an exhibition environment and a contained physical object; an object that lies entirely under the control of the observer.

Thanks to this familiarity, the image-object can better perform the enigmatic "strangeness" that assimilates it to a *wunderkammer* object. Due to this condition of *wunderkammer*, the installation can activate a reserve of meaning that does not limit itself to performing the only didascalic and didactic task for which it was also conceived.

Generalising these conclusions we might note that the development of digital media in artistic and scientific teaching still supports some of the (cultural) ways of enhancing the "immersive" experience gained in the tradition of scientific *mirabilia* of classic and baroque encyclopedism. The most effective contemporary installations are still aesthetic environmental machines – created to "make people test" - that make the border between two social domains very ambiguous: that of art and that of scientific learning.

These are, generally, devices whose essential semiotic functioning can be traced back to the "square of veridiction".

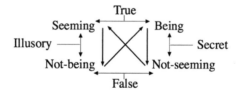

Typically, an observer evaluates the optical box in at least two times and belief schemes:

1 - Looking at the peephole, he sees the physical image of an interior that does not correspond to the empirical characteristics of the outer box, so, as a first factual judgment, he believes that the image is "Illusory" (i.e. not-being + seeming).
2 - Entering the fictional game of the image, he hypothesises possible referents and a cultural link between the surrounding environment and the image-object, which he judges as belonging to the order of the "Secret" (being + not-seeming) giving it further meaning.

References

Bachelard G (2006) La poétique de l'espace. PUF, Paris 1957 (trad. it., La poetica dello spazio, Dedalo, Bari

Griffero T (2010) Atmosferologia. Estetica degli spazi emozionali. Laterza, Roma-Bari

Leeman F (1976) Hidden images. Games of perception, anamorphic art, Illusion from the Renaissance to the present. H.N. Abrams, New York

Malraux A (1994) [1951] Il museo dei musei. Leonardo, Milano

Palmer SE (1999) Vision science: photons to phenomenology. MIT Press, Cambridge

Pierantoni R (2012) Salto di scala. Bollati Boringhieri, Torino

Stoichita V (1998) L'invenzione del quadro. Il saggiatore. Milano

Automatic Image Recognition.
Applications to Architecture

Igor Todisco[1], Geovanna Esther Menendez Giglio[2],
and Ornella Zerlenga[3(✉)]

[1] Igor Todisco Imaging, Via Prato Piternis, 5, 03044 Cervaro, Frosinone, Italy
mail@igortodisco.com
[2] Menendez Consulting, Naples, Italy
menendezconsulting@virgilio.it
[3] Department of Architecture and Industrial Design,
University of Study of Campania "Luigi Vanvitelli",
Via San Lorenzo ad Septimum, 81031 Aversa, Italy
ornella.zerlenga@unicampania.it

Abstract. Starting from digital technological innovation of automatic facial recognition (today proposed for control and safety operations), in order to increase information and architectural education through digital media, an innovative design inspiration is proposed: use this artificial intelligence for the automatic recognition of the linguistic elements of architecture.

Keywords: Architectural education · Digital media ·
Automatic image recognition

1 Introduction [IT, OZ]

Architectural video projection, digital catalogs, interactive immersive environments, reconstructions in virtual reality, dynamic maps, interactive multimedia panels: in a word, virtual architecture, a technological reality that today represents the most innovative and advanced frontier in the acquisition of knowledge as well as in the management and dissemination of information (Fig. 1).

What is more, there is no doubt that in the process of knowledge communication, the digital technologies have greatly facilitated the clarity of information (especially to non-specialized users) as well as the greater speed of acquisition, the reception of information both locally and remotely (Maschini 2011).

In this article we will refer to the advanced technology of facial recognition, more generally, of automatic image recognition to hypothesize intelligent systems able to decode material architectures in digital environments for education, arts and heritage.

© Springer Nature Switzerland AG 2019
A. Luigini (Ed.): EARTH 2018, AISC 919, pp. 106–115, 2019.
https://doi.org/10.1007/978-3-030-12240-9_12

2 Intelligent Technologies for the Management and Communication of Knowledge [OZ]

In general, the activation of disciplinary hybridization pathways favors better per-forming results than the purpose, especially in those projects in which the goal is the digital acquisition of knowledge. In this sense, if it is true that traditionally architects, in general, and representatives, in particular, are called upon to contribute to the methods of innovation of space description systems, it is also true that today they must also be interested in ways to transfer the architectonic information according to increasingly virtual and less physical contexts (De Luca 2011). At the same time, it is equally clear that the speed with which technological innovation proceeds makes obsolete solutions considered unimaginable only a few years earlier. In this sense, the relationship between digital media performance and information communication is a constant challenge. Among the most advanced digital technologies, the automatic image recognition appears today a significant frontier, able to revolutionize not only the processes of control and security but also capable of offering itself as a planning and methodological reflection for the advancement of artificial intelligence in the field of architecture.

Fig. 1. Digital systems for communication of cultural heritage.

Facial recognition (and, for it, automatic recognition) is constituting one of the frontiers of artificial intelligence which, more than any other, suggests great developments in the future not only in the field of security but also in a variety of other applications. As is known, this device proves to be more effective than a human being in recognizing a person's face in the midst of millions of faces, and in acquiring and processing further information through vision. Facial recognition is based on three phases: registration, archiving and authentication. More specifically, this biometric technology is organized according to three processes: during the first, one 'teaches' the system to recognize the face; therefore, the data are stored in security and always accessible from the system; finally, the system becomes 'able' to compare the image of the face with respect to a database (Fig. 2).

Recently, facial recognition technology has been associated with that of the latest generation drones, capable of activating automatic recognition, locating objects, being aware of the context and producing 3D mappings.

3 The Automatic Image Recognition [IT]

Into the late 1960s the *Star Trek* TV series was viral, in which races of humanoids from different planets coexisted on board the spaceship *Enterprise*. The series anticipated many technologies: tablet, GPS, voice assistant (SIRI, e.g.), voice translator, automatic doors, mobile phone. What would the Star Trek writers think about looking at facial recognition systems that work today, about 250 years ahead of the setting of the series?

Fig. 2. IT systems and current applications of automatic facial recognition.

From computer technology point of view, the concept of facial recognition is divided into two phases: identification (recognition of the subject starting from an image); validation (checking the identity provided by a subject through an image).

Nowadays, the facial recognition system is used in many airports to make automatic passport control: the gates open only if the photo on the document corresponds to the face framed in the camera. Most commonly, every time a group photo is uploaded to *Facebook*, facial recognition is activated with the automatic tag of the people portrayed. In addition, in the iPhone image galleries, the software allows you to split the photos depending on the person portrayed, recognizing among others. With the *i-Phone X*, then, facial recognition replaces the fingerprint scanner to unlock the smartphone.

But there's more. At the cinema, in many films, a facial recognition system is seen that identifies somebody in the crowd. The belief of viewers is that the system is not real but it is also being launched in Italy. The *Parsec 3.26* company, from Lecce, won the contract to supply the system to the State. The name of the system is *S.A.R.I.* (Automatic Image Recognition System) and from the company website we read that: «The *S.A.R.I.* system, realized by *Parsec 3.26* for the Ministry of the Interior, has positively passed the testing verifications. *Parsec* is satisfied with the result obtained and with the quality of the work carried out in the last year, which has allowed us to positively pass the verification tests of the *S.A.R.I.* Now we will proceed with the start-up phase that initially provides the provision of training courses to Police Forces throughout the country. It will start from the capital, while the roll-out in all other regions will be launched in the coming months» (S.A.R.I., Parsec 3.26 2018).

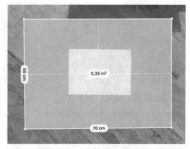

Fig. 3. IT systems and current applications of automatic image recognition.

As we read in the technical specifications of the contract, on the website of the State Police, *S.A.R.I.* is able to manage two operational situations. The first, *Enterprise*, is the one in which «an operator needs to find the identity of a face, within an image, by means of one or more facial recognition algorithms contained in a large database» (Riconoscimento facciale, Italy 2018). The database in question provides 10 million images and the output of the algorithm is a list of faces similar to the one sought. The second, *Real-Time*, serves in the case where, given a restricted geographical area, «the faces of the subjects taken by the cameras installed there must be analyzed in real time, comparing them with a *watch-list* whose size is of the order of the hundreds of thousands of subjects» (Riconoscimento facciale 2018). Through the use of augmented reality, the algorithm generates *alerts* on a screen when, in the video, individuals who are on the *watch-list* appear. The purpose of this system is to be «in support of territorial control operations during events» (Smartfiy 2018).

Face recognition, however, is not a simple operation because the software must be able to: find faces in a specific image; identify the face regardless of the brightness of the photo, expression and direction in which the head is turned; recognize the unique characteristics of each face; identify the face uniquely by comparing the characteristics of the other existing faces. So, summarizing, the procedure can be divided into several phases.

Fig. 4. Artificial intelligence, automatic image recognition and smart drones. *Parley SnotBot* project: collaboration between *Intel* and *Parley for the Ocean.*

The first consists in locating the presence of the face within an image. At the beginning of the computer experimentation, a solution adopted was based on the colors present in the image; therefore, the algorithm 'searched' the typical colors of the complexion but this method generated problems due to the presence of more skin colors. Therefore, they chose to work on the geometric character capable of recognizing the presence of the oval of the face. Once the face has been identified, the system proceeds to the second phase: identification of the main characters that distinguish it as eyes, an eyebrow arch, nose, mouth, etc. These elements have been called 'fiducial points' and a mesh is applied to them which allows to evaluate the dimensions, proportions and distances between the points. Through a database, which contains images, they proceed to the third phase: identification of the correct. Obviously, the quantity of sample images supplied and included in the description (*machine learning*) is directly proportional to the accuracy of the recognition system.

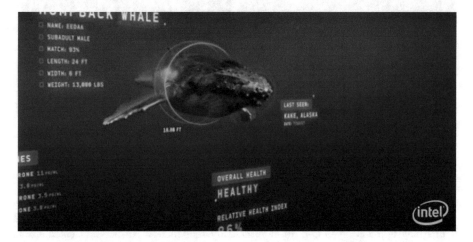

Fig. 5. Artificial intelligence, automatic image recognition and smart drones are becoming very useful for the study of the health of endangered animal species as whales (*Parley SnotBot* project).

But technologies seen so far have followed a development process that has not only stopped at facial recognition.

A demonstration is the presentation of *ARKit 2* platform that *Apple* presented together with the new operating system for smartphones and tablets (*iOS 12*).

From the *Apple* website we read that «*ARKit 2* allows developers to integrate shared experiences, persistent AR experiences tied to a specific location, object detection and image tracking to make AR apps even more dynamic. *Apple* is also unveiling the *Measure* app for *iOS*, which uses AR to quickly gauge the size of real-world objects, as well as a new open file format with *iOS 12*, *usdz*, which is designed to more deeply integrate AR throughout *iOS* and make AR objects available across the ecosystem of *Apple* apps» (ARKit 2 2018).

Apple declares that the new app *Measure* «uses AR to quickly gauge the size of real-world objects similar to a tape measure. The new app automatically provides the dimensions of objects like picture frames, posters and signs, and can also show diagonal measurements and compute area» (ARKit 2 2018).

Fig. 6. Livio De Luca. 40° International Conference of Representation Disciplines Teachers "Drawing as (in)tangible representation", UID: *Digitizing cultural heritage: between complexity and intelligibility* (Milan 2018, 13 September).

It may seem like science fiction until you try it but actually the application provides very precise data, here it is a test performed on a 50×70 card. It is easy to deduce that if this new application is able to automatically recognize a surface and calculate its measurements, then we can design an application based on the same platform which compares the measures of an architectural element (and therefore the proportions) with those of a database containing the various stylistic examples, thus identifying (in augmented reality or through photographs already taken previously) the architectural typology to which our subject belongs (Fig. 3).

4   Recognition Systems Based on Artificial Neural Networks [GEMD]

A mathematical-informatics model based on biological neural networks consists of groups of information interconnections, composed of artificial neurons. Neural networks represent an adaptive system, whose structure is based on information (external or internal) that flows through the network during the learning phase. These non-linear statistical data structures are organized as models in which digital images are acquired through a sampling and quantization process (Colantonio and Salvetti 2005).

Neural networks are useful in graphic-digital acquisition applications. Automatic recognition, description and classification of the information contained in the images are a matter of fundamental importance for the scientific disciplines and require the acquisition, treatment and transmission of information in a visual form or in images. Applicability to architecture is desirable to increase the effectiveness of automatic education programs for material and immaterial heritage.

Fig. 7. Livio De Luca. 40° International Conference of Representation Disciplines Teachers "Drawing as (in)tangible representation", UID: *Digitizing cultural heritage: between complexity and intelligibility* (Milan 2018, 13 September).

5   Conclusions [OZ]

Artificial intelligence, automatic image recognition and smart drones are becoming very useful not only for security against terrorism or for research expeditions in dangerous places but also for the study of the health of endangered animal species. For example, the collaboration between *Intel* and *Parley for the Ocean* gave rise to the *Parley SnotBot* project, «a technological platform based on *Intel's Machine Learning* able to recognize a specific animal and give indications about its health in real time» (Riconoscimento facciale 2018) (Fig. 4).

More specifically, with the application of this artificial intelligence, the marine experts of *Parley SnotBot* have recently completed a scientific expedition in Alaska, where «they successfully deployed advanced drone technology, artificial intelligence (AI) and machine learning tools to collect biological samples from whales and analyze data in real time [...]. Without leaving the boat and disturbing the whales, the research team used Intel technology to identify a whale from a past expedition, confirm pregnancy in another whale and gather real-time data on cetacean health. This expertise and innovative technology empowers researchers to make more timely decisions in their immediate mission, allowing them to act upon real-time data that informs the longer-term health of our oceans and humanity» (Intel and Parley SnotBot 2018). Thanks to this innovative technology, researchers have been able to conduct investigations in an indirect and effective way: «So far, *Parley SnotBot* has been used to collect spout water from blue whales, right whales, gray whales, humpbacks and orcas in oceans around the world. Artificial intelligence gives whales a voice to share the health of our oceans and the environment» (From Polar Bears to Whales 2018) (Fig. 5).

In this sense, by applying the digital criterion of automatic image recognition and developing a machine learning based on architecture with the definition of specific fiducial points, the system could be specialized in the digital image recognition to the architecture, identifying automatically the different typological elements of which architecture is composed, both in real time (through augmented reality) and through images provided subsequently.

Reflecting on the "digitizing cultural heritage: between complexity and intelligibility", Livio De Luca summarized an intelligent system for architecture: «an 'informative *continuum*' based of three essential features: a continuous 3D mapping and annotation process; a morphology-based data structuring approach; a flexible and scalable technology. A cloud computing service allowing the gathering, processing and sharing of semantically-enriched 3D data within online and onsite documentation scenarios» (De Luca 2018) (Figs. 6 and 7).

References

Anche l'Italia si è munita di un sistema di riconoscimento facciale. https://medium.com/ @ORARiccardo/anche-litalia-si-%C3%A8-munita-di-un-sistema-di-riconoscimento-facciale-4a6f4c4e4f3f. Accessed May 2018

Apple unveils ARKit 2. https://www.apple.com/newsroom/2018/06/apple-unveils-arkit-2/. Accessed June 2018

Arriva Smartify, la nuova app che riconosce in automatico le opere d'arte. http://www.artribune. com/progettazione/new-media/2017/03/arriva-la-app-smartify/. Accessed May 2018

Colantonio S, Salvetti O (2005) Categorizzazione automatica di immagini mediante algoritmi neurali. https://www.google.it/search?source=hp&ei=-3sAW9XRHMyssAHc_J-QBw&q= Categorizzazione+automatica+di+immagini+mediante+algoritmi+neurali&oq= Categorizzazione+automatica+di+immagini+mediante+algoritmi+neurali&gs_l=psy-ab.3... 3186.3186.0.4400.3.2.0.0.0.0.122.122.0j1.2.0....0...1c.2.64.psy-ab..1.1.120.6..35i39k1.120. 0NwLQ7AgDz8. Accessed May 2018

De Luca L (2011) Verso la caratterizzazione semantica di rappresentazioni digitali di artefatti architettonici: linee programmatiche di ricerca. In: DisegnareCON, vol 4, no 8, dicembre 2011. ISSN 1828-5961

De Luca L (2018) Digitizing cultural heritage: between complexity and intelligibility. In: Proceedings of 40° international conference of representation disciplines teachers "drawing as (in)tangible representation", UID, Milan, September 2018

From Polar Bears to Whales, Intel Pushes the Boundaries of Wildlife Research with Drone and Artificial Intelligence. https://newsroom.intel.com/news-releases/from-polar-bears-to-whales-intel-pushes-the-boundaries-of-wildlife-research-with-drone-and-artificial-intelligence/. Accessed May 2018

Il sistema S.A.R.I. realizzato da Parsec 3.26. http://www.parsec326.it/index.php?option=com_content&view=article&id=252:incontro-formativo-su-portale-digitale-la-presentazione-in-digitale-delle-pratiche-sue-&catid=43:news-parsec&Itemid=54. Accessed May 2018

Intel and Parley SnotBot Use Game-Changing Artificial Intelligence and Drones to Advance Whale Research. https://newsroom.intel.com/news/intel-parley-snotbot-use-game-changing-artificial-intelligence-drones-advance-whale-research/. Accessed May 2018

Maschini A (2011) Tecnologie digitali e comunicazione dei beni culturali. Stato dell'arte e prospettive di sviluppo. In: DisegnareCON, vol 4, no 8, dicembre 2011. ISSN 1828-5961

Riconoscimento facciale. http://pralab.diee.unica.it/sites/default/files/int_LXP122_18-23_login_biometrico.pdf. http://www.hertasecurity.com/it/tecnologia. Accessed May 2018

Riconoscimento facciale: che cos'è e perché sta rivoluzionando smartphone, sicurezza e sistemi di pagamento (Intel's Machine Learning). https://www.ai4business.it/sicurezza/riconoscimento-facciale/. Accessed May 2018

Kosmesis Design. Eco-nomica-logical Cultural

Maria Dolores Morelli$^{(\boxtimes)}$

Department of Architecture and Industrial Design (DADI),
University of the Studies of Campania "Luigi Vanvitelli",
Street S. Lorenzo 1, 81031 Aversa, Italy
mariadolores.morelli@unicampania.it

Abstract. Kosmesis Design (from the Greek words, kósmos «rule, decora-tion» and kósmesis «adorn»): is the totality of eco-nomica-logical, ethical actions with aesthetic value, aimed at the cultural development of the territory, resulting from the research project LANDesign®. Design surveys and products, enter into a relation with fashion, cosmetics, architecture, culture "to build new experiences with art and heritage towards an awareness of the protection of the creative expressions of civilizations". The kosmetic approach is linked to other styles: korporeo (from the Latin words, corporeus, der. from corpus -poris «body»), karismatico (from the Greek word, khárisma, der. from kháris «grace»), kostruttivo (from the Latin words, der. constructivus, past participle of con-struere «build») and kreativo (from Latin words, create from the Sanskrit origin KAR-TR «he who does»). The letter "K" whose origins derive from the Phoenician alphabet and meaning palm, appears as the first letter in each style. This research is aimed to broaden views and begin relations like *La main ouverte* of Le Corbusier as a symbol of "ouverte pour recevoir, ouverte pour donner" to give and take.

Keywords: Design · Kosmesis · Heritage · Artifacts · Economy · Ecology

1 Introduction

The applied LANDesign®[1], reasearch project, University of the Studies of Campania 'Luigi Vanvitelli' has organized the virtuous system [University + School + Fam-ily + Institutions + Companies] for the conception of processes and artifacts produced nearby, revealing the cultural identity and responding to the future consumers needs. LANDesign® has identified a method/tool that is able to make Design give happiness and well-being through custom-made products (cosmethics). Moreover, the need to join, share, and cooperate to design processes which can change social, cultural and environmental behaviors is what the WDO World Design Organization, defines as a mission: "As the international voice for industrial design, we advocate, promote,

---

[1] Project of Applied research LANDesign® (scientific managers Prof. Sabina Martusciello, Prof. Maria Dolores Morelli, Department of Architecture and Industrial Design, University of the Studies of Campania "Luigi Vanvitelli".

© Springer Nature Switzerland AG 2019
A. Luigini (Ed.): EARTH 2018, AISC 919, pp. 116–125, 2019.
https://doi.org/10.1007/978-3-030-12240-9_13

and share knowledge of industrial design driven innovation that has the power to create a better world".[2] The totality of eco-nomical-logical, ethical products with aesthetic value for the cultural development of the territory are shaped by the decor which is the refined form of the object, resulting from a suitable choice of each of its parts, corresponds to the *convenience*, the custom, the nature and can be defined with the contemporary term of ecology; whereas for the *oixonomia* that is the use of limited resources to meet the individual and collective needs reducing the costs, through a system of essential parts linking the form to the function, the *dispositio*, the order and the symmetry define the object in a weighted, proportional and harmonic way. All these parts together *concinnitas* showing us the usefulness and the value of an object through their communicative ability, are such to promote the empathic role of the object.[3]

2 Methods

The project "CULTIVARS: cultivating culture in art", third prize in the Competition "ARS - Art that creates social employment", sponsored by Accenture Foundation with a special mention from the Italian Ministry of Heritage and Cultural Activities and Tourism, is an example to illustrate clearly what has been said in the introduction. It is aimed to valorize a system of places of build heritage in Campania territory. For the participation in the competition have chosen two monuments: the first one is the Abazia di San Lorenzo ad Septimun in Aversa and the second one is the Mostra d'Oltremare in Naples. Both places have been selected because they are a historical and architectural highly prestigious heritage not completely appreciated from a tourist point of view even though close to the main tourist flows (historic centre of Naples and Caserta Palace). The Borgo San Lorenzo is in Aversa. In addition to the late-gothic church, also the seventeenth-century building, which was the accommodation of Benedictines, is part of the monumental complex. This build has a large two-level cloister (one of the few examples in Campania) and today it hosts the Department of Architecture and Industrial Design of the University of Studies of Campania "Luigi Vanvitelli". The wide wall also surround San Lorenzo Garden, a garden of agriculture used for a long time as a parking and the turned again into garden orchard open to schools and managed by the association Orto di San Lorenzo. The Mostra d'Oltemare was inaugurated in 1940 in 36 pavilions on 1.066.197 m^2. It is a large multifunctional park equipped with 720.000 m^2 of a prestigious tree, architectural and artistic heritage, which merges precious architectural works and urban green. The Mostra, with its urban scheme which is almost unchanged from its birth, has its international value. In both complexes, surrounded by walls, the green spaces and the land are structural elements within the architectural project: these characteristics allow the integration of the touristic and historical value of the buildings with the possibility to develop activities

---

[2] World Design Organization, *mission,* wdo.org.

[3] For further information Morelli (2018). How can we make sustainable design? ***BEYOND ALL LIMITS/2018.*** *International Congress on Sustainability in Architecture, Planning, and Design.* October 17-18-19, 2018. *Proceedings Book of The Extended Abstracts.* Çankaya University Press: Ankara.

and services linked to culture and "cultivations" of the Mediterranean diet and of Campania wine and food panorama. Cultivars has been preceded by actions concerning culture, nature and environment, the dissemination of products and projects and respectful initiatives that valorized cultural, rural and natural environment and propose to safeguard the rural, handicraft and wine and food local heritage, even throught agreements and co-operations with public and private companies in the organization of training activities for a culture of a new rural and urban agriculture which improves the territory: from the realization of the garden/orchard in the Abazia di San Lorenzo in Aversa, to 2011 with the Oscar Green of Coldiretti, to the cultural and educational initiatives directed to all schools, through creative and sensorial multidisciplinary workshops that stimulated the knowledge of elements and processes of agriculture and healthy diet. The students and researchers UNICAMPANIA also contributed to *extra-moenia* initiatives to organize educational gardens in schools (Fig. 1).

Fig. 1. CULTIVARS, ARS to make with EXPERIENCE. The aim is to associate the value of the architectural heritage with experiences of urban agriculture to innovate the roles of the tourist and the work.

CULTIVARS is aimed to activate a group of services in the selected architectural complexes to strengthen their attractiveness for tourism. The starting point is to turn tourists who passively consume their time and space into travellers who live and positively interact with places. The Building heritage must be an active and alive heritage which produces, (softly) changes and interacts with travellers. The project includes the utilization of green spaces to create gardens and settlings of urban agriculture that can be the core to realize workshops on the culture of the Mediterranean diet and Campania food and wine. The workshops will take place in three levels: STORICA_MENTE (HISTORICALLY): it is oriented towards the knowledge of the artistic and architectural context through a narration of places, the history of monuments and their connection with the land. A "widespread museum of work" will be able to improve and facilitate the access to information through digital resources and tools.

NATURAL_MENTE (NATURALLY): it includes workshops on sowing and/or harvesting, according to seasons, in the gardens and green spaces of the monumental complexes, to know the key elements of the Mediterranean diet. CREATIVA_MENTE (CREATIVELY): it is a workshop which allows travelers, in a convivial dimension, to learn to transform products who have been cultivated, harvested or sowed in the gardens and the green spaces of the involved areas. The project includes partnerships with third sector bodies to develop "extramoenia" agricultural services aimed to improve green areas. This model is scalable for other regions and architectural complexes containing areas to be turned into gardens and workshop spaces. Through various meetings and workshops this project is a network of third sector branches that can be involved both directly, in the management of artistic complexes and services, and to map skills, resources and new "art areas" in which to implement the CULTIVARS model for new services. Meetings and workshops with the third sector actors will be an opportunity for socializing in which to identify the necessary skills to set up the staff of experts who will plan the workshop contents and will train the operators. The project includes small operations to improve green areas, with the co-operation of associations in the different territories. These areas, called "tissues of urban agricultures", will be widespread in the cultural approach of the project and will also have the task to promote and communicate the in initiative. The third sector will be also involved in the development and production of memorabilia designed by design students and to be sold in the hop; partners who have handicraft productive skills will have the opportunity to apply for the production of memorabilia, even by networking to integrate their skills. In the final part of the project there will be workshops to identify new art spaces where to implement CULTIVARS services and laboratories and create partnerships between subjects who can manage the initiative in the territory. The project provides partnership with professional tour operators who are directed to an international public, as well as partnership with tour operators of cruising and hotel sector. This activity will be taken into care by the project marketing referee. Through CULTIVARS the different tour operators will be able to improve their offer by proposing a new and involving kind of travel which combines the artistic and historic dimension with the food and convivial one (which is strongly attractive for the foreign market and not fully exploited! (Fig. 2).

Fig. 2. The tourist turns from space and time consumer into traveller, and the work from contemplative to an active place interacting with persons and their region.

This offer is highly competitive in South Italy tourism, where advanced services for accurate and not trivial experiences are rare. The valorization of architectural works such as those of the Mostra d'Oltremare with specific services for language targets adds value and competiveness and shows an unusual vision of architectural heritage in Campania. The project CULTIVARS gives the development of a system of reception and services for cultural and linguistic targets with ad hoc communication and digital supports. Partnership with university departments of foreign languages and cultures and conventions encouraging students traineeship will allow an offer which is qualitatively adequate to the international market. The project develops web and new technologies through different solutions. (1) The project provides the creation and the installation of interactive video projections stimulating the user through a recreational and creative

Fig. 3. The three phases-structured workshops. Historically. Naturally. Creatively.

approach on three thematic levels corresponding to laboratories: storica_mente with artistic and cultural contents; natural_mente which concerns the garden care and management; creativa_mente with interactive installations stimulating the use of garden elements and artistic contexts for the virtual creation of products, recipes and narrations, suggestion. The installation will be dynamic works changing according to seasons and the intervention of users who can add and modify elements or information. (2) Widespread digital museum: the architectural complexes and their green spaces will be enriched with elements allowing, through smartphones and tablets, to use contents which will strengthen the access to information. (3) Web platform will be helpful both in managing the organizational phase, through reservation and services customization, and contents presenting CULTIVARS art places and exploring Campania and Mediterranean agri-food issues. This platform offers contents extending the user's experience, making accessible photographs, productions, contacts created during the user's real presence in CULTIVARS (For example the user can see the growth of the young plant he contributed to plant or cure.) (Fig. 3).

CULTIVARS considers the period of start-up and building of spaces and services as the opportunity of developing training laboratories for tutors and operators, the worksites of know-how. Training activities will be directed to tutors and operators and will be based on the action learning that is training combining theory and practice. Construction and activation of the spaces and the services will be the training worksite where operators will face critical issues and will find solutions in a participatory way. Through some "special editions" of workshops, the project CULTIVARS is aimed particular to emphasize the involvement of people with sensorial disabilities (both as users and as operators): for example, deaf persons will be directly involved in the tour of art places and in services for laboratories for deaf people, events in LIS (Italian Language of Signs) will take place. Blind persons can be involved in sensorial workshops about taste and touch. All laboratories will be open and accessible to people with different abilities, a specialized tutor will follow the activities of special users. The project will also facilitate some micro-operations for the valorization of green or agricultural spaces in all Campania, these "tissues of agricultures" will be activated in partnership with associations of the third sector that are active in the involved territory, in the selection of partnership to activate policies and practices directed to the work integration of persons from so-called "poorest categories" will be an advantage, as well as to involve poorest categories in the identification of those who will produce memorabilia. The project CULTIVARS has seen in the ancient city of Pompei the possibility of its development through the knowledge of the ancient city which admirably combines not only archaeology, architecture and art but also agriculture and food and investigates the roman house as agricultural company *ante-litteram*.

3   Conclusions

From CULTIVARS are born many products of Kosmesis design: "Video pulchre", a bracelet-glasses to see well and beyond appearances, born from the meticulous investigation of the Vesuvian territory, architectural and cultural resources (the Domus of Poppea to Boscoreale and its treasures to the Archaeological Museum of Naples) and the study of the jewels contained in the Museum of the Coral of Torre del Greco, highlighting the values and the valences of the territory and its products. The jewel (from Fr. Ant. joel, lat. iocalis, iocus agg. "Joke, game" Precious metal ornaments worked, finished with great care, masterpiece, gem), made of rubber and coral, it transforms from bracelet to glasses and through a kay-code allows the link to the specific information sites describing the characteristics of the places from which the substitute object (De fusco op. cit.) was born. The object responds to the 3 F (form, function, feasibility) and the 3 E (ecology, economy, empathy). The product shows "an increasingly complex interweaving between media and environments with the consequence that any artifact can be configured as a digital ecosystem … innovative ways of education to tangible and intangible heritage".[4]

Also "Aurea Mile" is a kosmesis design product, a jewelry collection, precious metal ornaments worked, finished with great care, made of coral, mother of pearl, turquoise, which infer their structure from the recognition of the Vesuvian territory and the its products. The Stones (lat. pĕtra, Gr. πέτρα) name that is commonly given to some compact rocks, especially those used as construction material through the historical, typological, functional study and the recognition of the typological sequences of the Vesuvian villas of the "Golden Mile" turn into gems (lat. gemma "Bud" and "gemstone") generic term for any appropriately faceted gemstone with or without incisions, animal and plant products. A jewel dress that is worn and broken up realized in synergy with the most important companies of the place in a collective and connective manner (Fig. 4).

"To build new experiences with art and heritage towards an awareness of the creative expressions of civilizations"[5], the LANDesign® Research group has designed and produced a sound event titled "Lull Between Sound, Fashion and Design" In the benedictine Abbey of San Lorenzo *ad septimum* at Aversa, site of the Department of Architecture and Industrial Design. The seventeenth-century cloister of San Lorenzo has hosted the vibrations of the Gong, the Tibetan bells and the sounds that evoke nature, produced by the skillful hands of Gianluca Pistoia, a master able to combine and experience relationships between music, fashion, design for the wellness. The Gong bath has guided the numerous participants, pupils of the schools, university students, faculty, technical and administrative staff of the Department, to the knowledge-but with different modalities: through the 5 senses and different points of view, View from the bottom, from the top, suspended-of the relationship between environment, architecture, housing and dress through 150 "artifacts antigravity" exhibited on display and made by design students (Fig. 5).

---

[4] #Earth 2018, Digital Environments for Education, A Heritage International and Interdisciplinary Conference Brixen 5-6/7.

[5] idem.

Fig. 4. "Aurea Milia", LANDesign® with Annunziata Cirillo designer.

Fig. 5. "Lull Between Sound, Fashion and Design" with Gianluca Pistoia and students of Department.

Acknowledgements. The activity presented in the paper is part of the research grant the project of applied research LANDesign® (scientific managers Prof. Sabina Martusciello, Prof. Maria Dolores Morelli), Department of Architecture and Industrial Design, University of the Studies of Campania "Luigi Vanvitelli" with Benecon Scarl Regional Centre of Competence for Cultural Heritage Ecology Economy Design Services, Department of Pharmacy UNISA, direction General Miur Campania, Department Europe and Foreign National Council of Architects landscape planners and conservatories and Regione Campania has obtained the mention COMPASSO D'ORO INTERNATIONAL AWARD 2015, is testimonial "The Universities for Expo 2015" and "Project School Expo 2015", winner "Special Participatory Design Prize" and "prize on Li-NE-Works Realized" section of the X competition Iqu 2015 (Innovation and urban quality); II Award International Design Competition Poli.Design "The 5 seasons 2015"; III Prize contest "Ars. Art that realizes social employment "Foundation Accenture Special mention Mibact" 2013; Prize "Oscar Green" Coldiretti" 2011.

References

Cappellieri A (2007) Moda e Design: Il progetto dell'eccellenza. Franco Angeli, Milan

D'Auria A, De Fusco R (1992) Il progetto del design, per una didattica del disegno industriale. Etas books, Milan

De Fusco R (1985) Storia del design. Laterza, Rome-Bari

Martusciello S (2012) LANDesign. La Scuola di Pitagora, Naples

Martusciello S, Morelli MD (2014) Cultivars: cultivating culture in art, best practice in heritage conservation management from the world to Pompeii. In: XII international forum, Le vie dei Mercanti, Aversa, Capri 12–14 June. La Scuola di Pitagora, Naples

Morelli MD (2012) Design mediterraneo. La Scuola di Pitagora, Naples

Morelli MD (2018) How can we make sustainable design? BEYOND ALL LIMITS. In: International congress on sustainability in architecture, planning, and design, proceedings book of the extended abstracts, October 17–19, 2018. Çankaya University Press, Ankara

Communication

Communicating the Heritage, a Transmedia-Driven Approach

Matteo Moretti[✉] and Gianluca Camillini

Faculty of Design and Art, Free University of Bozen-Bolzano,
piazza Università, 1, 39100 Bozen-Bolzano, Italy
{matmoretti,Gianluca.camillini}@unibz.it

Abstract. The sales of printed material are at a historic low, digital publications are growing at a constant rate. Concurrently, we are witnessing the development of a culture of print that dialogues with the digital, creating a converging relationship. With this premise, the paper presents the research project *Das Land* and *LP magazine,* a transmedia editorial project edited and published in a post-editorial context by the Provincia Autonoma di Bolzano.

Keywords: Post-editorial design · Transmedia storytelling

1 Introduction

Sales of printed material are at a historic low, while information and publications disseminated by digital media are growing constantly and exponentially.

At the same time, we are witnessing a phenomenon that goes against the tide: the development of an opposite culture centred on the printed medium. This culture is constituted by independent publishing companies and distinguished by the attention to the content by the authors and the construction of the product.

The crisis that has stricken the publishing world in recent years has led to a natural selection that has guaranteed the survival of publications that offer a high standard of information presented in various modes (Camillini 2015, 104).

As a consequence, all professional figures who work together to produce a printed magazine, must have a high-level professional profile, that enables them to interpret the themes they address from the standpoint of their own discipline, giving the product a new editorial homogeneity, in which the boundaries between design and content are increasingly blurred, allowing the latter to follow the reader in any place and at any time of day, with the help of technologies that dematerialize it. A relationship is thus established between the physical and the digital, which is not in competition but on the contrary convergent (Jenkins 2006).

The scientific literature taken into consideration on this issue (Striphas 2011; Cramer 2013; Ludovico 2012) shows that the relationship between publishing and technology need not be viewed as a diatribe or competition, but rather as a dialogical relationship between the parts with the purpose of combining the specificities that each of them has to offer the other, compensating as a result for their respective weaknesses.

© Springer Nature Switzerland AG 2019
A. Luigini (Ed.): EARTH 2018, AISC 919, pp. 129–137, 2019.
https://doi.org/10.1007/978-3-030-12240-9_14

The scenario described above is not to be taken as a catastrophe, what we are witnessing is the death of standard-format publications such as lifestyle magazines, for example. The productions that survive however are those that stand outside the mainstream market and its logic of quantity, publications in which the quality of the printing and the tactile element are essential, and which respect the logic of a concept that guides the entire editorial project all the way to its physical realization. To publish means not only to inform, but to propose and explain significant points of observation, to look at things from a particular angle, to convey a perspective view. Perhaps, superseding its function of information, dissemination or discourse, the act of publication is acquiring its own expressive and narrative function, not only in the content as has always been the case, but in the form and in the making.

Research, both technological and not, therefore plays a central role, providing the instruments and platforms needed to open new spaces for design, such as the integration and hybridisation of printed and digital publishing, to generate what are known as *augmented magazines:* not distant islands but facets of a more wide-ranging project that embraces traditional, digital and augmented audiences, thanks to the production and/or redesign of the content on the basis of technology. This gives rise to what Jenkins defines as a transmedia narration (Jenkins 2006). Every medium is a channel for new and distinct information, and contributes to the development of the story and the understanding of the narrated world. The user is thus stimulated to reconstruct the comprehensive meaning of a publication through the integration of various media. The hybridisation of forms, content and technologies thereby become the distinctive characteristic of what we may define as *post-publishing,* the editorial *third way.*

Based on this short premise, this publication describes and concludes the section of analysis and strategy development for the research project titled *Das Land,* dedicated to the revival of an institutional editorial project by the Provincia Autonoma di Bolzano, which failed after several years of publication. Following a methodology based on co-design (Fuad-Luke et al. 2015) the team, in synergy with the stakeholders and scientific partners included in the process, identified the primary critical issues that led to the failure. It then explored the possibilities offered by transmedia design, elaborating a design strategy that aims not only to revive the editorial project, but to open it to new audiences.

The aim of the research project is to explore new forms of utilization and storytelling that can not only connect the digital world with the print world, but also develop new relations with different audiences, stimulating their curiosity to explore new platforms and their respective forms of storytelling.

The sections that follow describe the design phases of the case study required for this exploration: Sect. 2 introduces the analysis of existing case studies, with particular attention to augmented publications. Section 3 describes the process of redesign and the consequent editorial choices that led to the determination of the need for a transmedia strategy, whereas Sect. 4 describes its substance. Finally, the conclusions describe the evaluations of impact and effectiveness that will be made after the first issues of the magazine are published.

2 Analysis of the Case Studies

The first part of the work involved a careful study of the publishing landscape, both print and digital, from an aesthetic and formal point of view, and in terms of the content and how it is conveyed and utilised, in different ways and on a range of media, analogical or digital.

A preliminary analysis showed that very often the typical end-user of a publication is constantly searching for news and information, a tendency that reveals the static nature of the print medium, and on the contrary, extols the simultaneity of online publications, which are dynamic and changing, and satisfy the constant need for new content, not only in terms of the substance but the form as well.

In the attempt to overcome this weakness, we observed how some magazines have adopted solutions that build actual bridges between the print and the digital worlds, to foster convergence (Jenkins 2006) rather than competition. One of the strategies used to sustain media convergence was augmented reality: this is a technology that makes it possible to overlay digital data in the form of images, videos and three-dimensional renderings over images framed by the reader's smartphone.

In fact, though not continuously, this device had already been applied to print publications with the aim of making them more dynamic by creating an interaction between the reader and the editorial object. This was the case of the *New Yorker,* which entrusted the interpretation of "The innovators' issue" (May 16, 2016) to creative professional Christoph Niemann who illustrated and animated the issue with augmented reality. The development of *Uncovr,* a dedicated mobile phone application, made it possible to point a smartphone at the cover to bring to life an animated cityscape that bursts three-dimensionally out of the paper object.

Since January 2017, the popular science magazine *Focus* has used augmented reality to offer photos that can be explored 360°, 4K videos and 3D renderings readers can interact with. By opening the application on a smartphone and pointing it at the page, the images come to life and emerge from the physical limits of the printed magazine.

A similar solution was adopted by the *Harvard Business Review,* the printed content of which is not only a key to access the digital content, but is extended and implemented when framed with a smartphone.

Apart from the initial excitement, the superposition and interaction between analogical and digital media generated by augmented reality creates a relationship between the observer and the printed page. Augmented reality exploits the tactile nature and physical specificity of printed material, to create a very real experience, that is revealed to be radically different from the classical linear mode of reading the content. This new publishing paradigm substantially changes the value, the perception and the way of using the printed copy, which from an object that is traditionally read and set aside, is transformed into an actual key to access a new augmented world. Content that would otherwise remain hidden is extended and/or integrated, de facto offering a longer life to the printed artefact and opening up a new and heretofore little-considered relationship.

3 *Das Land*, a New Post-editorial Model

3.1 The Original Magazine

The research project titled *Das Land,* of which the authors of this paper are the founders and investigators, aims primarily to re-design and produce a monothematic magazine, printed in 40,000 copies to be distributed free of charge across the territory of the Autonomous Province of Bolzano. The original publication, given the bilingual nature of readers in Alto Adige, was circulated in two distinct editions: *Das Land Sudtirol* the title of the German-language version and *Provincia autonoma* the title of the Italian-language version. Published for 40 years, from 1976 to 2016, and distributed free of charge to 40,000 readers, it informed the subscribers in the two language groups about local events focusing on the territory, the heritage, and its protagonists. In 2016, publication ceased, following a consistent loss of interest on the part of the public, which in the meantime had evolved. The analysis of the Provincia concluded that the project was unable to evolve, to understand the demands of the territory and its public, and so in the end it was often ignored. In a further analysis session with the research team, other critical points emerged: on the one hand, the content, which was thoughtfully selected but not very homogeneous, often lacking thematic coherence, and on the other the formal and aesthetic aspects. The poor quality of the printing, the free distribution and the substandard design positioned the magazine on the level of many free-press newspapers, disposable publications of little use to anyone.

3.2 The Re-design

In June 2018, after a period of reflection that lasted two years, the Provincia decided to bring new life to the project, formalizing its collaboration with the Free University of Bolzano in the research project *Das-Land*, presented in this paper. The primary objective was to explore new forms of design that could tell the story of the territory and its heritage in an innovative manner, that could stimulate and engage an ample and diverse audience. The research group formed for the project was composed of two researchers with a background in editorial and digital design, the authors of this paper, who coordinated the exploration and re-design of the magazine. The relationship with the client was approached as a co-design project (Fuad-Luke et al. 2015): the first months of work involved periodical meetings finalized towards a discussion of the needs, possibilities, ideas and design proposals. The practice of co-design fostered a continuous mutual discussion, facilitating the convergence of viewpoints and proposals regarding the visual aspect, as well as the content and strategy.

After 5 months of co-design sessions, the decisions that were made proved radically antithetical to the existing project, affecting every aspect of the design process, and were obviously critical to the future of the magazine.

The direction we chose was to enhance the object by making a product of superior quality, both from the point of view of the content, and the point of view of the form. From the point of view of the content, the magazine will be published every four months and not monthly, and each issue will be dedicated to a specific theme; this will make it possible for the team of journalists to dedicate greater attention to the texts, and to the entire approach to the theme. Similarly it will offer the reader a compact outlook on the theme, avoiding the problem of dispersive contents which emerged from the analysis of the previous experience. From the point of view of language, it will no longer be produced in two separate Italian and German versions, but in a single version with contents in one language, equally divided between the two (specifically three articles in Italian and three in German). The masthead will consequently no longer be printed in two languages, but in one. A series of co-design sessions were dedicated to this problem, leading the team to decide on the acronym LP, consisting of the L for Land, the German term for province, and the P for the Italian counterpart Provincia. The masthead thereby intends to embody the strong connection of the inhabitants to their territory, underscoring the importance of the integration between the Italian and German cultures that coexist in the Alto Adige region.

From a formal point of view, contrary to the practice of more common magazines, LP will rely on sophisticated solutions and materials: again to assert the importance of the territory, its content will be printed on apple-paper, a special paper produced by Frumat from the recycled waste of local apples. Each issue will feature special production techniques that will interpret the theme of the issue and dialogue with it visually and through the touch – using die-cutting, transparent varnishes, special colours such as metallic or fluorescent inks, and hot foil stamping that will make the magazine a non-standard, more precious publication that readers are enticed to hold on to.

In addition to redesigning the magazine, the team elaborated new forms of digital utilization that are particularly significant for the theme of this publication, such as the web and augmented reality. These will create a new system of communication that implements the transmedia strategy developed by the research team, which aims at reaching and interacting with different types of readers, and encouraging the interaction of readers with the different media, to produce an authentic informative experience.

4 Transmedia Strategy

During the co-design sessions, the heterogeneous nature of the target audience clearly emerged, with its distinguishing features: the existence of the two language communities, Italian and German, and its ample demographic spectrum. One of the needs expressed by the client was the importance of reaching the widest possible range of people, from teenagers to the elderly.

The first step was therefore to analyse the target audience. Currently the Alto Adige region boasts a population of 527,750 inhabitants, most of them between the ages of 18 and 64 (Table 1), of whom 73.7% use Internet, often on a mobile device (5 users out of 6) (Astat 2017), especially in the young and adult age groups, often to read newspapers and magazines online (Voltolini 2018) (Table 2).

The analysis shows an audience, or rather a series of audience groups, divided by age, who offer an interesting point of departure for a consideration on new methods of converging design. On the basis of its initial premises, the research group thus began to speculate on the relationship between medium, age and languages (both verbal and visual). The result was the delineation of the major audience segments (seniors, adults,

Table 1. Age groups in the population of the Alto Adige region

Age	0–17	18–64	65–74	75+
	19.2%	65.1%	9.5%	9.8%

Table 2. Use of Internet by age groups

Age	16–34	35–54	55–74	Total
	93.9%	83.1%	40.3%	73.7%

young people) who must address three different technologies and media (paper, digital, augmented). On the basis of the research team's design experience, a relationship between the two groups was imagined, postulating a preference of the young people for digital media (web and AR) and of adults and seniors for print; the latter, furthermore, switch effortlessly between printed and digital media (Fig. 1).

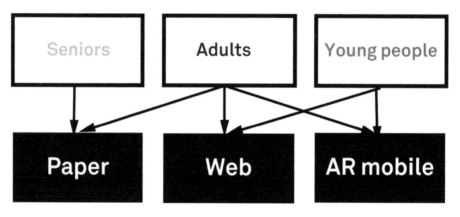

Fig. 1. Assumed correspondence between audience segment and medium

Assuming these relationships between audience and medium (scheme 1A), the research made further considerations in order to plan a strategy that could facilitate the interaction between the different audiences and the different media (Fig. 2).

The result was the development of a transmedia narration in which the three media, print, digital and augmented, contain a narrative project that unfurls interactively with changing content depending on the platform, and consequently on the audience that will use it. One of the key elements in a transmedia strategy is to arouse curiosity and encourage the reader to explore the content across platforms, by fragmenting a single narration into various levels and media (Herr-Stephenson et al. 2013). Two different types of decisions were enacted to pique the curiosity of the readers and push them to interact with the content: one based on the media, the other on the content.

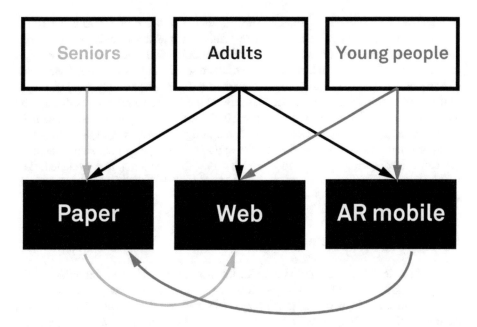

Fig. 2. Interaction between medium and audience segments generated by a transmedia approach

4.1 Media-Based Strategy

Following the transmedia model, the main content of each issue will be developed in different form and content depending on the medium. An example may be found in the project for the first issue, currently under development, on the theme of "Innovation", which will feature among other things the new technological hub in Bolzano. The story will be accessible in the traditional manner in print, in an article illustrated with photos. The web version will feature videos showing interviews with the protagonists, and finally, by scanning the opening photograph of the article with a smartphone, a three-dimensional model of the technological hub will appear: every space of it may be explored, with the visualization of information and data relative to the part that appears on the screen of the reader's smartphone.

The printed product becomes the key to access augmented content, thereby motivating the audience segments most resistant to the printed medium (young people) to acquire a copy of the magazine so that they can access the augmented version. Similarly, the adult audience segment (and perhaps even the senior segment) can read the content in print or view it and other new features such as videos, interviews and photo-galleries in the online version.

4.2 Language-Based Strategy

The original "Das Land" project, which was printed in two versions, Italian and German, essentially prevented the interaction between the two language groups. In view of a greater cross-pollination between the groups and between the printed version and the web, a second design strategy was implemented, based on the language of the content. In the printed edition, the articles will be published in only one language, either Italian or German. Each issue of the printed edition will therefore contain 6 major articles, 3 in Italian and 3 in German. Each of them will include two "bridge" elements: an abstract in the other language that summarizes the content, and a QR code that leads to the translated version online. The idea behind the bridge elements was dictated by the desire to use the abstract to create an initial engagement of the other-language reader, an engagement supported by the digital bridge offered by the QR code, which when scanned will take the readers of the opposite language to the same content by switching media, from printed to digital, so that they will not feel excluded. The language strategy involves every audience, taking readers from all three segments indistinctly from the printed magazine to the web.

5   Conclusions and Future Developments

This publication describes and concludes the part of analysis and definition of the strategy relative to the research project Das-Land, currently underway. The next steps will involve the design of the graphic elements and the design guidelines that will distinguish the first four issues, followed by a definition of the cycles for the assessment of impact and strategies. There will be two cycles of assessment, coinciding with the publication of the second and fourth issues using the model of research through design (Schon and DeSanctis 1986), a practice of thinking by practicing: the designer redefines and refines the design model through a series of cycles of assessment, followed by a theoretical reflection on the result achieved in relation to the starting assumptions and the research question.

The interest does not lie in a comparative assessment between the existing and the current design, but in gathering information about the interaction between the audience segments and the chosen media, to understand whether the transmedia strategies that were enacted had an impact on the audience and whether as a consequence each reader used more than one platform, and in that case, which ones. The assessment will be both quantitative and qualitative, based on the analytics provided by the web version together with those from the app in the augmented reality version. They will complete the answers to the questionnaires submitted to the readers on a dedicated page inside the magazine. The quantitative assessment will give an idea of the impact and utilization of the digital media, with particular focus on the age groups and geographic provenance, while with the qualitative analysis, the research team hopes to assess if and who used the printed version to access the augmented and web versions. This paper therefore represents the first step in a wide-ranging design and academic research project.

Acknowledgments.   The authors wish to thank the Provincia Autonoma di Bolzano for their collaboration and support.

References

Astat (2017). http://www.provincia.bz.it/famiglia-sociale-comunita/sociale/pubblicazioni-statistiche/pubblicazioni.asp?publ_action=300&publ_image_id=458253. Accessed 23 Aug 2018

Camillini G (2015) Beyond the book. Motives, economics and skills in contemporary publishing research. In: Progetto Grafico. Aiap Edizioni, Milan. N 28, Year 13

Cramer F (2013) "Post-Digital Aesthetics", Jeu De Paume, 1 May 2013. lemagazine.jeudepaume.org

Fuad-Luke A, Salokannel R, Keinanen K (2015) Return on Giving. Best mindset and practices for co-designing. LADEC, Lahti, Lahti Regional Development

Herr-Stephenson B, Alper M, Reilly E, Jenkins H (2013) T is for transmedia: learning through transmedia play. In: Los Angeles and New York: USC Annenberg Innovation Lab and The Joan Ganz Cooney Center at Sesame workshop, vol 10, p 2015. Accessed April

Jenkins H (2006) Convergence culture: where old and new media collide. NYU Press, New York

Ludovico A (2012) Post-digital print: the mutation of publishing since 1894. Onomatopee, Eindhoven

Schon DA, De Sanctis V (1986) The reflective practitioner: how professionals think in action. J Contin High Educ 34(3):29–30

Striphas T (2011) The late age of print: everyday book culture from consumerism to control. Columbia University Press, New York

Voltolini S (2018). https://www.salto.bz/it/article/09072018/web-generation-alto-adige. Accessed 23 Aug 2018

Representing Heritage on the Web.
A Survey of Online Platforms to Communicate Tangible Assets

Giovanni Caffio[(⊠)]

Department of Architecture, Università degli Studi "G. d'Annunzio",
Chieti-Pescara, Italy
giovanni.caffio@unich.it

Abstract. The main goal of this research is to identify the various forms of communication and representation of projects for the enhancement and protection of the artistic, architectural and cultural heritage present today on the net in order to create a classification and taxonomy that illustrates the state of the art from the point of view of the communicative, aesthetic and technological modalities. The paper also wants to focus on the specific case of heritage in Abruzzo highlighting, through the analysis of case studies, the strengths and weaknesses of the surveyed platforms.

Keywords: Web · Representation · Heritage · UX · Abruzzo

1 Introduction

Although the widespread use of web platforms for art and culture is broad and increasingly documented, the use of digital interactive systems to support the goals of cultural and natural heritage (UNESCO 1972), such as teaching and the knowledge of history, architecture and cultural traditions, or improving the experience of visiting museums and places of cultural interest, has not been considered with the same attention especially in local contexts where experiences, nevertheless interesting and praiseworthy, have not found the strength to evolve and keep up with the transformations imposed by technological and communicative progress. This, despite the obvious advantages of a communication that uses the net within the communication strategies and the most advanced digital technologies; the great information capacity, thanks to the multiple media resources that can be put in place (graphics, video, interactive 3D, infographics); the sophisticated systems of collaboration and interaction, to finally arrive at the integration with social sharing platforms. In this essay the focus is on the examination of the current state of theories, methods and technologies used, highlighting the strengths and weaknesses of the methods described and reporting unresolved problems and challenges. In addition, a case study will be presented illustrating the application of methods and technologies used in cultural heritage.

Through these examples, I want to give an answer to the questions from which the research starts, paying particular attention to the interface object of the websites, what today in the field of web design takes the name of User Experience Design or UX

A. Luigini (Ed.): EARTH 2018, AISC 919, pp. 138–146, 2019.
https://doi.org/10.1007/978-3-030-12240-9_15

(Triberti and Brivio 2017). The interface, conceived as a complex and coherent project using communication and information modes and written-graphic languages, can be used as a heuristic key, a useful tool to highlight the characteristics of a communicative form that, during a relatively short time, has been transforming, and is continuing to change, reaching today a uniform and conventional configuration. The web platforms, therefore, flank the previous communication systems for the knowledge and dissemination of the artistic and cultural heritage and redefine, according to different methods, a variety of tools used to represent the resources of a territory. The research methodology is based on a process that can be defined as "digital empiricism", where the theoretical structure is not established previously, i.e. imposed from above, but elaborated from below, starting from the examples and the results found on the field. The need to follow a "bottom-up" research line, going from the particular to the general, arises, finally, from the need to avoid a schematism that interprets the web platform as an automatic translation of established practices on a different medium (virtual museum as a digital copy of the real/analogue one) or, on the contrary, as a resolutive departure from the traditional model. In the first case, we would run the risk of not understanding the potential of the new support and tools, in the second case, we would risk accepting passively and uncritically the changes taking place. For this purpose, the websites of associations and institutions, that deal with projects safeguarding and enhancing local heritage, have been researched on the net and analysed, paying particular attention to those who explore both the fields of representation in an innovative way and the user experience design.

2 The Research Boundaries

As well demonstrated (McLuhan 1971; Bolter and Grusin 1999), the birth of a new medium determines, as a consequence of its own appearance and beyond the contents it diffuses, important transformations in social, economic and artistic behaviors: we are interested in highlighting how deeply they are also reflected on the culture of heritage, on the investigation and critical reflection that revolves around the theme, on the modalities of representation and dissemination of cultural and natural heritage. Determining in which specific forms, times and qualities this process is transformed by the advent of new information technologies and telematic networks is one of the many questions revolving around this research. To answer, we believe that it is essential to start the construction of an updated and detailed cartography of the multiple ways in which heritage is presented on the web. The realization of this thematic map is necessary the more the cultural, aesthetic, economic, collective and educational interests of the telematic networks appear inextricably linked to the communicative forms. The panorama of the experiences is manifold and varied: from an initial analysis, it is clear that, alongside the heritage websites created by museums, superintendencies, cultural institutions or professional associations, there are numerous websites produced by individuals or groups of people who share an interest in certain thematic areas of the heritage area.

The growth of websites about heritage causes not only a widening of access to documents and information otherwise unavailable, but also the conditions that anyone, having the necessary equipment and technical knowledge, can put on the web organized and packaged materials according to their taste and their passions linked to particular themes. On the Internet, and especially in the World Wide Web, a new global public space comes to light, in which the thematic sites represent a form of dissemination of the heritage, completely new, that we could define as "diffused" and "dotted". The communication of heritage then takes on various forms and invades new spaces: it can become a place for confrontation between opposing stakeholders on relevant topics; ground on which to seek the involvement of citizens with respect to some collective choices on the methods of conservation and protection; a dimension in which to cultivate narrative and communication methods through which to create and propose new protection practices. In the space of the web, not to mention the social networks with which would need an appropriate and in-depth reflection that goes beyond the aims of this essay (Giaccardi 2012), new paths of research start in connection with the heritage subject: there is a need to construct and define in a new way the relationships between institutions, scholars and public and private stakeholders. Let us try to point out the main categories within which we can summarize the many and varied forms that the relationship between heritage and the web can take.

Heritage on the Web: in this context, we consider the Internet and, in particular, the Web as a macro-support that conveys images, resources, historiographic materials, bibliographies, and so on, like a large library or, it would be more appropriate to say, a large archive. The metaphor of the library, although more immediate and understandable, could deceive if you think that materials about any subject present on the Internet, and therefore also the artistic and architectural ones, can hardly be framed and catalogued effectively. The metaphor of the archive can be more productive, if we reflect on the dynamic and not delimited, but at the same time orderable, nature of heritage materials on the Internet, and if it allows us to elaborate criteria for interpreting the devices regulating the elaboration and dissemination of documents. The enormous quantity of materials and sites prevents us from discussing this specific aspect of the net in this context, which it seems appropriate to postpone to a subsequent research.

Heritage Throughout the Web: while in the previous category the web is seen as a closed configuration as a support or deposit of already processed documents, in this category we consider the web as an open structure. Therefore, in this context, we do not consider the Internet as a means of transmitting predetermined contents, but as an environment for interaction, communication, cooperation and promotion. This category mainly includes social networks and, finally, those sites where some forms of commercial promotion emerge related to heritage and tourism.

Heritage of the Web: these are items, made up of information flows and graphic interfaces, thought and designed to remain virtual. In this case, we speak mainly of digital heritage, that is "unique resources of human knowledge and expression. It embraces cultural, educational, scientific and administrative resources, as well as technical, legal, medical, and other types of information created digitally, or converted into digital form from existing analogue resources. Where resources are 'born digital', there is no other format but the digital object. Digital materials include texts, databases, still and moving images, audio, graphics, software and web pages, among others" (UNESCO 2003).

3 Heritage on the Web: Cultural Heritage Websites in Abruzzo

With respect to the cases previously exposed, we focus our attention on the first of the three categories considering, in particular, the specific case of museum institutions. The numerous pages linked to museums of which the web is populated witness a process of widespread dissemination of the presence of museums in the cyberspace that, although extensive and detailed, has very different characteristics and qualities. Certainly, we are facing a panorama of cases in which there is a communication standard dictated by habits and uses of the web now rooted in users and designers. However, even in the more traditional and commercial sites, next to merely informative pages, we can find interesting experiments. In general, and at a basic level, museum websites are a means to present themselves, to self-promote themselves and to elaborate a specific communication on the web. The site becomes a sort of "business card" that contains essential contact information and a description of the collections and fields of study. Beyond these cases, in fact, there are well-known examples in which the website goes beyond merely promotional and communicative functions to the point of crossing the field of communicative research. Let's think about some examples of virtual museums that have made the history of the web (Galluzzi 2010) and have experimented with methods of observation and interaction with very sophisticated means (Ippoliti and Meschini 2011; Luigini and Panciroli 2018). Now the site is basically an indispensable means of communication whose realization requires specific skills and elaborated communication strategies, a process that, on the one hand, implies a continuous increase in the technical and graphic qualities of the websites, on the other, a flattening of information devices based on the most widespread and most successful standards. In fact, museums are increasingly appearing in a pedestrian style, with iconic patterns or interfaces borrowed from the more effective User Experience examples (Triberti and Brivio 2017) which, at the same time, are the more homologated. In our opinion, the sites that are most interesting are those where there is a more direct relationship between the vision of the museum and its digital communication project, or those websites where the proximity between heritage and new means of visual communication is strengthened.

An analysis of museum websites can be a useful way to understand some of the trends occurring in parallel on the web and in the dissemination of the heritage. The number of museum websites surveyed for this research phase is mainly derived from four web sources: Museo Italia, the portal of Italian museums and monuments (http://www.museionline.info); *Polo museale dell'Abruzzo*, born in 2014 with the reform of the Ministry of Cultural Heritage and Activities and Tourism, with the aim of enhancing and making accessible the cultural wealth of the state museums in the region (http://www.musei.abruzzo.beniculturali.it); the Museums section of the Abruzzo Region website (http://cultura.regione.abruzzo.it/); finally, the Abruzzo Museums section on the private portal In Abruzzo (http://www.inabruzzo.it/musei.html). In the first instance, field research focused on identifying and collecting the largest number of websites on the web, reaching a total number of 105 websites (Fig. 1). Subsequently, the museums' websites hosted on portals or general websites have been distinguished from the autonomous ones, in order to arrive at forms of classification and typological description useful for mapping a heterogeneous and, hopefully, expanding reality (Fig. 2).

Fig. 1. Map of websites dedicated to museums in Abruzzo organized by province. In bold the museums that are present with basic information on portals and general sites, with coloured background museums with autonomous websites.

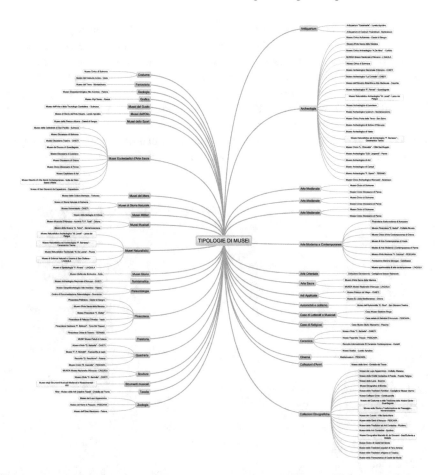

Fig. 2. Map of websites dedicated to museums in Abruzzo organized by type. Of the 40 typologies registered on the Museo Italia portal (http://www.museionline.info) the most significant number falls, in order, in archaeological museums, in ethnographic collections and in ecclesiastical museums of sacred art.

4   Website Analysis

The question deserves some preliminary clarification: it is clear that an analysis of the museum websites poses complex and delicate questions both in relation to the specific qualities of the medium and in relation to the disciplinary peculiarities. Wanting to deepen the criteria of analysis and declining them on the specific structure of the hypertextual structure, it is certainly helpful to start from the interpretative keys elaborated by Bettetini (2002) and based on the notion of space. These categories allow to reading the structure of a hypertext through three levels: the arrangement of contents, the dynamics of interaction and the iconic representation. Inspired by the methodology of Bettetini I previously (Caffio 2008) proposed an expansion of these levels of interpretation that I have called *topological structure*, *iconicity*, *interactivity* and *codicity*.

The first of the principles, *topological structure*, indicates the type of reticular organization by means of which the contents and the information are connected in a web of relationships such that the whole acquires a further significance with respect to the total of the individual components and changes according to the paths and mutual relationships. The *topological structure* is based on a logical disposition of the contents that, through the activation or deactivation of the links, creates a hierarchy among the nodes based on topological categories of above-below, near-far, centre-periphery. Moreover, it is possible to find general configurations that draw particular ratios both between single nodes and between larger sets: in parallel, as a tree, as a graph, and so on (Fig. 3).

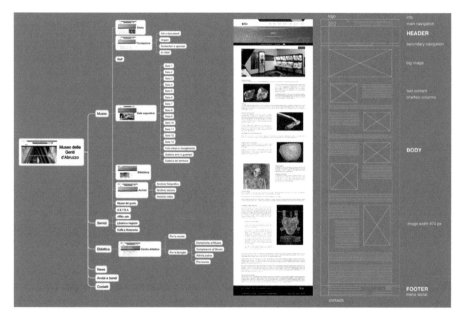

Fig. 3. Analysis according to the categories of topological structure and iconicity of the website of the Museum of the People of Abruzzo (http://www.gentidabruzzo.com). In this example, it is noted that the tree structure is rather branched in depth to the detriment of the users' achievement of the contents relating to the exhibition halls. These are described with a rich iconographic and textual repertoire organized according to a rather rigid two-column approach. There are no dynamic query systems like search engines and cross-links between materials on multiple rooms while the graphic representation is limited to the use of photographs. From the point of view of the code, the site is responsive, that is, it adapts in real time to different display dimensions (pc, tablet, smartphone).

The second principle, *iconicity*, concerns the display of contents, what today is properly defined as graphical user experience, in other words, the ways in which the information structure manifests itself to the user. We can highlight this principle fundamentally in the creation of navigation interfaces and in the design of digital pages where different codes and languages interact. The third principle, *interactivity*, concerns the presence within the connective architecture of a set of dynamics of use, of actions to be carried out in order to proceed in the knowledge. The goal of *interactivity* is not to communicate content but to stimulate actions that can take different forms: click, move, drag the cursor, but also travel and explore spaces. Finally, for the sake of simplicity, I indicate the importance of the software and the protocols used on the forms and operations of virtual spaces. In this treatment, therefore, *codicity* is the name given to the principle of materiality expressed by Cicognani (1998) when this is transferred from the physical to the digital world. This implies that in the design of digital spaces the rules of operation of the software must be respected with the same rigour with which the laws of physics apply to the material bodies.

5   Conclusions

Through the analysis of collected examples, it is possible to elaborate some general considerations. Although partial and extrapolated from a small number of examples on the net, these considerations bring to light the potentials and limits of the current websites of the Abruzzi museum spaces. It is important to recognize the website as one of the elements that contribute to defining and articulating the broader communication system. Within this complex and adaptive system, each medium interacts with the previous ones, continuously redefining limits, areas of influence, and communicative characteristics. The museum website, therefore, competes with other traditional media, such as specialized press and television, to conquer space and attention of an increasingly distracted public and is targeted by rapid and fragmented information. Compared to traditional media, the website has a series of undeniable advantages: in the face of relatively low-cost investment, it also allows small institutions to manage their own communication space; the audience that can be reached from a web page is virtually global; all the operations of updating the materials, modification and implementation of the organizational structures can take place in real time; finally, the website is scalable and expandable as a database, useful for storing, organizing and filtering materials collected and processed over time. On the other hand, compared to these undeniable potentialities, we are witnessing a rather bleak view of the total number of autonomous museums that, in the Abruzzo case, represent only 19% of the total, a very low number that reflects an equally modest national situation (Caprara et al. 2018). Moreover, apart from the brief description of the available materials, websites do not have virtual systems that, exploiting the digital communication and representation skills, work in synergy with the real exhibition spaces. To be penalized in these cases are mainly the dynamics of interaction, in which the navigator acts essentially as a passive reader, and the representation often flattens out on figurative formulas and trivial, if not simplified, graphic styles.

References

Bettetini G (2002) Gli spazi dell'ipertesto. Bompiani, Milano
Bolter JD, Grusin R (1999) Remediation: understanding new media. MIT Press, Cambridge

146   G. Caffio

Caprara B, Colombi A, Scala C (2018) I musei italiani nel Web: analisi, riflessioni e proposte didattiche. In: Luigini A, Panciroli C (eds) Ambienti digitali per l'educazione all'arte e al patrimonio. Franco Angeli, Milano, p 80

Cicognani A (1998) On the linguistic nature of cyberspace and virtual communities. Virtual Reality Res Dev Appl 3(1):25–33

Galluzzi P (2010) Museo Virtuale, voce in Treccani, Enciclopedia Italiana – XXI Secolo. Retrieved from testo disponibile in http://www.treccani.it/enciclopedia/museo-virtuale_%28XXI-Secolo%29/

Giaccardi E (ed) (2012) Heritage and social media. Understanding heritage in a participatory culture. Routledge, New York

Ippoliti E, Meschini A (a cura di) (2011) Tecnologie per la comunicazione del patrimonio culturale. Numero monografico di *DisegnareCon*, vol 4, no 8. Accessibile via DISEGNARECON. https://disegnarecon.unibo.it/issue/view/276/

Luigini A, Panciroli C (eds) (2018) Ambienti digitali per l'educazione all'arte e al patrimonio. Franco Angeli, Milano

McLuhan M (1971) Gli strumenti del comunicare, Il saggiatore, Milano (3 edn.)

Triberti S, Brivio E (2017) User experience. Psicologia degli oggetti, degli utenti e dei contesti d'uso, 1a edn. Apogeo Education, Santarcangelo di Romagna (Rimini)

UNESCO (2003) Charter on the Preservation of Digital Heritage, resolution adopted on the report of Commission V at the 18th plenary meeting, on 15 October 2003. http://portal.unesco.org/en/ev.php-URL_ID=17721&URL_DO=DO_TOPIC&URL_SECTION=201.html

UNESCO (1972) Convention Concerning the Protection of the World Cultural and Natural Heritage, adopted by the General Conference of UNESCO on 16 November 1972. http://whc.unesco.org/en/conventiontext

Caffio G (2008) Architetti nel web. In: Unali M (ed) Abitare virtuale significa rappresentare. Edizioni Kappa, Roma, p 54

Digital Exploration in Archival Heritage. Research for the Knowledge, Use and Communication of Architecture Archives Through Digital Representation

Caterina Palestini[✉]

Dipartimento di Architettura, Università degli Studi "Gabriele d'Annunzio",
Viale Pindaro 42, 65127 Pescara, Italy
palestini@unich.it

Abstract. The application of digital representation technologies in the archives of architecture is an important support for the knowledge, use and the most effective communication and enhancement of the documentary heritage.

In this sense the contribution proposes some research experiences aimed at the acquisition of graphic materials from private archives that risk disappearing without an appropriate systematization.

The goal is to present case studies that investigate the contribution that the drawing can offer as a tool for educational and popular analysis of these assets, in which cultural moments are summarized linked to different historical periods and different territorial realities that express the material values and intangible ones from which they were generated.

The acquisition in digital environment of collections of drawings, photos and other materials that accompany the compositional process developed by designers of different historical periods, allows, first of all, to transmit and consult in an interactive way the cultural heritage, procedures and professional experiences from which they derive, it also allows to retrace and analyze in detail the construction events of built and unbuilt architectures, also rediscovering the undisclosed experiments, remained on paper.

The study specifically examines the activities of designers who have worked in Abruzzo, between the nineteenth and twentieth centuries, highlighting the presence of unpublished materials from which merge figures of valid professionals and compositional events that deserve to be investigated and brought back to the internal of the national archival system.

Keywords: Digital representation · Heritage · Archives · Architecture · Communication

1 Introduction

Researching and bringing out the graphic-documentary patrimony held in the archives of twentieth century architecture is the goal of various cultural associations connected with public bodies and departments, among these the Associazione Archivi AAA-Italia, dedicated to the promotion of activities aimed at the knowledge and to the

© Springer Nature Switzerland AG 2019
A. Luigini (Ed.): EARTH 2018, AISC 919, pp. 147–153, 2019.
https://doi.org/10.1007/978-3-030-12240-9_16

valorization of design materials that risk to disperse in private and local situations. The coordination between the institutions and the researchers, among the persons interested in the study themes that investigate the architectural archives, has allowed gathering in a systematic collection, the work of professionals often ignored (Guccione, 2009).

From this synergy derives the research started and carried out in the university field that, in collaboration with the Archival Superintendence for Abruzzo, gradually adds cognitive elements to be brought back into the national archival system (Guccione, 2002).

The problems encountered are mainly related to the retrieval of data, to their systematization and to the precarious conditions of conservation, in particular, to private archives that are exposed to a progressive deterioration without attention.

In this sense, the initiative launched by the bodies responsible for protection appears to have been important, and they have undertaken the task of drafting and publishing, already in 2013, of a first catalogue of designers who worked during the twentieth century. On this occasion, the historical documentary values of 24 private archives, relating to engineers and architects who carried out their professional activity in the provinces of Abruzzo, have been made known. From this partial list, only 7 authors have converged on the portal of the national archival system that brings together the documentary corpus related to the Archives of Italian Architects (Toraldo, 2013).

In this direction, the digital acquisitions, the studies conducted through the representation that gradually evolve allowing progressive and ever increasing technological advances such as multimedia installations, interactive platforms and immersive experiences, have provided a collaborative support and continue to offer valid graphical support for analysis and comprehension of graphic materials, already archived or being acquired (Palestini, 2016).

2   Objectives and Methodology

The survey, conducted with the objectives previously exposed, proposes a repeatable operating methodology structured in various forms.

The survey therefore proposes different declinations and levels of detail that starting from a first overall analysis is directed towards the individual specificities of the archives examined. It is a vast and widespread work to be explored in different cases with cross-searches that allow to reconstruct the sources in an organic way to fully understand the composition and the idea for the realization (Palestini, 2017). The works and methods developed by the architects examined will then be traced back to the national platform, which will take on the task of making authors and projects available for consultation in a taxonomic manner to compare the various typological themes in their entirety and in relation to the distinct local realities.

The archives contain a myriad of technical drawings, photos, models, more or less complete information, often inhomogeneous between them that require specific keys for understanding the events, related to the construction or design of pieces that actually define the image of the contemporary city.

The realized projects allow comparison with the current image, those left on paper, the many solutions proposed and not materialized, allowing vice versa visualizing alternative scenarios, on which to be able to make new explorations, rethinking them to the built.

Fig. 1. Archive Antonio De Cecco, Borsa Merci Competition in Pescara 1958. Perspective view of the building. Original drawing tempera on table, Motto: "two for two"

3   Case Study: Competition for the New Commodity Exchange in Pescara

The contribution examines a case study shown to clarify the methodology adopted in the analytical rereading conducted through the drawing.

In this regard, digital representation technologies provide a contribution to communicate and make the original materials more usable, to understand and display in an alternative way the spatiality and the contents hidden in the many hypotheses left on the drawing sheets.

The analysis concerns in particular an unrealized project drawn up in 1958 in occasion of the National Competition for the new Commodity exchange in Pescara, to be built adjacent to the building of the Chamber of Commerce, built in the thirties on a project by Vincenzo Pilotti (Fig. 1).

The project rediscovered during the systematization and digital acquisition of the private archives of the architect Antonio De Cecco (1971–1971) who carried out his activity after the Second World War, between 1950 and 1970, mainly in the Abruzzo region and the Marche, reconstructs the vicissitudes of a public work in the city providing unpublished information and details.

Fig. 2. (a) Private Archive Antonio De Cecco, Borsa Merci Competition in Pescara 1958. Original drawings on watercolour table. Meeting room perspective; (b) View from the atrium (to the right of the trading room).

The drawings drawn up for the competition show an attention for the pre-existing structure that it joins by looking for a more modern stylistic language.

It is interesting to retrace through the graphs, products on gloss and paper, elaborated canons, plans, elevations and sections, which illustrate the rough 1:100 scale project which is accompanied by three perspective views that allow perceiving the three-dimensional image of the building. In particular, tables, made in tempera on cardboard, show in a corner view the two fronts of the new commodity exchange, proposed in a realistic inclusion in the city context, where it is possible to observe the graft with the neighboring Chamber of Commerce. Two watercolors further highlight the representative spaces of the interior, the entrance hall and the double-height first floor meeting room (Fig. 2).

This corpus of drawings made it possible to appreciate the prerogatives of the missing project, allowing it to be compared with the one produced by the architect Antonio Cataldi Madonna with engineer Giustino Cantamaglia, winners of the competition (Fig. 3).

Examining the plans drawn up by architect De Cecco, the close correlation with the adjoining building is evident, and is connected to it through the large double-height saloon, arranged in the central space of the internal courtyard. The ample space for the negotiations was the beating heart of the activities, the fulcrum of the project that foresees two accesses, the main one from via Conte di Ruvo, in continuation of the front of the Chamber of Commerce, and the side one from via Catullo. The latter is highlighted on the façade by the glazing of the meeting room framed by the original jutting parapet with decorated railing and bas-relief panels placed to mark the band between the first and second level. On the first floor, in addition to the meeting room, there were offices and service areas, while on the two upper floors, intended for the residence, there were apartments equipped with loggias.

The building finished with a modern terrace roof bounded by a shelter area supported by the succession of pillars.

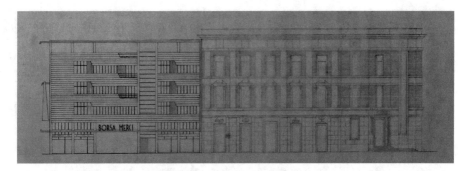

Fig. 3. Archive Antonio De Cecco, Borsa Merci Competition in Pescara 1958, original drawing.

Fig. 4. Survey and comparison between the building and the A. De Cecco project

A singular project for the linearity of its decidedly contemporary forms, exhibited in the effective perspective views of the inventors, best explored through three-dimensional study models that allowed visualizing and walking through a video the designed spaces that took shape in the digital dimension.

The three-dimensional analysis also allowed dissecting and breaking down the significant parts examined individually and as a whole.

It was then made an unavoidable comparison with the current reality with the project realized by Cataldi Madonna and Cantamaglia (Fig. 4).

The survey reveals the richness and the possibilities of dissemination contained in archival materials that, if analyzed, can provide information on the inventors, on the urban events of the city, on the historical moments, the cultural and architectural choices that led to the configuration of the contemporary image with its viewable alternatives (Fig. 5).

It is important to reiterate the documentary importance of the data deriving from the original projects that after an initial phase of acquisition, study and systematization of the materials, require appropriate multidisciplinary skills to be understood and communicated as in the specific case, through representation tools.

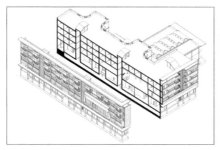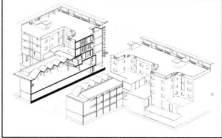

Fig. 5. Digital configuration of the original project, 3d sections

4 Conclusions

In short, the contribution that the methodologies and the increasingly extended formulas of digital design can offer in the analysis of architectural heritage, in explorations through three-dimensional models that exceed the boundaries of the drawing sheet, offer new semantic spaces to understand and disseminate with different approaches the precious inheritances kept in the archives of architects. The themes of the conference therefore constitute a moment of discussion and interdisciplinary debate on the educational communication of cultural heritage (Figs. 6 and 7).

Fig. 6. Digital configuration of the original project. Views of the three-dimensional model.

Fig. 7. Digital configuration of the original project. External view of the building

Acknowledgements. The research on the Antonio De Cecco archive was carried out with the collaboration of Tiziana Giura. A thank you goes to the Archival Superintendence of Pescara and the De Cecco family that allowed the consultation and acquisition of the original documents, in particular Mrs. Giuseppina Delle Ore, the architect's wife.

References

Palestini C (2016) Le ragioni del disegno come strumento di analisi e comunicazione per gli archivi di architettura del Novecento. In: Bertocci, Bini (eds) Le Ragioni del disegno. Pensiero, forma e modello nella gestione della complessità. Gangemi, Roma, pp 925–932

Palestini C (2017) Le frontiere del disegno per gli Archivi di Architettura. In: Territori e frontiere della rappresentazione. Territories and frontiers of representation, Gangemi, Roma, pp. 209–220

Toraldo F, Ranalli MT, Dante R (2013) L'architettura sulla carta. Archivi di Architettura in Abruzzo, Tinari, Villamagna Chieti

Guccione M (ed) (2009) Documentare il contemporaneo. Archivi e Musei di Architettura, Gangemi, Roma

Guccione M, Pesce D, Reale E (2002) Guida agli Archivi privati di architettura a Roma e nel Lazio. Da Roma capitale al secondo dopoguerra, Gangemi, Roma

PUDCAD Project. Towards a CAD-Based Game for the Implementation of Universal Design Principles in Design Education

Giorgio Buratti[1(✉)], Giuseppe Amoruso[1], Fiammetta Costa[1],
Margherita Pillan[1], Michela Rossi[1], Ozge Cordan[2],
and Demet Arslan Dincay[2]

[1] School of Design, Politecnico di Milano, Milan, Italy
{giorgio.buratti,fiammetta.costa}@polimi.it
[2] Interior Architecture Department, ITU Faculty of Architecture,
Istanbul, Turkey
{cordan,dincayd}@itu.edu.tr

Abstract. The notion of inclusive design and universal design principles are today widely recognised by most of the educational institutions, nonprofit organizations and particular authorities around the world. Within the subsequent legislations and obligations around the world, the awareness of universal design has reached a certain level to be placed in design education curricula. However, there are slight differences in teaching and practicing universal design principles in higher design education. Therefore, as educational outputs, these differences have a major impact on the students' knowledge of the universal design principles and implementing these principles into their design decisions in an effective way. In this regard, PUDCAD project (Practicing Universal Design Principles in Design Education through a CAD-based Game) aims to offers a CAD based game platform for undergraduate design students to learn and adapt universal design guidelines into spatial experience and design practice.

Keywords: PUDCAD · Education through digital media ·
Serious game and gamification · Universal design · Inclusion

1 Introduction

PUDCAD is a project founded by the European Erasmus + program which involves five European university institutes coordinated by ITU, Istanbul Faculty of Architecture. The other participants are Institute of Design and Fine Arts, Lahti, Finland; Detmolder School of Architecture and Interior Architecture, Detmold, Germany; Architecture Department, Università degli Studi di Firenze, Italy; School of Design, Politecnico di Milano; Turkish non-governmental organizations SERÇEV (Association for Well-being of Children with Cerebral Palsy) and Occupational Therapy Association of Turkey[1].

The project is part of European Union cooperation actions for innovation and sharing of good practices which provides, at systemic level, the modernization and activation of educational paths through cooperation with partners from other countries

© Springer Nature Switzerland AG 2019
A. Luigini (Ed.): EARTH 2018, AISC 919, pp. 154–162, 2019.
https://doi.org/10.1007/978-3-030-12240-9_17

and participatory approaches based on ICT. The activities supported by these key actions aim to acquire specific skills and to improve the students and young workers levels of preparation so that they can work easily in the different member states.

Among the actions promoted by Erasmus+ , acquisition of civic and social skills capable of fostering intercultural dialogue, social inclusion and non-discriminatory active citizenship is fundamental.

The development of critical thinking, the knowledge of computerized media and the creation of new or better practices, is intended to provide for the needs of disadvantaged social groups and to cope with the differences resulting from geographical, ethnic and economic disparities.

According to the European Disability Office in the face of an increase in people with disabilities, integration into a normal life in terms of employment, education and mobility is still lacking in many states.

Although there are many non-profit organizations and commissions that fight prejudice and discrimination, exclusion from normal social life for many people with disabilities begins with scholastic age. Based on these assumptions, the PUDCAD project aims to create a gaming platform based on CAD software which allows university students of the project disciplines (designers, engineers and architects) to learn and apply Universal Design principles in design practice. The term "Universal design" outlines a design method that provides for environments fruition and products use regardless of age, physical abilities and/or user social condition. This philosophy, that beyond a few nuances of meaning is also called Design for All or Inclusive Design, is due to Ergonomics. Ergonomics is an essential discipline for the implementation of the social inclusion and non-discrimination targets set by the EU, but often not taught or considered marginal in designers training. PUDCAD intends to remedy this gap providing an application that is configured not only as a tool for digital design, but as a real learning software. Through the implementation of playful dynamics, future designers will be able to internalize the principles of Universal Design and to develop solutions that consider different social groups skills and allow autonomy and equal opportunities for all. Participation of Occupational Therapy Association of Turkey and SERÇEV, organizations with extensive experience in rehabilitative clinical practice and in supporting children with cerebral paralysis (pathology that includes different forms of motor functions impairment), has oriented research towards secondary education institutions. In fact, this period is considered a crucial moment in ensuring employability and consequent social inclusion for people with disabilities.

2   Method

The project will last three years and it requires the involvement of 1000 people among researchers, students and consultants distributed among Turkey, Finland, Italy, Germany and Italy. The coordination among different nations' research groups is guaranteed by a program of transactional meetings, conferences and interdisciplinary workshops, where students actively contribute to implementation process. A task is assigned to each of the research institutes according to research specificity of each group. The program includes 6 phases:

1. *Analysis and documentation*
   The first activity is the comparative analysis of legislation and accessibility policies in the different participating states. In addition the different teaching methods and principles of Universal Design are evaluated.
2. *Pilot Research*
   This step involves the evaluation of each state's inclusion system. The research subjects are the secondary institutes, both as regards support practices through the evaluation of school environment accessibility and its correspondence to Universal Design principles.
3. *Scrutinizing the Game Database*
   In this phase, the parameters that determine the digital application feasibility and operating principles are specified. This step includes a cognitive and emotional mapping and the evaluation by students, specialists and researchers of individual capacity levels relating to specific disabilities.
4. *Developing the Infrastructure*
   This activity evolves the studied parameters in game inputs and it will allow the creation of first digital prototypes.
5. *Developing the Game and Its Supplementary Learning Materials*
   In this phase, an Information Technology company will be involved. This operator will help the research group in application developing, in creating additional teaching materials and in studying interactive experiences on different media (computers, tablets and smartphones).
6. *Implementing the Game into Universal Design Curricula in International Education tion Networks*
   This is the phase where, using also social media and technical conferences, the results and the application will be made known to the international didactic paths that train designers.

At the time this paper is written, the project is between the second and third steps. The pilot research activities, coordinated by the research unit of Politecnico di Milano led by prof. Fiammetta Costa, will be described below.

3   Results

The Milanese group was tasked with developing the pilot research. This step has been organized into several actions:

1. The construction of a survey and investigation method that, starting from the theoretical research carried out in the previous actions, makes it possible to verify the correspondence with the principles of the Universal Design of existing school buildings selected using different features of the school environment as measure.

2. The organization of first transnational meeting. These meetings purpose is the Universal Design principles dissemination and the creation of processes and methods intended for their learning and use in design practice.
3. The implementation of a Workshop involving 25 students from the 5 different Schools in a design competition. The students, organised in 5 international teams, are asked to design an inclusive high school environment encouraging students to develop innovative design ideas and to simulate the design process according to Universal Design principles.

The survey method is based on the adaptation of checklist ADA (https://www. adachecklist.org/). This tool was produced by Institute for Human Centered Design, and it has been developed as the first step in a planning process for readily achievable barrier removal. With the ADA accessibility checklist, you can quickly and easily verify that buildings are accessible by all individuals with disabilities. This case-by-case basis reporting tool checks for accessibility requirements and standards, such as checking for ramps, access to restrooms, pay phones and other structures, to support people with disabilities and to identify barriers to accessibility in order to provide reasonable accommodation. This tool has been adapted to Italian legislation and it has been simplified for the application in the workshop (Fig. 1).

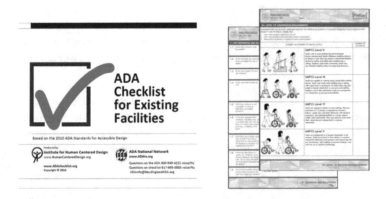

Fig. 1. ADA checklist (left) and the PUDCAD checklist (right)

The international workshop was scheduled for five days, with lectures and practical exercises alternating. The students were organized in groups of five people from five different countries.

Day 1 Empathy Day
The empathy day was designed to allow students to experiment with various types of physical disabilities and to understand the daily problems that a disabled person meets in a school environment. Physical problems have been simulated, such as lack of an arm or leg, or limited mobility and every student has experienced this state for a school day (Fig. 2).

Fig. 2. Empathy Day: students simulating disability experiences.

Day 2 Survey Day
The second day was dedicated to the survey. The different teams went to several secondary schools chosen on specific characteristics such as the building construction period (historical or modern building), the type of school (scientific, professional, etc.), peripheral or central location. Using the specifically prepared check list, each team verified the accordance of the buildings' features to Universal Design principles (Fig. 3)

Day 3 Storytelling Day
During this day students where encouraged to represent the knowledge acquired in the previous steps integrating elements observed in real context with direct experience. The different students group challenged the materials, debated the content, enriched them with their own knowledge and formulated their own opinions and research questions building their own ground for the development of design ideas. They organized the material in a storyboard to visualize their existing assumptions and each team produced a presentation summarizing the main school environments problem from the perspective of disabled people.

Day 4 Ideation Day
This was a full day of individual sketching and ideation around the selected opportunity areas, combined with sharing moments within the team to discuss and build upon each other's ideas. Participants chose which concept direction they wanted to work on further. Brainstorming allowed teams to identify a common design strategy and final concept directions (Fig. 4).

Fig. 3. Survey day. The survey was carried out in several schools chosen on the basis of different parameters: construction year of the building, type of school and location in the city. (a) Scientific and Linguistic lyceum "Guglielmo Marconi"; (b) High Education Institute "Enrico De Nicola"; (c) Classical lyceum "Tito Livio"; (d) High Education Institute "Falcone-Righi"-Lyceum "G. B. Vico".

Day 5 Project Day

This stage recreated typical professional pressures to deliver final design work on time to an expectant client. The teams needed to prepare a 20 min presentation of their final propositions. They had to resolve conflicting opinions and agree a plan, dividing tasks to produce their presentation materials in time. They had to choose which team members would present the story and how they would like to present it as a group. This step of the process offered participants the chance to develop essential design team skills, being able to identify and agree upon the key messages around a concept and tell a story that conveys the key benefits and value of a proposition convincingly in a given amount of time (Fig. 5).

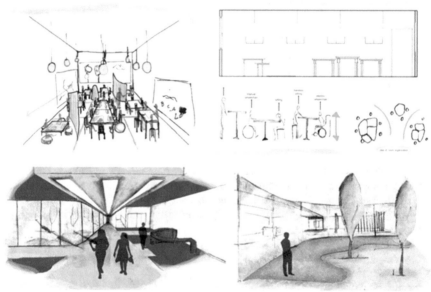

Fig. 4. Work in progress, teams develop ideas and identify the first concepts.

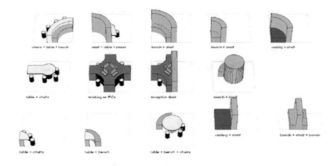

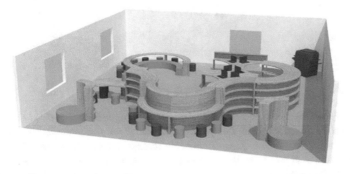

Fig. 5. The winning project: *Inganni, no more tricks on your way*. Andrea Zito, Anita Deckers, Rojda Edebali, Sabina Elena Quocchini, Mirka Pellikka. Modular furnishing elements for schools study rooms and libraries that can be used by both able-bodied and disabled people.

4   Conclusion

The intensive preparation phase enabled to complete a project in just five days, at an effective but challenging pace. Direct experience was fundamental: the survey results, the empathy day and the meeting with high school students and teachers, in synergy with the theoretical lectures of researchers from different countries, were the substratum on which the students developed the first digital models.

Five proposals for educational environments have been designed to highlight how, by considering disability issues already in a first design phase, and not considering it as a normative constraint, it is possible to obtain inclusive environments capable of perfectly meeting the needs of disabled and able-bodied users.

Projects submitted by different groups were evaluated by a jury of professors and researchers.

Acknowledgements. Authors of this paper wish to thank high schools staff for their contribution to this project: prof. C. Sequi and prof. A. Catalano, IIS "Enrico de Nicola"; Head Teacher A. Ferrario and prof. C. Costa, Liceo Classico "Tito Livio"; Head Teacher A. Rezzani and Head Teacher S. Bassi, IIS "Falcone-Righi"- Liceo Statale "G. B. Vico". And finally a special thanks

Prof. A. Rezzani and Prof. D. Di Lena, Liceo "Guglielmo Marconi", for their help in collecting so precious data.

ITU, Faculty of Architecture
  Dr. Ozge Cordan, Dr. Demet Arslan Dincay, Dr. CagılYurdakul Toker, Elif Belkıs Oksuz, Busra Gizem Vayva;
Institute of Design and Fine Arts
  Timo Sulkavo
Architecture Department, Università degli Studi di Firenze
  Antonella Sera, Francesca Tosi
Detmolder School of Architecture and Interior Architecture
  Ulrich Nether, Jan Philip Ley
Politecnico di Milano, School of Design
  Fiammetta Costa, Michela Rossi, Margherita Pillan, Giuseppe Amoruso, Giorgio Buratti
SERÇEV
  Kadir Ülger
Occupational Therapy Association of Turkey
  Gonca Bumin

ERASMUS+ KA203 2017 – TR01-KA203-046577

PUDCAD - Practicing Universal Design Principles in Design Education through a CAD-based Game Project is granted by the European Commission for the Erasmus+ Program KA203 conducted by the Center for European Union Education and Youth Programs (Turkish National Agency, http://www.ua.gov.tr) of the Turkish Republic Ministry of European Union. However, the Turkish National Agency or the European Commission cannot be held responsible for the opinions contained herein.

References

Blomberg J, Burrell M, Guest G (2002) An ethnographic approach to design. The Human Computer Interaction Handbook: fundamentals, evolving technologies and emerging applications. L. Erlbaum Associates Inc., Hillsdale, pp 964–986

Hall T, Meyer A, Rose D (2012) Universal Design for Learning in the Classroom. Uilford Press, New York

Hoegl M, Gemuenden HG (2001) Teamwork quality and the success of innovative projects: a theoretical concept and empirical evidence. Organ Sci 12:435–449

Kalbach J (2016) Mapping Experiences. O'Reilly, Newton

Lifchez R, Winslow B (1979) Design for independent living: The environment and physically disabled people. Architectural Press, Boston

Rose D, Meyer A, Hitchcock C (2005) Universally Designed Classroom. Harvard Education Press, Cambridge

Rosenberg N (1983) Inside the Black Box: Technology and Economics. Cambridge University Press, Cambridge

Rouse R (2001) Game Design: Theory & Practice. Wordware, Texas

Rubin J (1984) Handbook of usability testing: how to plan, design and conduct effective tests. Wiley, New York

Sanders EB, Dandavate EU (1999) Design for Experiencing: New Tools. In: Overbeeke CJ, Hekkert, P (eds) Proceedings of the First Int. Conference on Design and Emotion, TU Delft

Digital Heritage 1

3D Printing Technology, Video Mapping and Immersive Audiovisual Scenography for Heritage Museum Exhibits

Case Study: FSJ-3D Printing + Mixed Media Installation in the MuCEM

Franz Fischnaller[1](✉) and Francesca Fatta[2](✉)

[1] Accademia Albertina di Belle Arti di Torino, Turin, Italy
franz.fischnaller@albertina.academy
[2] Università degli Studi Mediterranea di Reggio Calabria, Reggio Calabria, Italy
ffatta@unirc.it

Abstract. This paper presents FSJ-3D printing + mixed media installation (FSJ-3D P + MI), a design combining 3D printed models, video-mapping, immersive audiovisual scenography and digital heritage storytelling. The installation is part of the Virtual Journey through the history of Fort Saint Jean (VJ-FSJ) Project, a permanent digital heritage exhibit, namely *Virtual Journey through the history of Fort Saint Jean,* a historical site in Marseille, to be open at the Musée des Civilisations de L'Europe et de la Méditerranée (MuCEM) in France, as part of the planned activities of the Center of Interpretation of the history of the FSJ in France.

Keywords: 3D printing · Video-mapping · Mixed media · Exhibit ·
Cultural heritage · VR technologies in museums ·
Digital narrative and storytelling · Historical monuments

1   Introduction

Premise: Project Background and Framework
The Museum of European and Mediterranean Civilizations in Marseille (MuCEM) [1], designed by architect Rudy Ricciotti [2] was unveiled together with the Villa Méditerranée conference center [3], designed by Stefano Boeri [4] on the occasion of the appointment of Marseille as the capital of European culture [5], where new cultural infrastructure (MP2013) was a key part of a larger, decades-long, multibillion-dollar development effort to revitalize the city [6]. This development and cultural activities took places between the framework of Marseille-Provence 2013 or MP2013 [7], was the year-long series of cultural events that took place in Marseille, France and the surrounding area to celebrate the territory's designation as the European Capital of Culture for 2013. In total, there were more than 900 different cultural events that attracted more 11 million visitors [8]. Marseille-Provence 2013 had an operating budget of approximately 100 million euros and more than 600 million euros in new

© Springer Nature Switzerland AG 2019
A. Luigini (Ed.): EARTH 2018, AISC 919, pp. 165–173, 2019.
https://doi.org/10.1007/978-3-030-12240-9_18

cultural infrastructures [6]. Dedicated to Mediterranean culture, the MuCEM complex was built at the entrance to the Vieux Port and is joined by a walkway to the Fort Saint Jean (FSJ) [9], a seventeenth century fortress full of history, built on the Roman memories of the city. The MuCEM encompasses three sites. Along the sea, at the entrance to the Old Port, the J4 building (Rudy Ricciotti's and Roland Carta's symbolic architectural creation) and the FSJ, a fully restored historical monument [10]. Five years after the inauguration, MuCEM is investing in the FSJ to inaugurate a "Center of interpretation of the history of this historical monument to be able to tell part of the complex history of this defensive structure. Within this context FSJ-3D printing + mixed media installation have been conceived and implemented. This paper presents an overview of the concept, the design, the production process and challenges encountered in successfully creating the installation to valorize the FSJ (Fig. 1).

Fig. 1. Musée des civilisations de L'Europe et de la Méditerranée, Photo: MuCEM

2   Research Framework

The ongoing new possibilities offered by the widespread diffusion and accessibility of digital tools and technologies are progressively empowering the cultural heritage practice in the research, documentation as well as the creation of quality projects, experiences, that are enhancing the communicability and the fruition of cultural content, making it more accessible to the global community. In this melting pot of innovation, the 3D printing technologies are greatly contributing to the cultural heritage field. There is a fast-growing community within the cultural heritage field using 3D printing technologies, techniques and tools. Apart from the industrial and commercial use of engineers and designers that have been using 3D printers for more than 30 years [10]. 3D printing is one of the hottest things trending in the tech world, and people have used it to create all kinds of things for entertainment, art, work, education, medical needs and more. We are slowly coming to grips with the potential that 3D printed materials can bring to the plate across multiple industries, including manufacturing, education, space, and even weaponry [11]. 3D printing is in a phase of rapid technological changes and promises more enhancing experiences for the field of cultural heritage. We expect that 3D printing will not only become vital in the field of reconstruction of objects, but also for research, documentation, preservation and educational purposes, and it has the potential to serve these purposes in an accessible and all-inclusive way [12].

3   Related Works

In the last several years 3D printing has been intensively used by in the cultural heritage field for preservation, restoration and dissemination purposes [13]. Many Europeans and North American Museums have purchased 3D printers and actively recreate missing pieces of their relics [14]. Scan the World is the largest archive of 3D printable objects of cultural significance from across the globe. Each object, originating from 3D scan data provided by their community, is optimised for 3D printing and free to download on MyMiniFactory. Through working alongside museums, such as The Victoria and Albert Museums [15] and private collectors [16]. The initiative serves as a platform for democratizing the art object. The Metropolitan Museum of Art and the British Museum have started using their 3D printers to create museum souvenirs that are available in the museum shops [17]. Other museums, like the National Museum of Military History and Varna Historical Museum, have gone further and sell through the online platform threading digital models of their artifacts, created using Artec 3D scanners, in 3D printing friendly file format, which everyone can 3D print at home [18]. During the last years, the application of 3D technologies to Cultural Heritage has provided successful results, with impact on preservation, valorisation and heritage transmission. Now, the emergence of 3D printers open new horizons for the heritage sector [19]. In this vein, this paper presents the conception and the production process of this case study.

4   Concept, Research Context and Motivations

FSJ-V3D Printing + MM Installation is a cross disciplinary installation, combining technology, digital media and tools intersected with cultural narrative (i.e. Digital heritage storytelling) 3D printed models and video mapping merged into immersive audiovisual scenography). It was designed to be an integral part of the exhibit: *Virtual journey through the history of Fort Saint Jean project* (VJ-FSJ), one of the outcomes of a cross-disciplinary framework research entitled: NEW GENERATION (Interaction in Cultural Heritage, Interactive Immersive Exhibitions (NGI-CH research) carried out by Franz Fischnaller [20], as artist and researcher in residence at the Institut d'études avancées - Exploratoire Méditerranéen de l'interdisciplinarité of Aix-Marseille University (IMéRA) [21], in partnership with the MuCEM [22] and the MAP Laboratoires [23]. Project outcomes were the result of a collaborative effort and support of institutions and experts from the fields of history, archaeology, architecture, design, social science, engineering, technology, storytelling, communications and management.

5   Research Context - Motivation - Goals

In the past two decades, museums have seen rapid changes in terms of the application of information technology, which has been used to represent their collections in new ways. Museums provide a public service and communicate through collections associated with information applications which create new visions of museum issues for the visitor [24]. NGI-CH research focuses on the intersection of Art, humanities and social sciences (history, archaeology and cultural studies) combined with leading technologies and advanced new digital media tools with the aim of empowering engaging and creative design solutions for the fruition of content and cultural heritage experience [25]. A major motivation behind the research is to envision experimental approaches for exhibit design solutions that can provide context for enhancing the creation of high quality digital heritage experience [26]. Digital Heritage works that can strengthen the European capability for the creation of new forms of digital entertainment and engagement based on cultural heritage, and that can promote the use of new technologies such as new media and new modalities of access making cultural heritage more accessible to the global community [27]. NGI-CH responded to the challenge of how technology and digital media can be effectively used to support the museums practice for the growing need to create DH experiences with richer interpretations of the past and enhancing the audience's knowledge improving the communicability and the fruition of cultural contents for a new understanding of the past while attracting a wider audience and public engagement [28].

6   Project Concept, Exhibit Space and Historical

Patrimony Context
FSJ-V3D Printing + MM Installation is integral part of the virtual journey through the history of the VJ-FSJ project, a new media permanent exhibition based on five Historical periods (49 BC, 1423, 1660, 1943 and today) of the FSJ and Marseilles. Initially the opening of the exhibition is expected for the end of summer 2018 in the FSJ Galerie des Officier in the FSJ at the MuCEM in Marseilles. VJ-FSJ Project was conceived as a twelve phase development. Phases one to eight, delivered prior to this paper has been completed by Franz Fischnaller in collaboration with MuCEM in- and out house with cross disciplinary teams. Phases 10 to 12 (i.e. Final content production, content and system integration of exhibit components on site, final exhibit set up, project closure and exhibit opening) is currently under development directed by the MuCEM.

VJ -FSJ Exhibition Concept
The exhibition offers to the visitors an audio visual multilayered immersion through historical key moments that shaped the history of Marseilles. It combines digital narrative and storytelling in physical and virtual architecture, bridging physical augmented and virtual architecture with digital content and mixed media interfaces, embedded in a historic building. The narrative and storytelling content inspired on the selected historical periods are presented in a holistic manner in the exhibit space and throughout the different rooms equipped with platforms, technical systems and devices among

which, video-mapping, augmented reality effects and optical illusions within real surfaces and virtual projections.

Exhibit Space: Virtual Journey Through the History of FSJ

The Exhibit space of VJ-FSJ Lower Officers Gallery is located in the central part of the FSJ, constructed at the time of Vauban. The Seigneur de Vauban and later Marquis de Vauban (1 May 1633–30 March 1707), commonly referred to as Vauban (French: [vobã]), was a French military engineer who rose in the service to the king and was commissioned as a Marshal of France [29]. Gallérie des Officiers is a linear structure composed of a gallery articulated by six identical rooms. Room O.01 to O.06 and a tunnel. FSJ-V3D Printing + MM Installations was design to be displayed in ROOMS O.01 and O.03 in the Exhibition Space (Fig. 2).

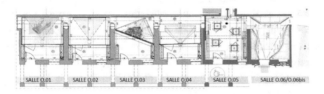

Fig. 2. FSJ Gallérie des Officiers (a) Division of rooms in Officier Gallery (b) - Photo: MuCEM.7

Historical Patrimony and Architectonic Heritage Context

Built by Louis who XIV decided to strengthen the city's defenses [30]. The FSJ has been a military complex and it was fundamental part of the history of Marseille. A complete restoration of this historical monument was concluded in 2013 and since then FSJ is linked by two thin bridges to the historical district Le Panier and to the MuCEM, the building named J4, designed by architects Rudy Ricciotti and Rolland Carta [31].

7   Project Description

FSJ-V3D Printing + MM Installation: Technology, Software Usage and Development Phases

The project is articulated by two large 3D printed models: A and B, made with mixed 3D printing systems with integrated interior lighting. **Model A** is the architectural reconstruction of the FSJ in a scale of 1:100 according to an ideal revival of the seventeenth century installed in ROOM O.03 of the exhibit. **Model B,** is a definition of the territorial structure aimed at illustrating the relationship between the history of the FSJ and the context and the urban area installed in ROOM O.01.

Model A: Development and Execution – Definition of the Scores

The complex articulation of the model A is spread over an area of about four square meters (43 ft^2) and concerns the great attack on the ground of the ramparts and the walls with the architectural parts that over the centuries have stratified on the large esplanade of the FSJ (210 × 190 × 30/54 cm) (6.8 × 6.2; 0.9×1.7 ft). The Reggio Calabria team designed the construction of the model according to a division into four pieces to facilitate its execution and transport. The model A-FSJ was built with mixed techniques, partly in polyurethane (structural part HD 65 kg/mc), partly in plaster (architectural parts with Project 660 Pro 3D System printer). In addition, some parts have been programmed to illuminate the hollow part, according to Fischnaller's concept. The assembly was carried out in two phases: the first involved the assembly of the four structural parts in polyurethane while the architectural parts, made separately, were subsequently collated. Two different methodologies were compared: milling (subtractive method of matter) and printing (additive method). Once the individual parts have been optimized, corrected and implemented, a manual treatment has been carried out for the final touch-up treatment with primer and acrylic paint, in order to uniform the color and grain of the polyurethane surfaces (more porous) and the powder of plaster (more compact). At the end of these treatments, for the completion of model A, there remained the installation of the lighting project of five parts of the fort, realized according to a high brightness LED system, for programming the sequences and for adjusting the timing in sync with the video projection of the exhibit.

Model B: Development and Execution
The territorial model where the FSJ insists has a dimension of 200 × 158 × 11 cm, (6.5 × 5.1 ft, h.4.21 inch) and is made entirely of polyurethane (HD 65 kg/mc) with surface treatment suitable for image projection with video mapping. Given the quality of the form, it was considered a two-part model cut and the realization and optimization times were considerably lower than the previous one.

Installation in Exhibit Space
The models have been positioned and contextualized in the physical space dedicated to Room O.01 and Room O.03 respecting the demands expressed by the design and upon the requirements of the rooms hosting the models and the exhibition.

Production Team
The team responsible for this project was articulated by the in- and out house staff (i.e. architects, engineers, experts in digital modeling) of the Università degli Studi Mediterranea di Reggio Calabria, Department dArTe, including specialist in mechanical prototyping. www.roboticom.it, Machined Science, SculptRob.

8   Conclusions and Lessons Learned

The steps taken from the digital model to the analog model were very demanding in terms of production, given the different systems and printing materials. The solids acquired according to the subtractive process have presented mechanical characteristics different from those printed with additive layers (tolerances, degrees of resistance, etc.). For this reason the intervention of manual correction was fundamental. The work was successfully concluded, however the project development and implementation was challenging. The fact is that although the tech panorama is appealing and offers great media tools of expression, it is filled of "traps"! for the practitioner. The use and application of digital tools required the necessary expertise of those who are working in the DH field. They shall have an understanding of the technologies and its principles in order of exploiting these fully and to respond to the challenges and demands when working in the field. Cross-disciplinary team collaboration in this type of project is fundamental (Figs. 3, 4, 5 and 6).

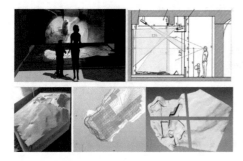

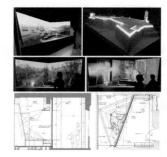

Fig. 3. Room O.01. (a) projection system – Model B, Photos: UNIRC.

Fig. 4. Room O.03. (b) scenography and tech solution, projection and display system: 2 video projector – hd – panasonic pt-rz670; ultra wide angle lens panasonic 0.38–0.40:1 and-dle030. Photos: UNIRC. Drawings: MuCEM

Fig. 5. Processing phases of model A + B (milling) Photos: UNIRC and MuCEM.

Fig. 6. Model B (a), Processing of 3D printing (b, c), Model A illuminated (d) – Photos: UNIRC

Acknowledgements. The authors wish to thank among others IméRA, Aix-Marseille University, Marseilles, MuCEM and MAP Laboratoires.

References

1. Mucem: Musée des civilisations de l'Europe et de la Méditerranée. http://www.mucem.org/en
2. Page index. http://rudyricciotti.com/
3. Villa Méditerranée. https://it.wikipedia.org/wiki/Villa_M%C3%A9diterran%C3%A9e
4. Home: Stefano Boeri Architetti. https://www.stefanoboeriarchitetti.net/
5. Marseille-Provence 2013, Capitale européenne de la culture - Ministère de la Culture. http://www.culture.gouv.fr/Actualites/Marseille-Provence-2013-capitale-europeenne-de-la-culture
6. Marseille-Provence 2013. https://en.wikipedia.org/wiki/Marseille-Provence_2013
7. Marseille-Provence 2013. Accessed 1 Oct 2014
8. 11 millions de visiteurs pour la capitale européenne de la culture. Accessed 1 Oct 2014
9. Architecture of the Mucem. http://www.mucem.org/en/the-mucem/architecture-of-the-mucem
10. The Mucem. http://www.mucem.org/en/the-mucem
11. Why is 3D Printing Important? https://3dsupplyguys.com/blogs/3d-printing-education/why-is-3d-printing-important
12. 9 Ways 3D Printing Is Changing The World–Hongkiat. https://www.hongkiat.com/blog/ways-3d-printing-change-world/
13. 3D Printing for Cultural Heritage: Preservation, Accessibility, Research and Education. https://www.materialise.com/en/blog/5-trends-3d-printing-for-2018
14. Scopigno R, Cignoni P, Pietroni N, Callieri M, Dellepiane M (November 2015) Computer Graphics Forum: n/a. https://doi.org/10.1111/cgf.12781
15. Museum uses 3D printing to take fragile maquette by Thomas Hart Benton on tour through the States. Accessed 17 Nov 2015
16. 3D Imaging in Cultural Heritage, Becky Knott Sculpture, Metalwork, Ceramics & Glass. https://www.vam.ac.uk/blog/news/3d-imaging-in-cultural-heritage. Accessed 7 Dec 2017
17. Inside private art collections with Scan the World. https://3dprintingindustry.com/news/inside-private-art-collections-scan-world-106451/. Accessed 23 Feb 2017
18. British Museum releases 3D printer scans of artefacts. https://www.independent.co.uk/life-style/gadgets-and-tech/british-museum-releases-scans-of-artefacts-to-let-you-3d-print-your-own-museum-at-home-9837654.html. Accessed 04 Nov 2014
19. Threeding Uses Artec 3D Scanning Technology to Catalog 3D Models for Bulgaria's National Museum of MilitaryHistory. http://3dprint.com/45699/threeding-artec-museum/ 3dprint.com. Accessed 20 Feb 2015

20. 3D printing applied to Cultural Heritage. http://www.digitalmeetsculture.net/article/3d-printing-applied-to-cultural-heritage/?upm_export=print
21. Fischnaller F. IMéRA – Institute for Advanced Study. https://imera.univ-amu.fr/en/resident/franz-fischnaller
22. Fondation IMéRA–Institut d'études avancées - Aix Marseille Université. https://imera.univ-amu.fr/
23. Mucem–Musée des civilisations de l'Europe et de la Méditerranée. http://www.mucem.org/
24. http://www.map.cnrs.fr/?p=3984
25. Fahy A (1995) New Technologies for Museum Communication. In: Hooper-Greenhill E (ed) Museums Media, Message, 82. Routledge Publisher, London
26. The power of intersection across art, architecture, interactive design, science and technology. https://imera.univ-amu.fr/sites/imera.univ
27. Imera.univ-amu.fr. https://imera.univ-amu.fr/sites/imera.univ-amu.fr/files/agenda/files/colloquefranz_fischnaller_mucem_imera_20_mai_2015_0.pdf
28. Fischnaller F. IMéRA - Institut d'études avancées. https://imera.Univ-emu.Fr/Fr/resident/Franz-fischnaller
29. Rfiea.fr. http://rfiea.fr/sites/default/files/newsletters/rfiea_annuaire_2008-2015_web.pdf
30. Sébastien Le Prestre de Vauban. https://en.wikipedia.org/wiki/S%C3%A9bastien_Le_Prestre_de_Vauban
31. History of Marseille. https://en.wikipedia.org/wiki/History_of_Marseille
32. Are the Mucem and the Fort Saint-Jean the same thing? http://www.mucem.org/en/are-mucem-and-fort-saint-jean-same-thing
33. Museums as places for intercultural dialogue: selected practices from Europe https://www.ne-mo.org/fileadmin/Dateien/public/service/Handbook_MAPforID_EN.pdf

Digital Survey and Parametric Representation. The Hypoglies of Civita di Bagnoregio

A. Maiolatesi[(✉)]

Department of Civil, Environmental and Mechanical Engineering (DICAM),
University of Trento, Via Mesiano 77, 38123 Trento, Italy
alessia.maiolatesi@gmail.com

Abstract. The research presents the study of an architectural and cultural heritage unique in the world, the village of Civita di Bagnoregio, in the province of Viterbo, known by all as "the city that dies", due to the progressive erosion of the tuff rock on which it is located. In particular, the study is carried out through surveying operations and the consequent restitution of the three-dimensional documents in the BIM (Building Information Modeling) environment. Relevant to the survey, data process acquisition was conducted through laser scanners and photographic campaigns and regarding the return in BIM environment, the software used for the representations is Autodesk Revit. The acquired data consists of a set of points as a cloud of points, which are appropriately discretized, scaled and processed for future parametric processing. The aim of the research, open and in continuous evolution, aims at the conservation and enhancement of the village of Civita di Bagnoregio through a precise analysis of the delicate historical-architectural heritage. The acquisition of construction and architectural data allows the preparation of the projects for structural monitoring and the planning of conservation interventions. After a general overview of the architectural and cultural condition of the village, the research focuses on the survey and consequent parametric and semantic restoration of a hypogean mill, present in the historical building, part of Civita.

Keywords: HBIM · Civita di Bagnoregio · Survey · Representation · Heritage

1 Introduction

The operations carried out during the research presented, have the main purpose to preserve and enhance the architectural and cultural heritage of Civita di Bagnoregio. The small village of Civita, unique in its kind, is continually threatened by the inexorable crumbling of the tuff rock on which it insists and it is known to the rest of the world as "the dying country". The study addressed during the research, aims at first analysis to promote a renewed reading of the "civitonic" environment and its cultural and architectural peculiarities, aimed at preserving the memory of the place. The data collected and meticulously organized in a semantic database, are used to structure a three-dimensional reconstruction of the case study, through digital simulations in the BIM environment. The use of advanced and constantly developing technologies, made available by digital

© Springer Nature Switzerland AG 2019
A. Luigini (Ed.): EARTH 2018, AISC 919, pp. 174–183, 2019.
https://doi.org/10.1007/978-3-030-12240-9_19

tools, offers an innovative and advanced approach compared to traditional systems of cognitive analysis and three-dimensional restitution of acquired data.

The survey of the chosen crusher, conducted by laser scanning, is structured as a partial experimentation of a work in progress for the digital preservation of the historical-architectural heritage of the entire village of Civita di Bagnoregio.

2 (H)BIM

When we talk about "HBIM" (Historical Building Information Modeling), we intend to say of a modeling methodology in the BIM environment of existing building organisms. These three-dimensional models, intelligent and interoperable, structure, within them, sets of data related to geometry, materials, construction systems and more. Therefore, an existing building elaborated in BIM environment, becomes a complex set of information that can be implemented and modified in real time and, considering its uniqueness, it can be configured as a "case-driver" for other similar buildings from the historical point of view and morphological aspects. In particular, by analyzing the peculiarities of the facades of Civita, "parametric" objects can be reconstructed which describe the recurrent architectural details; such intelligent objects are described by values that can be modified according to some parameters and for this reason, they can be adapted to each specific case. The advantage of this approach, it allows to create a semantic database from which it is possible to pick up the parametric object and adapt it according to the case in question, with similar characteristics from both the historical and the morphological point of view. The considerations that lead the use of BIM to built heritage, derive from the effective possibility of acquiring, storing and disseminating data in an intelligent manner, within models that become informative semantic databases. The particular case of Civita di Bagnoregio, becomes testimony of how the acquisition and return of information relating to the built of the fragile village, can be used to monitor the static consequences of the continuous crumbling of the rock of tuff.

Although HBIM is still a poorly applied methodological process in the redevelopment of the existing architectural heritage, the studies that are being encouraged are proving the effectiveness of this operational approach.

The Building Information Modeling applied to the existing scenario, promotes the dissemination and conservation of the historical-architectural heritage, through effective protocols of intelligent modeling of the acquired data, aimed at monitoring and recovery projects.

As the case-study presented in this research, the most interesting preliminary and cognitive aspect from the methodological point of view, concerns of the acquisition and the description of constructive information through "cloud of points model". This approach, obtainable through different methods, allows to acquire a large number of georeferenced points at high resolutions, so to obtain a detailed description of the object and they contain all the necessary information. Through the discretization and cataloging of the data, it is possible to obtain, in post-processing, a parametric and intelligent BIM model, as a basis for subsequent semantic representations.

This research traces the theoretical intentions indicated and attempts to represent a complex model in the BIM environment, by starting from the clouds of points acquired through laser scans. The experiments have the aim of structuring a work process that allows to create the complex and parametric three-dimensional models, composed of intelligent objects, classifiable and able to preserve the semantics of the reality they represent. Furthermore, the application of the BIM approach to the heritage built, can be used to structure three-dimensional models to be used for the most disparate purposes; in other words, starting from a HBIM model, it is possible to involve different professionals to guarantee technical insights, for the purposes of recovery and valorization. Moreover, if the three-dimensional model is aimed at the restoration and conservative recovery of existing artifacts, the advantage of a HBIM model consists in favoring different hypotheses of design intervention, all of which can be validated in real time and in a repeated manner.

The creation of a database of parametric information and intelligent objects, usable and adaptable to different needs, becomes essential for the structuring of semantic archives, which can be shared among the experts of the sector and continuously implemented. In conclusion, encouraging the experimentation of BIM on the existing heritage, which today represents the majority of the recovery interventions to be put in place, allows us to approach the redevelopment of the built in an intelligent, multi-disciplinary and multi-scale way.

During the cognitive phase of the photographic survey, structured in different stages, it is immediately shown the operational complexity that requires a village as delicate as Civita; a particularly compromised physiognomy that is opposed to an equally strong identity. A place to save, at least in its memory.

The relevant photographic campaign, preliminary to laser scanning, involved the entire village and subsequently, the focus was on the case study chosen, it concerns one of the characteristic underground oil mills present in the suburb of the village, perfectly preserved and a it is a destination for touristic itineraries.

This photographic survey operation, more accurate from the technical point of view and contextualized to the case study, is aimed at acquiring the point clouds through laser scanners, which will be discussed in the second phase of the research. The point clouds, to be inserted later in the BIM environment, form the basis for the representation of a parametric and semantic model, as a structured container of data and information deriving directly from the analyzes carried out on site.

As part of the detailed description of the built reality, the techniques and technologies for surveying and returning the acquired data, have reached a very advanced level of definition and complexity; what we want to develop is a work process, replicable, which it allows us to finalize this knowledge to the recovery and redevelopment of the historical architectural heritage.

With reference to the research presented, therefore, the aim is to present an applicative and experimental methodology, in order to create three-dimensional models of the existing architectural heritage, by using the innovations introduced by BIM. These semantic models, generated by a cloud of points acquired with laser scanners, are made up of intelligent and parametric objects, adaptable and repeatable, for a new description of reality.

The objectives proposed, made explicit in the course of the research and achieved in this first part of the work, concerned various thematic areas:

1. data acquisition and the generation of cloud of points from digital survey (high quality laser scanning); 2. the realization of the cloud of points in a three-dimensional BIM model; 3. the recognition of semantic and parametric objects that describe in detail the chosen building organism; 4. the structuring of digital meanings and signifiers within a repeatable and implementable database, from which to draw in recovery situations, they can be assimilated by geometry and type.

Using the BIM methodology, it is therefore possible to represent a complex model within different multidisciplinary information flows; it is also possible to implement and query the prototype created on historical, constructive, technological and other data. By analyzing the different temporal moments that punctuate the operating methodology, it is deduced that the survey is the operation through which, data and information relating to the selected product are acquired; the three-dimensional representation is the phase in which the acquired data is processed and displayed in a digital environment. In the specific case of experimentation in BIM environment, the acquired information is structured in a 3D database (which it coherently describes the reality) that can be implemented and shared; moreover, the possibility to use and disclose the data of a discipline such as the architectural one, made up of different professions often located in different places, making this methodology of work essential and innovative.

As anticipated, to fine tune the proposed theoretical intentions, it is chosen as a case study, a crusher present within the peculiar architectural fabric of the village of Civita di Bagnoregio. Despite the significant campaigns have been conducted on different pieces of the architectural aggregate, here is the example of the mill as it contains different stylistic typologies and structural emergencies.

3   Brief Description of the Case Study. The Oil Mill Called "Il Vecchio Mulino"

After describing photographically, the general configuration of the places, by including the dynamics typical of the historical-architectural tradition, what we want to tackle in this study, is an important experience of the underground oil mills of Civita, in particular of the one called "Il Vecchio Mulino". The survey of this mill is conducted by laser scanner, as partial experimentation work in progress, for the digital preservation of the historical-architectural heritage of the entire village of Civita di Bagnoregio. The premises of the oil mill used for the production of olive oil, can still be visited and preserve intact all the typical morphological characteristics; the caves dug into the tufa, have probably Etruscan origin and, they have been used in the past years in disparate uses and they were dedicated to the production of oil. The olives to grind were collected in the valleys below Civita and transported on the backs of the animals to the mills, where they were placed inside the machinery and squeezed by the millstones rotated, helped by the force of the animals themselves (Fig. 1).

Fig. 1. Instrumentation used during the work and photos of the hypogeum mill

4   The Survey with 3D Laser Scanner

The surveying operations carried out inside the Civita hypogeum crusher, were conducted using Laser Scanner 3D. This survey methodology uses light radiation to acquire an important amount of data and return three-dimensional point cloud. By using laser scanning processes, it is possible to acquire all the information that describes the geometry of the product, the consistency and, through a conscious discretization of the points, the technical data (plant sections, elevations). One of the greatest advantages of 3D laser scanner surveys, is the temporal factor. In a very short time a lot of information is acquired - complete and complex - compared to the traditional methods of survey. The aim of the survey campaigns applied to the case study presented in this research, is to create a digital base - to be progressively extended to the whole village of Civita - on which set up all future planning and static monitoring operations. Furthermore, the 3D laser scanning technology offers the possibility to acquire technological and structural information, as well as the cracking and degradation ones; all these factors constitute the greatest emergency of the urban area.

From the theoretical point of view, the survey method performed with laser scanning is based on the methodology defined as "active sensors". By this technique the light is used in the measurement process of the individual points detected. Through the emission of light, the precise position of the point in space is determined and an excellent level of detail, in the sampling of the recreated surface. From an operational point of view, the Leica HDS6100 Laser Scanner based on the "unlike phase" system, was used to perform the hypogeum crusher detection. This system calculates the distance of the individual points, comparing the phase difference between the transmitted wave and the wave received after the reflection on the surface of the object. Before scanning, the instrument is placed on a tripod that it is leveled; during acquisition, the support plane must be kept in a stable condition throughout the scan. This type of Laser Scanner, using the phase difference, takes very short time (about seven minutes each scan of medium quality) and for this reason, finds a wide use in the world of architectural and monumental survey, as well as entire pieces of the city.

5   The Applied Methodology: From the Digital Survey to the Three-Dimensional Restitution in BIM Environment

When approaching scientific research on an open and constantly evolving theme such as that of HBIM, it is not possible to define a certain and indisputable procedure; on the contrary, it could be better to propose an iterative and questionable approach, while it will be presenting the results obtained time after time.

In the proposed operational phase, a specific target is defined (survey aimed at preserving the crusher), definition of methods and measurements are identified (data acquisition by digital laser scanning), a working methodology is developed (data processing and representation in BIM environment) and the results are analyzed and discussed. Usually, this last phase is repeated as many times as the measurement process gets closer to the desired results.

Often it could be possible that we look back to the operational choices even after several months, to improve the methodology and to tune the results. This iterative and innovative approach, allows to add continuous knowledge and to ask new questions, to provide an answer through scientific research. The work presented is based on a methodological approach in which the hypotheses are explained through the representation of the results of the case study.

Once all the data have been acquired with laser scanning, we proceed to the representation of the point cloud in the BIM environment, where all the phases of the subsequent detailed modeling work will be set.

They will cover the future developments of this research and in the continuation of the study, therefore, we will work through the "inverse modeling" starting from the point cloud. By continuing the elaborations, the mathematics of the objects to be returned are deduced, directly from the model described by the point cloud, appropriately united and aligned.

In this delicate phase, a necessary operation is the verification of the management of the point cloud; if it was hard to work with the data, it is possible to choose and proceed to further discretization to check its size. The next phase is the meshing, in which a surface composed of triangles is calculated and in which vertices are located the same points of the cloud.

Through the creation of this skin, (skin more defined, more triangles are present), the object is described in a complete way. Once the mesh has been created, it is also possible to add the chromatic information, called textures, acquired directly from the laser scanner or from photographic campaigns.

In the specific case of the important work carried out on the crusher, the point cloud acquired by laser scanner, is imported into the Autodesk ReCap software. This software allows both to manage and to visualize the data to be extracted from the cloud of points for the construction of the model (elevation of points, radiance, reflexivity, measurements, specific sections and others). The choice of ReCap software, was requested by the desire to prepare the processed data for a subsequent import in BIM environment, through the software Autodesk Revit.

The operative modality adopted, is to work directly on the point cloud generated by the laser scanning, cutting it at various levels, to determine the correct position of the single elements present in the crusher. The typical methodology is to follow the profiles generated by the points belonging to the section plan, as a basis for the future creation of the BIM model. The creation of this surface on which to set the successive works, becomes the information container, within which to structure the classification of the semantic data that will become parametric objects in the BIM environment.

By this way, consistent object are obtained with the real considerations, not only from the geometric point of view, but also from the semantic point of view. With reference to the heritage built, it is particularly useful to have intelligent objects that describe the recurrent architectural elements. Often some components, including windows, doors, moldings, columns, are very similar to each other, with the exception of some small details; for this reason, to have a parametric and shareable database, it offers the possibility to use the same objects going to modify only the values that allow you to modulate its shape and size, preserving its semantics.

At the end, the purpose of the operations described, is the future creation of a BIM model to which to refer further relevant campaigns (for the monitoring of cracks and failures), to compare the results time after time and follow the changes over time. All the information (the surveys, the point clouds, the parametric objects, the structural and historical conditions) of the chosen artefact, are not replaced or lost each time, but they become a structuring part of the digital parametric archive contained in the three-dimensional model questionable (iterative process) (Figs. 2, 3, 4 and 5).

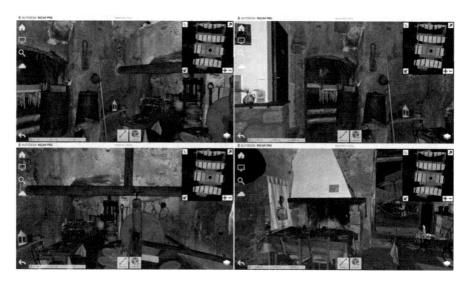

Fig. 2. Images of the clouds of points (ReCap)

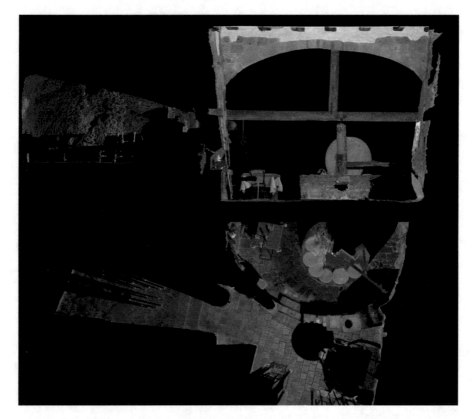

Fig. 3. Cross section and horizontal section of the point cloud

Fig. 4. General view of the point cloud (ReCap)

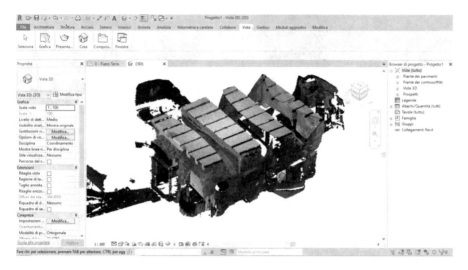

Fig. 5. Point cloud representation imported into Autodesk Revit for subsequent processing (Autodesk Revit)

6 Conclusions and Future Developments

As deduced from the considerations made, the research conducted and in progress towards further processing, focuses on the possibilities offered by the use of the laser scanner along with the BIM technologies applied to the existing historical architectural heritage of Civita.

Starting from the actual "as is state", passing through the elaboration of point clouds, in the future developments of this research we will arrive at the construction of a complex BIM model and specific libraries of parametric objects, elaborated for the construction of a model three-dimensional semantic.

The recognizability of the architectural elements of the hypogean mills, typical and recurrent in the architectural fabric of the village, offers the possibility of creating and classifying a series of digital and informative tools that can be continuously implemented. The results obtained will be used for the study, reconstruction, monitoring and conservation of a portion of the precarious architectural heritage of Civita di Bagnoregio.

Furthermore, the elaboration of complex, parametric and interactive three-dimensional models, lays the foundations for the development and implementation of technologies, such as those of Virtual Reality. By using these systems, it becomes possible to have access to an uncertain heritage, as is Civita, although not physically present on the site. Finally, if this village should be the victim of its own, precarious condition, its memory would become part of our precious heritage to be saved and disseminated.

References

Brusaporci S (2017) Digital innovations in architectural heritage conservation: emerging research and opportunities. IGI Global, Hershey

Caputi M, Odorizzi P, Stefani M (2015) Il Building Information Modeling - BIM. Valore, gestione e soluzioni operative. Maggioli Editore, Santarcangelo di Romagna

Ciribini ALC (2016) BIM e digitalizzazione dell'ambiente costruito. Grafill, Palermo

De Luca L (2011) La fotomodellazione architettonica. Rilievo, modellazione, rappresentazione di edifici a partire da fotografie. Flaccovio Editore, Palermo

Di Giuda GM, Villa V (2016) Il BIM: Guida completa al Building Information Modeling. Hoepli, Milano

Garagnani S, Cinti Luciani S, Mingucci R (2011) Building information modeling: la tecnologia digitale al servizio del progetto di architettura. Disegnarecon 4(7):5–19

Sacks R, Eastman C, Lee G, Teicholz P (2018) BIM handbook: a guide to building information modeling for owners, designers, engineers, contractors, and facility managers. Wiley, New York

A Journey of Valorisation from the Sacred to the Secular. The Oratory of Sant'Antonio Abate in the Village of Mele (Genoa-Italy)

R. Vecchiattini[1]([✉]) and C. Battini[2]

[1] Architecture and Design Department (dAD), University of Genoa,
Stradone Sant'Agostino 37, 16123 Genoa, Italy
rvecchiattini@arch.unige.it
[2] Department of Civil, Chemical, Environmental Engineering (DICCA),
University of Genoa, Via Montallegro 1, 16145 Genoa, Italy

Abstract. The Oratory was the expression of a community that, even with its strong sense of identity and wealth (deriving from the profitable local paper mills and ironworks), felt the need for a symbol, which could represent them; a morally enlightening space, spiritually transcendent, and socially prestigious. The development and the creation of the project allowed professionals in the fields of Restoration, Drawing, and Informatics to work together but mainly it created the opportunity to become acquainted with an ancient collective devotional culture, which has an undeniably fundamental value from an historical and anthropological point of view. The goal was to develop a mobile application which does not incorporate the use of 3D models, but was easily accessible by the visitor. Inside the app, information sheets and images of detail offer a more thorough understanding of Oratory, also thanks to using special sensors (Beacon) and graphic symbols (QRcode).

Keywords: Confraternity · Immaterial artefacts · Beacon · Application · QRcode · JSON

1 Introduction

In the village of Mele, located in Liguria within the forest of the Leira Valley, there hides a small treasure: the Oratory of Sant'Antonio Abate. Reconstructed in 1634 over a pre-existing building, the Oratory has an undisputed artistic value. It contains important eighteenth-century works of art (Fig. 1), among which: the stucco decoration in the *rocailles* style by Rocco Cantoni, which frames twelve paintings by Carlo Giuseppe Ratti; two processional floats, one of which is considered a masterpiece by the famous sculptor and ebony carpenter, Anton Maria Maragliano; silver *ramages* crucifixes and other significant artefacts deriving from the collective devotional culture in the seventeenth and eighteenth century (Bianchi 2013; Gavazza and Magnani 2000; Priarone 2012; Sanguineti 2012).

The Oratory was the expression of a community that, even with its strong sense of identity and wealth (deriving from the profitable local paper mills and ironworks), felt the need for a symbol, which could represent them; a morally enlightening space, spiritually

© Springer Nature Switzerland AG 2019
A. Luigini (Ed.): EARTH 2018, AISC 919, pp. 184–193, 2019.
https://doi.org/10.1007/978-3-030-12240-9_20

Fig. 1. The interior of the Oratory of Sant'Antonio Abate, Mele (Genoa) with the altarpiece attributed to Andrea Ansaldo and part of the magnificent stucco decoration by Rocco Cantoni.

transcendent, and socially prestigious. The Confraternity of Sant'Antonio Abate (Fig. 2), the existence of which is documented since 1536, has guarded and taken care of the artistic-religious treasures of the Oratory, according to tradition and collective devotion (AA VV. 1982; Galella 2014; Pareto 1908; Piana and Casanova 2004).

Fig. 2. Members of the Confraternity during the procession, which is the result of a secular stratification of practices and rites. (photo by M.L. Carlini)

A project for the valorisation of this building will shortly allow the general public access to its history rich of socio-economical, cultural, artistic and human facets, financed by the Compagnia di San Paolo (main supporter), the Confraternity, and Mele City Council.

2 The Project of Valorisation

When developing a plan to promote an artefact, it is vital to start by imagining its potential recipients so that the project will meet the interests of a heterogeneous public. In fact, the Oratory is a destination – or a passing point – for hikers, tourists, religious persons, students, or simply curious passers-by who find themselves walking along one of the most important historical pathways connecting the coast to the Oltregiogo, a mountainous region in Liguria. For this reason, three interoperable user options have been designed to offer a full experience of the area.

An app (*Melapp*) can be downloaded for free from the City Council website onto smartphone, tablets, and similar mobile devices and it provides maps and images of the Oratory as well as historical information on the building, the artists who worked on it, the surrounding area, the Confraternity, and the historical community of *paperai* (the local paper producers) (Arri 2012; Cevini 1995). The app also provides technical information on materials, pigments and the restoration techniques of the stuccos and the wooden processional float, as well as odd interesting facts and details woven in to enrich the visit (Fig. 3a and b).

Fig. 3. The support and participation of some *paperai* families was so important that even today in the Oratory traces remain of these profound social and religious ties. a: the paper mill *La Scaglia* painted in the landscape of Mele in the altarpiece. b: a paper mill with a water wheel represented in the upper part of one of the Crucifixes (eighteenth century).

A series of sensors, *Beacon* and *QRcode*, activate the application, which has been previously downloaded on the mobile device of the visitor, displaying the description of the work of art one is observing, as well as more detailed information, on the screen. *Beacon* and *QRcode* sensors were placed not only in the Oratory, but also in the surrounding relevant landmarks related to the Oratory, such as the church of Fado, the

Paper Museum of Mele, and the Sanctuary of Nostra Signora dell'Acquasanta in Genoa-Voltri. This Sanctuary is the destination of the solemn and grand procession which starts from the Oratory of Sant'Antonio Abate every 15th August. It is an important event that renews the sense of belonging of the whole community, from the old to the young – the latter preparing to continue their fathers' tradition.

Lastly, leaflets are available to visitors to guide them through the various points of interest: the area of Mele, the Confraternity and the solemn procession, the Oratory of Sant'Antonio Abate, the stuccos by Rocco Cantoni, the pictorial cycle by Carlo Giuseppe Ratti, and the processional float by Anton Maria Maragliano (Fig. 4).

Fig. 4. Garlands with flowers and fruit decorate the light-coloured background of the walls, referencing the traditional models of the Canton Ticino families' repertoire (photo by M.L. Carlini).

3   The App

The amount of information available on the World Wide Web and the number of users who use it annually record a strong increase. From a survey conducted by We Are Social (international agency for the development of creative ideas) and Hootsuite (platform of social media management more used throughout the world), it emerged that the number of Internet users in the world has surpassed the threshold of 4 billion people: a historical fact that tells us that today more than half of the world's population is online (Digital in 2018), exchanging data and information (Fig. 5). In the tourist sector, the modern Internet provides tourists with huge possibilities for searching interesting information and planning their activities. All this information can be particularly useful for those users wishing to visit a particular destination, in addition to stimulating the curiosity of the potential users and allowing remote access to those unable to visit these destinations. Information about travel destinations and their associated resources, such as accommodation, restaurants, museums or events, is the research that tourists perform to plan their trip. The tourism industry becomes one of the largest sectors in the world and generates about 11% of global gross domestic product (Kabassi 2010). In light of this, research into how information technology can support tourists becomes essential.

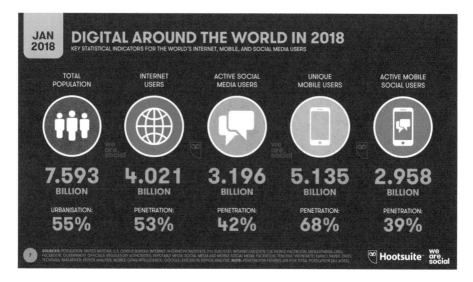

Fig. 5. Key statistical indicators for the world's internet, mobile and social media (image from www.wearesocial.com).

The recent developments in information and communication technologies allow today greater and easier retrieval of information from tourists during their travels. Smartphones are the mainstream in this sector with iOS and Android devices with over 700 million supports globally.

New research projects can be developed with the use of commercial platforms and open source tools, such as three-dimensional models, images, texts, and sounds to view and interact with the collected data. Many studies, such as the Archeoguide (Vlahakis et al. 2002), were able to create guided tours in augmented reality with head-mounted displays. Other projects, such as Virtual Rome, reconstructed the landscape of modern day Rome and that of Rome in the second century A.D. using common web browsers with three-dimensional online reproduction, including multimedia insights (Pescarin et al. 2009). However, the use of three-dimensional models often clashes with the non-perfect compatibility with the mobile tools on the market. In fact, these systems of representation need smartphones with medium-high technical characteristics, such as high RAM memory and video processors capable of displaying three-dimensional models and overlapping information in real time.

However, such a complex system can not be used by users with low-powered smartphones. The risk is to create an application can not be used by most users.

For these reasons it was decided to develop a mobile application which does not incorporate the use of 3D models, but that would be easily accessible by the visitor. Inside the app, information sheets and images of detail offer a more thorough understanding of Oratory, also thanks to using special sensors (Beacon) and graphic symbols (QRcode).

Other requests of the Confraternity were the ability to easily update information (text and images), and the possibility, in the future, to create an iOS version of the same application expected at this time only for Android.

The choice of the type of language and platform to be used is relapse into *Framework React Native*. The *Framework React Native*, chosen because it is reliable and guarantees the ability to be updated, as it is owned by *Facebook inc*, one of the most important companies in the world, that also makes use of this framework as do other companies such as *AirBnb*, *Skype* and *Instagram*.

React Native is a framework that allows to build applications (called native) specifically on iOS and Android systems using JavaScript. Among the main advantages is that of not building an application in HTML5 (language for the structuring of web pages used to simulate also native applications), nor a hybrid application, but to use the components that are actually made available by iOS and Android. By using this framework is it possible to build an application that has real components and uses JavaScript and React to move and to define the logic.

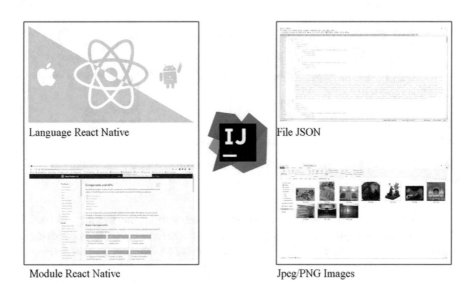

Fig. 6. Schema of the workflow adopted

Other fundamental characteristics of *Framework React Native* are its adaptability and the ability to modify textual contents and images in a simple way, even programmatically through customs scripts. In this way it was possible to provide a simple system to the members of the Confraternity to keep updated and/or add content to the application (Fig. 6).

The system involves the use of a JSON file (text file that can be edited with any text editor) placed on a remote server, which is downloaded and read every time the application is started. If there are changes within the JSON file, the application promptly updates the sections and contents, downloading and saving new information on the terminal. The built JSON file has been structured into objects with pairs of keys/values in it. In the project MelApp JSON file consists of a series of specific keys (Id, Major, tag, imageScr, title and description) that allow to dynamically load content in specific categories menu. Specifically, "Major" refers to the Beacon to which it is associated, "imageScr" to the connection of the image loaded on the remote server, "title" to the title of the content and "description" to the description of the specific content. Finally, the "key" tag implementation allows the division and the inclusion of content in specific menu items (Fig. 7).

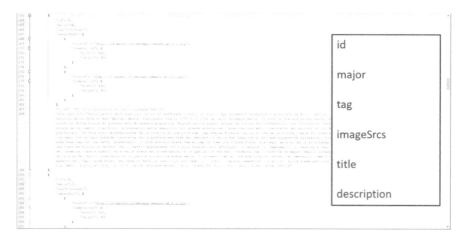

Fig. 7. Example of JSON file with indications of keys taken to populate the application of texts and images.

To promote greater usability of the application also in the territory, a specific section has been designed where it is possible to load a map of the territory of Mele and a series of points of interest that refer to specific detailed information sheets (Fig. 8).

Fig. 8. From top to bottom and from left to right: application menu automatically generated by the JSON file; main screen with the list of sheets; map of the area with indication of the thematic routes; credits screen.

4   Conclusions

The present contribution is the result of a research developed by authors working in close collaboration on different aspects of the project: Rita Vecchiattini worked on the analysis, historical reconstruction and the restoration with the aim of identifying the eventual contents of the appreciation project, while Carlo Battini worked on surveying and informatics to create the necessary tools for the project.

It was decided to develop a mobile application which does not incorporate the use of 3D models, but that would be easily accessible by the visitor. Inside the app, information sheets and images of detail offer a more thorough understanding of Oratory, also thanks to using special sensors (Beacon) and graphic symbols (QRcode).

The development and the creation of the project allowed professionals in the fields of Restoration, Drawing, and Informatics to work together but mainly it created the opportunity to become acquainted with an ancient collective devotional culture, which has an undeniably fundamental value from an historical and anthropological point of view.

Acknowledgements. The authors would like to thank the Compagnia di San Paolo (the main supporter of the project), the Confraternity di Sant'Antonio Abate, the City Council of Mele, The Mele Paper Museum and the Association Le Muse, the restoration company CoArt, the Superintendence of Archaeology, Fine Arts and Landscape in Liguria and everyone that enthusiastically collaborated to help realise the project.

References

AAVV (1982) La Liguria delle Casacce. Devozione, Arte, Storia delle Confraternite liguri. Cassa Risparmio Genova e Imperia – Genoa City Council, Genoa

Ardito C, Buono P, Costabile MF, Lanzilotti R, Piccinno A (2009) Enabling interactive exploration of cultural heritage: an experience of designing systems for mobile devices. Knowl Technol Policy 22(1):79–86

Arri ER (2012) Cartai e cartiere. L'antica arte dei "paperai". Associazione Culturale S. Donato, Varazze (Sv)

Bianchi S (2013) I cantieri dei Cantoni. Relazioni, opere, vicissitudini di una famiglia della Svizzera italiana in Liguria (secoli XVI-XVIII). Sagep, Genoa

Cevini P (1995) Edifici da Carta Genovesi. Secoli XVI-XIX. Sagep, Genoa

Digital in 2018 https://www.slideshare.net/wearesocial/digital-in-2018-global-overview-86860338. Accessed Oct 2018

Galella I (ed.) (2014) Sotto il segno di Antonio Abate. Arte e devozione a Mele (secoli XVI-XX). Sagep, Genoa

Gavazza E, Magnani L (2000) Pittura e decorazione a Genova e in Liguria nel Settecento. Sagep, Genoa

Kabassi K (2010) Personalizing recommendations for tourists. Telematics Inf 27(1):51–66

Nack F, Gordon AS (2016) Interactive storytelling. In: 9th International conference on interactive digital storytelling. Springer, Los Angeles

Pareto S (1908) Memorie della Parrocchia e Comune di Mele in Val di Leira (Voltri). ATA, Genoa, Reprinted in 2012

Piana PG, Casanova G (2004) Storia di Mele. O Caròggio, Arenzano (Ge)

Pescarin S, Palombini A, Calori L, Negri A (2009) Ambienti collaborativi 3D. Il caso di Virtual Rome. Archeol. e Calc. Suppl. 2:121–130

Priarone M (2012) Andrea Ansaldo 1584-1638. Sagep, Genoa

Sanguineti D (2012) Anton Maria Maragliano 1664-1739. Sagep, Genoa

Vlahakis V, Ioannidis N, Karigiannis J, Tsotros M, Gounaris M, Stricker D, Gleue T, Daehne P, Almeida L (2002) Archeoguide: an augmented reality guide for archaeological sites. J. IEEE Comput Graph Appl Arch 22(5):52–60

Project and Representation. A Dialogue for the Campania Hinterland

Lorenzo Giordano[✉]

Dipartimento di Architettura (DiARC), Università degli Studi di Napoli
"Federico II", Via Toledo, 402, 80134 Naples, Italy
lorenzo.giordano.lvd@gmail.com

Abstract. The analysis of urban realities, including valuable sites and degraded places close to each others, could result fundamental to program new reconfiguration strategies for diversified open type spaces of our contemporary. Those spaces, urban consolidated or peripheral places, as well as marginal or central areas and hybrid or atopic sites, propose themselves, especially in the light of unbridled globalization, as ambits, although disaggregated, able to accept design experimentations for a new contemporary city proposal able to measure itself with an innovative idea of quality, sobriety and naturalness, reflecting its own identity characters accumulated over the centuries. The thought over quality reconfiguration of urban central spaces, as well as those of small and medium dimension, should be measured with a reasoning capable to intervene on ways of constructing the different parts that make up the contemporary city as a whole, as well as the ways of connecting these parts to each other, in order to escape from a dangerous condition of trivialization. The project for the construction of the "School of excellence in hotels and agri-food" of Ariano Irpino is configured as a valid test bench to experience the "Technologies for digital representation" within their use closer to the needs of the civic community.

Keywords: Technologies · Digital representation · Architectural design · Contemporary

1 Introduction

Fifty years have passed since Aldo Rossi published "The Architecture of the City", a proper theoretical and scientific Manifesto, in 1966. A text able to collect and elaborate, in a unitary sense, the previous reflections addressed by the Italian architectural culture, in the second half of the Fifties, towards the territory, the city and history. The problem to return a disciplinary and social value to architecture, after anti-history International Style caesura, and the so called "naive functionalism", was one of the concerns of at least three leading figures in post-war architecture: Ernesto Nathan Rogers, who developed his theory of environmental pre-existence; Giuseppe Samonà, constantly tending towards the unity of architecture and urban planning; Ludovico Quaroni, particularly attentive to the morphological tradition of Mediterranean architecture. From this generation both the research on the design of the territory and geography understood as the story of Vittorio Gregotti took place, and, within the IUAV or the

© Springer Nature Switzerland AG 2019
A. Luigini (Ed.): EARTH 2018, AISC 919, pp. 194–201, 2019.
https://doi.org/10.1007/978-3-030-12240-9_21

University Institute of Architecture in Venice, the tradition of urban analysis by Carlo Aymonino and Aldo Rossi. With "The Architecture of the City", the milanese architect, starting from a critical urban concept of modern functionalism, addresses the view on western European city, redefining it as an archaeological artifact produced by man such as an autonomous structure of history. Out of this context the term permanency comes out again. According to Rossi, the permanents are the primary element of the city: monuments and housing areas, not just single replaceable buildings; they define the grow of the city within defined formal and typological rules, scientifically recognizable. Also new city projects have to follow these rules, which allow different combinations. This creates a link between analysis and project, between the examination of the existing and the invention of the new. The apparatus that makes this possible is the analogy: it detaches the typology from history and, thanks to the resulting abstraction, makes it available again. However, the dynamism of the global and spectacularizing society, of the late twentieth century, that is to say an economically, socially and structurally consumption reality, overlaps with the enlightenment of Aldo Rossi: energies, images, goods and unfortunately ground and territory consumption. The new global reality made impractical the rigid theoretical project of Aldo Rossi as well as, in his different design joints, was celebrated in 1973 by the so-called "Tendenza" during the fifteenth Triennale di Milano. This new architectural theory contested the concept of avant-garde, rejecting utopia and proposing a political and critical architecture committed with the real, influencing, abroad Italy, leading figures of the architectural debate such as Joseph Paul Kleihues and Oswald Mathias Ungers, from which The Dutch architect Rem Koolhaas was formed, able to promote the first real break of continuity in favor of discontinuity, through the concepts of generic city, Junkspace and Bigness. Also thanks to Koolhaas insight, at the end of the theoretical hypothesis time, tending to drop an urban order from above, it was no longer possible to pursue those efforts aiming to bring homogeneity and unity to the discourse on urban facts that, in the meantime, grew out of all proportion, placing themselves in a new dimensional, heterogeneous and fragmentary reality, defined as metropolis, anti-city or territorial city. Out of this scenario, in the last two decades of the twentieth century, only one winner emerged: the chaos or, as a Koolhaas exhibition reminds, the Chronochaos. Such chaotic dimension comes out within a karst current of Italian rationalism, known as the post-modernism of the eighties, fueled by the First Venice Biennale, titled by Paolo Portoghesi "The Presence of the Past" and focused on the realization of the Strada Novissima inside the spaces of Corderie dell'Arsenale; in addition, the subsequent spectacularizing logic of the Star System of the Nineties and, finally, the recent explosion of new pseudo-urban experiments in Middle Eastern countries and those of the Far East, have made actual and problematic the following question: does the city still exist or is it a disproportionate atopic place that has lost, irremediably, its identity character, its genius urbis, its very reason for existing? It is reasonable to answer this question trying to interpret and query the change involving the structure and the idea itself of the contemporary city from the point of view of the operational practice, taking into consideration the critical transmutation of a conceptual approach in relation to a personal analytical methodology that is inextricably linked to our contemporaneity. The demand for a common and shared language becomes necessary, where through physical construction it's easily to understand the true nature of the project, or the consistency of its ideas.

2 The Contemporary and the Technologies for Digital Representation

Out of this scenario, our contemporary present itself as an extremely interconnected society, society, thanks to ever more new ways of communication, information and mobility. Within these observations, even architecture has the responsibility to answer to those dynamics. It is fundamental to intend which are new instruments, in order to use them at their best, able to sustain the continuous design processes that make possible contamination first, then exchange and ultimately enrichment. Indeed technologies for representation and their instruments, such as BIM, Laser scanner, photogrammetry, virtual reality, 3D modeling, have the responsibility to approach the project of architecture according to a more closely use to the needs of the civic community, introducing and returning, in terms of design and digital representation, the different landscape, orographic and architectural qualities, in order to identify a representative path capable of loading an apparently ideal functional theme. It is precisely this aspect that risks to make these tools no longer a means and a fundamental contribution for architecture, but themselves a reason for composition. A tangible example of this working methodology can be observed in the architectural development that characterized the great majority of those architectures defined as spectacular, emblems of a purely consumpting society, capable of letting oneself be seduced by an image that no longer binds with that anthropic dimension of the city, but which is instead seduced by the logic of consumption in favor of an architecture that speaks only with itself. The proof of such an approach can be identified, above all, in the countries of the Near and Middle East and in the great Asian metropolises, where the great wave of consumpting globalization has become a concrete and tangible image. In contrast to these design methods, an increasingly consistent generation of European architects, adopts a culturally and ecologically sustainable design methodology, where digital representation becomes a means for architecture, aware of what are the parameters and the logic able to build in a constructive way towards the city and architecture. The communication of the project through digital representation thus assumes a fundamental role in the architectural production process, capable of translating into its different phases of elaboration a path that is prodigal for knowledge first, then study and finally the production of architecture, where representation is a conscious and necessary tool, in contrast with a vision that relegates, thanks to an unconscious use of technology, architecture no longer as a social producer but as a product of consumpting logics. Therefore, a critical revision of these modalities is necessary, which can only be implemented by architects and by their conscious use of technology.

3   A Dialogue for Campania Inland. Ariano Irpino "School of Excellence in Hotels and Agri-Food"

In response to these conditions, the project for the "School of excellence in hotels and agro-food" in Ariano Irpino is configured architecturally not only in functional terms, assuming and returning the different requests for the school, but also, and above all, according to a logic settlement able to optimize the typological, morphological and linguistic characteristics in relation to the urban and orographic characteristics of the site. A careful analysis was in fact supported thanks to the use of 3D models and the Point cloud image, in order to better understand what are the spatial characteristics of the site. The project therefore seeks to assume the different conditions of the two urban layouts, including a new building that presents, on Via D'Aflitto, a high basement on which there are five levels characterized by large glass surfaces of which, the last one, is defined by a structural truss, proposed as the constructive crowning of the building in question. The south-east facing facade intercepts the light by filtering through a series of curtains capable of filtering the sun's rays while preserving the transparency both inside and outside the building: an overstructure capable of dressing the building, protecting it from direct light. Vice versa, the facade looking on the overlying widening of Via Mancini is characterized by its sober sizing as well as for its linguistic muteness: a compact and articulated system of buildings that, in part, takes shape from the typological plant of the building body overlooking on Via D'Afflitto and assuming its autonomous configuration separated from the aforesaid main body, it is proposed as an architectural whole capable of dialoguing with the measures and the built forms of the traditional local architecture. A volume composed of three levels, emerging from behind the outline of the Pastoral Center of St. Francis of Assisi, characterized by circular rooms illuminating the flights of stairs of the underlying multi-storey building, connects through the cylindrical body of the main stairs of the "School of excellence in hotels and agro-food", to the body of the building located on the western side of the widening and defined by wide arched openings. All the structural issues have been effectively addressed with the support of BIM technologies, where thanks to a conscious digital support, it has been able to optimally define not only the issue related to loads, but also, and above all, the building language. The urban connotation of the facing outlooks on the open space is ensured not only by the language of the façades and by the articulation of the architectural volumes but also by the presence of a sloping pitched roof that represents the identity characteristics of the Irpinia small town. The two architectural systems are separated from each other by a court that acts as a zenith light interceptor for the hypogean laboratories located below the widening on Via Mancini. From the distribution point of view, the functions received in the multi-storey building, whose access is made possible both from the underlying Via D'Afflitto and from the overlying widening on Via Mancini, are mainly organized to accommodate the gym in the basement, the classrooms and the auditorium. Beyond the courtyard, beneath the open space in front of Via Mancini, are located the wine and food laboratories, the offices and the library. Ultimately a proposal capable of staging those that are, on one hand, issues related to a critical architectural design modality towards society and, on the other hand, to use at their best "Technologies for digital representation", with the aim of first perceiving the existing, then to conceive the modalities of action and finally to define the project, as return, therefore, of a conscious and anthropic vision of the contemporary design process (Figs. 1, 2, 3, 4 and 5).

Fig. 1. Planimetry

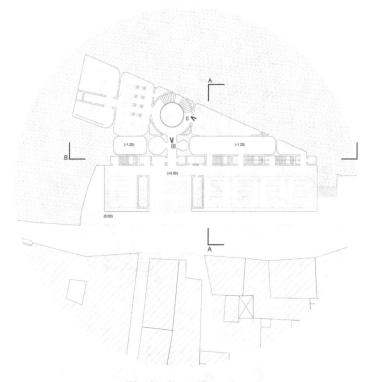

Fig. 2. Groundfloor plan

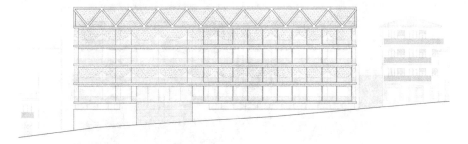

Fig. 3. Façade

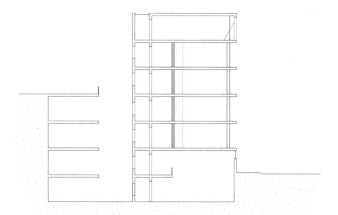

Fig. 4. Section

Fig. 5. Outside image

References

Agamben G (2008) Che cos'è il contemporaneo?. Editore Nottetempo, Milano

Agamben G (2017) Stato di eccezione. Bollati Boringhieri, Torino

Aureli PV (2016) Il Progetto dell'autonomia. Quodlibet, Roma

Bachelard G (2015) La poetica dello spazio. Edizioni Dedalo, Bari

Breitschmid M, Olgiati V (2018) Non-referential architecture. Simonett & Baer, Coira

Frank C, Pedretti B (a cura di) (2013) L'architetto generalista. Mendriso Academy Press, Silvana Editoriale, Mendrisio

Pedretti B (a cura di) (2016) L'atlante dell'architetto. Mendriso Academy Press, Silvana Editoriale, Mendrisio

Rykwert J (1991) La casa di Adamo in Paradiso. Adelphi, Milano

Vidler A (2012) Storie dell'immediato presente. Zandonai, Rovereto

The Digital Platform of the *Gabinetto di Fisica* of the Gymnasium School *Paolo Sarpi* in *Bergamo*: A Case Study Between Research and Didactic

Alessio Cardaci[1]([✉]), Antonella Versaci[2], and Pietro Azzola[1]

[1] School of Engineering, University of Bergamo, Viale Marconi 5,
24044 Dalmine, Italy
alessio.cardaci@unibg.it
[2] Faculty of Engineering and Architecture, University of Enna "Kore",
Viale delle Olimpiadi, 94100 Enna Bassa, Italy
antonella.versaci@unikore.it

Abstract. This paper presents the results of a project aimed at establishing a virtual museum of the scientific instruments collection, dating from the late 18th and early 20th century, hosted in the *Gabinetto di Fisica* of the state high school 'Palo Sarpi' of Bergamo, developed with the support of students.

Keywords: 3D architectural survey · Conservation and valorization · Digital platform · Gymnasium school 'paolo sarpi' · Bergamo

1 Introduction

The most effective tools for the dissemination of that part of cultural heritage, today wrongly defined as 'minor' are the opportunities ensured by the continuous development of Information and Communication Technology (ICT). The collections hosted in small museums of schools, universities and public institutions and/or private sets, often reduced in the number of pieces, are an expression of a precious cultural heritage, frequently unknown to the majority of people.

Today the Virtual Museum has transformed and expanded the means of knowledge and enhancement of these hidden treasures, also considering the new possibilities offered by the web 2.0. The current digital platforms allow a high level of interaction between the site and the user, by facilitating the editing and the sharing of texts, videos, images and 3D models. They permit online communication thanks to blogs, forums, chats and social channels; tools that have radically transformed the way in which the network is used. If the Internet was previously a 'static' structure, a large library in which it was simple to find information, it has now acquired a great dynamism and a wide flexibility in using contents. Everything that is hosted in an 'open site' can be both quickly communicated through drawings and images - in a few seconds between two clicks - and understood by the exploration of 3D models and the navigation of spherical images that guarantee an immersive and interactive experience and simulate the real

© Springer Nature Switzerland AG 2019
A. Luigini (Ed.): EARTH 2018, AISC 919, pp. 202–211, 2019.
https://doi.org/10.1007/978-3-030-12240-9_22

visit of a place. In this context, the action of 'sharing'–i.e. the publication on a social network of a content that has aroused our interest and or the use of the tags, likes, pins, etc.–allow the establishment of a participatory dialogue with other users making them the new diffusers of knowledge and the interpreters of original and innovative ideas.

These are the basis of the project of the digital museum of the scientific instruments collection, dating from the late 18th and early 20th centuries named *Gabinetto di Fisica* and jealously hosted by the state high school *Palo Sarpi di Bergamo*. The numerous initiatives aimed at visiting and opening the small museum to the public, as well as at producing numerous printed texts, show the pledge of the school in bringing citizenship closer to young people, in particular.

The new technologies for the acquisition and the capture of the reality finalized to the digital reconstruction of the objects and the creation of interactive didactic models, movies and computerized animations explaining the use of ancient machines and their physical meaning are valuable instruments of our time that can obtain a wider audience. Besides the use of AR (augmented reality), which can 'recreate' objects everywhere.

2   The History and the Architecture of Gymnasium School *Paolo Sarpi* and Its *Gabinetto di Fisica*

The edifice that accommodates the high school Paolo Sarpi is an important building of historical-architectural interest; a significant testimony of both the local identity and the history of public education in Bergamo. The glorious construction, from the hilly prominence on which it stands, dominates the southwestern spur of the city, integrating itself in the skyline in an organic, harmonious and perfect manner (Fig. 1). As it looks today, is the outcome of an evolutionary procedure that has translated the ancient monastery of the Poor Clare nuns of Rosate, in the Upper Town, into the current neoclassical complex. An event of significant cultural and urban importance that has matured in a historical context marked by two essential phenomena: the French presence in Lombardy with the consequent Napoleonic suppression of Orders and Religious Corporations and the profound urban transformation that, between 1845 and 1852, involved the *Colle del Rosate*. Actually, the city, following the changed political geography and the new role compared to the past - no longer a bulwark of the Duchy of Milan but a strategic hub of the emerging region of Lombardy-Veneto - underwent profound changes both urban and administrative (Belotti 1940). The educational institutions were reformed to adapt teaching methods to the educational needs of the age of the Enlightenment. In 1802, the Cisalpine Republic promulgated the law for the General Plan of Public Education in which the approach to knowledge became a prerogative of the state; a secular education aimed to advance the use of reason against superstition and the dogmas of religion.

The *Collegio Mariano*, the oldest educational institution in Bergamo founded in 1506 under the name of the *Scuola della Misericordia*, was suppressed to establish, on 15 November 1803, the Departmental High School of Serio. The school, thanks to the introduction of new disciplines and a renewed didactics, assumed a role of primary importance both in the creation of the new managerial class of Bergamo and in the training of educated and aware citizens (Medolago 2003).

Fig. 1. The gymnasium school *Paolo Sarpi* in *Bergamo* and the heart of the city.

The abbot Lorenzo Mascheroni, formerly a physics lecturer at the *Collegio Mariano*, was among the protagonists of this change by introducing the teaching, both of mathematical and scientific disciplines, and of the Italian language, which he considered on a par with Latin. A fervent supporter of the Enlightenment ideas and of the experimental method in the applied sciences, he was the founder of the *Gabinetto di Fisica* today after him named (Mirandola 1996; Serra Perani 2011).

The Departmental High School of the Serio was firstly located in the ex-convent of the Poor Clare sisters of Rosate. A proposal to adapt the old structures to the new requirements of the school was elaborated in 1815 by the architect Francesco Lucchini. The project, based on a simple reuse of existing premises, was never realized perhaps because unable to communicate the renewed role of the institution in the city context.

A new assignment was entrusted to the architect Ferdinando Crivelli, who designed a solemn building that stood on a high plinth with a wide staircase ending in a pronaos (Bocci 1995). The General Direction of Public Buildings of the Lombardy-Veneto kingdom, however, did not appreciate the first drawings. A new solution was therefore conceived, foreseeing the maintenance of some of the pre-existing structures and of the church. In addition, the project of a new urban public space, the current *Piazza Rosate*, at a lower altitude than the existing road level was incompatible, with the idea of an elevated building (Resmini 2018). The construction of the new building took place between the constraints and pressures of the municipal administration; the same Ferdinando Crivelli later emphasized with bitterness, the weak reception that his factory had met in the city environments (Fig. 2).

The Departmental High School of Serio, following the Constitution of the Kingdom of Italy, by an 1865 Royal Decree was named after the scholar and scientist Paolo Sarpi, an important philosopher and man of science that Galileo Galilei, his great friend, did not hesitate to define *Maestro*. In 1883, the church was deconsecrated and reused as the gym of the new high school, causing the loss of its furnishings now

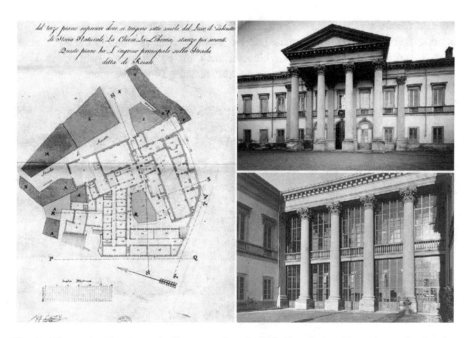

Fig. 2. The project by the arch. Francesco Lucchini (left) and the gymnasium school today following of the arch. Ferdinando Crivelli (right).

dispersed in other sacred buildings and noble houses. In the second half of the 20th century, the scientific laboratories and the library were recovered and partly modified (Tironi 1995).

The *Gabinetto di Fisica* is therefore closely linked to the institution to which it belongs and to the vicissitudes of Bergamo. The value of the laboratory is linked both to the peculiarity of the collection of instruments and to the historical and cultural value that the cabinet has had in the history of the city. A specificity, which a project of musealization cannot ignore and that was therefore used as foundation of the project's guidelines.

3   The Digital Platform for the Knowledge and the Valorisation of the *Gabinetto di Fisica*

The creation of the digital platform for the knowledge and the enhancement of the *Gabinetto di Fisica* is part of a broader research and didactic activity that involved both the University of Bergamo and some city schools. A project aimed at not only the creation of models and IT contents but also a careful study that - starting from the documents of the high school archive and the ancient inventories - has reconstructed the history of the laboratory allowing the historical and typological classification of the instruments.

The *Gabinetto di Fisica* still preserves today, within the original cases, over five hundred instruments dating from the late 18th century to the first half of the 20th century (Fig. 3); among them, the famous planetarium built by Giovanni Albricci in 1783, recently restored and jealously kept in a reserved wing of the presidency room.

Fig. 3. The *Gabinetto di Fisica* and its instrument.

The first inventory of about one hundred instruments dates back to 1793; subsequently, it was updated in 1804 and in 1817 following the new purchases. The document is a simplified list of the pieces in the collection, without descriptions but with valuable information on the manufacturers of the machines and the construction period. The first real catalogue, in which the pieces were filed and grouped into categories, was however drawn up only between 1851 and 1859 when the workshop moved to the new factory. The register, which was subsequently updated in 1871, in 1888, in 1914 and finally in 1955, remained unchanged in the structure until today.

The virtual musealization project, therefore, began with the creation of contents - by studying the instruments and assessing their state of conservation - to classify them in a way that is appropriate to contemporary needs. A part of them underwent a philological restoration to preserve their authenticity and to keep them in their original condition (Miniati and Brenni 1993). The intervention was conducted at the Science and Technology Foundation of Florence, under the direction of Dr Paolo Brenni.

The information has been updated, integrated and organized according to the current classification systems of scientific machines and, in an optimal way, both for the creation of a hardcopy archive and the implementation of a database to be consulted online. Each instrument has been identified with its own name, an alphanumeric code and a representative photographic image. Accordingly, for each one a sheet has been drawn up, mentioning the name of the constructor, the year of construction, the material, the overall dimensions and a detailed description of the instrument and its use; in many cases, when possible, a bibliographic note has been associated.

The consultation of the catalogue has been imagined in an interactive way, by allowing the virtual navigation within the laboratory environments. A spherical image that is oriented in the direction of the observer, allows visitors to see the instruments contained inside the cabinets. By entering the cases, it is possible to scroll each tool, to click on it and see the contents. An additional navigation menu, not visual but 'listed', has been imagined collecting tools in different areas of physics: astronomy, measurement, mechanics, fluids, acoustics, thermology, optics and electromagnetism. By selecting a category, users can access a list that can be clicked to obtain in-depth information box (Fig. 4).

Fig. 4. The navigation menus of the online platform (left) and the catalog sheets of the printed version (right).

The 3D models and the photographic animations of the laboratory experiences enrich the contents and allow a better understanding of the instruments and their functioning (Fig. 5). The short films, produced by the assembly of video recordings made in 'special' days dedicated to the realization of some of the best-known experiments in the history of physics and conducted with the ancient instruments, allow reliving the teaching of experimental physics as happened centuries ago (Fig. 6).

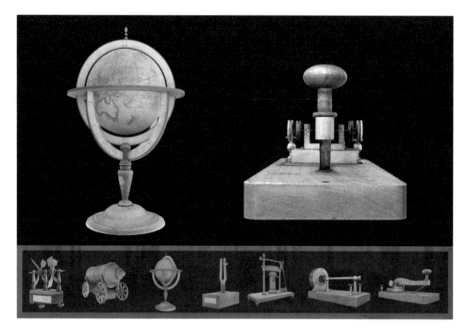

Fig. 5. The virtual models of some instrument.

Fig. 6. The short films of well-known experiments in the history of physics, made with the ancient instruments of the *Gabinetto di Fisica.*

4   An Experimentation Between Research and Didactic

The involvement of young people, to educate them to respect cultural heritage and to the importance of its understanding and safeguarding, was a fundamental component of the project. A course of study and training in which the teachers have thrilled and approached the students to the knowledge of the hidden heritage of their school. In fact, both during the course of the school year and during the summer thanks to a two-week summer school, numerous integrative activities linked to the themes of knowledge, preservation and enhancement of the artistic and scientific memoried of the past were organized (Cardaci 2017). Students were protagonists of the work aimed at preparing the digital platform, both in terms of content and structure (organization of the pages, HTML programming, the creation of 3D models, etc.).

This has provided them with a new competence (transversal to what is offered by their course of study) and has encouraged an addiction to the scientific disciplines and to the inventory and heritage conservation field with an inductive approach strictly connected to a real situation. A specific learning path - similar to a small master - that more than others has brought students closer to the professional context. A form of apprenticeship that allowed them to understand the aspects of an assignment bound to the respect of time, deadlines and quality standards.

Experienced tutors - chosen from former high school students who continue to collaborate with secondary educational institutions and/or doctoral candidates and university graduates - have assisted the teachers 'work in addressing students' activities.

The teaching methodology has overcome the archaic use of the classroom as a place dedicated exclusively to passive learning; the creation of multimedia content and the 'playing in cyberspace' have allowed children, through the playful and discovery aspect, to 'learn by doing'. In this context, the project included the production of some films by the same pupils. They, consequently, were the directors, set designers and actors of their own productions: short documentaries illustrating the scientific instrumentation and its physical meaning, as well as a living *reportage* of their personal experience (Fig. 7).

Fig. 7. The students describe the *Gabinetto di Fisica* and its experiments.

The films, in addition to increasing the curiosity towards the portal of the *Gabinetto di Fisica*, have allowed a creative growth of the group by means of brainstorming techniques used in the design phase of the plots. The integration between students from different schools and university students has also fostered interdisciplinary exchange and stimulated a dialogue between young people with a different cultural background, with the aim of increasing collaboration, complicity and feeling of belonging to a group of researchers in progress.

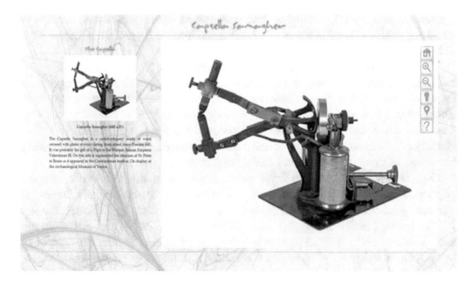

Fig. 8. The player 3DHOP: the sample of visualization of the instruments.

5   Conclusions

The project has taken advantage, in its technical aspects, of the use of the laboratories and the instrumentation of the partners involved but, above all, of the help of the Lab.S.A.B.E. (Survey and Analysis of Building and Engineering) of the University of Bergamo.

The laboratory has conducted both metric acquisitions with active sensor instruments, and photographic campaigns for the creation of an image repertoire that is contextually suitable for the preparation of the interactive catalogue and for the definition of virtual models with 3D image-based modelling techniques.

In fact, the digital platform had to support the display of virtual models through the 3DHOP (3D Heritage Online Presenter) player - an innovative iterative system developed by the Visual Computing Laboratory of the ISTI-CNR Department - as well as to improve the understanding of models thanks to Augmented Reality applications (Fig. 8).

The ministerial platform of the school, able to manage only static and non-dynamic models, has made it impossible to implement these contents, which are still not accessible remotely. The full potentials of the system remain, therefore, still unexpressed in the expectation of a hopefully fast software update of the MIUR platforms.

Acknowledgements. The digital platform of the Cabinet of Physics of the State High School "Paolo Sarpi" of Bergamo is the result of an educational-scientific collaboration (under the responsibility and coordination of Prof. Alessio Cardaci) between the School of Engineering of the University of Bergamo and the State High School '*Paolo Sarpi*' of Bergamo, with the participation of the State Institute of Higher Education '*Giacomo Quarenghi*' and of the FBK Center - Bruno Kessler Foundation. An important technical and scientific contribution was provided by the 3DOM group (3D Optical Metrology unit), directed by Prof. Fabio Remondino, of the FBK research centre - Bruno Kessler Foundation of Trento, an external project partner. The project is the winner of a national call of the Ministry of Education of the University and Research (MIUR), funded through the measures provided for by law L.113/91 (L.6/2000) for the 'Dissemination of scientific culture'.

References

Belotti B (1940) Storia di Bergamo e dei Bergamaschi. Ceschina, Bergamo

Bocci B (1995) Ferdinando Crivelli (1810–1855) Tesi. Ed. Politecnico di Milano, Milano

Cardaci A (2017) Il disegno, la 'Buona Scuola' e l'università: approccio didattico e esperienze negli insegnamenti del 'disegno'. In: Territori e frontiere della Rappresentazione. Gangemi, Roma

Medolago G (2003) Prima del Liceo, il nobile Collegio Mariano di Bergamo nel secolo XVIII. In: La Rivista di Bergamo, n. 36, dicembre 2003

Miniati M, Brenni P (1993) Restauro di strumenti storico-scientifici e filosofie di intervento. In: Masetti Bitelli L (ed) Restauro di strumenti i materialli: scienza, musica, etnografia edn. Nardini, Firenze

Mirandola G (1996) Il Gabinetto di Fisica del Collegio Mariano a Bergamo. In: La Rivista di Bergamo, n. 6, settembre 1996

Resmini M (2018) Scuole in piazza: nuovi volti per il liceo e l'università, in Percorsi e incontri sul Colle di Rosate: società, cultura, luoghi. Edizioni Ateneo di Scienze, Lettere, Arti di Bergamo, Bergamo

Serra Perani L (2011) Lorenzo Mascheroni e il Gabinetto di Fisica del Collegio Mariano. In: Gennaro E (ed) Lorenzo Mascheroni tra scienza e letteratura nel contesto della Bergamo settecentesca. Sestante, Bergamo

Tironi L (1995) Il Liceo Ginnasio di Bergamo, Notizie storiche. Edizioni dell'Ateneo, Bergamo

When the Future Is the Past. Digital Databases for the Virtualization of Museum Collection

S. Parrinello[1]([⊠]), F. Picchio[1]([⊠]), and A. Dell'Amico[2]([⊠])

[1] Department of Civil Engineering and Architecture (DICAr),
University of Pavia, Via Ferrata 3, 27100 Pavia, Italy
{sandro.parrinello, francesca.picchio}@unipv.it
[2] Department of Architecture (DIDA), University of Florence,
Via della Mattonaia 14, 50121 Florence, Italy
anna.dellamico@unifi.it

Abstract. The paper through an excursus on the technological development of virtual fruition systems, intends to reflect on the methods of communication and dissemination of cultural heritage, taking as a reference part of the results of research recently conducted on some case studies. The museum, configured in its new immaterial form and no longer as an exclusively physical place, amplifies the availability of space open to visitors, revolutionizing its role as cultural mediator in the extension of a potential connective that increases the dynamics of social development. The present research was aimed at programming a methodological protocol for the documentation and the virtualization of museum assets, collections and architectural heritage of tourist interest, based on a new approach to fruition of the space and the work of art in it contained.

Keywords: Digital survey · 3D database management · VR and AR systems · Virtual museum · Native Americans handicraft

1 Real-Virtual: A New Approach to the Documentation Process[1]

"…Painful as it may be sometimes, the reality remains the only place to eat a good meal. Because the reality is real. Can you follow me?…" Steven Spielberg, Ready Player One[2]

There is no future without a past: "planning" always involves comparing the experiences in progress with those already experienced, as well as the evaluation of behavioral models in order to undertake some fundamental procedural choices. In this way "the virtual" means how much more it does not exist and what can not be

---

[1] The Section 1 entitled "Real-Virtual: a new approach to the documentation process" and Section 4 Conclusions is edited by Sandro Parrinello, of Section 2 entitled "The use of digital technologies in the CH: the tools and the production of digital databases for the virtual" is edited by Francesca Picchio and Section 3 entitled "Content Virtualization and Museum Container: case studies compared" is edited by Anna Dell'Amico.

[2] The quote from the 2017 film refers to *"It's not that i'm going crazy about reality, but it's still the only place to eat a decent meal"* by G. Marx.

© Springer Nature Switzerland AG 2019
A. Luigini (Ed.): EARTH 2018, AISC 919, pp. 212–222, 2019.
https://doi.org/10.1007/978-3-030-12240-9_23

described precisely because, if described, if it is harnessed in an image, if represented, it will cease to be virtual, acquiring its own identity within what we consider "real", that is in all that it can be somehow perceived by a community of individuals.

The architect's profession deals with the transformation of virtual images into real images and how ideas can be made, based on experience, to become figures in the mind and finally a critical experience represented: in a few words Drawing.

Today the virtual can be associated with a second meaning, more commonly used, which more specifically relates to the experience of life in the digital world, simulated through specific interactions with what the digital graphic expression is able to recur in the real world (Levy 1997).

This creates a parallelism between real-material and virtual-digital, within which human experience is inserted to give life to new design scenarios. The implementation of meanings in the virtual context of digital expression implies giving a second life to the dimension of places, whose laws are dictated by computer science. This implementation of meanings also implies a substantial simplification of the complexities characterizing the real space, so that the process of image construction is able to replicate in all and for all the action of "drawing" and the elaborate products become tools from which he deduces simplified and critically interpreted information of what has been specifically described. Being a digital life experience, the interaction with these drawings or representations, in any case, involves the generation of a new awareness and, consequently, a new logic of learning. In this sense, living and enjoying the virtual means interconnecting data, explaining actions and designing analyzes and knowledge that, even at the unconscious level, qualify the understanding of a given phenomenon. It is well known that the image is entrusted with the task of adding the word within the narrative systems to allow a more effective projection and virtualization of the imaginative identity of what is narrated. The imaginative projection of one's own virtual identity and, at the same time, of the community and the community contextualizes the identity necessary to inhabit a place and live a certain environment.

The process of virtualization of history, which originates with the story, expresses this condition well, and it is easy to imagine what emotional tensions support the story that the Neolithic community, gathered around the hearth, received from the elderly about the events of the origins of the community itself. This story, which represents the origin of civilization and virtualization of a bygone era, was also proposed to us, as children, to educate the imagination and memory through the narration of stories.

This is why talking about the future necessarily involves talking about the past, qualifying it and reproducing it through virtual images, especially when the processes for their production are addressed, as then, to the teaching and dissemination of information.

The technological revolution and the dissemination of information started with the digital age has progressively transferred the sphere of drawing and representation towards an almost totally immaterial communication system, able to propose, through virtual images, an idealized future or a glorious past, as a witness to landscapes in continuous transformation. (Parrinello and Picchio 2017). The image is entrusted with the task of reproducing the characteristics of a given context by implementing its contents and meanings in the virtual dimension, often modifying the concept of reality in favor of greater emotional involvement on the part of the user. To the multiple utopian images associated with the "real", research in the field of drawing and representation is increasingly turning towards the development of new expressive systems, capable not only of telling the complexities of contemporary spaces but also of actively involving the viewer in the learning and dissemination of information collected. Within this field of technological experimentation and communication development, which includes contemporary cinematography, *serious games*, and *educational entertainment*, in recent years the museum spaces and the works that are part of the collections inside have also found their place also in favor of the promotion of a system of fruition of the culture increasingly projected towards sharing and global fruition.

2   The Use of Digital Technologies in the CH: The Tools and the Production of Digital Databases for the Virtual

In the definition "Virtual is a new form of reality that allows us to understand the real best" by the philosopher Philippe Queau, the link between virtual and image is clear, underlined by the use of the word form. (Queau 1993). The virtual we refer to today, 3D models, VR and AR applications, are the outcome of the technological development of a representative system, of how our ordering of space refers to computational models and how, despite the change in the medium, the unchanged remains the purpose of representing, of communicating, of transmitting knowledge effectively, which today corresponds to the qualities of speed and immediacy. On the basis of these reflections, the technological development of "representing" has gradually led to the elimination of barriers and distances between the user and the object used, making the virtual experience ever closer and more likely than the real one. The escape from the real took place through drawing and the use of the graphic sign as a total form of abstraction that allowed the user to immerse himself in idealized imaginations of the unrepresentable (an example is the first depictions of the amanuensis monks, combined with the texts of books sacred), from the mid-nineteenth century, following the construction of the first devices of "escape" from the real through systems for image amplification (among the first instruments are the stereoscope, the Kaiserpanorama[3] of Fuhrmann più the Kaiserpanorama of Fuhrmann and the more recent Tru-Vue e View Master[4]), is the tool to become a point of contact between virtual reality and the real world, establishing a new connection with the user by the amplification of the two-dimensional drawing (Fig. 1).

---

[3] Conceived by August Fuhrmann, in 1890 the Kaiserpanorama was an optical device that exploited the technology of the stereoscope, a machine around which could seat about twenty people and simultaneously view different stereo photography. Taken from the website: http://www.kabarett.it/kaiserpanorama-visore-stereoscopico-tra-divertimento-e-propaganda/.

[4] True-Vue, a Rock Island company founded in 1931, became famous for the production of the stereoscopic viewer by David Brewster. In 1951 it was then incorporated by the rival company Sawyer's owner of View-Master. Taken from the site: http://www.wikiwand.com/it/Stereoscopi_del_XX_secolo.

Fig. 1. From the left: a depiction of the Kaiserpanorama of Fuhrmann, and the two viewers systems in the center the Tru-Vue and to the right the View-Master.

From these types of instruments, ancestors of our viewers, to the first experiments of dynamic virtualization of the second half of the twentieth century with Ivan Sutherland and his "Sword of Damocles"[5] and the creation of the first interactive digital management system with the project by Andrew Lippman the Aspen Movie Map, anticipating 30 years of Google Street View, the interactive map of Google. (Biocca and Delaney 1995) In the '80s and '90s, some laboratories were set up to research and develop new technologies for virtual reality, creating new products such as Dataglove, NASA VIEW, Nintendo Power Glove, Virtuality 1000CS, SEGAVR, Nintendo Virtual Boy and many other fruition systems that have followed one another every year with the fast pace of an ever increasing vertiginous technological revolution that has led to the production of the current viewers on the market like Oculus Rift and HTC Vive.

Despite the change and the evolution of the medium, the goal remains to simplify the understanding of the user: technological development contributes decisively to the increase in user involvement through immersive systems, thanks to which the user it can interact and discover a certain place through different levels of interaction. These systems become necessary means for the communication and dissemination of culture and the use of spaces within a click; this is why the tendency, in the field of drawing and representation, is to increase project towards the development of new expressive systems capable not only of telling the complexities of contemporary spaces but also of actively involving the viewer in learning and disseminating the information collected. (Gerosa and Pfeffer 2006). The development of utopian virtuality has also been applied to museum spaces through descriptive systems for the works and collections contained in them. This configuration of the digital message shows its usefulness when it ascends to a communicative level that is not affected by cultural constraints but is often in line with the promotion of a system of fruition of the culture increasingly projected towards

---

[5] The Sutherland experiment, built in 1968, was the first prototype of augmented reality. Taken from the website: https://www.tomshw.it/storia-realta-virtuale-75901.

sharing and global fruition. In this cultural context, images take on a precise role in the development of learning, becoming the language we use to communicate information, mainly visual, and to establish the ways in which such information can be conveyed to be transposed to different areas. In this way, digital end up attributing to the images a new cultural dimension and unexpected perspectives of development, new cultural products that condition the type of experience, new meanings and different ways of constructing knowledge. Our society at *once and immediately*, built on ever more dynamic times and expectations reduced to a minimum, is necessarily forced to update its expectations and its communication needs, transferring training in information so that each individual can perceive the complexity of the real through direct channels.

The applications of virtual reality go to stimulate the curiosity and the attraction towards the discovery for the "new": they awaken emotions and sensations able to reach and activate our neurons and generate physical sensations that predispose to listening and reading more engaging and participatory.

It must be recognized how the advent of new digital media forces a change of perspective not only in the modes of communication but also in how those same contents, vehicles of information, are produced (Fig. 2).

Fig. 2. Access to the use of interactive virtual visits is necessarily conveyed by a material carrier, such as the viewer Oculus Rift, link between real and virtual space. These applications can be navigated through AR and VR visualization systems in situ and not, which allow to place and display information about the object, thus enriching the experience of visiting the museum.

The systems of production and use of this information make use of applications for virtual reality, augmented and mixed reality. Their accessibility is now within reach of the new generations of users, who are now increasingly young, growing in close contact with this type of reality, accustomed since childhood to immerse themselves in the virtual through digital devices and interactive platforms, catapulting themselves into scenarios and stories of the "cyber society"; a generation, belonging to a virtual context, which we can define as "digital native". Our whole existence is developing within digital environments, both to communicate information and to share and establish new "virtual" connections between individuals. Thus, part of our life is carried out only virtually, through our configuration as entities existing on social networks or on digital platforms, producing a cultural misunderstanding between what is imagined in the solitude of one's real experience, compared to what is communally transmitted as information.

The tool of digital models for the study and the thematic deepening, and therefore the creation of virtual spaces where to use the most varied information, goes to enhance the means of cultural diffusion through what is called *ubiquitous learning*[6] e *discovery-based learning.*[7] Elements that distinguish these new types of smart learning are the permanence of information, collected and always available thanks to the accessibility of digital databases, the ease and speed with which the user can access the various information data in any place through the digital network and the possibility of doing structured research based on the specific needs of the user: thanks to the interactivity of the tool, it is possible to outline the thematic analyzes based on the different user profiles, adapting the knowledge path to their learning needs. (Ogata and Yano 2004).

On the basis of these key points, even the museum complexes are opening the doors to new digital experiences trying to expand their spaces, no longer confined to the physical container detectable in the museum walls, but open their contents to new digital spaces, through virtualization of their collections.

The interaction with the virtual space, with the object or with the collection, transforms the drawing into a computational act that reaches its maximum programmatic expression with the awareness of the interaction between the various databases. Reproducing virtually every object and museum complex in a model involves defining "synthesis" strategies to organize the perceived and measured place semantically. To these 3d models, designed and complete with geometric and material information, it is possible to add further information, qualifying a metadata structure. From hypertext formats to further models, each digitized element is usable and able to interact with the user and with the context, real or virtual, in which it is placed.

---

[6] *Ubiquitous learning* is defined as a daily learning environment supported by the use of the pc and is intended to provide students with content and interaction anytime and anywhere. The learning process takes place through the virtual medium. The direct access to information always, in any place, and with any type of device is the characterizing element of a new generation of information systems identified with the term Ubiquitous Computing. In 1988 Mark Weiser coined this term, imagining computers placed in walls and in any other object of daily use (Hwang et al. 2008).

[7] *Discovered based learning*, a 21st-century experiential learning technique based on the study of theorists and psychologists Jean Piaget, Jerome Bruner, and Seymour Papert (Mayer 2004).

3   Content Virtualization and Museum Container: Case Studies Compared

The theme of digitization of public information and cultural heritage is, today, one of the priority themes of the European Digital Agenda[8] that encourages public administrations to invest in the potential of information. However, to date, some "homogeneous" museum policies that favor the integration of heritage and digital technologies are missing. Analyzing the statistical data[9] relating to the flow of museum visits in 2017, no Italian museum at international level is ranked among the top ten most visited museums in the world.

Among the first three are the Louvre museum, with 8.1 million visitors, the National Museum of China, with 8 million visitors and the MET in New York, followed by the Vatican Museums, the British Museum, and the Tate Modern. In the Italian scene, the recent data collected by the Mibact[10] statistical office record an increase in visits compared to 2017 and see the Colosseum among the first three most visited sites, with about 7 million visitors, the archaeological site of Pompeii and the gallery of the Uffizi.

Analyzing the largest museums in the world ranking, it can be observed that not by chance, are those who have already started to open their archives in digital mode is the example of THE MET that has networked the cataloging of 375,000 free photos from rights, and the British Museum that, in collaboration with Google Art Project, has designed an accessible virtual timeline of the works inside the museum.

The diffusion of digital technologies has led to a profound change in the use of art, which in addition to the static approach also includes personalized interactive, the museums while preserving their tradition of place for the protection and conservation of works with the advent technology are populated with new ways of learning and awareness to bring the user closer to the art and it does so through digital that today is the fastest way to get there.

This trend has allowed the development of museums that find their construction only in the digital world.

An example is the French project UMA (Universal Art Museum): officially inaugurated on December 5, 2017, the system works in all respects as a museum with temporary exhibitions, designed and organized by a real curator, in the idea of collecting, in a unique digital space, all the works of the world. And here the technology comes to their aid, giving the possibility to create a totally new, imaginary design environment, modifiable according to the organized exhibitions.

---

[8] The digital agenda presented by the European Commission in Brussels in 2010 sets targets to be achieved by 2020, aimed at boosting productivity and technological development and supporting social cohesion in the European Union (EU).

[9] Data taken from the world ranking compiled by the Giornale dell'Arte with The Art Newspaper.

[10] Data published on the website http://www.beniculturali.it/mibac/export/MiBAC/sito-MiBAC/Contenuti/visualizza_asset.html_249254064.html. Source: Mibact-Statistics Office, 2018 - provisional data subject to change.

Another similar experience is proposed by the "Virtual Museum of Iraq" which, however, does not claim to be a reconstruction of the Royal Museum of Baghdad, remembered for the events of 2003, which saw him victim of several looting during the Iraqi conflict, but it is rather a reinterpretation of the real museum presenting only a selection of the most significant works with 3D reconstructions offering an interactive, sound, visual approach and learning to the works.

This opens the reflection on the fact that in Italy there is still a lot of work to do to reach the world standard because today's museum is not just a container of collections.

In order to combine information systems capable of describing the museum spaces, within the research activities carried out by the Experimental Laboratory of Didactics and Research DAda-Lab of the University of Pavia, have been developed some projects that have had as their object the digitization of the heritage and museum collections for the production of 3D databases and interactive modes of use associated with them.

The activities of the laboratory are concentrating both towards the realization of a methodological process of digitization of the museum space (container) towards innovative forms of use of the museum space, and towards the study of a methodological process of acquisition of the museum collections (content) generating new experiences of visiting the digitized space and encouraging renewed systems of interaction between real and virtual with the aim of creating information systems in which the content is directly connected to its container. Through digital detection and the use of specific data management and processing software, databases have been produced organized according to different levels, dimensions, and data complexity, in which it was possible to collect all the data acquired to allow the extraction of a useful information. In particular, the digital survey produces point clouds that can be converted into models in which spatiality is re-proposed in its three dimensions (Parrinello and Picchio 2017) (Fig. 3).

Regarding the collections, a first case study saw the experimentation of Native American craftsmanship[11] carried out on a widespread heritage. The research has been involved in the production of highly reliable models from which to develop useful considerations for the construction of information systems and digital databases for collections that unlike others are not collected in a single museum structure, but diffused among the various private collectors and not Americans and Europeans, and therefore the creation of a virtual museum system that allows to organize databases to try to gather such widespread heritage in a complex information system (Parrinello and Dell'Amico 2018). The aim is to preserve the specific qualities of each material, deformations, alterations and imperfections, working on the geometry of the polygonal mesh in order to decimate as much as possible the number of triangles without altering the functional qualities to achieve the objectives for the investigation.

The models thus obtained, reliable and complete, can be used to define an information database on the morphological qualities of each work. With this in mind, the database becomes a sample of technical sheets describing craftsmanship through a census that links qualitative information to models that describe "quantitatively" in terms of measurement, the specifics of each work.

---

[11] The collection referred to is a private collection by Sergio Susani, an expert in the culture and art of Native American manufacturing.

Fig. 3. The digital model can be used to connect information, which can be viewed through mobile devices and interactive digital platforms.

The set of database information describes a digital archive that offers various development possibilities for the enhancement of the collection as well as for the management of the phenomenon (crafts of the natives) as a whole. A possible development for the use of the collection began with the design of a virtual museum on the natives, an all-digital architectural space that collects the different collections (Fig. 4).

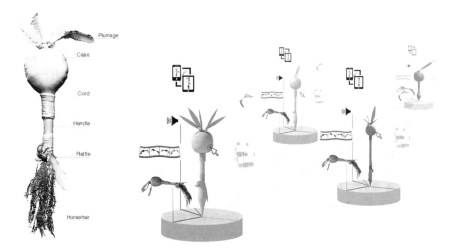

Fig. 4. The management of a database composed of a very large number of elements through a virtual stereotype to which multimedia files and information cards can be associated, in addition to the relative mesh model from which to be able to uniquely identify the work with all its formal characteristics three-dimensional.

A second case study is being developed within the laboratory hours of the court of Drawings Foundations and graphic documentation[12] held by prof. S. Parrinello and Dr. D. Bontempi: the course was aimed at experimenting with a photogrammetric survey for the design and the digitization of artifacts and works with historical-artistic value developing actions for the enhancement and conservation of cultural heritage, in detail addressed to museum collections and valuable exhibits belonging to the museum structures of the University itself, specifically saw the survey of a series of musical instruments belonging to the collection of the Department of Musicology of Cremona. The digital reconstruction of musical instruments, and scientific and technical instruments and their components, with the aim of obtaining two-dimensional drawings and detailed 3D models associated with a database of technical data sheets describing technical and historical information, conservation status and guidelines for the programmed management and restoration of the artifacts. Use of the archive material produced in a questionable database and with the possibility of updating data, through which to start initiatives and projects to enhance the objects of the various collections.

4   Conclusions

The research activities promote the creation of a heterogeneous data archive, updated with new information and accessible through virtual platforms. Localization systems refer the work to the container exhibition system while allowing a cultural connection with keywords and links that, through various access channels, animate the experience of remote use. This study is a reflection on the museum management systems in which space and artwork coexist within their virtual, dynamic transposition.

A database, in order to preserve the historical memory of the museum complex and of the cultural system that can become both an instrument for the management of the asset in terms of planning short, medium and long-term interventions and an enhancement tool. We could talk about databases for the planned exploitation where the use of immersive reality systems and digitalized space gives rise to a system of information that amplifies the potential and connections of 3D databases with different types of formats and information systems. Through digital if on the one hand problems of accessibility and diffusion of good are resolved, on the other hand the same work of art takes on a new expressive value, capable of renewing the glorious past through dynamic, audio aspects and explanatory contents aimed at enriching its identity and making it reacquire that original dignity too often hidden behind a closed glass case.

Acknowledgments. The research project concerning the documentation of the artifacts of Native American was made possible thanks to the collaboration between the experimental laboratory DAda Lab of the University of Pavia and the collector Sergio Susani. The project on the digitization of musical instruments was born from the collaboration between the DAda Lab Experimental Laboratory of the Department of Civil Engineering and Architecture and the Department of Musicology and Cultural Heritage of Cremona, University of Pavia.

---

[12] The course is part of the educational didactics offer of the single cycle degree course in Conservation and Restoration of Cultural Heritage (class LMR/02) a.a 2017/2018.

References

Biocca F, Delaney B (1995) Immersive virtual reality technology. In: Biocca F, Levy M (eds) Communication in the age of virtual reality. Lawrence Erlbaum Associates Publishers, Hillsdale

Gerosa M, Pfeffer A (2006) Mondi virtuali: benvenuti nel futuro dell'umanità. Castelvecchi editore, Roma

Hwang G-J, Tsai C-C, Yang SJH (2008) Criteria, strategies and research issues of context-aware ubiquitous learning. Educ Technol Soc 11(2):81–91

Lèvy P (1997) Il virtuale. Raffaello Cortina editore, Milano

Mayer R (2004) Should there be a three-strikes rule against pure discovery learning? the case for guided methods of instruction. Am Psychol 59(1):14–19

Ogata H, Yano Y (2004) Context-aware support for computer-supported ubiquitous learning. In: Proceedings of the 2nd IEEE international workshop on wireless and mobile technologies in education, pp 27–34

Parrinello S, Dell'Amico A (2018) The traditional crafts of the native Americans Procedures of survey and documentation for the creation of informative systems 3D. In: Proceedings of the conference 3D modeling and BIM, pp 394–409. Nuove frontiere, DEI Tipografia del genio civile, Roma

Parrinello S, Picchio F (2017) Databases and complexity. Remote use of the data in the virtual space of reliable 3D models. Archit Eng 2:27–36

Queau P (1993) Le virtuel: Vertus et vertige. Champ Vallon Editions, Ceyzérieu

Education

The Pollicina Project: A Collaborative and Educational Social Suite to Build Cultural Itineraries

S. Calegari[(⊠)] and M. Dominoni

Department of Informatics, Systems and Communication (DISCo),
Università degli Studi di Milano-Bicocca, Viale Sarca 336 Building 14,
20126 Milan, Italy
{silvia.calegari,matteo.dominoni}@unimib.it

Abstract. The Pollicina project is aimed at defining a collaborative coordinated learning environment, called Educational Social Network, to allow students to elaborate thematic cultural paths on the territory. The topic is addressed with the "flipped learning" methodology where the socialization aspect assumes a key role in the learning process: students can collaborate and share knowledge and their assessment is obtained as an aggregation of formal (i.e., grades) and informal activities (i.e., soft skills). The starting phase of the project consists in defining a common semantic schema of the heterogeneous material in order to facilitate the work of students when they access to the Educational Social Network. The Pollicina's e-learning platform presents several innovative services to build the customized itineraries according to the track defined by the teacher, e.g. the "ArtTour" service dedicated to the definition of the cultural paths, the "Magazine" service to collect the most interesting cultural itineraries, etc. The first one is the "Data Filling" service where students have to complete, in a collaborative way, the information of the cultural heritage objects provided by the cultural institutions (museums, churches, archaeological sites, etc.) joined to Pollicina.

Keywords: Education 3.0 · Flipped learning · Art and Teaching · Cultural heritage

1 Introduction

The goal of the Pollicina project (Calegari et al. 2017) is to build a collaborative coordinated social learning environment which allows to create knowledge itineraries and to bring the students closer to cultural heritages (museums, churches, archaeological sites, etc.).

The mission is to obtain an active participation in the cultural life; the younger users will approach the historical and cultural topics through direct involvement in pleasurable activities in order to share experiences and ideas. Collaborative teaching among peer groups can induce synergy for the active production of the paths. These are created according to the indications of teachers and experts of cultural institutions establishing a novel form of social learning dedicated to the art topic. Students can also enrich the

© Springer Nature Switzerland AG 2019
A. Luigini (Ed.): EARTH 2018, AISC 919, pp. 225–234, 2019.
https://doi.org/10.1007/978-3-030-12240-9_24

heterogeneous material (e.g., paintings, archaeological finds, statues, etc.) provided by the cultural heritage institutions that joined the project.

These paths are defined with the help of a recommendation system that suggests alternative paths based both on the location of the material inside the museum, and on the semantic correlation between the materials. This approach falls within the concept of Education 3.0 according to which the contents are proposed and articulated through interactive social channels, and they are processed by students in a collaborative way. In Pollicina, we are developing a learning environment called EduSN (Educational Social Network) to support collaborative teaching. EduSN is a Social LMS (Learning Management System) that integrates social networking, collaboration and knowledge sharing capabilities, as well as interactive elements that enable users to rate contents. These objectives are achieved by integrating aspects of a CMS (Content Management System) for the classification of the material, and of an Enterprise Social Network (for collaborative work) with a strong emphasis on the social aspects to extend the standard LMS platforms. EduSN is equipped with a dashboard to evaluate the itineraries created, both for teachers who propose the guidelines, and for the peers themselves who can use these itineraries to get closer to new cultural heritage according to the proposed topic. To support the visit to the cultural heritage sites, a geo-referenced system is defined with the intent to realize an augmented visit by providing more details on the materials.

As a result, it is possible to produce complex itineraries which include several cultural institutions, like museums, archaeological sites and churches. These itineraries will be reusable by the cultural institutions as a mean to promote their activities, attract more users, encourage a more flexible and collaborative use of the collections.

The paper is organized as follows. Section 2 presents an overview of the Pollicina project, Sect. 3 gives a panoramic of the EduSN's architecture, Sect. 4 defines the strategy adopted to represent the data model of the cultural material, Sect. 5 proposes the "Data Filling", the first service of our e-learning platform. Finally, some conclusions are presented.

2   A Brief Presentation of the Pollicina Project

The Pollicina project (https://www.progettopollicina.eu) follows the "flipped learning" paradigm (Filiz and Kurt 2015; Dalsgaard 2006; Michael 2006), where the use of technology supports the learning practices in order to: (1) stimulate the creation of learning communities - students can take notes and share their experience, (2) collaborative learning - students can improve their skills on the course/topic, interacting with colleagues and experts anywhere and anytime, (3) the adoption of new workspaces - students and teachers can join to virtual work areas to share projects, ideas, etc. A collaborative virtual work space leads the student to obtain greater cognitive awareness and increases self-esteem. Furthermore, the identification of the expert (Avogadro et al. 2016) plays a key role in the paradigm of "flipped learning"; indeed, the expert helps peers within the learning communities (Herling 2000). Figure 1(a) shows some learning features, in detail:

- Revision, students can check the work performed by peers in a collaborative way. The teacher supervises and comments the learning activities;
- Soft Skill, students are evaluated by the teacher according to their social capabilities;
- Role, students can have different responsibilities during a task in order to acquire learning awareness and improve their self-esteem;
- Multimedia, the tasks are performed thanks to the use of technologies such as smartphones, tablets, etc.; in addition, students can enrich the knowledge of each cultural heritage object with movies, pictures, musics during the definition of their cultural paths.

Figure 1(b) presents the logical division of the students in small groups where the members of each group collaborate and share knowledge to solve the task defined by the teacher. In the figure, we refer to a class that logically can be organized in groups, but in the flipped learning context the design can be extended to the concept of a large group (i.e., students who belong to different classes or schools, thus not only members of a single class) that can be aggregated in groups independent of their origin.

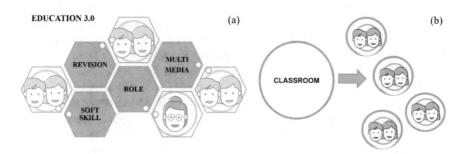

Fig. 1. Pollicina's elements: (a) social features, and (b) working groups.

The Pollicina project involves students starting from the primary school level, up to secondary schools, including the "alternanza scuola lavoro" (i.e., an Italian teaching method created in collaboration between schools and companies to offer students skills that can be used in the job market), in which the approach to cultural heritage can be translated into a moment of collective and individual cultural and emotional training. In this way, it is possible to achieve an active participation to the cultural life, which is suitable to the educational level of the groups. Younger users can approach the historical-cultural themes through a direct involvement in amusing activities that convey a reasoned learning of the contents according to a gamification paradigm. To achieve this goal, different methodological and technological approaches are used. In the first phase, the project involves 12 heterogeneous schools of all educational levels, for a total of about 900 users. There are 26 cultural institutions involved in the

Lombardy region. Approximately 300 secondary school students are involved in "alternanza scuola lavoro" activities, including aspects of user centred design. With the new academic year, we plan to enlarge the audience of users (both schools and cultural institutions), and to complete the development of the whole EduSN's features.

3   The Educational Social Network

The goal of Pollicina is to define an innovative Educational Social Network (EduSN), that combines standard aspects of an e-learning environment with social networking, collaboration and knowledge sharing capabilities, as well as interactive elements that enable users to rate contents. EduSN is developed as SaaS (software as a service) for giving the possibility of groups of students to elaborate the lessons anywhere and anytime. This section gives an overview of the architecture underlining the EduSN (see Fig. 2); it is important to stress that our architecture follows the principle of microservices, namely each service is an independent component that can be integrated in other platforms according to a few modifications related to the APIs aspects. In the starting phase of the project, we have conducted a survey by analyzing the existing opensource e-learning platforms not only as a baseline for our development but also to understand the motivations of a possible integration. To this aims, a deep analysis has been made with Moodle, and after a preliminary integration we understood that our EduSN presents a lot of innovative services and user's requirements. The outcome is that no integration with other e-learning tools can be possible for the Pollicina's objectives.

The data are provided by heterogeneous sources of information and this increases the complexity of the ETL (Extraction, Transformation, Process) process aimed at defining common schemas of the meta-data according to the specific EduSN's service that has to be invoked according to the user's request. In detail, the storage level collects the following information: (1) Social LMS (Social Learning Management System), it considers all the users' activities related to the ability to collaborate and share information to solve a task such as the information generates within a social wall, concurrent editing, comments, chat, etc.; (2) VLE (Virtual Learning Environment), it implicitly monitors the user's actions during his/her interaction with EduSN, for example, the material printed, saved, downloaded, viewed (video, images, texts), etc.; (3) Student Information System, it considers scholastic information related to a student such as ID number, formal grades, class and school to which he/she belongs, etc.; (4) Cultural Heritage Information, it stores the knowledge provided by the cultural institutions which have joined to Pollicina (for more details see Sect. 4). The "Learning Records Warehouse" component stores the knowledge acquired by the storage level within ad-hoc data structure/format as result of the ETL process.

The data elaborated are then used by ad-hoc methodologies, in detail: (1) Flipped Learning, the students are organized within editorial committees, and they have a specific role in the creation process of the itinerary. In detail, Pollicina adopts a *student-centered approach*, where students become engaged in "active learning" where a lesson goes beyond a passive listening and students elaborate the learning tasks starting from elementary materials and the guidelines from the teacher. (2) Gamification, the students' activities are monitored to assign the relative badge according to communication skills, interpersonal skills, problem solving capabilities, interaction with peers and leadership skills. (3) Recommender System, the user profile is analysed to find peers with similar interests in order to suggest useful learning materials (Re Depaolini et al. 2018). (4) Classification System, the definition of a novel algorithm of soft clustering (ref Vietnam) to mine data according to the user's information needs.

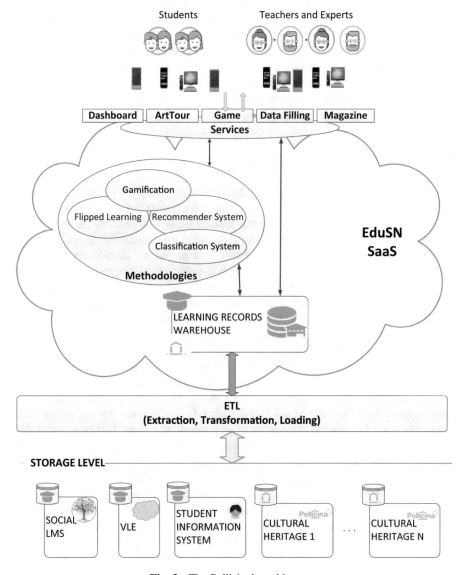

Fig. 2. The Pollicina's architecture.

A key level of EduSN is dedicated to the services that allow a smart communication between the users and the Pollicina's knowledge with the mediation of the ad-hoc methodologies previously introduced. In detail: (1) Data Filling, this service is the first one of the EduSN platform and it is propaedeutic for the definition of the personalized itineraries, and it is aimed at defining the knowledge that will be stored in the repository (see Sect. 5 for more details). (2) Dashboard, the system monitors the user's activities and elaborates the data acquired in order both to assign badges and define indicators to track the quantitative parameters such as accesses to the EduSN platform, execution time of a task, etc. (3) ArtTour, this service is dedicated to the definition of the customized itineraries thanks to the use of off-the-shelf technology. (4) Game, users are involved in pleasant learning activities to define their own cultural itineraries by using games like puzzle, quiz, word and image association, etc. (5) The Magazine service is dedicated to gathering and public the most interesting cultural itineraries.

Users (students, teachers, cultural experts) can access to the EduSN's e-learning platform thanks to the use of external devices (e.g., mobile, tablet, pc) and applications (e.g., Web Clients, Application Services, etc.).

4   The Data Representations in Pollicina

The starting phase of the project is dedicated to the gathering of the material provided by the cultural heritages (museums, churches, archaeological sites, etc.) that have joined to the Pollicina project. During this process we have tackled different problems ranging from the difficulties to manage heterogeneous material (e.g., paintings, archaeological finds, statues, etc.) to the lack of a partial or full digitalization of the material itself. To this aim we have analysed the cultural representations used in the literature in order to provide a unique schema for synthetizing the information for Pollicina. A need of this project is to guarantee a version of the material that is able to simplify the collaborative work of the students during the editorial phases of the data filling process. This goal is achieved by defining a unique meta-data schema representing the heterogeneous nature of the cultural heritage objects.

Figure 3 presents an overview of the methodology adopted to establish the data representations in Pollicina. In detail, we have identified 5 forms for Pollicina: author, cultural heritage object, cultural site, indoor space, and outdoor space, respectively. These forms are the outcome of our analysis after the study of certified guidelines used in the literature, i.e. SIRBeC (http://www.lombardiabeniculturali.it/sirbec/) and Europeana (http://www.europeana.eu), the European open source portal dedicated to the cultural heritage knowledge. SIRBeC is the information system of cultural heritage of the Lombardia Region (Italy) that follows the Italian standard of the ICCD (central institute for the catalog and documentation) institute. The more complex part of the work has been to analyse the schemas related to each type of cultural material; indeed, SIRBeC has about 24 forms (e.g., paintings, archaeological finds, statues, etc.) for the cultural heritage objects, whereas one for author and one for cultural institute site.

Our goal is to propose to the students a simplified knowledge of the cultural material, and at the same time this definition has to be exhaustive since such material is used by teachers to prepare the lessons. To this aim, first we have identified the SIRBeC form closer to our intent from the 24 ones (i.e., the "archeological" form), and then we have extracted the fields useful for Pollicina. Table 1 shows the number of fields dedicated to the definition of the three main forms, i.e. "Cultural Heritage Object Form", "Author Form", and "Cultural Site Form". In general, the Pollicina' forms have less fields than the SIRBeC ones in order to simplify the student's tasks as previously described. In particular, the "Cultural Heritage Objects" form has 121 fields of which 97 from the SIRBeC form, the remaining 33 fields are novel and proper of the Pollicina project (see Sect. 5); the "Author" form has 24 fields of which 14 are novel and proper of the Pollicina project (e.g., the place of death, biography website from Wikipedia, image, etc.); and the "Cultural Site" form has 32 fields of which 24 are novel and proper of the Pollicina project (e.g., weblink, ticket cost, contacts for visit, description of the indoor/outdoor location, etc.).

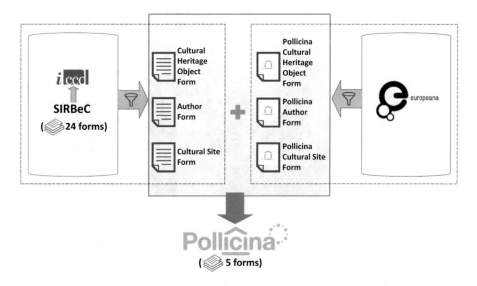

Fig. 3. The schema adopted for representing the Pollicina's meta-datas.

In addition, we have analysed the Europena's meta-data to consider novel attributes with respect to the SIRBeC and the Pollicina fields'. In detail, from the "Cultural Heritage Object" form, the attribute "concept" for describing the content of the material, "Author" form, the attribute "biography", and "Cultural Site" form, the attributes "GPS coordinates of the cultural site", and "the description of the indoor/outdoor location".

Table 1. Attributes used to define the material of the cultural institutions

	Cultural heritage object fields	Author fields	Cultural site fields
SIRBeC	278	64	43
Pollicina	121	24	32

5   The User Experience with the "Data Filling" Service

This section presents the "Data Filling" service aimed at bringing the students closer to the cultural heritage materials where the learning activity is proposed in a pleasant way with respect to standard methodologies of study such as books, Web knowledge, lessons in class with the teacher, etc. The "Data Filling" is the first service of EduSN and it is propaedeutic for the definition of the **personalized itineraries**. This service is aimed at defining the knowledge that will be stored in the repository as shown in Fig. 2. By using this service, the students can access to the assigned cultural form dedicated to a specific cultural material, and then fill the content. The proposed editorial process is supported by a novel workflow for managing the steps of the editorial process with a focus on the collaborative aspects, see Fig. 4 for the details of the workflow.

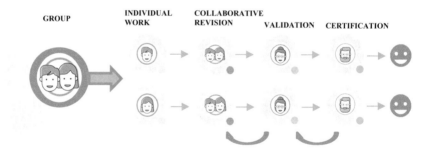

Fig. 4. The editorial workflow to certify the cultural material.

The staff of Pollicina is digitalizing all the material shared by the cultural heritage institutions that joined at the project. Then, thanks to the support of our cultural expert the content is opportunely modified and enriched. Once this phase is concluded, the secondary school students, during the activities of the "alternanza scuola lavoro", are expected to study in depth the material and enrich the content. This learning phase establishes a first coordinated and collaborative process where the students are divided into groups to enrich the information of the cultural heritage objects. A student (1) learns to search for information by several sources of knowledge, (2) summarizes the texts, (3) shares comments to improve the content of the attributes. The interactions among peers are supervised by the teacher and the new knowledge produced is assessed by experts of each cultural institution. Indeed, an expert can approve the completed schema, thus certifying the quality of the work, or can refuse it adding explanations. The certified material will be accessible to students in order to create the cultural itineraries and then obtain a flipped learning experience.

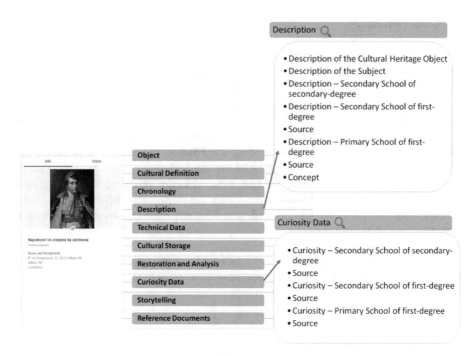

Fig. 5. An extracted of the fields used for the "Cultural Heritage Object" form in Pollicina.

Thanks to the support of our expert in Art and Teaching we have modified and elaborated the descriptions of the cultural heritage material from the SIRBeC forms. Indeed, the cultural knowledge must be accessible to all ages of the students involved allowing them to have textual descriptions according to their level of education. According to the scholastic institutions, we have filled in several attributes in order to help and support the students during the completion of the other attributes. At the end, for each school, we have assigned the schemas precompiled. Figure 5 presents the main fields of the "Cultural Heritage Object" form with a focus on the "Description" and "Curiosity Data" fields, that are some of the novel attributes added for the Pollicina's schema. During this phase, a student learns how to look for information from several sources of knowledge, for example, by using search engine in order to complete the "Curiosity" and "Description" attributes for the specified level of education, he/she summarizes the textual information by the reference website and by the given text within the assigned forms. In addition, he/she can edit the website used to take information and add the curiosity information logically linked to the material of the form that will be accessible during the augmented visit of users within the cultural institute. The site visits will also include scenarios for users who are visually impaired; the paths and applications will be equipped with the technologies enabling vocal tools supporting audio-guide.

6 Conclusions

The "Pollicina" project is aimed at defining a collaborative social suite called EduSN that follows the principles of the Education 3.0 paradigm. The goal is to obtain an active participation in the cultural life: users will approach the historical and cultural issues through a direct involvement in amazing activities sharing comments, experiences, ideas, social feedbacks. A first phase conducted by the staff of Pollicina has been to define ad-hoc data model representing the cultural knowledge taken inspiration by certified meta-data schemas used in the literature. Furthermore, this paper presented the "Data Filling" service that is dedicated to the digitalization of the cultural heritage material provided by the cultural heritage institutions that joined to the project. Students work on editorial committees, having both the role of editor and reviewer. They become the producers of knowledge, with peer help, under the guidance of teachers and experts of cultural institutions.

Acknowledgements. The Pollicina project is supported by the Regional Operational Program of the European Fund for Regional Development 2014–2020 (POR FESR 2014–2020).

References

Avogadro P, Calegari S, Dominoni M (2016) Expert students in social learning management systems. J Interact Technol Smart Educ 13(3):202–217

Calegari S, Meluso F, Avogadro P, Dominoni M (2017) A navigator for sharing cultural heritages in an educational context: the "Pollicina" project. In: 7th international conference, the future of education, Florence, Italy, 8–9 June. Edited by Pixel, pp 16–20. ISBN 978-88-6292-868-7

Dalsgaard C (2006) Social software: e-learning beyond learning management systems. Eur J Open Distance E-Learn (EURODL) 2:1–9

Filiz O, Kurt A (2015) Flipped learning: misunderstanding and the truth. J Educ Res 5(1):215–229

Herling RW (2000) Operational definitions of expertise and competence. In: Herling RW, Provo J (eds) Strategic perspectives of knowledge, competence, and expertise, Chapter 2. Berrett-Koehler Publishers, San Francisco, USA, pp 8–21

Michael J (2006) Where's the evidence that active learning works? J Physiol Educ 30(4):159–167

Re Depaolini M, Ciucci D, Calegari S, Dominoni M (2018) External indices for rough clustering. IJCSR 2018:378–391

The District as a Heritage Asset to be Explored. Pathways to Discovery and Appropriation in Bicocca

Franca Zuccoli[✉] and Alessandra De Nicola

"Riccardo Massa" Department of Human Sciences for Education (DISUF),
University of Milano-Bicocca, Milan, Italy
{franca.zuccoli,alessandra.denicola}@unimib.it

Abstract. This paper describes a series of projects conducted in the Bicocca district, the location of Milano-Bicocca university, with a view to disseminating and promoting the neighbourhood's heritage. The starting point of this programme was an exhibition on the work of Vittorio Gregotti, entitled "Gregotti e Associati 1953_2017", which was held in Milan at the PAC- Pavillion of Contemporary Art (a contemporary art museum) from December 2017 to February 2018: the exhibition inspired reflection on the Bicocca neighborhood, which in turn informed the design of new participatory initiatives with a digital component.

Keywords: Heritage · Education · Teaching and learning · Public ·
Visual culture

1 Starting from the "Gregotti Themed Walks"

The desire to promote the Bicocca district to the students and staff of Milano-Bicocca University, as well as to the residents of the city and the surrounding area, was born in 2017, inspired by an exhibition curated by Guido Morpurgo, entitled "Il Territorio dell'architettura. Gregotti e associati 1953_2017", and devoted to the work of Vittorio Gregotti, the architect behind the redevelopment of Bicocca.

It should be acknowledged, however, that for several years beforehand, academic staff from different departments of the university, albeit from different disciplines and pursuing different lines of inquiry, had already been organizing field trips to local heritage sites both on and off campus, explorations, *flâneries*, and walks in the streets around the university, with the aim of awakening interest in the neighbourhood.

To understand the prior lack of interest in the area, often perceived by the university students and staff themselves as mere spaces to be transited while en route to their classes, laboratories and offices, it is useful to review the history of how the university came to be

---

This paper reflects the joint thinking of the two authors, but the writing up was divided between them as follows: Abstract, Sect. 1 and Conclusions were written by Franca Zuccoli, and Sects. 2 and 3 by Alessandra De Nicola.

© Springer Nature Switzerland AG 2019
A. Luigini (Ed.): EARTH 2018, AISC 919, pp. 235–242, 2019.
https://doi.org/10.1007/978-3-030-12240-9_25

located here and the architectural genesis of its buildings[1]. The University of Milano-Bicocca, and its campus, were inaugurated in 1998, in a former industrial district that had historically been home to the Pirelli and Breda plants, but that had more recently been rezoned and completely redeveloped to the design of Gregotti e associati, the winners of an international architectural competition launched in 1985. "The international competition for the redevelopment of the 750,000 sq.m. Pirelli industrial estate in north Milan was announced in 1985. [...] The original concept was to make the area into a research hub, but from the outset it was deemed essential to come up with a multifunctional structure [which was to be] the specific identity of this "downtown of the suburbs", as we of the design team, somewhat paradoxically, defined it. Simplicity, order, organicity, and precision were the qualities required for this purpose." (Gregotti 2002, pp. 83–87). Those invited to take part in the competition included architects of the calibre of Gae Aulenti, Carlo Aymonino, Mario Botta, Giancarlo De Carlo, Gabetti and Isola, Frank O. Gehry, Gregotti Associati, Joaquim Guedes, Richard Meier, Renzo Piano, and Aldo Rossi (to name but a small selection). Each of the participants proposed an innovative plan for the redevelopment of the vast area. Much has been written about the competition, including numerous criticisms of how it was managed and of the ongoing changes to the project specifications, as well as a smaller number of positive commentaries. As observed by Luigi Mazza, in his introduction to an interesting book on the redevelopment of Bicocca published in 2003, this was such a large change, involving the redevelopment of such a vast area, that it engaged the city in a process of discovery, re-elaboration, connecting, and re-appropriation that was often challenging. A change that was also partly unpredictable in nature, given that the plans were also modified during the building phase itself: "Bicocca is the most important urban renewal project conducted in Milan in recent decades and, from an urban development point of view is a case of particular interest for many reasons, both political and technical. The Bicocca affair brought to light the local government's indecision concerning spatial strategies for Milan [...]." (Bolocan Goldstein 2003, p. 9). Thus, being a place in flux, partly already transformed and partly waiting to stably redefine its identity within the city of Milan - which should have begun to emerge by now - makes it difficult for those living or working in Bicocca to perceive or pin down its identity, negatively conditioning how they experience the neighbourhood.

Today, Bicocca still struggles to raise its profile, attract city goers, retain students, workers, university staff, etc. after business hours, or in general come across as a welcoming, characterful place where it is worth spending one's leisure time.

In particular, the choice of a "Morandian" architectural style (Morpurgo 2017) - with large-scale buildings, wide perspectives, strong vertical and horizontal linearity, angularity, etc. - appears to obscure the small details, the traces of a past deposited in "the nooks and crannies" that may be glimpsed here and there, but that will easily escape a hurried glance. It is as though the new architectural design, though respectful of the existing street network, has covered over the previous layout of the neighbourhood, making it unrecognizable, and concealing from view the area's links with the past.

---

[1] That the university students have failed to bond with the area is confirmed by the fact that they typically do not attend cultural events there, although they can avail of student discounts at leading cultural venues (including for example, Pirelli HangarBicocca and Teatro degli Arcimboldi). This is borne out by surveys conducted by the various venues over the years.

Bicocca's *genius loci* (Norberg-Schulz 1979) thus appears to have been partly suffocated by a drastic change, which is still in progress, and which obscures the traces of the anthropological, social and economic developments of previous centuries. At the same time, traces of new artistic features (Young 2014; Krause Knight 2008), of alternative appropriations of the area, or of newly developed or redeveloped green spaces suggest a vitality that is seeking to emerge and make itself known. With the twofold aim of bringing Bicocca closer both to those who already frequent the area and to those who do not, and contributing to the conservation of key memories that have partly been erased by the advent of a new architectural look and a radically different form of land use, themed walks of the neighbourhood were designed for a mixed audience.[2] These interactive field trips were divided into different steps, but designed to form an organic whole. Their purpose was above all to transmit the multifunctionality of the place, the multiple perspectives from which it may be seen and used, and the echo of different voices that have sounded here over time. The walks started out from the *former Pirelli headquarters*, then participants were invited to go up the cooling tower, observe the Bicocca of the Arcimboldi family, read historical documents, look at photo and film footage of the industrial adventure, and listen to the voices of eye witnesses and researchers. Interactive, material and digital resources were also then offered to facilitate exploration of the neighbourhood's history and the various narrative accounts. Throughout, we attempted to draw out and capture the voices of the audiences who were contributing to develop a different image for the area. The defining characteristics of the walks project included seeking to identify as many quality routes for exploring the neighbourhood as possible, attentively listening to the requests and opinions of participants, and making use of different languages (De Nicola and Zuccoli 2016). The search for suitable digital technologies to adopt, and researching other projects designed to foster exploration of territories, were also enriching and change-inspiring steps.

2 Looking at Bicocca Once More

As can be seen from the graph (Fig. 1), the interests and background of the groups participating on the walks was highly diverse. The characteristics of the audiences and the peculiar nature of the heritage explored suggested the need for different critical-theoretical tools with respect to the classical art theories. Thus, the main interpretive lens adopted was that of *visual studies* and more generally of *visual culture* (Berger 1972, 1980; Mitchell 2017), which focuses on the relationship between people's personal definitions of objects they can see and that which is visible. *Visual culture* not only investigates what has been created to be seen (for example, works of art), but also the invisible, or, that which is not immediately visually perceptible. As Arnheim argues, following Piaget, sight (along with hearing and smell) is one of the "distance" senses: "[These…] not only give a wide range to what is known, they also remove the receiver from the direct impact of the explored event" (Arnheim 1969, p. 23). To put this more

---

[2] Nota bene: the design of the themed walks was shared and agreed with the Pirelli Foundation, owners of the building from which the walks set out. Our grateful thanks go to Laura Riboldi and Martina De Petris of the Foundation.

simply, the visual process relies on a decoding of images that is informed by our prior experience and knowledge. Not by chance, one of the key areas of inquiry in this field concerns digital technology. For the purposes of the current study, one of the most salient aspects of *cultural studies* is that "They particularly concern themselves with intersubjective phenomena [and] the dynamics of seeing and being seen by others as constitutive of the social sphere" (Mitchell 2018, p. 21). According to Mirzoeff "For most people, seeing the world still means first and foremost seeing our own city: taken together, today's global cities make a world of their own. (p. 107). The new global city extends beyond the older concept of city limits (p. 108). [...] Seeing in the global city requires active self-censorship from its residents as part of a highly controlled environment" (Mirzoeff 2015, p. 109).

From this perspective, the aim of the "themed walks" is to provide participants with simple tools for looking at Bicocca with different eyes, and to help them overcome their sense of self-censorship towards places normally perceived as unwelcoming or alienating. Because "Seeing is not believing. It is something we do, a kind of performance. [...] The key places [...] are the global cities, where most of us now live. In these immense dense spaces, we learn how to see - and also not to see - potentially disturbing sights - as a condition for daily survival." (Mirzoeff 2015, p. 15) Thus at each stage of the walk, basic tools were used, such as, for example, postcards of a contemporary place, but also old postcards showing this place as it was in the past, seen from the participants' own viewing point or from a different viewing point. Gradually, the audience was guided to make observations, develop new perspectives, and home in on details that had normally escaped their attention because they self-censored them, did not understand them or simply did not notice them.

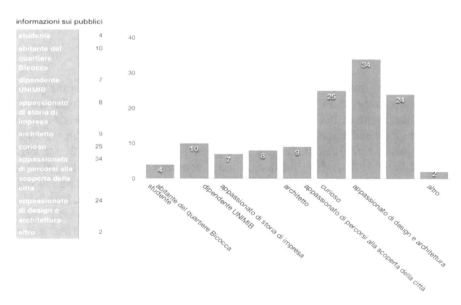

Fig. 1. A graph showing participants' self-declared social backgrounds and self-descriptions, which reflected their specific interest in the themed walk event.

Another tool that contributed to activating narrative visual processes was a set of photos from an album owned by a long-time resident of the district. The participants were offered a vivid fresco of the area and how it had changed, through the photographic images, this local woman's personal account of her family's history, and life as it used to be in the neighbourhood. A direct oral source is of immense value in helping people to "see a place" once more. In this case, the use of digital reproductions was avoided, so as to allow those attending the event to use their senses of touch, sight and hearing. As Arnheim reminds us: "Aristotle, in explaining the importance of memory, observed that without representations, intellectual activity would be impossible" (Fig. 2).

Fig. 2. "Themed walks": one frame of activities people is searching differences between different point of view from the suspense passage between two buildings of university (U6-U7)

3 The Introduction of Digital Instruments

Following the success of the "themed walks", piloted with over two hundred people as compared to the initial projection of 75 participants, we analysed the research data - our own field notes and the survey completed by many of the participants - and this helped us to identify meaningful directions for future explorations of the neighbourhood. At this stage in the project, we worked on adding to the tools of inquiry we had used up to then, specifically focusing on digital technology. We felt the need to expand our theoretical framework by drawing on media aesthetics, a discipline that unites reflection on sensory perception with the use of media tools which, as McLuhan pointed out, cannot exist without a message and are addressed to the mass society. This was because the key challenge of the project was to identify tools - or media to use the Latin term – with the power to awaken the senses and facilitate the appropriation of meanings. As early as 1967, McLuhan had famously observed that the medium is the message, pointing up the paradigm change brought about by the "electric media", especially in relation to the senses (McLuhan and Fiore 1967). Today, the design of educational activities on cultural heritage must not only attend to message and medium but also to the images that audiences have stored away as part of their stockpile of knowledge. The concept of image here is taken to include words, sounds and materials: it may be perceived with all the senses. Hence the need to develop connections between the cultural and the visual. Thus, on the basis of these reflections, we proceeded to review methods of moving in this direction. Inspired by the cover illustration of McLuhan's book on the "relatedness of the senses", which features the face of a man with an ear in the place of an eye, Adorno's expression "thinking with our ears" (Adorno 1972), and Rancière's "distribution of the sensible" (Rancière 2016), we set out to identify ways of exploring heritage assets that fostered reflection on the relationship between eye and ear, leaving aside at this stage in our inquiry, the relationship between hand and mouth. For example, the eye-ear relationship was a key focus of the Remote Milan city exploration experience organized by the cooperative RiminiProtokol: this was one of the first ever collective events in which the participants were isolated from one another by the sound they were hearing through their individual sets of headphones. Here, each participant individually experienced a collective experience; the explorers perceived that they were not alone, as voices and sounds guided their exploration of a place, inviting them to perform simple physical gestures to symbolically take ownership of the space, and thus leading them to discover in a given place - perhaps their everyday life context and for this very reason less appreciated and less familiar - the existence of new spaces and new dimensions. Another example of visual contamination was Caterina Moroni's project Un.Habitants, a theatrical performance staged in a number of different cemeteries, which are generally not viewed as cultural heritage assets but as entirely functional. A "psychosensory pathway through a graveyard, in which visual space and sound intersect and dialogue with one another. An invitation to spectators to expand their perceptions and create their own reality at the frontier between inner and outer vision." (from the artist's website). In this case also, participants were part of a group but received individual audio-guides (headphones). They quietly and serenely explored the tranquillity of a place that others were simultaneously experiencing as painful. Entering a graveyard is an act of courage (from childhood onwards), especially when it is unfamiliar to us, and this is why it was crucial to have other explorers with whom to share the experience. Aside from the specific theme of the project "which inquires how much the idea of death shapes our response to life", we selected Un. habitants as an example because of its ability to generate alternative and parallel spaces and the power of its digital sound to evoke images. Finally, the spirit of this project was to "invite the spectator to confront the taboo, to be inside things, and to revisit them from an alternative point of view".

Turning next to the mouth-hand relationship, we identified as meaningful the Nightwalks with Teenagers experience devised by the cooperative Mamalian Diving Reflex, a project that has travelled different continents and that involves inviting group of adolescents to take possession of their own district, usually a lifeless suburb. The young people receive basic guidelines on how to conduct the activity and are given the opportunity, outside of school hours, to design and organize a night stroll open to anyone who is interested. The walk is self-managed, but with adult supervision to ensure that the teenagers remain safe throughout. While participants may not find the contents of the event to be enriching, they should nonetheless benefit from taking part in an authentic experience with educational value for young people. Significantly, in the context of this project, the young participants chose to use the tools most familiar to them. In terms of digital technology, they exploited their smartphones and frequently used apps to play music, light their way (torch function) and take photographs (camera function) to share on their preferred social network. Another example, from the field of mixed explorations, was Nouvelles Flâneries. In this case, the artist Ettore Favini used the app Strava, normally used by cyclists and runners to facilitate their fitness tracking, to compare the routes of a group of flâneurs he formed to create a new - artistic - map of Parma.

Finally, we examined the potential of digital tracking systems, and specifically popular everyday applications such as Google Earth, Google Maps and Street View. Since the advent of GPS and the development of map tools by Google, never getting lost, and always knowing where we are - even if the place is strange to us - has become a reality. Thus, the maps in Google Earth provide us with an instant aerial view of an area - in our own case study, we applied this to the Bicocca district - while with Street View we can physically see places we plan to visit before going there, or even see places we do not intend to go. These tools use a so-called stitching system to sew together a vast quantity of individual photographic images, enabling the app to display an apparently seamless itinerary. While this is a wonderful facility, Brilli (2018) has pointed out that at another level it is likely to undermine our explorations by preventing us from truly discovering places. Hence, we adopted a strategy described by Brilli that is intended to reduce the risk of generating an empty experience: specifically, we invited participants to follow a trail laid down by others who had gone ahead of them along the route. As well as representing the Bicocca district in all the forms described up to now, we considered it of value to add two further aspects: digital sound and digital images. In the first case, we created a sound archive that offers users the opportunity to listen to the sounds of the past on the very sites where they would have been heard. In the second, we developed animated footage of historical photographs and documentaries.

4 Conclusions

As this brief account of our Department of Human Sciences project on exploring the Bicocca district suggests, one unexpected outcome was the high level of participation by the public. The audiences included many students and staff of the university who were intrigued by the new perspective being offered to them on a space that they had habitually perceived as ordinary and unexciting. A crucial role was played by the accounts of key oral sources and by visual and digital tools that could be used individually or collectively during the exploration events. Digital technology thus opened a new door on undervalued spaces, allowing them to be reinterpreted, and helping audiences to re-appropriate new and old stories that do not always have the strength to tell themselves.

References

Adorno T (1972) Critica della cultura e società. In: Prismi. Saggi sulla critica della cultura. Einaudi, Torino

Arnheim R (1969) Visual thinking. University of California Press, Berkeley, Los Angeles

Berger J (1980) About looking. Pantheon Books, New York

Berger J (1972) Modi di vedere. Penguin, London

Bolocan Goldstein M (ed) (2003) Trasformazioni a milano. Pirelli Bicocca direttrice nord-est. Franco Angeli, Milano

Brilli A (2018) Gli ultimi viaggiatori. Il Mulino, Torino

Brunetta GP (1997) Il viaggio dell'icononauta. Dalla camera oscura di Leonardo alla luce dei Lumière. Marsilio, Venezia

Dell'Agnese E (ed) (2005) La Bicocca e il suo territorio. Skira, Milano

De Nicola A, Zuccoli F (eds) (2016) Paesaggi culturali. Nuove forme di valorizzazione del patrimonio: dalla ricerca all'azione condivisa. Maggioli, Santarcangelo di Romagna

Dewey J (1934, 2005) Art as experience. Penguin, London

Falcinelli R (2017) Cromorama. Come il colore ha cambiato il nostro sguardo. Giulio Einaudi editore, Torino

Gadamer HG (2004) Thruth and method. Bllomsbury Academic, London/New York

Gombrich EH (1999) The uses of images. studies in the social function of art and visual communication. Phaidon Press Limited, London

Gregotti V (2002) Project bicocca. Progetto bicocca. In: Leotta N (ed) La nascita di una università nuova: milano-Bicocca. Dal lavoro di fabbrica alla fabbrica del sapere. Skira, Milano, pp 82–97

Krause Knight C (2008) Public art: theory, practice and populism. Blackwell Publishing, Oxford

Leotta N (ed) (2002) La nascita di una università nuova: milano-Bicocca. Dal lavoro di fabbrica alla fabbrica del sapere. Skira, Milano

McLuhan M, Fiore Q (1967) The medium in the massage. An inventory of effects. Bantam Books, New York

Mitchell WTJ (2017) Pictorial Turn. Saggi di cultura Visuale. Raffaello Cortina Editore, Milano

Mitchell WTJ (2018) Image science: iconology, visusl culture, and media aestetics. University of Chigago, Chicago

Mirzoeff N (2015) How to see the world. Penguin, London

Morpurgo G (ed) (2017) Il territorio dell'architettura. The territory of architecture. Gregotti e Associati 1953_2017. Skira, Milano

Norberg-Schulz C (1979) Genius loci: paesaggio ambiente architettura. Electa, Milano

Rancière J (2016) La partizione del sensibile. Estetica e politica. DeriveApprodi, Roma

Spirito G (2015) In-between places. Forme dello spazio relazionale dagli anni Sessanta a oggi. Quodlibet Studio, Macerata

Young A (2014) Street art, public city. Law, crime and the urban imagination. Routledge, New York

www.caterinamoroni.it/caterina_moroni/un_habitants.html

Children's Color Experience Across the Virtual and Material Dimensions. Reflections Based on Experimentation

A. Poli[⊠] and F. Zuccoli[⊠]

"Riccardo Massa" Department of Human Sciences for Education (DISUF),
Università degli Studi di Milano – Bicocca,
Piazza dell'Ateneo Nuovo 1, 20126 Milan, Italy
{annamaria.poli, franca.zuccoli}@unimib.it

Abstract. This paper explores how color experience in preschool and primary school contexts can become color education: specifically, through the use of digital technologies and an interdisciplinary approach, the experience of color can be expanded from the material dimension represented by colors of pigment to include the virtual dimension of colors of light.

Keywords: Color education · Digital education · Interdisciplinary approach · Virtual colors · Colors of pigment

1 Introduction

This paper makes a case for offering color education and digital technologies in childhood educational settings, with a view to introducing children to the virtual by designing and implementing pathways for exploring the multiple dimensions of color (Al-Saleh 2013) and the language of images.

The color education laboratories piloted to date and our teacher training experience have led us to revisit the lines of inquiry of the "Color Project" pursued by our research group in Play, Education, and the Teaching and Learning of Image and Color, which is based at the "Riccardo Massa" Department of Human Sciences and Education in the University of Milan-Bicocca.

Color is a highly versatile topic, which lends itself to a digital and interdisciplinary educational approach to designing new teaching-learning paths for 3- to 10-year-old children. Using digital technologies to engage children in novel activities relating to color and virtual design, combined with more traditional activities using paper, material colors of pigment, and colors of light has yielded positive outcomes and appears to offer strong educational potential, although continued theoretical analysis and practical experimentation is required.

A. Poli—This paper reflects the joint thinking of the two authors, but the writing up was divided between them as follows: Introduction, Section 2 and Conclusions were written by Annamaria Poli, and Section 3 by Franca Zuccoli.

© Springer Nature Switzerland AG 2019
A. Luigini (Ed.): EARTH 2018, AISC 919, pp. 243–248, 2019.
https://doi.org/10.1007/978-3-030-12240-9_26

2 The Evolution of the Color Project

The Color Project run by the "Riccardo Massa" Department of Human Sciences and Education at the University of Milan Bicocca began in 2008 with a preparatory training phase on the theme of color, offered to a group of educators from infant-toddler centers in Reggio Emilia, Italy who wished to develop their competence in the area of introducing color in early childhood education.

The first experimental phase of the project was implemented over the three-year period 2009–2012, based on a research collaboration agreement between the Department of Human Sciences and Coopselios, the cooperative running the four participating infant-toddler centers. The research group was then made up of, on the University of Milan Bicocca side, Annamaria Poli (researcher and professor of film and visual arts and project leader), Enrica Giordano (professor of physics teaching), and Francesca Zaninelli (researcher in early childhood education), and on behalf of Coopselios: Aldo Manfredi, Sabina Bonaccini, Elisa Bagni, Elisabetta d'Amore, and the remaining education staff involved in implementing the experimental activities with the children.

In all, the researchers were joined by thirteen educators both during the design of the experimental semi-structured teaching-learning path, and throughout the detailed planning and implementation of the project activities. The aim was to offer the children a first experience of color/light by introducing them to darkness, light, and shadow. The research was informed by the STEM education approach to teaching science to young children (Moomaw 2013). The researchers observed the actions of the thirty children who participated in the project, as well as evaluating their prior competence in terms of their basic scientific theories about light, shadow, and color/light.

The second phase of the research project has been ongoing since 2015, and has involved childhood education facilities in Milan, Italy: infant-toddler centers and nursery schools (specifically the "Primavera" infant-toddler center and a nursery school in via Stoppani, and the infant toddler centers and nursery schools in via F.lli Grimm and via Pini, to Milan, Italy).

Meanwhile the composition of the research group has changed somewhat, and the current members' different areas of expertise have prompted a shift in emphasis: the "Color Project" is now more focused on fostering children's visual perception of colors of pigment and colors of light and educating them in the many cultural aspects of color. The current members are: Annamaria Poli (researcher and professor of film and visual arts), Franca Zuccoli (professor of art education) and Alessandra De Nicola (research fellow specializing in the promotion of Italian cultural heritage).

In 2016 and 2017, new interdisciplinary pathways for the exploration of color and color/light were tested in selected childhood education contexts in Milan.

This has centered around an itinerant color workshop entitled Colors of light: adults and children share their personal experience of color across science and art. This laboratory was conceived as an innovative element of an overall educational strategy with a long-term perspective on cognitive development, which offers multimodal and plurisensorial exploratory pathways (Cytowic 2018) based on activities designed to link knowledge to meaningful experience.

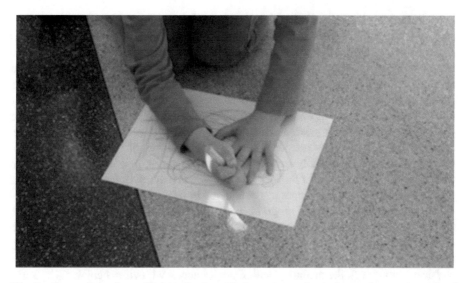

Fig. 1. Comparing colors of light and colors of pigment on a sheet of paper in a nursery school in Milan. The child discovering the colors of light into the rainbow and she doing the attempt to draw it on the paper

To gradually introduce children to the exploration of color/light, the laboratory was divided into two parts: the first involved experiencing being immersed in darkness, prompting discovery of the perceptual dimension of darkness in a room, artificial light, and colors of light. The second part, conducted outdoors, was about exploring being immersed in natural light, with a view to fostering the children's perception of colors of light and natural colors discovering the colors of rainbow (Fig. 1 shows the child discovering the colors of light into the rainbow and the attempt to draw it on the paper).

A short training course was provided for the adults involved, and professional development meetings were held with the educators at the end of the experimentation.

A further experimental program for early childhood education settings was launched in 2016: in this case, an interdisciplinary and multicultural approach is being brought to bear on the exploration of color and color/light with a view to introducing young children to virtual color.

3   Comprehensive Color Experience

As we have observed in the course of our own experimentation and as the educational research literature suggests, color is of great importance for children. Since the late 1800s (Ricci 2007), when children's graphic art first attracted genuine interest on the part of scholars, becoming a focus for research and theorization, color has always been a leading theme of inquiry (see Cannoni 2003; Cox 1993; Freeman 1980; Golomb 2004; Longobardi et al. 2012; Luquet 1969). Our research group in Play, Education and the Teaching and Learning of Image and Color has reviewed theoretical developments in the field alongside its own ongoing experimentation in educational settings. From the extensive research we have carried out in early childhood education centers and schools (both nursery and primary), a key finding has been that teachers predominantly make use of "real" colors, that is to say, colors of pigment, which are produced using an extremely limited range of materials, namely markers, colored pencils, and, to a lesser extent, paints (Poli and Zuccoli 2017; Poli and Zuccoli 2018; Zuccoli 2012). Our research data early made us aware of the need to extend the color experiences offered to children by experimenting with, and reflecting together with teachers and educators on, colors of light in addition to colors of pigment. In parallel, we also began to think about how to offer children digitally-mediated color experiences, in order to provide them with a comprehensive view of the infinite possibilities that the world of color can offer.

For example, at a color laboratory conducted in late 2017 as part of the University of Milano-Bicocca's master's program, participants first shared their personal ideas about color, before going on to: experiment with colors of light (using instruments such as: torches, light tables, prisms, and other light sources); revisit colors of pigment by working individually and collectively with finger-paints (hence engaging in direct physical contact with the medium); and, finally, interact with virtual color, using touch technology and specially selected apps.

After this, the participants were also given an induction in making natural colors and the nomination of colors using the Munsell Color System (Cleland 1921).

The participants were greatly struck by the contents of the training session, which were largely a novelty to them, and this prompted rich reflection on their part, especially in relation to how they might extend their teaching practices to offer children a more diverse chromatic experience and a more continuous art education.

After this brief experiential introduction, the theme of using color in digital environments was discussed, and the student teachers were invited to experiment with a set of apps, previously selected on the basis that they were available for free download and were age-appropriate for primary school children.

The apps selected were the following: Paint, Finger paint, Finger-paint Magic, and Drawing. The idea was that the students, having first tested the apps on themselves, could later use them with children in the school setting. The professional development and research group reflected together on the possibility/desirability of offering a dual "material-virtual" approach to color, that could involve moving back and forth between real-life finger paints and virtual applications. This could serve to draw out the differences between two possible modes of action, modification, and creative expression. In the discussion, much emphasis was laid on the key importance of stimulating the child's sensory system (from sight to touch and vice versa, from smell to taste and hearing, from perception via multiple sensory channels – synesthesia – to using the whole body), no longer from the point of view of replacing one kind of stimulus with another, but with the aim of adding as many different kinds of stimulus as possible, to yield rich, complex, multi-faceted, multidimensional, and multisensory learning opportunities.

4   Conclusions

The general lack of training in this area constrains educational offerings within the parameters of the better known colors of pigment, often in the limited terms of asking the children to stereotypically transcribe colors observed in reality, with the result of consistently failing to harness both children's and teachers' curiosity and desire to experiment with color.

In the present study, the idea of offering, and contributing to, digital education in early childhood settings through innovative explorations of color and the language of images stimulated interesting reflections and suggestions on the part of teachers and students teachers, which nonetheless require ongoing theoretical analysis and testing in the field.

Color remains a highly versatile topic that can also be built into children's digital education.

Our classroom experimentation to date and our work with teachers and student teachers prompt us to continue to research new approaches to color education for children aged 3 to 10 years.

The analysis of the observations have been carried out to evaluate some critical points in human perceptual terms during the experiences compared between the use of real tools (paper and color pigment) and the use of virtual tools (tablet and color/light).

Both our observations of children's encounters with the virtual and the queries, perplexities, and constructive criticisms we have received from teachers throughout the inquiry process confirm the importance of introducing, in preschool and primary school settings, new pathways devoted to exploring directly the color/light and gradually experiencing the virtual dimension.

Acknowledgements. The study presented in the paper is part of the research titled "Color Project" promoted and financed by "Riccardo Massa" Department of Human Sciences at the Università degli Studi di Milano-Bicocca, Italy.

References

Al-Saleh C (2013) Qu'est-ce qu'une couleur?. J. Vrin, Paris
Cannoni E (2003) Il disegno dei bambini. Carocci, Roma
Cytowic RE (2018) Synesthesia. The MIT Press, Cambridge
Cox M (1993) Children's drawings of the human figure. LEA, Hove
Cleland TM (1921) A practical description of the Munsell color system, with suggestions for its use. Munsell Color Company, Boston
Freeman NH (1980) Strategies of representation in young children. Academic Press, London
Golomb C (2004) L'arte dei bambini. Contesti culturali e teorie psicologiche. Raffaello Cortina, Milano
Longobardi C, Pasta T, Quaglia R (2012) Manuale di disegno infantile. Vecchie e nuove prospettive in ambito educativo e psicologico. Utet-De Agostini, Novara
Luquet GH (1969) Il disegno infantile. Armando, Roma
Moomaw S (2013) Teaching STEM in the early years, 1st edn. Redleaf Press, St. Paul (MN)

Poli A, Zuccoli F (2017) Education Through Color Il colore come linguaggio in contesti educativi. In: Marchiafava V, Valan F (eds) Colore e Colorimetria. Contributi Multidisciplinari, pp 505–520. Gruppo del Colore, Milano

Poli A, Zuccoli F (2018) The power of colour language in learning child. In: Hannes K, Dierckx De Casterlé B, Heylighen A, Truyen F (eds) ECQI 2018 Proceedings, Nomadic Inquiry. European Congress of Quality Inquiry, pp 296–303, Leuven

Ricci C (2007) L'arte dei bambini. Armando, Roma

Zuccoli F (2012) A scuola di colore. Pensieri e parole di insegnanti e di bambini. In: Rossi M, Siniscalco, A (eds) Colore e colorimetria. Contributi interdisciplinari, pp 733–740. Gruppo del Colore, Maggioli, Santarcangelo di Romagna

Art-Based Methods. An Approach to Educational Research

Elisabetta Biffi[1], Nancy Gerber[2], Jacelyn Biondo[3],
and Franca Zuccoli[1(✉)]

[1] Department of Human Sciences and Education, University of Milano-Bicocca,
Milan, Italy
{elisabetta.biffi, franca.zuccoli}@unimib.it
[2] College of Nursing and Health Professions,
Department of Creative Arts Therapies, Drexel University, Philadelphia, USA
ng27@drexel.edu
[3] Department of Creative Arts Therapies, Drexel University, Philadelphia, USA
jb859@drexel.edu

Abstract. In recent decades, art-based methods of formulating research questions, collecting data, and documenting research processes and outcomes have played an increasingly important role in educational research. The current paper calls for a review of art-based research tools, with a particular focus on digital environments. Within this framework, we present the early stages of a joint training-research project - involving the Human Sciences Department of Milano-Bicocca University and the Department of Creative Arts Therapies, Drexel University, Philadelphia – which will present art-based, including digital, methods of inquiry in a global classroom environment.

Keywords: Art-based methods · Artistic experiences · Student ·
Teaching and learning · Research

1 The Place of Art in Qualitative Research

Much recent qualitative research in the field of education has involved art in some capacity. In many cases, art is itself the research topic, while in others it serves as a mode of data collection or data analysis; in still others it may be used by the researchers as a medium of reflection. Documentation often totally or partially relies on artistic expression, viewed as suited to capturing the complexity and diversity of educational settings. Several scholars have examined the reasons for this growing interest in art-based research methods, identifying a set of key contributing factors: First, to cite Melisa Cahnmann-Taylor: "With the acceptance of postmodern approaches to educational research in the last few decades […] assumptions about what counts as knowledge and the nature of research have dramatically changed. Not only have multiple qualitative research methodologies gained more widespread acceptance, but also the tools we employ to collect data and findings have been diversified to include artistic as well as traditionally scientific methods." (Cahnmann-Taylor and Siegesmund 2008, p. 3).

A. Luigini (Ed.): EARTH 2018, AISC 919, pp. 249–252, 2019.
https://doi.org/10.1007/978-3-030-12240-9_27

Or in the words of Sullivan: "in an uncertain world, there is a need to develop more widespread means of exploring human understanding and [...] visual arts can play a key role" (Sullivan 2010, p. XXIII). Artistic approaches therefore appear to offer considerable potential for capturing less deterministic phenomena. It follows that they represent a key resource for educational research. "[...] challenging us to think creatively about what constitutes research, to explore even more varied and creative ways to engage in empirical processes; and to share our questions and findings in more penetrating and widely accessible ways." (Cahnmann-Taylor and Siegesmund 2008, p. 3).

To provide a snapshot, albeit imperfect and incomplete, of the current scenario, we now briefly review some examples of art-based research, in order to point up some of its main characteristics, while bearing in mind the words of Pablo Picasso: "I never do a painting as a work of art, it's all research" This position is close to that of visual anthropology, one of whose exponents, George Mills, called for all anthropologists to use art in their inquiry, as early as 1957. Mills argued that acts of artistic expression signal social change, while art objects can be sources of information that is not accessible in any other way (Mills 1957). A more recent development that draws on a participatory as well as an art-based framework is the Photovoice as Social Action Research Method (Chilton and Leavy 2014).

While much art-based educational research has drawn on more traditional art forms such as painting, sculpture, performances, photography, dance, and writing, more recently the potential of digital art has begun to come explicitly to the fore.

To begin to more systematically document this widespread use of hybrid research methods that include - at least implicitly and/or informally - an art-based component, we decided to survey the research practices of the academic staff and students at the Department of Human Sciences and Education as a basis for formal, shared reflection. To this end, we developed a questionnaire with both open-ended and closed questions, with a view to broadly mapping the state of the art in educational research.

2   An Example of Art-Based Research Involving the Use of Collage

The starting point for these initial reflections was our personal experience of applying art-based methods of inquiry in both educational and teacher education contexts. A representative example, which has been discussed at a number of international conferences, is the use of collage in teacher education. Collage, an established art-based research method, has proved highly effective in fostering intuitive and novel thinking: this outcome is associated with the semantic rereading of the materials used to produce the composition. The composition process itself is a form of thinking in metaphors, which condenses content and subjects it to a semantic shift. Even from a purely artistic point of view, collage is one of the techniques that has seen the most innovation and liveliest artistic experimentation. We drew on the work of Georges Braque, Pablo Picasso, Marx Ernst, Henri Matisse, and Mimmo Rotella, to mention but a few, to experimentally introduce different forms of collage to student teachers as a method of exploring educational topics.

3   The Global Classroom Project

Following a conference in Louvain on qualitative research and art-based methods in particular, the authors held a number of meetings to exchange their knowledge on these themes, and eventually decided to organize a joint course for the PhD students at their two university departments, to be delivered in a virtual digital environment, but with the opportunity to produce real artwork built in. Developing this pilot course involved identifying the artistic techniques to be used, the forms of documentation to be kept, and the precise use that would be made of digital technology. The resulting programme follows a mixed approach (virtual and in-person) and will be offered to PhD students in the field of Education and Care from both the Italian and the US universities, with a view to setting up a 'global' classroom for the teaching/learning of arts-based methods of inquiry. More specifically the course will cover: the various definitions of arts-based research in the US and Europe; philosophical, theoretical, and methodological approaches to ABR across multiple disciplines in the social sciences, education and healthcare; the social and cultural influences impacting the advancement of ABR; a global research agenda specific to ABR; and strategies for fostering the advancement of ABR on a global scale.

To this end, both partners will adopt the digital technology required to conduct distance videoconference classes and in-person intensives, at which faculty and students will meet to study the current status, trends, approaches, and social and cultural positioning for arts-based research.

The course will take place over the period October 2018–May 2019.

4   Conclusions

Our reflection on art-based research is prompting us to conduct a systematic review of what is known and theorized about ABR in the field of education and professional development. In this context, a shared digital space for exchanging ideas and jointly developing new contents will play a valuable role.

References

Arnheim R (1974) Art and visual perception: a psychology of creative eye. University of California Press, Berkeley, Los Angeles

Barone T, Eisner E (2012) Arts based research. SAGE, Thousand Oaks

Biffi E, Zuccoli F (2015a) Utilizzare il collage per ricercare l'educazione. In: Tarozzi M, Montù V, Traverso A (eds) Oltre i confini, lungo i margini. Dipartimento di Scienze per la Qualità della Vita, Alma Mater Studiorum – Università di Bologna, pp 69–74

Biffi E, Zuccoli F (2015b) Comporre conoscenza: il collage come strategia meta-riflessiva. FORM@RE 15(2):167–183

Biffi E, Zuccoli F (2016) 'It's not the glue that makes the collage' (Max Erns): training in educational research as an artistic process. In: Formenti L, West L (eds) Stories that make a difference. Exploring the collective, social and political potential of narratives in adult education research. PensaMultimedia, Lecce, pp 135–142

Butler-Kisber L (2018) Qualitative inquiry. Sage Publications, Thousand Oaks

Cahnmann-Taylor M, Siegesmund R (2008) Arts based research in education. Foundation for practice. Routledge, New York

Chilton G, Leavy P (2014) Arts-based research practice: merging social research and creative art. In: Leavy P (ed) The Oxford handbook of qualitative research. Oxford University Press, New York, pp 403–422

Knowles JG, Cole A (eds) (2008) Handbook of the arts in qualitative research. Sage Publications Inc., Thousand Oaks

Leavy P (2015) Method meets art: arts-based research practice, 2nd edn. Guilford Press, New York

Leavy P (ed) (2017) Handbook of arts-based research. Guilford Press, New York

McNiff S (1998) Art-based research. Jessica Kingsley Publisher, London

Leavy P (ed) (2018) Handbook of arts-based research. Guildford Press, New York

Mills G (1957) Art: an introduction to qualitative anthropology. J Aesthet Art Crit XVI(1):1–17

Schön DA (1983) The reflective practitioner. How professionals think in action. Basic Books, London

Sullivan G (2010) Art practice as research. Inquiry in visual arts. Sage, Los Angeles

Using Cinema and Digital Technologies in the Classroom to Construct Spaces for Learning About Cultural Heritage

A. Poli[✉]

"Riccardo Massa" Department of Human Sciences for Education (DISUF),
Università degli Studi di Milano-Bicocca, Piazza dell'Ateneo Nuovo 1,
20126 Milan, Italy
annamaria.poli@unimib.it

Abstract. This paper presents an experimental teaching and educational research project in which digital technologies and movie animation were used in the classroom to construct spaces for learning about cultural heritage.

Keywords: Digital technology · Cinema · Cultural heritage education ·
Digital education

1 Introduction

This paper presents a project that drew on digital applications and short animation to enhance the teaching/learning of cultural heritage and, more generally, to develop good media education practices for schools. The initial research question was: how might digital technologies and movie animation be innovatively used to teach and learn cultural heritage in educational settings?

As is well-known, digital technologies and digitalized contents have led to a sharp increase in the importance of visual communication via a wide range of devices and platforms. Indeed, digitalization has enhanced models of communication generally, across all cultural domains. Current examples include humanistic computer applications (Celentano et al. 2004), or the Digital Humanities, an area of study at the intersection of computing and the humanistic disciplines, as well as a branch of educational research whose aim is to develop other approaches to studying the human sciences (Berry 2012).

Digital art has become an artistic medium for making artistic and historical contents available to vast online audiences (Benjamin 2000). There are many examples to be found on the Internet: the online pages of museums, online art galleries, online heritage archives and libraries, and the web pages of researchers on Art, architects, painters, photographers, and other artists, to name but some. Going forward, ongoing commitment to the use of digital technologies is needed to engage learners in the humanities and to promote historical and artistic cultural heritage in both formal and informal educational contexts.

© Springer Nature Switzerland AG 2019
A. Luigini (Ed.): EARTH 2018, AISC 919, pp. 253–260, 2019.
https://doi.org/10.1007/978-3-030-12240-9_28

2 Using Digital Technologies to Construct Learning Spaces

I would like to begin by describing my own experience of contributing to pioneering research and teaching programmes that used digital technologies and movie animation to introduce culture heritage into the classroom following an interdisciplinary approach.

Why have I chosen this as my starting point? Firstly, to give an account of how digital technologies first came to be used in Italy to teach and learn cultural heritage in educational settings.

It all started in the 1990s at Politecnico di Milano, in the Faculty of Architecture and Design, with a research group composed of Professor Alessandro Polistina, a pioneer in Italian computer graphics and virtual environments, the architects Rossana Verona, Francesco Bellini, and myself.

After twenty years from the pioneering studies conducted by our group, authors from all over the world agree, and many observers note, the beneficial impact of digital technology on education. In this paper is not possible to mention all of them. However, of particular interest is Njoku (2015) who has claimed that exploiting the multimodal channels offered by ICT (Information Communication Technologies) enhances the quality of both teaching and learning in secondary schools. His analysis was based on a review of reports from a range of authors and institutions that bear witness to the positive role that ICT has recently come to play in education. Njoku Chris has also described the main ways in which ICT have been applied for educational purposes, as well as the many good practices identified by schools in developing countries in particular. He adopts the UNESCO 2002 definition of "Information Communication Technologies". The term "information and communication technologies" (ICT) refers to forms of technology that are used to transmit, process, store, create, display, share or exchange information by electronic means. This broad definition of ICT includes such technologies as radio, television, movies, DVD, telephone (both fixed line and mobile phones), satellite systems, and computer and network hardware and software, as well as the equipment and services associated with these technologies, such as videoconferencing, e-mail and blogs.

In another key study, Ivon and Kuscevic (2013) have explored the idea that learning is always a cultural activity, whether it takes place at school or outside of school, arguing that a school's peculiar cultural heritage environment leaves its mark on students. As is well known, the quality of early school experience places a key role in children's cognitive development (Dewey 1998; Fiorilli and Albanese 2008). Considering, in accordance with Dewey, art as a form of experience, if, indeed, the view of the artistic production is the lived experience, the documentation can be considered the way through which that experience can be understood. Similarly, education is a kind of experience which is lived in the here and now, while the documentation can be used in order to understand the educational lived process.

In a different field, during a recent interview, Stephen Laster – chief digital officer at McGraw-Hill Education – has stated that learning with digital technology transforms education and changes how we approach topics (https://www.bctpartners.com/single-post/2018/05/11/Three-Ways-That-Machine-Learning-Can-Make-Education-Smarter).

Alessandro Polistina already had these educational insights back in the 1990s, and thanks to his university teaching and research efforts, innovative computer labs were introduced into the Politecnico di Milano's degree courses in Architecture and Design.

At the time it was difficult to foresee the future outcomes of this move, but even our earliest experimental studies yielded positive results. In fact, only a few years later, in 1997, at the SMAU Industrial Design Awards – 5° Targa Bonetto, our group received special mention for *innovative methods in the use of information technology* (the Jury gave special mention to the project presented by the Politecnico di Milano - research team coordinated by Professors Alessandro Polistina, Francesco Bellini, Rossana Verona and Anna Poli). In retrospect, we might say that this was a sign that our efforts were in the right direction.

But as is always the case, when everybody is trying out everything with the same technological innovations, it is difficult to discern what exactly the right direction is. Alessandro Polistina and Maldonado (1992, 1997) were both key contributors to the lively debate then underway in Italy about the introduction of digital technologies into modern societies. There was much discussion concerning the potential offered by these technologies and likely future scenarios: we were asking what advantages and benefits would virtual, multimedia, hypertextual and interactive technologies bring to human existence, particularly in the educational, work-related, social and cultural domains.

This framework owed much to the ideas of both Alessandro Polistina and Tomás Maldonado. Polistina especially contributed far-reaching insights in relation to the potential applications of virtual representation technologies, bringing to bear an approach that was highly original and displaying a particular interest in using digital technologies to study cultural and architectural heritage reproducing digital models or part of their, while simultaneously engaging in well-thought-out and critical experimentation with innovative teaching methods. His work at the Politecnico di Milano, and subsequently at the IUAV in Venezia, made Polistina one of the leading pioneers of Italian computer graphics. Above all, I would emphasize the importance of his teaching method, which he generously passed on to his students and team members.

3   Teaching Students to Construct Learning Spaces with Digital Technologies

Our work with students was based on a truly experimental teaching method that involved the construction of virtual environments and the selection of existing objects for digital reconstruction. This creative and interdisciplinary approach introduced students to representation, in a digital 3D space, of topics as diverse as colour sensations, the culture of tea, the writer, the music room, the design room, etc. The students designed virtual environments using software for 3D modelling, digitalizing 2D images, and producing short animated movies (Fig. 1 shows a frame of walking thought in the classic ambience of a typical hard-boiled American mystery writer).

At that time Alessandro Polistina was already expert in most of the available software for design and computer graphics, with particular expertise in 3D modelling applications: he was looking for a 3D modelling package that was *flexible and user-friendly,* and therefore suitable for students with only basic computer skills. He chose

Fig. 1. This three-dimensional space represents the classic ambience of a typical hard-boiled American mystery writer (by Mario Locati and Grazia Cupolillo). Soft lighting, architecture, furnishings, textures and shadows are used to produce an evocative visual perception experience. The language of images is fashioned here from light, shadow, surfaces, colours, and the shapes of objects, all seen from the viewpoint of an observer.

formZ by AutoDesSys (http://www.formz.com). It was relatively easy for each students to learn how to use the instrument (hardware and software); this left them free to concentrate on the task of reflecting on and researching how best to use the software to design, construct, and represent original virtual spaces.

We worked hard during those exciting years to provide entire class groups with the required level of computer literacy: the research group organized ad hoc courses teaching students to apply digital technologies. The students used the technology as a tool for developing new competence in creating and communicating knowledge/information. Digital tools for automatic drawing and digital representation techniques and movie animations offered the students new opportunities to engage in new forms of learning the objects of human experience in the life: learning how to model an object in a virtual space is not a spontaneous and intuitive operation.

4   Digital Technologies for Learning About Italian Cultural Heritage

On the research front, our work was again experimental in nature. In part, it was devoted to studying methods of teaching computer science and digital graphic representation by observing and evaluating innovative ways of proposing digital technology as a means of designing learning spaces and performing creative tasks.

However, our main focus, pursued with the assistance of some of our undergraduates, was on an applied research program aimed at enhancing the communication of

Italian Cultural Heritage. More specifically, we chose fifteenth-century museums: the frescoed rooms of the Italian Renaissance. Why this particular theme? Because these museums are characterized by well-defined architectural spaces, whose frescoed walls teem with culture from the different branches of human endeavour: historical, artistic, literary, scientific and technological.

The virtual reconstruction of these architectural spaces, which began with real-life geometrical measurement and culminated in virtual rendering, gave students the opportunity to engage in a complex learning trajectory enriched with multiple cognitive experiences. Through applying this mode of analysis and study to different fields, students encountered additional opportunities for learning and came to attribute increasingly greater cultural value to this part of their heritage. At the same time, their new cultural awareness helped them to produce new "artifacts", or creative digital forms of communicating and promoting culture.

"Camera Picta" was among the first applied research projects in Italy to use virtual technology in the teaching and learning of Italian artistic and architectural Cultural Heritage (Polistina 1996; Polistina and Poli 1996).

What is more, Alessandro Polistina had identified Internet as the ideal "place" in which to share these virtual 3D explorations (Fig. 2 shows a frame of Virtual Camera Picta walking thought). With the digital reconstruction of Mantegna's "Camera Picta" and its publication on the World Wide Web using the VRML language, we inaugurated the web-based consumption of Italian cultural heritage – the year was 1996.

Fig. 2. Cameta Picta Project: "The impact of this research on the teaching of the new degree in Industrial Design at the Politecnico di Milano was immediate, although cyberspace teachers are only beginning to be trained" (Polistina 1996).

5   Digital Technologies and Spaces for Learning and Teaching

Tomás Maldonado in *Reale e Virtuale* examined the peculiar and innovative features of virtuality. He identified three different forms of virtuality: first, immersive-inclusive virtuality, in which the observer sees a digitally-generated three-dimensional space from the inside, second, third person virtuality in which the observer sees from the outside his or her own image interacting within a system-generated three-dimensional space – a definition which the author himself qualified strongly – and third, the low-level/threshold virtuality provided by the traditional desktop computer, in which the observer participates from the outside, simulating dynamic involvement in the space represented on the monitor. Maldonado emphasized the fact that the notion of virtuality or virtual reality is also assigned a far broader meaning: for example, virtuality is held to be present when the observer can dynamically intervene to modify aspects of an object represented via computer graphics, such as its position, shape and colour. Applications are currently available that offer augmented reality (AR) and augmented vision (AV) experiences, in which the observer uses a mobile device to see virtual objects or information of various kinds superimposed on the surrounding environment (Maldonado 1992, 1997).

In relation to virtual representation, Tomás Maldonado wrote that "computer graphic models take on a peculiar significance. They undeniably bring something completely new to the history of modelling, something that distinguishes them from earlier models. And that is to say: their syncretic nature. Indeed, they are the outcome of the convergence of three modelling techniques that up to a short time ago had always been used separately: replication (or emulation), simulation and mathematical formalization. Thanks to their syncretic nature, computerized models can offer all domains of scientific research and design, possibilities that they never enjoyed in the past."

And today, we can go even further to say that digital models can now be associated and supplemented with an infinite variety of interdisciplinary and multimedia contents, making it possible to expand and improve digital learning technologies and to finally increase our production of innovative learning objects, designed as part of increasingly effective, appealing and flexible learning pathways which can also facilitate, for example, the implementation of "student-centred learning".

Actually many scholars are asking how digital technologies can help us to create new learning objects/products and environments? And how these technologies may be exploited in schools to communicate cultural heritage?

Compared to twenty years ago, many more digital tools are available to us, with which to develop innovative modes of representation that we can use to showcase cultural contents from all over the world.

As Meschini (2011) has observed about the state of the art and future development prospects of digital technologies in the communication of cultural heritage, "three-dimensionality and virtuality are the key features of the new trend". This is because these are the features that maximise the potential of virtual images to elicit emotion, which plays a significant part in human cognitive processes driven by the visual-perceptive system.

As early as the 1990s, our research group had clearly grasped the appeal of digital and multimedial virtuality, and their power to command students' attention, focusing it on the represented contents or those to be represented.

It was surprising to observe the effort and determination with which students approached the digital "blank sheet". The opportunity to take part in our programme also stimulated competition among them, encouraging them in the constant quest for new knowledge, and novel contents, and new technical skills. Thus, we presented digital tools with a view to enhancing the students' knowledge and appreciation of cultural heritage by inviting them to represent it using new multimodal forms of communication, and each student created his or her own space of learning and knowledge.

Diana G. Oblinger, in her book *Learning Spaces* (2006), outlines principles, practices and case studies of learning spaces created using digital technologies in combination with traditional forms of learning and teaching. She offers guidelines to teachers on how to design and implement a Blended Learning Space with the potential to provide the student with an innovative learning experience. She also explains the fundamentals of Human-Centered Design and reflects on the pedagogical implications of the positive learning outcomes obtained by the students. To date, the digital industry has invested heavily in the production of multimedia products for entertainment purposes, but very little has been invested in the creation of multimedia offerings for teaching and learning (Miller 2012).

Currently, it is relatively easy to access software (e.g., Open Source) for the production of virtual environments using 3D and 2D modelling, animation, increasingly sophisticated multimedia hypertexts, and web platforms for constructing and connecting the databases. Newer developments include augmented reality systems using mobile devices and eye-glasses displays, hologram technologies for generating moving images, and the learning technologies underpinning multimedia books, of which the most recent spin-off are SmartBooks that actively tailor content to suit individual needs (Smartbooks by McGrawHill: http://whysmartbook.com).

6 Conclusions

Nonetheless, the educational potential of digital technologies remains little understood and little explored, while Italian teachers at all levels of schooling continue to have limited access to digital tools. Likewise, the value and educational benefits of using digital technologies and movie animation as an educational resource at school are largely unappreciated. The creative approach presented here demonstrates how digital technologies and movie animation may be used to teach and learn cultural heritage in educational contexts. As I mentioned earlier, the now substantial body of publications on digitally-mediated education confirms that our initial theoretical framework was appropriate.

Therefore all the technological tools that we have described up to now are actually cognitive tools, which can make an increasingly effective and valuable contribution to enhancing learning and teaching environments in schools. They are true educational resources, with the potential to carry students beyond the analogical dimension of the blank sheet of paper: we are all familiar with the limitations of the blank sheet and its sometimes oppressive two-dimensionality. All students have experienced, from their first days at school up to and including the present, the difficult of expressing their own personality, imagination and thoughts, and making them fit on the blank page.

All the more complex forms of representation invented by humankind have offered the opportunity to transcend the limits of two-dimensional space and today, the digital screen is the new blank page, it is the virtual space on which we can visualize images, film and animated content, sound, text and innovative forms of interaction between reality and virtual reality. The screen also allows students to transcend the boundaries of the classroom walls, by representing contents in all space and time dimensions.

At this point, we are not suggesting replacing the blank sheet of paper with the digital screen, but rather the integration of both instruments, and this with a view to enhancing the expression and sharing of cultural values communicated using both traditional and new learning spaces.

Acknowledgements. The study presented is in honor to Prof. Alessandro Polistina pioneer on the use digital technologies in the classroom to construct spaces for learning about cultural heritage.

References

Benjamin W (2000) L'opera d'arte nella sua riproducibilità tecnica. Einaudi, Milano

Berry DM (ed) (2012) Understanding digital humanities. Springer, New York

Celentano A, Cortesi A, Mastandrea P (2004) Informatica umanistica: una disciplina di confine. Mondo Digitale 4:44–55

Dewey J (1998) Experience and education. Kappa Delta Pi

Fiorilli C, Albanese O (2008). I processi di conoscenza dei bambini: credere, pensare, conoscere. Ricerche e riflessioni. Edizioni Junior, Bergamo

Miller Fayneese S (ed) (2012) Transforming learning environments: strategies to shape the next generation, vol 16. Emerald Group Publishing, Bingley

Ivon H, Kuscevic D (2013) School and the cultural-heritage environment: pedagogical, creative and artistic aspects. Center Educ Policy Stud J 3(2):29–50

Maldonado T (1992) Reale e virtuale. Feltrinelli, Milano

Maldonado T (1997) Critica della ragione informatica. Feltrinelli, Milano

Meschini A (2011) Tecnologie digitali e comunicazione dei beni culturali. Stato dell'arte e prospettive di sviluppo. Disegnare con, 16 Dicembre

Njoku C (2015) Information and communication technologies to raise quality of teaching and learning in higher education institutions. Int J Educ Dev Inf Commun Technol 11(1):122–147

Oblinger DG (2006) Learning spaces. Educause, Boulder

Polistina A (1996) Camera picta. Casabella, Novembre 1996

Polistina A, Poli A (1996) Camera picta, images et architecture de l'espace virtuel. In: Actes du Colloque Imara 1996, Session 2: Réseaux et multimédia, Monte Carlo, France, pp 81–85, 21 February 1996

Chromatic Dimensions as Heritage of the Project Culture. *Cromo*: Interactive Teaching Manual

Federico O. Oppedisano[1,2]([✉])

[1] School of Architecture and Design, University of Camerino,
62032 Camerino, Italy
direzione.sad@unicam.it
[2] Viale della Rimembranza s.n.c., 63100 Ascoli Piceno, Italy
federico.oppedisano@unicam.it

Abstract. Illustrating the progressive expression of colour in the project culture, this article describes the goals, objectives, and characteristics of an interactive teaching manual, *Cromo*, which is designed to introduce aspects of colour. The product is inspired by the *Colordinamo* manuals created by the Centro Design Montefibre in the first half of the 1970s, which, in a search for the primary design, investigated the immaterial dimensions of the quality of space. With their meta-project nature, the *Colordinamo* manuals were new operational tools for the project that concretely combined the scientific and emotional aspects of colour with theoretical assumptions and applications based on scientific theories developed between the nineteenth and twentieth centuries. These tools contributed to promoting a new chromatic culture and the entrance of colour in Italian production logic, thereby serving as a mediating factor between professional practice and theoretical development. With reference to this important experience, *Cromo* intends to favour infuse teaching with the understanding of different aspects that characterize the culture of colour and a conscious approach to designing colour, combining theoretical, historical, and bibliographic information with information about applications. This content is integrated with further information and investigated thanks to the integration of virtual material that can be accessed from digital devices.

Keywords: Art and heritage education · Education through digital media · Interactive digital publishing · Psychology of perception and attention · Psychology of arts and communication

1 Introduction: Chromatic Dimensions in the Project Culture

In today's project culture and the field of design in particular, colour represents a basic design parameter due to its implications for space, the sensory apparatus, and the properties of materials, as well as its connotations in the different fields of visual communication. The project dimension of colour is combined with continual, periodic revisitations in relation to scientific, social, cultural, and technological transformations. For centuries, colour has been the object of numerous reflections that have been renewed with the social, cultural, economic, and technological changes that have

© Springer Nature Switzerland AG 2019
A. Luigini (Ed.): EARTH 2018, AISC 919, pp. 261–270, 2019.
https://doi.org/10.1007/978-3-030-12240-9_29

occurred over time. Reflections on this theme are broad and organized into different areas of knowledge, from philosophy, art, and psychology to more strictly scientific fields. Thanks to chemical synthesis, the range of colours began to expand in the eighteenth century, continuing in the nineteenth century with the production of industrial-scale dyes and in the twentieth century with colours produced by electronic systems (1986, p. 195). Over the course of history, different theories have been developed that basically define two attitudes towards reading the phenomenon of colour: a "scientific" one and an "emotional" one. The two perspectives seem to have condensed after Wolfgang Goethe, largely opposing Newton's scientific view (1704), developed his theory of colours (1810) with the aim of bringing colour onto the emotional phenomenological plane. An initial attempt to reconcile this dichotomy came in the first half of the 1900s, especially through didactic and theoretical contributions, such as those by Kandinsky (1912), Klee (1945), Arnheim (1959), Itten (1961), and Albers (1963). We also recall that scientific interest in colour intensified in the 1800s and the beginning of the 1900s with the publication of different fundamental treatises on colour, such as those by Runge (1809), Grassmann (1853, von Helmholtz (1856–1867), Chevreul (1839, 1865), Maxwell (1872), Rood (1881), Ostwald (1916, 1917), and Munsell (1905, 1907, 1921).

In the world of design, advances beyond the purely decorative dimension of colour and its confirmation as a design factor have occurred relatively recently. In the modern concept of industrial products, the presence of colour seems to be connected mainly to the functionality of the object (Romanelli 1987). The prevalent tendency in architecture, however, is to avoid polluting the clarity of the compositional thought with colour, preserving the purity of the structure by using white or defining colours through processes of abstraction, connecting natural shades to the essence of primary pigments, the uniformity of chromatic rendering, the plane on which colour is delimited, and governing it through balanced compositional relationships among basic geometric shapes (Polano 1990). In *Grundbegriffe der neuen gestaltenden Kunst*, Van Doesburg maintains that the surfaces or lines in which colour is enclosed should be free of any emotionality to avoid altering its concreteness (Doesburg 1925). The project culture seems to be pervaded by a sort of widespread chromophobia (Batchelor 2001) anchored to rationalist thought that largely avoids colour due to its decorative implications and intangible, emotional, subjective, uncertain, fleeting nature, which makes it an uncontrollable immaterial factor that is difficult to assume as a design parameter. Thus, colour does not seem to be a primary application inherent in the nature of space and objects, but rather a "superstructure of the object" (Branzi et al. 1984, p. 24) (Fig. 1).

Since the end of the 1950s, the influence of colour in mass communication in the industrialized world has gradually grown to play an important role. At that time, rapid economic growth produced profound imbalances among different areas of the country, criticalities that are viewed as an effect of the delay in industrial development. While spreading the idea of defining an economy capable of healing the contradictions present in the country through gradual growth in the industrial sector, part of the project world, in line with the principles of the Modern Movement, was connected to the serial system and the production aspect with a vision that accepted technological progress but rejected the logic of consumerism (Branzi 2008, pp. 30–41). At the time, Edwin Land, the founder of Polaroid, was studying the connections the human perceptual system

Fig. 1. Theo Van Doesburg, Preliminary colour scheme for the ceiling and walls in the dance hall at Café Aubette, Strasbourg, France (1926–1928).

established among the colours, resulting in his Retinex theory in the 1970s (1959a, 1959b, 1964, 1977). According to this theory, the perception of shades is an automatic process carried out in a specific area of the brain where colour is recognized by comparing the spectral compositions reflected by all the surrounding objects. Still in the 1950s, various studies begun by Faber Birren in the 1920s while consulting for important American companies (Birren 1934, 1939, 1940, 1955, 1956, 1961) began to spread. These studies regarded the influence and effects of colour on the psychological level of employees and on sales activities.

Chromatic language, with the progressive shift of interest from production to the market, also became the products' seductive lexicon. In addition, the introduction of colour in nocturnal life and, starting in the 1960s and 70s, the spread of colour television and electronic media, multiplied the interaction with colours produced by additive synthesis, conditioning the chromatic languages of the following decade. The use of new plastic materials and experiences, initially from Radical Design and Design Primario and then from Memphis and Alchimia, favoured the extension of a new culture of colour and a new way of thinking about colour as connoting the objects. New lexicons were fed by the use of chromatic ranges with strong visual impact, found, as Sottsass states, "within zones where no one had worked before" (Radice 1984, p. 124). In effect, the development of the culture of immaterial aspects in the approach to design combined with social changes and emerging technologies. Prejudices about the chromatic universe inherited from a part of the Modern Movement were overcome and intangible factors such as colour became design parameters.

2   Colour as a Design Parameter

The confirmation of colour as a design parameter seems to have occurred concretely at the beginning of the 1970s with the search for the primary design. Up to that point, design had largely been conditioned by principles based on rationality, compositional balance, and the correspondence between form and function, as unique parameters of design correctness. The search for the primary design instead set the objective of moving attention from the structural correctness to other qualitative parameters of the environment, considering for the first time the effects of all those intangible, soft phenomena tied to physical perception, distinguishing them from the hard aspects pertaining to the structure. In this perspective, colour is dealt with for its emotional nature and re-evaluated as an immaterial parameter of space. We recall that in the 1970s, the economic recession, the oil crisis, and social tensions made the future uncertain, but simulated new approaches to design research. As Branzi states, people began to investigate "constructive subsets that were not a part of the classic modern planning skills" (2008, pp. 158–160). At the same time, the use of new plastic materials and design experiences that referred to radical design initiated and then consolidated a profound change in the approach to design and its relationship with colour. An important experience that allowed the principles of primary design to be concretely applied was begun in 1973 by the Montefibre company. The company, which produced synthetic fibres for the Montedison group, was then the leader in Italian chemistry and, in reaction to the oil crisis and its repercussions, founded the Centro Design Montefibre (CDM) in Milan. The company was in operation until 1977 and aimed to create and develop innovative products and services to apply in the textile field. The direction of the fashion department was entrusted to Elio Fiorucci while the design department was headed by Massimo Morozzi, Andrea Branzi, and Clino Trini Castelli. The research at CDM was aimed at identifying the immaterial factors tied to the different perceptual levels that characterize space, and the control of all the tools and parameters that are situated at the heart of traditional design, consisting of "selected information, semifinished products, reference manuals, and also new general problems capable of directing the work of the designer and the industry" (CDM 1975, p. 41).

The work to develop the culture of the sensory quality of space begins precisely with colour, which becomes the primary, strategic factor among all the intangible qualitative factors. With the aim of spreading the culture of colour in the industrial world, between 1975 and 1977, CDM developed the *Colordinamo* research program. The goal of the program to simultaneously offer tools and indications to enable coordination between the decor and chemical industries in order to address the question of colour, both in terms of design and with respect to marketing, involving specialists in the sector largely hailing from abroad (Fig. 2).

The *Decorattivo* and *Colordinamo* manuals were published as research products. These were aimed at operators in the industrial sectors and were also proposed as innovative tools to support designers, connecting cultural and historical aspects to purely technical and operational aspects. In particular, the three editions of the *Colordinamo* manuals (Branzi et al. 1975, 1976, 1977) present a chromatic range of forty colours organized into families along with a specifically designed operational

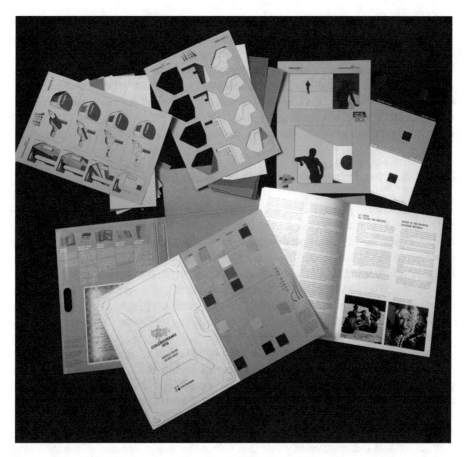

Fig. 2. Andrea Branzi, Clino Trini Castelli, and Massimo Morozzi, pages and tools from the 1976 *Colordinamo* manual for professional use, "Il colore presintetico", edited by CDM Centro Design Montefibre.

apparatus composed of an insulator and a colour simulator to compare the colours present in the folder and to industrially reproduce the shades. Created by Branzi, Morozzi, and Trini Castelli with the participation of Alessandro De Gregori and Franco Brunello, the series was conceived as a working tool to "design colours" (Branzi et al. 1976). The colour is built starting from an analysis of the sociocultural, psychological, and physiological implications that colours can generate, detached from any product, and without any intention of providing solutions to specific ergonometric or psychological problems or acting as a forecasting tool. Each manual is also integrated with a treatise on a specific theme, including historical notes that describe the chromatic trends and expressions of different periods. The topics addressed are: *The colours of energy* (1975), referring to the cathode colours of new media such as television; *Pre-synthetic colours, new colours for environments according to old dyers' recipes* (1976), illustrating the natural colours preceding the use of synthetic colours; *And colours of the environment* (1977), which addresses the chromatic set determined by the spread of consumer goods. This manual, awarded the Compasso d'Oro ADI in 1979, was an integral part of the *Fibermatching 25* system, and served as the connective tool between the Montefibre industry, producer of the raw material, and production industries. In fact, with these intentions, it was offered together with the raw material—the polypropylene fibre Meraklon—as a service to design the products' colours. It contained the conceptual premise for the ideal use of the product, and 600 colours reproduced and prescribed in illustrative folders (Trini Castelli 1977, p. 61).

3   *Cromo*, an Interactive Teaching Manual

The experiences in primary design made colour the mediating factor between professional practice and theoretical development (Moro and Castelli 2010, p. 204), introducing it into the industrial production system. The *Colordinamo* manuals, aimed at operators in the industrial sectors, were also proposed as innovative tools to support designers, connecting cultural and historical aspects to purely technical and operational aspects. As Trini Castelli states, "thanks to the fact that engineers can also deeply understand what happened in the world of emotional language […] it is possible to support a given chromatic language over another, proposing new views of the dynamics of colour" (Moro 2010, p. 204).

   With the confirmation of colour in the project culture, a growing interest in the dimensions of colour has developed in parallel in the field of designer education, playing a key role in identifying material and immaterial elements that qualify space and matter as well as elements of the lexicons of visual communication. Therefore, teaching chromatics and its related heritage of knowledge requires the codification of flexible tools that can provide a framework integrated with information organized such that the student can be correctly oriented within the vast panorama of the culture of colour. Based on this assumption and inspired by the *Colordinamo* manuals, the idea was to develop an experimental teaching tool, *Cromo*, that, using the manual formula, aims to become a mediating factor between the culture of colour and the practice of applying colour. *Cromo* is organized into three sections in which theoretical, historical, cultural, and bibliographic information converge and are combined with practical applications, implemented by additional content that can be accessed via digital devices. Overall, the sections aim to create an integrated system of information to favour the understanding of different aspects that characterize the culture of colour and a conscious approach to designing colour. In particular, the section "Introduction to the history and theories of colour" provides a summary of the main historical events regarding colour. The dates at the beginning of each chapter mark important moments, allowing the chronology of events to be better established and facilitating the understanding of the role of colour in the development of society. The section ends with a glossary to orient the reader within the chromatic lexicon and a basic bibliography of references. The section entitled "Reflections on colour" illustrates some projects, studies, and theories of colour, allowing the reader to visualize the results and conclusions of the research deemed most pertinent to the project culture in the area of colour (Fig. 3).

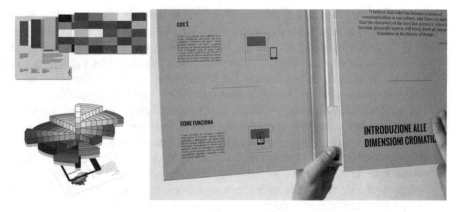

Fig. 3. *Cromo*, a teaching manual about colour with interactive content. *Laurea* thesis – *Laurea* course in Industrial and Environmental Design at the University of Camerino (IT). Student: Giulia Muscatelli, supervisor: Federico O. Oppedisano.

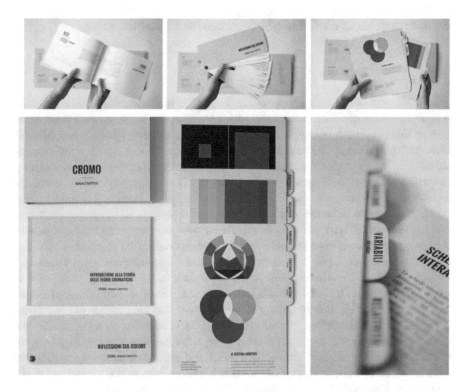

Fig. 4. *Cromo*, a teaching manual about colour with interactive content. *Laurea* thesis – *Laurea* course in Industrial and Environmental Design at the University of Camerino (IT). Student: Giulia Muscatelli, supervisor: Federico O. Oppedisano.

The section "Interactive teaching sheets", useful to practicing colour design, briefly follow the concepts developed by Itten (1961), Kandinskij (1912), Klee (1945), and Albers (1963) for teaching, and is useful for stimulating the sensory apparatus to the interactions that colours can activate. The sheets basically introduce the fundamental aspects that characterize colour, making the fundamental aspects tangible, such as, for example, the components and characteristics and related systems of classification (additive and subtractive), the geometric models of visualization (colour circle), perceptual phenomena, balances, and colour contrasts. A brief descriptive text is included in the sheet along with bibliographic references and a figure that, if viewed on a digital device, allows access to further virtual information regarding models and concepts of colour and numerous examples of applications related to chromatic phenomena (Fig. 4).

The product also represents an attempt to codify a flexible editorial formula that, open to possible digital integrations, does not reject the paper format, which is useful for providing the student with a concrete reference. *Cromo* also aims to highlight how colour is tied not only to strictly scientific and theoretical aspects, but also to symbolic aspects of the individual and of society. In sum, presenting itself as an introductory tool to chromatic aspects, it amplifies the awareness that colours, despite their semantic instability, have grown to play an important role in industry, becoming design parameters capable of qualifying space, products, and visual languages.

4   Conclusion

As Ezio Manzini observes, we have moved from a "solid world", one that is static, that foresaw the production of permanent goods in time, to a "fluid world" in which products have become services, experiences, and knowledge (Bertola and Manzini 2004, p. 20). In these circumstances, the orientations of knowledge have changed profoundly. The rigid scientific models of study and research are no longer sufficient to understand the possible directions of the transformations underway and to respond to the emergence of new, unexpected needs. Uncertainty, discontinuity, contradictions, and instability seem to be the terrain that has allowed design and the project culture to combine to form different realities. In this framework, in a social and cultural context undergoing continuous change, which tends to dematerialize the physical consistency of objects, to reduce them to concepts or turn them into imagery, the relationships between the project world and colour are expanded, often revealing themselves as design assumptions for the formulation of hybrid artefacts with blurred edges. Therefore, in teaching, it is necessary to follow paths that are capable of considering colour as a cultural heritage, making it an active element of design. *Cromo* was designed in this perspective with a content organization that aims to highlight the ongoing debate surrounding chromatic aspects and the consequent impossibility of framing colour in a single regime of thought. It also testifies to the formalization of a chromatic culture in design that is capable of transmitting design theories and practices regarding colour and how it has favoured the development of a holistic approach to the project.

References

Albers J (1963) Interaction of colors. New Harven, London

Arnheim R (1959) Art and visual perception: a psychology of the creative eye. University of Califonia Press, Berkeley

Batchelor D (2001) Cromofobia. Storia della paura del colore, Bruno Mondadori, Milano

Bertola P, Manzini E (a cura di) (2004) Design Multiverso. Appunti di fenomenologia del design. POLIdesign, Milano

Birren F (1934) Color dimensions: creating new principles of color harmony. Crimson, Chicago

Birren F (1939) The American colorist: a practical guide to color harmony and color identification. Crimson, Westport

Birren F (1940) Character analysis through color: a new and accurate way of revealing the hidden secrets of personality. Crimson, Westport

Birren F (1955) New horizons in colour. Reinhold, New York

Birren F (1956) Selling color to people: a book on how to sell color in commercial products and advertising to the American public. University Books, New York

Birren F (1961) Color psychology and color therapy: a factual study of the influence of color on human life. University Books, New York

Branzi A (2008) Il design italiano. 1964-2000. Mondadori-Electa, Milano

Branzi A, Trini Castelli C, Morozzi M (1975) Colordinamo 1975, Il colore dell'energia. Manuale per uso professionale. Centro Design Montefibre - Gruppo Montedison, Milano

Branzi A, Trini Castelli C, Morozzi M (1976) Colordinamo 1976, Il colore pre-sintetico. Manuale per uso professionale. Centro Design Montefibre - Gruppo Montedison, Milano

Branzi A, Trini Castelli C, Morozzi M (1977) Il colore ambientale degli anni '70, Manuale per uso professionale. Centro Design Montefibre - Gruppo Montedison, Milano

Branzi A, Trini Castelli C (1984) Le emozioni del bradisismo. Colloquio con Clino T. Castelli sull'educazione militare, le stranezze dei nomi, il design primario e l'agopuntura. Modo, vol 73, pp 24–27

Centro design Montefibre (a cura di) (1975) Il Design Primario. Casabella 408

Centro design Montefibre (a cura di) (1976) Il colore. Casabella 410, 33–40

Centro design Montefibre (a cura di) (1977) Operazione Colordinamo. Modo 1, 33

Chevreul ME (1839) De la loi du contraste simultané des couleurs. Pitois-Levrault, Paris

Chevreul ME (1865) Des couleurs et de leurs application aux Arts Industriel. Baillière, Paris

Van Doesburg T (1925) Grundbegriffe der neuen gestaltenden Kunst. Albert Langen Verlag, München

Von Goethe JW (1810) Zur Farbenlehre. Cotta, Tübingen

Grassmann HG (1853) Zur Theorie der Farbenmischun. Poggendof's Annaler der Physik und Chemie (series 3), vol 29, pp 69–84

Von Helmholtz H (1856-1867) Handbuch der physiologichen Optik. Verlag von Leopold Voss, Leipzig

Itten J (1961) Kunst der Farbe. Otto Maier Verlag, Ravensburg

Kandinskij W (1912) ber das Geistige in der Kunst, Insbesondere in der Malerei. R. Piper & Co., Verlag, München

Klee P (1945) Über die moderne Kunst. Benteli, Berlin

Land EH (1959a) Color vision and the natural image (part. I-II). Proc Nat Acad Sci 45:115–129, 636–644

Land EH (1959b) Experiments in color vision. Sci Am 45:84–99

Land EH (1964) The retinex. Am Sci 52:247–264

Land EH (1977) The retinex theory of color vision. Sci Am 237:108–128

Land EH (1983) Recent advances in retinex theory and some implications for cortical computations: color vision and the natural image. Proc Nat Acad Sci 80:5163–5169

Manzini E (1986) La materia dell'invenzione. Materiali e progetto, Arcadia, Milano

Maxwell JC (1872) On colour vision. Proc R Inst G B 6:260–271

Moro M (a cura di) (2010) Clino Trini Castelli e il Design Primario. In: Boeri C (a cura di) Colore. Quaderni di cultura e progetto del colore. IDC Colour Centre, Milano, pp. 190–207

Munsell AH (1905) A color National. G. H. Ellis Co., Boston

Munsell AH (1907) Atlas of the munsell color system. Wadsworth-Howland, Malden

Munsell AH (1921) A grammar of color. Strathmore Paper Co., Mittineague

Newton I (1704) Opticks: or, a treatise of the reflections, refractions, inflections and colours of light. Sam Smith and Benj Walford, London

Ostwald W (1916) Die Farbenfibel. Unesma, Leipzig

Ostwald W (1917) Beiträge zur Farbenlehre. Unesma, Leipzig

Polano S (1990) Il colore nello stile. Note sulla neocromoplastica architettonica di De Stijl. In: Celant G, Govan M (a cura di) Mondrian e De Stijl. Olivetti-Electa, Milano, pp 111–134

Radice B (1984) Memphis: ricerche, esperienze, risultati, fallimenti e successi del nuovo design. Electa, Milano

Romanelli M (1987) Clino Trini Castelli: Color Matrix Olivetti. Domus 685:7–8

Rood ON (1881) Modern chromatics with applications to art and industry. D. Appleton and Company, New York

Runge PO (1809) Von der Doppelheit der Farbe. unbekannt, Standort

Trini Castelli C (1977) Un manuale diverso per colorare. Più colori a minor costo nei tessuti con un nuovo sistema di colorazione delle fibre. Modo vol 4, pp 61–62

Semantic Models for Education. Representations, Between Research and Didactic, for Architecture and Design

Maurizio Unali[✉]

Department of Architecture, Università degli Studi "G. d'Annunzio",
Chieti-Pescara, Pescara, Italy
Maurizio.Unali@unich.it

Abstract. The elaborative form that we have called, in its general aspects, "3D Semantic Model", configures methods of representation, between research and teaching, for knowing, creating and transmitting cultural processes, ideas and forms preparatory to the project of architecture and design.

The main objectives of this method of representation, which over time we have been theorizing and experimenting on several occasions, are: to elaborate an ethical and conscious "aesthetic recycling"; to construct an interactive visual archive of memory fed by conceptual references, ideas, images and spatial hybridizations; to learn to draw, between survey and project, for solving "limits" pedagogically, both tracing and deleting them, at the same time.

Thus, the idea of a "cross-media" design (real, virtual, ideal, utopian, etc.) emerges, an outcome of personal creative elaborations, to help represent the complexity of contemporary culture.

Keywords: Architectural drawing · Semantic models · Hybridizations · Aesthetic recycling · Pedagogy of drawing · Representation

1 Introduction

The proposed study summarizes the last results of a long work (still underway), between research and teaching, on that particular visual-elaborative form that we have defined, in general, "3D Semantic Model".

It is an experimentation aimed at configuring "methods" of representation to know, create, transmit and elaborate cultural processes, ideas and forms preparatory for the project of architecture and design.

A model of representation emerges to elaborate habitable, real and virtual spatiality (but also ideal, utopian and radical), which are placed in a barycentric status between the survey of conceptual references and the project: a visual model that, like a conceptual map, allows to elaborate relationships between different issues.

The drawing that derives from this elaboration process can also be described as a personal "identity archive"; a pedagogical "visual library", implementable and available for subsequent reflections.

© Springer Nature Switzerland AG 2019
A. Luigini (Ed.): EARTH 2018, AISC 919, pp. 271–278, 2019.
https://doi.org/10.1007/978-3-030-12240-9_30

Through the medium of drawing we can, thus, experiment with cultural hybridizations, juxtapositions, critical issues and relationships between the different forms of knowing and doing.

2   Which Drawing?

But which drawing are we theorising?

First of all, we want to experiment a form of drawing (which can be defined conceptual), realized through mixed techniques (mainly digital), aware of the history of representation but also very personal (original), which allows the student (but not only) to elaborate and mature their own compositional process.

A drawing under the banner of "cross-media semantic" (keyword), intertwining and developing languages, detecting and designing visual alphabets, experimenting with techno-cultural convergences, highlighting references, etc.

Deepening this form of drawing (for simplicity, here defined as conceptual, theoretical, ideal and utopian), also means actualizing theories and techniques of the so-called "paper architecture" (experimented above all in Italy since the '70s) compared to the new visual territories now enlarged by the computer technology revolution.

A drawing that experiments with conformations coming from ethical "aesthetic recycling" (key word), intertwining and developing systems of signs, detecting and designing visual alphabets, visual morphemes, paradigms and "monuments".

A drawing to experiment with techno-cultural convergences, to highlight creative, educational, informative and entertaining activities, in different formats and techniques.

That's why we speak of an "ideal" form of drawing, in fact; a drawing that allows us to process and communicate ideas through a visual expression structured as an interactive model (outcome of a specific thematic structure of information); a representation that preserves forms and offers an archive of searchable sub-models.

Fundamental elements to prefigure habitable spaces in the contemporary culture, in its many forms.

3   Drawing Always Means "To Survey and Design" at the Same Time

Conceptually, drawing semantic models means to elaborate habitable spaces, of material and immaterial order, which are (culturally) always placed between survey and project.

In general, it is the constant real and virtual historical polyvalence of architectural design. In particular, the experimentation carried out has gradually led us towards a representation that moves between the knowledge of existing architectures and design prefigurations; an architectural drawing in which to develop that particular moment that anticipates the project, prefiguring the foundational aspects.

A visual laboratory to break up or recompose spaces ("matrioska" organisms that preserve models), to relate languages, to study the geometric characteristics of forms, to number groups of thematic elements, etc.

It is an editing process that starts from the hypothesis that all phenomena, even the most complex and immaterial, can be represented, then elaborated and communicated, according to shared disciplinary methods and techniques.

4 A Pedagogical Representation that "Reflects" on Other Images: A Meta-Conceptual and Cross-Medial Model

For a designer (but not only), to represent is a natural and pedagogical processing dimension; first of all, as a universal multidisciplinary, synthetic and direct language, a historical, theoretical and practical expression.

With specific reference to architectural drawing, the coincidence of metalinguistic order between the visual form (drawing) and the architectural form (whether real, virtual, ideal, utopian, metaphorical, etc.), experimented and conveyed in the graphic sign (be it iconic, symbolic, allegorical, etc.), makes the representation a natural place to elaborate ideas.

A model that, as we have seen so far, is also the outcome of multidisciplinary hybridisation processes, today particularly influenced by cross-media techno-cultures.

These considerations are also supported by the idea that the most interesting manifestations of contemporary creativity seem to be the result of converging disciplines that are changing and which, in some cases, also lose their traditional sectoral boundaries, which are now more and more liquid.

Designing semantic models (but not only), the "meta-design" and cross-media factors seem to play, therefore, a fundamental role, perhaps of a conformational nature.

We must also consider that one of the most interesting conformations of contemporary space seems to be the elaborative result of a conscious, and at the same time instinctive, intellectual action of multidisciplinary hybridization between multiple dialectical combinations.

This also means actualizing the pedagogical cultural practice which, summarizing a lot, consists in representing (in the sense of critically elaborating) dialectical "dual couples".

Let's think, for example, of some ideas presented in the didactic exercises: real and virtual, original and copy, true and false, known and unknown, finished and infinite, ephemeral and lasting, center and periphery, analogue and digital, tradition and innovation, etc.

A drawing that creatively develops dialectical couples that in our contemporary liquid culture can integrate, recognize and give rise to new representations; comparative-relational models, in which to represent apparently antithetical meanings.

Fig. 1. The image (detail), together with the next one (Fig. 2), illustrates the project of a virtual city composed (in the area called "red carpet") mainly by "semantic 3d models" (drawn through mixed techniques, mainly digital, and represented in isometric view) elaborated during the "Architectural Drawing" course, third year of the degree course in Architecture, Department of Architecture, "G. d'Annunzio" University, Chieti-Pescara (Unali 2014).

From the teaching point of view, this approach to architectural drawing helps to trigger open and dialectical processes, with a meta-conceptual and methodologically cross-media spirit.

Architectural representation (even if ideal, utopian, etc.) does not constitute a momentary and illusory "escape from reality", but a strengthening of it: virtual in architecture, as often theorized, means above all "widening the vision". This is one of our goals.

5 Conceptual and Visual References: Theoretical Drawings, Morphemes, Visual Alphabets and Paradigms

In general, the cultural references of the semantic models are multiple and multidisciplinary.

In particular, the main conceptual and visual references of the semantic models concern the history of the theoretical architectural drawing. Among these, just by way of example, we recall especially those representations that have elaborated morphemes, visual alphabets, paradigms, stylistic features, diagrams, etc.

Thus, the semantic models presented here express concepts, methods and techniques of representation that develop, actualize and reinvent theories and practices drawn from the history of architectural drawing, testifying to a new season fueled mainly by contemporary techno-cultures.

Fig. 2. The image (detail) illustrates the "conceptual entrance" to the virtual city described in the previous caption (see Fig. 1).

In the context of the history of architectural representation, for example, I point out a very short and personal "list" of references: the "morpheme" notation systems designed by Franco Purini since 1969; the images elaborated by Bruno Munari in the second half of the '60s using a Xerox 914 copying machine; Marino Auriti, *Encyclopedic Palace of the World*, 1950; the *Mendinigrafo* (1985), the graphic instrument used by Alessandro Mendini; the "Histograms of Architecture" (1972) by Superstudio and the drawings of the Florentine radical laboratories; *La Città Analoga* (1976) by Aldo Rossi; the drawings by Massimo Scolari; the diagrams by Peter Eisenman; Frank O. Gehry, in the role of Frankie P. Toronto, for the performance *Il Corso del coltello* (Venice 1985); the *Cretto di Gibellina* (1984–89) realized by Alberto Burri in the old city destroyed during the 1968 earthquake; the installation "Copycat. Empathy and envy as form-makers" by Cino Zucchi exhibited at the 2012 Venice Architecture Biennail; virtual living on the web, from social networks to virtual city; etc.

But the examples are endless. Representations that teach thinking, that feed the memory, that trigger regeneration processes to develop habitable, real and virtual spaces.

6 Towards an Ethical and Conscious "Aesthetic Recycling"

From what described so far, it appears evident that the drawing we are theorising is the result of an ethical and conscious process of hybridization of conceptual and visual references (chosen and studied), aimed at experimenting with further forms of "aesthetic recycling"; creative paths found in many contemporary creative expressions (composing, decomposing, reusing, re-signifying "things" and images to regenerate reality and represent imagination, to understand and recognize).

To describe the triggered design process, these references must be explicitly stated in an illustrative "tab". Thus, the experimentation of "aesthetic recycling" practices takes on a pedagogical, as well as an ethical, value. The documentation of conceptual and visual references contextualizes the project, places it in a historical path, giving it meanings and a memory. It is always important to place works and ideas in a historical perspective, highlighting affinities and relationships with the past, but also with the present. The exercise of reading, manipulating, transforming and communicating the chosen references is an important cultural act, at various levels. Very often, what we create derives from a natural, instinctive, empathetic and continuous process of "aesthetic recycling". In theory, we can also hypothesize that no work is in itself a *unicum*, but belongs to a cultural context; it is the result of a process of re-reading and updating works previously seen and studied, even at the unconscious level. It is not hazardous, then, to evaluate that to learn to design it is also important to knowingly and ethically "appropriating" the ideas we intercept, declining them in a personal lexicon and always quoting the sources. Between research and teaching, this is a theme that transverses contemporary cultural phenomena, a topic of great interest, which also concerns, in general, the comprehension, transmission and elaboration of ideas (Fig. 3).

Fig. 3. The image illustrates an initial detail of the so-called "red carpet of semantic models" (developed by the students) in the virtual city described in the first caption (see Fig. 1).

7   Conclusions

What is more virtual than a "formula" (Fig. 4) to conclude the description of the semantic models for education described here?

Provocatively (feeding the debate) I want to conclude the argument proposing the metaphorical and ephemeral "formula" to draw "semantic 3d models", taken from one of the didactic representations on the theme carried out "on the blackboard".

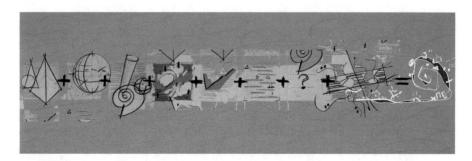

Fig. 4. The metaphorical and ephemeral "formula" to elaborate "3d semantic models", in an educational representation carried out "on the blackboard".

The "algorithm" procedure established by the ephemeral artistic "formula" consists, summarizing a lot, in choosing and elaborating the creative "substances" (the conceptual and visual references) useful to feed one's own representation project: the result is the semantic model, as described above.

It is an invitation to trigger, as already mentioned, a creative workshop in which to reconstruct spaces, relate parts, to show ideas to oneself and to others; graphic exercises that can be structured in visual methods to elaborate ideas.

Finally, as a teacher of architectural drawing, from the experience described so far, I think that to feed the students' creativity and to develop an ethical approach to the project, it is important to transmit these forms of representation.

A drawing that is aware that every "new idea" is the result of a plural path, which spreads and feeds through multiple hybridization processes.

A universe of relationships and ideas that come to life through free representations.

Acknowledgements. The activity presented in the paper summarizes the latest outcomes of a work (still ongoing), between research and teaching, on that particular visual-elaborative form that we have called "Semantic Model".

I would like to thank everyone who, to varying degrees, has made this research possible:
- first of all the students, intelligent observers of the techno-cultural revolution;
- my colleagues, an inexhaustible source of cultural dialogue;
- the designers and architects whose works are represented as fragments in this publication.

References

Unali M (2014) Atlante dell'abitare virtuale. Il Disegno della Città Virtuale, fra Ricerca e Didattica. Gangemi, Roma

European Digital Library for the Intercultural Dialogue. Interactive Environments for Education, Cultural Heritage and Civic Empowerment

Giuseppe Amoruso[1]([✉]) and Valentina Battista[2]

[1] Department of Design, Politecnico di Milano,
Via Durando 38/a, 20158 Milan, Italy
giuseppe.amoruso@polimi.it
[2] Materias s.r.l. c/o, Università degli Studi di Napoli "Federico II",
Corso N. Protopisani 50, 80146 Naples, Italy

Abstract. The European Digital Library project encompasses the establishment of a digital community library based on the use of new technologies for the knowledge dissemination in a European framework and the design of an experiential environment for education, cultural heritage fruition and, active participation in civic society. The project operates within the community libraries proposing the development of experiential services and digital applications. The initiative, promoted by the Puglia Region for the activation of *Community Libraries* within the regional territory, aims to set up an integrated creative environment supporting local development and socio-educational and tourism-cultural actions. In particular, the community library is dedicated to local activation and cultural cohesion, conceived as an advanced library model offering innovative services for the promotion of reading and culture.

Keywords: Digital heritage · Digital arts · Intercultural dialogue ·
Education through digital media · Interactive environments ·
Interactive digital publishing

1 Introduction: Learning, Technologies, Innovation

Technologies of knowledge are recognized as opportunities in terms of conservation, study and communication of heritage, but also of creation and dissemination of culture and awareness that are expressed in contemporary forms of sharing and dissemination. Lifelong learning should therefore be considered as the source of an increasingly innovative economy that becomes sustainable and produces a considerable impact if it reaches a substantial and diversified number of users and social subjects. The learning society represents a contemporary human condition linked to new social phenomena, in a society in which people perceive knowledge every day as the new capital (Stiglitz and Greenwald 2004). The learning society is an educational philosophy promoted by the OECD and UNESCO that fosters education as the key to a nation's economic development; according to its principles education should extend beyond formal learning

© Springer Nature Switzerland AG 2019
A. Luigini (Ed.): EARTH 2018, AISC 919, pp. 279–287, 2019.
https://doi.org/10.1007/978-3-030-12240-9_31

(conventionally based in traditional educational institutions: schools, universities etc.) into informal learning centres to support a knowledge-based economy. A learning society encompasses the actual process of learning as an 'activity, not a place' – that is, it takes place outside of regular educational institutions, and is thus also decentralised and deregulated, a tenet of globalisation theory (Cisco 2010). If lifelong learning is about the ability of the individual, then this is enabled through a Learning Society. It is the social and cultural process of individual lifelong learning, internalising the norms and ideologies of society and encompassing both learning and teaching (Oecd 2000). This vision is a structural basis for economics and social development: starting from Donald Schon's paradigm, *'learning, reflection and change'* translates into the promotion of creativity at all levels, creating a critical and civic awareness and inducing a social change process; it is currently aided through technologies at different level and the increasing focus on social networking, by using the shared learning experiences of individuals as a basis for a larger framework of education that encompasses both formal and informal environments (schools, universities, job-training, support, collaboration, feedback etc.).

In the Italian panorama it is interesting to analyse data presented by the *Osservatorio Innovazione Digitale nei Beni e Attività Culturali* of the Politecnico di Milano to understand how critical issues remain regarding access to heritage, culture education and the impact of culture producers on the territories.

According to the ISTAT report, *I musei, le aree archeologiche e i monumenti in Italia* (2015), Italy has 4976 museums, archaeological sites and monuments, 1 for every 12,000 inhabitants. In the country of widespread and omnipresent beauty, today the so-called digital transformation lives in an innovative or conventional form modifying the institutional communication tools of libraries and museums, website, social networks, newsletters, etc.

Analyzing the sample of museums, the *Osservatorio* reports that 52% of museums are present on social networks (mainly on Facebook), 57% have a website of which only half of these are translated into English and in 20% of cases there are services and activities aimed at particular categories of users; so if you turn the focus on services to users, the picture is quite critical with about 10% of the museums that do not even have the website. On the other hand, Istat data show lower adoption rates, less than 20%, for digital services linked to the use of collections, both on online sharing platforms (for example, an accessible online catalog and the possibility of virtual visits), and directly on the website (like QR-code targets and proximity systems, and applications for mobile devices).

In this panorama, in an increasingly multicultural society and in the age of migration, the challenges for the future are numerous; digital innovation can help overcome critical issues and introduce new methods of cultural mediation and socialization. Challenges are linked to technology transfer, digital skills practice, knowledge of national and regional heritage and the creation of efficient management models based on the opportunities of the digital universe.

Learning is to be considered as an economic expression of social well-being; it becomes sustainable if it reaches a large and diversified number of the population which benefits from it and returns it in the various forms of access to culture.

2   Experiential Design: The *European Digital Library* Project

The experiential design proposes a system of mediation between the territory, the cultural heritage system or the intangible heritage (memory, history, landscape) and the target community intended as a user, allowing multiple forms of representation of values and legitimizing their shared identity, access, use and appropriation differentiated, either directly or using technologies.

In this sense, the design process is not limited to the experience of use of value (economy of experience), but introduces an innovative vision of system and shared cultural heritage in all its forms; it also makes it possible to activate a participatory and inclusive learning path, of social well-being, which makes its diffusion in the community sustainable (and from the institution, to the cultural operator, to the different categories of users). The dissemination of digital skills can be combined with the need for innovation and technology transfer for the benefit of the territory, young people, start-ups and industrial districts.

The service economy in recent years has shown considerable potential by creating an innovative system of a social nature based on a particular type of economic performance. Goods and services are no longer sufficient as economic products; a new need has been created: through a design process, an integrated fruition project can be created, that is, the project of experience, leaving an experiential impression in people, that is, giving a sensorial and psychological form to the experience.

Experiences are the fourth form of economic offer, distinct from services, products and commodities but until now not recognized as such. When an experience it is chosen, it is accepted the economic value to spend time in enjoying a series of events that engage us directly. The oldest and most basic form of experience is that of the prolonged use of a product, ie the one for Pine and Gilmore defined as "*ing the thing: any can be inged*" (Pine and Gilmore 2011).

Experiences have always been the heart of entertainment, today we are talking about Edutainment. The introduction of this innovative engagement based on experience can be attributed to Walt Disney. After introducing innovative experiential effects in cartoons (synchronized sound, color, three-dimensional backgrounds, stereo sound, etc.) reached its peak in 1955 with the opening of Disneyland in California and the subsequent opening of Walt Disney World. The well-known park EPCOT stands for *Experimental Prototype Community of Tomorrow*; a utopian city of the future designed by Walt Disney, often exchanging "city" and "community". A project based on the experience of the future and other cultures of the world. In the first theme parks, visitors immersed themselves in the games and in the history that was taking place.

Nowadays the availability of low-cost technological resources makes it possible to use cultural heritage through the project of experience and the personalization of the relationship between the citizen and the cultural asset understood as a common value shared in a community. The library intended only as a cultural garrison and preservation of literary memory, historical social expands into a new immaterial dimension, of informal accessibility, of discovery, of integration of institutional training paths.

The *European Digital Library* (EDL) project addresses the establishment of a digital thematic library based on the use of new technologies for the dissemination of knowledge in a European context and the configuration of an experiential environment for education, cultural heritage fruition and active participation of civic society. The project is developing experiential services and digital applications for community libraries. In particular, within the extraordinary initiative promoted by the Puglia Region for the activation of Community Libraries in the regional territories; the program fosters community participation and cultural cohesion as an advanced library model offering innovative services for the promotion of reading and culture. The proposal aims to set up an integrated creative environment with the aim of supporting local development linked to socio-educational and tourism-cultural actions.

In the SMART-IN PUGLIA program (Support, Memory, Arts, Resilience, Territory, Intelligence) the Puglia Region promotes support to "school libraries, local authorities and universities, for interventions that deliver environmental improvement and enhance it through the recovery/restoration of interiors, encouraging their functionality through the appropriate and innovative tools and equipment". The experimental actions are aimed at developing original contents through the creation of educational experiences applied to cultural learning, to the incentive of reading through digital media, storytelling and interaction with digital environments, book crossing and gamification of history.

The aim is to generate an innovative cultural offer by providing a community library that addresses the memory of the territory and also including a library of Europe dedicated to European intercultural dialogue with particular reference to the macro Mediterranean region. The project integrates new technologies for the accessibility and knowledge of cultural heritage and its socialization through new media to promote, enhance and disseminate local collections and cultural heritage but also in relation to the processes of European integration.

The concept library develops its role as a cultural reference for the territory, including the functions of gathering place, cultural entertainment and digital assistance point to stimulate the widest civic participation and access to digital services.

The EDL therefore develops contents, services, cultural products for the benefit of community libraries. The project is based on the use of new technologies for the dissemination of knowledge and the socialization of new media to promote, enhance and disseminate the library and cultural heritage. It is planned to activate a series of laboratories interdisciplinary teaching, using experiential design techniques, representation, storytelling and contemporary communication languages to transfer knowledge and knowledge to young people skills to increase their cultural background and actively contribute to the realization of innovative goods and services. The proposal wants to configure an integrated and long-term planning environment with the aim of creating synergies and local development processes, linked to socio-educational and touristic-cultural services: the collection and processing of contents on the intangible heritage, memory and local traditions is aimed at the design and development of an APP dedicated to the collection and processing of contents on the intangible heritage, memory and local traditions also as a function of characterization tourist-cultural city.

The APP will allow the widest use of content both on personal mobile devices and on graphic stations and specific devices that will be installed at the EDL, at the project partners and at the affiliated cultural sites (museums, cultural containers, temporary events, etc.).

The operative proposal foresees the following phases: analysis and characterization of the tourist identity of the city starting from the research on the history and the local historiography; the cataloging of the forms of material and immaterial expression of cultural heritage; and to the selection of historical episodes that have influenced the formation of the social and cultural image; multimedia documentation, selection of sources and collection of information and historical data. In this phase the production of original architectural reliefs is important, carried out for the first time with advanced photogrammetry and 3D scanning technologies: these elaborations will form the core of a collection of three-dimensional models to be used for all subsequent applications required for EDL such as content processing for the WEB/APP, the production of images, animations and advanced graphic documentation. Will be produced architectural and thematic representations, construction models of the main monuments, architectural reconstructions of sites and monuments that have undergone transformations showing the evolution and the urban and architectural configuration of the sites of interest also using 3D printing systems and smart objects. Another technological development concerns the recovery of high-definition digital images for the production of immersive and panoramic virtual tours and subsequent audiovisual elaborations to be used for the development of the APP and the use of other experiential systems, immersive or on digital and social platforms; design of site-specific installations and materials to support the use of monuments and sites of interest along predefined itineraries and in synergy and coordination with other EDL initiatives, including temporary ones.

3   Interactive Environments for Education, Cultural Heritage and Civic Empowerment

The project explores the role of available technologies as a key for the experiential learning process. The community cultural engagement developed by the research is concerned with designing the value of processes, goods, environments and services, of increasing it and transferring it to society and to citizens.

According to the *Recommendation concerning the Protection and Promotion of Museums and Collections* (Unesco 2015), some primary functions are attributed to museums, including conservation, research, communication and education. On this last aspect it is emphasized that '*Museums engage in formal and non-formal education and lifelong learning, through the development and transmission of knowledge, educational and pedagogical program, in partnership with other educational institutions, notably schools. Educational program in museums primarily contribute to educating various audiences about the subject matters of their collections and about civic life, as well as helping to raise greater awareness of the importance of preserving heritage, and fostering creativity. Museums can also provide knowledge and experiences that contribute to the understanding of related societal topics*'.

Technologies in museums are thus recognized as opportunities in terms of conservation, study and communication of heritage, but also of heritage and common value creation, sharing and dissemination of knowledge.

Learning becomes a sustainable economy, if it addresses society needs and encompasses a large and diversified number of people; learning as an expression of social well-being, approaching one's own community, sense of identity and regeneration of memory (mnemonics).

It is very singular the case of the Young Fund on memory and mnemonics. It is one of the richest collections of books, articles and memorabilia on the subject of memory and mnemonics today. It belongs to the library of the University of the Republic of San Marino, which bought it in 1991 from the American collector Morris N. Young. Umberto Eco reminds us that memory is "a faculty thanks to which both individuals and collectives base their identity (the forgetful does not know who he is)" (Eco 1998).

In the age in which we live, technological systems tend to substitute themselves, with their apparatus, for our brain, which instead needs to exercise and process memories through material expressions, rituals and the recognition of symbols.

A sectoral study scope is that which analyzes the real and virtual, physical or digital nature of the museum: locally accessible information systems (multimedia workstations, touch screens located in the rooms of the royal museum); technological devices (iPad, smartphones, tablets, viewers, smart glasses …); technological environments (virtual museums, apps, video games …) that make information resources accessible via the internet in mobile mode.

The technologies have changed the exhibition space within museums and places for culture learning and fruition; rooms are transformed according to a virtual amplification perspective of the paths, interaction with collections is designed according to personalization (users can select contents), participation and sharing is allowed (users can create new cultural contents and share them with other users) moving towards new forms of active and participatory learning.

In this regard, Manovich has distinguished some specific cultural actions that are mediated by the new digital tools: creation, sharing of information and knowledge; creation, sharing and accessibility of digital artifacts representing aesthetic ideas and values; to the interactive cultural experience; textual, vocal and/or visual communication; participation in a sort of ecological information online (Manovich 2002).

In fact, in order to fulfill their educational mission, museums need to go beyond the tangible dimension of their architecture to communicate a heritage understood also as a process and as such intangible.

In the *Convention for the Safeguarding of the Intangible Cultural Heritage* (Unesco 2003) framework, the project is aimed in particular at the Intangible Cultural Heritage (ICH) - or the living heritage - which is the protagonist of the cultural diversity of humanity and its maintenance guarantee for continuous creativity. Intangible cultural heritage indicates practices, representations, expressions, knowledge, skills - as well as tools, objects, artifacts and associated cultural spaces - that communities, groups and, in some cases, individuals they recognize as part of their cultural heritage. This immaterial cultural heritage, transmitted from generation to generation, is constantly regenerated by communities and groups in response to their environment, their interaction with nature and their history and provides them with a sense of identity and continuity, thus promoting respect for cultural diversity and of human creativity.

The research project proposes to activate an innovative digitalization and dissemination laboratory in order to transfer to young people knowledge and skills to increase their cultural background and actively contribute to the realization of innovative application and digital services. The experiential design program is implemented through a plan of acquisition, data collection, production, consultation and dissemination of multimedia content and then, consequently, an itinerary of activation and experiential education.

The project applies exploitation methodologies and techniques whose scope is the cultural heritage system understood in its cognitive, social and symbolic dimension. The disciplines of representation interact with the multiple disciplinary specializations of design, proposing the definition of interpretative models for the analysis and representation of the historical, cultural, aesthetic and environmental values of a cultural asset and its material and immaterial meaning. The valorisation strategy produces advanced visualizations and informative and multimedia modeling. In addition, the experiential value, of emotional imprint and fruition are emphasized through immersive and interactive technologies. The applications allow a structured and flexible knowledge process also to simulate the forms of innovation and increase the social value of the transmission and sharing of cultural contents.

In fact, in order to fulfill their educational mission, the spaces of culture need to go beyond the tangible and common sensorial dimension to communicate and share a heritage understood also as a process of appropriation and as such also linked to the intangible dimension.

Among cultural actions that are related to new media and their language, the creation, sharing of information and knowledge but also the accessibility to heritage through digital artifacts that represent ideas, identities and values of belonging. To these Manovich also adds the interactive cultural experience, the opportunity to enjoy the experiences and cultural products by visitors and ways to recreate the exhibits, textual, vocal and/or visual communication and participation in a kind information that regenerates "ecologically" knowledge and its diffusion.

Participatory museum (according to Simon 2010) in which participatory processes are activated transform the museum into a socio-cultural platform able to connect different subjects and inform three use scenarios: the museum based on the personalization of the itinerary; the Matryoshka museum based on the multilevel deepening of the contents in relation to the degree of deepening; the ludico-experiential museum, which relies on the performative dimension of the visit in which the user is called to action and not only to contemplative activity.

Knowledge technologies, design techniques and tools for the image-based representation of complexity and interactive and haptic communication for the benchmark of ways of transferring the values and potential of heritage (graphic tools for territorial identity, social communication, information models, mobile applications based on graphic and immersive technologies, interactive virtual reconstructions of future and past oriented locations and habitats) (Amoruso 2009).

Fig. 1. SMART-IN PUGLIA_Community Library program, Regione Puglia. Comune di Brindisi, *History Digital Library*, Società di Storia Patria della Puglia, Liceo delle Scienze Umane e Linguistico "Ettore Palumbo" di Brindisi, Associazione Vola Alto.

Therefore contents representation inform a cognitive and exploratory investigation and orient results to a metaphorical and creative scope which is sharing a set of theories, tools and practices (Amoruso 2016); these projects are developed at strategic, functional, aesthetic and formal level and applied to the enhancement of cultural heritage but also in the design of communication platforms and artifacts and in the configuration of urban locations and public spaces of high qualitative value.

Finally, techniques and tools of representation and visualization will be decisive for the definition of ways of sharing and transferring the values and potentials of the asset through visual tools aimed at assessing its impact, fostering awareness, consent and participation and at the same time guaranteeing another degree of "instrumentality" and applicability to local actors through adequate and sustainable processes of involvement and training (Fig. 1).

4   Conclusions

Technologies are therefore changing the relationship between users and the fruition environment and cultural content in museums, libraries and learning places. The environments must be imagined and transformed considering also their virtual extension and also allowing a range of personalization linked to the selection of contents. Participation and sharing also mediated by the user can create new cultural content by opening up new forms of active and participatory learning. The applications here presented allow a structured and flexible knowledge process also to simulate the forms of innovation and increase the social value of the transmission and sharing of cultural contents. Knowledge technologies offer multiple opportunities and challenges to cultural and scientific practitioners; the challenge of involvement and experience is not only technological and design, but also and perhaps above all mental, of imagination.

Acknowledgements. SMART-IN PUGLIA program (Support, Memory, Arts, Resilience, Territory, Intelligence) is promoted by the Puglia Region (Italy) and it is part of the regional Strategic Plan for Culture. The Strategic Plan (PiiiLCultura in Puglia) is an instrument of planning and development in the short, medium and long term written and built with a functional and participatory method.

The *History Digital Library* is a community library and a non-profit public cultural project promoted by Comune di Brindisi and operated at the Casa del Turista by the Brindisi Virtual Library consortium: Società di Storia Patria della Puglia, Liceo delle Scienze Umane e Linguistico "Ettore Palumbo", Associazione Vola Alto.

Both authors developed the research concept and the library layout: Valentina Battista edited the *Introduction: learning, technologies, innovation* paragraph, Giuseppe Amoruso edited the *Interactive environments for education, cultural heritage and civic empowerment* paragraph, both the authors edited the *Experiential design: the European Digital Library project* and the *Conclusions* paragraph.

References

Amoruso G (2009) Il disegno per il design dei beni culturali. In: Bartolomei C (ed) Cultural heritage documentation, Disegnare Con vol 3, no 6

Amoruso G (2016) Handbook of research on visual computing and emerging geometrical design tools, vol 2. IGI Global, Hershey, pp 1–924

Cisco Systems Inc. (2010) The Learning Society. http://www.cisco.com/web/about/citizenship/socio-economic/docs/LearningSociety_WhitePaper.pdf. Accessed 15 Oct 2018

Eco U (1998) Fondo Young sulla memoria e la mnemotecnica. Presentazione del Fondo. http://web.unirsm.sm/young/eco.htm

Manovich L (2002) The language of new media. MIT Press, Boston

OECD (2000) Knowledge management in the learning society. OECD Publishing, Paris

Pine BJ II, Gilmore JH (2011) The experience economy. Harvard Business School Press, Cambridge

Simon N (2010) The participatory museum. Santa Cruz: Museum 2.0

Stiglitz JE, Greenwald Bruce C (2014) Creating a learning society: a new approach to growth, development, and social progress. Columbia University Press, New York

UNESCO (2003) Convention for the Safeguarding of the Intangible Cultural Heritage, Paris

UNESCO (2015) Recommendation concerning the Protection and Promotion of Museums and Collections, Paris

Visual Culture and Cultural Heritage: ViC-CH a Synthesis Between Digital Representation and Heritage Experience

A. Luigini[1]([⊠]), G. A. Massari[2], S. Vattano[1],
C. Pellegatta[2], and F. Luce[2]

[1] Faculty of Education, Free University of Bozen-Bolzano, Viale Ratisbona 16,
39042 Brixen-Bressanone, BZ, Italy
alessandro.luigini@unibz.it
[2] Department of Civil, Environmental and Mechanical Engineering,
University of Trento, Via Mesiano 77, 38123 Trento, Italy

Abstract. The dissemination possibilities offered by digital technologies provide multiple ways of reading and fruition of the cultural heritage. In order to define a visualization and communication strategy through images, the paper shows some of the results of the ViC-CH *Visual Culture and Cultural Heritage* workshop, which involved the University of Trento and the Free University of Bozen-Bolzano. The graphic elaborations focused on the Library of the Priest Seminar in Brixen; photomodelling, short films with drone shots and virtual visits have been some of the ways of manipulating the image for the animation and realistic visualization of a cultural heritage not easily accessible to date (The paper is to be attributed to Alessandro Luigini for paragraph 1, to Giovanna A. Massari for paragraph 2, to Starlight Vattano for paragraph 3, to Cristina Pellegatta for paragraph 4, and to Fabio Luce for paragraph 5).

Keywords: Cultural heritage · Digital representation ·
Image-based technologies · Virtual tour · Open source procedures

1 Visual Culture and Heritage: Access to Knowledge and Educational Possibilities

Finding a balance in the fragile relationship between the need for knowledge and use of heritage and its conservation, even in conditions of deterioration, is necessary to ensure that the heritage itself continues to maintain its meaning through generations. Very often archaeological excavations, or heritage in a state of abandonment, require significant interventions to achieve the goal of passing on what we have received as an inheritance, and in these cases digital technologies, evidently, allow the possibility of reconstruction and use of great potential and effectiveness. The potential of digital reconstructions, supported by direct and indirect surveying or archival research, are rapidly developing and each model can be structured for the only visualization or for the management of material or immaterial factors. The choice of a path to the detriment of another depends on many factors, but one of the main ones is the destination of digital reconstruction.

The case of heritage in good preservation conditions but not directly usable - due to inaccessibility of the location, to the risk of alteration of the delicate balance of works at risk of deterioration, due to lack of funds, etc. - is different because in these cases the relationship between digital representation and the artifact is mainly directed to enhancement needs. Reconstructing a digital model of the existing heritage, without prejudice to the legitimate need for documentation, takes on value when the phase of visualization and communication ensures a deepening of knowledge of the artifact, beyond what is visible.

In these cases, the potential of digital representation technologies is boosted by all those image-based technologies that allow the deferred and increased use of heritage. Panoramic photography - either by single-shot or by stitched frames taken by a camera on a panoramic head - aerial shooting - internal or external - moving shots and multi-resolution images are some of the tools available for documentation and communication of heritage. The relationship between the subject and its digital representation based on photography is a mimetic relationship able to reproduce exactly the appearance of the work, to the advantage of a documental efficacy and its deferred fruition: a single shot of a 360° camera allows to generate virtual tours that can be easily transmitted over the Internet and can be accessed by an ordinary smartphone and a Cardboard that costs few euros. This (sometimes apparent) simplicity is totally symmetrical to a multiplicity of uses that involve more and more entertainment systems, how the many projects in the exhibition and museum area demonstrate, which in recent years have developed processes of valorization also through the experience-design and interactive-design. Moreover, the historical-artistic heritage has a preferential relationship with the visual media because of the need to transmit the exteriority of the works as carrier of the deeper meaning of the works themselves. And it is always through visual media that in the educational field, whatever it is, it is possible to experience the collections of museums, works of art and the environments that contain them. Therefore it seems to be outlined the trajectory that must be followed, starting from the heritage, passing through its visual representations, to arrive at the valorization of the heritage and at the education to it. After all, it is clear that this aim is "a formative, formal and informal activity that, while educating in knowledge and respect for goods, adopting responsible behaviors, it makes heritage the concrete object of research and interpretation, adopting the perspective of recurrent and permanent training of everyone for an active and responsible citizenship" (Bortolotti et al. 2008).

The workshop described in the following paragraphs is based on these assumptions and aims to build a structured path that can be the basis of institutional courses to be included in similar study courses: from the degree course in Engineering to the degree course in Education, from the degree course in Environmental Preservation to the degree course in Communication Science.

The present section presents some theoretical assumptions, the second one presents the project of the ViC-CH workshop, the third introduces and contextualizes the case of study, the fourth and the fifth paragraphs explain the techniques and the modalities through which students achieved the required results.

2 The ViC-CH Project: A Formative Path Between Sciences and Arts

The visual narration in ancient works of art, made largely through serial figures used for stories of various kinds, shows what relevance the image reception and, consequently, the access to the meanings of represented stories has always had for the public (Brilliant 1987). In the passage from oral to written tradition, it was soon realized that, in front of a visually usable message, the observer can enjoy not only a greater freedom of choice than the listener or the reader, but he can transform himself into a narrator and he can elaborate an internalized form of verbal expression, starting from the figures. Despite the distance that separates us from the painters and the sculptors of antiquity, some of the demands of their work are preserved in the use that our society makes of the image: for example, the presence of a descriptive content selected starting from reality, even if only thought; or the creation of scenes useful to bring the public to the interpretation and continuity of an action; finally, the use of compositional syntax as well as codification mechanisms for the transmission of adequate information.

The images that accompany the entire essay are the outcome of the five days of intensive workshop held in Brixen from 22 to 26 January 2018, thanks to the funding obtained from the University of Trento (DICAM) and the Free University of Bozen-Bolzano (Faculty of Education) as part of the 'Euregio Mobility Fund' project, launched in 2014 by the European Group of Territorial Cooperation 'Euregio Tirolo - Alto Adige - Trentino' formed by the autonomous provinces of Trento and Bolzano and the Land Tirol.

This project supports the activities of the three Euregio universities (Trento, Bolzano and Innsbruck) aimed at enhancing mutual knowledge as well as cultural exchange and mobility between students and teachers. The ViC-CH 'Visual Culture and Cultural Heritage' proposal, funded for the 2017–18 academic year, involves five professors and twenty two students from the two universities in lectures, field operations and laboratory exercises[1].

ViC-CH topics concern image processing, graphic composition, visual communication and multimedia representation for knowledge and enhancement of cultural heritage, implemented with the exclusive use of free and open source digital procedures. In this field these procedures offer very interesting alternatives to commercial products and they make it possible to direct the increasingly scarce economic resources

---

[1] The working group of the University of Trento is composed by: Giovanna A. Massari (scientific coordination), Cristina Pellegatta, Fabio Luce, Davide Bassetti with the students Franco Aassila, Sara Alberti, Monica Bersani, Marika Ciela, Elisa Fratton, Furio Magaraggia, Elena Margesin, Hanns Oberrauch, Michele Odorizzi, Simone Orsolin, Luis Antonio Pederzini Velazquez, Andrea Tavella, Virginia Trinco, Monica Vedovelli. The working group of the Free University of Bozen-Bolzano is composed by: Alessandro Luigini, Starlight Vattano with the students Sophie Bidell, Jenny Cazzola, Silvia Cunico, Michele Flore, Beatrice Fusari, Sophie Hartmann, Federico Pontarollo, Matteo Redaelli. The two lectures dedicated to 'Panoramic images and virtual tours' and 'Web-based communication tools' were carried out respectively by Daniele Rossi (University of Camerino) and Daniele Villa (Politecnico di Milano).

towards the indispensable purchases of hardware equipment and to the need for continuous training of operators (Ballarin 2014 and Empler 2008).

ViC-CH targets are the pursuit of cross-curricular educational activities in the fields of scientific and humanistic knowledge; the definition of responses to the growing demand for teachings that combine practice with theory; the assumption of methodological awareness as an indispensable tool for building and transmit thought through image. Today the languages that replace visual messages to words seem more appropriate both to new technologies and to the needs of society, not only for their immediacy but above all because they entrust communication to the visual perception, in other words, a quick and natural mechanism of reading and interpreting. However, the image as an aesthetic result and informational vehicle must be constructed as such to be a carrier of knowledge and it is in this specific experimental field that the experience of Brixen develops.

The outputs produced to illustrate the Library of the Major Priest Seminary are of various kinds: manipulations of the single photographic shot, photo-compositing of current views and historical images, posters and flyers for different purposes, interactive panoramic images, virtual tours, complete short films (assembly of heterogeneous materials, opening and closing titles, audio track), sharing maps on the web, 3D models for animation and realistic visualization. As a whole, they bear witness to how much in the daily life of scientific research the multiplicity of skills and interests is a resource, not a limit.

Anyway, ViC-CH is not a circumscribed experience to the workshop: it is an E-learning initiative whose first results are expected for the beginning of 2019, when some of the lessons and the corresponding exercises will be usable in the didactic on line Moodle platforms of the two universities (Chiarenza 2017). The computerization of a course in English language, with modular contents to be developed over time and to be directed to an ever-wider pool of users, will allow us to describe and apply the most widespread digital techniques in the field of graphic representation and of visual communication, thus allowing interested users to acquire the skills necessary for the design and the creation of digital images that are able to establish a form of dialogue between cultural heritage, digital culture and society.

Fig. 1. On the left, view of the seminar, F. Gatt, 19th century approx.; on the right, the seminar after enlargement in 1900.

3   An Iconographic Path Among the Historical Representations of the Major Priest Seminary of Brixen

The survey on the historical iconography of Brixen and of the Major Priest Seminary concerned the sights already realized starting from the second half of the 16th century through which it is possible to recognize some of the architectural elements that determined the expansion and the morphological structure of the urban fabric of this town. The settlement of the city dates back to 901 A.D. and from 1004 it became the main residence of the prince-bishop of Brixen, remaining for the following centuries under ecclesiastical domination. The first buildings of the original urban structure were built in correspondence of the market square, while the main axis of the city corresponded to the Tratten street; this one constituted the link between the areas in which the Clarisse and Franciscan foundations were found (Flachenecker et al. 2000). The historical sights realized by Burglechner, Kessler, Braun and Hogenberg, Prunner's engravings and Gatt's watercolors give back the look of a fortified city: both the river on one side and the curtain of buildings on the other one establish the morphological elements that contain urban development. A comparison among historical views let to recognize each single town fragment incorporated into a network of hospices built on Alpine pass, which became strategic points of the religious itineraries of the twelfth century. The study of urban evolution of Brixen proceeded with the identification of the construction phases of the Major Priest Seminary, tracing its relations with the other architectural signs that determined its location, becoming, over time, one of the most important site on the pilgrimage ways directed to Rome, Gerusalemme and Santiago (Gummerer 1994).

In 1721 the prince-bishop of Brixen, Caspar Ignaz von Künigl obtained the hospital building and after the restoration of the cathedral, in 1778, bishop Leopold von Spaur dedicated himself to the *ex-novo* erection of the seminary. Regarding the architectural style, the prefect Georg Tangl, who followed the work of the entire building, undertook a series of trips to Austria, Bavaria, France, Swabia and Italy to study the baroque configuration adopted in the restoration and furnishing of the seminars (Gruber 1991).

The iconographic research on the constructive vicissitudes of the seminar, through the retrieval of historical plants, has brought to light some of the compositional and spatial aspects of the building, not only in relation to urban context, but also in relation to historical events concerning the ancient medieval hospital complex in which the building was later erected. A quadrangular plan with the library located on the first floor (Baur 1975), the seminar was completed in 1766, becoming an architectural reference for the other churches built in Brixen. The addition of the eastern wing and the overlapping of a level, as shown by archival images in the late nineteenth and early twentieth centuries, will be from the following century. A further study focused on the library of the seminary with the integration of bibliographic and archive research relating to interior decorations, frescoes and spatial configuration (Heiss et al. 2006). Built in correspondence of the main entrance, on the first floor, the library hall is characterized by a rectangular layout and it is developed on two levels. Two marble columns placed on the axis of symmetry of the plant symbolically represent the bases of theology, 'Scripture' and 'Tradition'. The six lowered domes are decorated with

Fig. 2. The building and its context: above, the seminar related to the surrounding urban area; below, the inner courtyard and a detail of the main façade. Aerial shooting by UAV DJI Phantom III standard.

stuccos through which Zeiller represents biblical, ascetic, dogmatic and moral science, jurisprudence and retorica (Gelmi 2007). The production of images through the use of open-access software and the mapping of the strategic points of the city were integrated with the data collected through iconographic research to provide graphic and historical-evolutionary information about both the seminar and the inside library. In this process of place reading for the knowledge of the architectural good, the dimension of historical iconography is combined with the digital one, providing new images designed for the promotion of cultural heritage and the enhancement of the major seminary and the library.

4 Communicating Built Heritage: Methods and Criteria for Image Design

Built heritage is a tangible and material common good that can be enjoyed in every moment and also in its absence through images that make it visible and then 'present'.

Fig. 3. The library of the seminar, three levels of description: the architectural space, the book heritage and the frescoes decorative apparatus. Terrestrial shoots by Canon EOS 70D reflex digital camera.

This happens thanks to the representation, act of interpretation and form of knowledge, which supervises the putting into picture of every form of space whether it is constructed or only hypothesized. Visual communication of this patrimony is configured as "dissemination action of the knowledge of the good" and it involves the identification of specific tools and operating procedures, from time to time chosen *ad hoc*, according to themes and purposes that direct both the design aspect both the realization of images production. In fact, the development of popular images implies the definition of a sequence of operations that aim to realize, with awareness, effective visual products. The identification of the procedural paths and the forecasting of the methods of implementation involve a critical approach to the theoretical and practical foundations of images and the recognition of high professional skills.

First of all, in order to define realization methods and procedures it is necessary to have a clear understanding of the image construction process, from the initial phase of data acquisition to the last one, that is to say, the diffusion.

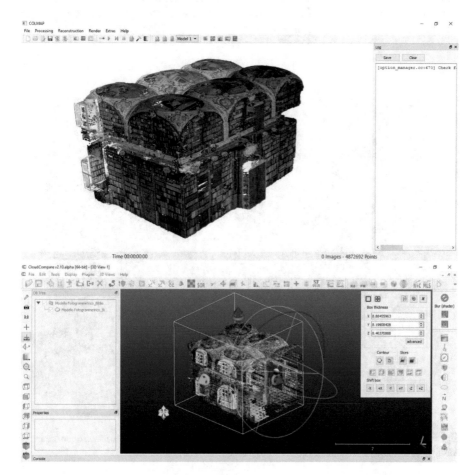

Fig. 4. Image-based 3D digital model construction made via *Colmap* and *Cloud Compare* software: screenshots of processing phases (F. Aassila, E. Fratton, F. Magaraggia, E. Margesin).

The procedural analogy with the thematic design process, of which Ugo (1994) writes, speaking about surveying, is clear; here it is to be understood in its widest sense of knowledge of the artifact that allows to acquire and transfer 'information'. This is what is demanded in the moment in which we want to divulge a work; knowing the object to communicate and replicate this knowledge through images.

The operations that take place belong to the scope of the survey, which can be recognized here in its declination of qualitative cognitive importance of the built heritage; for this reason, in the drafting of the work process the three macro phases of data acquisition, processing and communication can be recognized, operative procedures that require specific and specialist skills, both theoretical and practical. Thus it becomes necessary the design of the complex path of image processing by identifying the most suitable ways of collecting information, processing sources and disseminating outputs because each choice must be the result of a weighted decision about it. The clarity of the result to be pursued makes it possible to trace the most appropriate path to reach it: topics, tools, objectives.

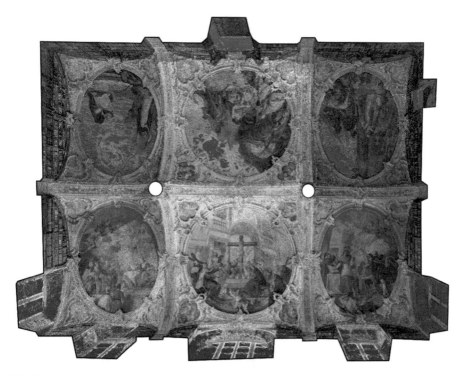

Fig. 5. Perspective zenithal view of the point cloud produced via *Cloud Compare* software (F. Aassila, E. Fratton, F. Magaraggia, E. Margesin).

ViC-CH experience has been exactly developed from this reflection. The theme of the final product requested to the students was "unveiling" the Library of the Major Priest Seminary of Brixen: let us know a lesser-known architectural object hidden within a well-known one. "Stories" have been designed at different scales, following multiple levels of reading and designed for different modes of diffusion and use: videos, virtual tours and navigable panoramas, shared paths, website, qualitative 3D models, printing products for dissemination. After the selection of outputs to be managed by representation models, the methods of acquisition and processing to be implemented were identified. The conscious use of the available equipment has allowed us to carry out a targeted data collection campaign: outdoor and indoor shooting videos by drones; general and detailed photographic recognition[2]; photographic sockets to produce a 3D image-based model; photographic sockets, with tripod and panoramic head, for the elaboration of a spherical panorama; photographic sockets with spherical digital camera[3].

Fig. 6. Construction of a 360° panorama. Acquisition with Manfrotto QTUR spherical 303SPH tripod and head, and Canon EOS 600D reflex digital camera; processing by *Hugin* 2017 software (M. Odorizzi, S. Orsolin).

'Themed' acquisition has unambiguously defined the workflow of data processing and manipulation. The processing of static and dynamic images was carried out with the help of open source applications, according to procedures that respect the criteria for constructing images and which identify the constitutive elements of the image in the geometric structure, in the graphic configuration and in the communication techniques. Final products, obtained through this process, record and show the implicit programming of the followed procedural path and the 'measurement' of the obtained results proves that the control of the ideational and productive process, of the image processing modality (determination of the structure, identification of tools and processing techniques, models construction) and their realization allows the achievement of an effective and aware final product, a mediation between an efficient communication message and a conscious use of data and tools.

---

[2] There are two UAV systems used: a standard DJI Phantom III quadricopter with a 12 Mpx camera and a 2.7 K video resolution; a DJI Spark LT 300 gr quadricopter with 12 Mpx camera and Full HD video resolution (1920 × 1080).

[3] The digital photography equipment used are: a Canon EOS 600D digital SLR camera with 18 MPX camera and Full HD video resolution (1920 × 1080); a Nikon D5300 digital SLR camera with 24 Mpx sensor and Full HD video resolution (1920 × 1080); a Manfrotto tripod with a traditional head and a Manfrotto QTUR spherical 303SPH panoramic head; a Ricoh Theta V spherical camera with tripod and steady cam support; three iPad pro 12.9″ with standard and third-party app.

Fig. 7. Photographs by Ricoh Theta V spherical camera and steady cam support. Above, internal recovery of the library (A. Luigini); below, outdoor shot of the courtyard (A. Tavella).

5   Communicating Built Heritage: Open-Source Tools for Image Processing

Nowadays a correct communication of historical heritage is conditioned in equal measure both by a full awareness of the procedures and criteria for the construction of effective images, and by a technological know-how of digital tools for their use. Moreover, in a historical moment in which the free accessibility to historical-archival heritage contents as well as the will of the public administrations to free themselves from the use of commercial software have become increasingly binding, the experience gained within ViC-CH has tried to respond by promoting the experimentation of contemporary multimedia languages, also suitable for shared fruition, and supporting the use of free and open source software thanks to the construction of skills useful for the conscious use of these digital tools.

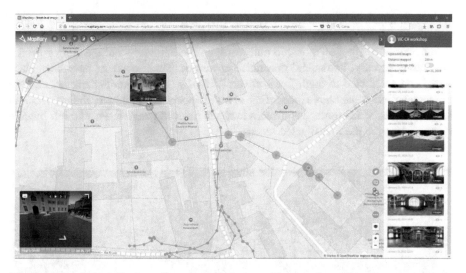

Fig. 8. Construction of urban tale: spherical photographic shots located on the map using the sharing and participation *Mapillary* application (F. Magaraggia, E. Margesin, M. Redaelli, A. Tavella).

As mentioned previously, the basic objective was to illustrate to tomorrow's professionals the majority of the consolidated and innovative ways of communicating and enjoying cultural heritage: from traditional printed brochures to static synthesis images, from aerial shots through UAV systems to popular videos, from immersive panoramic images to participated maps. All forms able to bring a wider and wider audience to the historical-artistic heritage with new eyes.

The first area of study concerned the digital tools for the management of vector graphics; the answer to this need was provided thanks to the use of the *Inkscape*[4] application. It is, in fact, an open source vector graphics editor that uses the native SVG (Scalable Vector Graphics) format. This tool has been used mainly for the construction of the graphic layout of posters and brochure and, in particular, for the construction of an infographic image aimed at illustrating the results of the workshop and the contributions of each participant.

The only vector graphics, however, cannot solve all the needs related to the processing of a digital image: with *GIMP*[5], an open source, multiplatform and freely developable software, in fact, it was possible to provide the participants with an effective application for the management of raster graphics. The use of this program allowed to become familiar with the basic graphic aspects (image formats, color models, tools for photo-editing and photo-compositing), both for the construction of new images and for the manipulation of acquired photographs by digital cameras.

---

[4] *Inkscape*, version 0.92, available at https://inkscape.org/it/.

[5] *GIMP*, version 0.92, available at https://www.gimp.org/.

The photographic acquisition did not involve only terrestrial procedures but, thanks to the use of UAV systems, it was possible to describe from an aerial viewpoint, with shoots and videos, the relationship both between the Seminary and the city of Brixen and among Library, books and decorative apparatus. These contents have been elaborated and assembled through free software *VideoPad*[6]; a program characterized by a simple interface to assemble, according to a previously projected storyboard, archival images, shoots, video footage and audio tracks in order to generate a useful informative video to describe the investigated places.

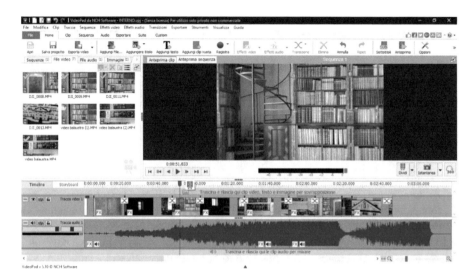

Fig. 9. Synthesis construction movie about library internal space: screenshot of the processing phases using the *VideoPad* application (F. Aassila, D. Bassetti, B. Fusari, F. Magaraggia, L. Pederzini, M. Redaelli).

Photography and communication of cultural heritage establish a pair of necessary dependence, especially if one looks at the great potential offered by photographic acquisition tools and digital processing procedures. The workshop, in fact, devoted ample space to the deepening of the techniques of acquisition and processing of photographic images in order to obtain 3D digital visual models and immersive photographs. In the first case the sequence of operations for the construction of a 3D image-based model was illustrated thanks to the use of the *Colmap*[7] and *CloudCompare*[8] programs. In the case of immersive images, that is to say, 360° panoramic images through which the user has the sensation of being inside the space to study, two

---

[6] *NCH Software VideoPad*, version 5.10, available at https://www.nchsoftware.com/software/it/video.html.

[7] *Colmap*, version 3.4, available at https://colmap.github.io/.

[8] *CloudCompare*, version 2.9.1, available at http://www.danielgm.net/cc/.

alternatives have been proposed: one, more rigorous, based on the stitching operation carried out with the *Hugin*[9] software in order to obtain the panorama following the assembly of numerous single frames; another, more expedient, based solely on the acquisition by camera for spherical photographs and videos such as Ricoh Theta V. In order to offer richer cognitive routes, the web-based software *Alvire*[10] and *Marzipano*[11] were deepened, with the objective to create virtual tours, in other words, spherical images placed in connection through sensitive points (hotspots) according to a precise cognitive path.

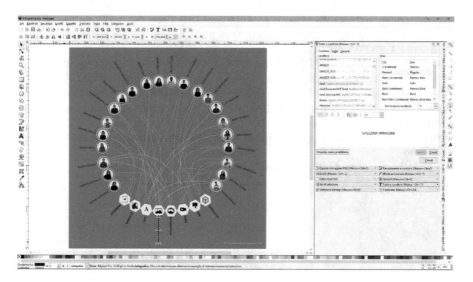

Fig. 10. Infographics about authors and results of the Euregio ViC-CH workshop experience 2018.

The last act of the training phases has led students to experiment with some procedures for sharing produced outputs; a simple yet easily accessible hypertext created with *WordPress*[12], a software platform for personal publishing and content management, and the design of guided paths to use urban fragment surrounding the Seminar through the use of *Mapillary*[13], a web service based on crowdsourcing methods, for sharing conventional and geolocalized panoramic photographs.

[9] *Hugin*, version 2017.0.0, available at http://hugin.sourceforge.net/.

[10] *Alvire*, available at http://www.alvire.com/.

[11] *Marzipano*, available at http://www.marzipano.net.

[12] *WordPress*, version 4.9.4, available at https://it.wordpress.org/.

[13] *Mapillary*, available at https://www.mapillary.com/.

References

Ballarin M (2014) Software gratuito per l'Architettura e l'Urbanistica. Maggioli Editore, Santarcangelo

Baur J (1975) Das Brixner Priesterseminar, Ein Blick in die Geschichte. Brixen

Bortolotti A, Calidoni M, Mascheroni S, Mattozzi I (2008) Per l'educazione al patrimonio culturale: 22 tesi. FrancoAngeli, Milan

Brilliant R (1987) Narrare per immagini. Giunti Editore, Firenze

Chiarenza S (2017) E-learning tools in the teaching of drawing: a frontier between didactics and research. Territories and frontiers of representation, 14–16 Sept, Naples

Empler T (2008) Software libero per la progettazione. DEI Tipografia del Genio Civile, Rome

Flachenecker H, Heiss H, Obermair H (2000) Stadt und Hochstift. Città e Principato. Abteilung Denkmalpflege Südtiroler Landesarchiv

Fuchs B, Heiss H, Milesi C, Pfeifer G (2004) Die Geschichte. Athesia/Tappeiner, Bolzano

Gelmi J (2007) Pietas et scientia. 400 Jahre Priesterseminar Brixen, 1607–2007. Weger

Gruber K (1994) Il Seminario Maggiore di Bressanone. Tappeiner Editore, Bolzano

Gummerer H (1994) Brixen 1867–1882 Die Aufzeichnungen des Fäbermeisters Franz Schwaighofer. Folio Verlag, Bolzano

Heiss H, Milesi C, Roilo C (2006) Brixen Kunst, Kultur, Gesellschaft. Athesia/Tappeiner, Bolzano

Ugo V (1994) Fondamenti della rappresentazione architettonica. Esculapio

Augmented Reality

Remediating the Historical City. Ubiquitous Augmented Reality for Cultural Heritage Enhancement

S. Brusaporci[1(✉)], F. Graziosi[2], F. Franchi[2], and P. Maiezza[1]

[1] Department of Civil, Construction-Architectural and Environmental
Engineering, University of L'Aquila, Via Giovanni Gronchi 18,
67100 L'Aquila, Italy
stefano.brusaporci@univaq.it

[2] Department of Information Engineering, Computer Science and Mathematics,
University of L'Aquila, Via Vetoio, Coppito, 67100 L'Aquila, Italy

Abstract. The chapter presents the outcomes of an experience that rises from the realization of L'Aquila Smart City (Italy). Its realization roots on the possibly given by the realization of a smart tunnel with a net of optical fibers and by 5G mobile networking. This system of real time and diffused data computing and transmission allows the project of a ubiquitous Augmented Reality (AR) application. It favors the relationship between buildings and urban spaces with different kind of information, mainly of visual nature, such as 3D models, images, videos, texts. This interdisciplinary study gives the opportunity to develop a theoretical and methodological reflection on AR as mixed-media and on the relation that it establishes between tangible heritage and information, also in relation with the current post-digital approach to cultural heritage.

Keywords: Augmented Reality · Digital culture · Cultural heritage

1 The Reality-Based Turn of Virtuality

With the rising of ICT, digital systems have become an inescapable component of our everyday life. Instruments have changed and are continually changing the media, according to a pervasive dimension of continuous interrelation (Brusaporci 2017b). In our on-line state (The Onlife Manifesto 2015), the concept of "digital natives" and "digital migrants" (Prensky 2001) tends to blur (Jenkins 2007). It is not simply for the advancing of generations but also because – on one hand – devices and applications have immersed the everyday life of everybody in a ubiquitous digital dimension, and because – on the other hand – the visual and tactile way of devices use has become intuitive, easy and accessible for everyone. Consequently, the way we perceive and interact with the environment that surrounds us has changed and it is still changing.

In this context, the visual media plays a central role. For example, Virtual Reality (Sutherland 1965) aims to a total immersion in an artificial environment, where computer-generated perceptions – first of all visual ones – aims to reduce replaced external ones. Obviously, the synthetic images are seductive, according to an aesthetics

© Springer Nature Switzerland AG 2019
A. Luigini (Ed.): EARTH 2018, AISC 919, pp. 305–313, 2019.
https://doi.org/10.1007/978-3-030-12240-9_33

end in itself, a charm of visual seduction (Brusaporci 2018). These reflections are interrelated with the so-called "visual turn", a typical aspect of our time (Mitchell 1994). According to Mitchell (1996), this focusing on "visuality" can produce an "iconic panic" of modernity, that is a fetishist obsession: images produce increasingly macroscopic social reactions, often reactivating ancient fears and ecstasies.

Baudrillard (1976) predicted that the reality would be threatened by the simulation, with the rise of the "Hyperreality", or the "more real" of the real, with the spectators who would no longer be able to distinguish the "replica" from the "reality". However, from post-modern experiences, this phenomenon has developed in a more complex way than Baudrillard anticipated. The current "Post-digital" dimension (Berry and Dieter 2015; Brusaporci 2017a) has among its roots the phenomenon of "New Realism" (Ferraris 2011). According to which, the lesson of the post-modern and of the hermeneutic is not lost, but it reassesses the observation of reality understood as an actual presence, on the basis of a resumption of importance of the role of perception, that becomes a reference of an external with which the observer is called to confront.

In this cultural context, reality comes back in a role of primary importance; nevertheless, it does not aim to overcome digitality. In this sense, thanks to ICT and digital apps – in particular with reference to Mixed and Augmented Reality –, Hyperreality moves toward what we could define with a neologism "Hypervirtuality" – or "post-virtuality" –, i.e. "over the virtual". People perceive reality together with synthetic images, but they are conscious of what they are looking, and of the different nature of the objects they are seeing through digital applications (Fig. 1).

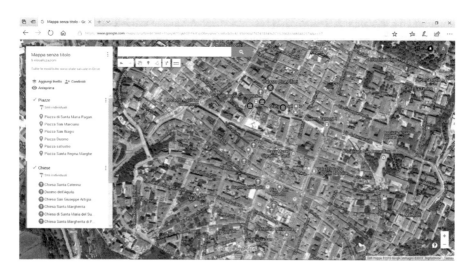

Fig. 1. The interactive map of the historic center of L'Aquila indicating the Churches and squares.

2   Augmented Reality as Mixed-Media

According to the assumption that all media are "mixed media" (Mitchell 1986), the concept of "mixed reality" – as defined by Milgram and Kishino (1994) – returns central. It describes the different states of the digital representation within the "Virtual Continuum", mainly described by six states, between the "only-real" and the "completely virtual environments". Their concept of "Extent of Presence Methapor" is of particular interest, related to the quality of the perception, or to the level of "presence feeling" of the user compared to the perceived environment. As Murray (1997) points out, in every representation the intrinsic aesthetic quality of the medium is very important, and therefore in every medium a stimulating narrative similar to a virtual reality can be experienced, because our brain is programmed to tune with the stories according to an intensity that can exclude the world around us (p. 98).

Recalling the idea of "Re-Mediation" of media by Bolter and Grusin (1999), there is a double correlation between "Immediacy" and "Hypermediacy": VR and graphical interfaces favor the logic of transparent immediacy, that is "[…] the user is no longer aware of confronting a medium, but instead stands in an immediate relationship to the contents of that medium" (p. 24). On the other hand, media multiplies itself: "The multiple representations inside the windows (text, graphics, video) create a heterogeneous space, as they compete for the view's attention. Icons, menus, and toolbars add further layers of visual and verbal meaning. […] Unlike a perspective painting or three-dimensional computer graphic, this windowed interface does not attempt to unify the space around any one point of view. Instead, each text window defines its own verbal, each graphic window its own visual, point of view […] The multiplicity of windows and the heterogeneity of their contents mean that the user is repeatedly brought back into contact with the interface, which she learns to read just as she would read any hypertext. She oscillates between manipulating the windows and examining their contents, just as she oscillates between looking at a hypertext as a texture of links and looking through the links to the textual units as language" (p. 32–33).

Augmented Reality AR applications increasingly widespread in the field of cultural heritage and they are promising of important developments (Bonacini 2014; Clini et al. 2016). Augmented reality establishes a game of re-mediation between reality and digitality (Brusaporci et al. 2017). Digitality certainly plays an important role thanks to visual fascination – augmented by the amazing presence of reality (instead of virtuality) – and it is able to capture the user's attention evoking edutainment mechanisms. However, reality does not blur in a game of mirrors with digitality, but maintains its ontological status: with AR the eyes of the user don't replace the reality itself. It is not a new form of "Hyperreality", but AR can be intended as a new form of Digital Heritage (UNESCO 2003): it is a DH related to reality, with the superimposition of visual information to the world. Information becomes an attribute of reality – an adjective – useful to increase its knowledge, understanding, and enhancement (Fig. 2).

In this sense, AR is a media, not a mere support, but it is a network for relations (Brusaporci 2015).

Fig. 2. Augmented Reality application: screenshot of the realization process (a); visualization of the unrealized façade of the church of Santa Margherita (17th century) via mobile device (b).

3   Ubiquitous AR for L'Aquila Smart City

The project INCIPICT (Innovating City Planning through Information and Communications Technology), funded by the Interministerial Committee for Economic Planning (CIPE) with the intention of offering an instrument to "support productive activities and research" in the process of the post-earthquake reconstruction of L'Aquila, aims at the development of solutions oriented to a living laboratory for smart city applications by leveraging on specific research skills of the local University and on proper vocations of the city.

Coordinated by prof. Fabio Graziosi, the project has an interdisciplinary management committee, with prof. Stefano Brusaporci as coordinator of activities related to the enhancement of cultural heritage through ICT technologies.

Through the use of Information and Communications Technology (ICT), we want to create interactive applications aimed both at scholars and not, which make it possible to enjoy the architecture and urban spaces, thus facilitating the interpretation and communication of the values of L'Aquila's cultural heritage.

The INCIPICT project is well integrated with the 5G experimentation in progress in the city of L'Aquila. The 5th generation mobile networks, abbreviated 5G, is the proposed next telecommunications standard beyond the current 4G/IMT-Advanced standard. 5G planning aims at higher capacity than current 4G, allowing a higher density of mobile broadband users, and supporting device-to-device, ultra-reliable, and massive machine type communications and also aims at lower latency than 4G and lower battery consumption, for better implementation of the Internet of things, the future where all our online-enabled objects will quietly pass on data to our tech overlord of choice.

Facilitating the use of mobile networks by connected or autonomous cars, remotely controlled industrial robots, telehealth systems, and smart city infrastructure are also all expected to figure large in 5G thinking. AR applications for cultural heritage, originally proposed as one of the pilot actions of the INCIPICT project, have been considered one of the potential killer applications for 5G and a specific use case has been designed for the ongoing 5G trials in L'Aquila.

4 AR-UNIVAQ

The experimentation of Virtual/Augmented Reality is based on the definition of the following main functionalities: 3D streaming service for VR viewers; Service of reconstruction of 3D environments for VR/AR viewers and smartphones; VR navigation system based on 3D engines.

A fundamental component for the creation of services aimed at enhancing cultural heritage through ICT is the definition of methodologies suitable for the dynamic and sustainable creation of three-dimensional models to be used in VR/AR mode.

AR/VR applications based on these platforms make it possible to correlate the views to the current state of the places, overlapping both didactic and user-shared information. Compared to classical applications of augmented/virtual reality, the proposed applications are characterized by the requirement to dynamically integrate heterogeneous data, produced by different sources distributed throughout the city.

For these reasons, the development of these applications involves all the layers that characterize the architecture of the system, from the infrastructural or network ones to that of retrieving, processing and interpretation data, publication, up to the application services by which the user interacts directly.

Since the main purpose for augmented reality is to enhance the reality with virtual content, it is important to make sure that virtual objects are correctly registered to the real scene. This can help users view the virtual content as part of the real world.

Correct registration can be obtained by estimating the pose of the camera (for video see-through) or user's view point (for optical see-through).

The registration process usually consists of two parts. In the first part, fiducial markers or feature points are detected, using marker-based methods or marker-less methods (Huang et al. 2013). Then the second part estimates the pose and map 3D virtual objects through proper projective geometry.

Maker-less method is the one chosen for the experimentation. It helps the AR system detects the scene in a more natural way.

In the feature extraction step, the goal is to find areas of interest in input image that can be served as unique and reliable markers.

There are lots of feature detection and extraction algorithms based on different single or combination of features, such as edges, corners, blobs, ridges. For example, corner-based detectors focus on the rapid change of image gradients, using the first or second derivative of gradients along different directions.

As part of this thought, an application of AR apt to a ubiquitous use in the historical center of the city was developed (Fig. 3).

The use case related to the enhancement of cultural heritage through ICT technologies can have 2 different behaviors: on the one hand an historical building, a museum, a monument or an archaeological site require the deployment of an environmental sensors network for monitoring, that define the use case as mMTC. On the other hand, considering the possibility of extending the tourist experience by exploiting the potential of VR and AR solutions, the same use case is connoted as capable of representing the eMBB segment of the 5G scenario.

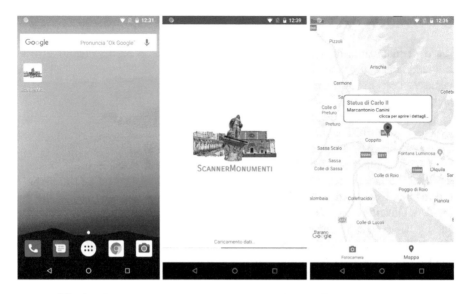

Fig. 3. *"ScannerMonumenti"*: Augmented Reality app for mobile devices.

5   AR for the Historic City

The historical city is characterized by profound phenomena of modification and stratification. Therefore, the city is constantly recreated both as a result of exceptional events - such as earthquakes - and the daily action of the communities.

Therefore, the study of the city history takes on particular importance. It is carried out through two fundamental approaches: firstly, the architectural survey of buildings and urban spaces and the correlation with historical information - previous studies and archive documentation -; secondly, the realization of synchronic and diachronic historical reconstructions, related to significant moments of the transformations and representative of the values, of the events and of the architectural cultures that occurred over time.

The goal is not only a virtual reconstruction of scenarios no longer existing, but it is a scientific process for the history study by means of a temporal sequence of events that led to the current configuration.

The augmented reality makes it possible to relate, on-site, cultural assets with different types of information, such as archival documents or 3D models of past configurations. This allows us to understand the current historical values, and this knowledge is a precondition of the conservation of architectural and urban assets.

New digital models of city use are developed, which facilitate the understanding of the historical transformations of the urban fabric. Through the use of 3D models, it is possible to visualize the architectures in their different historical phases, reconstructed on the basis of the survey and of in-depth historical-critical analysis.

A key role is played by the experiences of mixed reality by which the user can easily access the heterogeneous content about the cultural heritage (multimedia or not), which are part of the information system on which the entire application is based (Fig. 4).

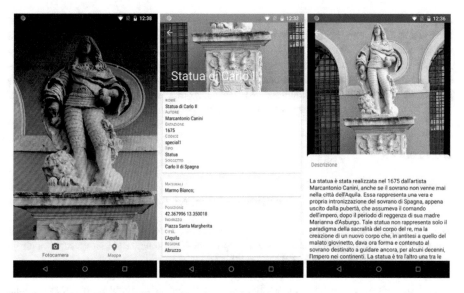

Fig. 4. *"ScannerMonumenti"* App: Framing of cultural asset by camera (a); recognition of the asset and visualization of the information sheet (b); description of the artifact (c).

Since the knowledge of a place is intertwined with the culture of who live in those spaces, this interactive system is a valid instrument for the formation of a new collective awareness of places, after the forced interruption due to the earthquake.

The 5G technology will be used to show virtual reconstruction of the city before the earthquake and also in different era via Augmented Reality and Virtual Reality. Those reconstructions will use the high bandwidth offered by the 5G technology.

6 Conclusions

Digital applications and ICT renew the relationship between people and "images". It is a new perspective, the so called "pictorial turn" (Mitchell 1994; Mitchell 2017; Purgar 2017), where visual paradigms merge with verbal ones, without conflicts but in cohabitation and collaboration. In this context, all media become "mixed media", and Augmented Reality applications are paradigmatic of this phenomenon (Brusaporci 2018).

With ICT, the role and presence of the real and the virtual are combined but not confused. According to this new relationship with visual experiences, synthetic images marries the reality born ones through media devices (Brusaporci 2017a). The screen allows this meeting, with the enrichment of heritage with information without touching, altering, or put in danger its materiality, that is its intrinsic constitutive matter that bear and embody historic and aesthetic values. AR consent a new dimension of IoT, without physical modifications of heritage, without cybercultural hybridizations. A line toward forms of Smart Heritage and Smart Places (Brusaporci et al. 2018), where ubiquitous communication favors a discussion on cultural values, but material (i.e. historic) values are preserved.

Acknowledgements. The research has received funding from the Italian Government under Cipe resolution n. 135 (Dec. 21, 2012), project INnovating City Planning through Information and Communication Technologies (INCIPICT).

Although the paper was conceived unitedly, S. Brusaporci wrote the paragraphs "The reality-based turn of virtuality", "Augmented reality as mixed-media" and "Conclusions; F. Graziosi is the author of paragraph "Ubiquitous AR for L'Aquila smart city"; F. Franchi wrote "AR-UNIVAQ" while P. Maiezza is the author of the paragraph "AR for the historic city".

References

Baudrillard J (1976) L'echange symbolique et la mort. Gallimard, Paris

Berry DM, Dieter M (eds) (2015) Postdigital Aesthetics. Art, Computation and Design. Palgrave Macmillan, Basingstoke

Bolter JD, Grusin R (1999) Remediation – Understanding New Media. MIT Press, Cambridge

Bonacini E, (2014) La realtà aumentata e le app culturali in Italia: storie da un matrimonio in mobilità. Il capitale culturale, vol IX, pp 89–121

Brusaporci S (2015) On visual computing for architectural heritage. In: Brusaporci S (ed) Handbook of research on emerging digital tools for architectural surveying, modeling, and representation. IGI Global, Hershey, pp 94–123

Brusaporci S, Ruggieri G, Sicuranza F, Maiezza P (2017) Augmented reality for historical storytelling. The INCIPICT project for the reconstruction of tangible and intangible image of L'Aquila historical centre. In: Proceedings IMMAGINI?, 27–28 Nov, Brixen. ISSN 2504-3900

Brusaporci S (2017a) Della rappresentazione in epoca post-digitale. In: Luigini A (ed) Lineis Describere. Sette seminari tra rappresentazione e formazione. Libria, Melfi, pp 47–59

Brusaporci S (2017b) Digital innovations in architectural heritage conservation: emerging research and opportunities. IGI Global, Hershey

Brusaporci S (2018) Advanced mixed heritage: a visual turn through digitality and reality of architecture. Int. J. Comput. Methods Heritage Sci. 2:40–60 ISSN: 2473-5345

Brusaporci S, Maiezza P, Tata A (2018) For a cultural-based smart city. In: Salerno R (ed) Rappresentazione materiale/immateriale - Drawing as (in) tangible, pp 73–80

Clini P, Quattrini R, Frontoni E, Pierdicca R, Nespeca R (2016) Real/not real: pseudo-holography and augmented reality applications for cultural heritage. In: Ippolito A, Cigola M (eds) Handbook of research on emerging technologies for digital preservation and information modeling. IGI Global, Hershey, pp 201–227

Ferraris M (2011) Manifesto of New Realism. SUNY Press, Albany

Huang Z, Hui P, Peylo C, Chatzopoulos D (2013) Mobile augmented reality survey: a bottom-up approach. arXiv preprint, arXiv:1309.4413

Jenkins H (2007) Reconsidering Digital Immigrants. www.henryjenkins.org/2007/12/reconsidering_digital_immigran.html. Accessed 15 Nov 2016

Milgram P, Kishino F (1994) A taxonomy of mixed reality visual displays. IEICE Trans. Inf. Syst. E77-D(12):1321–1329

Mitchell WJT (1986) Iconology: image, text, ideology. University of Chicago Press, Chicago

Mitchell WJT (1994) Picture Theory. University of Chicago Press, Chicago

Mitchel WJT (1996) What do Pictures 'Really' Want? October 77:71–82

Mitchell WJT (2017) Pictorial Turn. Raffaello Cortina Editore, Milan

Murray J (1997) Hamlet on the holodeck. The future of narrative in cyberspace. MIT Press, Cambridge

Prensky M (2001) Digital natives, digital immigrants part 1. Horizon 9(5):1–6

Purgar K (ed) (2017) W.J.T. Mitchell's Image Theory. Routledge, London

Sutherland I (1965) The ultimate display. Proc IFIP Congr 2:506–508

The Onlife Manifesto (2015). https://ec.europa.eu/digital-agenda/en/onlife-manifesto. Accessed 15 Nov 2016

UNESCO (2003) Charter on the Preservation of the Digital Heritage

Digital Interactive Baroque Atria in Turin: A Project Aimed to Sharing and Enhancing Cultural Heritage

V. Palma[1], R. Spallone[2(⊠)], and M. Vitali[2]

[1] FULL, Politecnico di Torino, Via Agostino da Montefeltro 3,
10134 Turin, Italy
valerio.palma@polito.it
[2] Department of Architecture and Design, Politecnico di Torino,
Viale Mattioli 39, 10125 Turin, Italy
{roberta.spallone,marco.vitali}@polito.it

Abstract. Turin Baroque atria, characterized by complex vaulted systems, are a unique case in the architecture of the time. These atria have been realized with particular spatial schemes that present: unified spaces, absence of intermediate pillars, and composite vaults made of brickwork masonry. Three main types of vaulted systems established: the "star-shaped" vaults, the "planterian" vaults, and the "a fascioni" vaults. It is a Cultural Heritage of great interest but it is little known and visited by the public, especially if intended as an urban system. To spread knowledge of over 70 examples found, and to enhance Cultural Heritage Tourism, the authors are setting up a digital collection and AR experiences that present the results of surveys and geometric interpretations of these artifacts. The aim of this action is mixing and merging real and virtual documentary materials and fruition experiences.

Keywords: Baroque atria · Vaulted systems · Digital modeling ·
Digital archives · Augmented reality

1 Introduction

Between the 17th and 18th century in Turin, a highly innovative architectural season emerged, which, in the field of civil architecture, demonstrated unprecedented and pleasing spatial configurations of access spaces as well as distributions of noble buildings. These were conceived as a spectacular fulcrum at the acme of the ceremonial entrance.

The atria realized with such spatial schemes present unified spaces, absence of intermediate pillars, and spaces covered by composite vaults made of brickwork masonry. These were characterized by a remarkable geometric complexity, which gave them dynamism and airiness, allowing at the same time, whenever necessary, the use of rather small rises (Fig. 1).

The interest of these spaces has been evidenced, among others, in the pages of Norberg-Schulz dedicated to the late Baroque palace, in which the Turin solutions are widely described (Norberg-Schulz 1980).

© Springer Nature Switzerland AG 2019
A. Luigini (Ed.): EARTH 2018, AISC 919, pp. 314–325, 2019.
https://doi.org/10.1007/978-3-030-12240-9_34

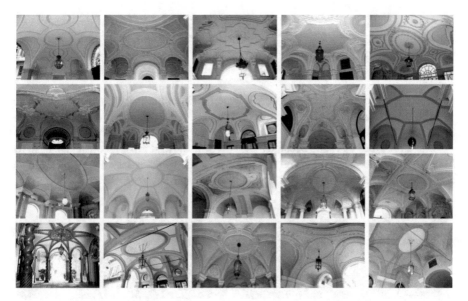

Fig. 1. Star-shaped vaults, planterian vaults and "a fascioni" vaults in the atria of the historic city centre of Turin

Three main types of vaulted systems established: the "star-shaped" vaults (following the Guarinian model), the "planterian" vaults (so called from the name of their inventor Gian Giacomo Plantery) and the "a fascioni" vaults.

2   The Vaults in Turin Baroque Atria as an Architectural Paradigm

The first example of star-shaped vaults was designed by Guarini in the atrium of Palazzo Carignano (from 1678), which represents a baroque evolution of the lunettes vault on rectangular plan, typical in the Renaissance palaces.

The star-shaped vaults triggered the phenomenon of diffusion of the unitary complex vaults and were built in a small number of cases. They generally had an elliptical or oval plan covered by a main surface cut by radial planes and completed by groins that generates a radio-centric scheme.

The planterian vaults conversely had a great spread in the historic city, from the first decade of the Eighteenth Century. They were mostly set on a rectangular plan and were formed by a main vault in which the axial groins and the angular vaults are inserted, creating schemes in which the two longitudinal and transverse axes prevailed.

The "a fascioni" vaults were already presented in the Architettura Civile by Guarini (posthumous 1737) who attributed to himself the paternity of this kind of which make most noble sight, and leave great spaces for painting. These were designed to circumscribe the space of very wide rooms in areas to be covered with single vaults separated by large arches. They were built at the same time of the planterian ones, representing an alternative adopted in a dozen of palaces by famous architects as Juvarra.

While it is possible to observe a sequential and evolutionary process between the star-shaped and planterian vaults, the "a fascioni" vaults develop as a parallel phenomenon to the latter.

The three types of vaults became in a short time the system of recurring cover in the halls of the noble palaces located in the areas of the three expansions of the baroque city and in the reshaping tissues of the ancient square city (Fig. 2).

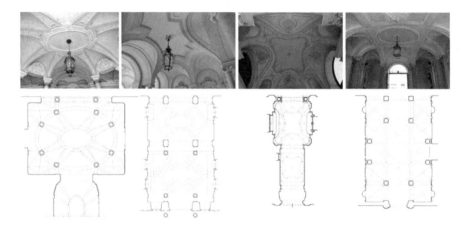

Fig. 2. Star-shaped vaults (Guarini), vaults attributed to Plantery, vaults reinterpretation of the planterian scheme, "a fascioni" vaults: the plan analysis highlights the different spatial configuration shown by the photographs. From left to right: Palazzo Carignano, Palazzo Cavour, Palazzo Riche di Coassolo, Palazzo Coardi di Carpenetto

A recognition recently realized by the authors of this paper (Spallone and Vitali 2017a) has allowed to catalog in the historical city center over seventy atria having such characteristics, highlighting the ability of the Turin architects both to invent new solutions and to propose a series of variations on the theme (Fig. 3).

In this previous work, a short record describes each atrium, which has been localized on the digital map of the city and has been identified through the current address and, when documented, the family name of the owner, the name of the designer, the date of construction, and the archival and bibliographic references. Moreover, the main dimensions of the atrium, impost, and keystone height of the vault allow categorizing them in exceptional, large, medium, and small. Finally, an extended text shows the relationships between the atrium and the palace, the geometrical interpretation of the vault, and the architectural features.

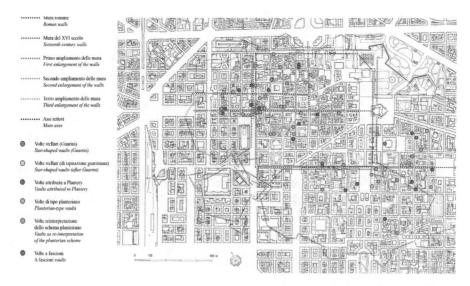

Legend (reading from top to bottom, left column):

Mura romane
Roman walls

Mura del XVI secolo
Sixteenth century walls

Primo ampliamento delle mura
First enlargement of the walls

Secondo ampliamento delle mura
Second enlargement of the walls

Terzo ampliamento delle mura
Third enlargement of the walls

Assi rettori
Main axes

Volte stellari (Guarini)
Star-shaped vaults (Guarini)

Volte stellari (di ispirazione guariniana)
Star-shaped vaults (after Guarini)

Volte attribuite a Plantery
Vaults attributed to Plantery

Volte di tipo planteriano
Planterian-type vaults

Volte reinterpretazione
dello schema planteriano
*Vaults as re-interpretation
of the planterian scheme*

Volte a fasci005
A fascioni vaults

Fig. 3. Identification of the different types of atria analyzed within the historical city centre of Turin, with representation of the expansion phases of the fortified walls

The atria identified as formal archetypes and some of the most interesting variants have been more in depth studied, through the survey, intended as open system of knowledge including documentary and archival research, measurement and the two and three-dimensional graphic synthesis of the cognitive and interpretative process.

In particular, the recognition of the geometric models underlying the formal conception, indispensable after the geometric systematization of the vaults by Guarini (Guarini 1671, 1674, 1737), led to the creation of digital interpretative models of the constitutive elements and the composition processes of the vaulted systems.

Furthermore, real themes and lines of shaping inspiration have been recognized which have led to the hypothesis of different fil rouge of connection between an atrium and the other. This last aspect has made possible to imagine possible routes within the historical city, already experimented on a theoretical level and in didactic function in the PhD course in Architectural and Landscape Heritage and in the Laboratory of Drawing and Survey of the Degree course in Architecture of the Politecnico di Torino.

Indeed, in 2017 the authors were required to set a route in the baroque Turin addressed to specialists and lovers of mathematics by the editor of "The Mathematical Tourist", published by the international journal The Mathematical Intelligencer (Spallone and Vitali 2017b).

This led us to think of creating other thematic routes dedicated not only to an audience of specialists, but also to citizenry making it aware and participating to a common heritage, and to the tourists who, more and more, are looking for unusual cultural itineraries. Therefore, it is a Cultural Heritage of great interest but it is little known and visited by the public, especially if intended as a system.

3   Project Lines for Enhancing Cultural Tourism

Using the tools offered by the digital revolution we are working in the direction of an enhancement, valorization and sharing of this heritage, mixing and merging real and virtual documentary materials and fruition experiences.

Indeed, the desire and the will to communicate, share and spread the values of this heritage and the results of the investigations carried out were the motivations for undertaking two different and complementary actions, currently under development.

On the one hand, the collection is being inserted into a website dedicated to the communication and dissemination of Cultural Heritage Tourism; on the other, AR applications which allow, during on-site visits, to display short descriptions, icono-graphic documents, bibliographic references, geometric models of the vaults, and survey drawings, as well as to connect to the portal for further deepening, are being experimented (Fig. 4).

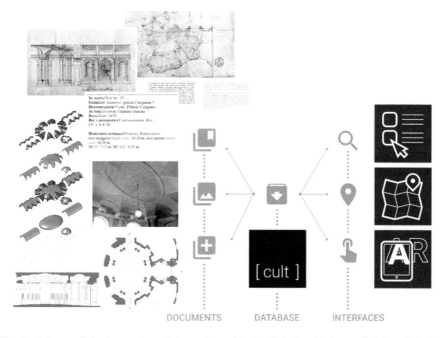

Fig. 4. Scheme of the interaction of the project with the digital archiving tool Cult, originally developed by the University of Padua. The input documents are texts, data sheets, photographs, architectural drawings, interpretative 3D models and archive materials (examples on Palazzo Carignano). The output interfaces are meant to make the Cult database accessible through different means, such as web pages, GIS tools and mobile apps with AR capabilities.

We believe that these two tools have to be considered for their synergistic poten-tials, so their features have to be accurately set.

Moreover, we would like to involve users more effectively, tracing their paths and asking them to share their experiences. They will then be able to make their personal itineraries available for visits, their comments and suggestions, photographs, etc. They will also be able to suggest useful materials for the implementation of the website pages, which will be evaluated and eventually added through the monitoring and management operations. In this sense we intend to stimulate interest in the work both by a public that is simply interested in Cultural Tourism, and by the community of scholars involved in specific research topics.

As a corollary of the proposal, there is the objective of using open source software and low-cost display devices, normally available to users.

From the point of view relating to the organization of content for the structuring of the website pages, in its different versions (desktop and mobile devices), the topic is particularly stimulating as it brings together heterogeneous materials and documents which must be proposed to the user in such a way as to structure and support different actions: visits and experiences of augmented reality, in-depth research, remote exploration.

The creation of in-situ visit paths offers users different thematic itineraries, built in relation to the time available for the visit, to the opening times and accessibility of the atria, to specific interests. For example, paths were hypothesized related to:

- the transformation over time of the entrance and distribution spaces of the noble palaces of the city in relation to the evolution of construction techniques, to changes in the requirements linked to the entrance ceremonial, to the change in architectural taste
- the architectural production linked to a specific period in the wider arch of reference or to a single type of vaulted atrium (star-shaped, planterian or "a fascioni")
- the production of a specific author (for example: Guarino Guarini, Gian Giacomo Plantery, Filippo Juvarra, etc.).

4 Digital Interactive Baroque Atria in Turin: Methods and Tools Aimed to the Project Development

4.1 Digital Collections

Digital tools for surveying, processing, and representing are increasing the amount and the details of information on Architectural Heritage, and the possible levels of analysis. The construction of a virtual archive of late-baroque vault systems in Turin can be a field-test to cope with several open problems related to information and communication technologies (ICT) and for testing new systems to access information.

In the first place, the collection aims to respond to content management needs: different types and formats of documents should be accepted, and these should be organized and connected through their information set. Moreover, on the one hand the system should update itself dynamically in order to deal with a growing information flow. On the other hand, it must guarantee the long-term accessibility of data, and therefore it should remain compatible with the development of new data retrieval tools.

A second theme concerns the usage of the collection and the possibility of a multi-disciplinary target and different professional or non-professional levels to access specific information, with purposes ranging from research, documentation and management to dissemination, tourism, and recreation. In short, we address the problem of identifying different paths of knowledge within new and complex "information topologies".

Therefore, it is needed to take into account the characteristic heterogeneity of cultural heritage to support data integration (the homogeneous representation of different types of documents), the interoperability of the contents (the possibility to access and edit data through different devices and software) and the scalability of the tools used, therefore a flexibility over time with respect to the quantity and type of input (Kakali et al. 2007).

4.2   Storage Tools

The project aims to make accessible through different devices a collection of data sheets concerning 71 Baroque halls in Turin, which include photographs, vector drawings, three-dimensional interpretative models and reproductions of selected archive documents.

In the choice of the digital archiving tool, we selected "Cult" (Bortot et al. 2017; Cecchini et al. 2018), a web service developed by the ICEA department of the University of Padua (Principal Investigators Andrea Giordano and Luigi Stendardo, web-designer Valerio Palma). Cult is a project for the cultural spreading oriented to Cultural Tourism.

Cult allows the user to upload texts, images and models, to associate metadata to documents, to establish relationships between elements, to explore resources through text queries or geographic queries. The service is entirely based on free and open source software, which supports information sharing, in addition to containing costs (Scianna 2013; Cerutti et al. 2015). Among the available software, the following is used: PostgreSQL and its spatial extension PostGIS for the management of the geographic database, Python and the Django framework for the website and other web services. Furthermore, Cult metadata are organized on the basis of the Dublin Core Metadata Initiative scheme (DCMI 2018), which is a good starting point to take standards into consideration, aiming at interoperability and data integration (Kakali et al. 2007; Haus 2016).

Cult information sheets are well suited to the description of monuments and documents: the 15 entries of the DCMI Element set are used (title, creator, subject, description, publisher, contributor, date, type, format, identifier, source, language, relation, coverage, rights) as well as some refinement terms, such as the role of contributors, a spatial coverage (in "well known text" format geometries, or WKT) and the type of relationship between one document and another.

We verified the compatibility of Cult with the needs of the collection, and we performed and planned some upgrade.

At present, some limits of the instrument are connected to the metadata that can be inserted. In Cult the wide-ranged possibilities offered by Dublin Core are restricted by some conventions applied to the web interface for data entry, which, for instance, does not always allow to choose more than one definition per field, or limits the input to a list of values. The insertion of Turin's database allowed a revision which includes, among other additions, increased options for the type of document (from the three categories of images, texts and models to the 12 entries of the DCMI Type Vocabulary) and increased types of relationship between documents (again in this case using the DCMI specifications, namely the refinements of the relations in the DCMI Term set).

A page dedicated to the atria collection has been added to the website, and it is replicable for other projects that may contribute to a further expansion of the portal. For the future development of these pages, we propose integrating maps to suggest thematic readings of the archive (e.g.: the evolution of taste, spatial organization, construction techniques, or a specific author or period…), to consult documents through paths not allowed by simple database queries, and to suggest, where possible, directions for in situ tours.

4.3 Visualization Tools

In order to broaden our consideration of some of the aspects introduced for the digital archive, we conducted some experiments in the exploration of digital archive documents.

The research addresses critical issues about the integration of digital archiving tools and augmented reality (AR) techniques, considering the technological advances required and the relationship with standards for information sharing.

The valorisation of cultural heritage is increasingly employing the digitalization of the physical form of objects and monuments. Examples are connected to the possibility of obtaining accurate 3D reproductions through laser scanning or photogrammetry techniques (Younes et al. 2016).   While we can record a state of a building and make it remotely available, the detail of spatial data makes it possible to put the information network in continuity with real documents and environments.

In the present case, we intend to make the digital works produced by the research group viewable on site, using AR applications that allow superimposing a digital informative layer to images of the real world (Amin and Govilkar 2015).

AR techniques need to work in real time and to get an accurate estimate of the position of the observer, as discussed in detail by Yang et al. (2013) and Younes et al. (2016). To obtain these results also on largely diffused mobile devices, different approaches bring together computer visual techniques (capable of recognizing remarkable points in the series of images taken by a video camera) and the information from the motion sensors of the device (Apple Inc. 2018; Google Inc. 2018).

The authors have identified some software development kit (SDK) that enable the production of low cost and easily deployable AR applications, also for devices with a monocular camera.

A first SDK is Vuforia, a commercial product that offers free solutions for developers, and allows the creation of multi-platform apps through software such as Unity. The research group has already worked on other Vuforia applications based on tracking two-dimensional images (Palma et al. 2018), but the current version can also track 3D objects (PTC Inc. 2018). The ability to scan the reference model through a support mobile app was considered for this study, even if tracking from a pre-existing 3D model is also possible.

Similar possibilities are offered by Apple's software. The software development application Xcode incorporates the augmented reality framework ARCore, which provides for the tracing of 3D models (Apple Inc. 2018). Here too, an app to build the digital reference model is available.

Other packages for developers are produced by Google. Google's ARCore allows the analysis of the 3D characteristics of a scene, but the tools are presented as particularly suitable for the detection of flat surfaces to make digital elements interact with (Google Inc. 2018), so these were not further considered for this phase of the research.

Due to the more limiting needs of the Vuforia scanning app (15 × 10 cm are the recommended dimensions of the tracking object, and a printed target image is required for the scanning operation), we decided to use Apple's software for the first experiments of the project, although a more detailed comparative study would be necessary.

The tools were tested in the atrium of Palazzo Carignano. Inside the sample scanning app made available by Apple, a virtual bounding box anchors itself to the environment, and it can be freely scaled and moved to frame the object to be scanned. Then, the app proceeds to the scanning process, which consists of framing the box from several points of view, in choosing the origin of the reference system (it will serve to position the virtual part of the scene), and in verifying that the model can be recognized.

Scanning only starts in good lighting conditions and, in the present experience, if the object is less than 3.5 m away. In this case, since the impost vault is about 7 m high, we scanned the base of two coupled columns supporting the vault (Fig. 5). Several parts of the atrium, illuminated by natural light from the court of the building, were found to be too dark to make the app detect a sufficient number of points.

Fig. 5. Screenshots of the scanning phases of the reference model for the atrium of Palazzo Carignano. Left: arbitrary definition of a virtual bounding box; the app keeps the box anchored to the environment and detects features inside the box (the yellow dots). Right: positioning of the reference system origin needed to correctly place the digital model to be visualized in the AR app. These and the following figures are produced using software by Apple Inc. (Xcode v10.0 beta 4, ARKit Scanner, v1.0, iOS 12.0).

The reference model produced with the scanning app was moved into a simple augmented reality app project and tested with a geometric model of the vault surface. As a result, despite just a small part of the atrium is used to anchor the digital model, we consider the obtained superposition as sufficiently stable and accurate for a dissemination application (Fig. 6).

Fig. 6. Screenshots of the AR app prepared by the authors, as tested in the atrium of Palazzo Carignano. Left: digital interpretation of the surface of the vault superimposed on the images of the camera in real time. Right: view of the reference object (marked with a white frame) from the opposite side of the atrium. Even if the reference object is just the basis of two coupled columns (marked with a white frame), the AR framework manages to keep the digital model stable and quite accurately placed.

However, we encountered many different problems. The presence of repetitive elements can confuse the recognition system, as demonstrated during some tests in which the model detected the wrong column of the couple. In addition, the limited scanning distance does not yet allow using the entire atrium as anchoring object, and the lighting problems are still to be addressed with greater attention and dedicated tests, to understand how much the user experience can be affected.

This limited experience leads us to argue that AR technologies can and should be used to reflect on the role of digital models in the organization and access to the digital information on the architectural heritage, and in particular to study the conventions that can be adopted to record and share the contact points between virtual and physical reality.

5   Results and Conclusions

Two main results characterize the current development phase of the project.

On the one hand, we have produced an extension of the Cult web service, verifying that it remains homogeneous about materials, data, products, and intents.

On the other hand, we started to create a mobile application able to associate a digital model to be visualized with a physical space for "anchoring", but we still need to deepen and insert the kits available on the market and open source apps for AR in a comparative evaluation process, updating our studies according to rapid technological progress.

Future developments of the project should evaluate how to insert in the digital collection the information to enable the applications of AR, and integrate into the interactive experience the other materials of the archive.

The continuing project aims to contribute to the creation of a widespread museum that does not isolate buildings and documents from the urban context (Stendardo 2015), but is rather a dynamic source of knowledge, based on the actual use of the architectural heritage.

The architectural heritage can become the privileged access point of the specialized information collected, for an immediate and effective use. The use of the digital collection and the space of the city can intertwine, and can contribute to the sustainability of services and to the enhancement of knowledge and heritage.

Acknowledgements. Although the proposal is the result of a shared research among the three authors, it must refer to the specialist work of: Valerio Palma the paragraph 4, Roberta Spallone the paragraph 2, Marco Vitali the paragraph 3. Valerio Palma, Roberta Spallone, and Marco Vitali together are the authors of paragraphs 1 and 5.

References

Amin D, Govilkar S (2015) Comparative study of augmented reality SDK's. Int J Comput Sci Appl 5(1):11–26

Apple Inc. (2018) https://developer.apple.com/documentation/arkit. Accessed 15 Sept 2018

Bortot A, et al (2017) TU-CULT. Architectural revelations in the Churches of Santa Giustina and Santa Maria dei Servi in Padova. In: Territori e frontiere della rappresentazione - Territories and frontiers of representation. Atti del 39° Convegno internazionale dei docenti delle discipline della rappresentazione, 14–16 Sept, Gangemi Editore, Naples

Cecchini C, Cundari MR, Palma V, Panarotto F (2018) Data, models and visualization: connected tools to enhance the fruition of the architectural heritage in the city of Padova. In: Graphic Imprint. The Influence of Representation and Ideation Tools in Architecture. Proceedings of the XVII EGA International Conference, 30–31 May, 1 June, Alacant. Springer

Cerutti E, Noardo F, Spanò A (2015) Architectural heritage semantic data managing and sharing in GIS. In: GISTAM 2015 1st International Conference on Geographical Information System Theory, Application and Management, 27–30 Apr, Barcelona. SCITEPRESS - Science and Technology Publications, Lda

DCMI (2018) http://dublincore.org. Accessed 10 May 2018

Google Inc. (2018) https://developers.google.com/ar/discover. Accessed 15 Sept 2018

Guarini G (1671) Euclides adauctus et methodicus, matematicaque universalis. Typis Bartholomaei Zapatae bibliopolae S.R.C, Torino

Guarini G (1674) Modo di misurare le fabriche. Per gl'Heredi Gianelli, Torino

Guarini G (1737) Architettura Civile. Gianfrancesco Mairesse, Torino

Haus G (2016) Cultural heritage and ICT: state of the art and perspectives. DigitCult - Sci J Digital Cultures 1(1):9–20

Kakali C, et al (2007) Integrating Dublin Core metadata for cultural heritage collections using ontologies. In: International Conference on Dublin Core and Metadata Applications, 1–4 Sept São Paulo. e-LIS

Norberg-Schulz C (1980) Architettura Tardobarocca. Electa, Milano

Palma V, Lo Turco M, Spallone R, Vitali M (2018) Augmented iconography. AR applications to the fortified Turin in the Theatrum Sabaudiae. In: Marotta A, Spallone R, Defensive architecture of the mediterranean, vol. IX. Proceedings of the international conference FORTMED - modern age fortification of the mediterranean coast, 18–20 Oct. Politecnico di Torino, Torino

PTC Inc. (2018) https://library.vuforia.com. Accessed 15 Sept 2018

Scianna A, Gristina S, Sciortino R (2013) Integrazione di sistemi GIS FOSS e modelli dati 3D PDF per la fruizione multimediale di beni monumentali e archeologici: il Castello di Maredolce a Palermo. In: Stanco F, Gallo G (eds) Free, libre and open source software e open format nei processi di ricerca archeologica, 8th edn. Archaeopress, Oxford

Spallone R, Vitali M (2017a). Volte stellari e planteriane negli atri barocchi in Torino - Star-shaped and Planterian Vaults in Turin Baroque Atria. Aracne, Ariccia

Spallone R, Vitali M (2017b) Baroque Turin, Between Geometry and Architecture. Math Intell 39(2):76–84

Stendardo L (2015) Self explaining city. Merging city and art, through thick and thin. In: Proceedings of the XIII international forum of studies 'Le Vie dei Mercanti' heritage and technology. Mind, knowledge, experience, 11–13 June Aversa and Capri. La scuola di Pitagora editrice

Yang MD, Chao CF, Huang KS, Lu LY, Chen YP (2013) Image-based 3D scene reconstruction and exploration in augmented reality. Autom Constr 33:48–60

Younes G, Asmar D, Elhajj I, Al-Harithy H (2016) Pose tracking for augmented reality applications in outdoor archaeological sites. J Electron Imaging 26(1):011004

Representing and Communicating the Cultural Heritage Construction of Virtual Urban and Architectural Scale Places for Learning

Alessandra Meschini$^{(\boxtimes)}$ and Ramona Feriozzi

School of Architecture and Design "Eduardo Vittoria" (SAAD), University
of Camerino, Viale della Rimembranza snc, 63100 Ascoli Piceno, Italy
alessandra.meschini@unicam.it

Abstract. This contribution addresses the opportunities that technological innovations offer to expand accessibility to knowledge. The goal is to verify how the organization of specific content, together with the use of identified technologies, are factors that significantly influence the relationship between users, the curators of the transmitted information, and the institutions appointed to conserve and enhance various cultural heritage. In particular, two experimentations centred on using augmented reality/virtuality and interactive media were made to verify the potential of their use and application to two different types of cultural heritage. Both experimentations have the common goal of identifying and initiating new cognitive processes based mainly on inquiry in an active, exploratory way, that is, allowing users to interact with the information tied to the cultural heritage, offering broad, multi-sensory use.

Keywords: Cultural heritage · Virtual environments · 3D reconstruction ·
Immersive navigation · Interactive interfaces

1 Introduction

Contemporary reality has for some time demonstrated that procedures to digitalize content and the use of various applied technologies can determine important modifications with regard to cultural activities, that is, the quality of presentation and the use of resources. This is also true in terms of positive user feedback and renewed collaborations between institutions entrusted with enhancing the various goods in the heritage and the curators of the transmitted information (Irace et al. 2013).

Therefore, if the common objective is, more simply, to facilitate and expand access to knowledge, one of the decisive aspects for the innovative redesign of cultural activities is to focus attention on new forms of both presentation and the spread of content.

Within this framework, this contribution presents two experimentations made in relation to two different types of cultural heritage. Two areas are closely tied to reaching the objectives identified in the two case studies presented: augmented reality/virtuality and interactive media (Ippoliti and Meschini 2011). More specifically, the experimentation regarded products pertaining to tools for visual-tactile interaction,

© Springer Nature Switzerland AG 2019
A. Luigini (Ed.): EARTH 2018, AISC 919, pp. 326–335, 2019.
https://doi.org/10.1007/978-3-030-12240-9_35

technological devices for immersive navigation, and explorable 3D interfaces, concentrating on the identification and study of ad hoc systems to create different levels of interactiveness/immersion.

Both experiences begin with two intentions: building paths capable of easing but also stimulating—even emotionally—curiosity regarding the knowledge; and preparing dynamic modes of fruition based on the 'visual correlation' between searchable content and the three-dimensional presentation of real places (object/topic of study) to which the information refers. This favours the immediateness given by this representative/communicational form, that is, trying to limit the need to activate more tiresome processes of abstraction. In addition, with both experimentations, an attempt was made to identify additional alternative systems of presenting the cultural content correlated with the specific theme of interest, trying as well to use open-source digital applications as much as possible.

2 Study for an Interactive Map for Augmented Visual Exploration

The focus of the first experimentation is interventions in reference to the Regulations of the so-called "Pubblico Ornato" that slowly transformed the minor building fabric of the historical centre of Ascoli Piceno in the historical period of the 1800–1900s. In brief, these regulations—three in particular, referring to the years 1885, 1902, and 1907 —aimed not only to oversee building activities and regulate the growth of the city, but also to preserve the urban decor, guiding private initiatives in the process of renewing buildings in the historical centre and improving the design of the city. Standards of intervention were indicated for the composition of façades, street alignment, definition of building prominences, mergers, and demolitions.

Evidence for the modifications made to the different building units were composed of exclusively non-digitalized paper materials stored in large folders at various city archives (Archivio di Stato, Archivio Settore Edilizia privata del Comune, Archivio Storico Iconografico del Comune), with current access still following the classical means of search, request, and *in situ* viewing.

Therefore, the objective identified and addressed with this specific experimentation was to 'modernize' the means of consulting cultural resources stored over time at the institutions dedicated to their protection, looking for and proposing forms of organizing and communicating/visualizing the content that are centred on innovative, fluid, interactive fruition.

2.1 Research and Analysis to Identify the Interventions

As is clear, the first phase of study centred on retrieving any possible documentary source through specific searches made at the Archives mentioned above. This first step highlighted an entire series of problems, such as; the lack of interaction among the archives, the lack of organization of the archived sources, the absence of some data in the sources (street numbers, owners' names, etc.), the sometimes difficult comprehension of the written texts in the documents (exclusively handwritten), as well as changes in the toponymy of the street names or sequential numbering, the difficulty of identifying some cadastral particles, and the difficulty in recognizing some façades caused by further later transformations. In each case, all the material retrieved was appropriately digitalized.

With regard to these problems and in order to identify all the buildings within the historical centre that were the object of modifications in the time frame considered, it was even more necessary to make further investigations and consistent correlated actions in rereading the maps. In other words, a search was made for any mention of the properties by studying the urban historical land registry as well as quick, on-site photographic and metric surveys. This additional research led to more complete knowledge of the topic and the identification of 39 different interventions that could be located in the historical area of the city.

In the second phase of each study, the heterogeneous data was subjected to careful critical analysis and documents were collected/processed for each individual building/intervention. In this phase of reprocessing the information obtained, it was especially important to build a focused classification of the types of interventions, organizing them based on the different modifications made and recognized on site (Fig. 1a), creating adequate catalogues of the interventions and defining appropriate data sheets for the buildings affected by the transformations (Fig. 1b). All of this helped to construct the necessary ordered frame of reference useful for reaching the goals.

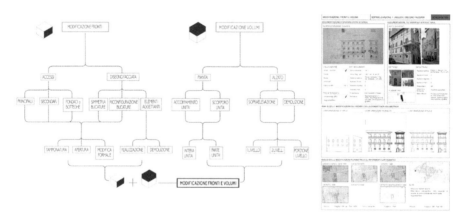

Fig. 1. Systematization of the different categories of building modifications (a) and example of a catalogue sheet of interventions organized into three sections (b).

2.2   Preparation of Content and Applied Experimentation: The Map

Due to what was underlined above, the third phase of the research could only concentrate on the subsequent, fundamental construction of the content to make it usable. Therefore, in order to facilitate understanding of the modifications for each of the 39 interventions identified, in addition to the cataloguing sheets, the following content was made available: an animated visualization (stop-motion video) of the changes made to the façades (moving between states before and after the work) (Fig. 2a) and a three-dimensional reconstruction (appropriately discretized) of the volumetric modifications (before and after work) that could also be visualized with spherical panoramas (Fig. 2b).

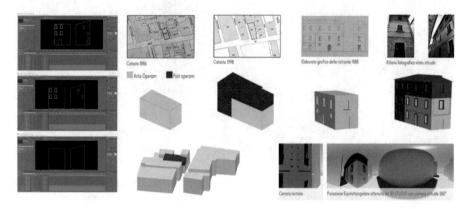

Fig. 2. Screen shots of the animated visualization of the transformation of the façades (a) and 3D reconstructions before and after the volumetric modifications (b) of one of the 39 interventions identified.

Finally, with regard to the means of organizing and sharing the constructed content, the most adequate choice to pursue should be based on the possibility of allowing immediate identification and visualization of the spatial location of each intervention within the historical centre (Boyer and Marcus 2011). Starting from this assumption, the research identified the representative means of a 'map' as the most effective medium to respond to this intention. With this scope, the studies were aimed at identifying and using suitable 'free' applications that could allow the digital content related to each individual case of intervention to be organized and make available starting from an urban-scale representation. The goal was to turn the representation into an interactive map with augmented viewing in order to organize and communicate the relationship between the parts and the whole, that is, between the places/buildings of intervention and the entire historical centre. In particular, one of the applications allowed each content item to be traced to an online satellite view of the city.

In the final result of the experimentation, therefore, the plan of the city becomes the 'place' both for organization and for flexible access to the different types of data. In other words, a "user-friendly" interface allows users to 'visually' consult the heterogeneous, organized content composed of 3D reconstructions of before and after states, 2D drawings, catalogue sheets, brief stop-motion explanatory videos, and 360° panoptic views. Finally, since one of the objectives at the basis of the research was to identify multiple alternative systems of presenting cultural content related to the specific theme of interest, an attempt was made to experiment with and make available two different dynamics for using the map.

The first means of fruition/accessibility proposed was based on an interactive search of the content, which is connected to the map shared on the network through visual/tactile devices such as touchscreens, PCs, smartphones, and tablets (Fig. 3).

Fig. 3. Interactive consultation of the online map via touch screen. Examples of some viewable content: panoramic 3D reconstruction and stop-motion video of the façade modifications.

The second means of use was instead based on building a 'physical' map that would allow for augmented-reality visualizations of the content that could be accessed through tablets and smartphones. This form of augmented visualization was studied to be useable not only on a reproduction of the map printed in a suitable graphical scale (AR based on recognizing the portions used as markers) but also in the real place in the city (AR based on georeferencing of 3D content) (Fig. 4).

Fig. 4. Augmented reality on printed map (left). Examples of use of some contents (right): stop motion video of the transformations and augmented reality of 3D models on site.

3   Project for Immersive/Interactive Navigation

The object of study for the second experimentation was the Church of the Resurrection, the remaining part of an ancient Farfa monastery built in the tenth century on Mount Matenano (Province of Fermo).

After a series of modifications made over the centuries, its current structure can be traced to the Baroque transformation made after a partial demolition carried out in 1771. In particular, the church conserves the so-called Oratorio degli Innocenti, a small space entirely frescoed with stories and characters drawn from the Gospels, which constitutes a cherished 'document' of a fifteenth-century school of art that flourished within the monastery.

This church constitutes an emblematic example of the large quantity of buildings of recognized value spread throughout the Italian territory that national organizations and foundations such as FAI aim to maintain and recognize. More generally, this heritage contributes to ensuring that Italy ranks at the top of nations with the most UNESCO sites.

Therefore, the first choice made in the experimentation was to identify a case study that, being exemplary of this reality, would address the theme of identifying 'renewed' means of enhancement for these myriad small and mostly unknown buildings that constitute the historical/artistic and architectural richness of Italy.

In this case, the most appropriate means of pursuing this objective was to propose a broad approach to the knowledge, creating appropriate 3D reconstructions referring both to the current configuration of the church overall, and to a hypothesis of virtual reconstruction of its conformation in the state preceding the partial demolition in the 1700s. The goal was to allow them to be experienced with wide use, that is, through interactive/immersive navigation of these models.

3.1   Investigations and Surveys of the Church of the Resurrection

The work in this second experimentation was also carried out in phases.

In the first phase of historical/archival research, the bibliographic and iconographic sources useful for reconstructing the numerous modifications made to the building over the centuries were identified.

Among the resources traced and studied, two documents were particularly useful: a drawing contained in the 1765 Inventory (Archivio capitolare di S. Vittoria) and a description by the scholar Crocetti (1997).

From the comparison and analysis of the information contained in the Inventories of the era, it was possible to identify the portion of the church that remains today with respect to the original conformation and to build a reconstruction hypothesis of the church before the demolitions (Fig. 5a).

At the same time, appropriate geometrical/metric surveys were made on site in order to obtain a correct representation of the current state. In addition, a photogrammetry survey was made of the Oratorio degli Innocenti with the aim of rendering the particular nature of the frescoes.

The comparison between the results of the surveys and the documentary sources allowed us to hypothesize what the previous configuration of the church was (Fig. 5b).

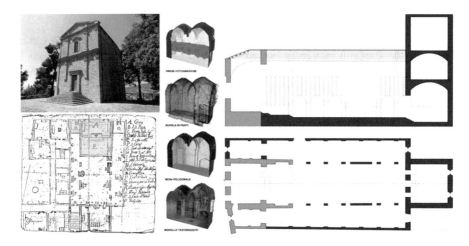

Fig. 5. The church today and the 1765 drawing (a); results of the surveys inserted in the reconstruction hypothesis of the church before 1771 (b). The portion highlighted in yellow corresponds to the current state.

3.2   Preparation of Content and Applied Experimentation: 3D Models

The results of the overall studies made possible the two three-dimensional reconstructions.

The first 3D model corresponds to the current conformation of the church where particular attention was placed on correctly texturizing of the surfaces of the oratory space in order to make further analysis related to the components present in the composition of the frescoes.

The second 3D model has been created in order to propose a virtual reconstruction of the church in the state preceding the partial demolition in the 1700s (Fig. 6).

Therefore, in this second experimentation, the usable content, that is, the representative means designed to achieve the objective of enhancement, primarily concentrated on three-dimensional reconstructions (Ippoliti and Meschini 2010).

In fact, these 3D models constitute the main focus through which a dual intent was realized: make the comparison between the current and 'no longer existing' states capable of being visualized and used virtually; allow users to interact - always in a virtual way - with the frescoed space of the oratory, making it possible to examine the different characteristic figurative and geometric/decorative aspects (Ma et al. 2013).

Fig. 6. 3D navigable models: the hall of the church before and after the Baroque transformation (left); the Oratorio degli Innocenti with the fresco texture (right).

Operationally, the most suitable software application for arranging the virtual environment was identified. The aim in this experimentation as well was to propose two different means of navigating the models, that is, two alternative systems of accessing the content while keeping in mind the variety of possible users: a virtual desktop-type system (Fig. 7a), and another immersive one that uses a 3D visor (Fig. 7b).

The latter, in particular, allows for an engaging perceptual experience capable of achieving a 360° view of the virtual environment (appropriately optimized for this viewing means) and therefore to use the space as if one were really found within it, enjoying a system that simulates possible movements through a naturally intuitive interface (Desai et al. 2014).

Both means of using the organized 3D content allow the church to be navigated both at the current state and in its reconstruction before the demolitions. The result is to facilitate understanding of its transformations and make an analysis of the oratory frescoes possible, definitively building a virtual place for learning about the spatial quality of the building.

Fig. 7. Virtual desktop navigation: examples of exploring the church before and after the transformations (a) and immersive navigation with visors: examples of interactive visualizations of the frescoes (b).

4   Conclusion

The two different experimentations presented show how the potential of augmented reality/virtuality allows specific digital environments to be constructed, thereby triggering new cognitive processes for heritage education (Meschini et al. 2016).

Through these environments, the institutions charged with the various tasks of conservation, protection, or exhibition of goods with cultural value can offer forms of fruition that, if appropriately characterized by different levels of interactiveness and immersion, can be oriented at satisfying the needs of a varied public that ranges from simple everyday consumers of culture to studious experts.

Acknowledgements. The research activities presented here were made thanks to the participation of two young Master's degree students at the SAAD, University of Camerino: Mila Fares (first case study) and Matteo Iachetti (second case study).

References

Boyer D, Marcus J (2011) Implementing mobile augmented reality applications for cultural institutions. In: Proceedings of museums and the web, archives. Museum Informatics, Toronto

Crocetti G (1997) Quaderni dell'Archivio Storico Arcivescovile di Fermo, vol 23

Irace F, Ciagà G, Lupo E, Trocchianesi, R (a cura di) (2013) Design & cultural heritage. Electa, Milano

Desai PR, Desai PN, Ajmera KD, Mehta K (2014) A review paper on oculus rift-a virtual reality headset. Int. J. Eng. Trends Technol. 13(4):175–179

Ippoliti E, Meschini A (2010) Dal modello 3D alla scena 3D. Prospettive e opportunità per la valorizzazione del patrimonio culturale architettonico e urbano. Disegnarecon 3(6):77–91

Ippoliti E, Meschini A (2011) Tecnologie per la comunicazione del patrimonio culturale. Disegnarecon 4(8):1–138

Ma N, Laroche F, Hervy B, Kerouanton JL (2013) Virtual conservation and interaction with our cultural heritage: framework for multi-dimension model based interface. In: Proceedings of digital heritage international congress, 28 October–1 November, Marsiglia, France. IEEE Publisher

Meschini A, Rossi D, Feriozzi R (2016) La Basilica in una scatola. Proposta per una wunderkammer contemporanea. Disegnarecon 9(17):1–10

The Augmented Reality as an Instrument for the Representation/Visualization of Architecture

Mirco Cannella[✉]

Department of Culture del progetto, Università IUAV of Venice,
Dorsoduro 2196, Cotonificio veneziano, 30123 Venice, Italy
mcannella@iuav.it

Abstract. This paper deals with issues related to the representation/visualization of architecture and its narration through the augmented reality tools. Specifically, the possible scenarios and the different strategies to address the problems related to the application of AR platforms in the field of cultural heritage are presented.

Some case studies will be analyzed and the use of augmented reality applied to museums and archaeological sites including the Museum of the *Cité de l'architecture et du patrimoine* in Paris, the Regional Archaeological Museum A. Salinas in Palermo and the archaeological site of Selinunte.

Thanks to these exemplary cases, the potential and critical aspects of the latest AR technologies developed by Google applied to indoor and outdoor contexts will be analyzed.

Keywords: Augmented reality · 3D modeling · Cultural heritage · Education

1 Introduction

In recent months we are witnessing the release of a large number of applications that take advantage of augmented reality. The implementation and launch of new development platforms such as Apple's ARKit and Google's ARCore certainly favoured this growth, in fact, their compatibility with a substantial number of mobile devices currently on the market has potentially generated a new market made up of millions of users.

This research starts from a series of tests conducted over the past few months using different AR platforms, which confirmed how in the architectural field and archaeological and museum areas the augmented reality may offer a new and powerful tool for the fruition of cultural heritage through uncharted methods.

This paper seeks to define the processes and operational practices that led to the construction of 3D models, aimed at integration and visualization through augmented reality applications.

© Springer Nature Switzerland AG 2019
A. Luigini (Ed.): EARTH 2018, AISC 919, pp. 336–344, 2019.
https://doi.org/10.1007/978-3-030-12240-9_36

2   Strategies for Developing AR Applications

2.1   Displaying 3D Model in the Augmented Reality

The complexity of digital models and their level of detail is one of the key aspects in developing an application for mobile devices. In fact, it is impossible not to take into account some factors of primary importance, such as the need to download the application on the move from the store. Furthermore, considering the different performance levels of the smartphones, very complex 3D models can negatively affect the performance.

Analysing the AR virtual reconfiguration of an urban block into the Acropolis of Selinunte, it has emerged the need to subtract from the visualization, in a dynamic and real-time way, of specific areas of the digital model corresponding to architectural elements that from time to time are interposed with the user (Fig. 1).

As is well known, virtual models displayed in augmented reality are superimposed to a video stream acquired from the smartphone camera and it is necessary to use a specific shader assign to specially designed surfaces, in order to partialize the visualization of the 3D model.

The decision to keep visible the ruins of the site during the AR experience imposed such necessity, therefore the digital mesh model of the actual state, realized with 3D laser scanning and photogrammetric data and used as a support for virtual reconstruction too, it was used for this purpose.

This model was appropriately optimized so that the number of triangles did not interfere negatively with the performance of the mobile device. It is not directly visible but its effects are perceived in those areas characterized by a significant changes orientation of surfaces. E.g., let's consider one of the pillars of the porch that characterize these housing units; this is formed by five visible faces and without considering the area of attack on the ground, of eight edges. It follows that the digital model that describes this element, and which will act as a 3D occlusion mask, must have a high level of geometric detail close the edges, while the planar faces can be characterized by a few numbers of triangles. This solution, adopted for all the architectural elements such as walls and floors, allows to obtain an ideal optimization of the mesh model.

Fig. 1. Visualization in augmented reality of the virtual reconstruction of the urban block FF1 in the Archaeological Park of Selinunte.

Some considerations on visualization and representation techniques of 3D models for augmented reality can be made by analysing the experience carried out at the Antonio Salinas Regional Archaeological Museum of Palermo and in particular on the metopes of the Temple E, exhibited in the hall of the former refectory of the Filippini Fathers.

On the wall at the back of the room, we find a reconstructed portion of the frieze where 4 of the metopes that once decorated the upper part of the outer walls of the *naos* are placed (Fig. 2).

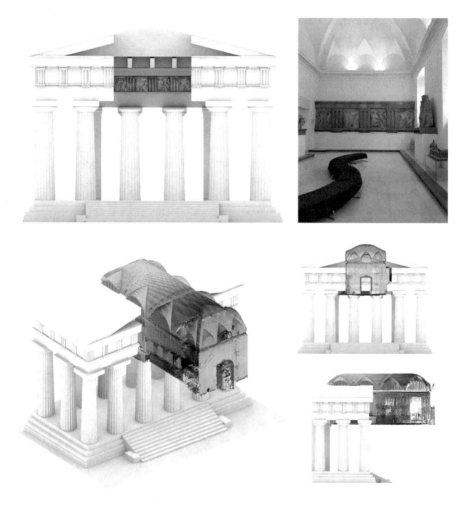

Fig. 2. Virtual positioning of the Temple E inside the Filippini Fathers hall in the Regional Archeological Museum "A. Salinas" of Palermo.

The goal of this experimentation was to be able to view a portion of the temple in augmented reality, allowing the visitor to understand its dimensions and proportions.

The lower part of the frieze is located at a height of about 1.50 m from the floor, a condition that places the visitor's gaze corresponding to the height of the lower edge of the metopes. It is clear that originally the point of view of these sculptural configurations was very different, in fact, if we consider the highest level of the crepidoma the lower part of these was above 11 m. It follows that if we want to make the metopes are placed in the original location in the temple visualized in the augmented reality, we get a virtual point of view located well above the level floor of the museum hall. This condition, which is not entirely natural and which may disorient the user at first, offers interesting thing. In fact, it is possible to observe a Greek temple from a privileged position, and thus grasp the sculptural details that often are not perfectly visible from below (Fig. 3).

Fig. 3. Palermo, Regional Archeological Museum "A. Salinas". Displaying in the augmented reality of Temple E inside the museum hall.

To be able to virtually be placed the temple within the museum space was necessary its metric knowledge. In fact, both the museum hall and the Temple E, which has been reassembled for anastylosis and shows off on the eastern hill of the Archaeological Park of Selinunte, have been surveyed using laser scanning techniques. The two surveys allowed the construction of two discrete models, in particular, the temple's 3D model was made with the aim of obtaining a mesh characterized by a minimum number of triangles. The definition of a unique reference system allowed to orientate the temple digital model inside the hall, making the position of the metopes coincide with the top of the wall of the *naos*.

The front of the Temple E is 26.60 m. wide and 20.35 m. high, while the hall measures respectively 8.20 m. and 10.50 m. in the highest part. This implies, even if virtually, the impossibility of the space dedicated to containing the model of the temple and the arising of some questions: how to treat model surfaces that go beyond the walls of the hall? Can characterizing these surfaces with different materials help the user to have a better perception of space and an easy understanding of dimensions?

The tests have shown that the visualization of the model of the temple in the augmented reality without a differentiation of what is inside compared to that which goes beyond the perimeter, determines a disorientation and a difficulty in understanding the real position of the model inside of the hall. This condition has therefore imposed a differentiation of the surfaces and the decision to limit the depth of the model to the first three columns, interrupting it on the front wall of the *naos*.

Different tests were carried out: in the first instance, the part of the model included in the room volume was separated from the rest, the two central columns are cut from the floor in correspondence of the echinus, while the pediment is divided into three parts.

The first solution adopted was addressed to the assignment of a transparent material to the surplus surfaces, while a controller allows the user to decide the level of opacity of the middle part.

In order to obtain a more consistent volumetric perception of the model, texture baking was performed in advance, which allowed to generate maps containing ambient occlusion information and to simulate a diffused illumination of the 3D model (Fig. 4).

Fig. 4. Palermo, Regional Archeological Museum "A. Salinas". Virtual reconstruction of the Temple E within the museum hall. Displaying with and without transparent effect of surfaces.

In the areas of virtual intersection between the 3D model and the actual surfaces of the room, have been arranged planar surfaces parallel to the walls and the floor, textured with maps calculated with the texture baking technique which allowed a slight shading to be simulated. This solution made it possible to better highlight the digital model intersection with the hall walls.

The second proposal studied does not intervene on a different treatment of surfaces but proposes their dematerialization, adopting a wireframe visualization. This solution does not propose the adoption of particular shaders but opts for a materialization of the edges of the model through a conversion of lines in mesh surfaces of the 3D model parts located beyond the hall. An augmented reality visualization of such model gives the user the idea of being in front of a three-dimensional pen drawing. The effect thus obtained makes it possible to perceive with greater emphasis where the front of the temple goes beyond the walls of the room and in addition allows a clearer perception of what lies beyond the model itself thanks to the evanescence of wireframe viewing (Fig. 5).

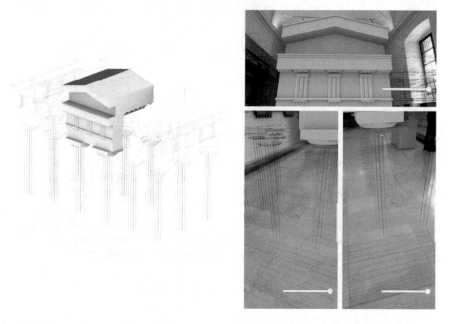

Fig. 5. Palermo, Regional Archeological Museum "A. Salinas". Virtual reconstruction of the Temple E. The parts that cross the walls and the floor are displayed in wireframe.

The third solution investigated instead focuses on subtraction. In this specific case, the central part of the model is eliminated by determining a cross-section of the temple. The surfaces that delimit the section are characterized by burgundy colour.

Taking advantage of augmented reality, the user remains virtually at half height, can walk inside the temple and approach the real metopes that will be embedded within the model, allowing it to view details of the roof covering system consisting of a grid of wooden beams (Fig. 6).

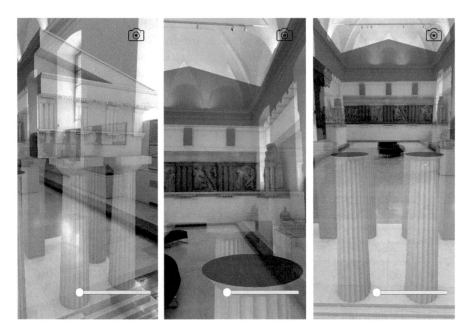

Fig. 6. Palermo, Regional Archeological Museum "A. Salinas". Virtual reconstruction of the Temple E. The middle part was removed.

2.2   Access to Digital Content in the Augmented Reality

Part of the research was directed to the study of the AR applications experience for cultural heritage. It is in fact known that virtual and augmented reality applications can be very disorienting for users who are not accustomed to the use of 3D visualization technologies.

The goal of making the application of augmented reality a valuable tool for common use for visiting cultural contexts requires a targeted design of both the graphical interface as well as the ways of accessing and viewing 3D content.

Thanks to localization processes, even in indoor spaces, offered by the most recent platforms for augmented reality, and already investigated in previous studies (Cannella 2018; Cannella 2017), it is possible to provide a system that allows accessing the correct multimedia contents according to the user's position in a specific environment.

This solution greatly simplifies the approach to the visit, reducing the need for direct intervention by the user in the search for information of interest. This approach has been tested at the Museum of the Cité de l'architecture et du patrimoine of Paris (Cannella and Gay 2018). For example, will be enough to approach an artefact displayed inside a museum hall to see appear, in overlapping, specific pop-ups on the monitor, from which it will be possible to access additional digital contents. Similarly, the display of this content will be inhibited after it has gone away.

Augmented reality offers a further possibility that allows, in a simple and effective way, to guide the user during the visit. The possibility of visualizing in augmented reality and real time the useful indications to reach a specific place gives the possibility to study and suggest the best route aimed at making the understanding of a particular cultural heritage more effective (Fig. 7).

Finally, these new tools can also provide important information to site managers, through the registration and transmission of data regarding the paths followed by users or time spent in specific places. These data, collected in respect of privacy, can be used, for example, to identify any critical issues that may interfere with an optimal site visit.

Fig. 7. Paris, Museum of the Cité de l'architecture et du patrimoine. A virtual button appears on the display when approaching the portal in the moulages gallery.

3 Conclusions

It is evident that in the field of cultural heritage, applications for visualization in augmented reality today are able to provide a powerful and unprecedented tool for reading artefacts and architectures. Its innovative character opens new branches of research in the digital representation, aimed at communication and transmission of knowledge on architectural studies.

Acknowledgements. The activity presented in the paper is part of the research grant supported by University of Venice IUAV and the Archaeological Park of Selinunte.
I thank the architect Chiara Scarnò for providing me with the digital model of the Temple E.

References

Cannella M (2018) La realtà aumentata come strumento interattivo per la diffusione della conoscenza: l'isolato urbano FF1 nel Parco Archeologico di Selinunte. In: Rappresentazione/Materiale/Immateriale. Atti del 40° convegno dei docenti della Rappresentazione. Gangemi Editore, Roma, pp 389–396

Cannella M, Gay F (2018) Ambienti aumentati e archeologia dei media. In: Luigini A, Panciroli C (eds) Ambienti digitali per l'educazione all'arte e al patrimonio. Franco Angeli, Milano, pp 64–78

Cannella M (2017) Per un teatro dell'architettura e della città: teorie e pratiche di realtà aumentata alla Cité de l'architecture et du patrimoine al Palais de Chaillot (Parigi). In: Territori e frontiere della Rappresentazione. Atti del 39° convegno dei docenti della Rappresentazione. Gangemi Editore, Roma, pp 1691–1699

Bertocci S, Arrighetti A, Valzano V, Bartolomei C (eds) (2015) Survey and documentation for archaeology. SCIRES-IT Sci Res Inf Tech 5(2) (special Issue). http://caspur-ciberpublishing.it/index.php/scires-it/issue/view/756

Gaiani M, Benedetti B, Apollonio FI (2011) Teorie per rappresentare e comunicare i siti archeologici attraverso modelli critici. SCIRES-IT Sci Res Inf Technol 1(2):33–70 http://caspur-ciberpublishing.it/index.php/scires-it/article/view/9549/8918

Digital Cultural Heritage: From Educational Experience to the Artefact in Augmented Reality

C. Panciroli[✉], A. Macauda[✉], and L. Corazza[✉]

Department of Education Sciences "G.M. Bertin", University of Bologna,
via Filippo Re 6, 40126 Bologna, Italy
{chiara.panciroli, anita.macauda,
laura.corazza}@unibo.it

Abstract. Several national and international research studies have highlighted important aspects linked to the application of augmented reality in the educational contexts, with particular reference to education concerning the cultural patrimony. The augmented reality ambients indeed offer different training opportunities: some with cognitive finalities others in terms of active participation, others, again by means of the realisation of experiences of an expressive-creative kind with high coefficients of imagination. Specifically speaking, this contribution aims to propose the results of research carried out on three case studies, relating to school projects that are situated in the field of a process of knowledge, participation and recreation of the cultural patrimony in ambients of augmented reality through the construction of new digital artefacts.

Keywords: Education · Artefact · Heritage · Augmented reality · Digital environments

1 Introduction

Several studies have shown the educational potential of the digital ambients (virtual, augmented and hybrid), in which each student can experience concrete learning models of a cognitive and socio-relational nature. In this regard, the mediation of educational contents in ambients of augmented reality represents an innovative research field (Rivoltella 2010; Rossi 2013; Ranieri and Pieri 2014; Billinghurst and Duenser 2012; Brown 2015; Diegmann et. 2015; Guerra and Rossi 2016; Hills-Duty 2017…), with particular reference to education in the cultural heritage (Bacca et al. 2014; Smith 2016…). The design and construction of digital ambients in augmented reality for education in heritage falls within the actions of the PON – National Operative Program "For the school, competences and ambients for learning 2014–2020" (MIUR 2017) that

---

This contribution, fully shared by the three authors, was drawn up as follows: paragraphs "Introduction", "Ambients of augmented learning" and "Conclusion" by Chiara Panciroli; paragraph "Augmented reality and digital heritage" by Anita Macauda and paragraph "Augmented reality and educational experience" by Laura Corazza.

© Springer Nature Switzerland AG 2019
A. Luigini (Ed.): EARTH 2018, AISC 919, pp. 345–354, 2019.
https://doi.org/10.1007/978-3-030-12240-9_37

support the need to sensitive the students in regard to their own cultural, artistic and landscape heritage to construct full citizenship. In particular, the public notice for the enhancement of cultural heritage education recognises among the significant project proposals also "the access, exploration, knowledge and valorisation, also digital, through technological experimentation, of the heritage." In this perspective, the schools are trying out new experiences with the heritage, oriented to the diffusion of a digital culture, for the knowledge and valorisation of the cultural assets through forms of digital artistic creation (i.e. performing arts) and digital communication (i.e. digital media, e-learning).

2 Ambients of Augmented Learning

The scientific literature shows how in the educational ecosystem physical-virtual didactic spaces and different languages are interwoven in an the increasingly natural way within a multimodal perspective (Kress 2004). The reference is to the ubiquitous ecologies as emerging systems in which old and new media, physical and digital ambients are designed, realised and enjoyed as a homogeneous whole (Rosati 2013). In the specific case of school teaching, the digital ambients can take on the role of mediators as a function of a renewed and expanded knowledge: they allow the student to converse with the world and with knowledge and to build bridges between different levels of the same knowledge (Damiano 2013). Furthermore, the digital ambients represent a privileged context of re-elaboration and creation (Panciroli 2017): they allow the user not only to access the information but also to experience and create new artefacts bearing original meanings in an ecosystemic perspective. Indeed, each artefact carries with it a series of visible and invisible connections with other elements of experience and with other artefacts that constitute the actual added value of that product.

Hence, with the spreading of visual wealth provided by technology and the development of the possibilities of interaction, the digital ambients become the place in which both the manifestations of creativity and expressivity can be connected in the educational ambient and those of design and experimentation. "The new technological instruments and their application are capable of offering concrete potential only is they are put at the service of critical models of didactic mediation and are developed within a precise educational, mindful and coherent project" (Panciroli 2016). Specifically, augmented reality can be used for visual forms of learning, capable of producing a significant impact on the experiences, enhancing them in terms of knowledge and re-elaboration (experiential amplification). Indeed, unlike the virtual reality, in the ambients of augmented reality it is possible to continue to see what surrounds the user via digital data that are overlapping and enrich the real world (Rossi 2013), providing new learning experiences. The immediate reference is to the distributed character of knowledge, with the possibility to access multiple informational resources. By means of augmented reality we have a shift in focus from instructing to learning transforming the spaces of knowledge from places for codified knowledge to laboratories for the acquisition of knowledge (Bonaiuti et al. 2016). The student therefore is not an acritical consumer of knowledge but rather a constructor and interpreter. The experimentations of the last few years in the school domain have been made possible above all by the growing use both of the smartphone (hand-held display) equipped with powerful microprocessors, cameras, accelerometers and sensors as well as digital compasses and GPS, and applications based on the video-see-through technique that allow one to superimpose virtual graphic elements upon the real environment.

Specifically, the experiences of augmented reality are the result of the combination of several elements: the application, contents, interaction, physical ambient and participants. The application is the programme that allows for the organisation and the control of the different aspects of the augmented reality experience, amongst which the recognition of the physical world with reference to the digital contents and the synchronisation between physical and virtual world, so as to add the digital elements to the user's vision. The augmented content, the digital layer, includes all the objects, the idea, the stories and the sensorial stimuli and can appear in different formats (texts, images, video and animations). The interaction allows the user to observe the digital layer from different points of view or perspectives. Also, each experience of augmented reality is closely tied to the physical ambient in which it is realised and to the real object that is augmented with virtual information. Those participating in the experience have a central role, because their needs, actions and movements influence the whole system of creation and recreation of the contents of augmented reality (Herrington and Crompton 2016; Hills-Duty 2017). Hence, by means of augmented reality technologies virtual objects and real objects end up coexisting in another space, an ≪intelligent distributed space in which it becomes ever more difficult to distinguish between real and virtual and where the mobile technologies mediate the experience of a new sense of space, which we can call augmented≫ (Ranieri and Pieri 2014, p. 22). In this new space, several subjects can collaborate and construct new digital artefacts composed of fragments, each one of which not only maintains its own autonomy and identity but, being inserted in a shared system, can converse with other artefacts. In this sense, the experience with these artefacts is configured as a process, that is an evolution in space and time, facts and behaviours tied to one another.

3 Augmented Reality and Digital Heritage

Recent studies attest to how the "Sciences and Humanities & Arts are the fields of education where AR has been applied the most" (Bacca et al. 2014). Indeed, vis-à-vis the heritage, augmented reality is configured as a "stimulating agent" which leads, according to original approaches, to discovering, knowing, narrating and reinterpreting the cultural objects and elaborating new ones, in turn, to convey and share with the community (Arduini 2012; Di Serio et al. 2013; Ranieri 2015; Smith 2016; Chen et al. 2017; Gabbari et al. 2017). The experiences that some pilot schools have carried out in the past few years can provide some significant elements for a reflection on some fundamental aspects tied to the experimentation of didactive pathways on the heritage in augmented reality. In particular, here we shall examine three case studies relating to experiences with the heritage developed by secondary schools. These projects fall within the scope of events and/or cultural events and expositions that promote the cultural heritage via the digital (Global Junior Challenge, Competition Crowddreaming: the young co-create digital culture," Monumenti Aperti, Settimane della cultura Digitale, Biennale dei Licei Artistici…). Some of these initiatives can be traced back to the DiCultHer - Digital Cultural Heritage, Arts & Humanities School, a network agreement finalised, as regards the educational sphere, to "endowing the pupils with a series of cultural and scientific instruments addressed to stimulating interdisciplinarity (…) and developing a digital culture in the conservation and the valorisation of the cultural heritage in the arts and the human sciences" (DiCultHer 2015).

First Case Study "Hostel Project"
The "Hostel Project" (https://www.progettohostel.it/) was realised by the Liceo Artistico Musicale Foiso Fois of Cagliari in the school years 2016–17 e 2017–18 (referent Prof. Beatrice Artizzu) and involved fifty students from the third, fourth and fifth years, besides some former pupils. The project's main aim was to make known, through the digital technologies, the transformations that in the course of the centuries have characterised the ambients of the Complesso Monumentale di Sant'Antonio di Cagliari: ancient convent before, already starting from the 15th century, it was converted into a hospital; in the second half of the 20th century, the rooms of the ancient convent were transformed into a school building and then, in more recent times, the current hostel was built. These spaces have been reproposed by the students through the planning, realisation and setting up of a virtual museum, a space of continuous work-in-progress correlated to the platform DiCultHer and accessible by means of augmented reality technologies. Specifically, via augmented reality the virtual museum user can access the three-dimensional reconstructions that show the transformation of the ancient monumental complex, the previous planimetries and the animations with period photographs. By means of this project, the students have been able to gain skills in the environmental, naturalistic, territorial, urban, architectural, artistic, historical-literary, chemical, physical-mathematical, computer, musical fields, through a series of creative laboratories that have seen the disciplines taught at the secondary school interact according to different moments of the sharing of intents (Fig. 1).

Second Case Study "Discovering Hidden Paths Through Augmented Reality"
The project "Discovering hidden paths through augmented reality" (http://www.gjc.it/it/progetti/alla-scoperta-dei-cammini-nascosti-attraverso-la-realt%C3%A0-aumentata) was realised by the Istituto di Istruzione Superiore Alberto Castigliano of Asti in the school years 2016–17 and 2017–18 and continues to be developed in the school year 2018–19 (referent Prof. Maria Stella Perrone). The project, which took part in the international competition Global Junior Challenge on the innovative use of technologies in education, involved twenty students from the fourth and fifth years for the realisation of a historical-geographic pathway of valorisation of the Piedmontese territory. The students first of all tried out new techniques of representation through augmented reality; subsequently they collected information, also with the collaboration of experts from institutions and associations. Lastly, they started to construct digital pathways in augmented reality addressed to illustrating the historical, social and economic peculiarities of some "hidden routes," "ways and paths" that cross Piedmont and that, with the passing of time, have been forgotten (Perrone 2017).

Fig. 1. Hostel project: digital pathways in augmented reality.

Third Case Study "Augmented Music"
The project "Augmented Music" (http://www.museumreloaded.it/musica-aumen tata-parma-passeggiata-pubblica-restituzione-del-progetto/) was realised by the Liceo Musicale Attilio Bertolucci of Parma, in the school year 2017–18, and involved twenty-six first year pupils (referents Prof. Maria Chiara Iemmola, Agnese Ferrari and Alessandra Mancino).

The objective of the project, which has won the tender "Future Present" promoted by MIUR and UNESCO Young Professionals, was to rediscover one's own city, starting from the ideas produced by the texts and the tunes of the songs that describe it. The students went on the discovery of new viewpoints of the city, guided by the words of different performers and singer-songwriters. In a first phase, the students graphical re-elaborated a specific place described in a song, each one according to his/her own vision, new and original. In a second phase, through augmented reality, the illustrations were overlapped with the real places, thus transforming the public spaces into scenarios of a personal imaginary.

Comparative Analysis of the Case Studies
From a comparison of these case studies, the educational potentials of augmented reality emerge in the field of the valorisation of the material (libraries, archives, museums, archaeological and architectural heritage) and immaterial heritage (demo-ethno-anthropological assets), in regard to three main dimensions: knowledge, participation and re-elaboration.

In the first case study, the "Progetto Hostel", the augmented reality is tied to a strongly cognitive educational dimension, which has ed the young generations to know, deepen and reconstruct the architectural heritage of their own territory of belonging, by means of hypermedia creations and projects of urban regeneration. As highlighted by the project referent, Prof. Beatrice Artizzu: "Augmented reality has helped to compose a history of the monument by encompassing the different plans of the students according to a unitary project, but with different ways of interacting with the public and different digital media, reviving the relationship of proximity with beauty."

In the second case study, "Discovering hidden paths through augmented reality," the participative dimension of the heritage is valorised. The rediscovered "routes," described and communicated by means of augmented reality, are made accessible not only to the inhabitants of the territory but also to tourists and cultural, economic and political operators. Augmented reality has thus fostered the cohesion and the social integration, promoting both the rediscovery of a 'hidden' and 'forgotten' heritage, and the sense of belonging to the community. The students have indeed been able to deepen the history of the territory in which they reside, keeping alive its historical memory and the traditions, and sharing it also with their companions coming from other territorial realities and from other countries. Through these digital itineraries both the material heritage has been rediscovered, experienced and shared, and the immaterial contents and values bound to the territory.

In the third case study proposed, "Augmented Music," the students discovered/rediscovered the material assets of the heritage (certain places of the city) through immaterial goods (the texts and the melodies of the songs). Of these assets, the students provided their own personal interpretation, through a graphic re-elaboration, digitally transposed and communicated with the applications of augmented reality. Each place/asset of the city has thus been enriched through the augmented reality with new meanings constructed by the students and shared with the whole city through a perspective of a diffuse and involving cultural heritage. These artefacts in augmented reality, as explained by the referents of the project, have led to "creating a full-fledged virtual map, a digital exposition of street art works of the future in which the visions of the students will be stratified upon the reality."

4   Augmented Reality and Educational Experience

By projecting and developing digital and augmented environments, it is possible to improve communicative and digital skills in the production and dissemination of images and in knowledge of art and the heritage.

The digital environment can not only be used as a simple means of transmitting contents but it can also help us experience spaces and things. This is possible thanks to particular techniques for the production of sounds and moving pictures, which allow us to have real, sensory, cultural and artistic experiences. In any case, they can be thought of as educational experiences because the person develops knowledge and skills thanks to the relationship with objects, ideas and sensory and emotive perceptions.

According to John Dewey's philosophy of Pragmatism, aesthetic experience is more than a bare observation of reality because it leads to real processes of knowledge. For this to happen, experience has to be the result of interaction between the body and the environment and must develop strong emotive and aesthetic perceptions.

Emotions, in particular, lead to knowledge processes by generating meanings.

An emotive situation, which can be created by both an artist and a teacher for didactic purposes, can develop new perceptive and cognitive modalities. According to Dewey, objects or only intellectual thoughts can generate an experience.

In order to create knowledge, however, there has to be a proper balance actions and feelings. Therefore, Dewey compares teachers to artists. The former, indeed, are able to create situations where both what is being learned and the learner, through situations and tasks, play an important role. To sum up, the quality of the experience and its emotive power determine the quality of the learning ability itself (Dewey 1949, 1951, 1954).

Dewey's philosophy leads us to rethink the relation between art and technology. In the case of augmented reality, which makes use of visual arts and media language techniques, interactive and virtual media play the role of re-projecting reality. The latter has more than a merely contemplative function, because thanks to art, it acquires the role of mediator. These media are iconographic and make use of moving images.

Therefore, audiovisual language is widely used. Both cinema and these types of media have a strong relationship with art, on one hand, and education, on the other.

According to Dewey, art and education create a common space, which can be occupied by many different realities such as cinema and its languages, forms and knowledge-mediators (Fig. 2). This is an active dimension that contains structures and ideas of both worlds, ending up looking a little like one and then a like the other.

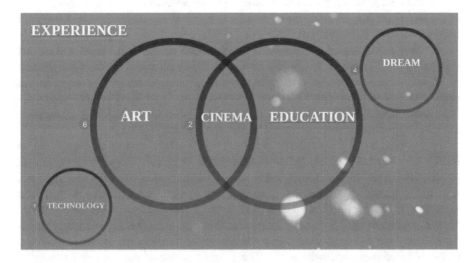

Fig. 2. Experience between art and education

In the 20th Century, the so-called "philosophy of cinema" demonstrated that cinema is art. A movie is considered art form because it gives rise to emotion and thoughts, questions and different worldviews (Carroll 2011). Central to this is the concept of experience, because a movie is a cultural product. Furthermore, it is a strong experience for the public because it transmits temporality and dynamism and offers a strong emotional impact.

Cinema has the incredible ability to show several points of view, first and third person at the same time, with different filming techniques, photography and sound editing (Cabrera 2000). Viewing becomes an artistic rather than a technological experience. Like any other form of art, it withstands time, and any type of technological innovation (Casetti 2005, 2015).

The connection between cinema and technology is shown in the picture as a separate bubble together with experience and the dream, which is another typical element of art, education and cinema. Cinema is the expression of soul and feelings. It shows the soul of things and artists show their soul in things (Godard 1971).

Cinema is inspired by poetry and dreams are its major component. The "Cinema of poetry" is the artistic and metaphorical experience of past and emotions (Pasolini 1979). According to Pier Paolo Pasolini, cinema is an artistic language because it plays the role of a parabola and it is not a direct philosophical expression. It belongs to poetry and not to the novel or drama. Cinema contains an irrational element that cannot be removed. The attempt to turn cinema into pure technology has the effect of leading the unconscious and the dreamlike element back into the background, making it invisible to a superficial view. This allows people to use cinema inappropriately and to seek rationality through specific formats, that is, a production of commercial and standardized movies.

On the contrary, a film director who aims to produce an arthouse film knows that an unconventional glossary is needed, in order to express his ideological and poetic vision of reality. Therefore, cinema can exist only as a metaphor. Reverie plays a huge and important role in it (Pasolini 1972).

Pasolini often highlights the audiovisual nature of cinema, which means that images are as relevant as words and sounds and they all make up the final product. Their connection, in the overall editing, creates a huge amount of stylistic and expressive possibilities. The viewer, on the other hand, is required to have good skills in understanding and interpreting the audiovisual product that modifies, as a narration, the relation between viewer and what he/she sees (Manzoli 2001).

Augmented Reality is similar to cinema. Their production and their enjoyment are similar to production and enjoyment of audiovisual products. Their strong multimedia connotation needs the same knowledge of multimedia and audiovisual language as a film. In the collective imagination, a movie is easier to understand than a book. That is not actually true. Never mind. The reason is that audiovisual narration fascinates the viewer and makes us live a captivating cultural experience. This is particularly true in our contemporary society, where there are even more and different spaces and chances to use video contents (Casetti 2015). The Internet is one of these spaces, as well as mobile apps and Augmented Reality software that reads and rebuilds narratives through images and sounds. We believe that the characteristics of the cinematographic and aesthetic experience as well, together with the language of poetry and emotions of art, make these experiences educational.

5   Conclusions

The augmented digital environments highlight the complex structure of the skills to be put on the web, facilitating the integration between different disciplinary fields (literary, historical, artistic, archaeological, philosophical, anthropological, scientific…), along with the re-elaboration and reinterpretation in a creative way of the heritage, through new means of participation. In the case studies taken into examination, the ambients of augmented reality become suitable spaces for the creation and production of artefacts that reinterpret, also in narrative form, the objects of the cultural heritage. The real objects enriched with digital contents allow the youngsters to describe and tell their own experiential context and share it with others. If indeed every digital artefact is part of an ecosystem, then it should be conceived and analysed as part of a complexity and not as an isolated entity, with particular reference to the co-creation of digital culture. In this regard the Digital Cultural Heritage "identifies entities, processes and phenomena whose essence, manifestation and expression lie in the transferability and reproducibility in space and time of the assets that categorise, identify and qualify the history and the existence of the communities with their social and cultural context" (DiCultHer 2017). In this sense, the artefacts of augmented reality, constructed by the youngster starting from the direct relationship with the cultural objects/gods, also by means of the language of art and specifically that of cinema, reinterpret the heritage creatively and allow the aesthetic experience to be enjoyed to the full.

Acknowledgements.   The activity presented in the paper is part of the research grant.

References

Arduini G (2012) La realtà aumentata e nuove prospettive educative. Educ Sci Soc 3:209–216
Bacca J, Baldiris S, Fabregat R, Graf S, Kinshuk (2014) Augmented reality trends in education: a systematic review of research and applications. J Educ Technol Soc 17(4):133–149
Billinghurst M, Duenser A (2012) Augmented reality in the classroom. Computer 45(7):56–63
Bonaiuti G, Calvani A, Ranieri M (2016) Fondamenti di didattica. Teoria e prassi dei dispositivi formativi. Carocci, Roma
Brown P (2015) How to transform your classroom with augmented reality. EdSurge News. https://www.edsurge.com/news/2015-11-02-how-to-transform-your-classroom-with-augmented-reality. Accessed 21 Apr 2018
Cabrera J (2000) Da Aristotele a Spielberg. Capire la filosofia attraverso i film. Mondadori, Milano
Carroll N (2011) La filosofia del cinema. Dino Audino, Roma
Casetti F (2005) L'occhio del Novecento. Cinema, esperienza, modernità. Bompiani, Milano
Casetti F (2015) La Galassia Lumière. Sette parole chiave per il cinema che viene. Saggi Bompiani, Milano
Chen P, Liu X, Cheng W, Huang R (2017) A review of using augmented reality in education from 2011 to 2016. In: Popescu et al (eds) Innovations in smart learning. Springer, Singapore
Damiano E (2013) La mediazione didattica. FrancoAngeli, Milano
Dewey J (1949) Esperienza e educazione. La Nuova Italia, Firenze 1938
Dewey J (1951) L'arte come esperienza. La Nuova Italia, Firenze 1934

Dewey J (1954) Il mio credo pedagogico. Antologia di scritti sull'educazione, trad. it. a cura di Lamberto Borghi. La Nuova Italia, Firenze

DiCultHer (2015) Accordo di rete in Digital Cultural Heritage, Arts and Humanities. https://www.diculther.it/accordo-di-rete/. Accessed 19 June 2018

DiCultHer (2017) Il Manifesto "Ventotene Digitale". https://www.diculther.it/blog/2017/03/24/il-manifesto-ventotene-digitale/. Accessed 19 June 2018

Diegmann P, Schmidt-Kraepelin M, Van Den Eynden S, Basten D (2015) Benefits of augmented reality in educational environments. A systematic literature review. http://www.wi2015.uni-osnabrueck.de/Files/WI2015-D-14-00036.pdf. Accessed 12 Apr 2018

Di Serio Á, Ibáñez BM, Kloos CD (2013) Impact of an augmented reality system on students' motivation for a visual art course. Comput Educ 68:586–596

Gabbari M, Gagliardi R, Gaetano A, Sacchi D (2017) Comunicazione e apprendimento "aumentati" in classe – Fare lezione a scuola con la realtà aumentata. Bricks 1:8–30 SIe-L - Società Italiana di e-Learning

Godard JL (1971) Il cinema è il cinema. Garzanti, Milano

Guerra L, Rossi PG (eds) (2016) Come le tecnologie cambiano la scuola, come la scuola cambia le tecnologie, *Pedagogia oggi*, no. 2

Herrington KS, Crompton H (2016) Augmented learning with augmented reality. In: Churchill D, et al (eds) Mobile learning design. Springer, Singapore

Hills-Duty R (2017) Technology in education - the effect of VR and AR. VR/Focus. https://www.vrfocus.com/2017/08/technology-in-education-the-effect-of-vr-and-ar/. Accessed 12 Mar 2018

Kress G (2004) Multimodalità. Un approccio socio-semiotico alla comunicazione contemporanea. Progedit, Bari

Manzoli G (2001) Voce e silenzio nel cinema di Pier Paolo Pasolini. Pendragon, Bologna

MIUR (2017) Avviso pubblico per il potenziamento dell'educazione al patrimonio culturale, artistico, paesaggistico. http://www.istruzione.it/pon/avviso_patrimonio-artistico.html. Accessed 12 June 2018

Panciroli C (2016) Le professionalità educative tra scuola e musei. Esperienze e metodi nell'arte. Guerini, Milano

Panciroli C (2017) Ecosistemi digitali. In: Corazza L (ed) Apprendere con i video digitali. Per una formazione online aperta a tutti. FrancoAngeli, Milano

Pasolini PP (1972) Empirismo eretico. Garzanti, Milano

Pasolini PP (1979) Il cinema in forma di poesia. Edizioni Cinemazero, Pordenone

Perrone MS (2017) Didatticamente immersi nella realtà aumentata nella realizzazione di un progetto divertente. Bricks 1:31–39 SIe-L - Società Italiana di e-Learning

Ranieri M, Pieri M (2014) Mobile learning. Dimensioni teoriche, modelli didattici, scenari applicativi. Unicopli, Milano

Ranieri M (2015) Bring your own device all'università. Un'esperienza di storytelling con i dispositivi mobili. TD Tecnologie Didattiche 23(1):46–49

Rivoltella PC (2010) Oltre il virtuale: la nostra è una 'realtà aumentata'. Vita e Pensiero 5:102–108

Rosati L (2013) Ecosistemi fisico-digitali: progettare e produrre contenuti per i media integrati. Problemi dell'informazione 1:12–24

Rossi PG (2013) Realtà aumentata e mediazione didattica. In: Persico D, Midoro V (eds) Pedagogia nell'era digitale. Menabò, Ortona

Smith D (2016) Augmented reality in art education. The University of Arizona Libraries. Estratto da. http://arizona.openrepository.com/arizona/handle/10150/621860. Accessed 12 May 2018

SAR for Kids: Spatial Augmented Reality as Tool for Art Education

Daniele Rossi[✉]

School of Architecture and Design "E. Vittoria",
University of Camerino, Camerino, Italy
daniele.rossi@unicam.it

Abstract. This article, after describing some possible developments of spatial augmented reality (SAR) in urban areas since the first experiments by Bruno Munari, will present two SAR experiences into public spaces for cultural heritage education of school-age children. These experiences were aimed, on the one hand, to verify the potential of live drawing on large dimensions and on the other to represent one's own personal graphic interpretation of an urban façade on the basis of suggestions deriving from a specific event: the passage of the Giro d'Italia.

Keywords: Video-mapping · Spatial augmented reality · Sketching · Cultural heritage

1 Introduction

When the book *Painting Photography Film* was published in 1925, the artist and theoretician Lazslo Moholy-Nagy dedicated a chapter to what he called "Domestic pinacotheca". In it, the author tried to imagine the future developmental results of techniques to reproduce texts, images, and sounds. Ten years before Walter Benjamin's celebrated essay "The Work of Art in the Age of Mechanical Reproduction", Moholy-Nagy spoke of the possibility of developing an "image-transmission service via radio" that would allow for a further increase in the spread of photographic reproduction, which was already profoundly modifying the relationship of the masses with works of art. "It is probable that future development will place great importance on projecting kinetic compositions, which could even very likely be obtained from the mutual intersection of rays and coloured masses freely fluctuating in space" (Moholy-Nagy 1925).

In the new techniques of reproduction and the wireless transmission of images and sounds he therefore saw a factor capable of notably modifying the relationship between art and the public (Somaini 2017).

In 1954 Bruno Munari designed about a hundred compositions created with the most varied materials inserted in slide frames. The resulting projections, built with "transparent, semitransparent, and opaque materials, brightly or subtly coloured, with physical materials that are cut, torn, burned, scratched, melted, etched, crushed; with animal and plant tissue, with artificial fibres, with chemical solutions" [*trasparenti, semitrasparenti e opachi, violentemente colorati o a colori delicatissimi, con materie plastiche tagliate, strappate, bruciate, graffiate, liquefatte, incise, polverizzate;*

© Springer Nature Switzerland AG 2019
A. Luigini (Ed.): EARTH 2018, AISC 919, pp. 355–363, 2019.
https://doi.org/10.1007/978-3-030-12240-9_38

con tessuti animali e vegetali, con fibre artificiali, con soluzioni chimiche] (Munari 1954), eliminate the physical nature of the material fragments and, projected onto large surfaces, render a monumental, spectacular aspect.

One of the goals of the experimentation was to bring artistic production, all contained in the exclusive circuit of galleries and museums, down to a private domestic scale. The glamourization of anonymous projected elements should create a creative short circuit that carries with it the fun and games necessary to involve spectators.

Spectators would be able to use a private art gallery projected on the walls of their rooms at home. In this respect, he states: "Modern living has given use music on disks (and no one thinks about calling an orchestra to their home in order to listen to music): now it gives us projected paintings; and everyone close to the disco can have their own projected art gallery, made, however, of originals and numbered copies" [*Il vivere moderno ci ha dato la musica in dischi (e nessuno pensa di chiamare una orchestra in casa per sentirsi una musica): ora ci dà la pittura proiettata; e ognuno vicino alla discoteca, può avere la sua pinacoteca fatta però di originali e di copie numerate, da proiettare*] (Munari 1954).

In 1959, Munari designed a game in a box for direct projection called "Scatola" for the company Danese in Milan. In the brochure, Munari specifies that the kit contains: "...all the material necessary to make small transparent compositions for projection in colour (like those that Munari projected in New York and Stockholm, in museums and private houses), a new technique for visual arts" [*...tutto il materiale occorrente per fare piccole composizioni trasparenti da proiettare a colori una tecnica nuova per l'arte visiva*] (Fig. 1).

Fig. 1. "Scatola" for direct projections by Munari (left) and direct projection on a wall (right)

In a similar way, works by Claes Oldenburg and Coosje van Bruggen follow the concept of art as a social function in a pop context. In particular, the large-scale projects — monumental sculptures in architectural scale or incongruous buildings in a sculptural key — aim to solidify the relationship between individual and community, between private and public, through operations of gigantism applied to small objects taken from daily life that become monumental in the true sense of the word.

Therefore, if enlargement for Munari was an exploratory action capable of upsetting the sense of projected material fragments, for Oldenburg, the outsized object was an act of rejection towards a society that had made the object an idol to adore.

What unites the two approaches is the willingness to "see better", to observe and discover unexpected characteristics and details or simply reject their presence, enlarging them innumerable times until one becomes immersed within them.

2 Spatial Augmented Reality

More than fifty years after Bruno Munari's experiments with projection, a form of contemporary art also based on the projection of light and the magnification of images allows for educational experiences in the form of interactive/immersive fun entertainment: spatial augmented reality (Bimber and Raskar 2005). Spatial augmented reality, which is found in public places in shows better known as video mapping (Antonelli and Mordenti 2011; Maniello 2014), represent first of all a new means to communicate and enhance the architectural heritage. Video mapping allows augmented reality experiences to be made in the absence of appropriate viewing devices (glasses or head-mounted displays), through video projections on large surfaces, which is capable of programmatically changing the architectural connotation and making the user participate in the representation of a virtual depiction in a real space (Ippoliti et al. 2012). The content of these projections can be more or less philologically and scientifically tuned according to the reference public and the goals of the event. In most shows that have populated the squares of small and large urban centres in recent years, the main goal is to emotionally involve the public/visitor, who thereby becomes immersed in another dimension of time (Leila Ciagà 2013). The repertoire of pertinent effects are those deriving from motion graphics (CGI sequences usually depict fragmentations, explosions, systems of particles, the effects of physical simulation, and digital clothing). Due to the ephemeral character of the show, there is limited time (between 7 and 15 min) in which a series of content aimed at pure visual entertainment, the understanding of plastic intelligence, and the history of the building on which it is projected must be concentrated. As of writing, the use of Google Trends to compare the three terms most used to identify this type of show, i.e., 3D mapping, projection mapping, and video mapping, sheds light on some facts (Fig. 2).

The first is that on the date of first detection in 2004, the use of the three terms was very distinct, a symptom of the novelty of the medium, which was freed for the first time from the pioneering activities of university laboratories or the R&D departments of large companies (e.g., Disney). The second is that on the contrary, after more than twenty years, the three terms are used interchangeably, as can be seen from the superposition of the lines, without any term in particular having the upper hand. The third is that the trend of the three terms, that is, the recursiveness of the query on Google is in slight decline, a sign perhaps that this type of show has partly exhausted its attractiveness tied to the surprise effect of seeing a live show for the first time. With regard to the latter point, it is clear that the medium may be exhausting its innovative

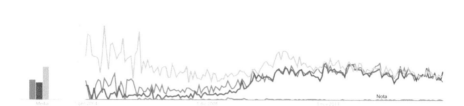

video mapping
Termine di ricerca

projection mapping
Termine di ricerca

mapping 3D
Termine di ricerca

spatial augmented …
Termine di ricerca

Fig. 2. Google trends diagram comparing three terms referred to spatial augmented reality

strength and that it should therefore be reinvented and remedied through other forms of entertainment. Watching videos on the Internet that are published daily on video-sharing platforms, one can see a general trend in the use of video mapping in commercial areas specifically dedicated to marketing and publicity. Another trend relates to shows that are produced to include elements for public interaction, engaging a public that usually passively watches a show in silence (often with the smartphone camera pointed at the illuminated façade), in the same way people might view a fireworks show or a theatre performance. Low-cost 3D sensors and scanners, infrared cameras, and a series of high-tech wearable accessories natively designed for gaming now allow projectable content to be personalized, choreographing the show based on the spectators' behaviours and gestures (Rossi 2013).

3   SAR for Kids

In recent years, these performance demonstrations of graphical calculus and electronic intelligence have been combined with secondary events aimed at educating and entertaining a public of children, usually between 5 and 10 years old, making sheets as large as an entire building available through the use of Munari's projective enlargement.

In Italy, some examples include (Fig. 3):

3.1   Glow Festival

Glow Festival, an International video-mapping festival, designed and realized in Ostuni (LE) by Studio Glowarp under Donato Maniello and Visual Designer Luigi Console. In the four years it was held (2013–2016), different activities dedicated to children were incorporated, including a section called Mapping4Kids. In this way, children would be able to send the organization their designs on a printed outline of the surface where it would be projected. In fact, as the call reads: "This year the GLOWFestival opens the door to the kids! We provide the paths (black and white) that will be printed on a A4 sheet (do not in any way distort the image when printing and scanning). At this point the imagination of the little ones will do the rest! The designs will transform the facades

Fig. 3. Spatial augmented reality events for kids in Italy

of the buildings through the imagination. Use any technique you want, the important thing is to respect the constraints imposed by the drawing that we provide. When you're finished, seeking help from someone older than you, scan the A4 image that you create and send it by mail with the form filled out by your parent".

3.2   Fotonica

At Macro in Rome, in December 2017, the agency Flyer Communication, which had already designed the LPM Live Performers Meeting, one of the largest events related to audio visual digital arts, organized the FOTONICA Audio Visual Digital Art Festival. The festival hosted events tied to contemporary audiovisual performance. Light installations, NetArt, Vj sets, lectures, and workshops characterized the festival programme. Some of the workshops included Video Mapping for Kids, run by Gianluca Del Gobbo. "During the workshop the kids will create a visual-sound project that will be shown that same evening. They will be invited to work on paper, creating colourful shapes out of it. They will use them to create sounds by putting them on a big interactive screen which will be projected on the facade of L'Aquila cinema. The sound synthesis is generated in real time from the arrangement of forms on the screen, producing melodies that children can invent simply by changing the arrangement of forms". In this case, therefore, visual performance is combined with the spontaneous design of an accompanying audio track.

3.3   Kidsbit

The Kidsbit festival in contrast, held in May 2018 in Perugia, was created expressly as an event dedicated to children. In fact, the slogan was "Creatività digitale per famiglie del 21esimo secolo" [Digital creativity for 21st-century families]. The festival was organized by Associazione ON, which is dedicated to favouring the training, education, and personal and professional development of both children and adults, especially in relation to the tools offered by new technologies. One of the events, *La Città Che Vorrei* [The City I Would Like] held in Piazza IV Novembre on the façade of the Palazzo dei Priori, was dedicated to a video-mapping show for the whole family. In this case, the organization Antica Proietteria, following the example of Mapping4kids in Ostuni, made available the entire layout of the Palazzo. The instructions in the call then summarize all the steps necessary to participate: "…(2) Print it on a normal sheet of A4 paper. (3) Use any colours you want to draw what comes to mind: heroes, heroines, princes, princesses, monsters, aliens, or abstract compositions. (4) VERY IMPORTANT: Sign your drawing with your name. (…). (6) Come, together with all your family, Friday 25 May at 9:30 p.m. in Piazza IV Novembre!" Of particular note is the emphasis on the importance of the signature, which is probably aimed at a hypothetical phase wherein parents share their photos, proud to see their son or daughter's name projected in block letters on one of the main monuments in the city. In this case, the theme for developing the drawings was not open; the call was expressly dedicated to stimulating children's imagination, requesting drawings of their ideal city, composed mostly of some iconic childhood elements (hearts, coloured flowers, rainbows, etc.).

4   Case Studies

Within this cultural framework, the present article presents two experiments with spatial augmented reality for children. The goal is twofold: verifying the potential of live large-scale drawing through direct projection (Senigallia, Piazza Roma 2015) and representing the graphical interpretation of an architectural façade based on suggestions deriving from a specific theme, the Giro d'Italia passing through (Osimo, Piazza Marconi 2018).

4.1   Fosforo 2015

The first experiment took place in Senigallia in May 2015 at the Fosforo: Festival delle Scienze, organized by the cultural association Next. Integrated with a canonical video-mapping show organized by the University of Camerino, a projection system was set up to project children's drawing activities made in the square onto the city hall of Senigallia in real time.

The system was basically composed of a web cam affixed to the column of a copy stand. The web cam was directed downwards where the drawing paper in A3 format containing the outline of the building's façade was situated on the support platform. The part of the sheet between the bulk of the drawing and the edges was filled with black to prevent it from containing any part of the drawing, given that the projection of that part, outside the façade, would not be projected (Fig. 4).

Fig. 4. Set-up of the copy stand

A jig was fixed onto the platform of the copy stand in the mapping phase so that the sheet would not move by itself, thus losing the spatial coordinates to register the drawing with the architectural partition of the façade.

The sheets with the layouts were given to each child during the evening. The children then approached the table and had about 5 min to complete their drawing while spectators directly observed the growth of the drawing and, contextually, the simple gestures of the children, who could act freely using various materials (coloured pencils, felt-tip pens, crayons, etc.), including finger paints. Finger paints wound up being the preferred tool for this type of activity since they are capable of amplifying the performance aspect of live drawing (Fig. 5).

Fig. 5. Some pictures from the event in Senigallia.

4.2   #fotofinish 2018

In Osimo, instead, a different approach was taken, asynchronous and similar to the activities experimented with in Mapping4kids in Ostuni or Kidsbit in Perugia. The opportunity was based on the Giro d'Italia passing through Osimo in 2018 and the events organized by the city administration to celebrate the event. Alongside a video-mapping contest called *Il Giro sui Muri* aimed at students and professionals in the sector on themes tied to the Giro and to the world of cycling in general, a slide show entitled "#fotofinish" was created to be projected on the façade of the Nuova Fenice Theatre in Osimo in Piazza Marconi. The slide show was composed of a series of drawings made by students at some schools in the district of Osimo. For this activity, some schools were involved organically in order to create collective, non-personal class drawings. Art teachers were equipped with A3-format sheets of paper containing line drawings of the façade of the theatre.

The theme on which the representations were to focus in some way allowed students, with free techniques and teacher guidance, to synthetically depict some symbolic elements evocative of the Giro d'Italia and cycling in general. The collective drawings therefore represented a unifying moment to build knowledge both of the sporting event and the architectural heritage with which the drawings were to interact.

The analysis of the resulting drawings shows some dominant colours: pink, that is, the colour of the jersey of the winner of the Giro, and the green, white, and red of the Italian flag. The same drawings also contained some recurring figures that depicted the shape of the Italian boot and bicycles stylized with different degrees of detail, as well as a series of block letter texts used to sign the drawing.

Around half of the resulting drawings left the white background of the sheet, while in the rest, the architectural partitions of the nineteenth-century La Nuova Fenice Theatre were coloured in order to differentiate each part of the building (Fig. 6).

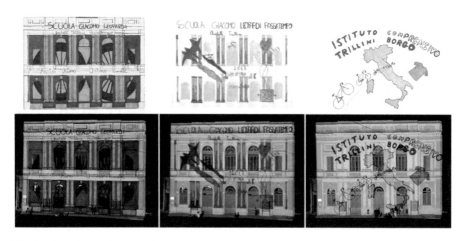

Fig. 6. Comparison between the original drawings and projections on the façade of the Osimo Theater

5 Conclusions

Magnifying drawings and images during a public video-mapping show on urban façades means experimenting with new educational forms aimed at a variegated public composed of adults and children, experts in artistic subjects or simple occasional tourists. Children's drawings, direct and spontaneous, unmediated by digital processing, thus move from a real, manipulable aspect to another that is more abstract and strange. One immediately relates to the individual architectural partitions without scaled mediation.

From scribbles to more complex and primitive human depictions, each drawing presents an unconventional aspect for the child, mediating the step from one reality to another, more extended one, thereby activating an involuntary process of cognitive appropriation of the architectural building.

The playful experience of seeing one's own drawing projected on a large scale represents an approach to knowledge of the artistic and architectural heritage through gesture and action.

Acknowledgements. The activities presented in the paper were promoted by the University of Camerino in collaboration with Fosforo, Senigallia (AN, Italy) Science Festival, and the municipality of Osimo (AN, Italy).

References

Antonelli E, Mordenti A (2011) La videoproiezione architetturale. In: DisegnareCon, vol 4, no 8

Bimber O, Raskar R (2005) Spatial augmented reality. A K Peters, Wellesley

Ippoliti E, Meschini A, Moscati A, Rossi D (2012) Interfacce e tecnologie visual 3D per conoscere, condividere e valorizzare il patrimonio culturale. In: DisegnareCon, vol 5, no 10

Leila Ciagà G (2013) Riproduzioni e ricostruzioni digitali tra ricerca storica, divulgazione e spettacolo. In: Irace F, Ciagà GL, Lupo E, Trocchianesi R (eds) Design & Cultural Heritage. Electa, Milano

Maniello D (2014) Realtà aumentata in spazi pubblici: tecniche base di video mapping. Le penseur

Moholy-Nagy L (1925) Malerei Fotografie Film

Munari B (1954) Le proiezioni dirette di Bruno Munari. In: Domus, no 291, Milano

Rossi D (2013) Smart architectural models: spatial projection-based augmented mock-up. In: Digital heritage international congress 2013, vol 2, pp 677–684. IEEE

Somaini A (2017) Da Dioniso alla televisione" Archeologia dei media e ruolo storiografico del disegno nel progetto ejzenšteniano di una "storia del cinema". In: Faietti M, Nardoni P, Schmidt ED (eds) Ejzenštejn. La rivoluzione delle immagini. Giunti

Art upon Art: The Spatial Augmented Reality as New Value for Contemporary Art and Educational Tool for Art History

Donato Maniello[(✉)]

Studio Glowarp, Expert in Spatial Augmented Reality for Cultural Heritage,
Via F. Crispi 26, 76012 Canosa di Puglia, Italy
info@glowarp.com

Abstract. Contemporary Art is not always well acknowledged even when work of successful talents. Forgotten, if not abandoned by its own community, it is often not recognised as Art by the potential users, as the Italian educational system does not always provide the right tools for its understanding. This paper focuses on two case studies which final aim is to increase the value of Contemporary Art and its educational foundations using the Spatial Augmented Reality (SAR), well known as video mapping, a performative action that allows to "augmenting" the existing contents. Today this artistic form is undergoing a split: on the one hand a growing graphic data processing are turning into independent performance whose immersiveness recalls that of gaming, on the other its use as a means of enhancement and education for Art, including the contemporary one, without taking anything away from the artistic performance. Here we want to show two preparatory performances made recently by the Studio Glowarp that follows the second mentioned front.

Keywords: Spatial Augmented Reality · Video mapping · Contemporary art · Valorization · Edutainment

1 Introduction

The video mapping (Maniello 2014) can be used to highlight goods not always properly appreciated with excellent results. The first case study examines "All Bands" artwork by Sol LeWitt, donated by the author in 2003 to the city of Bari and exhibited in the Spazio Murat. The work (5 × 8 m) placed on the background wall of the Spazio Murat, was underestimated and of difficult fruition for several years even though the original intent was to be the cultural and artistic catalyst of the location. In that unfortunate position, the work was the background of several events for many years and it turned out to be hard to read in the eyes of citizens who often used it at odds with its original value and purpose. In 2013, the Studio submitted a draft of enhancement of the work using video mapping, to raise the citizenry awareness of the work by the means of a multimedia performance. The abovementioned project did not see the light but in 2016, it was decided to "de-contextualize" it and to pay tribute to it during an event created and curated by the Studio Glowarp dedicated to the SAR (Raskar et al. 1998) for the enhancement of the territory: the GLOWFestival (Maniello 2018a). The work was reproduced to scale and an

© Springer Nature Switzerland AG 2019
A. Luigini (Ed.): EARTH 2018, AISC 919, pp. 364–373, 2019.
https://doi.org/10.1007/978-3-030-12240-9_39

international call started. The challenge was to recreate depth in a large and colourful bi-dimensional work together with its enhancement. It was achieved by imposing a black and white or grey scale performance to the participants, veiling and unveiling the original colours in order not to apply new ones.

The second performance was shown during the Kernel Festival in Messina in September 2015, a "classic" video mapping performance but with a new educational purpose. By the combination of Analogue and Digital (Maniello 2018b), the gothic façade of Messina cathedral turned into a support means to give a lecture on contemporary art history that captivated adults and children by the projection on the façade of works loosely based on the 20th century most famous artist's styles. It can therefore been concluded that the connection between art and video mapping as art at the service of art, is far from over and inspiring for the future (Borriaud 2004).

2   Give Depth to a Contemporary Artwork

In 2003, the great master of American Minimalism Sol LeWitt donated one of his "wall drawings" called All Bands to the city of Bari (Fig. 1) and realised it at Spazio Murat (Fig. 2). As often happened for his other works, All Bands was a Sol LeWitt's drawing completed by others by the will of the same artist. The work, placed at the end of the great hall, was the background of several events for many years and it turned out to be hard to read in the eyes of citizens who often used it at odds with its original value and purpose (Fig. 3).

Fig. 1. Master Sol LeWitt at work

A bureaucratic foolishness further complicates matters, or rather the missing certification that attests the authorships of the work. To this day, it has only an emotional and historical value but not the artistic one. It was useless affixing a transparent plexiglas framework by a committee of cultural associations, that hosts the caption of the work and the author's biography in several languages and enforces the respect of a distance from the wall without altering the vision of the work.

These praiseworthy but not effective contributions wanted to focus the attention on the importance of rediscovering, enhancing and defending a part of the city heritage.

Fig. 2. Exterior and interior of the hall

Fig. 3. The work of Sol Lewitt in its original location and how it was awkwardly enjoyed

Even this action seems not to have had the desired effect. Its position have not certainly helped its discernment and is often difficult the coexistence of Sol LeWitt's work and temporary exhibitions. In 2013, the Studio Glowarp submitted a draft for the enhancement of the work by means of video mapping, in order to raise the citizenry awareness of the work by the means of a multimedia performance. Indeed, the promotion measures were not merely video mapping performances but the project provided for a chapeau, a short film that should have to explain its meaning. Unfortunately, the project was not realised in Bari, where the work is located, but the Studio Glowarp decided to "decontextualize" it four years later. A scale model was created by printing four overlapping strips of about 10 cm and then gluing them on multi-layer panels, reaching the video projection dimension of 4 × 2,5 m. The reproduction of the work was positioned at Largo Stella, one of the locations of the IVth edition of the GLOWFestial (Fig. 4).

Fig. 4. The reproduction of the work at Largo Stella, Ostuni

Decontextualizing was a provocation: if the work was not enhanced locally, it would be better to do it elsewhere. This wholly proper precondition explains why the performance was shown during an event, which attempted to revamp the local cultural Heritage, not forgetting to experiment. The work is bi-dimensional and colourful, not a traditional mapping for sure (3D and grey scale or black and white surfaces are usually used). Several challenges had to be met: the performances had to recreate a full three-dimensionality, use black and white or grey scale videos and not least respect the work enhancing it.

It has been used Sanyo PLC-XF70 XGA 9.000 Al video projector, 1,35-1,8 optics, which projected an image of about 5 × 3,7 m on the wood panel at the limit of the frame from a distance of 10 and a height of 2 m. The warping consisted in matching the four corners. The abovementioned matching is possible when the video mapping works on surfaces not volumes, allowing to the real and virtual models to be perfectly overlapping by modifying the positions of the four corners. Creating a grey scale video was actually successful because it created visual effects whose result was the overlay of analogue and digital media. In some cases, the work achieved a deep three-dimensionality, exceeding expectations and adding value to the work.

The technique used to give depth to the work is called 2.5D or pseudo 3D and it were used two types of effects (Maniello 2018c): the 3D effects that recreated the illusion of volume using different grey shades and the 2D effects whose forms breathed life in the background colours (Fig. 5). The interest in this art installation was then demonstrated by the participation of many visitors, especially children, fascinated by the structure and its colours and that read the playful aspect and novelty of the performance (Fig. 6).

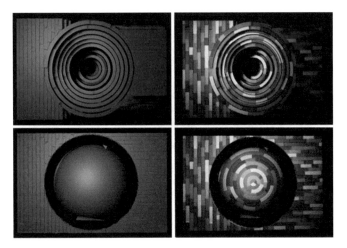

Fig. 5. Rendering and final video effect projected on replica

Fig. 6. The children were fascinated by the result

3 Educating While Having Fun: Mixed Art on Messina Cathedral

In 2015, the Studio Glowarp received an invitation to attend to the Kernel Festival held in Messina. Messina cathedral (Malaspina 2008) has a salient façade (Fig. 7) with sloping roofs placed at different heights and the battlements on their top. Its underbelly is decorated with polychrome landscape oriented inlaid marbles, while the top is totally made of stone and has three gothic monofores and a rose window, both enhanced by elegant transennas. There are three aisles over the three gothic gates; the original gates were designed and chiselled by Polidoro Caldara da Caravaggio. The central gate made by Antonio Baboccio da Piperno in 1412 has a solid and harmonious framework decorated with spiral columns with decorative trim and on both sides, overlapped niches with saint statues. In the architrave, there is the statue of Christ among the Evangelists. In the ogive lunette, frescoed by Letterio Subba in 1840, is placed Giovan Battista Mazzolo's statue named "Virgin Mary an Infant Jesus" dating from 1534, underneath a rich pinnacle adorned by "Virgin Mary's Coronation" medal, work of Pietro de Bonitate dated in 1268. The side gate lunettes has the portrayal of St. Placido and Virgin Mary.

Fig. 7. Duomo of Messina

A double row of two-tone windows marks the sides of the cathedral, while the battlements and the light frame, supported by small corbels, give rhythm and coherence to the whole. The structures are in reinforced concrete, infilled with bricks. Interesting is Messina astronomical clock, part of the cathedral. Built by Strasbourg Ungerer company in 1933, is part of the church bell tower (rebuilt at the beginning of the century after an earthquake), of which is the hallmark. The mechanisms are similar to the ones of Strasbourg's astronomical clock. The astronomical clock of Messina is the biggest and most complex in the world.

4   The Performance Conception

The accurate study of the Messina Cathedral's architecture was a crucial step for the storyboard design that helped organising the contents based on a 3D model and layer masks provided by the organization. The new storyboard element was the use of analogue techniques converted to digital techniques. The façade layout, previously simplified, was printed on a 300gr A3 watercolour paper and then the artist Prof. Buonaventura Maniello illustrated the façade thirteen times as per 20th century avant-garde styles using a mixed technique (Fig. 8).

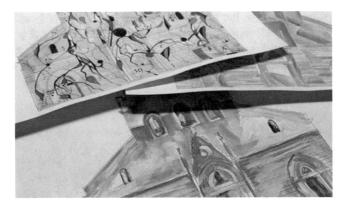

Fig. 8. Part of the works revisited by the artist inspired by the avant-gardes of the 20th century

The drawings are fourteen and only one of these is a digital illustration inspired by Glith Art. A source of inspiration was the work of a well-known Italian artist Mario Mariotti, who in the 80 s had intervened on the façade of the Chiesa di S. Spirito in Florence, left unfinished by Filippo Brunelleschi. He had asked to famous artists, friends and student to work on some projections of the church and to draw the missing parts of the building following their imagination. In those years, the artist had already foreseen how this technique could be used to enhance a cultural asset, catching the glimpse of the evolution of a new artistic frontier, born by merging painting, noble art par excellence, and video mapping.

After having painted each image following the different avant-garde styles, we moved on to scanning the figures in order to start the digital post-production. Each scanned image was about of 8 MB and 300 dpi and was subsequently reduced, until it matched again with the mapping file, to the same video projection resolution parameters of 72dpi (1920 × 1778 px). The digital means used in an analogue context paves the way for a new language and method of use of Art, allowing the final user to dive in new experiences and amplify the senses.

The pictorial projection together with the digital effects allow us to explore and to get the hands on the brush strokes and the colour surveys, giving us new suggestions and making us immerse in the unique visions of the twentieth century artists. The façade sheds its painting skin thanks to the video mapping technique, donating an original viewing to the audience. It proves how analogue and digital can live in beautiful symbiosis, extending the painting concept. Giving a painting life to architecture was a Studio Glowarp's goal too.

The viewer is completely immersed in scenarios that refer to Cubism by Picasso, Action Painting by J. Pollock, Impressionism by C. Monet, Fauvism by H. Matisse, Abstract Painting by V. Kandinsky (Fig. 9), Graffiti Art by J. M. Basquiat, Abstractionism by P. Mondrian, Pop Art by R. Lichtenstein, Pointillism by G. Seurat, Surrealism by J. Mirò (Fig. 10), Spatialism by L. Fontana, Metaphysic by G. De Chirico (Fig. 11), Graffiti Art by K. Haring (Fig. 12), Pop Art by A. Warhol and lastly Glith Art. The musical notes of Peter and the Wolf by Prokofiev accompanied the performance, giving it a hint of irony, result of a contemporary action like clicking on a device.

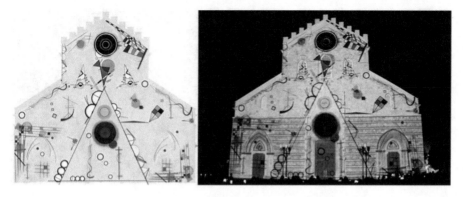

Fig. 9. Work inspired by the abstract painting of V. Kandinsky

Fig. 10. Work inspired by Surrealism by J. Mirò

Fig. 11. Work inspired by the metaphysics of G. De Chirico

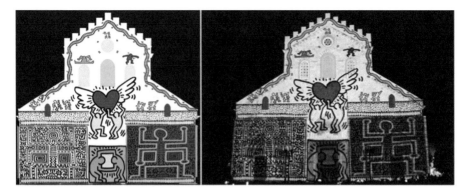

Fig. 12. Work inspired by Graffitiism by K. Haring

The performance's name Souvenir d'Artista#Messina (vimeo.com/glowarp/souvenir) is ironic too, remembering the 80 s trend of giving plastic cameras as souvenir.

The set up of the performance followed the below data sheet: two Christie Roadster HD20 K-J 3-chip DLP video projectors, lens 1.16–1.49:1, distance 45 m, height 6 m. Using the painting techniques of the most famous avant-guard artists, we paid tribute to the modern and contemporary art history turning the cathedral façade into an extemporaneous piece of art. The audience had the opportunity to take home a piece of the performance, going beyond its virtual aspect. The original figures realised, starting point of the performance, have been framed and now are unique art pieces.

5   Conclusions

The choice of using this particular kind of mapping comes from the curiosity of implement the trials started by Mario Mariotti during the 80 s, as well as the chance of studying the new-born relationship with the audience, because it feeds back unknown experiences for first time viewers and not.

The children, who, although not aware of the different artistic styles, revise into the work a perceptive familiarity, thanks to the drawing, a means connected to their playful activity and their enthusiastic comments are proof of this. This artistic test follows and recalls those experimentations already started in the 60 s by artistic movements like Dadaism and Surrealism or, for example, Fluxus, an artistic trend that considered the game and its creative makings the key of the dialogue between artwork and viewer; gaming became a cultural learning or completing process too. In fact, the public, that usually contemplate the artwork passively, now gets involved in its physical reconstruction thanks to today technologies (Carbone 2014).

Interaction should not only be understood as the use of a technology that makes possible to match a process to an action (an event that has now become almost dominant) but also as a mutual influence of the observer elaboration of the concept and the message (Bruno 2016).

McLuhan and Fiore (2011) were already convinced of this when they talked about man's change in thinking and acting in relation to the new media and his consequent perception of the world. The active involvement of the observer is a relatively new experience – for centuries the eyesight prevailed on the other senses – in an age where the cold media, as defined by McLuhan (2015), are dominant, media that involve more sensory organs but transfer limited information. The interactive artistic research is part of this improvement, especially when McLuhan, talking about the figure of the "authentic artist", attributed him the capacity of facing technology as aware of the changes of perception. Any work exists in relation to the men who contemplate it and the art, the games, or even the media are not different.

The artistic avant-garde styles used in the Studio Glowarp's performance were also a tribute to those artistic movements that first had expressed interest in the creative potential of the game, understood by not only the observer but also by the performer, who used the analogical medium thus reinforcing the message then reworked in digital form. The performances on the reproduction of Sol LeWitt's artwork and on Messina Cathedral, demonstrate SAR infinite communicative potentialities when applied to complementary areas; two forms of art that interact with digital tools.

References

Borriaud N (2004) Postproduction. Come l'arte riprogramma il mondo. Postmedia book, Milano

Bruno G (2016) Superfici. A proposito di estetica, materialità e media. Johan & Levi, Monza

Carbone M (2014) Lo schermo, la tela, la finestra (e altre superfici quadrangolari normalmente verticali). Rivista di Estetetica. (numero monografico: Schermi) Univ. Torino Dipartimento Discipkune Filosofiche, pp 21–34

Malaspina F (2008) La Cattedrale di Messina. Antonino Trischitta

McLuhan M, Fiore Q (2011) Il medium è il Messaggio. Corraini

McLuhan M (2015) Gli strumenti del comunicare. Garzanti, Milano

Maniello D (2014) Augmented reality in public spaces. Basic techniques for video mapping, vol 1. Le Penseur

Maniello D (2018a) Augmented Cityscape: the GLOWFestival case as valuator of the territory cultural heritage. In: #EARTH2018 Digital environments for education arts and heritage, 5–6 July, Bressanone, Bolzano

Maniello D (2018b) Tecniche avanzate di video mapping: spatial augmented reality applicata al bene culturale, vol. II. Le Penseur

Maniello D (2018c) Improvements and implementations of the spatial augmented reality applied on scale models of cultural goods for visual and communicative purpose. In: Salento AVR 2018. Vth international conference on AR, VR and CG, vol 2, Issue 2, pp 303–319

Raskar R, Welch G, Fuchs H (1998) Spatially augmented reality. In: Proceeding of the first IEEE workshop on augmented reality, pp 63–72

Augmented Cityscape: The GLOWFestival Case as Valuator of the Territory Cultural Heritage

Donato Maniello[✉]

Studio Glowarp, Expert in Spatial Augmented Reality for Cultural Heritage,
Via F. Crispi 26, 76012 Canosa di Puglia, Italy
info@glowarp.com

Abstract. Studio Glowarp gained experiences into the application of the Spatial Augmented Reality (SAR) that allowed creating a cultural exhibition called GLOWFestival (www.glowarp.com/glowfestival.html) whose aim was the revaluation of the cultural heritage set in Ostuni, using digital technologies. The enhancement, intended not as a substitute of the historic and cultural value, provides an alternate use through a multimedia installation. The light and its linked technologies promote the culture sustainability infused in an interested audience. Thought as a four-year festival come to an end in 2016, it evoked an event totally dedicated to light as artistic medium. The web had a fundamental role as mean of sharing and diffusion that helped to start important inter-disciplinary collaboration in the ICT area. The share of the event via social network had made possible the involvement of artists from all over the world who merged into an environment open to sharing digital skills. The decisions made brought different age groups closer to the expressive potential that this medium offers as a show through the form of the artistic edutainment. The participation of artists from all over the world was free of charge. This paper wants to show the results, the findings and potentialities of the GLOWFestival.

Keywords: Festival · Spatial Augmented Reality · Video mapping · Enhancement · Augmented heritage · Cultural heritage

1 Introduction

Today the architectural cultural heritage is often devaluated and perceived as a real "urban empty space", which is inherent to the common idea of heaviness and steadiness of some buildings. Their features are big volumes and "classic" shapes that make the buildings invisible to the citizen consciousness. SAR technique (Oliver and Raskar 2005), commonly known as video mapping (Maniello 2014), or augmented heritage (Maniello and Amoretti 2016), when adopted to enhance our cultural heritage open our eyes to a new urban awareness of the architectural heritage (Trocchianesi 2014). It vests itself of a virtual intangible skin; the edifice loose its materiality in order to model itself following new artistic forms and dimensions, enhancing that goods that are usually perceived as not functioning and that now emotion the public. All this permits the good enhancement elaboration and consequently its inclusion as element of the

© Springer Nature Switzerland AG 2019
A. Luigini (Ed.): EARTH 2018, AISC 919, pp. 374–383, 2019.
https://doi.org/10.1007/978-3-030-12240-9_40

citizens' identity. It becomes a medium through which urban experience is integrated and completed (Bruno 2015), not going beyond the real world but simply telling absence through artistic forms of entertainment. The augmented heritage turns the surfaces into media iper-surfaces, whose communicative possibilities are almost unlimited (Maniello 2018a). The aims of the GLOWFestival needed to include the ones established by the law on the cultural heritage and on their basis we took actions that allowed it to grow in the short term. In 2013 year of the first edition, it did not exist a Festival that used the communication technologies as social aggregator in a historical location in Southern Italy. The choice of Ostuni old town (Fig. 1) as urban staging and also of indoor and outdoor locations, perfect settings for the union of ancient history and contemporary technologies, were the strengths for the diffusion and the fortune of the other editions.

Fig. 1. Ostuni, old town

Technical sponsorship together with the contribution of Ostuni municipality supported the festival financially. An artistic panel that decided the winner videos selected the artists. The artists were called to compete in five different sections: video mapping (Fig. 2), mapping 4kids (Fig. 3), artistic installations (Fig. 4), 3D printed gadget (Fig. 5) and the last one for the volunteers. The last two editions established an invitation section related to the installation and the last edition hosted one of the most famous video mapping installation entitled Le petit chef by the Belgian duo Skullmapping (Fig. 6). The success of the GLOWFestival was also due to the press office that disseminated the news before and after the event.

Fig. 2. The surfaces of projection

Fig. 3. Projection on the San Francesco's Cloister for the mapping 4kids section

Fig. 4. Third edition selected installation entitled "Ostuni Windows" by Chilen artists

Fig. 5. 3D printed gadget from last three editions

Fig. 6. Le Petit Chef installation by Skullmapping

2   Augmented Heritage and the Group Social Use

Until a few years ago, Augmented Reality was mostly associated to the QR codes, that used to redirect to a link or to overlap a 3D model but without any enhancement of it. In 2014, Google Glass invaded the market early showing the limits of its usage. It created visual layers untied from the space around rather than augmenting the reality and even if it represented the cutting-edge research into its field, it was fast substitute for Microsoft Hololens or similar systems, today in development kit. The speed with which new technologies have been experimented helps us realize how today augmented reality can develop. Just think about the holograms or the augmented spatial reality systems that deform the video in real time thanks to the eye tracking, creating the impression of full three-dimensionality no longer tied to a single point of view. These communication systems are imposing into the museums becoming a new and effective engine of cultural growth capable of modifying and enhancing the dynamics of engagement and learning. However, the aforementioned current and impactful technologies have a limit of usage related to the device/user formula. When these systems are appropriately compared with the SAR, it appears that in the field of the augmented heritage some issues related to the direct experience are overcome; the observer is through a collective and device free participation. This technology, from which the GLOWFestival fully draws on its purposes, is showing infinite and adaptable communicative potentialities, especially when it becomes creator of stories in images through the use of the visual storytelling that while not necessarily guaranteeing quality, emotion and involvement, makes the audience active and participatory (Bryson et al. 1997).

3   The GLOWFestival Settings

The places chosen for video projections followed an accurate expansion plan. The first location was San Francesco's Cloister (Fig. 7) and then every year other locations were added along the main street of the old town, in order to visit all the settings along a single main route. They were the Baroque altar of Martyred San Vito's Church (Fig. 8) and Scoppa's Arch (Fig. 9). In the last edition, a 1:2 scale reproduction of Sol LeWitt's All Bands (Maniello 2018b) was placed at Largo Stella experimenting the impact would have had an augmented artwork on the public. Since it was completely neglected for years in its original location (Fig. 10), we decided to experiment and evaluate the impact that the same piece of artwork would have had on the public with the use of new technologies (Maniello 2018c), once it was renovated (Fig. 11). The original ambition scope was to turn the old town into a great scenography devoted to new technologies. And finally a mobile installation entitled Fish Eyes was created, which projected various animations on the white surfaces of the historic center (Fig. 12).

Fig. 7. San Francesco's Cloister

Fig. 8. The Altar siting in Martyred San Vito's Church, branch of Southern Murgia's Pre-classic Civilizations Museum

Fig. 9. Scoppa's Arch

380   D. Maniello

Fig. 10. Sol LeWitt's artwork in its original location and the proposed enhancement action

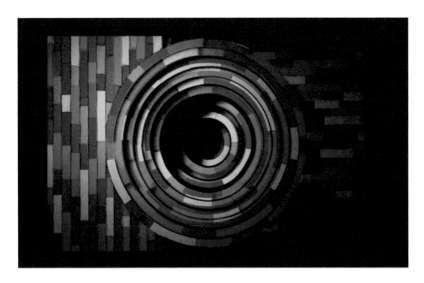

Fig. 11. The transformation of Maestro Sol LeWitt's artwork with the video mapping

Fig. 12. Fish Eyes, mobile installation

4   Effects and Result of GLOWFestival

In these years, important achievements have been reached in the field of the cultural heritage enhancement thanks to the use of the SAR, especially in an area where, even if it was not well known by the public, it was really appreciated. Having extended the calls not only to the video mapping, allowed embracing a wider audience. Beyond any analysis of the goals reached, it is impossible to ignore the secondary effects it produced, such as the growth of cultural diversity, the urban promotion, the social inclusion and the involvement of citizens.

Unfortunately, this last aim has not been fully achieved although over the years the creators of the event tried to raise the audience awareness on its position as centre of the cultural heritage definition, whose vitality depends on the ability of means and people to recreate and revitalize the intangible elements of our heritage, as underlined by appropriate agreements. These agreements are expression of the same points that the web has brought to the fore once used as a means for the transmission of knowledgment and creative groundwork: the active role of everybody for shaping the definition of Heritage and the recognition of its intangible dimension as integral part of the social and cultural life of the territory (Balzola and Rosa 2011).

The web enabled different communities to meet in Ostuni to give life to interdisciplinary collaborations, finding and sharing data and services. The measuring of the abovementioned relationship is a precious wealth of knowledge; an intangible heritage, that today can be shared and used for creating persuasive and sustainable forms of fruition and enhancement by the means of new technologies. These objectives, which are difficult to measure, were part of the Festival plot, a forum where the effectiveness of the proposed action was established by the meeting of setting and audience and whose aims were the glue to have the right overview.

The Festival thus takes on with a symbolic meaning because of the involvement of art and culture, new formidable means of sharing. However, there are still problems. Especially during the last edition, the territory was set of a multitude of events and the GLOWFestival, while carving out a certain audience in the panorama of the local culture festivals, managed to maintain its uniqueness with many difficulties. Regarding the financial viability, no structural choices resulted in the impossibility of planning a multi-year event.

The gradual planned inclusion and the support of the city were never fully realised preventing the actualization of the innovative project behind the GLOWFestival, at the detriment of the participation and involvement of the public that the event managed to build up during the years. Even though we do not have any certain data on the visits, because of the free entry, we could monitor the web data. In conclusion, the GLOWFestival can be considered as a container of activities gravitating around the concepts of creativity, sustainability, technology, mobility, innovation, tourism, enhancement and business' ideas and their relationship (Fig. 13).

Finally, the participation of the artists to the various calls did not increased significantly during the various editions despite the increased number of available locations. It was the evidence of how the Festival, even if attracting artists, could not compete with the rewards offered by other events for both the selected and the winning performances.

Fig. 13. The GLOWFestival's activity and its purposes

5   Conclusions

The GLOWFestival was an event, which showed a great potential on the national and international stage. The intuition of mixing ancient and contemporary in a small historical center was successful, because it offered a different approach to the use of the cultural asset, attracting artists from all over the world that worked on a different territory and culture.

The natural effect was a great attention obtained by the involved locations and, as result, the widespread in Italy and abroad of the different activities on social media. The initial intuition was also confirmed by the great participation of the public in the years, even if in these days the critical issue are still multi-level: associative, municipal and regional.

Therefore, having planned a four-year event has allowed us to evaluate the results and postpone a new edition as long as we have favourable and changed conditions.

References

Balzola A, Rosa P (2011) L'arte fuori di sè. Feltrinelli

Bruno G (2015) Atlante delle emozioni. In viaggio tra arte, architettura e cinema. Johan & Levi

Bryson S, Zeltzer D, Bolas MT, de La Chapelle, B, Bennett D (1997) The future of virtual reality: head mounted displays versus spatially immersive displays. In: SIGGRAPH 1997 conference proceedings, annual conference series, ACM SIGGRAPH. Addison-Wesley, pp 485–486

Oliver B, Raskar R (2005) Spatially augmented reality. Merging real and virtual world. A K Peters, Wellesley

Trocchianesi R (2014) Design e narrazioni per il patrimonio culturale. Maggioli

Maniello D (2014) Augmented reality in public spaces. Basic techniques for video mapping, vol I. Le Penseur

Maniello D, Amoretti V (2016) Interference ancient-modern: new strategies for digital enhancement for museums. In: VIIth international conference: diagnosis, conservation and valorizazion of cultural heritage, pp 22–32

Maniello D (2018a) Spatial augmented reality. La progettazione dell'edutainment negli spazi digitali aumentati, vol III, Le Penseur

Maniello D (2018b) Art upon art: the spatial augmented reality as new value for contemporary art and educational tool for art history. In: #EARTH2018 Digital environments for education arts and heritage, Bressanone, Bolzano, July 5–6 2018

Maniello D (2018c) Improvements and implementations of the spatial augmented reality applied on scale models of cultural goods for visual and communicative purpose. In: Vth International Conference on AR, VR and CG, Salento AVR 2018, vol 2(2), pp 303–319

Digital Heritage 2

Digital Museums, Digitized Museums

M. Lo Turco$^{(\boxtimes)}$ and M. Calvano

Department of Architecture and Design (DAD), Politecnico di Torino,
Viale Pier Andrea Mattioli 39, 10125 Turin, Italy
massimiliano.loturco@polito.it

Abstract. The research project, still in progress, developed a proposal procedure to visualize a 3D models of an hidden collection of Museo Egizio in Turin. The prototype procedure exposed is focused on the visualization of 3D objects shapes and additional information by networking the enriched 3D model. This preliminary output is part of a broader purpose that aims to make a dialogue between container (museum) and content (museum collections). The use of building information modeling (BIM) tools and technologies could not only apply to the building's life cycle, but in this case, it could be deeply connected to its museum collections which themselves contribute to the continuous museum's transformations. The consequence of the new relationship between container and content is also the development of procedures to support the set-up project.

Keywords: Museum · Container · Content ·
Collection Information Modeling · Visual Programming Language ·
Data enrichment

1 Museum Experience Today

Today, the museum is understood as a place of interaction, where its intrinsic nature of exchange between cultures is realized. The information is offered to the user in an apparently passive way, but, it can help to define the relationship with the data. The same behavior that the user has with the artworks, the nature and the degree of interaction, suggests a system of iterations structurally recursive but constantly modified by the actions of the user. The physical limitation of the spaces, together with the fragility of the materials of the artifacts, can be overcome by transforming it into data that can be interpreted in different ways, suitable for carrying out the bidirectional and colloquial transfer of information between the broadcaster (the artifact) and the user; in this way the museum becomes virtual.

The virtualization of the museum experience takes place by acting on its main components (Fig. 1):

- the museum building;
- the collected objects;
- the visitors.

© Springer Nature Switzerland AG 2019
A. Luigini (Ed.): EARTH 2018, AISC 919, pp. 387–398, 2019.
https://doi.org/10.1007/978-3-030-12240-9_41

The other subjects and/or components exist in the museum to maximize the relationships between container, content and user, making possible the maximum enjoyment of the Good, also through "participatory" cultures (Jenkins 2009).

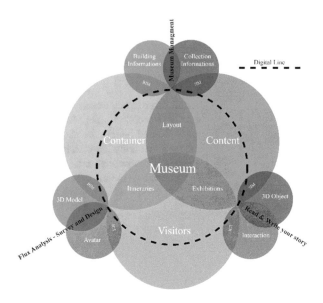

Fig. 1. Diagram that summarizes the museum experience. Internally the main components, externally the evolution of the concept with the advent of digital.

In the contemporary museum, the exhibition becomes the moment in which the visitor relates with the contents displayed within it. During the exhibition, the collections are placed in the rooms of the museum building according to a story, a story created by the curator of the exhibition. The exhibition makes possible the relationship between the container and the visitor, who moves along the thematic paths proposed to enjoy the contents displayed.

Today, digital technologies for cultural heritage allow experiences of "augmented" knowledge, supported by devices and apps that propose the overcoming of contemporary understanding, often entrusted to in-depth textual and multimedia works. The new tools, on the other hand, allow access to contextualized and critical areas, offering visitors multiple levels of in-depth study of the goods displayed.

2   Interacting Models

The new experiences are based on the heterogeneous information that comes from the collections, both of a historical-critical nature and of a managerial nature. The first ones, if opportunely communicated, allow to deepen the knowledge of the exposed contents, the second ones (managerial) allow to assure the well-being of the artwork in time and in its possible movements (lifecycle).

The digitization of collected objects and related information allows the creation of small-scale informed models whose potential goes beyond the greater communicative possibilities expressed by this artifact (Hervy et al. 2014).

Even more can be done by proposing a virtual environment in which the exchange of information between container and content is triggered. We are therefore in a situation in which the main actors are the information models. This is certainly the case with the museum building, since the editing of architectural models will increasingly converge on BIM (Building Information Modeling) approaches, while the area to be explored is the digitization of information models for the collections (Collection Information Modeling - CIM). The interconnection of data between the two models in a digital environment makes it possible to combine the tools for the knowledge of the collections with tools to support the museum setting up project.

2.1 BIM for the Container

Generally, through the BIM procedures, the information system associated with parametric models characterized by building components is expanded and structured. An informed architectural model proposes the creation of a relational database, in which the formal, functional, technological and topological aspects of environments and architectural components can be identified. The proposed procedure also involves enriching the model with information contained in the Building Sheet and in the Environment Sheet to be used for the Facility Report.

2.2 CIM for Content

The drafting of information models for the description of museum collections (CIM) involves the digital acquisition of the object, acquiring its form and size. The result is a multifaceted representation (mesh) with topology optimized for web diffusion. The 3D model, as previously mentioned, must be combined with historical information in multimedia format. For a correct maintenance and management of the finds, it is also necessary to combine the information present in the Conservation Sheet of the object (Manoli 2015) that accompanies, often in paper format, the object collected describing the actions for conservation, the interventions for prevention and further information of a logistical nature (Condition Report).

3 Case Study and Methodology

The procedure is validated by its application on some case studies belonging to the Egyptian Museum of Turin. Although the museum has about 10,000 m^2 of exhibition space, it still preserves many artefacts in the storerooms waiting for new spaces to be set up.

Some of these are 11 physical models in scale (maquettes) of Nubian temples that stood between Abu Simbel and the Aswan dam; the reproductions are made of wooden material, generally composed of two halves to allow the view of the interior. The construction of these artefacts dates back to the beginning of the 19th century, (Bruwier et al. 2014; Einaudi 2016) before the buildings were dismantled and reassembled in other places outside Egypt to protect them from the flooding of the Nile caused by the construction of the Aswan dam in 1960.

Fig. 2. Wooden model of the temple of Nefertari at Abu Simbel.

Some of the models are on display, others preserved in the storerooms; the first digitization operations were concentrated on the wooden model of the Nefertari temple at Abu Simbel (Fig. 2). For the digitization of the model and the information enrichment (CIM), the following operational protocol has been implemented:

- Metric relief of the model.
- Restitution of the 3D model aimed at web diffusion.
- Document collection (historical-critical data; data for management).
- Digitization and hierarchization of the collected data.
- Data enrichment of the 3D model.

The digitalization of the displayed models, together with the digitization and information enrichment of the museum building, allows the pursuit of objectives capable of improving the conditions of management and enjoyment of the museum. Below is a list of the expected results:

- Make part of the heritage not accessible to the public accessible - through the virtualization of the exhibits stored in the warehouses;
- Create a database to Manage and Maintain content and container, in which the digital replicas of real models are responsible for receiving a compendium of information useful for their proper classification, management and maintenance.
- Analyze and prefigure the flows of visitors in order to prepare new tools to support the curator and the fitter of the museum spaces.

4 From 3D Model to CIM

The research has defined a procedure for the acquisition and digitization of the museum object that involves the use of modern surveying techniques. The 3D object obtained is the result of an excellent compromise between the speed of acquisition and the subsequent creation of accurate models, correctly retopologized (low number of triangles on large flat surfaces, greater segmentation in more irregular areas) and ready to be semantically enriched with useful information for the management and communication of the asset in the museum. The information enrichment of the model took place through an initial stratification of the data in relation to the documentation collected. In the field of document archiving, the impact of new digital technologies has led to the consequent use of computer science then the definition of formal ontologies applicable in the field of computer science and for the semantic organization of the web (Lo Turco et al. 2018).

The preservation of cultural heritage, over the years, has produced an ever-increasing number of archives and databases that today have considerably implemented the activity of archiving on the web. This digitized information must be organized according to classifications, which require a computer ontology, i.e. a series of conceptual distinctions in a machine-readable format that are transversal and interoperable (Bruseker et al. 2017). For this reason, the research focused on the definition of an ontology based on the CIDOC-CRM (CIDOC Conceptual Reference Model) standard for the documentation of cultural heritage in museums (Carboni and De Luca 2016).

Following the CRM model, the 3D model can be considered as a representation of a real object and it is assumed as the result of a digitization process. Then it is possible to declare three kinds of information structure:

1. Physical model (maquette) description:
   (a) Information concerning the maquette and its historical background;
   (b) Data about the life cycle of the object considering it as part of a museum collection.
   Digital data description: recording the provenance information of the digital 3D object
   Depicted subject: description of the Temple

Information 1a and 3 are used to create explicit contents to be offered to visitors through the development of responsive devices with which to disseminate multimedia information (explicit data).

Point 1b represents information of a managerial nature that does not have any formal feedback for the public but gives the possibility to develop design applications to support the design of the exhibition (implicit or latent data).

Point 2 aims to trace the process of acquisition of the object for the purposes of the research project.

The correct cataloguing within one or more specific databases is one of the objectives of the research aimed at developing an ontology based on CIDOC-CRM and its extensions to organize the complexity of the information that characterizes the museum collections.

The correct cataloguing of information allows the 3D model to be enriched with data through efficient and robust procedures; the CIM procedures return an informed and queryable model with the aim of achieving a more complete knowledge of the artifact (Fig. 3).

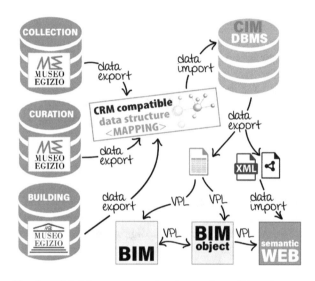

Fig. 3. CIM data management system and possible outcomes.

5   VPL Procedure for Model Enrichment

The information enrichment, in this phase of work, has been done by creating a prototype of a procedure explicitly controlled through Visual Programming Language procedures. The collected data (still partial) are collected in a simple database (spreadsheet). The simplified tools for programming and cataloguing make it possible to put two phases of the research in parallel: the collection and cataloguing of the data and the elaboration of the enrichment procedure. This is possible after an initial understanding of the panorama of available data that become open strings within the procedure; such strings that can then be filled in. The stated assumptions allow us to develop some enrichment logics compiled in a VPL environment (Casale and Calvano 2018).

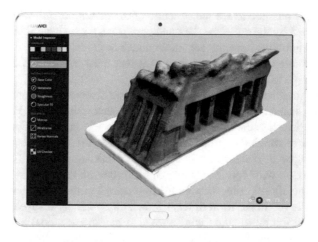

Fig. 4. Digital model of the Nefertari temple that can be navigated and interrogated using mobile devices.

The surveyed model is initially implemented by primitive geometries with which to generate hotspots for the sharing of further multimedia information. Attributes can also be external links to digitised photo documentation and media files stored in online servers. In this pilot procedure the hotspots are modelled inside the CAD space with primitive geometries appropriately enriched using the tools available in the drawing software used for the experience (Rhinoceros 6) (Fig. 4). The first series of activities is carried out by linking the surveyed model to the spreadsheet where information from the various disciplines is collected and then linked to the model using VPL procedures.

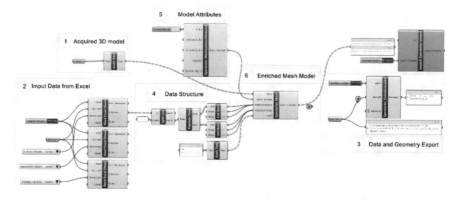

Fig. 5. Prototype of procedure to create the relationship between the database containing the data and the model acquired.

In Fig. 5 it is possible to see the structure of the definition with which the detected model is enriched by the collected data and opportunely translated into web language. Before the definition we have the acquired numerical model (1) to be enriched and the external data coming from the spreadsheet (2) that must be connected and translated into web language (3).

The use of stratified data, which can describe the diversified contents of the model, must be manipulated in such a way as to be correctly structured. Part of the VPL definition is dedicated to the management of "Data-flow" to match alphanumeric values to the attributes to which they refer. The components clustered in the group (4) of the above figure allow to connect the hierarchized information of the Excel file to the model. The model, with special components (5), can be further enriched by formal attributes that qualify the color through the re-proposal of the material acquired during the survey, preserved in the form of textures and appropriately mapped on the vertices of the mesh. All the information converges in a new mesh model to which the data processed in a structured form is linked (6). The enriched items are ready to be written to a .json file initially saved locally (3).

6 Responsive Models

The enriched model through CIM procedures can now be used for the different purposes listed above, including the possibility of creating design tools by triggering a dialogue with the data of the museum building in a virtual environment.

The information coming from the digitization of the Object Sheet attached to the model allows, in a virtual environment, the dialogue with the spaces in which the object will be placed. Let's assume therefore the presence of the BIM model of the museum under examination, obviously constituted by the joining of parametric architectural instances, informed with customizable attributes concerning the conditions of thermo-hygrometric well-being.

On the opposite side we have the collected objects that in a digital environment are also enriched by the data contained in the Conservation Sheet (condition report).

In a digital environment it is therefore appropriate to create a comparison and an analysis between the content and the container so that it can become a support for the exhibition project. A first prototype of the procedure has been designed again in the VPL environment (Fig. 6). The figure shows the actors of this operation: a schematic model that represents in BIM a museum and a geometric instance that collects the digitized properties of the Conservative Sheet. In both models two parameters are extrapolated as an example: the temperature and the specific humidity that on the container side represent the acquired values, on the contained side are parameters of object well-being described in the conservation sheet. A space described in the BIM environment is composed of parametric objects that constitute the envelope (walls, curtain walls, floor) and adaptive geometries that summarize the enveloped spaces. While the first contains information about the construction technique and the functional elements of the juxtaposed objects, the adaptive geometries are used exclusively to host attributes, therefore environmental parameters. An informative management model of a building could provide that the adaptive geometries previously described, can be enriched by changing data, constantly updated by sensors connected to the represented spaces.

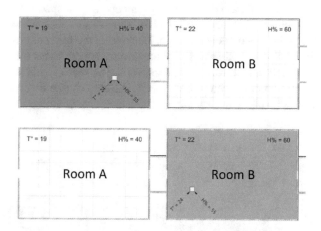

Fig. 6. An example of a relational interface for setting up museum spaces. Above, the collected artefact is placed in a space that is not suitable for its conditions of well-being (red). Below, the collected artifact is placed in a space appropriate to its conditions of well-being (green).

This would allow the digital model to be as close as possible to the real model in terms of information. This condition allows extremely accurate design prefigurations for the installation.

The VPL procedure designed proposes two levels of programming for:

– detection of the inclusion condition (in which room the object is located);
– comparison between selected attributes (once the location is understood, the dialogue is triggered).

Again, through visual programming procedures, models are deconstructed into synthetic geometries and attributes. The spatial relationship between geometric components allows the detection of inclusion conditions so we can understand if the model representing the artefact is within a given environment. Once the inclusion condition has been verified, the objects taken into consideration will be able to compare their attributes. In the simulation we have taken as an example the temperature and the relative humidity, important parameters for the thermo-hygrometric well-being of the collected objects: the materials and the degradation conditions of an artifact often require a controlled environment. The designer must therefore consider procedures that facilitate the design phase, immediately considering the possibility for a piece to be in a environment with adequate conditions.

7   Analysis and Prefiguration of Fluxes

Each object belonging to a collection, over time assumes values that characterize it from the historical, artistic, critical, social and media aspects. The weighted relationship between these values helps to create an attractive weight of the artwork within the collection of which it is part. The involved elements are the space set up, the whole collection and the single object belonging to the collection. The space set up generates a domain of action in which events happen. The events are triggered by the displayed artworks that in relation to their weight (influenced by the attributes mentioned above) create a field. The field, in the way we understand it, is a space characterized by events that configure a non-homogeneous area in which the entities (the objects collected) are able to influence the path of the visitors.

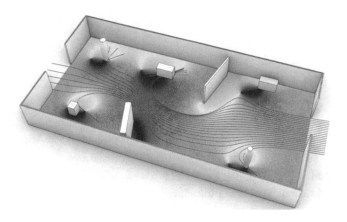

Fig. 7. Graphic output for displaying of the flux analysis.

In an ideal condition, assuming an empty exhibition hall in which we place the entrance and exit on the opposite walls, the possible foreshadowing of the flows will take place along a straight direction that will join the entrance to the exit of the space under examination. This is because the visitor's interest is mainly directed towards elements of perceptual perturbation. We are therefore in the presence of an almost "isotropic" field, in which the perceptive interest does not change in any direction.

As soon as the artworks are introduced into the space under examination, into the exhibition hall, they become attractive elements that create perceptive perturbations, so that the field becomes "anisotropic": the eye is no longer directed in one direction but moves attracted by the elements on display and looking for works that are known or particularly interesting for the visitor.

The fluxes of visitors move within a layout defined by the designer of the museum space but following trajectories and walking times strongly influenced by the weight of the works on display (Fig. 7). The design of procedures that collect and automate the considerations expressed makes it possible to avoid significant problems of visitor flow in the rooms, limiting the enjoyment and knowledge of the exposed artworks.

8 Conclusions

With a view to the technicalities deriving from the arrangement of effective procedures for the digitization of works, the question arises as to the development of a virtual system that reproduces objects and collections related to the museum and that allows the system of relations between the content and the container of the exhibition space to be explored.

The methodological approach is based on the awareness that an accurate critical apparatus developed in support of the relevant project can guide the process of knowledge of the exhibition environment, extracting the significant information that represents it and making it available in a digital model, qualified by means of intelligent semantic structures.

It is therefore defined as an instrument in which the dichotomy between container and content reaches a "meeting point" in the exchange of information between two worlds that, even if apparently disjointed, find themselves coexisting and dialoguing with each other. The result is a final synthesis perceived by the user who, in discovering the content, experiences the harmony of the container.

The construction of digital models can have different purposes, even if dialoguing with each other: through the organization of multidisciplinary processes of information processing and exchange, the acquisition of metric, geometric and material data of museums and their collections are codified in interconnected tools for the management and enhancement of the heritage, until they themselves can be used to record what happens during an event (survey) or to prefigure future exhibition scenarios (project).

Last but not least, the process of digitization and collection of data useful for management purposes will be followed by reflections on a wise use of recent digital technologies for popular purposes, in the direction of greater inclusiveness: in this sense, digital environments are particularly attractive not only for the new generations, but also for those of older age who show their curiosity in an attempt to fill their knowledge gaps in technologies when experiences with high digital content are related to the viewing of works of art (Lampis 2018), perceptions completely unknown until recently, but nevertheless convey great opportunities to understand the complex symbolism of the artistic heritage (Ferri 2011).

Acknowledgements. The activity presented in the article is derived from research project named B.A.C.K. TO T.H.E. F.U.T.U.R.E. (BIM Acquisition as Cultural Key TO Transfer Heritage of ancient Egypt For many Uses To many Users REplayed) The research project aims at defining a new methodology in which the Information Modeling tools can be used for unconventional purposes, to realize 3D databases of small objects, especially those belonging to large museum collections.

References

Bruseker G, Carboni N, Guillem A (2017) Cultural heritage data management: the role of formal ontology and CIDOC CRM. In: Heritage and archaeology in the digital age. Springer, Cham, pp 93–131

Bruwier M-C, Claes W, Quertinmont A (2014) La description de l'Egypte de Jean-Jacques Rifaud (1813–1826). Editions Safran, Bruxelles

Casale A, Calvano M (2018) Represented models and typological algorithms. The role of parametric models for the design of the product. In: Rossi M, Buratti G (eds) Computational morphologies, design rules between nature model and responsive architecture. Springer, Cham

Carboni N, De Luca L (2016) Towards a conceptual foundation for documenting tangible and intagible elements of a cultural object. Digit Appl Archaeol Cult Herit 3:108–116

Ferri P (2011) Nativi digitali. Mondadori, Milano

Jenkins H (2009) Culture e competenze digitali. Media education per il XXI secolo. Guerini, Milano

Lo Turco M, Piumatti P, Rinaudo F, Tamborrino R (2018) Back to the future. Informative models & virtual museums. In: XL convengno internazionale dei docent delle discipline della rappresentazione, Milano, September 13–15

Luigini A, Panciroli C (2018) Ambienti digitali per l'educazione all'arte e al patrimonio. FrancoAngeli, Milano

Manoli F (2015) Manuale di gestione e cura delle collezioni museali. Le Monnier Università, Firenze

Hervy B, Laroche F, Kerouanton J-L, Bernard A, Courtin C, D'haene L, Guillet B, Waels A (2014) Augmented historical scale model for museums: from curation to multi-modal promotion. In: Laval Virtual VRIC 2014, Laval

Einaudi S (2016) Drovetti e i modellini del Museo Egizio di Torino. Studi Piemontesi, vol XLV, n. 2, dicembre

Drawing and Project at the *VChUTEMAS*. Graphic Interpretations

Francesco Maggio[1] and Starlight Vattano[2(✉)]

[1] Department of Architecture, University of Palermo, Viale delle Scienze,
Edificio 14, 90128 Palermo, Italy
[2] Faculty of Education, Free University of Bozen, Viale Ratisbona 16,
39042 Brixen-Bressanone, BZ, Italy
starlight.vattano@unibz.it

Abstract. The article deals with the graphic study of the project for the Kominern Palace designed in 1929 by Lidija Komarova, one of the students of the Russian Laboratories known by the acronym VChUTEMAS, founded in 1920 in Moscow. Strongly characterized by the revolutionary atmosphere that was delineating the artistic progress based on the synthesis of all the plastic arts, the Russian Laboratories attributed to the architecture a position of the first order, a perfect association between the scientific possibility and the art technique. The redrawing of this project allows to deepen the compositional principles of the new architectural formation of the Eastern European avant-garde, providing digital images of a graphic heritage, that characterizing the teaching of VChUTEMAS, of which only a few traces are its testimony. Through the graphic reading and redrawing of the project for the Komintern palace, this study sheds light on the facts that characterized the aesthetic culture of the post-tsarist revolutionary Russia and of a technical-industrial school a year prior to the foundation of the Bauhaus.

Keywords: Drawing · Avant-garde art · VChUTEMAS · Project · Digital modeling · Redrawing

1 Introduction

In the years between 1917 and 1923 there was the transition from the school of Painting, Sculpture and Architecture to the Moscow Technical-Artistic Laboratories, better known with the acronym VChUTEMAS, a teaching attempt by the socialist society to form a joint path between professional art and productive art (Kopp 1987). In the same revolutionary, artistic and cultural context the Constructivism started to configure its principles, as an avant-garde movement with a direct influence on social transformation, in harmony with the new public initiatives and the didactic action aimed at a close confrontation between the practical and theoretical elaborations of architecture and art (Rowell and Znder Rudenstine 1981).

A. Luigini (Ed.): EARTH 2018, AISC 919, pp. 399–410, 2019.
https://doi.org/10.1007/978-3-030-12240-9_42

The themes emerged as a result of the development of radical left artistic move-ments, Cubism, Futurism, Cubo-Futurism and abstract figurative art, brought into the field essential reflections which abandoned the surface of the plan to build an objective world in the space of the three dimensions, in the solids' volume and in the structural composition of the form (Finizio 1990).

The message of the new aesthetics proposed by the Russian laboratories was the result of that Trotskyist theory according to which «the proletariat takes the power in order to end once and for all with all the class cultures and to open the way to a culture of humanity» (Komarova 1996, p. 33), that is, a vision of the project and industrial process that takes into account the implication of the creative labor force in the mechanized collectivism of the new social state.

The revolutionary creed that distinguished the actors of the School of Art and Architecture of Moscow matched with the equal recognition system between teachers and students, on a creative level, of the design and artistic aptitude combined with the study of the form and architectural expression; in fact, both the teachers' and the students' works were published indistinctly on the constructivist journal «SA»[1]. With the aim of bringing to light the cultural heritage represented by the architectural experiments together with some of the design approaches that defined the didactic method of the VChUTEMAS, the article deals with the study of the project designed by Lidija Komarova for the Komintern building, in 1929, in the laboratories of Aleksandr Vesnin (Fig. 1), taking into account the intimate interaction between the participation in political issues and the creative research of art that in that period characterized the education of each student (Elia 2008).

Thus, in fact, Komarova remembers: «the Komsomol members' students assigned to the work group also partly took care of the edition of the mural newspaper: they wrote articles, but above all, they adorned the mural newspaper with caricatures and drawings, recruiting students to this work still not member of the party» (Komarova 1996, p. 115).

Together with the negation of academicism, perceived as nihilism of art, students were then introduced to new systems of investigation of the form on scientific and ideological bases directly intervened on the teaching approach, inspiring to the objective values of the psychoanalytic method and the aesthetic-formal problems of architecture.

---

[1] The constructivist journal *SA* (Contemporary Architecture) was published for the first time in 1926 directed by A. Vesnin e M. Ginzburg with the objective of doing propaganda to the progressist soviet architecture. Cf. Michelangeli, L. (2004). *Avanguardie russe.* Giunti Editorie, Firenze-Milano.

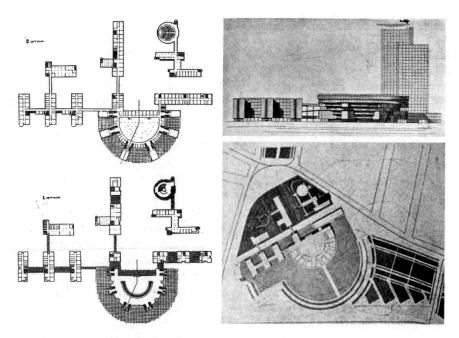

Fig. 1. Plan of the first floor, facade and general plan of the building for the Komintern.

2   The Drawing in the Pedagogy of the VChUTEMAS

«Art, which reaches higher levels of quality, must first of all serve the industry, as well as the mechanical mass production of objects necessary from the social point of view» (Finizio 1990, p. 48). As stated in the deliberation of the Soviet of the People Commissioners on the foundation of the Moscow Higher Technical-Artistic Laboratories of 1920, the clear intention to train "artist-builders" able to understand the new needs of the working class translated into the architecture and in the so-called vešči (= objects of daily use) reproducible in series, in reduced times and costs, determining profound changes not only in the culture of the project, the configuration of the form and its perception in space, but also in the process of conception and representation of the object investigated. Many questions raised concerning the relationship between volume and space, between surface and color, in other words, between mass and properties of the form, considered necessary for the understanding of the plastic possibilities of architecture.

In this new perspective the drawing was the starting point of the reflections on the spatial rhythm, on the geometric combinations and on the visual movements of the observer in the perception of the represented object, through the experimentation of different methods and techniques in the courses offered by the didactic program.

In this regard, recalls Sokolov, one of the students of the Moscow laboratories: «I almost do not believe my eyes when I find in my college transcript the signatures of eminent artists such as L.A. Bruni and P.V. Miturič: they did not simply teach us how to draw, but they made us understand how the artistic content of a drawing can be vast.

In this sense the half-naked paintbrush drawing lessons were particularly useful to get used to the idea that the drawing was not made of a thin line that snaked along the sheet of paper, but which, with the help of this line, had to be included also the shape and the chiaroscuro of a nude» (Komarova 1996, p. 103). Add to the artistic and cultural revolution implemented by the VChUTEMAS the strong link with the left artistic circles, such as the INChUK, the Institute of artistic culture, through which some issues were explored, including: the materiality and weight of the object; geometric translation in simple forms of complex volumes; the relationship between the color and the material/body/weight of the object; the decomposition of the form into parts that sharpen its perception and rhythmic structure (Komarova 1996).

Through the exploratory possibilities offered by the drawing, the attention was turned towards the materiality, or *faktura*, of the objects, their spatiality and the volume of the form, enabling the artist-technician to define new contrasts, new rhythms, new expressive forces. In this context, the mysticism of Vasilij Kandinskij allowed to develop an education methodology based on the actuality of the object itself, rather than on the mere graphic description, as also in the case of the extreme abstraction by Malevič that was very close to the combinations of simplified architectural volumes (De Micheli 1999). The two methods, together with the studies on the surface in space of Vladimir Tatlin's *counter-reliefs*, were sharply criticized by the teachers of the laboratories of Moscow because of the extreme abstract connotation assumed by the vision of the three artists, even if Aleksandr Rodčenko elaborated a synthesis between abstract art and architecture, in favor of the so-called "productive art", with the clear intention of producing objects useful to the nascent society. The abstract graphic exercises, treated without a defined functional purpose, developed according to four compositional themes related to the surface, mass and weight, the volumetric composition and the space-depth composition.

Although moving in a purely theoretical field, the students investigated the questions of the form on a scale of representation similar to that of the architectural project; in fact, the next step was that of the so-called "productive themes", practical design exercises through which the compositional-formal processes of architecture were dealt with.

3 Graphic Analysis of the Project for the Palace of the Komintern by Lidija Komarova, 1929

The social question within the Moscow laboratories was also addressed by Vladimir Tatlin who, interested in a sort of plastic appeal in relation to the cubist lesson on the organic combination of form, light and color, composed and modulated his spatial dynamics. The drawing became a dynamic expression of structures through a total form of design in which the spirit of art converged with the needs of community life.

The attention was then directed towards the social role of architecture, the propaganda for new building techniques and the standardization.

Following the total rejection of any historical reference, the need to develop new contents and new values arose, which gave rise to a radical reconstruction of the Soviet nation, starting from the planning reflections on the ideal cities, on the potentialities of new materials and on the construction of the future.

Students were asked to work on the themes of large social buildings, museums, libraries or entire cities, thought as suspended airships with spaceships designed for residential or social use (Figs. 2 and 3).

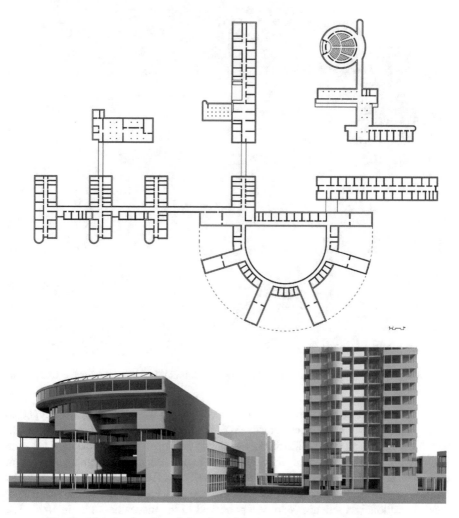

Fig. 2. Digital redrawing of the plan of the type-floor and perspective view.

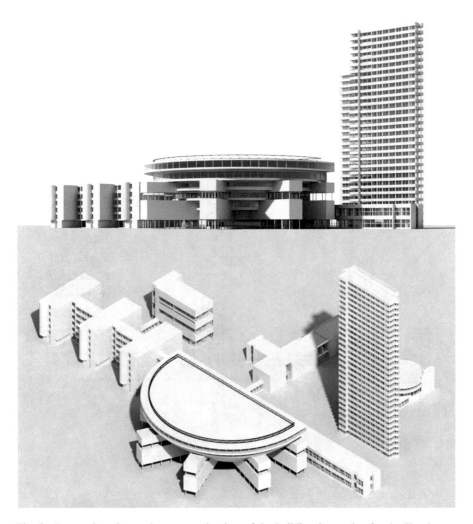

Fig. 3. Perspective view and axonometric view of the buildings' complex for the Komintern.

In the context of this attitude of Soviet architecture towards what was defined as "exploratory planning", projects aimed at a future time, often unreal, were promoted, as it was for the flying city of Kutrikov; the young students of the VChUTEMAS were involved in the expression of the Soviet ideo-logical content through the design of architectural forms such as the Soviet palace, the Town Hall and the socialist city. The proposal by Lidija Komarova on the building complex for the Komintern was part of these educational experiences and was published in the magazine «SA» in 1929. The graphic elaborations on which the redrawing was based include a plan of the first floor, a plan of the floor-type of the other levels, a façade, a perspective view and a general plan of the whole complex of buildings (Figs. 1 and 7).

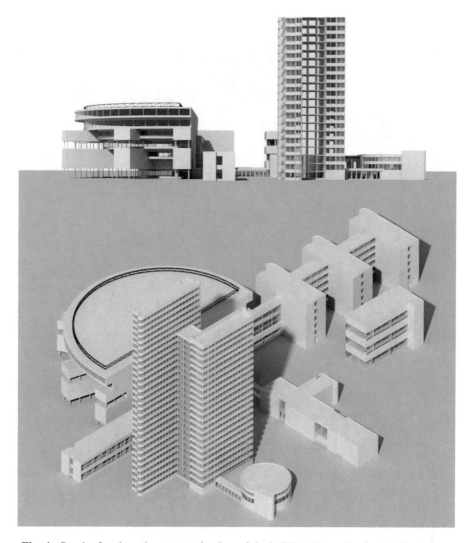

Fig. 4. Render facade and axonometric view of the buildings' complex for the Komintern.

The principle around which the project is developed is that of the international political forum where to build a spatial harmony between inside and outside through the interpenetration of volumes differentiated in height and proportions, with the aim of declaring, by means of the composition itself, the different functions (Fig. 4). A large public square generated by the expedient of the dynamic increase of buildings, starting from the main building, a hub of the urban system consisting of seven semicircles that correspond to the galleries of the congress hall (Fig. 5).

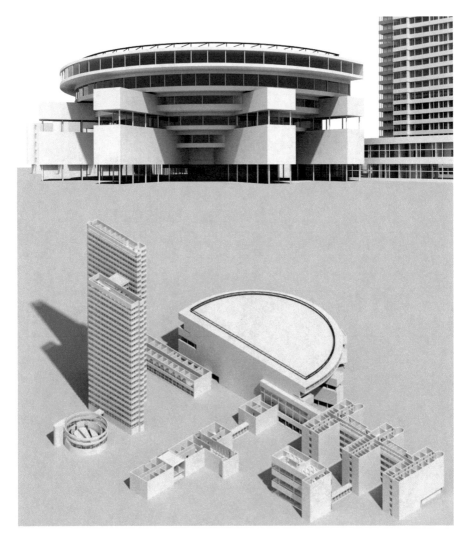

Fig. 5. Perspective view and axonometric exploded of the buildings' complex for the Komintern.

As it can be seen from the comparison with other contemporary projects realized by the students in response to Soviet ideological questions, the increasing development of the steps is one of the graphic-geometric values investigated during the volume and mass courses of the VChUTEMAS. The themes of rhythm, modeling of emptiness and plasticity of the movement, together with the sinuosity of the semicircular curve, provide a dynamic connotation to the Komarova project, through the annular concentricity that widens upwards. This movement also reflects the repetition of the six parallelepipeds arranged according to a radial development and grafted into the large funnel volume of the congress hall: probably the result of those reflections conducted by the students within the courses of «Volume» and «Space» on the interaction between curved and broken lines generating dynamic solids.

To underline the strict logic of the function, inherited from the laboratories, the six radial volums declared their social significance outside: balconies that were jutting onto the square like stages assembled during proletarian manifestations and raised from the ground on pilotis (Fig. 6).

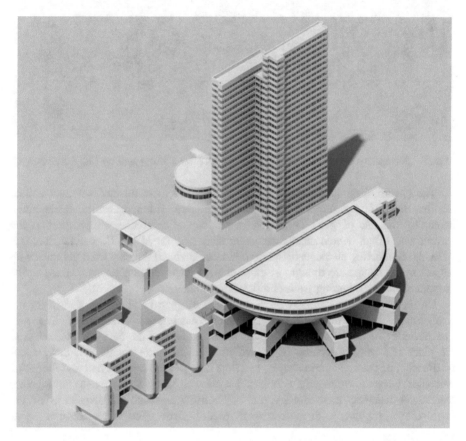

Fig. 6. Axonometric view of the buildings' complex for the Komintern.

The whole complex of buildings, as represented in the perspective view (Fig. 7), seems to respond to the Soviet social question of those years. In fact, reading some of Komarova's reflections regarding her experience at the VChUTEMAS, one gets the feeling of recognizing in the Komintern project that Red Square of the October Revolution that expressed the student spirit of the new era: «I remember the Red Square at that time. I was lucky enough to see its during the solemn and austere funeral of the victims of the October Revolution fights. Forever I will remember May 1919 on the Red Square. That day I saw Lenin: he quickly passed from one to the other small stands installed on the square, uttering a short speech, accompanied by the charac-teristic expressive gesture. The sun was shining, the animation of the party and the desire for general progress reigned all around» (Komarova 1996, p. 111).

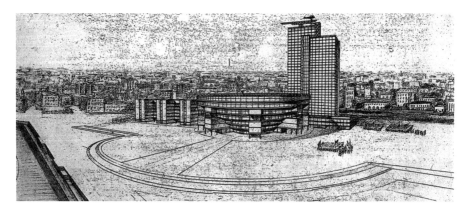

Fig. 7. Perspective view of the buildings' complex for the Komintern by Lidija Komarova.

The system of the large square was characterized by two turreted volumes, a clear manifestation of technological progress and standardization processes, made trans-parent by the use of glass and steel: two points of reference with respect to the surrounding urban development that underlined the role of the Bolshevik ideology. Also, the connecting elements between the foreground and the backward volumes with respect to the square are thought as glass tunnels suspended on pilotis or fixed to the ground, as devices passing from one function to another.

On the roof of one of the two tall buildings, Komarova places an airstrip for the airplanes: further imprint of a future vision on the nascent proletarian society in power. The plasticity of the buildings' complex, the dynamism of the façades obtained from the placement and orientation of the volumes in the large square and the gradual progression of the concentric shapes, as in the case of the congress hall and the radial balconies, were the architectural choices that allowed Lidija Komarova to put together the Soviet teaching methodology, on the construction and understanding of the form/volume, together with the constructive and artistic ideas of the Russian avant-garde.

In this regard, in his book on the Soviet architecture, Kirillov wrote: «the most striking thing about this project was the architectural solution of the congress hall, articulated in seven concentric semicircles that spread upwards, giving it an absolutely unusual funnel shape. The steps of the semicircular foyers surrounding the hall cor-respond to the gradual rise and widening of the galleries of the amphitheater» (Komarova 1996, p. 121).

In line with these values, the student used the architectural expedient to "organize life" thinking of the need for revolutionary society to use "expressions of movement, of dynamics!" (Komarova 1996, p. 64). The question of dynamism applied to architec-ture, in fact, constituted the plastic synthesis between artistic aspiration to technological progress and the new didactic programs adopted by the VChUTEMAS.

Add to this the eclectic character of Komarova, as one reads from the reflections of Nikolaj Sokolov, one of the classmates: «enthusiastic about unusual designs, which she herself created with a constant affectionate smile, activist, tireless organizer» (Komarova 1996, p. 105).

The future architecture explored by Komarova, presents many of the architectural and urban elements which previously interested Rodčenko, as in the case of turreted and light buildings, bridges, paths or transparent roofing to configure the new facade concept: a real dynamic system, observable from the outside, understanding the material to read the modeling of the internal vacuum. A plurality of the point of view from above that was probably affected by the development of aeronautics, as evidenced also by the inclusion of the airstrip obtained in one of the two skyscrapers of the project by Lidija Komarova.

Fig. 8. Facade and planivolumetric of the buildings' complex for the Komintern.

Also, Rodčenko dealt with a "façade seen from above", as a result of a multiplicity of the points of view gained as a result of the dynamic character of the emerging Soviet architecture (Fig. 8).

4   Conclusions

The intense and multidisciplinary vision of the Moscow laboratories addressed the students to the formation of an autonomous artistic-scientific vision of reality, contributing, at the same time, to the definition of an ideological awareness that intervened directly on the architectural thought. The redrawing of this project, left on paper as many of the projects realized by Komarova and the other students of the VChUTE-MAS, allowed us to deepen the compositional principles of the architectural education organized within the Eastern European avant-garde.

The possibility provided by the digital drawing to bring to light the cultural heritage represented by the architectural experiments of the Moscow didactical-productive laboratories allows to catalog new images that demonstrate the design and cultural contribution of the models of technical-artistic schools based on the interaction between different aspects of art and scientific-engineering training, in parallel with what was happening in the same years in the Bauhaus.

The exercises conducted by the students of the VChUTEMAS on the properties of volume and space, through the redrawing of the few archival works and the digital modeling as a way of visualizing the architecture, establish a system of images borrowed by means of the compositional possibilities of the drawing and at the same time purged from the obligation of its realization. These are testimonies of an educational methodology aimed at the investigation of architecture through the values of the Soviet artistic avant-gardes that, at the suspended stage of the project, declare their belonging to the possible dimensions of the drawing.

References

De Micheli M (1999) Le avanguardie artistiche del novecento. Universale Economica Feltrinelli, Milano

Elia M (2008) VChUTEMAS design e avanguardia nella Russia dei Soviet. Lupetti editore, Milano

Finizio LP (1990) L'Astrattismo costruttivo. Suprematismo e costruttivismo. Editori Laterza, Roma-Bari

Komarova L (1996) Il VChUTEMAS e il suo tempo. Testimonianze e progetti della scuola costruttivista a Mosca. Editori Kappa, Roma

Kopp A (1987) Città e rivoluzione. Architettura e urbanistica sovietiche degli anni Venti. Silvestri G. (trad. it.), Battisti E. (cur.). Feltrinelli, Milano

Rowell M, Znder Rudenstine A (1981) Art of the avant-garde in Russia. Selection from the George Costakis collection. The Solomon R., Guggenheim Museum, New York

Coherence of Visual and Epistemic Elements in Multimodal Artifacts for the Cultural Heritage Education. The Case Study of the Vitruvian Man by Leonardo da Vinci

Giampiero Dalai[1], Berta Martini[2], and Luciano Perondi[3(✉)]

[1] Alpaca Società Cooperativa,
via Giuseppe Garibaldi, 5, 44121 Ferrara, FE, Italy
[2] Dipartimento di studi umanistici, Università degli studi di Urbino Carlo Bo,
Via Bramante, 17, 61029 Urbino, PU, Italy
[3] Dipartimento Pianificazione e Progettazione in Ambienti Complessi,
Università IUAV di Venezia,
Santa Croce 191 Tolentini, 30135 Venice, VE, Italy
lperondi@iuav.it

Abstract. In this article we hypothesize that, in an interactive system for the representation of the knowledge related to a work of art, it is possible to detect a relation between visual coherence (in particular, the coherence of the number of constituent traits in graphical elements) and epistemic coherence (in particular, the coherence of the forms of knowledge), and that this relation affects the readability and the understanding of specific contents of the work of art. This article describes an experimental design which is conceived for verifying the validity of the research hypothesis. The planned research allows to describe a valid criterion for the development of a system of signs and contents related to a work of art.

Keywords: Visual rhetoric · Synsemia · Constituent traits ·
Epistemic coherence · Visual coherence · Cultural heritage education

1 Introduction

If we consider the works of art as signs (Antinucci 2004), educating people to art and cultural heritage implies to make the cultural object "readable" (Nuzzaci 2006) before everything else. This can be done by transmitting the knowledge related to the cultural object (Martini 2012).

From an educational point of view, in order to make the knowledge accessible to the reader, the knowledge needs to be put in relation with the perceived reality of the cultural object. This can be done by designing representations that make those elements of knowledge more suitable to be taught and understood (Martini 2016).

In this article we propose an hypothesis about what the structural elements of a model for the representation of the knowledge related to a cultural object can be.

© Springer Nature Switzerland AG 2019
A. Luigini (Ed.): EARTH 2018, AISC 919, pp. 411–421, 2019.
https://doi.org/10.1007/978-3-030-12240-9_43

These structural elements are specific variables of visual coherence and epistemic coherence, which once combined they allow to design effective representation systems.

We hypothesize that, in order to ensure high levels of readability and understanding of the cultural objects, the model needs to take into account systematically the visual coherence and epistemic coherence combinations.

2   Designing the Coherence Between the System of Signs and the System of Contents

In the proposed model and in relation to our research areas, we hypothesize that the concepts of communication coherence and epistemic coherence are divided into:

(1) communication coherence
   (a) rhetoric (Bonsiepe 1995; Migliore 2007)
   (b) graphic
       (i)   constituent traits (Eco 2016)
       (ii) visual variables (Bertin 2011; von Engelhardt 2002)
(2) epistemic coherence
   (a) reduction to essential elements (Martini 2005)
   (b) incomplete autonomy (Martini 2011)
   (c) knowledge organisation (Gnoli et al. 2006; Novak 2001)

2.1   Communication Coherence

We defined two fundamental areas basing on which we can describe the communication coherence: the rhetoric area and the graphic area.

The "rhetoric" area concerns the set of rhetorical figures in the metalogic area (the tropes of the classical rhetoric) These rhetorical figures are related to the signified – in particular to the meaning of a unit (Migliore 2007), since in this article we are dealing with graphic/semantic elements. Since this area of the rhetoric is related with the contents, it is independent from the form and to the modes of expression. We referred also to Bonsiepe (1995) and to Bonfantini (2000), in regard to the comparison between the rhetorical figures and the modes of expression.

The "graphic" area concerns the set of graphic choices which lead to the development of a communication artifact.

2.1.1   Rhetoric Coherence

Analogy

The analogy is a rhetorical figure which has great relevance in the design of representations; we elaborated on the definition provided by Bailer-Jones (2002, p. 110), defining an analogy as the association of two domains through the resemblance of at least one pertinent trait for each of the domains.

In our analysis the analogy is the key figure of speech, since it is possible to detect also metonymy and synecdoche in it (which are the other rhetorical figures we consider, but also the metaphor for example), as shown in Fig. 1.

Fig. 1. Pictogram for the Berlin 1936 Olympics. Athletics.

In Fig. 1, the analogy is described as "run as if you had wings on your feet", which is clearly inspired by the representation of Hermes/Mercury. The domain of destination of the running (human motion) is associated to the domain of start of the animal motion through the usage of the pertinent trait of the speed of flight compared to the other kinds of motion.

Metonymy

It is the association of two domains through a logic or consequential relation (causal, temporal, biological), regardless from the direction (for example, the cause for the effect or the effect for the cause), related to a pertinent trait.

In Fig. 2, the two crossed hammers signify "coal", therefore they signify the material through the representation of the tools for extracting it. Moreover, the ball of cotton wool still attached to the plant is used to signify the cotton fabric, therefore the raw material is used to signify the final product.

Fig. 2. Examples of metonymy a system of Isotype pictograms. "Export Drive", Isotype for Future Magazine, 1947, pp. 50–51.

Synecdoche

It is the association of a domain with a part of itself, which is also in this case independent from the direction (the whole for the part or the part for the whole).

Fig. 3. Examples of synecdoche in a set of pictograms for the Mexico 1968 Olympics.

A significative example is the set of pictograms designed for the Mexico 1968 Olympics (Fig. 3), in which a detail of the athletic action or of the sport equipment are used as pertinent traits in order to signify the sport in its whole.

food

Fig. 4. Examples of the combination of metonymy and synecdoche. "Export Drive", Isotype for Future Magazine, 1947, pp. 50–51.

Often the rhetorical figures are presented in combination. Figure 4 shows, for example, a pictogram which uses a combination of metonymy and synecdoche: the tin container is used to signify the content (i.e. the food – metonymy), and at the same time the canned food is used to signify the domain of the food in its whole (synecdoche).

2.1.2   Graphic *Coherence*
The graphic coherence concerns the design of the visual aspect of signs. In this article, we focused on the number of constituent traits.

The concept of the constituent traits is related with the concept of pertinent traits as described by Eco (Eco 2016, Chapter 1). Eco distinguishes between the pertinent trais and the facultative variants, but he states that while the reader processes of an icon, the 'relevance' or 'facultativeness' of a trait acquire meaning just in relation to the local and individual conventions. We have no intention here to debate Eco's descriptions, nevertheless it is useful to break down the graphic artifacts into discernible constituent traits, even if the operation is arbitrary.

By describing the number of constituent traits and their visual aspect (through the visual variables) it is possible to create aggregates and semantic hierarchies, basing on the coherence or incoherence.

We hypothesize that the number of constituent traits is a feature of a synsemic communication artifact, together with the visual variables, the reference frame, etc. (as described in Bonora et al. (in press), as the constituent traits describe the number of traits but not their aspects, neither their organization nor their relationship with the context.

Constituent Traits
In order illustrate what the concept of the constituent traits is, we can observe that in the Chinese writing the number of strokes which are the "traits" that constitute the single glyphs varies within a predetermined range, and its variation can be considered a rhetoric feature as well (Lussu 2003).

The matter of traits is a fundamental aspect of writing, also because it is closely related to the performance of writing (the etymology of term "trait" is the metonimia of the process of calligraphic execution "trahere", the Latin word for "to pull", while in Italian the words for trait and stroke can be translated by the word "tratto").

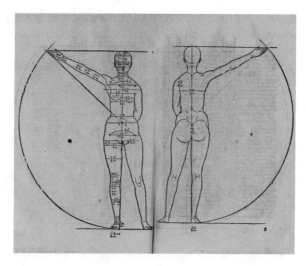

Fig. 5. Albrecht Dürer, Menschlicher Proportion durch Albrechten Durer von Nurerberg, 1528. Table K. Retrieved at https://archive.org/details/hierinnsindbegri00dure

Therefore, the constituent traits include both the pertinent traits and the facultative variants of Eco (2016, Chapter 1). For example, the presence of serifs in a latin typeface increases the number of constituent traits, without increasing the number of pertinent traits.

Here it follows an example in which the regularity of the density of constituent traits is evident, and this regularity makes the sign system coherent even in the case in which the iconic–representative component of the artifact is predominant, by comparison with the alphabetic component.

In the plates presented in Fig. 5, the human figure is rendered by a set of relatively monolinear (but non-rectilinear, geometrically complex) lines, while the dimensions, the proportions and the strokes connecting the joints/articulations (hips and shoulders) are rectilinear or geometrically simple lines.

The visual variables used by the two sets of lines are the same (two different stroke thickness), the difference between "simple" and "complex" stroke is given by the different density of the number of traits composing the lines. The two sets of lines make readable two semantic aggregates.

Visual Variables
As for the definition and description of visual variables, see Bertin (2011), von Engelhardt (2002), Bonora et al. (2017).

2.2   Epistemic Coherence

The knowledge associated with a cultural object constitutes a system of knowledge that can be referred to that object and which are related to each other. Such knowledge is usually of different types (e.g., declarative, factual, conceptual, procedural). Even the relationships that exist between these kind of knowledge can be of different types: logical (for example, inferential relations) or semantic (for example, relations of epistemic proximity).

According to our hypothesis it is possible to confer epistemic coherence to a set of elements of knowledge following these criteria:

(a) reduction to essential elements

Definition: it consists in detecting the object or the structures of the knowledge that build the interrelated system of the epistemological dimensions of a field of knowledge, by following a specific description of that field (Martini 2005). This means that the elements of knowledge which need to be associated with a cultural object need to be selected basing on their type (factual, conceptual, procedural) and on their relevance in the field of knowledge.

(b) incomplete autonomy

Definition: with reference to the representation of the knowledge of a discipline according to the network model, the autonomy consists in the possibility to arrange the elements of knowledge basing on their epistemic proximity: elements of knowledge which are epistemically close form groups highly interrelated inside and weakly interrelated outside (Martini 2011).

This means that the elements of knowledge which need to be associated with a cultural object constitute clusters elements which are epistemically close and maybe connected to each other (therefore they become relatively autonomous).

(c) knowledge organization

Definition: it consists in the detection of the logic or semantic relations between the elements of knowledge (Gnoli et al. 2006; Novak 2001).

This means that the elements of knowledge which need to be associated with a cultural object need to be arranged in accordance to logic relations (e.g., hierarchies/non-hierarchies) which express inferential relations between elements of knowledge (analogies, inductions, deductions), or semantinc relations (e.g. through the usage of schemes and mind maps) which express the epistemic proximity of the contents.

It is relatively easier to reach graphic and semantic coherence when dealing with a narrow domain, which is also semantically coherent, as the Olympic sports (Fig. 3). However, the semantic coherence imposes to represent all the pictograms as on the same hierarchical level, either of "visual energy" (Bertin 2011), graphic composition and rhetoric composition. When the domain is semantically more articulated, as in the case of the complete communication artifact from which Figs. 2 and 4 have been extracted, the number of relations between elements is so wide that it is difficult to keep a high degree of graphic and rhetoric coherence. In these cases, it could be useful to break down further the domain into semantic sub-categories, which can be represented by using similar rhetorical figures.

3   Description of the Work

In this work we study the effect of the combined and systematic application of the visual and epistemic coherence. In particular, we transpose into an interactive environment a part of the contents of the video clip made for the exhibition *Perfecto e virtuale, l'uomo vitruviano di Leonardo*[1], which was developed by the Centro Studi Vitruviani. We prepare a set of graphic elements which are applied to the representation of the Uomo Vitruviano, in order to test our hypothesis.

The objective is to understand if, while transposing some contents of the cultural object, the consistency of the number of constitutive traits with the type of the elements of knowledge (which are always epistemically close) affects the reading and the understanding of the cultural object.

The elements of knowledge can be of different types and they can be interrelated by logic or semantic relations. Therefore the variables of epistemic coherence can be described as a combination, which generates the following matrix of possibilities (Table 1).

Table 1. Variables of epistemic coherence

	Semantic relation (epistemic proximity)	Logic relation (inference)
Elements of knowledge of the same type	Elements of knowledge of the same type and with epistemic proximity	Elements of knowledge of the same type and with logic relation
Elements of knowledge of different type	Elements of knowledge of different type and with epistemic proximity	Elements of knowledge of different type and with logic relation

Every combination can be considered as an aggregate of elements of knowledge which we assume it is epistemically coherent.

In order to uncover the relation between the visual features and the epistemic aggregates, that we describe as visual coherence and epistemic coherence, we plan to proceed with an experimentation.

The experimental design consist in manipulating the two variables of epistemic coherence (type of elements of knowledge) in relation to the variables of visual coherence (difference in the number of constitutive traits) in order to test their impact on the understanding of the elements of knowledge (Table 2).

---

[1] The exhibition was held in Fano, in the period 24.10.14–06.01.15, the curator was Annalisa Perissa Torrini, the ideation and the coordination were by Paolo Clini. https://www.centrostudivitruviani. org/comunicato-stampa-3/.

Table 2. Combination of the considered variables of visual and epistemic coherence.

	Elements of knowledge of the same type and with epistemic proximity	Elements of knowledge of different type and with epistemic proximity
Difference in the number of constitutive traits non significative or none	coherence (v1)	incoherence (v3)
Significative difference in the number of constitutive traits	incoherence (v2)	coherence (v4)

We define arbitrarily for which values the difference in the number of constitutive traits is considered significative or non significative, since at the moment we are not aware of studies on the critical magnitude of this variable, for which we should expect a different elaboration from the reader.

We design four interactive variations of the same communication artifact, in which the visual elements aid the learning of specific contents of the Vitruvian Man. The four variations are made to accommodate the four variables in Table 2.

In the interactive system the visual elements are shown to the reader at first, and then after an adequate interval of time they are hidden. Afterwards, we will ask a question to the readers in order to test their understanding.

The impact on the readers' understanding of the artifact can be done by measuring the levels of understanding of the coherent/incoherent visual and epistemic aggregates.

The experimental design consist in detecting four groups which are comparable to each other. The fact that they are comparable is verified through a pre-test.

Afterwards, we apply to each group a series of visual elements which explicit the combination of visual and epistemic coherence. For each one of the combinations, we ask the reader a question (which we tried out before to ensure its functioning). The question is aimed to verify the legibility and the understanding of the elements of knowledge.

The combinations of visual and epistemic variables which we consider are the following:

V1 We consider elements of knowledge of the same type and with epistemic proximity, which are represented by visual elements with a difference in the number of constitutive traits that is non significative or none. This combination generates **coherence** of visual and epistemic variables.

V2 We consider elements of knowledge of the same type and with epistemic proximity, which are represented by visual elements with a significative difference in the number of constitutive traits. This combination generates **incoherence** of visual and epistemic variables.

V3 We consider elements of knowledge of different type and with epistemic proximity, which are represented by visual elements with a difference in the number of constitutive traits that is non significative or none. This combination generates **incoherence** of visual and epistemic variables.

V4 We consider elements of knowledge of different type and with epistemic proximity, which are represented by visual elements with significative difference in the number of constitutive traits. This combination generates **coherence** of visual and epistemic variables.

The two elements of knowledge with epistemic proximity and of the same type (declarative) which we plan to transmit during the experiment are:

1. "le misure dell'omo sono dalla natura distribuite in questo modo: cioè che 4 diti fa 1 palmo, et 4 palmi fa 1 pie, 6 palmi fa un chubito, 4 cubiti fa 1 homo";
2. "dal di sotto del mento alla sommità del capo è un ottavo dell'altezza dell'omo"

By designing the visual elements for the communication of these elements of knowledge with a coherent/incoherent number of constitutive traits, we highlight the kind of relation between the visual coherence and the epistemic coherence (as described in Table 2). Table 3 provides visual examples for each of the four representations.

The legibility and the understanding are evaluated by the following question:
"How many cubits measures the head of the man?".

The question implies to use elements of procedural knowledge (how to calculate an unknown measures from known measures). The declarative knowledge explained above and this question constitute different types of knowledge (with epistemic proximity).

4 Discussion and Expected Results

If the results of the experiment support a better understanding of the V1 group compared to the V2 group AND a better understanding of the V4 group compared to the V3 group, we could confirm the hypothesis that a combination of coherence of visual and epistemic variables exerts a positive effect over the understanding of the elements of knowledge. Therefore we could exploit this combination in order to create a system of signs and contents to associate with the cultural object, which should enhance its understanding.

If the hypothesis will be verified, we can affirm that this form of coherence has a semantic function and we could attribute it a role in a model for the design of cultural artifacts and in the transposition of the elements of knowledge which are associated with the communication artifact.

On the contrary, if groups V1 and V2 score higher on their opposites, or other way around, it would mean that the different types of elements of knowledge provide an advantage (or disadvantage) for the understanding of the artifact independently from the visual coherence.

Table 3. Examples of graphic artifacts showing the combination of the considered variables of visual and epistemic coherence.

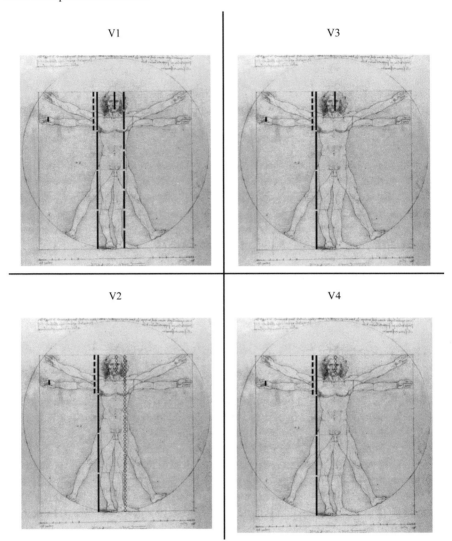

References

Antinucci F (2004) Comunicare nel museo. Editori Laterza, Roma-Bari

Bailer-Jones D (2002) Models, metaphors and analogies. In: Machamer P, Silberstein M (eds) The Blackwell guide to the philosophy of science. Blackwell, Oxford, pp 108–127

Bertin J (2011) Semiology of graphics: diagrams, networks, maps. Esri Press, Redlands

Bonora G, D'Ugo R, Dalai G, Rosa DD, Imperato A, Martini B, Perondi L (2017) The project "interactive topography of Dante's inferno". Transfer of knowledge and design of didactic tools. Proceedings 1(9):875. https://doi.org/10.3390/proceedings1090875

Bonora G, Dalai G, Rosa DD, Imperato A, Martini B, Perondi L (in press) Sinsemia as a tool for designing interactive artifacts for teaching. The case study of the topography of Dante's inferno and the detailed definition of reference frame. In: Proceedings of the 2CO2 Communicating Complexity International Design Conference. La Laguna – Tenerife, Spain, 23–25 November 2017

Bonfantini M (2000) Breve corso di semiotica. Edizioni Scientifiche Italiane, Napoli

Bonsiepe G (1995) Dall'oggetto all'interfaccia: mutazioni del design. Feltrinelli, Milano

Eco U (2016) La struttura assente: La ricerca semiotica e il metodo strutturale. La nave di Teseo, Milano

von Engelhardt J (2002) The Language of graphics: a framework for the analysis of syntax and meaning in maps, charts and diagrams. institute for language, logic and computation. Universiteit van Amsterdam, Amsterdam

Gnoli C, Marino V, Rosati L (2006) Organizzare la conoscenza. Tecniche Nuove, Milano

Lussu G (2003) La lettera uccide. Storie di grafica, 2nd edn. Stampa Alternativa & Graffiti, Viterbo

Novak JD (2001) L'apprendimento significativo. Erickson, Trento

Nuzzaci A (2006) Musei, Pubblici e Didattiche. La didattica museale tra sperimentalismo, modelli teorici e proposte operative. Edizioni Lionello Giordano, Cosenza

Martini B (2016) Il museo sensibile. Le tecnologie ICT al servizio della trasmissione della conoscenza. Franco Angeli, Milano

Martini B (2012) Il sistema della formazione ai saperi. Soggetti Oggetti Istituzioni. Tecnodid, Napoli

Martini B (2011) Pedagogia dei saperi. Franco Angeli, Milano

Martini B (2005) Formare ai saperi. Franco Angeli, Milano

Migliore T (2007) Introduzione. In: Migliore T (ed) Gruppo μ. Trattato del segno visivo: per una retorica dell'immagine. Bruno Mondadori, Milano, pp XII–XIII

Interactive Installations and Suggestive Experiences. A Project for the Home of M. Obellius Firmus in Pompeii

M. Capone and D. Palomba$^{(\boxtimes)}$

Department of Architecture (DiARC), University of Naples Federico II,
Via Forno Vecchio 36, 80134 Naples, Italy
{mara.capone, daniela.palomba}@unina.it

Abstract. The contemporary cultural context has become increasingly fascinated by the multiple cognitive systems dedicated to Cultural Heritage. The
development of often captivating methods of communication, the possibilities
offered by increasingly innovative and sophisticated technologies, encourages
experimentation as well as the development of alternative forms of communication and education. There are various professionals interested and involved in
this sector. IT specialists, artists, architects, engineers, archaeologists, art and
architecture historians, all take part in the conception of new communication
models in tune with contemporary iconographic culture. This paper discusses
the project of a temporary multi-sensory installation designed for the Roman
Pompeian *domus* of M. Obellius Firmus, developed as part of the DiARC
Master of Science in Design for the Built Environment. Images, sounds, videos,
physical and virtual installations are used to guide the visitor in a cognitive
experience of the *domus*. The main theme of the installation, interpreted in
different ways, is the water path in the *domus*. The installation aims to highlight
the high technological content as well as the application of the bioclimatic
principles present in a Pompeian house dating back to the late Samnite age.

Keywords: Pompeian Domus · Anamorphosis · Installations · Virtual reality

1 Introduction

Today's culture shows a great deal of interest in the multiple projects of fruition and
knowledge aimed at the "enjoyment" of Cultural Heritage in general and archaeological ones in particular.

One of the main characteristics of an archaeological site is the lack of integrity it
has, thus making it essential to design a communication project capable of filling the
communication gap and therefore the *shortcomings*. The aim of the knowledge and
valorisation projects, which affect these contexts, is to either make the heritage readable
and interpretable or able to convey the cultural significance of which it is a testimony.
A cultural meaning that can be understood by heterogeneous users through the integration and reconfiguration of images, places and recognizable contexts. Places characterized by the extreme difficulty of interpretation of the *traces* and often also exposed
to serious forms of degradation (Cirafici and Palmieri 2018).

© Springer Nature Switzerland AG 2019
A. Luigini (Ed.): EARTH 2018, AISC 919, pp. 422–431, 2019.
https://doi.org/10.1007/978-3-030-12240-9_44

Several studies have been carried out by the authors on these issues, in which different methodologies of analysis, representation and use of archaeological contexts have been experimented, and not only.

With the common aim of identifying effective tools, the methodological paths initiated have been defined following similar procedures. The acquisition and processing of morphometric data, preceded by an in-depth documentary and bibliographic cognitive survey, followed the identification of interpretative and re-constructive hypotheses, along with documenting the current state of the places. The contents were conveyed both through *Virtual Reality* and *Augmented Reality* systems and, by focusing on the user's involvement, by designing installations with which users are invited to interact.

From a conceptual point of view, interactive communication systems can be divided into two categories: those that allow for *remote* study and analysis of the virtual visit of the site, and those systems that are *on-site*, usable during the actual visit. The first category includes immersive images, which allow to structure more or less complex virtual tours, and 3D PDFs, based on the interactive use of easily navigable 3D models, as well as three-dimensional digital models elaborated by photogrammetric techniques; while systems based on the application of *Augmented Reality* belong to the second category. These latest information systems can also include, if referring to the condition of access to *on-site* contents, all those systems and/or installations that create *semantic spaces* by means of different methods, linked to the possibility of enjoying suggestions and emotions experienced at direct contact with the place. As part of projects that can be defined as *analogic augmented reality*, the construction of plexiglass panels, to be placed in the archaeological site, upon which to reproduce images of the constructive hypotheses that, overlapping the reality, allow to reconfigure the original forms (Capone 2015; Palomba 2015) (Fig. 1).

The project discussed here refers to different communication languages. The object of the experiment is a temporary multi-sensory installation designed for a Roman Pompeian *domus*. Images, sounds, videos, physical and virtual interfaces are used to guide the visitor in a cognitive experience of the *domus*. The common thread is water and, following its path, the visitor discovers secrets, goes beyond the visible, understanding the working of the domus and also visualises the image of the house of M. Obellius Firmus in its original configuration.

The possibility and the will to create virtual three-dimensional models, through which to reconstruct the image of places, raises several questions. The need to identify the most appropriate and effective way to represent the lost parts and elements cannot be neglected. However, it is obvious that the degree of fidelity, rather than referring to a more reliable scientifically valid reconfiguration, is linked to different factors ranging from the level of conservation, to the profound knowledge of the good or analogous realities (Fig. 1).

This experiment has two main objectives. On the one hand, work was carried out to restore and reconstruct the image of parts and elements that no longer exist, making it possible to understand the spatiality investigated, while on the other, to identify and construct an installation through which to describe a specific theme, that of collecting rainwater, which becomes the means to tell the story not only of the place in particular but of Pompeian culture.

Fig. 1. Temple of Apollo in Cuma. "Analogical AR": you can see the reconstructive hypotesis, overlapped on reality, from a fixed point od view.

If for the first experience, the increasingly common perceptive experiences that see the use of other devices or viewers to observe the digital reconstructions was *succumbed* to, for the second, temporary installations were *set up* with which to interpret the theme.

2   The Case Study

For more than two centuries, the ancient city of Pompeii has continued to be highly suggestive and fascinating to the visitors who, upon entering the domus and walking along its streets and the forum, rather than walking in the places of the *spaectacula*, the sacred and thermal buildings, among the shops and public buildings, are transported to places that were once lived in, almost unlikely, more than two thousand years ago. A place, that of ancient Pompeii, which is testimony to the intense life of an entire city, an important colony of the Roman Empire. It is here that it was chosen to experiment with some systems of communication and exploration of cultural heritage in general, applied to the archaeological heritage in particular. The objective of the project is to immerse the visitor in a typical Pompeian residence through a multi-sensory experience, aimed at satisfying, in an alternative and innovative way, the desire for knowledge of the place through instruments connected both to tangible and intangible assets. The site chosen is the home of *M. Obellius Firmus*, one of the largest and most articulated in Pompeii, dating back to the late Samnite period. Situated in Insula 14 of Regio IX, in the area to the north-east of the city, it is located along Via di Nola and has two floors. The house, home of a local aristocratic family, was excavated at the beginning of the last century between 1903 and 1911. The singularity of this *domus* lies in the presence of two halls: a tetrastyle, monumental and representative, in which four fluted Corinthian columns are preserved, and a second Tuscan, both with an independent entrance from the main street. The first is characterized by the imposing, tall tuff columns, with refined marble furnishings. Placed in line with the entrance, there are two pillars in the *impluvium*, which supported a statue of a Satyr, a puteal with grooves to access the underlying cistern and a marble table with lion feet. Going through the *tablinum* leads to the peristyle with four different sized paths, opening onto the private garden. The second atrium, probably built after the first, welcomed the *clientes* and gave access to the both the service and private areas, such as the small private spa. A survey of the current state of the places, together with the identification of the historical and documentary sources, made it possible to realise a representative model of what there is today, as well as a re-configurative model of the domus. The latter was realized following the hypotheses elaborated by Vittorio Spinazzola, director of the excavations in 1911, and depicted by A. Sanarica through images of plants, sections, axonometric views and watercolour perspectives (Spinazzola 1953).

Three-dimensional mono-material models were realised, in which it was chosen to represent, without exceeding in detail, the substance of the architectural forms, with the understanding that the philological reconstructions are only possible hypotheses (Fig. 2).

RECONSTRUCTIVE HYPOTESIS

Fig. 2. M. Obellius Fimus recontructive hypotesis: 3D model

If, on the one hand the objective is to reconstruct the image of the house of *M. Obellius Firmus* on the basis of philological studies and reconstructive hypotheses, on the other, the main aim of the project is to show the engineering capabilities of Romans who established themselves not only through their great works, but also in the designing of their homes. The architecture of the domus responded not only to representational aspects but also, and mainly, to functional factors. The exploitation of the bioclimatic principles, linked to the use and collecting of rainwater, is based on the apparent simple system of the *impluvium* and *compluvium*, which in reality is a highly ingenious system. The collection method not only guaranteed water in the house, it was also used to cool the rooms in the hot seasons.

The system was designed for rainwater to be collected in the *impluvium* as well as the cistern below. The conformation of the *compluvium* and the closed court atrium limited the sunshine in the hottest period, ensured the entry of light and favoured the generation of air currents that, thanks also to the presence of water, cooled the rooms.

3   The Installation

The imagined temporary installation is designed to be realised in the tetrastyle atrium, with the idea of giving shape to elements of the past through physical and perceptive elements that use a contemporary language.

What considerations were made at the beginning of the project? The first aspect was to hypothesise an experience that could be experienced exclusively on site, which therefore involved the user once having reached the chosen place, through *immersive* and engaging experiences. Secondly, what to communicate and how to do it was considered. It was chosen to focus on both the temporary installations through which to *reconstruct* the path of the water conceptually, but also to use Computer Vision to make it possible to see the domus virtually reconstructed and appreciate those places in possible original forms as hypothesized.

3.1   References

Before describing the project and the components of the installation, there are some cultural and artistic references that provided suggestions for the concept.

The research related to the identification of projects and artistic experiences that directly involve the users as well as use contemporary languages, while paying attention and respect to the places with which they interact.

The work of Edoardo Tresoldi, the Italian sculptor, is effective, with him giving shape to his art through the use and modelling of metal meshes. Sculptures that are realised in the forms of architectural elements, which blend with the architectures and contexts in which they are inserted. The project for the Basilica of Siponto expresses all the poetics and communicative power of his language. Ephemeral and evanescent signs, albeit made with metal structures, outline and describe the three-dimensionality of the places that were. Works that reconstruct time, as they have been defined, a time made of other places capable of generating a strong fascination. A work designed to be crossed, enjoyed, observed by multiple points, internal and external to it.

Even the artistic installations that make the perspective artifice the instrument through which to realise and stage singular and surprising perceptive inventions, have been sources of inspiration.

Architectures, rather than parts of cities or landscapes, become the canvases, the supports upon which to build the installation. The reference starts from here to all those works that are translated through anamorphic projections (De Rosa and D'Acunto 2002). From the famous spatial optical illusions of Felice Varini to those of Georges Rousse, to the exceptional works of artists who create 3D street-paintings. Perceptive suggestions in which the observer recognises and reconstructs the theme of figuration, conquering the only possible point of view.

If with these works, sight and touch are the senses involved, artistic expressions in which other senses are stimulated have also been considered: multi-sensory installations in which hearing, along with the sense of smell, are involved. The sounds amplify the suggestions and the involvement of those who assist and participate in the performances, often containing sounds, videos, static and dynamic projections. Forms and ways to rethink artistic expressions designed by Studio Azzurro. It is with the realisation of what are known as *Sensory Environments*, were it is possible to witness the participation of the spectator in the work, which can mutate and change in a certain place and in a certain time thanks to his choices, actions and interactions.

3.2   The Project

In the planned temporary installation, there are different components, two of which are dedicated to the theme of channelling rain water. The first is an installation that conceptually alludes to the falling of water from above, visually enhancing the function of the *impluvium*. A sculpture composed of two surfaces to be realised with nets tied in four points. With the dual purpose of re-configuring the original integrity of the columns, but also of creating a structure that could help to support surfaces, the columns are caged by cylindrical surfaces made from electro-welded metal nets, just over six meters high.

Symmetrically placed close to the longitudinal axis of crossing the *domus*, the sculpture is placed between the pairs of columns of the tetrastyle atrium.

The symmetrical surfaces are portions of a hyperbolic paraboloid generated as a function of the slanted quadrilateral, whose configuration has been defined in relation to the anchoring points. The intelligent use of geometry makes it possible to construct an object capable of enhancing a principle, that of collecting, and evoking an operation, collecting water in the cistern. The flat projection of the double curved groove is in this case a square, the rectilinear generators allow to easily construct the object that presents a single plane of symmetry that contains the main parabola, represented, in the first image, by the diagonal of the square. The main parabola conceptually represents the path and channelling of water (Fig. 3).

During evening visits of the archaeological site, scheduled for the presentation of the event, the parabolic curve will be made visible thanks to a strip of warm LED lights. The design surfaces, made with an elastic nylon membrane, are anchored with adjustable tensors in correspondence to the four vertices of the aquifers. Two connect the surfaces to the metal structures that surround the columns of the atrium, while the other two supports are positioned, one in *the impluvium* basin and the other, which also acts as ballast, to a support anchored to the ground.

The composition is designed to be crossed and observed from multiple points. The user is forced to move below it to access the other rooms of the domus. The movement the mesh of the nets gives unprecedented visual impressions due to the overlapping of the lattices of the membranes. The idea is to create an emotional event that stimulates the observer to interactively explore all the components of the installation upon reaching the atrium, the first representative area of the *domus* that is entered upon passing through the vestibule.

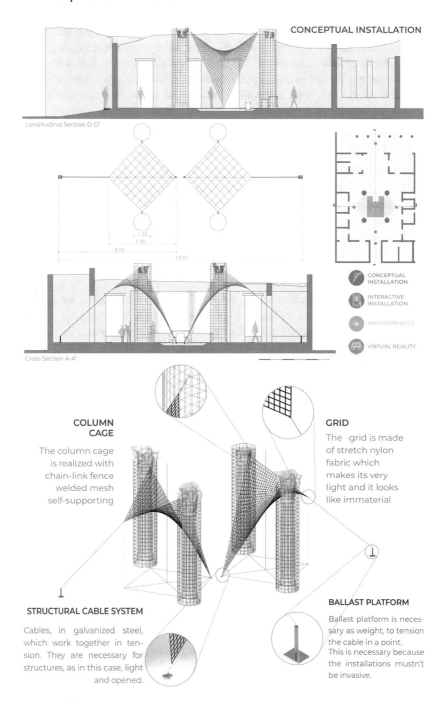

CONCEPTUAL INSTALLATION

Longitudinal Section D-D'

Cross Section A-A'

CONCEPTUAL
INSTALLATION

INTERACTIVE
INSTALLATION

ANAMORPHOSIS

VIRTUAL REALITY

COLUMN CAGE

The column cage is realized with chain-link fence welded mesh self-supporting

GRID

The grid is made of stretch nylon fabric which makes its very light and it looks like immaterial

STRUCTURAL CABLE SYSTEM

Cables, in galvanized steel, which work together in tension. They are necessary for structures, as in this case, light and opened.

BALLAST PLATFORM

Ballast platform is necessary as weight, to tension the cable in a point. This is necessary because the installations mustn't be invasive.

Fig. 3. Temporary installation concept: the water cycle in domus

It is at the end of the vestibule that the visitor meets, upon entering the domus, the first element of the temporary installation. A totem composed of a corten vertical sheet, 1.90 metres tall, inserted into an iron base that acts as a trapezoid. On the panel, there is a map of the area with the path of the exhibition upon which the *points of interest* (POIs) are indicated, which have been suitably designed to be immediately identified during the visit. The laser cut sheet is characterized by the installation logo, *Living Pompeii*, at the bottom. The upper edge recalls, with its irregular profile, the irregularity of the walls of the archaeological site.

A QR code, placed at the beginning of the visit path, invites to download the App that manages the virtual visit, the components and the multimedia contents.

The icon is a laser-engraved stylized eye that suggests to the user to look beyond the panel, where the other installation dedicated to the theme of collecting water is revealed: an anamorphosis created on a plexiglass panel arranged horizontally and installed in the *impluvium*, with the underlying tank and water collected in it are depicted. The perceptual experience is accompanied by a sound experience. When the user enters the totem platform, loudspeakers are automatically activated by weight sensing sensors that emit sounds of water. The installation makes the spectator a *spect-actor* since the events are generated as a consequence of his possible actions. Originated from a projective transformation, the deformed anamorphic image reveals its essence only if observed from the only privileged point that allows to recognise and reconstruct the figuration.

The last component of the installation refers to the POIs and the virtual contents accessible from an appropriately prepared App. The points are indicated with circular iron plates, with a diameter of 80 cm, upon which some corten plates are placed, engraved with the image of an electronic device and the eye alluding to the virtually accessible perceptual experience. Once again, the communicative power of images is used, in general, and pictograms in particular, in which the semantic content can also be understood by individuals of different languages and cultures. These elements, positioned on the ground along a hypothetical tour route, give access to virtual reconstructions. Through the App, it is possible to see videos and reconstructions of the reconstructive hypotheses of the *domus* that can be appreciated from those particular *points of interest*. The *spect-actor* walks over metal sheets and activates sounds, such as water falling into the cistern, as well as that of a receptacle being dropped from the puteal to draw water, which are activated thanks to the presence of sensor speakers for vertical sound diffusion (Fig. 4).

Fig. 4. Temporary installation elements

4 Conclusions

The project is part of a field of research and experimentation connected to the identification of methodologies capable of transmitting cultural content to a wider and heterogeneous public, without however yielding to the often sterile spectacle connected to the use of digital technologies. In other words, the concept tends to favour interactivity, without however exhausting itself in the exclusively recreational use of the installation. The use of ancient techniques and methods, such as anamorphosis, are integrated with the most innovative technologies, viewers, sensors, etc. with the aim of spreading the cultural content of the artefact. Therefore, not a trivial *storytelling* capable of representing the image of the reconstructive hypothesis, but rather a communicative system capable of transmitting the immaterial values of the Pompeian house through a multi-sensory experiential fruition able to stimulate suggestions.

Acknowledgements. The illustrated project was developed under the co-ordination of the authors by Maria Taurisano as part of her Master's Degree thesis in Design for the Built Environment of DiARC entitled *Living Pompeii. A "site-specific" installation performing Obellio Firmo Domus.*

References

Spinazzola V (1953) Pompei alla luce degli scavi nuovi di Via dell'Abbondanza (anni 1910–1923). La Libreria dello Stato, Roma

Capone M (2015) Teorie e metodi per la rappresentazione del patrimonio archeologico su piattaforma digitale. In: Giovanni M, Arena M, Raffa P (eds) Spazi e culture del Mediterraneo 4. La Scuola di Pitagora, Napoli, pp 556–567

Cirafici A, Palmieri A (2018) Lacune apparenti. La 'reintegrazione dell'immagine' nell'esperienza del patrimonio archeologico. In: Salerno R (ed) Rappresentazione materiale/immateriale, Atti del 40° Convegno internazionale dei Docenti delle discipline della Rappresentazione quindicesimo congresso UID. Gangemi Editore, Roma, pp 1043–1050

De Rosa A, D'Acunto G (2002) La vertigine dello sguardo. Tre saggi sulla rappresentazione anamorfica, Cafoscarina

Palomba D (2015) Il Tempio di Diana. In: Giovanni M, Arena M, Raffa P (eds) Spazi e culture del Mediterraneo 4, Costruzione di un Atlante del Patrimonio Culturale del Mediterraneo, Conoscenza, Comunicazione, Governance. La Scuola di Pitagora editrice, Napoli, pp 89–94

The Drawing and the Virtual Model of the Monastery of Archangels Michael and Gabriel in Kosovo. Survey and Modeling

Luigi Corniello[1]([✉]), Enrico Mirra[1], and Gëzim Hasko[2]

[1] Department of Architecture and Industrial Design (DADI),
Università degli Studi della Campania "Luigi Vanvitelli",
Via San Lorenzo, 81031 Aversa, Italy
luigi.corniello@gmail.com
[2] Faculty of Civil Engineering (FCE), UPT Polytechnic University of Tirana,
Mother Tereza Square, Nr. 4, Tirana, Albania
g_hasko@yahoo.com

Abstract. The research is focused on the study of the monastery of the Archangels Michael and Gabriel. The contribution, through the theoretical foundations of the survey and the representation of the urban scale on tradition and innovation, aims to compare images of the territory, of the current reality and virtual reconstructions.

Keywords: Monastery · Kosovo · Drawing · Survey · Virtual reconstructions

1 Introduction (E.M.)

The research is focuses on the study of the Archangel Michael and Gabriel monastery, located in southern of Kosovo, built on the ruins of an ancient church between 1343 and 1352 by order of Tsar Stephen Uroš IV Dušan. The place where the monastery was erected, on the left bank of the river Bistrica, in an audience formed by the fast course of the river, was the site on which stood a church dedicated to the Archangels Michael and Gabriel. The territory was protected by the walls of an ex-fortress and, for such architectural features, the monastery took over the task of controlling the city of Prizren. Through the theoretical foundations of survey and representation on an urban scale between tradition and innovation, the contribution proposes images compared to the territory, to current reality and virtual reconstructions, both interpreted with the scientific detection of places and aimed at conservation and protection as cognitive elements that tend to search for material and immaterial values (Fig. 1).

© Springer Nature Switzerland AG 2019
A. Luigini (Ed.): EARTH 2018, AISC 919, pp. 432–438, 2019.
https://doi.org/10.1007/978-3-030-12240-9_45

Fig. 1. The monastery of the Archangels Michael and Gabriel in Pritzren. View of the ruins of the Arcangeli church. (Corniello 2014)

2   Historical Notes on the Monastery of the Archangels Michael and Gabriel (G.H.)

Crossing the narrow and winding valley at the foot of the fortress, following the course of the river Bistrica, towards the east we find the monastery of Archangels Michael and Gabriel, built on the ruins of an ancient church, between 1343 and 1352, by order of Tsar Stephen Uroš IV Dušan. The place where the monastery was erected, on the left bank of the river Bistrica, in an audience formed by the fast course of the river, was the site on which stood a church dedicated to the Archangels Michael and Gabriel. The territory was protected by the walls of an ex-fortress, which contained a large part of Mount Sara. The monastery, for these architectural features, performed the task of controlling the city of Prizren. The head of the building was the Abbot Metropolita Jacob.

The monastery became one of the most important of the Balkans and came to host more than 200 Orthodox monks. The Tsar Dušan, who at the end of his life was buried in the main church of the monastery, gave to the visitors of this monastery 93 villages, a mine in Toplica, some vineyards and fields to be cultivated. Many of the products, in addition to being used for the sustenance of the monastery itself, were sold to the Prizren market (Fig. 2).

Fig. 2. The monastery of the Archangels Michael and Gabriel in Pritzren. Territorial framework of structures.

With the crisis of 1455 and the arrival of the Turks in the Balkans, the monastery of the Archangels was besieged. The historical sources and some archaeological excavations highlight the decline of the monastery and its total destruction in the second half of the sixteenth century. The church of the Archangels was completely demolished by Sinan Paša and its ruins were used to complete the Prizren Mosque. After the devastation of the monastery only the floors and walls of the former fortress remained unearthed during the recent archaeological excavations.

3 The Survey of the Monastic Structures (L.C.)

The main church, dedicated to the Archangels Gabriel and Michael, was one of the largest in Serbia, now visible from the surface occupied by the floor. It was a monumental structure 28,5 m high and 16,75 m wide with a cross shaped foundation and narrow side aisles, an unusual feature in buildings of this type. On the eastern side there were three apses: the one at the center the larger one is more protruding with a pentagon shape. A large dodecagonal dome of 6,40 m in diameter surmounted the building and was supported by four pillars. The facades were covered with white and

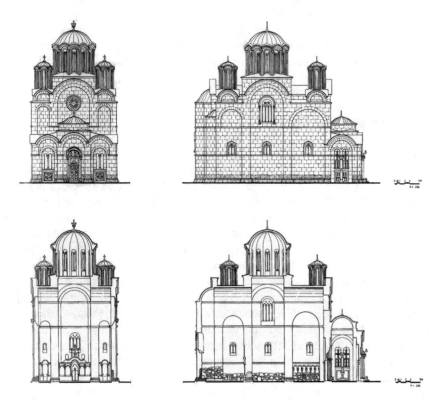

Fig. 3. The monastery of the Archangels Michael and Gabriel in Pritzren. Survey and graphic reconstruction of archival documents of the Church of the Archangels.

red marble and divided into three levels by some layers of decorated stone; the floor consisted of blocks of marble from central Europe. There were mosaics and frescoes depicting geometric shapes, mythical animals, griffins, lions, birds and fish. The interior of the church was almost completely frescoed and the capitals, the portals, the windows and the furniture were richly decorated.

The Chapel of St. Nicholas, however, was erected near the main church. It was much smaller (measuring 13,20 m in height and 7,00 m in width) but it was similarly decorated. It was a building consisting of a single nave with an apse in the eastern wall. The dome was supported by four pillars, two in the main room of the church and two in the sanctuary; furthermore, another dome overlooked the western wall. Both churches were decorated with statues of different materials and dimensions. About 1,700 fragments of sculptures depicting angels, saints, human and animal figures and floral decorations were found during archaeological excavations. Many of the sculptures preserved in the museum of the Archangel monastery come from the medieval period. In some artefacts found there are characteristics very similar to those of religious paintings painted in the coastal towns of Montenegro and Croatia. In 1970 the monastery was rebuilt and is still used today: life in the monastery takes its example from that conducted in medieval places of worship; the rule of eremitic isolation is in force and religious functions are regularly performed. The works were interrupted by the war that struck Kosovo but did not cause the monks to abandon the monastery. The existing structures were renovated, treatment that also suffered the walls, while an additional area was used as a residential area. The first monks arrived in the monastery of the Archangels in 1998 and, from that moment, play an important role in the spirituality of the Serbian population, and in particular in the area of Prizren (Fig. 3).

4   Conclusions (E.M.)

The activity of representing of the monastery of the Archangels Michele and Gabriele was, therefore, set up by providing, in an initial phase, the execution of a basic survey extended to the architectural organisms; subsequently, in a second campaign of survey and return, the digital model was finalized aimed at the knowledge and use of the places. Adequate photographic documentation was also produced in addition to bibliographic, archival, and iconographic surveys. In this representation, the photographic image, in addition to constituting a database value that can be used even after the survey phase, is evident in the possibility of interpolating this static figurative datum with dynamic informatic elements. For the activities of knowledge of the site, we took into account the laser instrumentation Ryobi applied on portable computer support, both tablet and smartphone, which allows an immediate view of the relevant data on the photographic image taken by the support, transforming it into a dynamic datum. The use of this photographic technology becomes the main instrument of importance and knowledge since it contains both the measurement data and the geographical coordinates connected to the device used, as well as information on the date and time of the execution of the survey campaign. The virtual model, built on the basis of graphic information collected with the relevant campaigns and iconographic sources, is a fundamental tool for the knowledge of the monastic site as it is questionable on the dimensional level, but at the same time allows non-professionals to enjoy a good, today in a state of ruin in some of its parts, otherwise unknown. The tools that have accompanied the various stages of knowledge, from the survey to the model, constitute a precious aid to the conservation, protection and digital dissemination of places as cognitive elements that tend to the research of material and immaterial values (Fig. 4).

Fig. 4. The monastery of the Archangels Michael and Gabriel in Pritzren. Three-dimensional model of the church of the Archangels

References

Corniello L (2013) Memoria, misura e armonia del patrimonio eremitico in Costa d'Amalfi. In: Conte A, Filippa M (eds) Patrimoni e siti UNESCO. Gangemi Editore, Roma
Corniello L (2016) Città e paesaggi d'Albania. Disegni e immagini. In: Carnevalis L (ed) Linee di ricerca nell'area del Disegno 4. Ermes Edizioni Scientifiche, Roma
Corniello L, Maliqari A, Vozza VMB (2016) Il disegno delle strutture religiose tra Montenegro e Grecia settentrionale. In: Bini M, Bertocci S (eds) Le ragioni del Disegno. The reasons of drawing. Gangemi Editore, Roma

Docci M, Gaiani M, Maestri D (2011) Scienza del Disegno. Città Studi Edizioni, Novara

Giordano P, Corniello L (2014) Atlante Grafico e Teorico Amalfitano. La conoscenza e la modificazione del paesaggio costiero. La scuola di Pitagora editrice, Napoli

Kindersley A (1976) The Mountains of Serbia: travels through in land Yugoslavia, Murray

Perica V (2002) Balkan idols: religion and nationalism in yugoslav states, Oxford University Press

Vignoli G (2000) La tutela delle minoranze nella ex Jugoslavia: il caso del Kossovo, Genova, ECIG

Zerlenga O (1997) La forma ovata in architettura. Rappresentazione geometrica, Napoli, CUEN

Amazon Mechanical Turk

Francesco Cervellini[✉]

School of Architecture and Design, University of Camerino, Camerino, Italy
francesco.cervellini@unicam.it

Abstract. In the technological inflation of a phantasmagoria of useful tools and/or accessories (and never indispensable) that want to be visible (for example the smartphone), it is not possible to see the signs of thoughts able to read and outline the emerging horizons. Great potential can be glimpsed but also great vulnerabilities. First of all the creation of new exploitation phenomena.

Keywords: New media · Digital player · Market place

1 Introduction

The Seminar offered stimulating possibilities of digital elaborations. A lot of they referred to the *integrated modeling*, to the so-called artificial intelligence and to applications of the *Net socialized*.

Nevertheless, the particularity of the center - privileged place of reflection on the education to the knowledge - I would like to also arouse a critical reflection on the awareness of the quality of the digital job. According to me such reflection is very *weak*, because it prevails online today often an unarmed delivery to the Web's great technologies (the famous 4 or 5, Amazon, Facebook, Google, Apple, Twitter…).

So the proposed occasions are ambivalent: from a side they offer a field of interesting experimentations, but at the same time they cannot live without *the hard dirigism* of the mechanisms of operation of the digital marketplace.

To well to see in the names, and in the ways of the proposed themes it shines through that we are living a transformation very acts and a little thought.

In the technological inflation of useful utensils e/o accessories (and never essential) that they want above all to be visible - (for *antonomasia* the smartphone) - I don't perceive in fact the signs of thoughts able to read and to outline the emergent horizons, sees great potentialities but also great vulnerabilities.

Before among the whole creation of new phenomenons of exploitation.

AMZ is an example of it and is a quotation that would like to be ironic but it is bitterly cynical.

Bezos, on purpose recalling the false automaton, (in reality a dwarf hidden in the piece of furniture), invented by von Kempelen to have a good time in the chess Maria Teresa of Austria, it still hides equally inside the cars some new rag dolls for that digital programs non computationally profitable for some assignments superior operativo/cognitivi; only that they are *the Providers*, (if attention is paid to the names of Bezos) or of the **paid workers to job contract** for that same assignments.

© Springer Nature Switzerland AG 2019
A. Luigini (Ed.): EARTH 2018, AISC 919, pp. 439–443, 2019.
https://doi.org/10.1007/978-3-030-12240-9_46

Wikipedia states: *"AMZ: it is a service internet of crowdworking that allows the computer planners (requester) to coordinate the use of human intelligence to perform assignments that the computers, to today I am not able to do. It is one of the suites of Amazon Web Services. The Requesters can publish objective known as HIT (*Human Intelligence Tasks*), as to identify the artists in a musical cd, the best photos of a shop, the writing of the descriptions of a product. The **Worker** (workers or **Turker**, can informally seek among the existing objectives and to complete them in exchange for a payment decided by the requester"*.

It is really in similar circumstances that it is visible that weakness of conscience, which I mentioned. But as it does him not to be radically against the fact that the human intelligence that the delicious ability offers to recognize images, sounds and gestures, to express judgments on the same, to formulate comparisons and analogies, to recognize differences and similes - and as such it is the product of a collective acquisition - can be paid to job contract? (Mogno 2018).

Through a diffused form of crowdsourcing - or of third part recruitment worker-crowd's - the mission of AMZ is that to purchase and to hardly sell the collective intelligence in a fragmentation not recomposed of small duties of any wealth property material neither intellectual.

Never as today it is necessary to submit to criticism *"is the political rationality of the innovation both his/her scientific rationality or the rationality of the algorithm, with his pretension to correspond objective time to a naturalization to turn all the phe-nomenons into states of necessity"* (Pennacchi 2018).

Today, in the third phase of the digital one the same crowdsourcing e/o the crowdworking they are the true formalities wished by the optimists to the Paul Dauggherty of *Meet the middle guru* (the review of digital culture unwound in June to Milan).

This as others are the conventions of the flat and uncritical *tecnoentusiasmo*. *"You cannot be returned back, to the* luddismo" it is their slogan - (for engraved me I don't sustain at all such a position). But the true objectives of such optimists it is both to reassure the minds of those people that have invested in the advanced capitalism of the bases - (according to the refrain *incontro/inclusione/business*) - both to contemplate, as form of show, also to the culture. To the first aspect, the expectations have more than a base, in how much today the data are worth more than the money. From one century and a half it was the money that made to make money. Instead they are today the data.

This is an informative super-money of the revolution of the documentation, con-sistent in synthesis in the accumulation of documents and in the generalization of the media - today each of us is a medium or as minimum as effective communicator can be equipped. The intersection between documents and media (*documediale*) it produces the *big data - that they pick up information on everything of all - and for this they are worth more than the money - and they are the interpreters of those information, that is the only ones in degree to interpret them in that dimension* (Ferraris 2018).

And here it is worth to underline a paradox, (what such is in comparison to the classical political economy): the today's capital doesn't consist more therefore in the ownership of the means of production, but in those of interpretation. The data in fact I am the fruit of the production of every of us that to such end it purchases the mean of production of the same datum - (computer or smartphone) and a consistent part of his job of production, over that of the retrieval and of the elaboration of the datum, it consists really in to transmit (to load) that same in one of the big data that they free appropriate some right of interpretation and use of the same, or without any remuneration or with a derisive remuneration as in the case of AMZ.

The new contradiction between capital and job is deceitfully in this formed relationship, deceitfully because in many cases (I would say the *most*) the job is not even recognized as such, because he has been gotten (extorted) through a voluntary contribution, that does even him to competition to furnish in different circumstances.

Anything else other than exploitation of the patrimony! Anything else other than sophisticated experimentations on the *heritage…*!

I believe that never as today is necessary to submit to criticism *"is the political rationality of the innovation both his/her scientific rationality or the rationality of the algorithm, with his/her pretension to correspond objective time to a naturalization to turn all the phenomenons into states of necessity."* Today the ritualizzazione is conclusive the *magicità* that accompanies their use. It is important the *decostruzione* of that Gillbert Simondon calls *"tecnofania"* (*to es. the legends and the mystery that it accompanies the algorithm* page rank *of Google)*; *tecnofania* that consolidating hides the order of the discourse, almost that the procedures for the resolution of a problem are comparable to objective, natural, phenomenons.

Also the possibilities could be other of which will mention only an exemplification: more and more often who works with the images (especially in movement) you/he/she can incur in experiences realizzative that assembles in itself different *undisciplined saperi* with inclinations and manifold ability, mixing.

Then the expressiveness, that is yes autonomous - but that you can always be unfolded however fully and only in a *confusione* - allowed by the experimental mastery (once unthinkable) of the digital chain *intuizione/captazione of immagine/montaggio/ deformazione* and editing of the figure, change the specific prerogatives of the author, sometimes going beyond its specialismis, and instead making to acquire him a fluidity in the use of languages others, in a practice of a nomadism that virtual is not alone allowed by the nets, but rather that solicited by an unbelievable acceleration and mnemonic amplification of the associations of ideas, (**the true incubation of the knowledge**, as it was in a lot of the poetic ones of the avant-garde).

Then reality would not be sought alone *iperrealisticamente augmented* but you could fancifully become *multiplied*. (Cfr. *"The small utopia - Ars Multiplicata"*, 2012 Show to Ca' edited by Corner Venezia German Celant, whose the title made reference to the dream, already of the historical avant-garde, of an inexhaustible multiplication of the ideas and the objects of art.

Well, anything else other than the *augmented realities*, with banal explanatory reconstructions of monuments and finds that owe their greatness really to their incompleteness, as taught us Rodin!

(Moreover their analytical value is almost always incoherent, to es. it doesn't distantly resemble to the systematic cultural ri-construction of an ideal of classicità what that transmitted us by the various WincKelmanns, etc.)

Well, anything else other than elaborations for virtual museums (immersivamente in 3D, is understood!) and shows useful Ghostbuster only to increase the intellectual dismay of the visitors. (For engraved the really important show this year you/he/she has been: ***Art and culture in Italy among the two wars*** to the Foundation Prada).

The only museum (or library) that each has to build with systematic and constant effort it is that **imaginary** (and anthological) that picks up in her mind, also undisciplinedly and without Google, her options for her forms.

Forms that concretely we will be able to study and to furnish to objects in a perspective of imagination, planning and direct figurative production and not for an execution of others. A model to es. as that pointed out by André Gorz of a handicraft digital production that allows to manufacture anything has three dimensions.

The evolution of the digital technology has already passed through two phases.

The **first** you can be made to depart from the same Alan Turing you/he/she has been *statuale,* public and very tied up to the academic world, in the best sense.

The second, after 1989 (meaningful!) it goes from Silicon Valley and it is express in the slogan: *the strengths of the market have to act unmolested.*

Its upsettings have been positive (p. es. the increase of the connettività between people and researchers of every Country, the analysis of the genetic code through the big given) etc. but also negative (p. es. the diffusion omologante of myths and styles of life you deteriorate and the zero resetting of a lot of traditional social and economic activities) etc.

We are now entering another phase, the third one, in which it needs to take a stand:

– **or we will make to resurface the public values** (in particular way, that interests above all me, for all of this that concerns the knowledge and his/her learning);
– **or we will allow to prevail the hardest logics of the capitalism of the digital bases**.

The objective of the digital bases is, to the fund, the construction of a "*algorithmic man that is of a human according to the principles of the real coomputability*" (Vecchi 2018a, b). Their the man interests especially in his lapels as *produttore/utente*, they don't interest if not marginally the contents that man proposes.

"*The* Weltanschaung *that from Silicon Valley he is radiating all over the world - it is a miscellany of white suprematismo, social darwinismo, cult scientista of the cars, meritocracy and unshakable faith in the free market. Therefore a conception of the social relationships that divides the human ones between winners and losers.*

The first ones, the only ones that deserve to survive to the progressive automation of the human activities, are separated in castes. For the others, enough some charity or miserable forms of guaranteed income. And if this explains the conversion to the income of citizen of many entrepreneurs of the Silicon Valley and the capitalism of the bases, more meaningful it is the miscellany among science fiction, fantasy, economic liberismo, where you finish as I risk, rhetoric of the frontier to conquer before and to consider a limit to subsequently force" (Vecchi 2018a, b).

To you the choice, and for those, the minority I believe, that will choose still the first one with courage, ancient, perspective the weight of a conflict also learns but *ineludibile*.

References

Ippolita (2017) Tecnologie del Dominio, Meltemi, Sesto S. Giovanni, Milano

Mogno C (2018) Ho lavorato come Turca Meccanica. In: Alias in il Manifesto 23 April 2018

Pennacchi L (2018) Lavoro e tecnologie nel modello di sviluppo per l'epoca digitale. In: il Manifesto 3 May 2018

Ferraris M (2018) Il reddito minimo? Ce lo dia Google. In: la Repubblica 4 July 2018

Vecchi B (2018) L'algebra di classe che domina la Rete. In: il Manifesto 6 July 2018

Vecchi B (2018) Un mondo distopico in salsa di silicio. In: il manifesto 21 July 2018. recensione critica del libro di Eric Sadin, La siliconizzazione del mondo, Einaudi, Torino 2018

Art Mistakes

The Aestheticization of Error in Digital Art

Valeria Menchetelli[(✉)]

Department of Civil and Environmental Engineering (DICA),
University of Perugia, via Duranti 93, 06125 Perugia, Italy
`valeria.menchetelli@unipg.it`

Abstract. The progressive reappraisal of creative errors in all fields of knowledge, together with the digital revolution and its consequences, have led to the birth and development of new artistic forms. Among these, glitch art, based on the intentional but casual application of distortions to digital images, lends an aesthetic value to an error, offering an unprecedented interpretive key of the artistic heritage. The paper is aimed at contextualising the phenomenon of glitch art and particularly focuses on its declension related to glitch of existing artistic-visual heritage; it also aims at exemplifying it, investigating the functioning and the effects of a few online softwares for the application of glitch to digital images, suggesting a critical interpretation accordingly.

Keywords: Error · Digital art · Glitch art · Creativity · Artistic heritage · Visual arts

1 Creativity of Error

The creative process that leads to the realization of any project work (from architecture to design to art) is generally marked by errors, the occurrence of which generates a feedback procedure which is iterated up to the convergence towards a definite project solution. The error, whose authenticity and spontaneity distinguishes every human activity, can sometimes have catastrophic effects, but often manages to determine unforeseen developments of the ideational path instead, capable of introducing significant methodological innovations and unexpected successes. The main ingredient of creativity lies in the error itself: in it, quoting Umberto Eco, the *ars combinatoria* is intrinsic or, in other words, the unprecedented combination of already known facts or elements (Eco 2004).

The error is extremely important in sciences and in the arts in general. It is no coincidence that many scientific discoveries that have progressed knowledge in a revolutionary way were made by randomness or errors (Boncinelli 2010): from microwaves to nitroglycerin, from X-rays to penicillin, just to cite a few emblematic cases. And, not by chance, there are numerous occasions whereby an often priceless value of a work of art is conditioned and increased by a series of misunderstandings, accidents and deviations.

A. Luigini (Ed.): EARTH 2018, AISC 919, pp. 444–455, 2019.
https://doi.org/10.1007/978-3-030-12240-9_47

The diagnostic investigations of works of art produced during the course of history, which are carried out with increasing diffusion (for example, preparatory to interventions of conservative restoration or restoration of the original conditions of the work itself), continue in fact to bring to light authentic discoveries: erroneous attributions of paintings, intentional counterfeits aimed at deceiving buyers or traders, transformations due to the successive overlapping of pictorial layers to "align" the style of the piece to the tastes of the eras crossed. An unusual review of these revelations was presented, for example, during the exhibition, *Close Examination: Fakes Mistakes & Discoveries*, held at the National Gallery in London in 2010 (Wieseman 2010), which allowed the famous museum to correct its acquisition errors while at the same time scientifically making the most of them (as well as marketing them). For example, the X-ray inspections carried out on the pictorial film of the *Portrait of Alexander Mornauer*, purchased from the National Gallery as *Portrait of Martin Luther* attributed to Hans Holbein the Younger, showed how the piece was conveniently and skilfully altered to resemble a painting by Holbein, through the superimposition of different pigments and the variation of the shape of the headgear. The incident of the *Resurrection of Christ* preserved in the warehouses of the La Carrara Academy of Bergamo, is different. The painting, that for years was mistakenly considered a copy, thanks to extensive research has recently been attributed to Andrea Mantegna, whose *Descent of Christ to Limbo* makes up the lower part of what was originally conceived as one entire canvas. On the other hand, the preparatory drawing of a work of art often reveals reconsiderations, variations, different conceptions of the work itself, both when the same is directly analyseable because it is available as a separate document and when it is possible to trace it back by way of targeted analysis thanks to the use of modern technological instruments. And it is exactly from the analysis of these reconsiderations that artistic culture draws new lifeblood every day.

2 Inappropriateness of Error

In most of the situations that we experience on a day to day basis, errors seem to us almost always to be occasional, mostly incidental facts: as a rule we tend to avoid them and to avoid their effects. At most, we limit ourselves to reevaluating the scope of errors after they occur, trying to learn from them.

In many technical fields, in fact, errors can compromise the reliability of a study, since they affect the accuracy and precision of a measurement; therefore, probabilistic analysis makes available calculation methods to determine the incidence of errors on the procedures carried out and to correct the consequences, limiting negative repercussions. The theory of errors is based precisely on the intention to ideally remove measurement errors, specifically "random" errors, i.e. those due to factors that cannot be controlled beforehand (while "systematic" errors, due to defects in the measuring devices used, are generally not detectable and "rough" errors, due to oversights or poor attention during the measurement phase, have less impact and are easily detectable).

Errors messages are sentries that warn us every day of the malfunctioning of the website we are consulting or of the software we are using: we are so driven to look for the causes and are thus guided towards self-correction. It is through the warning of an error that we learn and improve, in an evolutionary path ideally aimed at perfection. Our cultural background is in fact completely oriented towards achieving an "ideal" behaviour: an aesthetic ideal (just think of the widespread and standardizing use of plastic surgery), an efficient ideal (in which productivity is not undermined by unnecessary downtime), but also an ethical ideal (which at least we pretend to pursue, but then resoundingly reveal our fallibility).

This is also true of technology. The multiple apps that we use on our devices on a daily basis are constantly updated by the manufacturers to eliminate bugs that cause them to crash or to have inefficiencies, in the continuous search for an operation that is most compatible with every operating system and, possibly, perfect. However, this frenzied aspiration to perfection, albeit physiological in the third millennium, coexists with an awareness that shows its current relevance in an increasingly evident manner and which, in a relatively recent era, comes to be formulated from a theoretical point of view.

3   Art of Error

In fact there are numerous cases in which the error (unintentional or random) and its effects are not only re-evaluated but even valued and celebrated. This awareness develops transversally around the middle of the twentieth century, both in the arts and (exemplarily) in the pedagogical and educational fields: in this sense, in Italy, the famous *Libro degli errori* (*Book of errors*) by Rodari (Rodari 1966) definitively paved the way for the importance of failure in growth and positive evolution of thought, highlighting the need for it.

Digital revolution and technological innovation have also in this case brought about epochal changes, offering a new wide range of possibilities to avoid errors and to control the flow with a deterministic precision and, at the same time, an equally new wide range of possibilities to intentionally commit errors, which has fueled the birth and progressive development of unprecedented forms of creativity. This is the case of digital arts, created as experimentations of the limits of technology but now widely used and established as autonomous forms: entirely produced with the use of computer devices, they can be considered on the one hand the technological evolution of traditional arts (for example when through the use of available devices in dedicated software they allows us to simulate the realization phases of drawings, paintings or sculptures, to the coating of virtual colours on a flat surface to the modeling in an equally virtual space of three-dimensional shapes). On the other hand, however, technology allows us to produce works of art in which creative thinking takes place solely through the action carried out by the device, delegating the artistic act to the automation (and sometimes to the randomness) of its operation.

In this passage there is a radical change in the approach to creative error. If it is now established that the error can be elevated to an artistic gesture, the deeper meaning has changed, in this case from unintentionality to intentionality. That is, in the case of unintentional errors, the artist, the bearer of creative thought, transforms the error into a work of art, loading it with symbolic meanings and elevating it to the embryo of his own work. In a vast sector of digital art, the error is intentional, deliberate, and the artist establishes the assignment of creative thought to the *medium* constituted by the device: chance intervenes actively in the production of the work of art, without this negatively affecting its value.

4 Glitch Art

One of the areas whereby the creative attitude of the error is exalted to the maximum power is that of "glitch art". By borrowing its meaning from the word "glitch", which in electrical engineering indicates a temporary alteration of the transmission of information due to an unpredictable error, glitch art consists in submitting digital images (or videos), whether they already exist or are made *ad hoc*, a voluntary process of introducing a random error that alters its computer coding: a sort of bug that irreparably compromises the file by changing its visual appearance. The effect, completely unpredictable, is a "disturbance" of the image, which consequently may appear aged, distorted, stretched or blurred, through which an imperfection is artificially produced, whose aestheticization becomes an artistic language.

From a theoretical point of view glitch art, whose innovative needs move from the musical field to then involve the visual arts sphere (Cascone 2000; Menkman 2011), has been divided into two categories that include "pure glitches" and impure ones known as "glitch-alike" (Moradi et al. 2009): in the first case the error is actually incidental and there is no artistic post-production, in the second it is the artist or the graphic designer to draw specific glitch effects. These categories, however, tend to merge into an open and hybrid artistic practice, which arbitrarily contaminates the two approaches, promoting an expressive transversality that is more concerned with the perception of the phenomenon by the viewers and critics rather than dwelling on rigid technical positions, as professed in *Glitch Studies Manifesto* (Menkman 2011).

From a critical point of view, glitch art seems to want to embody a nostalgic tendency of taste to return to the technological imperfection of first generation devices, as if to "humanize" a technology that now aspires to the absolute perfection of performance. But its deeper meaning embraces the philosophical acceptance of error and its transformation into a productive occasion: according to the theory of Sylvere Lotringer and Paul Virilio "Malfunction and failure are not signs of improper production. On the contrary, they indicate the active production of 'accidental potential' in any product" (Lotringer and Virilio 2005).

The process has become within everybodys reach: all you have to do is own a smart-phone to experience the wide range of apps aimed at the application of digital glitches to images or personal videos. Not surprisingly, the community of glitch artists is constantly growing, this phenomenon can be seen in blogs, websites, Facebook pages and Flickr groups dedicated to sharing these digital artifacts. However, just to cite some examples, first the initiative *GLI.TC/H* (Chicago 2010, Amsterdam-Birmingham-Chicago 2011, Chicago 2012) and then the provocatively titled artistic project *Glitch art is dead*, which gave rise to the homonymous exhibition held in 2015 in Krakow and in 2017 in Minneapolis, have called the main representatives to gather in order to provide an organic, structured and cogent response to the rampant practice

448   V. Menchetelli

of the do it yourself glitch, showing the expressive and cultural potential of visual and sound manipulation with artistic purposes (Pienkosz and Plucienniczak 2016).

Among the countless, varied outcomes of glitch art, some experiments use images and videos as "raw material" that have consolidated cultural heritage as the key figure: the glitch thus takes on a strong evocative power, providing an unprecedented key to the reading of classical works of art that goes beyond their own meaning. In a historical moment in which the risk of material destruction of the historical-artistic and architectural heritage is particularly present (Ciccopiedi 2018; Cormier and Thom 2016), a few glitch artists thus prefigure alterations and deliberate disruptions of the image of the heritage itself, taking on, at the same time, the role of authors of its destruction and amplifiers of its semantic bearing, so much so as to compel a profound reflection on the concept of heritage and its value in modern society. If Salvatore Settis, sharing the positions of Dieter Roelstraete, affirms that the contemporary artist shows a

Fig. 1. Giacomo Carmagnola, *Caligula*, 2015. http://giacomocarmagnola.tumblr.com/post/156891454024/twentycentgroup-gennaio-2017-giacomo

retrospective attitude by using, transforming and sometimes inventing layers of history (Settis 2018), it is therefore evident that such a form of "immaterial iconoclasm" like that represented from what could be defined "glitch heritage art" raises very current questions. Delighting our eyes with a variety of "digital ruins", the artist carries out a seemingly contradictory conceptual action, that flaunts the devaluation of the work of art to push us to reconsider the heritage, recalling it to our memory and admonishing us on the new frontiers of its transience. At the same time, indulging the aesthetics of the ruins of which European culture is permeated (Augé 2004), we are called to ideally restore the perfection of the original work, hoping for its resurrection (Settis 2018).

The incessant dialectic relationship between the art of the past and the art of the present emerges clearly in the works of digital artist Giacomo Carmagnola, whose language makes prevalent use of the effects of "pixel sorting" obtained by isolating single lines of pixels in the photographic image. The effect is a "waterfall" of pixels that appear to simulate the snapshot of the progressive collapse of the artistic work and that actually stages the spectacle of destruction, forcing the observer to assist in this action. Another emblematic element is the "stretching" of famous Renaissance paintings artificially created by the Chilean designer, Javier Jensen, whereby an un-likely stretch of the canvas involves the definite loss of portions of the painting necessary for its complete comprehension, generating a visual and, at the same time, iconographic gap. Just like the iconic proliferation that, starting from the theoretical considerations of Benjamin (Benjamin 1966), transformed the most famous works of art first into icons and then in commercial gadgets (Bonazzoli and Robecchi 2013) continues to fuel itself and, rather, draws new lifeblood from the phenomenon of the glitch art: just think of the umpteenth alteration of Leonardo's *Mona Lisa* recently became a glitch t-shirt. But the range of possible alterations is wide and diversified and also includes sequences in which the sculptural works are animated by repeating, obsessively but uselessly,

Fig. 2. Javier Jensen, *Renaissance Glitch*, 2016. https://www.behance.net/gallery/34699881/Renaissance-Glitch

Fig. 3. Search results of images of glitch effects applied to classical art.

movements aimed at claiming some form of autonomy and integrity; an ordinary search for images on the web flaunts the multiple variations of glitch applied to antique art (Figs. 1, 2 and 3).

5 Technique of Glitch

A comprehensive review of the technical possibilities through which, from an IT point of view, glitches, which are intrinsic to the different image file formats, was presented by Rosa Menkman (Menkman 2010). In this regard, the author lists the characteristics of the compressed and non-compressed formats with a handbook approach, experimenting and consequently defining the multiple possible alterations and their reversibility or irreversibility. Any arbitrary variation of the coding of data in the image files corresponds in the decoding phase to a compromised aspect, which becomes irreversible if compression algorithms are applied to the image: these variations can be implemented by cutting, modifying or adding information to the code which describes the image itself. For this reason, even starting from uncompressed formats, the result of a glitch operation is often returned in compressed formats such as .jpeg or .gif, which also document the impossibility of restoring the original conditions.

The portal of the international webzine *Glitchet* presents a wide range of tools available to experiment with the technical methods through which glitch art is expressed (http://www.glitchet.com/resources): the tools (software or apps, most of which open source) can be organized (and selected) according to the operating system or the chosen interface. The "corruption" of the original file can be implemented in different ways, for example through text editor or sound editor: after opening the image file, the process of databending (which consists in processing a certain format with a software created to manage different formats) allows you to arbitrarily change the code; the subsequent overwriting makes the alteration permanent, determining the glitch effect. However, images and videos can also be edited using image editor, which allows you to intentionally apply glitch effects to the entire image or to its portions, configuring itself as sophisticated operations of photo editing. Among the main effects that are widely used in glitch art the previously mentioned pixel sorting stands out, which can be tested using free user-friendly applications (for example http://larixk.nl/experiments/sort/, which allows to vary the result by setting a few basic parameters such as intensity and the threshold value), but also the generation of fractal geometries with the use of special softwares (for example Mandelbulb 3D or Fractal Lab) or the application of different types of filters (for example https://snorpey.github.io/jpg-glitch/) or of selective triangulation effects of portions of the image (for example http://polyshaper.co/). The outcome of the operation also varies according to the possible iterations of the procedure: the parameters of some of the available applications allow you to set the characteristics and the number, so as to determine the overlap of a series of glitch steps and the consequent combination of a few effects. The interface of many of these applications is immediate, so as to make the process within reach of anyone who wants to have a shot at being a glitch artist experimenting with the results. The main risk that this ease of access and use leads to, however, is represented by the execution of a mere technical exercise, which deprives the process of critical depth: it is in this aspect that the distinction between the glitch artist and the technician of the glitch resides in.

With a view to offering an examination, albeit decidedly partial, of the technical possibilities through which the range of digital image processing can be expressed through the application of glitch effects, the results of the analysis of the functionalities offered by a sample consisting of five free utilities are presented below, available online and designed for this use. To assist with the comparison, in the exemplification the effects are applied to the same starting photographic image, chosen as a symbolic tribute to the election of the serial reproduction in the form of an autonomous art implemented by Andy Warhol (https://en.wikipedia.org/wiki/Andy_Warhol#/media/files:An-dy_Warhol_by_Jack_Mitchell.jpg).

The application *Image Glitch Tool* (https://snorpey.github.io/jpg-glitch/) allows you to alter a user-selected image through a few *ad hoc* adjustable parameters: the adjustment of these parameters facilitates the control of the effect obtained. The alteration is greater when the *amount*, *seed* and *iterations* parameter values are increased and the values of *quality* reduced. The *randomize* function allows you to make random changes, effectively renouncing the check on the result. The output can be downloaded only in .png format. Some of the possible results are shown in Fig. 4: the matrix always shows the original image at the top left.

The utility *Photomosh* (https://photomosh.com/) allows you to apply a significantly higher number of effects; each of them can be customised by setting the value of a few significant parameters. Starting from an input file, which can be an image in jpeg or .png or a short video in .mp4, the application generates images in .jpeg, animated gifs or videos in .webm. The function *mosh* randomizes the process of glitch combining a series of basic effects. Some of the possible results are shown in Fig. 5.

The tool *ImageGlitcher* (https://www.airtightinteractive.com/demos/js/imageglitcher) offers extremely basic functionality that allows you to set the overall glitch effect and the average brightness of the resulting image. An additional check allows you to

Fig. 4. Alteration of an image with the use of the application *Image Glitch Tool*.

Fig. 5. Alteration of an image with the use of the application *Photomosh*.

activate or deactivate the *scanlines* filter which alters the image by inserting a regular horizontal scan. The input image can only be in .png format. Some of the possible results are shown in Fig. 6.

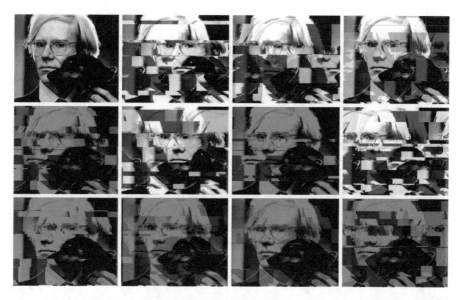

Fig. 6. Alteration of an image with the use of the application *ImageGlitcher*.

The utility *Glitchy3bitDither* (http://jkirchartz.com/Glitchy3bitdither/index.html) is presented as an abacus of the possible obtainable ranges starting from the same image file and offers the possibility to make a direct comparison between them. After selecting the image file, a series of algorithms alters it and show its effects individually. Some of the possible results are shown in Fig. 7.

Fig. 7. Alteration of an image with the use of the application *Glitchy3bitDither*.

The application *Glitchatron* (http://www.errozero.co.uk/glitchatron/) provides a unique alteration mode, which you can set the level (*low, medium, high, extreme, destroyed*), adding the possibility of amplifying the result of the glitch by overwriting the image of a text set by the user, whose size, alignment and colour can be defined. The output is supplied in .png format and can be cut out according to circular or triangular windows. Some of the possible results are shown in Fig. 8.

The result of applying these functionalities to digital images can naturally be a prelude to successive phases of artistic post-production, whereby the control of the final result is determined from time to time by the graphic processing tools used.

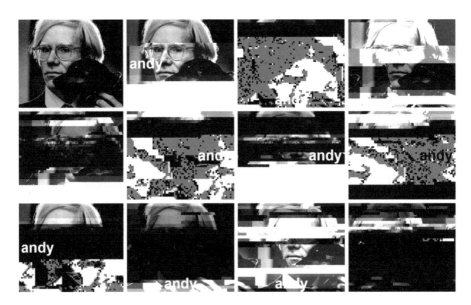

Fig. 8. Alteration of an image with the use of the application *Glitchatron*.

6 Concluding Comments

Since the fifties of the twentieth century, the semantic scope of the error has gone through a phase of renewed critical interpretation, which determined its definite rehabilitation elevating it to an event necessary for the evolution of thought and in many occasions to autonomous and recognisable expressive modality. This rehabilitation, which pervades numerous fields of knowledge, has encountered a decidedly fertile ground in the visual arts, both traditional and digital. In this last sector, glitch art stands out in a specific way for its declared cultural position, which elects the error (intentional or unintentional) in an independent artistic form and which occupies a prominent position on the international scene. There glitch art, which becomes a collective phenomenon also thanks to the widespread diffusion of apps and utilities by which anyone with a mobile device such as a smartphone or tablet can experience the potential of the deliberate compromise of encoding image files, retains a strong symbolic and evocative power when applied to images of the consolidated artistic heritage –which could be defined as "glitch heritage art"–, shedding new light on its identity value and its own definition. The analysis of the innumerable technical modalities through which a computer error is deliberately grafted into the representations of works of art causes a plethora of considerations, whose depth ranges from the concept of heritage to that of the permanence of the heritage itself and at the same time of its perishability, suggesting that in the danger of destruction an up-to-date glance may be included, more aware of the original value. The images made by glitch artists are thus presented as anticipations of future scenarios, foreshadows of a progressive devastation which nevertheless appears a harbinger of new ways of appropriating cultural identity. The glitch applied to the work of art, also reiterates the communicative power of the representation which, putting on stage the work and its infinite possible transformations, puts on stage itself, reaffirming its own unsurpassed sovereignty in determining the cultural evolution.

References

Augé M (2004) Rovine e macerie. Il senso del tempo. Bollati Boringhieri, Torino

Benjamin W (1966) L'opera d'arte nell'epoca della sua riproducibilità tecnica. Einaudi, Torino

Bonazzoli F, Robecchi M (2013) Io sono un mito. I capolavori dell'arte che sono diventati icone del nostro tempo. Electa, Milano

Boncinelli E (2010) Come nascono le idee. Laterza, Roma-Bari

Cascone K (2000) The aesthetics of failure: "post-digital" tendencies in contemporary computer music. Comput Music J 24(4):12–18

Ciccopiedi C (ed) (2018) Anche le statue muoiono. Conflitto e patrimonio tra antico e contemporaneo. Franco Cosimo Panini Editore, Modena

Cormier B, Thom D (eds) (2016) A world of fragile parts. La Biennale, Venezia

Eco U (2004) Combinatoria della creatività. http://www.umbertoeco.it/CV/Combinatoria%20della%20creativita.pdf. Accessed 8 May 2018

Lotringer S, Virilio P (2005) The accident of art. Semiotexte, New York

Menkman R (2010) A vernacular of file formats. A guide to databend compression design, Amsterdam. https://www.slideshare.net/r00s/rosa-menkman-a-vernacular-of-file-formats-4923967. Accessed 26 June 2018

Menkman R (2011) The Glitch Moment(um). Institute of Network Cultures, Amsterdam. Network Notebook 04. https://networkcultures.org/_uploads/NN%234_Rosa.Menkman.pdf. Accessed 15 June 2018

Moradi I, Scott A, Gilmore J, Murphy C (2009) Glitch: designing imperfection. Mark Batty Publisher, New York

Pieńkosz A, Płucienniczak PP (eds) (2016) Glitch art is dead. Hub Wydawniczy Rozdzielczość Chleba, Krakow. https://archive.org/details/GLITCH_ART_IS_DEAD. Accessed 15 June 2018

Rodari G (1966) Il libro degli errori. Einaudi, Torino

Settis S (2018) Resurrezioni. In: Ciccopiedi C (ed) Anche le statue muoiono. Conflitto e patrimonio tra antico e contemporaneo. Franco Cosimo Panini Editore, Modena, pp 9–19

Wieseman ME (2010) A closer look: deceptions and discoveries. National Gallery Co., London

Museum Ideas

Inclusive Memory. Museum Education to Promote the Creation of a New Shared Memory

Antonella Poce and Maria Rosaria Re[✉]

Department of Education, University of Roma Tre,
Via Castro Pretorio 20, 00185 Rome, Italy
antonella.poce@uniroma3.it,
mariarosaria.re@runiroma3.it

Abstract. This paper describes the design and implementation by CDM (Centre for Museum Studies – Roma TRE University) of a museum teaching and learning project, *Inclusive Memory*, aimed at supporting disadvantaged categories' inclusion processes, through a shared memory development, in contexts of cultural heritage fruition within the city of Rome. In the first phase of the project pupils from a secondary school based in Rome participated in the activities proposed. The group was characterised by a high rate of immigrant, disabled or disadvantaged pupils. Specific learning paths have been designed at the Museum of Rome - Palazzo Braschi to reach the project objectives. The city of Rome and its representations were the starting point for guided and in-depth discussion activities on issues such as social differences, urban and cultural transformations of the city, social aggregation, the relationship between the city and the countryside, the politics of consensus, with a view of promoting the participants' critical thinking skills. Ad hoc assessment procedures were carried out in order to evaluate the effectiveness of the *Inclusive Memory* project.

Keywords: Museum education · Inclusion · Critical thinking ·
Assessment and evaluation

1 Introduction

The *Inclusive Memory* project, carried out by the Centre for Museum Studies of Roma Tre University, aims at promoting the building of a common shared social memory realised through a museum based social inclusive system. The core idea stems from the potential benefits of the cooperation between Higher Education Institutions, Museums and High Schools, as a strategic partnership to advance in museum education as well as in museum fruition. The project wants to promote a different strategy for social inclusion, derived from the use of innovative teaching methodology, the use of digital tools and based on the development of cross sectional competences in museum visitors, especially socially disadvantaged categories. *Inclusive Memory* is based on seeing museums as teaching and learning environments, and Universities as active social actors, strengthening their role of cultural integration facilitators.

© Springer Nature Switzerland AG 2019
A. Luigini (Ed.): EARTH 2018, AISC 919, pp. 459–468, 2019.
https://doi.org/10.1007/978-3-030-12240-9_48

This paper presents the results of the first experimental phase of the project, which took place in Rome during the academic year 2017/2018.

2 State of the Art

The idea for this project is rooted in the consideration that museums are increasingly regarded as educational places, not only in terms of the permanent and temporary exhibitions they offer, but also with reference to their collections and the idea of social and cultural integration. For many years the strong attention paid by museum education to visitors, the different social targets which interact in such spaces and the demand for individualized teaching and learning (Parry 2010; Nardi 2014) contribute to define visitors' experience and all its implications as the focus of present research in the field. At the same time, the definition of learning no more referring just to the acquired knowledge, but especially to the competencies developed and lifelong employable allowed for the start of researches and use of new learning methods, which see teaching and learning as a wide, complex and especially social process.

The role of museums as social drivers can be accomplished when museums become educational environments, where all the social categories (different as regards age, cultural background and social status, people with special educational needs) can interact and develop competencies such as critical thinking, communication, cooperation and participation skills (Sandell 2002; Nardi 2014; Poce, Iovine 2015). Not by chance, recently, the idea of putting such museum characteristics at disposal of specific museum visitor targets has come forward. Previous researches, such as the one carried out by Outside in Pathways at V&A museum, entitled "Our lives", can be an example of such use, especially as regards accessibility and disabilities.

The lack of a valid educational contribution on the matter and the marginal role of Universities in relation to Museum initiatives is one of the reasons of the scarce culture of the territory among our population and, consequently, of the wrong perception of the value of the society and the culture as a whole. Furthermore, refugees, first and second generation migrant children and disadvantaged categories are too often excluded from the cultural life of their territory. As a result, they cannot contribute to the building and sharing of the collective memory of the region and, more in general, of the country they live in. The low level of participation in the social life and the exclusion from places in which culture is promoted, such as museums, leads to the worrying exclusion of some from active citizenship, with direct consequences such as marginalisation and social tensions.

Starting from these assumptions, the Centre for Museum Studies – CDM research group, based at University of Roma Tre, in cooperation with the University College of London (UK) and Museo di Roma – Palazzo Braschi, has developed the *Inclusive memory* project, whose aim is the promotion a new shared memory built on a new social inclusion process within the museums' systems. The first experimental phase of the project was carried out with the involvement of a secondary school in the city of Rome. This allowed the participation of a group of pupils from different backgrounds, as well as members with physical or mental disabilities or with special education needs. For the pupils involved, the *Inclusive Memory* project was an opportunity of visiting a museum and of participating in learning paths based on innovative didactic methodologies; for the teachers involved, the project turned out to be a moment of professional training in the field of promotion of transversal skills and inclusion, as well as the opportunity to observe their pupils in a new didactic context.

3 Methodology

Museo di Roma – Palazzo Braschi has been identified by CDM as the heritage institution in which *Inclusive Memory* learning paths were to be created and implemented. These learning and innovative didactic paths purposely created for the context of the Museo di Roma – Palazzo Braschi aim at developing target users citizenship and social inclusion competences thanks to the employment of up-to-date teaching and learning methods, such as *Object Based Learning* (Durbin 1990; Lane and Wallace 2007; Wiley 2002) and *Visual Thinking* (Bowen et al. 2014; Desantis 2009). For the *Inclusive memory* project, the following exhibition areas thematic were identified for the activities :

1. *And there the river flows.* The image of Rome between the XVII and the XIX century is perpetuated through numerous paintings showing landscapes that often have the same point of view. Themes developed: artistic topoi, cultural stereotypes; the point of view from an artistic perspective; self-respect and understanding of others.
2. *Street festivals.* Of all the themes useful to describe Rome from the XVII to the XIX century, the most famous and inherent in the consensus politics promoted by the Popes is that of the festivals of all kinds. Themes developed: festival as a moment of social gathering; festival as celebration of diversity; Knowing oneself and the others.
3. *Political changes and new society.* Over the period going from the Restoration to the decision to make it capital of the Kingdom of Italy, Rome faces deep transformations. The urban structure changes, at times completely, also due to economic transformations as well as social and political ones. Themes developed: social, cultural and political changes; the city as a monument to historical change.

The target group of the *Inclusive Memory* first experimentation phase was a third-year class from Domizia Lucilla Agricoltural Secondary School, in Rome. The class, composed of 21 pupils (15 boys and 6 girls) was very heterogeneous: it included 7 pupils with Specific Learning Disorders and 3 pupils with physical disabilities.

On the first visit, pupils were divided in 3 groups, welcomed to Museo di Roma by the researchers. Each pupil attended one of the tours proposed by CDM researchers and participated in one of the three activities proposed. Thanks to non conventional learning methodologies, pupils enhanced their reflection competences, supported by the observation of the museum object and by discussion groups. At the end of the first visit, participants self assessed the experience through the Wellbeing Measures Umbrellas developed by researches from University College of London – UK (Thomson and Chatterjee 2016).

The experience was carried out a second time with the same class, about 2 months after the first visit. Students were divided into the same three different groups, singled out during the first visit, but each group took part in another activity among the three main ones proposed. At the end of the second visit, a focus group was organised in order to deeply evaluate the whole experience (Fig. 1) .

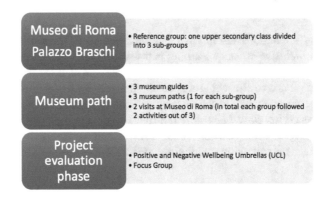

Fig. 1. Scheme of the inclusive memory first experimental phase

4 Evaluation Tools and Phases

The overall experience was evaluated through the use of different quantitative and qualitative evaluation tools in order to identify the project objectives achieved and to compare evaluation results. In particular, the research group used the following instruments: the UCL Museum Wellbeing Measures Toolkit, a Focus Group content analysis tool and a Critical thinking dispositions and skills observation grid.

1. *UCL Museum Wellbeing Measures Toolkit* (Thomson and Chatterjee, 2016). The toolkit is composed by a set of scales of measurement useful for assessing levels of wellbeing arising from participation in museum and gallery activities. In particular, the CDM research group used two kind of Wellbeing Measures Umbrellas, *Positive younger Adult* and *Negative*, to assess the psychological wellbeing as an indicator of the mental state of the project participants. The Umbrellas have a hexagonal shape with six sections of different colours. Each section contains a word related to a particular wellbeing mood or emotion and a numbers scale from 1 to 5. Users are required to circle the number corresponding to the level of emotion felt: 1 = "I don't fell", 2 = "I feel a little bit", 3 = "I feel fairly", 4 = "I feel quite a bit" and 5 = "I feel extremely". The *Positive Wellbeing Umbrella - Younger Adult* presents the following six mental state or emotion: Friendly, Interested, Lively, Motivated, Positive and Talkative. The six words for *the Negative Wellbeing Umbrella* are Distressed, Irritable, Nervous, Scared, Unhappy and Upset.

The two kind of Wellbeing Measures Umbrellas were distributed among pupils at the end of the activities in Museo di Roma – Palazzo Braschi. All the quantitative data acquired for each museum path (And there the river flows, Street festivals, Political changes and new society) have been analysed through the use of basic statistical analyses.

2. *Focus Group content analysis.* The Focus Group objective is to evaluate the level of inclusion of learning paths created for the participating class, as well as to carry out an overall evaluation of the experience, both from the point of view the acquired knowledge and the competences promoted through the activities.

At the end of the second visit, the pupils participated in the Focus Group led by a CDM researcher assisted by an observer. The Focus Group was recorded; then, the pupils' answers were transcribed and analyzed from a qualitative point of view, using the Morgan (1998) approach.

3. *Critical thinking dispositions and skills evaluation.* In order to evaluate critical thinking skills promotion during the activities, an observation grid was designed and implemented. The grid indicators are the critical thinking skills and dispositions defined in Facione, 1990. The observer had at his disposal a scale of three points, from 1 to 3, to evaluate the level of skills/disposition presented during the museum learning paths: 1 = skill/disposition not present or observable; 2 = skill/disposition partly present or observable; 3 = skill/disposition present or observable. The presence of three level for each indicators has been identified taking into consideration the construction of competences evaluation tools guidelines in Castoldi, 2009.

Each learning path (*And there the river flows, Street festivals, Political changes and new society for the three classes participating*) has been evaluated with the critical thinking dispositions and skills observation grid. Basic statistical analysis and frequency distribution were carried out on the quantitative data collected.

5   Analysis and Findings

The first evaluation phase, carried out employing UCL Wellbeing Measures Umbrellas tools (Thomson and Chatterjee 2016), shows positive results in each learning path. The average positive wellbeing index for each student is quite high: 3. 5 points for "And there the river flows" and "Political transformations and new society" paths; 4.2 points for "Street festivals" path. The modal value is 4 for "Interested wellbeing mood" in all activities and 5 for "Friendly", "Positive" and "Motivated" in 2 out of 3 learning path. The frequency of distribution of the positive wellbeing values shows a J distribution curve, defining the overall positivity of the learning experience. The assessment of negative wellbeing mood or emotion of participants confirms the results obtained through the use of the "Positive Wellbeing Umbrella": the distribution curve of negative feelings shows high frequencies in relation to low scores (1–2) in all three paths carried out, with points of minimum score for the emotions associated with the words "Scared" and "Upset"; the overall average of the negative feeling ranges between 1.2 and 1.4 points (Fig. 2).

The second evaluation phase was carried out at the end of the second museum experience at Museo di Roma – Palazzo Braschi. The class repeated the experience

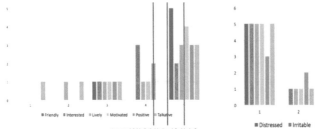
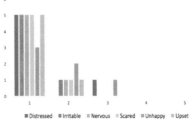

Fig. 2. (a) Frequency distribution of positive wellbeing for *street festivals path*. (b) Frequency distribution of negative wellbeing for *and there the rivers flows*.

about two months later. Students were divided into the same three different sub-groups, singled out during the first visit, but each group took part in another activity among the three main ones proposed. At the end of the second visit, a focus group was organised in order to deeply evaluate the whole experience. The class met in a room of the above-mentioned museum and participated in the Focus Group, without the accompanying teachers. The general Focus Group objective was to assess the quality of education and inclusion paths created for the participating class, as well as to carry out an overall evaluation of the experience, both from the point of view of the acquired knowledge and the competences promoted through the activities.

The Museum of Rome - Palazzo Braschi has been visited in the past by a very small number of students. Although it is a place of the culture and history of Rome, it is excluded from many school curricula. According to the answers given during the Focus Group, the perception of the city of Rome changed after the activity. The activity at the museum allowed the students to become aware of the historical and social changes in Rome, which have strongly renewed the city from the artistic and urbanistic point of view. The streets, the buildings, the cultural centres of Rome are the tangible expression of changes that have affected not only the inhabitants but Italian society as a whole. This awareness has led the students to develop a deeper reflection and analysis related to their past and future life experiences.

In general, the students' answers underline the high level of participation in the proposed activities, a participation that has led to the building of a common and shared knowledge. Arguing together about the works' details and the events that they portrait has encouraged a common and multisided reflection regarding the museum object itself and the context (historical background and society). The different points of view emerged, during the discussion, allowed, furthermore, the questioning of their own arguments and, at the same time, the acknowledgement of various perspectives. These attitudes are specifically linked to critical thinking abilities.

During the Focus Group, a student stated: "To see Rome and how the citizens in early times lived the city made me think a lot. In the past, like in the feasts on the streets, citizens met all together. Today, with the use of technology we are isolated. Communication is reduced". The present reflection about the different relationship of the single citizen with the community and between the community itself and the city places is an example of critical thinking analysis. The young student highlights the different typologies of contemporary relationships and communication: the advent of technology, even if it allows communication at a distance, is considered as reason for the isolation of a city community (Table. 1).

Table 1. Critical thinking observation grid

Skill (Facione 1990)			
Indicators	Description (Facione 1990)	Marks	Score
Interpretation	To comprehend and express the meaning or significance of a wide variety of experiences, situations, data, events, judgments, conventions, beliefs, rules, procedures, or criteria	Outstanding Good Inadequate	3 2 1
Analysis	To identify the intended & actual inferential relationships among statements, questions, concepts, descriptions, or other forms of representation intended to express belief, judgment, experiences, reasons, information, or opinions	Outstanding Good Inadequate	3 2 1
Inference	To identify and secure elements needed to draw reasonable conclusions; to form conjectures & hypotheses; to consider relevant information & to reduce the consequences flowing from data, statements, principles, evidence, judgments, beliefs, opinions, concepts, descriptions, questions, or other forms of representation	Outstanding Good Inadequate	3 2 1
Evaluation	To assess the credibility of statements or other representations that are accounts or descriptions of a person's perception, experience, situation, judgment, belief, or opinion; & to assess the logical strength of the actual or intended inferential relationships among statements, descriptions, questions, or other forms of representation	Outstanding Good Inadequate	3 2 1
Explanation	To state and to justify that reasoning in terms of the evidential, conceptual, methodological, criteriological & contextual considerations upon which one's results were based; & to present one's reasoning in the form of cogent arguments"	Outstanding Good Inadequate	3 2 1
Self-Regulation	Self-consciously to monitor one's cognitive activities, the elements used in those activities, and the results educed, particularly by applying skills in analysis, and evaluation to one's own inferential judgments with a view toward questioning, confirming, validating, or correcting either one's reasoning or one's results	Outstanding Good Inadequate	3 2 1

(*continued*)

Table 1. (*continued*)

Disposition (Facione 1990)			
Indicators	Description (Facione 1990)	Marks	Score
Truth-seeking	Being eager to seek the best knowledge in a given context, courageous about asking questions, & honest & objective about pursuing inquiry even if the findings do not support one's self-interests or one's preconceived opinions. The truth-seekers remain receptive to giving serious consideration to additional facts, reasons, or perspectives even if this should necessitate changing one's mind on some issue. The truth-seekers evaluate new information & evidence	Outstanding Good Inadequate	3 2 1
Open-mindedness	Tolerant of divergent views & sensitive to the possibility of one's own bias. Valuing tolerance & understanding of the beliefs & lifestyles of others	Outstanding Good Inadequate	3 2 1
Analycity	Prizing the application of reasoning &the use of evidence to resolve problems, anticipating potential conceptual or practical difficulties, & consistently being alert to the need to intervene	Outstanding Good Inadequate	3 2 1
Systematicity	Being organized, orderly, focused, & diligent in inquiry. Organized approaches to problem-solving & decision-making are hallmarks of a thoughtful person regardless of the problem domain being addressed. The inclination to approach problems in an orderly & focused way	Outstanding Good Inadequate	3 2 1
Self-confidence	Trust the soundness of one's own reasoned judgments & inclination to lead others in the rational resolution of problems	Outstanding Good Inadequate	3 2 1
Inquisitiveness	One's intellectual curiosity and one's desire for learning even when the application of the knowledge is not readily apparent	Outstanding Good Inadequate	3 2 1
Cognitive maturity	Approach to problems, inquiry, & decision making with a sense that some are necessarily ill-structured, some situations admit of more than one plausible option, & many times judgments must be made based on standards, contexts & evidence which preclude certainty. Making complex decisions involving multiple stakeholders, such as policy-oriented and ethical decision-making, particularly in time-pressured environments	Outstanding Good Inadequate	3 2 1

The analysis of students' critical thinking skills and dispositions shows the presence of high level skills, as far as *Interpretation*, *Analysis* and *Inference* are concerned: these skills were promoted by all museum learning path, thanks to argumentation, museum objects interpretation activities and continuous comparisons between the society represented in works of art and today's world. Also *Explanation* skill is quite present in critical thinking evaluation, showing the effect of activities in which pupils had to present, state and justify their reasoning. In general, critical thinking disposition are little or not at all present, both because these characteristic can not be assessed only through an observation grid and because of the short duration of museum meaning paths (2 h at maximum) (Fig. 3).

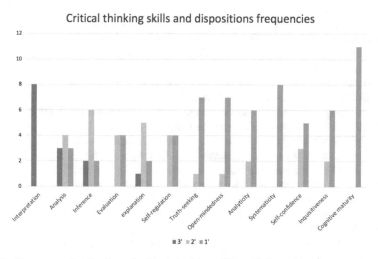

Fig. 3. Frequency distribution of critical thinking skills and disposition assessment marks

6   Conclusions

On the whole, the experience is positively evaluated by the students. The objectives of interactive activities are achieved: inclusion issues and common reasoning have been encouraged, as well as the reflection and the interest towards topics considered "new" by the participants. The Focus Group qualitative analysis confirms, as a result, pupils' self-assessment carried out through UCL Wellbeing Measures Toolkit, highlighting the activity effectiveness defined through moments of shared creation of knowledge and critical thinking enhancement in relation to broad issues discussed. The Critical thinking skills and dispositions evaluation shows the effectiveness of argumentation, analysis, interpretation, and discussion activities in promoting critical thinking competence. The above results support further development and replication of the activity with different group of disadvantaged individuals, refugees and immigrants in particular.

Acknowledgements. A. Poce coordinated the research presented in this paper. Research group is composed by the authors of the contribution that was edited in the following order: A. Poce (Introduction, State of the Art, Methodology, Conclusions), M. R. Re (Evaluation tools and phases, Analysis and findings).

References

Bowen DH, Greene JP, Kisida B (2014) Learning to think critically: a visual experiment. Educ Res 43(1):37–44

Desantis K (2009) Report to the education department of the Isabella Stewart Gardner Museum on the 8th grade school partnership program Visual Thinking Strategies adaptation 2008–2009. Visual Understanding in Education, New York

Durbin G, Morris S, Wilkinson S (1990) Learning from objects: a teachers guide. English Heritage, London

Facione PA (1990) Critical thinking: a statement of expert consensus for purposes of educational assessment and instruction—The delphi report. California Academic Press, Millbrae

Lane J, Wallace A (2007) Hands on: learning from objects and paintings: a teacher's guide. Scottish Museums Council, Glasgow

Morgan DL (1998) Focus group as qualitative research. Sage Publications, Newbury Park

Nardi E (2014) Musei e pubblico. FrancoAngeli, Milano

Paris SG (ed) (2002) Perspectives on object-centered learning in museums. Routledge, New York

Parry R (2010) Museums in a digital age. Routledge, New York

Poce A, Iovine A (2015) From cultural to socio-economic capital: lessons from a postgraduate course in 'standards for museum education'. In: Chatterjee H, Hannan L (eds) Engaging the senses: object-based learning in higher education. Ashgate, Farnham

Sandell R (ed) (2002) Museums, society, inequality. Routledge, London and New York

Thomson LJ, Chatterjee HJ: UCL museum wellbeing measures toolkit (2016). https://www.ucl.ac.uk/culture/sites/culture/files/ucl_museum_wellbeing_measures_toolkit_sept2013.pdf. Accessed 2 May 2018

Wiley DA (ed) (2000) The instructional use of learning objects. Indiana Association for Instructional Technology, Bloomington

In Search for Recovered Object. Creative Heritage as the Aesthetic, Pedagogical and Desire-Related Outcome of "Fake" Museum Art

Emanuela Mancino[(⊠)]

Department of Human Sciences for Education "R. Massa", Università degli Studi di Milano-Bicocca, Piazza dell'Ateneo Nuovo, 1, 20126 Milan, Italy
emanuela.mancino@unimib.it

Abstract. Cultural heritage can take and be displayed in many forms. It can be in the form of a collection, a set of archaeological exhibits, or an invented narrative.

The links between memory, archaeology and narrative may be fruitfully analysed in relation to two imposing expressions of "fake" art: Pamuk's *Museum of Innocence* and Damien Hirst's *Unbelievable*.

Keywords: Educating in aesthetic participation · Narrative fiction · Mythological-narrative heritage · Virtual museum and fake museum · Art and heritage education

1 Introduction

Cultural heritage can be displayed in many forms. It can be in an archaeological collection exhibits, or an invented narrative. The links between memory and narrative may be analysed in relation to two imposing expressions of "fake" art: Museum of Innocence and Damien Hirst's Unbelievable.

2 The Strength of Object

Cultural heritage can take many forms. It can also be displayed. And this may be done using the format of a collection. Or of a set of archaeological exhibits.

Indeed, memory, the unconscious, and archaeology share both practices and a lexicon (as observed and demonstrated by Freud).

The act of remembering or narrating lost or forgotten pieces - which in some cases may have been cast into oblivion as a matter of necessity - can entail a range of actions, from excavation to re-emergence, from immersion in deep or repressed recesses to recovery and reconstruction, to telling a story, outlining a narrative, or building meaning. The outcome may be the creation of archives, or transcriptions of scattered traces.

A. Luigini (Ed.): EARTH 2018, AISC 919, pp. 469–475, 2019.
https://doi.org/10.1007/978-3-030-12240-9_49

This resurfacing of the past also offers us a glimpse of maps that are dotted across the territory of time, marking out connections and ties.

Clearly, bringing to light that which is hidden or lost metaphorically evokes the exploration of ancient time or of one's own personal and intimate past time.

Indeed, that which comes to us from the remote past belongs to cultures whose languages we need to decipher to access their hidden messages, which are often cryptic and inevitably mysterious and full of charm.

The past features in the commemoration of an Antiochene freedman, who lived between the middle of the first and the beginning of the second centuries A.D., and on becoming wealthy, successfully put together an invaluable collection of statues and other relics of various ancient cultures. He loaded these treasures onto a huge ship, the largest ever seen in the ancient world, which was named the Apistos, or "The Unbelievable".

This naval and artistic marvel was shipwrecked, giving rise to 2,000 years of legend, before re-emerging from the abyss and being brought back above water thanks to a ten-year project of recovery, inventorizing, archiving and documenting, which culminated in the showing at an Italian museum not only of the artworks rescued from oblivion, but also of the story of their discovery, narrated using video documents and multimedia tools designed to engage visitors in this exhibition of mystery, wonder and the unbelievable.

This took place in Venice in 2017.

A past marked by marine growth, encrusted coral, and the ravages of time was displayed and narrated by Damien Hirst via monsters, coins, and statues, which were covered in layers not only of time, but also of meaning, truth, and fiction.

By staging not only a representation or reproduction of a legend but also the exhibition's own internal dispositive - that is to say, its discovery, care, and assignment to the place-museum as a place of art, culture and tradition - Hirst created precisely what we expect of a legend: something mysterious, inconsistent, almost beyond unbelievable.

And when the unbelievable appears in its most blatant form and the artist's playful intent to uncover the narrative mechanism becomes clear to us, we cannot but experience a degree of satisfaction in taking part in the *mise-en-scène*, as active spectators of a story that comes true as we consume it.

Hirst made the whole thing up: he did not rediscover a past; he created it *ad hoc*. In a sumptuous fictitious account of a documented myth, Hirst led us before the first *monstrum* in the exhibition, which inhabited Palazzo Grassi for several months.

Hirst issues a caution to us that recognizes what is due to the *monstrous*: he tells us to look at it (Figs. 1 and 2) .

And as we look, knowing that we are taking part in a lie, a wonderfully contrived narrative deception, we too realize that we may choose to treat it as a work of art (and therefore criticize it, judge it, deem it illegitimate), but that we cannot in any way deny its sensible reality.

Hirst proclaims an unbelievable story, while exhibiting the gap that is generated between that which we can narrate and that which we can display as we produce, bring forth, or restore our narrative to the world by telling it.

Fig. 1. Hirst's demon in Palazzo Grassi

Fig. 2. Hirst's demon in Palazzo Grassi. The head.

Why do we go along with this game of deception? Why does a narrative that is so obviously false appeal to a part of us, to the extent that we forgive the one who was skilful enough to create a magnificent and powerful narrative style that is threatening to the point of being disturbing (see the monster at the entrance and the monsters scattered across the lagoon in parallel with the exhibition) and unlikely to the point of being irritating? It is clear to us that we are looking at a fake, at a false narrative.

But we must not confuse clarity with openness. That which is clear has a profound impact on us, and above all, it helps us to perceive the interrogating force of our own gaze. The more the monster insists on narrating its presence to us, on insinuating to us that we are looking at it, the more we overcome our passivity and feel that we are sinking into an abyss.

The Spanish philosopher Maria Zambrano used the term entrails, *entrañas*, to describe a living and profound subject, that precedes or, perhaps we might say, is more powerful than the need for a *logos*, for a form of thought that openly declares Hirst's treasures of the unbelievable to be fakes.

Our participation in the artistic event is vital and sensory in nature even before it is logical.

If the wonder generated by the art sustains persistent nostalgia for a past that, albeit fake, manages to mask our immediate and intimate identification with a deep stratum inviting us to rediscover it, as spectators we will admire the inspiration that enables the work to be dynamically consumed in an ongoing process that cannot be reduced to establishing differences between what is true or false, but is experienced as immersion in the museum-artistic installation at a deeper level (Figs. 3 and 4).

Fig. 3. A frame from the video of the fake discovering under the sea (people could assist to the video in Palazzo Grassi, Venice)

The story of that which is true and that which is recognized as worthy of being deposited in the archives of time does not map onto our need to retrieve something forgotten from the past.

We experience this again when we shift Hirst's *mise en abyme* to another museum, moving from Venice to Istanbul.

Going from the art of deception to Orhan Pamuk's museum-novelesque narrative.

The holder of the 2006 Nobel Prize for Literature took that which existed in his novel *The Museum of Innocence* and gave it physical, material substance, creating a space to be explored, and giving life to the Museum of Innocence in the shape of a multiform and composite set of objects. The main character in his novel, Kemal, is in

Fig. 4. A frame from the video of the fake discovering under the sea (people could assist to the video in Palazzo Grassi, Venice)

love with Fusun. The young people's love cannot be brought to fulfilment as they desire: Kemal is obliged to forego the woman he loves. To appease his sorrow, the young man begins to collect objects that he associates with his memories of her.

Each object preserves a lost moment in time.

With the obsessiveness of the compulsive collector, Kemal gathers object after object and, as he is dying, entrusts to the writer Pamuk, his friend Pamuk, the duty and desire-testament to create a museum of innocence drawing together all his lost memories.

Thus, Pamuk set up the museum in the building where Fusun "formerly" lived (Figs. 5, 6 and 7).

The museum is now a leading venue for tourists to the Turkish city: here the literary imagination overlaps with the material reality of objects, which visitors can interpret while enjoying the experience of immersing themselves in a place of memory.

Pamuk shows us the space that is given to the things, whose evocative power leads us into the intimate space of the uncovering of the dispositive underlying the story: that which confined us between *logos* and *pathos*, between aesthetic-emotional participation and logical decoding, in the unbelievable work of Hirst.

We are inside. We are accomplices to the narrative.

The object substitutes what is not there. It institutes a dialogue between presence and absence.

Fig. 5. The museum is organized by little windows-display: here some details

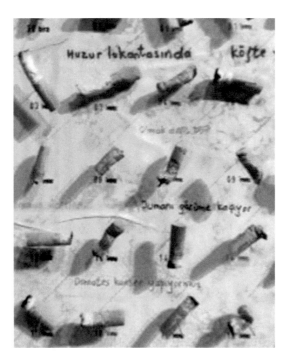

Fig. 6. Some of all the cigarettes (a selection) mostly smoked by Fusun

Fig. 7. Clothes, details.

Feeling the charm of a process - albeit fake - of rediscovery of a distant shipwreck and emotion - albeit fake - for a love preserved in memories of happy moments teaches us that our nostalgia implies an irresistible attraction to the unbelievable. And it tells us that perhaps we also like (and desire) the unbelievable because it comes to or calls to us from afar.

References

Agamben G (2017) Autoritratto nello studio. Nottetempo, Milano
Auster P (2010) L'invenzione della solitudine. Einaudi, Torino
Bachelard G (1993) La poetica dello spazio. Dedalo, Bari
Bodei R (2014) La vita delle cose. Laterza, Bari
Rigotti F (2004) Filosofia delle piccole cose. Interlinea, Novara
Pamuk O (2009) L'innocenza degli oggetti. Einaudi, Torino
Pamuk O (2015) Il Museo dell'innocenza. Einaudi, Torino
Rigotti F (2013a) Nuova filosofia delle piccole cose. Interlinea, Novara
Rigotti F (2013b) Il pensiero delle cose. Apogeo, Milano
Starace G (2013) Gli oggetti e la vita. Donzelli, Roma
Zambrano M (2004) Chiari del bosco. Mondadori, Milano
Zambrano M (1991) Verso un sapere dell'anima. Cortina, Milano

Through the Museum.
New Models of Communication

Francesca Guadagnoli$^{(\boxtimes)}$ and Elena Ippoliti

Dipartimento di Storia Disegno e Restauro dell'Architettura (DSDRA),
Università Sapienza, Piazza Borghese 9, 00186 Rome, Italy
`francesca.guadagnoli@uniroma1.it`

Abstract. This contribution reflects on some key aspects of the "museum" (intended in its broadest sense) in order to evaluate its history, formation, and evolution, which today offers a counter-narrative appropriate for overcoming stereotypes and prejudices. This is a new basis for finding a way to care for museums, including their present and past history. In this context, digital technologies are playing a key role in this change, generating new languages and experimentation that multiply the levels of telling about cultural artefacts, introducing new temporal dimensions and new installation paradigms. This contribution analyses the current changes, pausing on some international experiences and the different approaches they have chosen to take with the technological potential. This is, on the one hand, technology in relation to the space, the content, and play, generating other models of interaction; on the other hand, it is the visitor–museum relationship in a scenario wherein digital technologies act as tools that enable the change.

Keywords: Contemporary museum · ICT · Learning environment · Cultural ecosystem · Virtual dimension · Interactions

1 Introduction. The Museum - Frontier Theme

Today, museums are taking on a new role and presenting a new institutional mission. This modification process has abandoned the traditional museum model, which is no longer closed, but rather the expression of the world to which it belongs and the society that has designed it, beyond the building, beyond its aesthetic quality. This change, which has already begun in some of the most important museums in Europe, has facilitated the symbolic transition of museums. Contemporary museums are devices for images and things, a place for entertainment where events occur; as such, they are diminished under the profile of symbolic meaning but supercharged with communicational meaning. The contemporary museum as a mediating event is aimed at a generic public of users of various ages and cultures (no longer just art consumers in search of entertainment), who are approached by proposing ideal visits with explanatory interactions and on-demand visibility to satisfy the expectations of making a mental trip and thereby creating subjective memories of distant works. Therefore, the place of interaction is not a building; the contemporary museum is elsewhere, where digital technologies are making museums without walls possible, anywhere and

A. Luigini (Ed.): EARTH 2018, AISC 919, pp. 476–484, 2019.
https://doi.org/10.1007/978-3-030-12240-9_50

everywhere. This is the framework of the relationship between scientific research and the possibilities offered by the contemporary market of digital technologies, in particular, techniques for simulating three-dimensional space with the related integrations between real and virtual space, to encourage perceptual/motor exploration of the reconstructed spaces.

2 The Museum as a Product of a Historical Process - Origin and Function

For a long time, museums, as institutions, have played their conservative role according to a chronological rule crystallized in a historical concept, a process that has therefore laid down, photographed, and expressed *a posteriori* a place that instead should be viewed as animated by the continuous change of artistic creation. To understand the current change in museums, it is necessary to first construct an adequate historical framework in which the birth of the system of museum communication is recognized, knowing how to conserve "history's passing over the works" [il passaggio della storia sulle opere] (Brandi 1963).

The modern name *museum* derives from the Mouséion in Alexandria in Egypt, which did not correspond to our current idea of museum; it did not store or display objects, but operated as a library and cultural welcome centre for scholars in the Hellenic world. During the sixteenth and eighteenth centuries, the concept and structure of museums were influenced by a unique category of expository structures of "strange" and wonderful objects: the *Wunderkammer*—Cabinets of Wonder—"special" precursors of modern museums that determined part of the oldest history of museums and represent a sixteenth-century phenomenon whose roots lie in the Middle Ages. The *Wunderkammer*, found especially in the Nordic countries, can be considered the first phase in development of the concept of museum display and one of the first forms of collecting, aimed at enhancing the "fantastic" content displayed.

These represent just one aspect of what would be the development of the modern museum, which derives, in its first stage, from organizing the rare private collections of nobles, popes, and civil institutions and opening them to the public. The initial aim of the modern museum was to represent and transmit the prestige of power through exceptional works that testify to continuity in the artistic tradition, from the classical past to the present, developing specific exhibition sites for these collections.

3 The Museum and its Social Role

Over the years, *attention for the exhibition frame* that highlighted the monuments displayed fully corresponded to the *care in the organization and promotion of the museum itself*. The clear distinction between museum, historical/artistic, and even archaeological site and architectural container of shows and events was willingly lost, with the aim of enriching urban spaces and hosting public and private services. The varied configuration of the museum structure has, in fact, modified the normal destination from a museum place to a centre of cultural attraction, as has occurred for some

European museums such as the Centre Pompidou and Musée du Quai Branly in Paris, the Guggenheim Museum in Bilbao, the MAXXI in Rome, etc. Here, the attraction for visitors lies not only in the works displayed, but especially in the shows and architectural container (Criconia 2011).

It follows that with the Centre Pompidou, the museum divests itself of its traditional decorative clothes in order to bring to light the structural grid, the mechanical systems, and the coloured pipes, that is, the structure and function of the museum. With the MAXXI (Fig. 1), Guggenheim (Fig. 2), and the Musée du Quai Branly (Fig. 3), the museum builds an image of the city, becoming a symbol and sign of the territory, an attractor that seems to challenge the content.

Fig. 1. Centre George Pompidou-Beaubourg Paris 1977 R. Piano

Fig. 2. Guggenheim Museum Bilbao 1997 F.O. Ghery

Fig. 3. MAXXI National Museum of 21st-century Arts] 2009 Z. Hadid

Whatever the historical process of transforming the museum system, which is anyway still active, its expository function for cultural aims remains trapped in time. Already starting in the second half of the 1900s, the idea of the museum, undergoing constant change, represented <u>something</u> broader and less definable, in which a certain component was anyway present—the quantitative and qualitative attraction of visitors —in fact helping to increase tourism in the territory where the "museum" stands. This phenomenon of attraction, however, has been contaminated in the past by the anachronistic image of the museum still intended as a simulacrum of art and therefore capable of being appreciated by few, but used by masses of visitors who have inevitably become an indistinct set of people with little consideration for individuals. An example of this is (Fig. 4), which shows the crowd of visitors in a room of the Louvre.

Today this standardization, composed of unifying pressure that has persisted over time, is faced with a museum institution that is distinguished by a typical perception of the present, which can be summarized in the title of a book by Nicholas Serota, *Experience or Interpretation*. In the book, the author reflects on the influence that contemporary society has on the museum's role with respect to the past: from an analytical/interpretational approach to one guided mainly by the senses, since now the museum and its content is aimed at immediately stimulating the spectator's emotions before the mind. The museum therefore aims to be transformed not necessarily into a building (in the usual sense), but, in more general terms, into a defined spatial area where knowledge is built by establishing a familiar relationship between the user and the museum. This user-museum intimacy, viewed as a new social behaviour, supports individuals in overcoming standardization, expressing themselves individually with regard to the cultural context.

Therefore, museums, as complex entities, are seeing a renewal in their essential communicational characteristics. A new museum experience is being built through forms of personalization, interaction, and content enrichment, the true expression of the world to which it belongs and the society that has designed it. New progress is being made in redefining the museum's role as a "new" educational institution, opening other perspectives for the creation of an "enlarged cultural ecosystem" that involves the political, economic, social, and cultural worlds (Lotto 2017).

Fig. 4. Crowd - Louvre

In this context, museums are undergoing regeneration in their highest sense of transmission, dialogue, and collaborative work between institution and community. The reasons for the change respond to the museum's basic need to be a tool for understanding cultural artefacts and therefore to play a public education role. We are found in a new situation of "proximity to things" (Antinucci 2018); there is no longer that distance that has always characterized the visitor from the place-museum that, initially a simulacrum, becomes an environment for repository learning of visible values proposed as shared collective memory. In (Fig. 5) a brief representation of the new condition of the visitor in relation to the museum.

Fig. 5. From the exclusive space to sharing collective memory

It is interesting to recall G.C. Argan, who, according to his analysis from thirty years ago on art museums, proposed his idea of the museum of the future: "an active laboratory for reflection and interference with contemporary things, where the sacredness of the works is replaced by a set of services for culture. A sort of universal archive of the present, a malleable, plastic, ephemeral, transient, anti-volumetric container" [un laboratorio attivo di riflessione e di interferenza con la contemporaneità dove alla sacralità delle opere si sostituiscono un insieme di servizi per la cultura. Una sorta di archivio universale del presente, un contenitore plasmabile, plastico, effimero, labile, anti volumetrico] (Argan 1982).

If the analysis focuses on the social role of the museum—that is, the relationship between museum and its natural target, the public—the latter, from an entirely undifferentiated subject becomes the protagonist. At the root of this different viewpoint is a willingness to create an immediate relationship (even physical) between the museum and the public, which finds itself being called to participate in first person. The analysis focuses on the need to win the loyalty of visitors, creating a new public through varied solutions in which different types of expressiveness coexist. The objective is to present the solutions to the public and make the museum assume a multi-faceted aspect that includes art, architecture, cinema, dance, music, design, and fashion, underlining its cultural value as a place for the aesthetic manifestations of creativity.

One example of this is the installation *Put your head into gallery* by the Georgian artist Tezi Gabunia (Fig. 6). Gabunia proposes a reflection on the contemporary world by presenting miniature copies of famous exhibit spaces in which spectators are invited to rest their heads. In this way, he intends to upend the spectator's normal role, "bringing" the gallery to the spectator and not vice versa.

Fig. 6. Performance *Put your head in to gallery* Tezi Gabunia 2016

This transformation process, influenced by numerous contemporary proposals, has seen the gradual abandonment of the traditional typological model of museums—in which they are confined to a role of passive conservation—and the step from a closed place to a place for interaction. It is in this "change of state" that the question of going beyond the border with different realities becomes key: a place that opens into other places, generating participation and developing familiarity with the user through emotional involvement in constructing thoughts and theories.

4 The Museum—Tangible Experience

Today the answer an architect can provide to this idea of museum is to offer a formal solution to architecture's less prominent role, that is, representing the individual in space. The aim is to establish contact with the place-museum in order to dispel the disorientation and unfamiliarity that has long conditioned the visitor in the museum, responding as well to the human need to recognize oneself in a place and to act towards others as individuals.

The architect's awareness of this ancient and new functional need ties people to the museum space because it is a place dedicated to displaying how much collective culture has produced best. Basically, it can be defined as an institution operating in service of society, which follows and interprets the transformations.

In Tokyo's Museum of Contemporary Art, in (Fig. 7) the basic idea of "*Haunted Play House* is an example of the possibility of viewing the museum differently, where the traditional rules of the place are overturned. This provocative, engaging attitude was chosen by Torafu Architects, where art is manifested under the form of a "spectacle", even if according to specific methods. A different key to interpretation may therefore be the "repositioning" of the museum within the cultural context, losing the traces of its original meaning. This new form of museum certainly foresees a different relationship with the wider, varied public, which wants to be emotionally intrigued and surprised. This is a tangible experience that initially tries to entertain the user and then immediately requires a mental obligation, a reflexive effort oriented at reality.

Fig. 7. *Haunted play house* Museum Of Contemporary Art Tokyo Torafu Architects

5 The Museum's Times

Museums have always had a curious relationship with time and the society in which they are situated. This was seen in the past when the need to find a place to deposit the values of shared collective memory led to the institution of museums, places in which cultural objects were inserted and slowly absorbed with an abstract character, becoming part of a unique whole and thereby losing their singular nature. It was a place designed specifically for cultural objects where the quality of the individual work risked being undermined by the visual quantity.

As Umberto Eco observed: "as well organized and divided by era, genre, or style it may be, the modern museum becomes a place where anyone who wanted to see everything there is would see nothing, and if he even looked, would not be able to memorize. It is true that the real enthusiast visits a museum piece by piece; others do what I do when I find myself in Amsterdam, for example, and I dedicate half an hour to the umpteenth visit to the Rijksmuseum. I pass quickly through all the rooms, over-looking even Rembrandt, and I dedicate my time to my favourite painting, a church by Saenredam. Half an hour of intense contemplation saturates the spirit. Then I leave, so I do not lose what I have maximized" [per quanto sia ben organizzato e suddiviso per epoche, generi o stili, il museo moderno diventa un luogo dove, chi volesse vedere tutto quello che c'è non vedrebbe nulla, e se pure guardasse non potrebbe memorizzare. È vero che il vero appassionato visita un museo pezzo per pezzo, altri fanno ciò che io faccio quando capito per esempio ad Amsterdam e dedico una mezz'ora a un'ennesima visita al Rijksmuseum: percorro di corsa tutte le sale, trascurando persino Rembrandt, e mi dedico solo al mio quadro preferito, una chiesa di Saenredam. Mezz'ora di intensa contemplazione satura lo spirito. Dopo esco, per non perdere ciò che ho capitalizzato] (Eco 2001).

As mentioned above, the destination of the museum institution has changed over time; in today's environment-museum, cultural artefacts are removed from their quiet state to be "interrogated".

This is a new perspective that proposes the "museum outside of museums" in the role of an institution that has broad, ambitious objectives with regard to both the cultural heritage and the public-visitor. This is realized with the conscious, intelligent use of digital and multimedia technologies, thanks to which forms and languages of communication are being experimented with via applications that are characterized variously by degree of use, interaction, and interface-device to test new cognitive and emotional relationships.

6   The Museum Outside of Museums

The expression "virtual dimension" is being used with increasing frequency with regard to museum communication. The goal is to generate interaction between the place, physical and digital artefacts in the collections, and users, as protagonists and interpreters of these new relationships. One expression of this virtual dimension is the project Google Arts & Culture, where ICT have the task of not only integrating information, but, especially, building cognitive and educational narratives for the collections displayed in numerous museums throughout the world. The goal is to offer new opportunities to expand and deepen the means of learning.

Google Arts & Culture collaborates with more than 1200 museums, galleries, and institutes in 70 countries to make the exhibitions available online, becoming a container of copious content and thereby organizing the information on a global level, making it universally accessible to all. In this cultural project, two dimensions coexist that, while remaining distinct, interact continuously: the creation of a new space for education, and conservation of the collections (in its most contemporary meaning). Offering a wide choice of tools and devices, this online platform allows anyone to explore the greatest collections in the world of art and craftsmanship displayed with high-definition details. The user can visit the most important exhibits, enlarging the works of art to see the tiniest details, and create personal galleries of works to share on Internet, becoming actively engaged in the production and sharing of content through a personalized, user-centred dynamic dialogue with the museum collections.

7   Conclusions. The Virtual Dimension of Museum Communication

In light of what is illustrated above, it is clear that the characteristics of the place-museum have changed from a physical container that gathers the objects in the collection into an environment to build other relational systems. The term "virtual dimension" is being used increasingly, in which uncommon interactions (in real life) between user, cultural artefact, and scene or environment are being verified to experiment with new cognitive and emotional relationships. In this real-virtual blend, a dynamic communicational model is realized, composed of a constant, that is, its use, and variables, such as the scene and collections. This model of communication is therefore capable of returning indexed data, gathering content of different types, and allowing for a more refined and deeper data-user-scene interaction.

   The possibility of connection strengthens the use, acting more forcefully on the imagination; new perspectives are therefore opened to view and unexpected comparisons are revealed (Manovich 2008).

References

Argan GC (1982) Rapporto tra museo e allestimento. In: Il pubblico dell'arte, a cura di Mucci E, Tazzi PL, pp. XI–XX Sansoni, Firenze, Editore
Antinucci F (2018) Comunicare nel museo. Edizioni Laterza, Rome-Bari
Brandi C (1963) Teoria del restauro. Einaudi, Editore
Criconia A (2011) L'Architettura dei musei. Carocci editore, Roma
Eco U (2001) Il museo del terzo millennio. Conferenza tenuta al Museo Guggenheim di Bilbao
Manovich L (2008) Il linguaggio dei nuovi media. Editore Olivares, Milano
Lotto B (2017) Percezioni. Come il cervello costruisce il mondo. Bollati Boringhieri editore

Museums in the Era of Digital Revolution. Persuasive Communication and Multimodal Approaches for Overcoming the Digital Divide

Francesco Gabellone[1(✉)] and Maria Chiffi[2]

[1] National Research Council (CNR), Istituto per i Beni Archeologici
e Monumentali (IBAM), Prov.le Lecce-Monteroni, 73100 Lecce, Italy
`francesco.gabellone@cnr.it`
[2] Techné s.a.s. Museum Communication, Via Michele Gaballo, 26,
73048 Nardò, Lecce, Italy
`sastechne@gmail.com`

Abstract. The museum, intended as a mere container aimed only at the conservation of objects, has long since given space to activities of cultural production and promotion that have finally allowed the entry of new forms of communication. Based on dynamic storytelling and multimodal information, they propose to implement an effective dialogue with the anthropological, economic, social and cultural context, activating a set of various activities aimed at conveying complex and constantly evolving messages. From the simple linear and didactic communication mode, we move toward informative, persuasive and educational communication. But the most interesting aspect of this evolution is that it has strongly modified the exhibition logics and the ways in which cultural contents are used by the public. Based on these premises, we present in this article the results of some methodological approaches experimented in different museum installations. They consider different criteria, from passive to active visit, from serious games to immersive enjoyment.

Keywords: Museum communication · Virtual · 3D · Multimodal · Persuasive

1 Introduction

The museum communication makes use of methods and processes implemented in relation to different purposes, contents and targets, through the use of an extremely articulated system of languages and communication techniques. The museum, intended as a mere container aimed only at the conservation of objects, has long since given space to activities of cultural production and promotion that have finally allowed the entry of new forms of communication (Mantovani 2001). Based on dynamic storytelling and multimodal information, they propose to implement an effective dialogue with the anthropological, economic, social and cultural context, activating a set of various activities aimed at conveying complex and constantly evolving messages. The forms and the ways that museum communication takes depend on the actors involved, on the reference context and on the set of languages and tools employed from time to time. From the simple linear and didactic communication mode, we move on to

A. Luigini (Ed.): EARTH 2018, AISC 919, pp. 485–495, 2019.
https://doi.org/10.1007/978-3-030-12240-9_51

informative, persuasive and educational communication. But the most interesting aspect of this evolution is that it has strongly modified the expository logics and the ways in which cultural contents are used by the public (Fox and Henderson 2001) (Figs. 1 and 2).

Fig. 1. Calvello museum, 3D rendering of project layout

Fig. 2. Medieval and greek ceramics. User experience and final stage of the game

2 Persuasive Communication

For example, the impulse of new technologies has imposed new forms of representation, strongly characterizing the cultural activities with the use of digital technologies and languages that require the active participation of the public. All this has made more attractive museums based on non-traditional expository logics, which have seen the number of visitors increase and, most likely, have gained a greater understanding of the cultural information communicated. Multimedia, the prevalence of the iconic information on the written word and the freedom of use allowed by new technologies, radically change the perceptual and cognitive processes: from analytical, structured, sequential and referential, they become generic, global, simultaneous and holistic.

Based on these premises, we present in this article the results of some methodological approaches experimented in different museum installations. They consider different criteria, from passive fruition to active fruition, from serious games to immersive enjoyment. In some cases the integration of criteria that is the multimodal approach, has shown that "pervasiveness", understood as communicative efficacy, is in direct relation with a greater understanding of the communicated object. Increasing interest in some issues, through any form of communication, means gaining greater public awareness. A significant example in this sense assume immersive technologies and "persuasive" storytelling, two apparently distant approaches, the first active and the second, in general, totally passive. Immersiveness of active type, realized with VR viewers, produces a strong sense of presence in the virtualized environment: the realism of the representation and the almost physical interaction with the three-dimensional elements produces a natural and direct understanding of the architectural elements, of the figurative apparatus and of the spatial articulation of the ancient contexts. In "persuasive" movies, on the other hand, the passivity of the vision is compensated by an emotional approach that involves the visitor in an informative path in which, despite the inactivity of the fruition, he is a participant in some way, because he is emotionally involved (Titthasiri 2013) (Fig. 3).

Fig. 3. Pompei's docudrama. A context scene (forum) in which virtual actors will play

This type of vision does not require computer skills and is integrated with the different media, even traditional, in a "light" but effective learning logic. In this sense, the multimodal approach produces benefits also for those who are not familiar with the use of IT tools and the Internet, so the diversification of the media and the use of simplified languages allow everyone to understand the message communicated, but also to achieve a better response to the different tastes of visitors. This reflection should not lead us to consider active technologies as too complex or difficult to use, on the contrary. It goes in the direction of a museum identity, intended as complex communicative machine, as a center of cultural production and promotion, whose task is not limited to the sole activity of preservation of objects, but in its ability to establish an effective dialogue with the social and cultural context, as a primary tourist-cultural attractor The evolution of the methods of communication in the museum environment is a consequence of the general changes in the languages used in social communication. Since the forms of persuasive communication seem more adherent to the logics of an attractive, convincing and emotional presentation than those purely informative and explanatory, they are closer to the tastes of visitors. Persuasion is achieved through the adoption of techniques that aim to achieve emotional reactions, rather than purely rational arguments. In the specific field of archaeological museums, this type of strategy is recognized in the contents that mainly seek to promote the value of archaeological research itself, the protection and conservation of museum artifacts, the uniqueness or the high value of historical-cultural testimony of objects covered by the communication. More specifically, this is achieved through an argumentative speech that, for example, emphasizes the preciousness of the discovery context, the rarity of the find, the exceptional nature of the data. Objectives mediated by the exhibition, realized through the use of hyper-realistic 3D representation, of the animated effects that allow the immediate compression of the transformations over time, of the contextualization of objects, of dynamic presentation, of movie-like storytelling (Gabellone et al. 2017) (Fig. 4).

Fig. 4. Pompei's docudrama. A context scene in the Casa del Fauno

3   Case Studies: Serious Game and Emotional Storytelling

The integration of communication criteria based on the image and on the use of interactive, immersive and participatory technologies in the projects shown here, is based on some assumptions. Before the written word, seeing was not a structured decoding of graphic signs, but only a perception of images, experienced in a more sensorial way. In the "image society", with the pervasiveness of television and multimedia tools, the cognitive process returns to be the one based on the image. This process has however led to the consolidation of the so-called cultural divide, the cultural gap that separates those who are familiar with books, newspapers, magazines and other information and dissemination tools, and those who have television as the only reference from the communicative point of view. But if it was once the cultural tools compatible with the means of the social class to define this nuanced line of demarcation, today they are the work done or simply the personal predisposition: for a few years the further dividing line of the digital divide has emerged, between those who have the possibility and skills to use the new information technologies and those who are cut off from it. The determining factors in this sense are above all the age and the work carried out, which often favors the use of IT tools and the Internet. On the other hand, familiarity with IT equipment is a necessary but not sufficient condition to guarantee the acquisition of culture and information. As previously mentioned, the use of passive media and interactive technologies with minimum usability requirements, not only promote use by everyone, but promote cross paths and unexpected connections in a spirit of cultural serendipity (Huizinga 1973) (Fig. 5).

Fig. 5. Pompei's docudrama. Villa dei Misteri, outside

The first of the examples illustrated here, concerns a small town in the province of Potenza, Calvello, where a project of restoration and refunctionalization of the Castle, among other actions, involved the construction of a ceramics museum. Until a few years ago, the small town was the custodian of an ancient tradition of ceramics production. In the fitting out project, an articulated section is dedicated to the knowledge of ceramics, processing techniques, technologies and colors used by Calvello faenzari. A multimodal approach, which includes several applications, two immersive stereoscopic videos and an interactive serious game intended as an "enabling platform", allow the learning of the executive techniques and the peculiarities of ceramics in a precise historical period. The set of these devices, on which complementary contents have been developed, address the peculiar themes of the museum with different approaches and levels of study. Serious games, in particular, represent a real revolution in education strategies. Thanks to their ability to simulate different aspects of the experience, they are an effective tool for the acquisition and enhancement of learning in different sectors. The simulation of serious games allows users to make experiences, that is to concretely represent what we know only on a theoretical level. The simulation aspects allow us to get in touch with the knowledge through our senses, our body and not only at the abstract level (Zyda 2005). Compared to other methods used in education and communication, they involve the user in a motivational way, since the design of the game must primarily meet this requirement. Motivating the user in the training process means, for example, earning scores, completing missions, starting competition mechanisms between different players. Furthermore, it has been widely demonstrated that positive emotions such as interest, curiosity, exploration and a sense of challenge exert a strong influence on the ability to memorize the contents transmitted, both in quantity and quality. More specifically, serious games are able to capture our resources related to attention and focus on the task we are performing (Fox et al. 2001; Anderson and Phelps 2001). Attention is one of the many cognitive processes that allows us to relate with the external environment, we can consider it a basic psychic function. Without attention, in fact, we could not store information, manipulate and finally return it, we could not organize our commitments and solve problems promptly (Schooler and Eich 2000) (Fig. 6).

Fig. 6. Scene of the docudrama: Abalo in the Temple of Jupiter

For all these reasons, serious games can be considered the best instrument in the most effective forms of transmission of knowledge and culture, because at the same time they emotionally involve the user and "impose" learning. It is from this indirect imposition that depends the level of satisfaction obtained (gained) in the game. The more I understand, the more I gain, the more I go forward, the more I win (Michael and Chen 2006). A simple addiction, which in this specific case has very positive effects on learning. Because of their ductility and adaptability to different fields of knowledge, they can be more and more integrated into the traditional learning path for users of all ages, cultural levels and, if made with simplified user experiences, for every type of computer skills (Fig. 7).

Fig. 7. Scene of the docudrama: the torcularium for the grape pressing

Specifically, the learning mode of serious games developed for Calvello is based on simple questions that require a knowledge base. This knowledge base is acquired by playing and interacting with the application itself. The player has fun and learns, in a logic of edutainment game. In a collaborative environment, the visitor must assemble the various pieces according to some levels of completion. In association with these levels of completion, a message appears describing the various classes of pottery and the errors made. Since the game requires the involvement of only one person at a time, a large projection has been introduced to allow other visitors to follow the game, give suggestions, collaborate. In addition to medieval pottery, the player will have to recognize the food used in the same historical period, i.e. before the discovery of America. From the technological point of view, the game was developed completely in Lingo, an old language implemented many years ago by Adobe, still fully functional, but poorly supported. The programming is managed by three main behaviors, which assigned to the projections of the game allow to manage their absolute position with a trigger event. A second behavior allows the elements of the scene to be moved and placed in their hidden position. The sprite will compare its "loc" to a "targetLoc", if this is within the acceptable target range, the sprite locks into place. A last behavior is active when the object is in position. If this event is true, the object disappears:

```
on beginSprite me
sprite (me.spriteNum).visibility = TRUE
END
```

Other behaviors control specific sounds and events, for example a message warns in case of an error (Fig. 8).

Fig. 8. Scenes of docudrama. Below the *lararium* of the Casa del Fauno

Next to the game, of course active but simplified, the visitor has the possibility to extend his knowledge with a passive approach, according to emotional and persuasive communication logics. The same methods of approach to museum communication have been used for many other museums, where the various media interact with each other, telling the same contents in different forms. The value of the immersive animation, among all, deploys the maximum emotional impact, reaching in the shortest way the goal of "persuasiveness". In a case study of ancient Pompei, we have tried not to emphasize the reconstruction of material culture, developing the basic theme on a life story, which is intertwined with the tragic events of the eruption. To this end, an interdisciplinary team of scholars produced stereoscopic docudrama in 3D computerized animation "Pompei. A Buried Story", a 26 min film, in full HD, which describes a fantasy story. A series of original artifacts, discovered in some key places in Pompei, such as the Villa of the Mysteries, the Casa del Fauno and the Forum, have been placed in a virtual context dominated by the conflict between two characters, Abalo and Ottimo, digitally recreated. The philological reconstruction of those ancient places has become the virtual stage for the representation of a small drama. This narration centered on man, in which Pompei is only the background, offers an immersive experience in which the public is emotionally related to the protagonist, in a scenery dominated by the power of images, sounds, soundtrack, special effects and historical reconstruction.

Acknowledgements. Thanks to Niki Masini for having strongly supported the communication project of the castle of Calvello and to Davide Tanasi for the archaeological consultancy in the docudrama on Pompei. The 3D modeling of the docudrama was made with the contribution of Massimiliano Passarelli and Claudio Germinario. Special thanks to Federica Gabellone, for English translation.

References

Anolli L, Mantovani F (2011) Come funziona la nostra mente. Apprendimento, simulazione e Serious Games. Il Mulino

Corti K (2006) Games-based Learning; a serious business application. PIXELearning Limited. www.pixelearning.com/docs/games_basedlearning_pixelearning.pdf

Fox NA, Henderson HA, Rubin KH, Calkins SD, Schmidt LA (2001) Continuity and discontinuity of behavioral inhibition and exuberance: Psychophysiological and behavioral influences across the first four years of life. Child Dev 72:1–21

Mantovani S (2001) Infant toddler centers in Italy today: tradition and innovation. In: Gandini L, Edwards CP (eds) Bambini: the Italian approach to infant/toddler care. Columbia University Press, New York, pp 146–183

Michael D, Chen S (2006) Serious games: games that educate, train, and inform. Thomson Course Technology, Boston

Rashty D, Neign B, Chen B, Nitsani U (1997) Traditional learning vs. e-learning. Israel Government Internet Committee

Schooler JW, Eich E (2000) Memory for emotional events. In: Tulving E (ed) The oxford handbook of memory. Oxford University Press, Oxford, pp 379–392

Titthasiri W (2013) A comparison of e-learning and traditional learning: experimental approach. Int J Inf Technol

Zyda M (2005) From visual simulation to virtual reality to games. Computer 38(9):25–32

American Psychiatric Association (2000) Diagnostic and statistical manual of menthal disorders-text revision, 3rd edn. American Psychiatric Association, Washington, DC

Barkley RA (1990) Attention-deficit hyperactivity disorder: a handbook for diagnosis and treatment. Guilford, New York

Huizinga M, Dolan CV, van der Molen MW (2006) Age-related change in executive function: developmental trends and a latent variable analysis. Neuropsychologia 44:2017–2036

Huizinga J (1973) Homo ludens, Einaudi

Gabellone F, Lanorte A, Lasaponara R, Masini N (2013) Development of a serious game on the history of a medieval village based on remote sensing. In: Proceedings of the 4th EARSeL workshop on cultural and natural heritage "earth observation: a window on the past", Matera, Italy, 6–7 June 2013. ISBN 978-8-88-9693254. http://www.earsel.org/SIG/NCH/4th-workshop/proceedings.php

Gabellone F, Lanorte A, Lasaponara R, Masini N (2017) From remote sensing to a serious game: digital reconstruction of an abandoned medieval village in Southern Italy. J. Cult. Herit. 23:63–70. https://doi.org/10.1016/j.culher.2016.01.012

The Professionalism of the Museum Educator Between Heritage Competences and Digital Competences

Chiara Panciroli[✉], Manuela Fabbri[✉], and Veronica Russo[✉]

Department of Education Sciences "G.M. Bertin", University of Bologna,
Via Filippo Re 6, 40126 Bologna, Italy
{chiara.panciroli,m.fabbri,veronica.russo6}@unibo.it

Abstract. The hereby paper aims at focusing on the profession of the museum Educator starting from a reinterpretation of heritage and digital competences which, alongside the evolution of contemporary museology, are more and more shaping this profession.

Keywords: Professionalism · Competence · Educator · Museum · Heritage · Digital

1 The Museum as Public Service: What Recognition for What Professionalism?

In the early years of the new century, along with the greatest social, economic and cultural movements that crossed western societies – also in relation with the development of democratization processes – the museum has come to be defined, also in Italy, as a public cultural institution. As evidenced in fact by the International Council of Museums (ICOM) the museum is "a non-profit, permanent institution in the service of society and its development, open to the public […] (1986; 2001; 2004; 2007); a "structure […] organized for the preservation, valorization and public use of collections of cultural heritage" (Legislative Decree n°490/99 co.2 lett.a) destined to public use, performing a public service of social interest (Decree 42/2004 art. 101 co.3, co.4). The concept of the museum as a public space – from the Latin "publicus", "belonging to all people" – has determined a radical change in the promotion and development of the right to culture for all citizens – as established by art.9 of the Italian Republic Constitution – carrying on a vibrant and productive discussion which also investigates its educational role. In this sense, the museum intended as relational (Bodo 2003), of lifelong learning, lifewide and lifedeep (Sani 2005; Gibbs et al. 2007; Panciroli and Russo 2015), participative (De Biase 2017), social and inclusive (ICOM Report 2017; Caldin et al. 2017) has put at the center of its interest the public engagement, becoming a space intended to "[…] acquire, conserve, research, communicate and exhibit the tangible and intangible heritage of humanity and its environment for the purposes of education, study and enjoyment" (2007). In this respect, visitors studies (Solima 2000; Sani and Trombini 2003; Nardi 2004; Bollo 2008; Comoglio 2010; De Biase 2014), which spread in the early 20th century in the Anglo-Saxon context, represent a

© Springer Nature Switzerland AG 2019
A. Luigini (Ed.): EARTH 2018, AISC 919, pp. 496–506, 2019.
https://doi.org/10.1007/978-3-030-12240-9_52

significant framework of studies and analysis, primarily for the quality improvement of the museum experience starting from space design, time, methods, tools and educational actions, addressed to different audiences (children, young people, adults, old people, families, tourists…).

The attention given to museum as an educational space for all people and for each person however seems not to go alongside cultural, economic and political recognition which, in the national and international context, is dedicated to museum professions and specifically to museum Educators who, among their main activities, mediate the museum material and immaterial heritage. On these premises, the Italian Ministry of Cultural Heritage (MiBAC) has drawn some policy documents stressing out the importance of investing in museum professions to work for the improvement of the complex quality of institutions and services, also through a museum process of self-assessment, "certifying this way the organization from the inside and highlighting strong points and critical aspects, analyzing progress in time, involving the museum staff in pursuit of a shared modus operandi" (Panciroli and Russo 2015, p. 142). In particular, the Ministerial Decree of 10 May 2001 (*Guidelines on technical-scientific criteria and museum functioning and development standards, sector 4, Personnel*) has recognized the necessity for museums to avail themselves of qualified professionals to perform their functions properly and to satisfy minimum quality requirements or standards; moreover, MD of 21 February 2018 (*Adoption of uniform minimum levels of quality for museums and culture places of public belonging and activation of the national museum System, attached file 1, 5, Personnel*) has evinced that "the presence of specific professional figures in an institute organization represents a crucial aspect to ensure the proper management of a museum and the capacity to define a valuable cultural project, coherent with the museum mission and with adequate actions of fruition and valorization". Also from the point of view of continuous training, the *national Plan for education to cultural Heritage* (MiBAC 2015) has established specific actions for museum professionals training and updating aimed at studying heritage in its pedagogical dimension, which means in the direction of a recognition of its training values and the acquisition of cultural and professional instruments for its didactic transposition in a multidisciplinary perspective (ibidem, p. 14). In addition, the important documents elaborated by ICOM and ICOM Italia, in representation of museums and their professionals, have become a major inspiration for Italian ministerial politics; MD 2001 has in fact been defined starting from ICOM's ethical code that introduced and released the concept of minimum standards for museums in 1986. Already since 1971 ICOM has elaborated the *Basic Syllabus for professional museum training* – then revised in 1996 by ICTOP (International committee for the training and professional development of ICOM's museum personnel) – which, in cooperation with UNESCO, has drawn up a very detailed and precise list of themes and issues to be included into a museum training program. Syllabus was later reassessed in favor of *Curricula Guidelines for museum professional development* – approved by ICOM in 2000 – which acknowledge that museum professionals training rests on a dedicated and disciplinary formation obtained through university career and working experiences. Organized into 5 macro-areas, subdivided into minor areas, Curricula Guidelines focus on needful requirements to work into a museum, from general ones (professionalism, communication, information technology, project, relationships…) to museology, public programming (including competence in education), information and collections management and care and management, according to a multilevel in-depth study structure. Also, ICOM Italia, during the Permanent Conference of Italian museum associations (2005) has drawn up, starting from MD 2001 of MiBAC, the *National Charter of museum professions* – finally adopted in 2006 – which represents an instrument to claim a higher presence of museum professionals (Garlandini 2007, p. 129), pointing at "reaffirming the centrality of museum professions within museums and sooth the chronic lack of definition of museum professions, on which museums can rely in order to fulfill their mission and perform their functions" (ICOM National Charter 2008, p. 3). The Charter defines 20 professional profiles with their responsibilities, domains, roles and requirements for job application, among which: research, care and collections management, "services and public relations", management, finance, administration, structures and safety. In the specific of section "services and public relations" the profession of a museum Educator is defined as the "fulfillment of the museum programmed educational actions, adapting to the characteristics and needs of different audiences" (p. 23) and having the task of relating to different audiences by means of educational actions – in relation to permanent collections and temporary exhibitions – carrying out didactic activities by using multiple strategies, from more traditional ones as the guided visit to those more interactive as workshops, setting up the museum spaces, participating to research, programming and cooperating for new educational projects and lastly, ensuring that the experience gets appreciated through visitors analysis and assessment of activities (ibidem). Therefore, museum Educators commit with a wide range of ages and competences, fostering relations with the community in order to attract visitors and make museums accessible and inclusive. The museum Educator is thus seen as a cultured professional with a university education of 1st and/or 2nd level in disciplines related to museum, besides the study of art and heritage didactic and the participation at training courses and/or master in heritage pedagogy, not to mention knowledge in other fields, like those related to scientific and technologic knowledge. Moreover, the museum Educator should master linguistic skills, with at least one foreign language. In conclusion, the debate on professions, thanks to ICOM Italia's national Charter, has widened and enriched but the path towards an ultimate acknowledgment of museum professions, and in particular of museum Educators, is still struggling, confirming what emerges also in the international context.

2   The Museum Educator: Studies and Researches in the National and International Context

Still nowadays in Italy, despite the promulgation of the *national Charter of museum professions* there is a shortage of statistics that can offer a precise framework of how many people work in about 5000 museums in the national territory (Istat, Museums, archeological areas and monuments in Italy 2016). The Court of Auditors in a "Report on the control of Museums of local institutions" (Deliberation n°8/2005) has made a survey on a national scale of public and private museums "to compensate the absence of a recent census of the whole museum system[..]" (Polito 2006, p. 61). The survey tells that out of 1184 museums, the average number of employees is almost eight: in two regions, Veneto and Sicily, the average is way higher, with 15 and 12 employees per museum, respectively, some of whom with a permanent or temporary contract, others employed as external personnel (freelance or counsellors, workers at associations, cooperatives and profit or nonprofit companies) and again as volunteers. However, in Istat survey (2016) the average of museum employees seems to halve: we find about four employees per structure, an average of one every 2400 visitors. We must add to them those given by external companies and associations, about one for each institute, and volunteers, about 18000 (p. 10). Quantitative data – definitely reliable however sometimes "too" generalizable – must later be correlated to other variables which inevitably have an effect on the presence, more or less relevant, of professionals inside museums, among which: territorial lack of homogeneity, the number of visitors and offered services as well as the planning of opening hours and space design.

If we also consider scientific literature in this field, while experiences of good practice made inside museums both in Italy and abroad are widespread, on the contrary researches on how museum Educators work and what knowledge and competences are applied are few. Just relatively to this aspect, we find in fact multiple critical points due to the fragmentation of this role and work duties. In this respect the international study of Zbuchea (2013) – on 309 museums and 45 countries around the world – has found that museums have an average of four full-time employees and that only 61% of museums has an education Department. Also in Italy the situation is quite the same mainly in small museums. Here the absence of an area dedicated to education, to which an overlapping of roles can be added, force people working in these museums to dedicate their time to duties not always in line with those typical of a museum Educator, who has trained in this context. The lack of professional encouraging is followed by a shortage of investments on initial and continuous training and the difficulty to access the profession, in part due to the absence of economic funds. Considering financial limits, how can museums afford qualified Educators? How valorize professionalism of young employees who, trained in an educational context, work in the domain of culture under adverse conditions? To these questions, already in the mid-80 s, researchers like Eisner and Dobbs (1986) tried to give answer, describing museum Educators as "second class citizens", deprived of institutional power and at the bottom of status hierarchy, stressing out how museum education is a "gold mine of unexploited possibilities", but also a unique resource for the development of creative approaches in education, theory and research. Museums educational role is therefore an object of discussion: many people refute the lack of resources and professional development, an unclear vision of pedagogical priorities and again, a role ambiguity of these professionals (Munley and Roberts 2006; Kley 2009; Garcia 2012; Reid 2013; Kristinsdòttir 2017).

3 Digital Innovation and New Professions: The State of Art and New Perspectives for Museum Educators

In Italy new technologies in the museum context have hardly been accepted and trusted in the beginning due to high costs of devices and the fear of jeopardizing collections (Symbola 2018, p. 172). This has generated, above all in the national context, the lack of a widespread digital culture and the absence of a policy able to foster heritage and technologies integration (Russo 2015). Often, the digital sphere in the museum context is not thought as part of a strategic programming, but the presumed innovation is many times confined to website management and communication on social media. By MD of 21 February 2018, MiBAC has established that Italian museums can obtain accreditation by gaining minimum quality levels; for what concerns technology, museums should possess a web site and set goals for improvement, such as monthly newsletter updating and the creation of a blog or a social network with weekly updating. Indeed, the shortage of investments in the digital sphere is evident in the Italian context: museums are still poor in technologies, and when available they are not used at full potential. As reported by Istat (2016), online museums are a little over the half (57,4%), only 13,4% provides a digital catalogue and 18,6% of institutes offer guests Wi-Fi connection, while on the other hand social media are increasing (40,5% of museums have a social account). For small museums under 1000 visitors, which can be found also in small towns, mainly belonging to municipalities (47,4) or religious institutions, (13,9%) only 38,9% has a website (ibidem). Yet, it must be said that there cannot be any technological change before cultural change: in fact, when we consider museum professions in Italy references to digital competences requirements are still few when hiring new employees. If we think about the latest MiBAC competition of 2016 for the recruitment of 500 new museum professionals, the requirement of digital competences was unmentioned. Also in the context of continuous training we can see resistance and perplexity; in fact, as evidenced by Istat report (2016) despite 43,9% of museums has declared the programming of training and updating courses for employees in the last five years, only 0,8%, in case of a 10% budget rise, has confirmed the will to use them and carry out training programs (p. 10). It must be said that available data do not tell the kind of training being provided and precise contents taken into account. To sum up beyond stats, "still few Italian museums are working in the direction of a work quality improvement with the digital sphere, and the perplexities underlying this phenomenon can also be associated with the necessity to train professionals who can work "with" and "on" the virtual context by acquiring different competences" (Panciroli et al. 2017, p. 5). The European project Mu. Sa – Museum Skills Alliance, 2016–2019 (to which countries like Italy, Portugal and Greece have participated in cooperation with Symbola foundation and the Istituto per i beni artistici, culturali e naturali - IBC of the Region Emilia Romagna) has worked on the link between professions and digital competences in relation to heritage digitalization and public involvement, pointing out how important are investments in museum professions training in order to overcome cultural resistances (Silvaggi et al. 2016, p. 21). In detail, "if all museum aspects can rely on new technologies development all staff is asked to know and be aware of opportunities given by their use (ivi, p.37). Therefore, instead of concentrating on single actions of digitalization, most times expensive and surrogates of real museum visits, we should work transversally by creating a bottom-up organizational-project model to highlight cultural growth and organizational sustainability goals, thus involving the whole museum staff. All personnel should get involved in training paths and development of basic digital competences, acquired and developed according to one's role and specific functions and duties. It is necessary to reconsider museum as an institution able to promote a change in terms of vision of services; "in the future digital competences required by the Italian system will be numerous and diversified, mainly with reference to two macro-areas: heritage digitalization and public involvement (ivi, p. 33). In this direction it is clear that the area of audience development also includes competences related to museum didactic. Therefore, if digital is the means to access culture it is mandatory that technology answers differently to each user's capacities and needs. In particular, the absence of a didactic-pedagogical approach in technology significantly reduces the possibility for museum Educators to work in first person with the digital resource and alongside museum professionals or external consultants with competences in computer science, marketing and communication. In this sense, designing didactic environments, starting from a didactic-pedagogical approach in the context of museology and virtual museography, would mean mediating the museum material and immaterial heritage to foster collaborative learning experiences also on the digital sphere, still insufficient nowadays.

4 Digital Competences of Museum Educators: What Theoretical Framework of Reference?

It is widely believed that in the present society of knowledge new digital technologies can contribute to alter the way we operate and conceive knowledge (Rossi 2016a) with an ever increasing impact on cognitive processes but also on social, cultural, economic and political processes within formal and informal contexts of human experience (Masterman 1985, 1997; Buckingham 2006; Jenkins 2007; Simondon 2009). In the museum context, assuming that it is necessary to reinforce the whole personnel knowledge of digital competences, it is evident that digital modernization must be intended as a multifaceted cultural process, dynamic, systemic in consideration of a potential expansion of different audiences to whom is now highly advisable to address, and of educational dimensions put in practice thanks to the application of new instruments to museum didactic. Technological innovation can contribute to a substantial enrichment of training offer made by museum institutions, opening up democratically to all citizens. In particular, the museum must be considered a training resource able to compete with other territorial realities and work in synergy with them (Frabboni and Pinto Minerva 2001), able to rise society cultural quality, offering citizens training occasions indispensable to build up transversal competences of identity, civilization, society, value and citizenship – which make them critical and responsible actors. In this framework, the valorization of museum heritage should take place through the creation of specific digital *artefacts* (Rossi 2016b), real *didactic environments* in continuum with those real (Panciroli 2016). The starting point which guides this paper is the following: inside real and virtual museum environments, adaptable and intentionally training, users are able to *perceive, know, build, acquire* cultural heritage by personalizing learning paths and the resignification of their own learning also thanks to the others' contributions (Calvani and Varisco 1995; Wenger 1998; Calvani 2005; Rossi 2009), with a view of empowering the individual, cultural and social identity, integrating new knowledge and gained competences with those pre-existing. On these premises, it seems appropriate to train professionals able to foster *reflexivity, critical sense, participation and active construction* of the users' own knowledge.

Once the national and international professional and normative framework of the museum Educator has been defined, intended as an *in-situation* researcher and mediator who "builds up a reciprocal relationship with different audiences through a negotiation-sharing of meanings and practices, aiming at finding a sense of museum experience which is different for each person" (Caldin et al. 2017, p. 6) we can make our proposal. It goes in the direction of finding a possible theoretical framework for the programming of training paths to *digital competences*. This framework derives its basis and cultural scenario from the theoretical-conceptual reference framework of TPACK (Technology, Pedagogy and Content Knowledge, Mishra and Koehler 2006) *distributed* (Nore et al. 2010; Di Blas et al. 2014; Phillips 2016); and from the *problematicistic pedagogical* approach (Bertin 1968; Gattullo et al. 1985; Guerra 2002). This design is based on documents proposed in the European context, such as the *Digital Competence Framework for Citizens* (DigComp 2017), *Digitally Competent Educational Organizations* (DigCompOrg 2017) and *Digital Competence Framework for Educators* (DigCompEdu 2017), especially the latter as it shows the European framework of digital competences for teachers and educators who operate at different levels in the territory (Fig. 1).

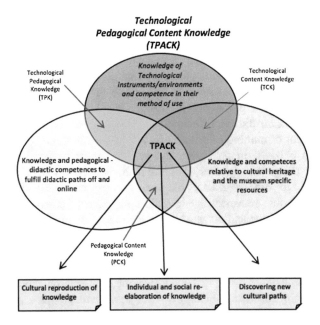

Fig. 1. TPACK model (based on the TPACK Image) in the museum context connected to problematic technological model (Guerra 2002).

Digital competences of museum Educators should intersect those relative to the knowledge of cultural contents belonging to the specific museum institution on one hand (on a disciplinary and interdisciplinary base), and on the other hand meet pedagogical-didactic competences (psycho-pedagogical, didactic-organizational, relational) relative in particular to a *situated* didactic planning (Rossi and Toppano 2009) and *personalized*, for different audiences, in accordance with training needs and taking into account different learning interpretations (*experiential, constructive, by discovery*, Guerra 2002, 2010). Education technological models that draw on the *problematicistic* approach aim at providing the museum Educator with needful competences to choose, case by case, the most proper (also) technological strategies to fulfill educational objectives with respect to a specific reference target. In other words, one of the main skills required to a real professional working consciously in the context of training processes is represented by the ability (associated with theoretical and technical knowledge) to integrate didactic different strategies and techniques with the planning of museum paths in accordance with the peculiarities of declared and fulfilled training goals (Di Blas et al. 2018). These objectives, on the cognitive level, can be grouped into three main learning perspectives, intertwined, which may be proposed in a museum context. At the first level we find *monocognitive* paths, with particular attention to knowledge dimension as cultural reproduction of scientific and artistic knowledge within the museum context in continuum between real and virtual environment. At the second level, *metacognitive* paths, inside of which we find dimensions of subjective cultural re-elaboration of the museum heritage together with the sphere of participation with other users, aiming at building up a fruitful confrontation, an exchange of different points of view to find out similarities and differences in reality perception. Lastly, *fanta-cognitive* paths, conceived as possibilities of exploring adventure educational dimension of adventure both on an individual and social level, where finding out new cultural paths becomes the purpose, always open and never definable beforehand.

Author Contributions.   Chiara Panciroli and Veronica Russo (paragraph 1); Chiara Panciroli (paragraph 2); Veronica Russo (paragrah 3); Manuela Fabbri (paragraph 4).

References

Bertin GM (1968) Educazione alla ragione. Armando, Roma

Bodo S (2003) Il museo relazionale: riflessioni ed esperienze europee. Fondazione Giovanni Agnell, Torino

Bollo A (2008) I pubblici dei musei. Conoscenza e politiche. FrancoAngeli, Milano

Buckingham D (2006) Media Education: Alfabetizzazione, apprendimento e cultura contemporanea. Erickson, Trento

Caldin R, Dainese R, Panciroli C (2017) Didactics towards a bottom-up museum approach. In: Proceedings of international and interdisciplinary conference IMMAGINI? Image and imagination between representation, communication, education and psychology, Basel, MDPI, vol 1, no 9, p 1108

Calvani A (2005) Rete, comunità e conoscenza: costruire e gestire dinamiche collaborative. Erickson, Trento

Calvani A, Varisco BM (eds) (1995) Costruire/decostruire significati. Ipertesti, micromondi e nuovi orizzonti formativi. CLEUP, Padova

Comoglio M (2010) La letteratura italiana sui museum visitor studies: una rassegna critica. Fondazione Fitzcarraldo, Torino. http://www.fizz.it/sites/default/files/allegati/articoli/pdf_articoli_completi/comoglio_2010.pdf. Accessed 20 Aug 2018

Di Blas N, Fabbri M, Ferrari L (2018) The TPACK model and teacher training in digital skills. Italian legislation and pedagogical implications. Ital J Educ Technol 26:24–38

Di Blas N, Paolini P, Sawaya S, Mishra P (2014) Distributed TPACK: going beyond knowledge in the head. In: Searson M, Ochoa M (eds) Proceedings of SITE 2014-society for information technology and teacher education international conference. Association for the Advancement of Computing in Education (AACE), Jacksonville, pp 2464–2472

De Biase F (2014) I pubblici della cultura. Audience Development, Audience Engagement. FrancoAngeli, Milano

De Biase F (2017) Cultura e partecipazione. Le professioni dell'audience. FrancoAngeli, Milano

Eisner EW, Dobbs SM (1986) The uncertain profession: observations on the state of museum education in twenty American art museum. A report to the J. Paul Getty Center for Education in the Arts, Santa Monica, The J. Paul Getty Trust

Frabboni F, Pinto Minerva F (2001) Manuale di Pedagogia generale. Laterza, Bari

Gattullo M, Bertolini P, Canevaro A, Frabboni F, Telmon V (eds) (1985) Educazione e ragione. La Nuova Italia, Firenze

Guerra L (ed) (2002) Educazione e tecnologie. I nuovi strumenti della mediazione didattica. Junior Edizioni, Bergamo

Guerra L (ed) (2010) Tecnologie dell'educazione e innovazione didattica. Junior, Parma

Jenkins H (2007) Cultura Convergente. Apogeo, Milano

Garcia B (2012) What we do best: making the case for the museum learning in its own right. J Mus Educ 37(2):47–55

Garlandini A (2007) La carta nazionale delle professioni museali. Genesi, risultati, prospettive. Museologia Sci. 1:129–139

Gibbs K, Sani M, Thompson J (2007) Musei e apprendimento lungo tutto l'arco della vita. Un manuale europeo. Edisai, Ferrara

Kley R (2009) Recessionary layoffs in museum education. Survey results and implications. J Mus Educ 34(2):123–128

Kristinsdòttir A (2017) Toward sustainable museum education practices: confronting challeges and uncertainties. Mus Manag Curatorship 32(5):424–439

ICOM (International Council of Museum) (1971) Basic syllabus for professional museum training

ICOM (2000) Curricula guidelines for museum professional development

ICOM Italia (2008) Carta Nazionale delle professioni museali. http://www.ufficiostudi.beniculturali.it/mibac/multimedia/UfficioStudi/documents/1261134207917_ICOMcarta_nazionale_versione_definitiva_2008%5B1%5D.pdf. Accessed 20 Aug 2018

ICOM (2017) Annual Report. http://www.icom-italia.org/wp-content/uploads/2018/06/2055_ICO-RA-2017-180x270-En-web.compressed.pdf. Accessed 20 Aug 2018

Istat (Istituto nazionale di statistica) (2016) Musei, i Monumenti e le Aree Archeologiche in Italia. https://www.istat.it/it/files/2016/12/Report-Musei.pdf?title=Musei+e+monumenti+in+Italia+-+19%2Fdic%2F2016+%20+Testo+integrale.pdf. Accessed 20 Aug 2018

Fondazione Symbola & Unioncamere (2018) Rapporto Io Sono Cultura. L'Italia Della Qualità e Della Bellezza Sfida la Crisi, Io Sono Cultura; Quaderni di Symbola. http://www.beniculturali.it/mibac/multimedia/MiBAC/documents/1529596696147_io_sono_cultura_2018.pdf. Accessed 20 Aug 2018

MiBAC (2015) Piano nazionale per l'educazione al Patrimonio culturale. http://www.dger. beniculturali.it/index.php?it/21/news/6/piano-nazionale-per-leducazione-al-patrimonio-culturale. Accessed 20 Aug 2018

Mishra P, Koehler M (2006) Technological pedagogical content knowledge: a framework for teacher knowledge. Teach Coll Rec 108:1017–1054. https://doi.org/10.1111/j.1467-9620. 2006.00684.x

Masterman L (1985) Teaching the Media. Comedia, London

Masterman L (1997) A scuola di media. Educazione, media e democrazia nell'Europa degli anni '90. La Scuola, Brescia

Munley ME, Roberts R (2006) Are museum educators still necessary? J Mus Educ 31(1):29–39

Nardi E (2004) Musei e pubblico: un rapporto educativo. FrancoAngeli, Milano

Nore H, Engelien KL, Johannesen M (2010) TPACK as shared, distributed knowledge. In: Gibson D, Dodge B (eds) Proceedings of SITE 2010-society for information technology and teacher education international conference. Association for the Advancement of Computing in Education (AACE), San Diego, pp 3920–3925

Panciroli C (2016) Le professionalità educative tra scuola e musei. Guerini editore, Milano

Panciroli C, Russo V (2015) I musei come luoghi per l'educazione permanente: l'esempio del MOdE-Museo Officina dell'Educazione dell'Università di Bologna. In: L'educazione permanente a partire dalle prime età della vita, «EDUCAZIONE PER TUTTA LA VITA», 2016. FrancoAngeli, Milano, pp 404–413

Panciroli C, Russo V, Macauda A (2017) When technology meets art: museum paths between real and virtual. In: Proceedings of international and interdisciplinary conference IMMAGINI? Image and imagination between representation, communication, education and psychology, Basel, MDPI, vol 1, no 9, 913, pp 1–14

Phillips M (2016) Re-contextualising TPACK: exploring teachers' (non-) use of digital technologies. Technol Pedag Educ 25(5):555–571

Polito MT (2006) L'indagine della Corte dei Conti sui musei di enti locali. In: Notiziario del Ministero per i beni e le attività culturali, Ufficio studi, n. 80-82, gennaio-dicembre

Reid NS (2013) Carving a strong identity: investigating the life histories of museum educators. J Mus Educ 38(2):227–238

Rossi PG (2009) Tecnologia e costruzione di mondi Post-costruttivismo, linguaggi e ambienti di apprendimento. Armando Editore, Roma

Rossi PG (2016a) Dall'uso del digitale nella didattica alla didattica digitale. Atti Convegno SIREM

Rossi PG (2016b) Gli artefatti digitali e i processi di mediazione didattica. Pedagogia Oggi 2:11–26

Rossi PG, Toppano E (2009) Progettare nella società della conoscenza. Carocci, Roma

Russo V (2015) Il progetto "Formare al Patrimonio della scuola": per un'indagine sulla qualità delle esperienze educative. In: Panciroli C (ed) Formare al Patrimonio nella scuola e nei musei, Bolzano, QuiEdit, pp 136–172

Sani M (2005) Musei e lifelong learning. Esperienze educative rivolte agli adulti nei musei europei. Istituto per i Beni Artistici Culturali e Naturali della Regione Emilia Romagna

Sani M, Trombini A (2003) La qualità nella pratica educativa al museo. Editrice Compositori, Bologna

Silvaggi A, Pesce F, Surace R, (a cura di) (2016) Musei del futuro. Competenze digitali per il cambiamento e l'innovazione in Italia, Progetto Mu.SA - Museum Skills Alliance 2016–2019, Erasmus + European Commission

Simondon G (2009) Entretien sur mecanologie. Revue de synthèse 130(6):103–132

Solima L (2000) Il pubblico dei musei: indagine sulla comunicazione nei musei statali italiani, Ministero per i beni e le attività culturali. Ufficio studi, Roma

Wenger E (1998) Communities of practice: learning, meaning and identity. Cambridge University Press, Cambridge

Zbuchea A (2013) Human resources management in the education departments of museum: a worwide survey. Manag Mark Chall Knowl Soc 8(3):479–510

Calculating the Social Impact of Culture.
A SROI Application in a Museum

Federica Viganó[1]([✉]) and Giovanni Lombardo[2]

[1] Faculty of Education, Free University of Bolzano,
viale Ratisbona 16, 39042 Brixen-Bressanone, Italy
Federica.vigano@unibz.it
[2] Management and Business Engineering Department,
University of Genoa, Genoa, Italy

Abstract. The paper presents an application of the SROI method to the case of culture and the social impacts of cultural institutions. The methodology is based on qualitative and quantitative evaluations and develops measurement proxies that refer back to financial measures, allowing to calculate the return in euros of a cultural investment.

Keywords: Social impact · Culture · Social Return On Investment

1 Introduction

The topic of impact measurement within the cultural sector, on both an individual and cultural level, dates back to the 1980's. Myerscough's study, "The economic importance of the Arts in Britain" (1988) is considered a cornerstone that started the evidence-based assessment of the economic impact of the cultural sector.

Until the 1980's the cultural sector had an auxiliary role within economic policy making at a local and international level, which confined culture to a secondary role, particularly with regards to resource generation. At the end of that decade, however, a series of studies on impact were conducted. These studies were mainly commissioned by local authorities and other public funding agencies that had an interest in understanding how this sector could play a larger role, especially in close connection with other strategic sectors such as tourism.

In the 1990's, particularly in Great Britain and the United States, it became increasingly important to prove that cultural values not only generated economic impact, but, crucially, social impact (as well as the traditional esthetic, spiritual, historical and symbolic impacts). The importance of the social impact of culture was evidenced by Françoise Matarasso, author of "Use or Ornament? The Social Impact of Participation in the Arts" (1997). Matarasso identified 50 different types of social impact within the cultural sector. His research gave impetus to the development of measurement techniques of these impacts, and in particular indicators relevant to the sector. These studies have enabled the identification of culture and cultural policies as an important area for policy agendas, while at the same time helping to counteract the tendency to exploit culture for political ends.

© Springer Nature Switzerland AG 2019
A. Luigini (Ed.): EARTH 2018, AISC 919, pp. 507–516, 2019.
https://doi.org/10.1007/978-3-030-12240-9_53

The last decade has been characterized by more holistic research and approaches, which in turn have increased the valuation of culture through the inclusion of new factors such as the environment and sustainability. David. C. Throsby, in his "Economy and Culture" of 2001, painted a very clear picture of the link between culture and sustainability, emphasizing how culture, like the environment, represents a resource (both tangible and intangible) that must be preserved for future generations, from both an inter-generational and intra-generational perspective. In recent years, the debate on measurement of culture has further diversified: studies on the evaluation of social impact have been developed by institutions such as museums, libraries, and individual cultural institutions, on events and festivals in municipalities, regions, and provinces – with a focus on culture-led development policies.

However, the question of measuring the impact of culture remains a big challenge both for the development of activities designed with a clear social purpose by cultural institutions, as well as for the continuing need for training and methodologies suitable for the cultural sector. This is due to the difficulty – and not just in of the field of culture - in establishing a direct causal link between actions taken and the social benefits achieved.

Coming to museums, there has been an increase in the scope of their purpose and role in recent years, which requires a greater effort to create awareness and to communicate that the value generated in society is of a multidimensional and complex nature. In particular, understanding and managing social significance is becoming increasingly relevant to inform both stakeholders (from visitors to employees and funding agencies) and policy makers on new evaluation systems that cultural institutions are using to provide concrete evidence of their work.

Amongst the different types of impacts created by the museum, social impact remains the most ambiguous and difficult to define, in comparison to economic and environmental impact. If on one hand, impact in the broad sense is explained by the change produced as a result of the work of the organization, the "social" impact should refer to the social consequences (in terms of education, health, social inclusion, urban revitalization) of different types of interventions and actions following interaction with the museum. Properly understood cultural effects should be associated with particular outcomes, such as a better understanding of the surrounding social environment, an increase in the propensity to participate in art/culture forms, or the growth and inner development of individuals.

2   The SROI Approach

Impact measurement is a topical issue for the company-organizational context, aimed at measuring the performance of companies in the economic, environmental and social fields.

Speaking of culture, the two most relevant concepts regarding the evaluation are those of impact and value. The theme of the "intrinsic value" of culture, connected to the difficulty of its measurement, is very actual, and in this vein lie the most recent methodologies for measuring cultural impact (Scott 2002, 2006; Selwood 2010). The difficulty lies in the capacity to find good proxies for intangible aspect, as it is not just a matter of collecting and monitoring data (Holden 2004) or calculating only the number of visitors, which, however important, it is unsuitable for expressing the multi-dimensional nature of the impacts generated by culture (Hooper-Greenhill 2004; Armbrecht 2014).

The SROI methodology, Social Return On Investment, is gaining ground as it gives quantitative evidence to intangible factors such as social and cultural impacts. There have not been many attempts to apply it in the cultural sector; its use can still be defined as pioneering. SROI has been adopted by cultural institutions that have incorporated social goals into their mission or where there is a strong social return on activities.

The SROI can be both evaluative and forecasting. The evaluative SROI is conducted retrospectively and therefore it is based on results already achieved. Meanwhile, the forecast SROI is used to predict how much social value will be created if the activities meet their outcomes. The latter can be very useful in the planning phases of one or more activities. It can help highlight how the "required" investment can maximize impact and is useful in identifying what should be measured once the project is in progress.

SROI methodology consists of five standard phases:

1. Defining the field of analysis and identifying and involving stakeholders.
2. Creation of an Impact Map, which is modeled through stakeholder engagement.
3. Highlighting outcomes and assigning them a value.
4. Impact Calculation. This phase allows us to estimate the risk of overestimating the tipping point analysis, thus ensuring that the impact evaluation is a precise and considered calculation.
5. The SROI calculation.

The general philosophy of this evaluation process passes through some principles: (a) the involvement of the interested parties in the evaluation; (b) some proxies with a quantitative definition are defined to express at the best the social value created; (c) a profile of "realism" is maintained in selecting the parameters and making evaluation choices; (d) the commitment to transparency and rigor of data evaluation; (e) the identification of monetary proxies; (f) the verification of the results (Arvidson et al. 2010a; Nicholls 2012; Millar and Hall 2012; SROI Network 2015; Whelan 2015).

The analysis uses mix methods, combining qualitative, quantitative and financial information to estimate the amount of "value", of mental health or well-being created or destroyed by a single activity or by a project or by the overall operation of an organization (Nicholls 2012; Paddon et al. 2014; Whelan 2015).

SROI is based on the so-called "Theory of change", oriented to explore how social change is achieved and what is the value created (Arvidson et al. 2010a). The challenge of applying this method lies in trying to quantify what can be hardly quantified, such as the trust generated by the work of an organization or an individual, the effects in terms of psychic and physical well-being, the attitudes on present and future behaviors.

The approach proved to be particularly advantageous in the museum sector because of its participatory nature and also because the application of the principles is often reflected in the mission and objectives of a museum. Furthermore, the methodology allows museums to give evidence of their responsibility - in line with the concept of social responsibility - and to offer a valuable learning opportunity as the greatest effort is concentrated on the identification of impacts that generate social value, and this result can be further embedded into the organizational culture (Rauscher et al. 2012).

Mostly the application of the SROI took place in the voluntary and community sector (Arts Council England 2012; Hull 2011; Museums of East Anglian Life 2011; SROI Network 2015; Wilson and Whelan 2014; Whelan 2015). In England there are significant examples of such application in the case of the museums of East Anglia (MEAL), Liverpool and Manchester.

Many museums, however, conducting the evaluation of SROI, often identify areas of activity that are purely social in nature and not related to the "core" activities of a museum (O'Brien 2010).

3 The Application of the SROI Method to the MUS.E Museum Association in Florence (Italy)

In 2017 the Florentine association MUS.E, which takes care of the enhancement of the heritage of the Florentine Civic Museums - including the Museum of Palazzo Vecchio, the Museo del Novecento, the complex of Santa Maria Novella, the Brancacci Chapel, the Fort of Belvedere and the Murate - and more generally of the city of Florence has undertaken the process of calculating its impacts (economic, social and environmental outcomes, meaning with these terms the effects on third parties and societies of the activities developed by the museums).

The desire to undertake this path has been strongly desired by the MUS.E Association, being an "in house" association, and thus part of the Museums themselves.

With regards to the MUS.E's socio-cultural and environmental impact, we refer to the economic, immaterial, social and environmental effects stemming from the activities carried out by the Association. There are both internal and external beneficiaries (for example, employees, visitors, local businesses, the environment, the local community, future generations, schools, families of students and other entities) that benefit from the cultural mediation activities conducted by MUS.E staff.

These effects are termed "externalities": costs and benefits that are not accounted for in the organization's balance sheet, falling on third party individuals or legal entities.

The latter, in turn, may have accounted for some of the effects of MUS.E's activity in their own financial statements (as in the case of suppliers) but, more frequently, external parties have had difficulty in providing a quantitative assessment of the costs or benefits derived from the existence of MUS.E. Culture in particular is seldom subjected to a qualitative estimate of the benefits it brings, in terms of well-being or health, and people are barely aware of the intangible costs and benefits produced by the system, networks, and "pivotal" external entities like MUS.E.

In the MUS.E evaluation, researchers have tried to develop proxies for the measurement of impacts deriving strictly from cultural activities. The overall scope of the proxy is the appetite for the consumption of cultural goods, which was verified through a series of semi-structured interviews. These interviews led to the shared development of more specific proxy assessments.

As part of the impact assessment, we interviewed a sample of various stakeholder groups in order to create a significant number of in depth accounts to assess the effects of "cultural mediation" on visitors, in the context of "change theory".

In the calculation of outputs and outcomes, it was necessary to interview the beneficiary stakeholders of the activities that were being analyzed.

The Social ROI returns an absolute value in Euros, which states how many Euros have been generated for every Euro invested. This is the actual value of the sum of the quantitative benefits experienced by parties other than the MUS.E Association (internal and, above all, external). Qualitative effects are converted into quantitative by using proxies, that is, variables that allow you to make a comparison by which you estimate the value of an underlying asset.

The impact has been categorized primarily in "economic", "social" and "cultural" terms.

For each type of survey, an appropriate "proxy" assessment was chosen and, in the context of the estimated impact, the effect over time was evaluated (duration).

The monetization methods used were "Cost-price based" (Incurred Losses Method, Hedonic Price Method, Cost Prevention Method, Travelling Costs Method) and "Value-price based" (contingent evaluation).

We performed a dead-weight analysis for each item, i.e. the impact or outcome calculation for each activity, and the value of the outcome without the associated activity. Equally, the weight of other factors in determining the outcome (attribution) and the reduction of the impact over time (drop-off) were also included (Table 1).

Table 1. Stakeholder, proxies and impacts

Initiatives/stakeholder	Measure of change	Impact generated (Euro)	Impact generated (%)	Type of impact
School Workshops	Out of approx. 30000 students, 5% are willing to increase the number of museum visits (from 2 a 4 per year, out of MUS.E's scope) and 10% are willing to pay up to 5 Euros per ticket, up from 2 Euros per ticket	13.119,00	0,52%	Economic/ cultural
"Musem in a Suitcase" for Elderlies' Institutes	80 senior citizens would be willing to pay to have access to the initiative and 40 have found value in similar experiences	9.720,00	0,38%	Social/cultural (wellbeing)

(*continued*)

Table 1. (*continued*)

Initiatives/stakeholder	Measure of change	Impact generated (Euro)	Impact generated (%)	Type of impact
Effects on hospitality and transport	The increase in the number of seats for lunch and dinner, use of public transport and overnight stays on guided tours of "secret paths", equal to 1 Italian person per day on Bank Holidays and 1 foreign person per day abroad, in a year	128.000,00	5,04%	Economic/ cultural
Attitudes to the consumption of cultural	The 1% of 87,000 visitors per year who changed their attitudes to the consumption of cultural goods, consisting of an increased number of days dedicated to culture and a rise in related spending	407.595,00	16,04%	Economic/ social/cultural
Institutional trust and new investments	The likelihood of increasing investment in MUS.E was used as a proxy for institutional trust and regard for skill levels of staff (from 10% to 50%)	1.558.550,00	61,32%	Economic/ cultural
Welfare and work/life balance	The inclination to spend more money, increased levels of calm, a decrease in use of medication, visits to a psychologist, use of baby sitter to deal with the fear of work contract not being renewed (10 people) other career benefits (marketability, time and money savings, increase in work/life balance) for 93 employees and/or contractors	424.528,00	16,70%	Economic/ social/cultural
Total impact		2.541.512,00	100,00%	

In relation to schools and young people, the appetite for cultural consumption increased and there is a willingness to pay a higher price for the same or equivalent service. This was evidenced in the evaluation by the increase in the number of structured visits managed by MUS.E, the increase in requests for teachers to plan museum visits in other cities, and the difference in the amount individuals were willing to pay for a ticket (in Euros). The estimate is very cautious, and significant deadweight, attribution and drop-off rates have been included in the calculation, as a sample could not be used in this first analysis that would ensure complete statistical relevance.

With regards to Elderlies' Institutes, where the "Museum in a Suitcase" initiative was carried out, we estimated the corresponding value of equivalent initiatives or other goods or services that would provide users with the same level of wellbeing, as well as the willingness to pay for a similar service. With about 120 respondents, the analysis has been significant, and the results essentially indicate how important it is for some elderly people to participate in interactive events such as cultural mediation. They are unique, generating psycho-physical well-being capable of reactivating the potential of the elderlies.

In the estimation of the effect on hospitality and transport, caterers, hoteliers and transport workers were interviewed, enabling us to profile the local Italian visitor, the family member who stayed for more than one day, and foreign users, who had a higher propensity to consume food and drink than Italians. Even then, this first evaluation is very conservative and, in the calculation, significant deadweight, attribution and drop-offs were included. The data seems to suggest that more focus should be placed on cultural mediation initiatives, as they are the source of a remarkable positive externality for traders in the historic center and the suburbs of Florence.

The fourth stage of analysis is crucial for an institution such as MUS.E, precisely because it is related to its mission: attitudes to the consumption of cultural goods in tourists. In short, we assessed the inclination to invest in culture after having benefited from cultural mediation and guided tours from MUS.E. The findings indicated a change in the mindset of tourists, who decided to allocate a proportion of monthly budget to pay for more museum visits than in the past (taking into account salary and other lifestyle choices). This directly correlates with the Theory of Change in that the experience of cultural mediation has affected the user to such a degree as to that they will increase their spending on other similar experiences. This applies to the city of Florence, the rest of Italy and the world, generating a multiplication factor for the whole sector.

With regards to the fifth part of the assessment, the members' trust in the management, administration and operation of the institution was assessed through interviews. Based the good results of MUS.E's "mediation" initiatives, members were willing to entrust additional services to their Association to such an extent that contributions would increase by up to 50%. In the final calculation, however, the researchers included several deductions to arrive at a conservative estimate that would articulate the real depth of impact, or how much change has been affected in the city's institutions, so as to modify municipal planning and to increase the tasks entrusted to a well-known entity trusted by internal and external stakeholders.

In addition to cultural mediation initiatives, we have attempted to estimate the impact of initiatives on internal stakeholders, at the core of the above-mentioned activity. These activities could not be delivered without a suitable workplace. The employee is the most important stakeholder in certain respects. Individuals perform at their best when they have a good work/life balance, when they are recognized for their achievements and commitment to their work. By identifying "employee welfare" initiatives, work/life balance, career progression and the stabilization of contracts we evaluated - in this case with interviews - the effect of the management's initiatives in support of mothers and male employees who, in response to MUS.E's proposals, have changed the way use their free time, their fuel consumption, level of well-being, saved time and improved their skills and marketability.

The impact generated in 2016 by "cultural mediation", valued in Euros, is the sum of the components above and the increased profits made by the difference between the revenues of the mediation activities and the respective costs (staff and overheads). From the impact assessment conducted with the use of proxies, a figure of approximately € 3 million was reached, compared to the €1 million required in order to generate the impact. The final estimate of the SROI has been as follows: for each Euro invested in MUS.E, a benefit of three Euros has been generated (or more precisely, a "Social ROI" of 2.8).

4   Conclusions

The challenges in the application of SROI are far-reaching and, as with other methods of economic evaluation, its use has been criticized due to some aspects of methodological controversy, and for the ambition of restoring a monetary measure social impact (Arvidson et al. 2010a; Pathak and Dattani 2014).

Some of the aspects most criticized in the literature are related to the discretion in the choice and definition of the indicators; the quantification of the value of the benefits that may affect an entire service or just one aspect and rarely the entirety of the factors that produce the impacts, leaving a preference share agreed between the parties involved. However, as in Arvidson et al. (2010b), there are also advantages in this methodology that he defines as "pragmatic" and "flexible": it can be applied in many sectors and even in single initiatives, provided that it is correctly defined and transparent the type of impact that we want to measure, without pretending to estimate the totality of the social impacts generated.

The research frontier on these methodologies is extremely lively and evolving because on the one hand it reflects the state of continuous experimentation in the field of impact measurement, on the other it is generated by the need of some specific sectors, including the cultural one, to find effective methods to report and measure the effects of their work.

Acknowledgements. The activity presented in the paper has been developed in close collaboration with the staff of MUS.E in Florence, with which the researchers are in debt.

References

Armbrecht J (2014) Developing a scale for measuring the perceived value of cultural institutions. Cultural Trends 23:252–272

Arts Council England (2012) Measuring the economic benefits of art and culture. Arts Council England, London

Arvidson M, Lyon F, McKay S, Moro D (2010a) Briefing Paper 49: the ambitions and challenges of SROI. Third Sector Research Sector, Birmingham

Arvidson M, Lyon F, McKay S, Moro D (2010b) Valuing the social? The nature and controversies of measuring social return on investment. Third Sector Research Centre, Birmingham

Holden J (2004) Capturing cultural value. How culture has become a tool of government policy. Demos, London

Hooper-Greenhill E (2004) Measuring learning outcomes in museums, archives and libraries: "the learning impact research project (LIRP)". Int J Heritage Stud. 10:151–174

Hull D (2011) Assessing the value and impact of museums. Northern Ireland Assembly, Belfast

Matarasso F (1997) Use or ornament? The social impact of participation in the arts. Comedia, Stroud

Millar R, Hall K (2012) Social return on investment (SROI) and performance measurement. Public Manag. Rev. 15:923–941

Myerscough J (1988) The economic importance of the arts in Britain. Policy Studies Institute, London

Museums of East Anglian Life (2011) Investing in culture and community. Museums of East Anglian Life, Stowmarket

Nicholls J (2012) A guide to social return on investment. SROI Network, Liverpool

O'Brien D (2010) Measuring the value of culture: a report to the department for culture media and sport. Department for Culture Media and Sport, London

Paddon HL, Thomson LJ, Menon U, Lanceley AE, Chatterjee HJ (2014) Mixed methods evaluation of well-being benefits derived from a heritage-in-health intervention with hospital patients. Arts Health: Int J Res Policy Pract 6:24–58

Pathak P, Dattani P (2014) Social return on investment: three technical challenges. Soc Enterp J 10:91–104

Rauscher O, Schober C, Millner R (2012) Social impact measurement and social return on investment analysis. New methods of economic evaluation? In: Working paper. Wirtschafts Universitat, Vienna

Rotheroe N, Richards A (2007) Social return on investment and social enterprise: transparent accountability for sustainable development. Soc Enterp J 3:31–46

Scott C (2002) Measuring social value. In: Sandell R (ed) Museums, society, inequality. Routledge, London, pp 41–55

Scott C (2006) Museums: impact and value. Cultural Trends 15:45–75

Selwood S (2010) Making a difference: the cultural impact of museums. Sara Selwood Associates, London

SROI Network (2015) What is SROI? http://www.thesroinetwork.org/what-is-sroi

Throsby D (2001) Economics and culture. Cambridge University Press, Cambridge

Tyne and Wear Archives and Museums (2012) Young people surprise city centre shoppers with creative flashmobs. http://www.twmuseums.org.uk/latest/watch-listen/young-people-surprise-city-centre-shoppers-with-creative-flashmobs.html

Whelan G (2015) Understanding the social value and well-being benefits created by museums: a case for social return on investment methodology. Arts Health 7(3):216–230

Wilson K, Whelan G (2014) An evaluation of house of memories dementia training programme, midlands model September 2014. Institute of Cultural Capital and National Museums Liverpool, Liverpool

Immersive

Travelling Salesperson in an Immersive Virtual Environment: Experimental Evaluation of Tracking System Device

D. Basso[1,2(✉)], C. Saracini[2,3], P. Palladino[4], and M. Cottini[4]

[1] Cognitive and Educational Sciences Lab (CESLab),
Faculty of Education, Free University of Bozen-Bolzano,
Viale Ratisbona 16, 39042 Bressanone, Bolzano, Italy
demis.basso@unibz.it

[2] Research Center in Neuropsychology and Cognitive Neuroscience
(CINPSI Neurocog), Universidad Católica del Maule (UCM), Talca,
Avenida San Miguel 3605 – Laboratorio de Psicologia,
Edificio Parque Tecnologico UCM, 3460000 Talca, Maule, Chile

[3] Vicerrectoría de Investigación y Postgrado (VRIP), Universidad Católica del
Maule (UCM), Avenida San Miguel 3605 – Laboratorio de Psicologia,
Edificio Parque Tecnologico UCM, 3460000 Talca, Maule, Chile

[4] Department of Brain and Behavioral Sciences, University of Pavia,
Piazza Botta 11, 27100 Pavia, Italy

Abstract. Nowadays Virtual Reality (VR) is an extremely versatile technology capable to cope with many areas of human life, and its fast development requires constant evaluation and validation. Cognitive models of human behavior play a central role in this evaluation, aiming at obtaining high quality, safe and usable products. A problem currently faced by VR users inside immersive Virtual Environments (iVEs) consists in the Simulator-induced Sickness (SS), a particular kind of motion sickness evoked by the simulated visual motion. SS can reduce subjects' performances, and bias data collected with VR. Although Tracking Systems (TS) were thought to reduce SS symptoms, their effective contribution is not clear. A task based on the Traveling Salaperson was implemented in an iVE to investigate whether TS (a) evoked less SS symptoms and (b) facilitated performance in participants with respect to a control condition without TS. Results showed that TS allowed reduction of many SS symptoms, but this did not produced clear benefits on the cognitive performance, mainly true for female subjects. While TSs may facilitate enjoyment of iVE reducing SS, the higher susceptibility of females suggested that VR designers and producers should consider valuable a certain training before using the iVEs.

Keywords: Tracking System · Visuospatial planning · Navigation ·
Simulator sickness · Immersive virtual environments · Gender

© Springer Nature Switzerland AG 2019
A. Luigini (Ed.): EARTH 2018, AISC 919, pp. 519–529, 2019.
https://doi.org/10.1007/978-3-030-12240-9_54

1   Introduction

Virtual Reality (VR) is a cutting-edge technology currently supporting several fields of human knowledge and application thanks to its possibility to create nearly infinite safe, controlled and versatile Virtual Environments (VEs). Apart from the entertainment industry, which is one of the most fruitful application of VR products, its use for Virtual Trainings (VTs) is common in many professional areas (Hansen 2008). In facts, they allow a safe simulation of complex operations and dangerous situations or machineries diminishing many costs for the same kind of trainings in real life. As Burdea and Coiffet (2003) defined it, "Virtual Reality is a high-end user interface that involves real-time simulation and interactions through multiple sensorial channels. These sensorial modalities are visual, auditory, tactile, smell, and taste" and contribute to the the three "I"s: Immersion, Interaction, and Imagination. Despite the fact that fruition of this technology involve human interaction, the majority of studies performed on VR belongs to other fields than psychology, mainly focusing on technical (e.g., engineering, design) or applicative fields (e.g., architecture, medicine).

Possible risks when technology for human people is developed without considering cognitive aspect consist in obtaining superficial results or producing unusable products (Norman 1988). A diffuse problem amongst the VR designers and implementers is related to unwanted side-effects (called in general "cybersickness", or "Simulator-induced Sickness": SS). VR tools such as the Head Mounted Displays (HMDs), allow completely filling people's Field of View (FoV) with a virtual scenario. They are referred to as "immersive Virtual Environment" (iVEs), which produce a very strong "sense of presence" (IJsselsteijn et al. 2000) that could lead to the complete perceptual immersion in the artificial environment. These features surely entail big advantages but also drawbacks, as they convey higher SS symptoms rates amongst users. Some people are indeed extremely sensible to the simulated optic flow inside the VS, and they might experience a very unpleasant set of symptoms ranging from nausea and vomiting to cold sweating, pallor of varying degrees, increases in salivation, drowsiness, headache, and even severe pain (Lackner 2014). By means of a Visualization System (VS), people may experience a condition defined as visually induced Motion Sickness (MS: Kennedy et al. 2010). MS is a complex syndrome originated by a physiological mis-match between what is perceived by the visual system at any moment, and how proprioceptive and kinesthetic information is being processed in a brain area called Vestibular Nucleus (VN), which give *online* information about the position of the body and body parts allowing an anticipated "internal model" (Tal et al. 2014). The VN has been suggested to play a role in visual-vestibular sensory conflict and possibly in forming that "internal model" (Roy and Cullen 2004). This "sensory conflict and neural mismatch" theory has been confirmed by following studies (see Zhang et al. 2016 for a review). A recurrent result showed gender differences in susceptibility to MS, which may be related to linear components of imposed motion (Koslucher et al. 2015). The SS problem has been considered in high-end graphics computers, and a series of technical developments tried to eliminate it. In particular, the use of Tracking System (TS) has been proposed to be a satisfactory solution to the SS, since it is able to continuously collect the position of users' body and, accordingly, to project in real-time the appropriate visual perspective of the virtual scenario (Villard et al. 2008). The benefits of reducing cybersickness symptoms in an iVE are of great importance when data are collected in VR, since discomforts may alter participant's performance, and this could produce biased data and results. A special kind of iVE with respect to the above mentioned VSs is represented by the Elbe Dom in Magdeburg (Germany), which allow the use of movement tracking for VEs presentation. In "normal" conditions (i.e., without TS), subjects stand on the platform in a static position and have to turn left and right with a joystick to navigate inside the environment and decide where to go (similarly to a first-person 3D game), generally reporting SS symptoms as the 3D scenario moves around them to fit the direction they want to walk through. By using the TS device, they can decide the direction by rotating their bodies and heads left, right and back to. They just need to use the "forward" command of the joystick to move forward, and the optic flow will be simulated according to their current position. According to the literature presented above, this is supposed to reduce the mismatch between the visually perceived optic flow and the proprioceptive feedback of the users, thus limiting MS symptoms.

The present experiment involved navigation in the iVE and has been run to evaluate (a) use and benefits of the tracking device for interaction and navigation in iVEs, and (b) whether TS may reduce SS symptoms. A cognitive experimental task a 3D version of the Maps Test (Basso et al. 2001) has been used. The 3D Maps Test has already been tested in computerized versions (3D graphics and desktop presentation: Saracini et al. 2008, 2010), and involved cognitive processes such as visuospatial planning and working memory and survey-to-route navigation. We hypothesized that the use of TS would reduce SS symptoms and, in turn, improve performance in the cognitive task. Gender differences were also expected, considering that both SS susceptibility and 3D Maps Task (Saracini et al. 2008) have shown that females produce higher affection and worst result, respectively.

2   Materials and Methods

Participants. The sample consisted in 24 participants (10 males, 14 females), age range: 19–32. All of them had normal or corrected-to-normal vision, gave written informed consent for participation to the study.

VR 3D Maps Task. The Maps Task (Basso et al. 2001) is an open version of the Travelling Salesperson Problem (TSP). The goal consists in visiting all the proposed spatial locations on a map, performing the shortest route in the shortest time. The 3D Maps Test offers the same task in an environment allowing first-person navigation inside the VE. The task consisted in two stages: at the beginning of each trial, a survey map of the environment made of a regular grid was shown to participants to let them plan their own strategy for an optimized route through the subgoals. Each one of the 20 trials showed a different configuration of the subgoals, located onto the 2D space. When the participant was ready, she was presented with the tridimensional view of the same map navigating in route (or "first-person": see Fig. 1) perspective, and started to move into the environment. In the virtual version of this task (VR 3D Maps) used in the present study, subjects had to collect 7 blue balls until the final red ball. The green ball represented the starting point, and was depicted in the 2D representation only. After achievement of the red target, the participant left the map, and a feedback about the performed route was presented in survey perspective.

Fig. 1. The sequence of the task is shown: (a) the survey view of the Map, showing the targets (balls) configuration when the participant could plan her route; (b) then the 3D iVE was presented and she navigated in first-person (route) perspective through the maze until she reached (c) the ending point; (d) after leaving the Map, a feedback was given to the participant with a red line showing the path actually performed.

Paper and Pencil Tests. Before starting the experimental session, participants filled in an anamnestic questionnaire with general questions (age, time spent at the computer, videogames experience) and performed the following paper and pencil cognitive tests: the Trail Making Test (TMT, both A and B versions; Reitan 1958), the Corsi Block Tapping Test and the set I from the Raven's progressive Matrices (Raven 1938). After the virtual experience, all the participants answered to another set of questionnaires. The Simulator Sickness Questionnaire (SSQ: Kennedy et al. 1992) involved 16 items, whose values ranged from 0 (no presence at all of the symptom) to 3 (abnormal presence of the symptom), according to their current physical state. The Immersive Tendencies Questionnaire (ITQ: Witmer and Singer 1998) produced 3 scales by using 18 items (range 0–5): Focus, Involvement and Games. The Presence questionnaire (PQ: Witmer and Singer 1998) produced 4 scales through 19 items (range 0–5): Visual fidelity, Involvement, Adaptation/immersion, Interface quality.

Elbe Dom and Tracking System. The Elbe Dom is a 360° quasi-cylindrical projection system of 6.5 m height and 16 m diameter spanning an approximately 330 m^2 surface area built from the Fraunhofer Institute. The wall is an enormous screen where VEs were projected in a realistic high-quality images of 1:1 dimension with respect to the observer, who stand on a circular platform in the center and had the illusion of ground projection thanks to a constriction of the lower portion of the screen. A cluster of 7 high-end PCs controlled the image generation of each of the projectors, the seventh also supplying the geometry and kinematics data for the other nodes and synchronizes them. The system allows both an "untracked" and "tracked" presentation of VEs. TS was realized by twelve MX-13 IR cameras and a tracking cap/collar with three passive IR markers give the possibility to the participant to simply rotate with her body in order to perform a rotation (left or right) in the virtual environment and use the "forward" joystick key to move forward.

Experimental Procedure. Each subject entered the Elbe Dom and received a brief explanation about the VE materials. They read and signed the informed consent where aims, procedures and eventual risks of the study were exposed. Then they were faced with the anamnestic questionnaire and with half of the paper-and-pencil questionnaires (randomly rotated between participants). After that, the experimenter explained the task and the joystick functioning, while participants assigned to the "Tracking" condition were also prepared for the tracking cap (factor Device, two levels: Tracking and noTracking). Two familiarization tasks were performed as a training for the participants, before starting with the experimental session. Each participant performed a series of 20 VR 3D Maps, which lasted from 30 to 50 min (depending on participant's speed). At the end of each path, participants were asked whether they followed the planned route or changed the plan during execution (binomial variable: Plan). At the end of the experiment, they were asked to fill in the SSQ, and were invited to take a rest and sit down as long as they needed to wait for any discomfort to completely vanish. After that time, they were asked to fill in the other half of paper-and-pencil tasks, which were not administered before. In the end, they received a short debriefing, describing methodology and goals of the experiment. The total duration of the procedure was approximately of 2 h for each participant.

Data Analysis. The computerized VR 3D Maps test automatically recorded, for each trial, the path executed by the participants. From the videos, the following measures were collected: initial preplanning time (IPT, that is: the time between the appearance of subgoals and the first movement), execution time (that is, the time from the first movement to the achievement of the final goal), the intermediate time and distance between every couple of subgoals an array of 2×8 values) and, consequently, the order in which sub-goals were achieved. The intermediate distance between sub-goals considered the corner-to-corner distance only, not including, e.g., variability due to inaccurate movements. This decision was made in order not to count this source of variability two times, since it is already included in the execution time (in facts, a series of corrections in the path, due to feedback-feedforward cycles always result in higher time). Additional variables of interest were calculated upon the previous measures. The total distance produced the StepPAO variable, which was calculated as the percentage distance above the shorter distance required to execute that path. Therefore, the more

StepPAO approximates to zero, the closer is the corresponding trajectory to the optimal solution. A planning index (PI) was calculated dividing the intermediate time between each sub-goal of the path by the corresponding number of intermediate distances. PI was created to obtain a series of measures (one for each sub-goal, excluding the first and the last one) weighted by the relative distance of the sub-goals in the situation. Then, a mean (meanPI) and a variance (varPI) of the PI were calculated for each path in order to summarize the PI array. MeanPI was considered an estimate of the cognitive effort devoted by participants to plan and execute the path, including additional information on the motor execution, while VarPI was associated to the variability of this effort during the path (for additional details: Cazzato et al. 2010).

A $2 \times 2 \times 2$ between-subjects ANOVA was run aimed at determining differences on the total score of SSQ due to Device, modulated by Gender and Experience. Then, performances in the VR 3D Maps task were analyzed through a series of mixed-effects regression models, by using the lme4 package in R (Bates et al. 2014). The following measures taken from the Maps task were considered as dependent variables: IPT, Execution time, StepPAO, MeanPI and VarPI, and a series of mixed model (one for each dependent variable) was fitted using the following structure. The five fixed factors were: Gender (two levels: males, females), Device (two levels: noTracking, Tracking), their interactions, Experience and Plan (no, yes). Then, the twelve continuous fixed-effect predictors were: visuo-spatial Working Memory (vsWM: results of the Corsi block tapping task), TMT-A (visual search), TMT-BA (divided attention), Raven (global intelligence), the total score of SSQ, the three scales of the ITQ, and the four subscales of the PQ. The random effects considered in the model were Trial (to control for the various stimuli presented) and Participants (to account for individual differences). Each model started by including all the variables listed before; then, the fitted model was submit to the automatic backfitting function "step" (lmerTest package version 2.0-33: Kuznetsova et al. 2015) in order to reduce the list of predictors to just the significant ones.

3   Results

The ANOVA run on the total score of the SSQ showed the significant main effects of Device: $F(1, 60) = 7.951$, p. < 0.01, $\eta_p^2 = 0.12$ and Gender: $(F(1, 60) = 70.119$, p. < 0.01, $\eta_p^2 = 0.54$, while neither Experience, nor their interaction were significant. The amount of discomfort was lower in the Tracking condition than the control condition, and in males than in females (Tracking-males $= 0.18 \pm 0.04$; Tracking-females $= 0.48 \pm 0.04$ NoTracking-males $= 0.25 \pm 0.04$; NoTracking-females $= 0.64 \pm 0.04$).

The Tracking condition produced significantly lower scores than the no-tracking condition in all four variables, while Gender produced mixed results. Given that their interaction was significant, it is worth to describe it instead of the single predictors.

Four participants (all females, balanced for Device) were not able to complete the tasks in the iVE, thus they were excluded from the following analyses. The results obtained from the five mixed-models are represented in Table 1.

Table 1. Results of the mixed-models for the five dependent variables. From the left to the right: Initial Planning Time, Execution Time, StepPAO, MeanPI and VarPI. We reported the beta value (positive coefficients indicate higher values for the dependent variable; when associated to factors they indicate an adjustment to Intercept, whereas when associated with continuous variables they indicate an adjustment to the slope), the associated standard error, the t- and p-values. If a main effect was part of significant interaction, it is represented regardless of its significance level. SE = Standard Error, SD = Standard Deviation.

Fixed effects	Initial Planning Time			Execution Time			StepPAO			MeanPI			VarPI		
	β(SE)	t	p	β(SE)	t	p	β(SE)	t	p	β(SE)	t	p	β(SE)	t	p
Intercept (Device=noTrack, Strategy=Constant, Gender=Males, Experience=No, Plan=No)	10.231(0.421)	24.349	<0.001	10.888(0.385)	28.282	<0.001	0.173(0.119)	1.451	0.167	8.551(0.153)	55.969	<0.001	7.686(0.816)	9.416	0.003
Device=Track	-0.115(0.103)	-1.120	0.325	-0.424(0.077)	-5.487	0.012	/			-1.160(0.080)	-14.431	<0.001	-1.498(0.303)	-4.948	0.016
Gender=F	0.014(0.175)	0.083	0.938	-1.192(0.105)	-11.405	0.002	/			-1.103(0.059)	-18.579	<0.001	-1.281(0.244)	-5.261	0.014
Experience=Yes	-1.161(0.230)	-5.057	0.007	-1.211(0.142)	-8.555	0.003	/			-0.066(0.024)	-2.683	0.008	-0.792(0.282)	-2.808	0.068
Plan=Yes	/			-0.094(0.030)	-3.101	0.002	-0.087(0.023)	-3.750	<0.001	0.178(0.015)	12.048	<0.001	-0.362(0.106)	-3.431	0.001
ITQ_focus	0.137(0.057)	2.413	0.073	0.192(0.026)	7.395	0.005	/			-0.079(0.007)	-11.246	<0.001	/		
ITQ_invol	-0.068(0.026)	-2.607	0.060	-0.084(0.012)	-6.762	0.007	/			-0.041(0.008)	-5.186	<0.001	/		
ITQ_games	0.130(0.019)	6.686	0.003	-0.036(0.014)	-2.597	0.081	/			-0.029(0.005)	-6.373	<0.001	/		
PQ_visfid	0.269(0.050)	5.381	0.006	0.209(0.033)	6.246	0.008	/			0.197(0.019)	10.386	<0.001	0.413(0.119)	3.459	0.041
PQ_invol				-0.031(0.007)	-3.934	0.029	/						-0.095(0.031)	-3.088	0.054
PQ_adapt	-0.059(0.020)	-2.893	0.044				/								
PQ_ifqual	-0.181(0.026)	-6.867	0.002	-0.208(0.018)	-11.513	0.001	/			-0.206(0.010)	-20.062	<0.001	-0.280(0.049)	-5.767	0.011
SS_tot	/			/			/			/			-0.155(0.027)	-5.672	0.011
TMT-A	-0.039(0.013)	-3.048	0.038	-0.033(0.006)	-5.254	0.014	/			-0.040(0.004)	-11.044	<0.001	0.081(0.021)	3.859	0.031
TMT-BA	/			/			/			0.004(0.001)	5.723	<0.001	/		
Raven	-0.173(0.047)	-3.686	0.021	-0.181(0.021)	-8.707	0.003	/			-0.153(0.012)	-12.950	<0.001	-0.181(0.056)	-3.213	0.049
GenderF × DeviceTrack	0.667(0.193)	3.458	0.026	1.092(0.145)	7.512	0.005	0.1407(0.094)	1.501	0.135	0.873(0.083)	10.572	<0.001	1.881(0.445)	4.230	0.025
Random effects	SD			SD			SD			SD			SD		
Trial	0.117			0.035			<0.001			0.023			0.140		
Participants	0.046			0.054			0.070			0.000			0.154		
Residuals	0.348			0.166			0.128			0.136			0.580		

All the models fitted, indicating that the set of predictors were able to explain a significant part of the variance of the dependent measures. Importantly, when a variable was excluded during the backfitting procedure, it should not be considered as relevant predictor. Moreover, the significance of random effect for Trial and Participants throughout all the models indicated significant variability in the overall performance of each participant, and between the various stimuli. These sources of variability were taken into account, producing an improvement for the fit of the models.

In all models (except the one with StepPAO as dependent), many variables achieved the significant threshold. In order to increase readability of the models, we decided to split the description of results describing first the interactions between Device and Gender separated for the dependent variable (on IPT, execution time, meanPI and varPI), and then evaluating results of the paper-and-pencil tests.

The four patters are presented in Fig. 2. The difference on IPT between males and females was higher in the Tracking condition than in the control condition. The effect size estimated for the model on IPT was $r^2 = .76$. Males' execution time was higher than females in the NoTracking condition but was lower in the Tracking condition while, in general, the execution time was higher in the former than in the latter condition. The effect size of the model on execution time was $r^2 = .86$. Both mean and variance of PI were higher for females in the Tracking condition rather than in the males and in the control condition. In the control condition, while the meanPI was not different between genders, the dispersion of values was higher in males than in females. The effect size of the models was $r^2 = .89$ and $r^2 = .53$ for meanPI and varPI respectively. The factors Experience and Plan emerged as significant predictors in all models except for StepPAO and IPT, respectively. Higher prior experience with 3D games produced lower values in the variables. When participants told to have followed the plan created before execution, the values for execution time, StepPAO and varPI were significantly lower, while they increased for meanPI. Indeed, the factor Plan was the only significant predictor for the model using StepPAO (the effect size was $r^2 = .40$).

In the ITQ questionnaire, no subscale was able to predict varPI. Focus was positively related to IPT and execution time, while negatively with meanPI; Involvement was inversely related to all three dependent variables, while Games was direct predictor of IPT but inverse predictor for execution time and meanPI. In the PQ questionnaire, the subscales Visual fidelity and Interface quality predicted, respectively, a positive and a negative relationship with all four models. Other negative relationships were found for Adaptation and IPT, and for Involvement with both execution time and varPI. While visual search (TMT-A) was positive predictor for varPI, it was negatively related to the other three dependent variable. Instead, divided attention (TMT-B) was positive predictor for meanPI. Fluid intelligence (Raven) was a negative predictor in all four models. Finally, the total score of SSQ was a negative predictor for varPI only.

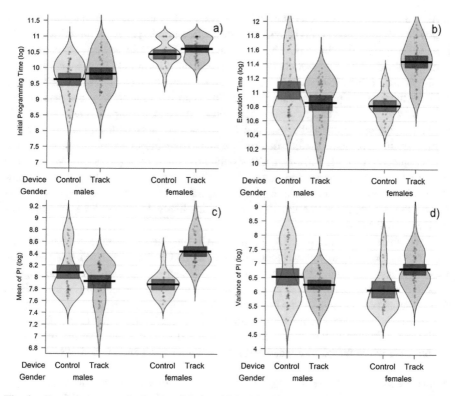

Fig. 2. Graphs represent the four models in which a significant interaction between Device and Gender was found. For each condition, boxplots indicate median (black line) and quartiles. The width of the shaded area for the violin plots represents the proportion of data located there. Gray points represent each single value for all participants.

4 Discussion

Results of the present study confirmed the hypothesis that TS can mitigate SS symptoms while navigating in an iVE. Participants in the Tracking group performed better throughout the several variables with respect to the group that did not use that device. SS symptoms were experienced less in the Tracking than in the NoTracking condition. Similarly to previous evidence, females were more likely to experience SS symptoms than males, therefore confirming the higher susceptibility in women to suffer from SS in iVEs. It is worth noting that, due to the discomfort, 4 females decided to quit the experiment, irrespectively to the device used.

A certain impact of the device was produced also on the performance of the VR 3D Maps task. In males the results in the Tracking condition was slightly better than in the NoTracking one, for all variables. In the female sample, the Tracking condition was worse than the control condition. This result may not be explained by personal factors such as the previous experience in playing similar videogames. Notwithstanding the pattern of results are consistent to Grön et al. (2000), in which women would show worse performances with respect to men in spatial tasks (and, in particular, navigation). A possible explanation could be based on the switch of perspective required when they have to navigate, after that a plan has been prepared on a 2D survey representation. For example, the cognitive cost of changing reference while turning left/right with the body could produce higher execution times. In a future study, this hypothesis could be tested by investigating the personal ability in dealing with the route/survey perspectives. In the meanwhile, the several subscales obtained by the paper-and-pencil tests showed to explain a relevant part of the variance for many measures of the planning task. In particular, involvement, quality of the interface, fluid intelligence and visual search exerted general a facilitation effect. Consistently to Fanini et al. (2018), higher usability of the iVE can improve performance. On the contrary, visual fidelity generally produced higher times and intermediate need of planning (meanPI): it may be possible that those who evaluated better the iVE were more likely to spend time on attributes irrelevant to the task.

Two main conclusion could be proposed. On the one hand, the use of a Tracking System showed a significant reduction of symptoms. On the other hand, this reduction was not reflected on the performance with a clear pattern. In general, we would suggest sensitive people/females to take a testing/training phase before entering in the iVE, so that personal reaction/symptoms could be either detected or mitigated. On how to use the interaction device should be included. As a concluding remark, psychological evaluation of devices showed to produce relevant data about the man-machine interaction, e.g., while people are faced with technologies such as iVE and VS.

Acknowledgements. The activity presented in the paper was part of a BMBF framed project research, namely the ViERforES project (www.vierfores.de), from the Fraunhofer IFF in Magdeburg. We thank Dr. Eberhard Blümel and the other collaborators from the Virtual Development Training Centre for the support and cooperation.

References

Basso D, Bisiacchi PS, Cotelli M, Farinello C (2001) Planning times during traveling salesman's problem: differences between closed head injury and normal subjects. Brain Cogn 46(1–2):38–42

Bates D, Maechler M, Bolker B, Walker S (2014) lme4: linear mixed-effects models using "Eigen" and S4. https://cran.rproject.org/web/packages/lme4/lme4.pdf

Burdea GC, Coiffet P (2003) Virtual reality technology. Wiley, New York

Cazzato V, Basso D, Cutini S, Bisiacchi PS (2010) Gender differences in visuospatial planning: an eye movements study. Behav Brain Res 206(2):177–183

Grön G, Wunderlich PA, Spitzer M, Tomczak R, Riepe MW (2000) Brain activation during human navigation: gender-different neural networks as substrate of perfor-mance. Nat Neurosci 3(4):404–408

Fanini B, Pagano A, Ferdani D (2018) A novel immersive VR game model for recontextual-ization in virtual environments: the μVR model. Multimodal Technol Interact 2(2):20

Hansen MM (2008) Versatile, immersive, creative and dynamic virtual 3-D healthcare learning environments: a review of the literature. J Med Internet Res. 10(3):e26

IJsselsteijn WA, de Ridder H, Freeman J, Avons SE (2000) Presence: concept, determinants, and measurement. In: Human vision and electronic imaging V, vol 3959. International Society for Optics and Photonics, pp 520–530

Kennedy RS, Drexler J, Kennedy RC (2010) Research in visually induced motion sickness. Appl Ergon 41(4):494–503

Kennedy RS, Fowlkes JE, Berbaum KS, Lilienthal MG (1992) Use of a motion sickness history questionnaire for prediction of simulator sickness. Aviat Space Environ Med 63:588–593

Koslucher F, Haaland E, Malsch A, Webeler J, Stoffregen TA (2015) Sex differences in the incidence of motion sickness induced by linear visual oscillation. Aerosp Med. Hum Perform 86(9):787–793

Kuznetsova A, Brockhoff PB, Christensen RHB (2015) lmerTest: tests in linear mixed effects models. https://cran.r-project.org/web/packages/lmerTest/lmerTest.pdf

Lackner JR (2014) Motion sickness: more than nausea and vomiting. Exp Brain Res 232 (8):2493–2510

Norman D (1988) The psychology of everyday things. Basic Books, New York

Raven JC (1938) Raven's progressive matrices. Western Psychological Services, Los Angeles

Reitan RM (1958) Validity of the trail making test as an indicator of organic brain damage. Percept Mot Skills 8(3):271–276

Roy JE, Cullen KE (2004) Dissociating self-generated from passively applied head motion: neural mechanisms in the vestibular nuclei. J Neurosci 24:2102–2111

Saracini C, Basso D, Olivetti Belardinelli M (2008) A rTMS study of planning using the 3D maps task. In: Hölscher C (ed) Spatial cognition SC 2008 conference proceedings SFB/TR 8, Freiburg, pp 41–44

Saracini C, Masik S, Wienert O, Basso D, Blümel E, Olivetti Belardinelli M (2010) Influences of different visualization systems on performances in a planning and way-finding test. In: Spatial cognition 2010 doctoral colloquium proceedings, Mt. Hood, Portland

Tal D, Wiener G, Shupak A (2014) Mal de debarquement, motion sickness and the effect of an artificial horizon. J Vestib Res 24(1):17–23

Villard SJ, Flanagan MB, Albanese GM, Stoffregen TA (2008) Postural instability and motion sickness in a virtual moving room. Hum Factors 50(2):332–345

Witmer BG, Singer MJ (1998) Measuring presence in virtual environments: a presence questionnaire. Presence 7(3):225–240

Zhang LL, Wang JQ, Qi RR, Pan LL, Li M, Cai YL (2016) Motion sickness: current knowledge and recent advance. CNS Neurosci Ther 22(1):15–24

Displaying Performing Arts. The *Dumb Type* Case at Centre Pompidou-Metz

G. Peressini[✉]

School of Doctorate Studies in Architecture, City and Design, Track in Design
Science, Università Iuav di Venezia, Santa Croce 191, Venice, Italy
g.peressini@iuav.it

Abstract. The aim of this paper is to discuss the act of rethinking the theatrical play within an exhibition context. The framework of reference is that of the technologically-mediated scene, which places at its core the interaction between body, space and technology and which requires new methods for its analysis and development. This paper will analyse two case studies: the Digitalife 2017 exhibition in Rome, Italy and Dumb Type. Extra-Sensory Odissey, at the Centre Pompidou – Metz, France. These two examples represent potential strategies to exhibit and re-organise the technologically-mediated performance without one of the key elements of live performance: the presence of both audience and actors. We witness a change in the framework, moving from the idea of exhibition to that of environment (seen as an immersive space, built to reinforce the audience's experience of perception). In the last part, I offer three coexisting dimensions to think about such environments in theatre: active design, expositional and educational dimensions.

Keywords: Dumb type · Exhibition · Immersive environment ·
Education through digital media

1 The Question of Exhibition Within Performative Arts

While theatre is changing rapidly towards a more technological, interactive and digital form, the instruments to analyse what we observe are not evolving as quickly. The transition implies a new relationship between the space and performers-actors and the audience, but it should also involve the researchers and their methods. The points touched by this paper come from an act of rethinking live arts within exhibition spaces. An argument that is necessary precisely for the increasingly frequent mixture of disciplines, arts and knowledge. The researcher quite often still has to analyse such practices using books, photographs, frontal videos, which limit the fruition of the contemporary scenic experience, which, on the other hand, thanks to technology, entails a direct involvement of perception and of the audience's experience. It is clear that there is a need to find new ways to study performative arts, not to mention the necessary analysis of contemporary scene materials. Here we describe 'scene' as a broader definition of *live art*, as the vast and complex realm of theatre outside its 20-th century boundaries, which encompasses theatre, performance, installations, interactive multimedia landscapes, etc. The boundaries of such space are always fluid and changing.

© Springer Nature Switzerland AG 2019
A. Luigini (Ed.): EARTH 2018, AISC 919, pp. 530–535, 2019.
https://doi.org/10.1007/978-3-030-12240-9_55

The play is always an exhibition, therefore it is interesting to establish a new way of documenting the play, which is exhibitive. As it is obvious that it is impossible to exhibit the play itself, one needs to shift the focus to the objects that interact/have interacted with the play and, as such, gain new meaning and strength. In accepting exhibitions as real centres for study and documentations, we accept the absence of the performer, but we also reinstate the importance of live fruition by the spectator. The *remediation* (Bolter and Grusin 1999) of theatrical play should take as a core element the experience of audience perception. It is necessary to elaborate a new critical thought for the technologically- mediated scene.

The scene uses, plans and creates innovative technology that can influence the mood and a wide range of materials, either texts, objects, wearables or artefacts. Nowadays the question is made more complicated because materials are always more intangible, virtual and obsolescent. We move from a system of physical and identifiable objects, to a continuum of communicative, virtual and real landscapes. Such materials can become, in best case scenarios, installation environments, at once immersive and interactive for the audience, invented specifically for the exhibition. We present two recent experiences that allow us to rethink the role of documentation within the landscape of contemporary scene practices, by linking it to the question of exhibition. The first example is *Digitalife 2017* (Palazzo delle Esposizioni, Rome, 7th October 2017–7th January2018),[1] part of the RomaEuropa Festival of contemporary and per-formative arts. *Digitalife* now at its 8th edition, wants to explore new technologies through digital art by presenting six maxi installations and by rethinking the spaces of the Palazzo delle Esposizioni as if they were immersive architectures, six theatres engulfing the spectator. Among the installation, it is worth noticing <360> , the environment created by Austrian collective Granular-Synthetis (active between 1991–2003). First presented in 2002, the work is shown across 15 screens as a new form of virtual theatre.[2] The work is a 3D creation for AVIE (Advanced Visualization and Interaction Environment), a multi-media, cylinder-shaped architecture that engulfs the visitors within a 3D audio-visual universe. The spectators find themselves in a world that is made of colour, sound and visual noise. In order to make the most of the environment, the spectator needs to wear special 3D glasses and to stand up, moving and interacting with the space. In this way the spectator's ear enjoys the spatialisation of sound and, conversely, the eye enjoys the regimen of pure vision. The physical experience of the audience becomes part of the creative project, becoming the object of the work itself. Another exhibition from *Digitalife 2017* is Dumb Type *Memorandum Or Voyage*, soon to be discussed in this paper as part of the second case study: *Dumb Type. Extra-Sensory Odissey*.

---

[1] https://romaeuropa.net/digitalife-2017/.

[2] http://www.granularsynthesis.info/ns/?goto=360.

2   Materials from an Exhibition: Dumb Type at the Centre Pompidou-Metz

Dumb Type. Extra-Sensory Odissey (Centre Pompidou-Metz, 2th January–14th May 2018)[3] is a retrospective dedicated to the work of Dumb Type, a Japanese collective made of visual artists, video makers, performers, architects, designers and sound engineers. The collective was born in Kyoto in 1984 and it is one of the first examples of new media performance, which over the years gave birth to an experimental form of theatre, in which body and technology have interacted in the search for hybrid languages as a means to analyse how the overabundance of data and digital signals structures the contemporary mind and body.[4]

The *Dumb Type* exhibition rethinks the materials coming from the scene. Five installations showcase the collective's history and plays to advance a context of museum-like fruition. One of the installations was created specifically for the spaces of the Centre Pompidou in Metz. It comprises of three archival works that re-enact the performances of the collective prior the death of Teiji Furuhashi, who co-founded the group with Ryoji Ikeda and Shiro Takatani. The materials come from: *PleasureLife* (1988), then renamed *Playback* - twelve record players that play random fragments of voices, speeches and sound from transparent vinyls, which recreate the alienation of communication in the age of globalisation; *pH (*1990), where a large machine, similar to the scanner of a giant photocopier with neon pipes that is constantly moving slightly above the ground, as a metaphor of the continuous and extreme control of society over the individual; *S/N* (1994), the peak of Dumb Type's experience, Furuhashi's confession of his homosexuality and HIV diagnosis, of which remains a screen/gravestone with the words "love", "sex", "death" and "money" running on it. The three different shows are brought together to represent the poetic and aesthetic paradigm of the collective, which is characterised by the presence of electronic music and Japanese minimalism.

Lovers (1994) is an interactive installation by Teiji Furuhashi. The real-life size naked bodies of nine performers are projected on the walls of a square room, while moving, running or walking. Some markers detect the presence of the spectator and alter the movement's sequence accordingly; men and women cross paths and overlap, mimicking an impossible embrace. Another installation is *Data.tron* (2007) which is a visual installation by electronic music virtuoso Ryoji Ikeda. Every pixel of this installation is the result of the combination of mathematical principles and data available online. *Toposcan* (2013–2016) shows an Irish landscape on eight hi-res screens, which is deconstructed in the form of the pixels composing the image itself.

Lastly, *MOV* (2004) encompasses three of the collective's theatrical works following Furuhashi's death: *Memorandum* (1999), about the relationship between memory and technology, *[OR]* (1997), a reflection on love and death from an original idea by Teiji Furuhashi, *Voyage* (2002), about Darwin's diaries. A 16-metres long

---

[3] http://www.centrepompidou-metz.fr/dumb-type.

[4] For a deeper analysis of Dumb Type's work, see the recent Eckersall, P., Scheer, E., and Shintaro, F. (eds.) (2017). *The Dumb Type reader*. Museum Tusculanum Press.

screen shows the history of the collective with today's technologies, constituting a device to re-introduce Dumb Type's memory.

The exhibition itself becomes a large, unique immersive environment in which the spectator's perception is overstimulated. A large maze of black linoleum, lit only by the videos' strobe lights, in which each installation gains power when interacting with the others, both on a visual and on a sound level. The exhibition that is installation, going further from the documentary, to offer a visual and perceptive experience in which materials are re-introduced in a new device. The above-presented experiences put the immersive and environmental experience of the visitor at their centre. As Dernie (2006) writes: "thinking about such exhibitions in terms of movement, activity and interaction challenges conventional approaches to museum and exhibition design, not as an aesthetic alternative but in terms of new strategies for communication and learning experience". We witness a paradigm shift, from exhibition to environment.

3 From Exhibition to Environment

Let's stop to think about the word "environment" or "ambience". Stemming from *ambire*, a Latin term indicating air and fluids revolving around something, the environment is an encompassing space, it is invisible matter that at once surrounds and wraps us. It is a dimension that implies an interaction. The spatial structure becomes the main characteristic of the environments, which conversely plan the space and "put it on the scene" for a spectator that physically interacts with it. Describing the environment in its scenic form means thinking of it as a spatial model that is generated by the expansion of technology and digital media. Technology and media have redefined the traditional rules of frontal representation by multiplying, juxtaposing and bringing together space and time.[5] The environment is not just a space but also a system, a melange of relations that entail the experience (Quinz 2014) of the space and empathy towards it (Mallgrave 2013). The environment is a holistic device which is not just the sum of the technologies it employs, but which also creates an amplified dimension of being, acting retroactively on the quality of the spectator's perception (Pitozzi 2016). If the role of technology is to push the boundaries of perception, then technology itself needs to become the environment, allowing the rise of a new dimension of invisible, virtual matter, which is by no means less real, affecting the senses of the audience. The environment becomes the interface – and this is the direction towards which the space needs to be restructured, in the quest for a spatiality that is material yet intangible, whose perception is imposed by the conditions of the space itself and which affects the senses and the interaction between tangible bodies, experience and the virtual, the

---

[5] The development of the environment is the result of the convergence of two fields of intervention. On one side, we have the reformulation of the idea of contemporary scene, which starts from utopian set designers who sought to *retheatricalize the theatre* in the early 1900s and continues with the works of the Avant-gardes and the development of the performance (art), which place the theatre in a hybrid territory. On the other side, we find the development of interaction design practices that focus on the development of a dialogue between human beings and computer systems and that has found in the artistic field a fertile ground for project experiments.

potential of technology. The goal is to communicate meaning and sensorial experience using one's imagination (Ring Petersen 2015).

Dumb Type. Extra-Sensory Odissey eschews from the traditional definition of exhibition and thus provide an important opportunity to think about the status of the contemporary scene and on the ways to document, archive and exhibit the play and what remains of it. Now more than ever the touch points between scene and technology offer experiences in which the spectator's perception is fundamental, and in which the audience is part of the environment itself. If we forget this aspect, we cannot fully appreciate the work itself. It is useful at this point to briefly go through Dernie's analysis (2006), which poses three typologies of exhibition space: (1.) *narrative space*, with a linear, episodic structure; (2.) *performative space*, the evolution of the former space, focusing on the spectator and its relationship with the exhibits, allowing for an active interaction with the process, especially thanks to the mediation of technology (audio guides, tablets, apps…); (3.) *simulated experience*, a space in which the real and the virtual spaces overlap and allow for immersive environments, which draw the spectator in a form of total design that uses theatre as a design and communicative tool. The last typology is the most relevant within this paper and it shows how maybe it is the word 'exhibition' itself to be in crisis and not be completely pertinent as it implies a frontality and a stark separation between the spectator and the object within the exhibition space. New technologies, such as sound spatiality systems and panoramic/landscape screens alter this relationship. Stepping in an installation or in an environment, whether interactive or not, makes us enter the realm of the virtual space. We are as immaterial in the processes that generate the virtual, such as binary codes, software, mathematical and logical abstraction, as we are in the results they generate. The real and the virtual enter one another and become part of the same entity. A good example of this process is the recently-opened "MORI Building DIGITAL ART MUSEUM teamLab Borderless" in Tokyo, Japan, a 10,000-sq.m. museum entirely dedicated to installations and environments by teamLab, a Japanese collective of digital professionals who, using the digital world and digital media, works on the creation of new spatial relationships.

On an abstract level, we can assume the coexistence of three dimensions within this context, three ways of analysing the rethinking of the technologically-mediated scene for the exhibition. The first level is about the active design and construction of installations and environments for the play. In relation to *Dumb Type. Extra-Sensory Odissey,* this level of analysis poses a very close relationship between technological and creative thoughts: the technological development works for a frame of thoughts that could not exist otherwise. In other words, it is the creative process that manipulates technology and not vice versa. Even if technology already exists, its application is not enough to claim an aesthetical value, it has to respond to a specific project. A process of remediation has to be applied in order to rebalance the potentials of the technology within an operational-aesthetic context. From this starting point, we enter the second dimension: exposition. We are in a situation in which technology becomes invisible, so, if we step into an installation and the interaction with the space and the environment is intuitive, this means that a process of thinking about the technology itself occurs; this is different from the fruition for which the machine was created. The technologies change the spatial perception: one no longer goes to a performance, or an exhibition, to watch or see it but to perceive it. Without the fundamental component of live performance, which is the presence of the performer's body, all the creative attention moves to the spectator, who becomes a key figure in the production of the performance and the exhibition space, which comes to life with the movement and the interaction of bodies and bodies and machines. We would like to reiterate, once again, that the perceptive involvement of the spectator is not an add-on but becomes a key part of the process of creation and of design of the environment. The last dimension, which is the educational dimension, is a result of the first two dimensions and refers to the observations made at the beginning of this paper about the need to update the study methods and about how necessary practical experience is to work on the theory. It is from the observation of the practical experience that implicit and explicit theoretical information emerge, information said by artists or read on works, from which it is possible to start elaborating theoretical frames. We need to thoroughly understand that things communicate with us.

Although it may seem that these three dimensions move on different tracks, as the first one is a design dimension, while the other two focus on the spectator's fruition, it is important to state that, within the contemporary context, they move in the same direction. The next step is to understand how, starting from these three dimensions, which are important in practice and for the project, we can theorize and abstract a frame, even an aesthetic one, that create digital environments for the theatre that renew the day-to-day relationship with the study tools. A prototype model of contemporary performing arts diffusion.

References

Bolter JD, Grusin R (1999) Remediation: understanding new media. MIT Press

Dernie D (2007) Exhibiton design. Laurence King Publishing

Dixon S (2007) Digital performance: a history of new media in theater, dance, performance art, and installation. MIT Press

Eckersall P, Scheer E, Shintaro F (eds) (2017) The dumb type reader. Museum Tusculanum Press

Jones CA, Arning B (2006) Digital performance: a history of new media in theater, dance, performance art, and installation. MIT Press

Mallgrave H.F (2013) Architecture and embodiment: the implications of the new sciences and humanities for design. Routledge

Montani P (2014) Tecnologie della sensibilità: estetica e immaginazione interattiva. Raffaello Cortina Editore

Quinz E (2014) Il Cerchio invisibile. Ambienti, sistemi, dispositivi. Mimesis

Pitozzi E (2016) Al limite del visibile. Dispositivi installativi e scena performativa contemporanea. In: Borgherini M, Mengoni A (ed) Sul mostrare. Teorie e forme del displaying contemporaneo, Mimesis, pp 199–212

Ring Petersen A (2015) Installation art. between image and stage. Museum Tusculanum Press

Immersive Experiences in Staircases. The Geometric System as Sensorial Stirring

Vincenzo Cirillo[✉] and Pasquale Conte[✉]

Department of Architecture, Università della Campania "Luigi Vanvitelli",
Via San Lorenzo, 81031 Aversa, Italy
vincenzo.cirillo@unicampania.it,
conte.pasquale1@gmail.com

Abstract. Currently, the gap between forms of representation and perceived reality has disappeared. In fact, a new form of communication and visualization, the simulation, appears more and more established. In this sense, the present contribution proposes an experimentation that evaluates the staircases geometric system as an element of sensorial stimulation through immersion with *Virtual Reality*.

Keywords: Simulation · Immersive spaces · Staircases ·
Geometrical configuration

1 Introduction [VC]

In contemporary society the gap between forms of representation (as an interpretive model of reality) (De Rubertis 1994) and perceived reality has been annulled. In fact, a new form of communication and visualization of these models, the simulation, appears more and more established. This latter allows us to inhabit a specific scene at a sensory level and not just to visualize it with our eyes, abstracting the sense of sight from others. Consequently, this form of communication introduces man into a prevalently perceptual dimension, where the context, the scene or the reconstruction of specific sites constitute the interpretative model of reality (specific of representation). In this sense, this represent a model that facilitates the understanding of itself by being 'in-habited' (Luigini and Panciroli 2018). Living the models is now possible available thanks to the use of the most modern technologies such as *Virtual Reality*, able to guide users in contexts that can be explored through the construction of specific paths or practicable thanks to the use of *joy-sticks*. Through this immersion the users could 'interact' with the given scenes, observing and perceiving the reconstructed 'model' (Ippoliti and Casale 2018).

The staircase (here, object of study and beyond to be understood exclusively linked to the function of overcoming differences in height) is one of the most pertinent design examples to exhibit itself both as a design model (linked to the 'mental shape' translated into sign) that as a model of perceptual space derived from its distance with the continuous change of points of view offered to the viewer (Zerlenga 2017).

© Springer Nature Switzerland AG 2019
A. Luigini (Ed.): EARTH 2018, AISC 919, pp. 536–542, 2019.
https://doi.org/10.1007/978-3-030-12240-9_56

Although the scientific and psychological debate is still underway, the perception (Foglia 2011) has always been a design element used into installation of numerous staircases, especially since the 15th century when this latter enjoys of the gradual transition from an element linked to the functionality of going up to an architectural representative space (Cirillo 2017).

Consequently, to give to staircase considerable architectural prestige, architects have always measured themselves through the adoption and experimentation of various solutions ranging from simple planimetric use of elementary geometrical figures (Docci and Migliari 1992) to more complex ones obtained from their concatenation.

2 Geometrical Configuration and Model: The Neapolitan Eighteenth-Century Residential Staircases [VC]

Following the arrival in Naples (Italy) of Charles III of Bourbon, in the eighteenth-century Neapolitan palaces were interested by renovations, such as the re-design of the façade, the portal and the staircase. These last are the object of singular planning operations and spatial-perceptual-temporal relationships, which give the staircase an additional value in the redefinition of the architectonic type (Zerlenga 2000).

The reason for which design attention is given to the staircase body lies mainly in the presence of narrow road sections, which characterize the axis of travel of the historical city of Naples and which prevents the use of figurative value in the façade. Not being able to guarantee the presence of a valid point of view functional to the perception of the entire façade design, the architectural project of noble residence concentrates its maximum expressive value in the predisposition of a 'mouth-scene' (Pane 1939), consisting on the spatial succession of portal, entrance hall, courtyard and staircase. The latter, in addition to the functional role of vertical connection between the different altimetrically levels of the building, during the 18th century the actual façade of the Neapolitan palaces constituted during the 18th century. This peculiarity (through the plastic-figurative attractor of portal and furnace of the entrance hall) has attracted the sight of the passers-by on the innermost fifth wall of the courtyard, corresponding to the staircase. These, often placed in an axial position, surprised the look of the passer by the rich articulation of the ramps and, often, for the existence of a back garden.

The most general investigation on the geometric matrices of the 18th Neapolitan residential staircases was conducted in the field through the architectural survey of some notable examples and their consequent cataloging through synoptic tables, in which the planimetric and structural shape can be easily deduced, with 'free well' or 'pillars'. Specifically, the staircases examined can be traced back to the geometrical shapes of the square and the circumference, variously manipulated, as well as to the oblong shapes derived from them such as the rhombus and the oval/ovule. Moreover, apparently more complex space systems can be traced back to polygonal profiles, variously irregular and similarly to 'free well' or 'pillared' structures.

The first eighteenth-century architect to confer this scenic role to staircase of the noble Neapolitan residences was Ferdinando Sanfelice (1675–1748) (Gambardella 1968). Mathematician, set designer, architect, urban planner (De Dominici 1744), this latter in the architectural project focused on the creation of spatial systems «implanted on unusual planimetric configurations of pillars, arches, vaults and ramps with an unequaled structural ease» (Zerlenga 2015), conceiving two different models of staircase: on pillars and cantilever. The first model, including the one defined as 'gullwing', consists on the adoption of an ordered series of pillars which allows both a considerable transparency of the back walls, and a multiplicity of points seen inside-outside and such as to define this model as 'extrovert' (Zerlenga 2014). Some of these models can be found into the palaces: Sanfelice, 6 (by Sanfelice); Spagnuolo; Fernandez; Trabucco; Sala Grifeo (by Sanfelician derivation) (Fig. 1). The second model, due to the presence of walls closed along the perimeter of the staircase and often connoted by a light that invades the space from above through the empty area, generates an introverted visual scene. Some of these models can be found into the palaces: Palmarice and Bartolomeo di Majo (by Sanfelice); de Sinno and Persi-co in via Duomo, Solimena and Santoro (by Sanfelician derivation).

Ferdinando Sanfelice possessed a deep knowledge of geometry, so much so that the planimetric system of the staircase he designed were conceived by a creative use of elementary geometric shapes and based on the manipulation of their properties and relationships.

The geometrical generative figures of the multiple spatial invasions are substantially two: square and circumference. For its regular quadrilateral properties with congruent angles, the geometrical figure of the square can be easily articulated into ramps and landings (dismount or rest), immediately distinguishing two types: with three ramps or four, giving to the latter a more circularity (Fig. 1a). If the square is rotated by 45° with respect to the axis of access to the staircase, this solution returns greater perceptive dynamism to the spatial configuration (Fig. 1b). In fact, the 45° rotated square projects, for of all, projects the staircase on the courtyard, creating an overhang that is often formally curved; in this case the arches opened in this front are of the fourth order. Finally, by the rotated arrangement of the square, if the staircase is open on the courtyard, the view of the same appears more dynamic as the ramps are perceived as scraps and not frontal. Exemplary examples of this model are the palaces Palmarice and Persico. If the square rotated by 45° cut along an axis, this solution generates the model by triangular matrix as verifiable in the staircase in Via (street) Tommaso Caravita, 6 (Fig. 1c).

On the other hand, if the square is flanked by one of equal size, overlapping a ramp for each of them, the so-called 'gullwings' model is created with a double well (Fig. 1d) and symmetrically oblique ramps in the façade, which in the staircase open on the courtyard generate a notable dynamism as in the palace: Sanfelice, 6; Spagnuolo; Trabucco; Fernandez; Sala Grifeo. If the squares of the same dimensions are rotated by 45°, the composition creates an irregular hexagon (Fig. 1e). This solution is a figurative matrix, for example, of the Palazzo Capuano (by Sanfelice) as well as of the double ramp staircase built in the Reggia di Capodimonte. The geometric manipulation criteria applied to the square matrix staircases models are like those for the circular shape. In this sense, the most common types concern the simple staircases with ring-shaped ramps interrupted by landings (dismount or rest), both entirely circular and semi-circular as well as at a free well or with pillars. A more complex model is used by Ferdinando Sanfelice in his palace (number 2). In this case the two circumferences of the same radius are approached, and the ramps are arranged according to a bilateral

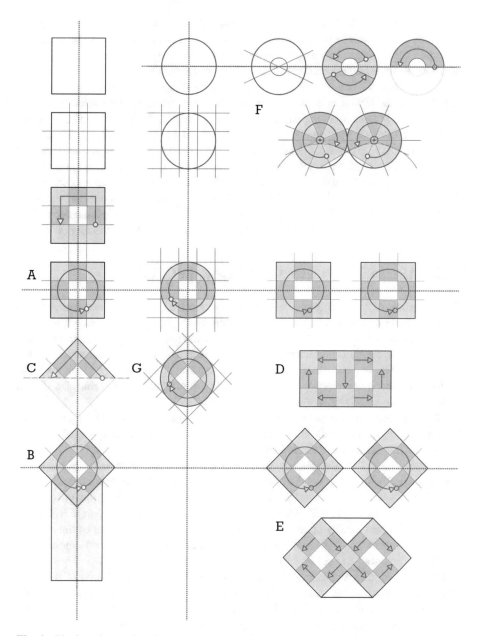

Fig. 1. Planimetric matrix of square, triangular and circular shape with three or four ramps (drawing by Vincenzo Cirillo).

symmetry (Fig. 1f). In these models, the definition of steps and landings occurs by radial genesis compared to the center of the circumference and, consequently, the treads of the steps have a smaller dimension towards the well and greater along the perimeter of the staircase's wall. If, instead, the circumference is inscribed in a square while the wall remains circular, the ramps follow the axial directions of the square and the treads are all parallel to each other. This scheme, if rotated by 45°, re-proposes the same perceptive dynamism of the square model, previously described (Fig. 1g), as in the case of the Maciocco staircase (numer 98), by Sanfelice.

Further formal developments derived from the square or circumference are, respectively, the oblong matrices of the rhombus or of the oval and ovolo. In the first case, relapse, for example, the staircases of the palaces Di Majo and de Sinno, where the straight sides of the rhombus are replaced by linear concave-convex trends that affect both the ramps and the landings. In the second case, the ovate profile (which in analytic geometry approaches the equation of the ellipse, i.e. the geometric place of the points of the plane for which the sum of the distances from two fixed points, called fires, remains constant) (Zerlenga 1997; Dotto 2002) characterizes the staircases of the palaces Di Majo (Piazza Vittoria, by Sanfelice) and Santoro (by Sanfelician derivation) while the staircase of the palace in Via Paladino, 9, returns planimetrically an ovule.

3   Immersive Experiences in Staircases [VC, PC]

The modeling of the proposed schemes, here elaborated, and the subsequent visualization of these models through appropriate axonometric or perspective views, has been more than a useful operation to the critical representation of the spatial characteristics, favoring an immediate understanding to the specialists of the sector and not only (Migliari 2003). In this sense, the conducted experience shows that graphic visualization takes on a noteworthy result and fulfills a powerful strategic role, i.e. that of giving voice to creativity, knowledge and communication.

The use, then, of the most contemporary digital media and visual culture of representation implements this knowledge, offering further and new types of multidimensional visualizations (Salerno 2018).

Virtual reality, for example, has radically transformed entertainment as we know it. Wearing a VR visor catapults the user into a new dimension of entertainment, characterized by experiences that seem real. In cinematic entertainment, the public is a spectator of a story, while with videogame technology we are an active part of it (Ippoliti 2010). The Virtual Reality takes a further step forward, creating the perception of them physically present in a virtual world as if it were real, just like the world around us.

In this direction, a small experiment was conducted based on the digital immersion of scaircases by different geometric matrix to show how the latter is one of the main and peculiar components that predisposes the user to the perception (Massironi 2007) of different sensorial stimuli (Cervellini 2011). To cite a few examples, the distance of a square-shaped planimetric staircase is different from a circular plan. The first generates continuous and sudden changes in travel in correspondence with the pavement planes arranged along the longitudinal axis; the second, on the other hand, offers the viewer a journey from the most sinuous movement with a gradual perception of the space that results in the eyes of the enveloping user.

Besides the geometric peculiarity, the sensorial data is strongly stimulated also by the constructive characteristics of the staircase. A staircase with pillars offers a different perception than the empty one in the center. This latter, in fact, arises due to the absence of visual disturbance elements (such as the pillars), which offers continuous and uninterrupted visions. To obtain a Virtual Reality visualization of the different staircase installations from the triangular, square, circular and hexagonal planimetric shape, the relative three-dimensional models have been imported into an open source software predisposing the latter to the communication with the software which regulates the functioning of the - sore for VR by integrating scripts. Having done this, it was possible to navigate within the architectural re-projections to analyze the perceptual experience offered by the different staircases planimetric plans (Fig. 2).

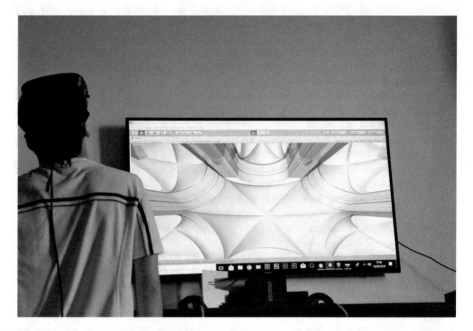

Fig. 2. Immersion VR in the staircase with a square geometric matrix (V. C. with Pasquale Conte).

4 Conclusions [VC]

This contribution reflects on the possibility that the staircase, due to functional, structural, geometric complexity, can constitute a significant architectural element where sensory exploration returns a highly relevant perceptual experience.

Based on this assumption and with today's possibility of recreating virtual scenes thanks to the modern technologies of Virtual Reality, we investigate how the perceptual phenomenon can be intimately linked to the basic geometrical system and, therefore, to the sensorial experience. In this sense, the geometry would be influenced by the sensorial experience of the viewer immersed in digital environments.

References

Cervellini F, Rossi D (2011) Comunicare emozionando. L'edutainment per la comunicazione intorno al patrimonio culturale. DISEGNARECON 4(8). ISSN 1828-5961

Cirillo V (2017) Istruzioni diverse di modelli e forme del salire. La scala fra teoria, principi e maestri. Territori e Frontiere della Rappresentazione. Gangemi, Roma, pp 301–310. ISBN 978-88-492-3507-4

De Dominici B (1744) Vite dei pittori scultori ed architetti napoletani, 1846 edn. vol IV, Napoli, pp 494–529

De Rubertis R (1994) Il disegno dell'architettura. La Nuova Italia Scientifica, Roma

Docci M, Migliari R (1992) Scienza della rappresentazione. Fondamenti e applicazioni della geometria descrittiva. Carocci Editore, Roma. ISBN-13 978-8843004140

Dotto E (2002) Il disegno degli ovali armonici. Le Nove Muse Editrice, Catania

Foglia L (2011) Percezione visiva. Prospettive filosofiche ed empiriche. Franco Angeli, p 12

Gambardella A (1968) Note su Ferdinando Sanfelice architetto napoletano. Istituto Editoriale del Mezzogiorno, Napoli

Ippoliti E, Casale A (2018) Rappresentare, comunicare, narrare. Spazi e Musei virtuali: riflessioni ed esperienze. In: Ambienti digitali per l'educazione all'arte e al patrimonio, First edn. Franco Angeli

Ippoliti E, Meschini A (2010) Dal "modello 3D" alla "scena 3D". Prospettive e opportunità per la valorizzazione. DISEGNARECON. ISSN 1828-5961

Luigini A, Panciroli C (2018) Ambienti digitali per l'educazione all'arte e al patrimonio, First edn. Franco Angeli

Massironi M (2007) La percezione. Psicologia generale. Carocci editore, Roma, p 63. ISBN 978-88-430-3847-3

Migliari R (2003) Geometria dei modelli. Rappresentazione grafica e informatica per l'architettura e il design, Kappa, Roma

Pane R (1939) Architettura dell'età barocca in Napoli. Editrice politecnica, Napoli

Salerno R (2018) Drawing as (in)tangible representation. In: 40th International Conference of Representation Disciplines Teachers. Gangemi, Roma

Zerlenga O (2017) Disegnare le ragioni dello spazio costruito. Le scale aperte del '700 napoletano. Diségno 1:45–56

Zerlenga O (2015). Le scale sanfeliciane a Napoli. Spazi e culture del Mediterraneo. Costruzione di un atlante del patrimonio culturale mediterraneo, vol 4. La Scuola di Pitagora, Napoli, pp 237–244

Zerlenga O (2014) Staircases as a representative space of architecture. Best practise in Heritage Conservation Management from the world to Pompeii | Le vie dei Mercanti. XII Forum Internazionale di Studi, Aversa-Capri 12-13-14 giugno 2014, Napoli, La scuola di Pitagora, Napoli, pp 1632–1642. ISBN 978-88-6542-347-9

Zerlenga O (2000) Criteri e metodi per rilevare, conoscere e rappresentare livelli differenziati di complessità. Il sistema degli accessi al costruito storico residenziale napoletano. La normazione nella rappresentazione dell'edilizia, Roma 22/24 settembre 1994, Roma, Kappa, pp 307–310. ISBN 88-7890-376-0

Zerlenga O (1997) La forma ovata in architettura. Rappresentazione geometrica. CUEN, Napoli. ISBN 88-7146-376-5

Interactive/Participatory Designing
the Experience of Contemporary Maquettes

Marta Magagnini[✉] and Nicolò Sardo

Scuola di Architettura e Design, "Eduardo Vittoria" – Università di Camerino,
Viale della Rimembranza, 63100 Ascoli Piceno, Italy
{marta.magagnini,nicolo.sardo}@unicam.it

Abstract. This essay investigates the changes and modulations between analogue and digital aspects of the architectural model, with regard to its peculiar nature as a device to convey three-dimensional information in both teaching and communication. Distinguishing between models on the architectural and urban scales, this contribution briefly reviews the development and some of the uses of this artefact as a unique medium that bridges the current cultural and social step from vertical transmission to the horizontal communication of knowledge. The models are considered important devices to learn and transmit thoughts about architecture and the landscape, even within museum institutions. Their historical importance for representing urban spaces and the territory is also analysed. In recent years, physical models have taken on original value thanks to the implementation of new technologies. These technologies not only expand the models' functions, but also promote a use that renews and updates the relationship between object and user, increasing the participatory aspect.

Keywords: Architectural models · Teaching and technologies for museums ·
Augmented or mixed reality

1 Introduction

Physical models have always been a very effective communication tool, and not just in architecture. Their three-dimensional nature allows them to be directly investigated by all subjects for two reasons: a) they are not mediated by any specific technical language; and b) they are tangible and can be inspected, aspects that allow for haptic—and not just visual—experience when learning information. In this sense, physical models are still considered current today, in their coexistence with virtual models and sometimes also integrated with digital media.

But that is not all. In contemporary society, limits and roles are much less rigid than in the past. In commerce, one good example is the hybrid figure of the prosumer: the user who is no longer a consumer, but an active part in defining the merchandise, i.e., a producer. In the world of mass media, informational content is publicized less and less through vertical transmission (TV, print media), because the voluntary implementation of users (radio, Internet, social media) has grown and become systematized. New technologies play an incisive role in this cultural transition towards communication

© Springer Nature Switzerland AG 2019
A. Luigini (Ed.): EARTH 2018, AISC 919, pp. 543–552, 2019.
https://doi.org/10.1007/978-3-030-12240-9_57

"in which each participant co-informs and coincides" (Dolci 1988). And the model is the "natural" place where contemporary communication is applied and matters.

2 A History of Transmitting Knowledge. Analogue Models, Between Teaching and Communication

The physical model has always been very important in teaching about and communicating architecture: "Its fascination surpasses any interpretational uncertainty due to the quality it has always shared with the construction: being definitively the best representation of the building. And for this reason, its quality was the tool of initiation for generations of architects that, in creating objects in the form of small buildings, prepared to build large ones" (Scolari 1988, p. 16). The relationship between the model and the referent is a special relationship inherent in its being an "iconic production": "a production of signed structures that hold a relationship of similarity with their referent" (Maldonado 1998, p. 102).

But it is a relationship with reality that is always highlighted in a rather compositional way: "Only the destination of the original, existing or not, can indicate whether the model, as we perceive it, in addition to itself, also refers to what it would want: the model is distinguished from the original by its structural phenomenology (in a machine, its operation) or by its phenomenology of relation with the user (in a building, its quality/function)" (Serralunga 1985, p. 58).

The presence of models is at the very root of the idea of "museum of architecture". In 1704, Clement XI collected models of the construction of Saint Peter's in the Vatican. Just as fascinating is the collection of nearly 800 architectural models of ancient buildings promoted by Louis-François Cassas, exhibited in Paris in 1806, and then acquired by the École des Beaux-Arts.

Already starting in the 1800s, notable collections of architectural models of historical buildings were usually found in museums and art schools. One might think of the Galerie des modèles d'architecture that formed part of the Musée de la Sculpture comparée in Paris organized beginning in 1878, or the models presented in the Gabinetto di Architettura antica and Tecnica degli stili at the Turin Polytechnic, assembled beginning in 1885 and considered fundamental for the education of future engineers. Used for teaching purposes, the maquette, with its innate communicational capacity and its three-dimensional entity, makes it "resemble" the object represented and is a favoured tool to communicate that building that participates in the education.

Even beyond teaching purposes, the model with its three-dimensional clarity also lends itself to presenting a non-specialist public with architectural works and other products in which the three-dimensional nature of the depiction is capable of increasing its understanding, surpassing the need for knowledge of essential "codes".

It seems obvious that the model is also capable of representing "symbolic functions", thereby turning its analogue relationship with reality into something more complex and multiform. This is the case, for example, of some of the models that Le Corbusier realized for the Unité project in Marseille: realizations—modular and equipped with a functional synthesis—appropriate for clarifying the constitutional logic of the "*machine à habiter*".

But models may also be capable of highlighting entirely unexpected aspects. This is the case of physical models—such as those designed by Luigi Moretti—that, by overturning positive and negative, represent that internal space of some buildings as materializing what is "empty" (Moretti 1952–1953). Of particular interest as well are the models of Michelangelo's buildings that Bruno Zevi had his students at the University Institute of Architecture in Venice create in 1964 to mark the four-hundredth anniversary of Michelangelo's death: not analogue, descriptive representations, but rather tools for critical interpretation (Zevi 1964) (Fig. 1).

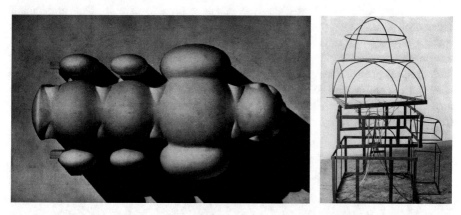

Fig. 1. (**a**) Guarino Guarini, Project for the church of Santa Maria della Divina Provvidenza, Lisbon. Model edited by Luigi Moretti. (From: Moretti 1952–1953) (**b**) Michelangelo Buonarroti, Medici Chapel in San Lorenzo, Florence. Model created by the students of IUAV, Venice, edited by Bruno Zevi. (From: Zevi 1964)

Topographic and urban models have also been very important. They have been made for strategic, defensive, celebratory, and naturally design purposes since antiquity and their use has accompanied models for buildings.

The capacity to "realistically" represent the orography and become—with a change in the point of view—an ideal tool for presenting a complex depiction capable of carrying out various functions may be meaningful. It is also important to note the close relationship that exists between the model's depiction and the "military perspective", that is, oblique axonometric projection (Scolari 1984): the search for "objectivity" often makes the two methods of representation interchangeable. The models are also configured as overcoming the difficulties inherent in representing the orography of the terrain. Graphical solutions—the use of colour and then the rigour of the contour lines—make a clear analogy with the topographical models capable of being used in a more articulated way thanks to the possibility of changing the observer's point of view.

Nor should some mechanisms implemented in the relationship between observer and scale reproduction be forgotten. As Levi-Strauss observes, the "quantitative transposition grows and transfers our power onto a counterpart of the thing: through this, the item can be gathered, weighed in the hand, grasped with a single glance" (Levi-Strauss 1996, p. 36).

From the models of forts—which have been documented since the sixteenth century—to the plan-reliefs of French cities made especially in the seventeenth and eighteenth centuries, one of the most important uses of urban scale models is for military architecture. These models are capable of indicating the execution of military engineering with a capacity to overcoming the eventual difficulties in understanding the graphical representations.

However, the documentary and teaching vocation of many urban models, as in the case of the great model of Constantine's Rome realized by Italo Gismondi and exhibited at the Museo della Civiltà Romana in Rome, should not be forgotten.

This large-scale model was also the means chosen to exhibit some emblematic urban projects in contemporary architecture, as was begun many times by Le Corbusier —for example with the *Ville Contemporaine* (1922), the *Plan Voisin* for Paris (1925), the *Projet Obus* for Algiers (1931), *Chandigarh* (1950)—and by Frank Lloyd Wright with the project for *Broadacre City* in 1935. But it also presented large utopian cities after the Second World War. It is enough to think of the many models for urban projects by the Japanese Metabolists or as in the case of *New Babylon* (1959) by Constant or *Motopia* (1961) by Geoffrey Alan Jellicoe (Fig. 2).

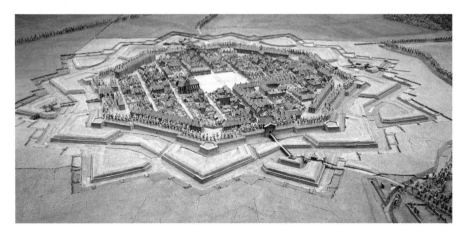

Fig. 2. Plan-relief of Neuf-Brisach, France (Musée des Plans-reliefs, Paris), 1703-1706. (Credits: ph. Lomita/Wikimedia Commons)

3 Communicating Knowledge: Interactiveness and Participation in the Contemporary Approach Between the First and the Third Worlds

In a relatively recent era, public administrations have begun to systematically use physical models as a tool to share information between designers and government institutions and between these and the final users, the citizens. The most meaningful examples include the large model of New York—*Panorama*—commissioned by the New York City public official Robert Moses for the New York World's Fair in 1964.

At a scale of one inch to 100 feet, it was meant to display the public works of the city and, according to its creator, it should be kept continuously up to date with the enclosure of new buildings and infrastructures. In reality, the last modifications were made in 1975 with the addition of the two World Trade Center towers. Today it forms the centrepiece of the collection at Queens Museum, where it is conserved as a piece of the city's history (Miller 1987) (Fig. 3).

Fig. 3. *The Panorama of New York City* located at the Queens Museum of Art, New York. (Credits: ph. OptimumPx/Wikimedia Commons)

The value of Moses' work is historicized in an era in which co-information between administrators and citizens was approaching, but still based on mechanisms that today, deriving from the world of computers, we define as vertical scaling, that is, which can be modified by a single hand. In the contemporary age, instead, the traditional physical model was turned into a potential Internet-based platform, that is, a system that acquires information from a collaborative network of users and which can therefore be implemented "horizontally". This participatory aspect means that contemporary physical models can be counted among the "revolutionary" communication tools of our time (Rifkin 2011) (Fig. 4).

The first to change their appearance were large-scale physical models. This is because the excessive increase in the amount of geographical and georeferenced information, territorial data first centrally controlled but increasingly available online

Fig. 4. The Interactive scale model for the Rotterdam Information center developed by the Dutch Rnul interactive studio. (Courtesy of Rnul interactive)

and to all sectors of the market, has meant that the means of visualizing and communicating maps and models on an urban and territorial scale required innovation (Magnaghi 2001). As well, it was not only the information that increased, but the way the information changes over time. As an extreme example, some geographical information regarding "borders" is not static in time, as recognized by the Italian legislature, which, in 2009 introduced the concept of "moving border" with regard to the border between Italy and Austria. This is defined as the watershed of the glaciers in the Alpine peaks, but because of recent modifications due to climate change, the line of demarcation between the two countries has contracted sharply and continuously continues to change. In the Monditalia section of the 14th International Architecture Show at the Venice Biennale, the installation *Italian Limes* (Folder 2014a, b) was presented for the first time. This research and monitoring project visualizes and maps this geographical oscillation of the border in real time, starting with a model of the valley and the watersheds of the Alpine section in question and with the help of an automatic pantograph connected to a GPS.

The production of physical models has increased significantly in the last two decades and new technologies applied to maquettes—interactive digital and augmented reality—are still increasing demand, as confirmed by the communicational effectiveness of this tool in transmitting not only geographical knowledge in schools, museums, and large public exhibits (Fig. 5).

Fig. 5. Participatory 3D Mapping for Cameroon's Forest Monitoring and Conservation Management; the model was presented on May 30 2016 in an official ceremony at the Southwest Regional Delegation of Forestry and Wildlife (MINFOF). (Photo and courtesy Arend De Haas)

For example, at the entrance to the info-point in Rotterdam, an interactive information system was installed in 2017 on the model of the centre of Rotterdam, designed and developed by the Dutch communication studio Rnul Interactive. Beyond learning historical news about the buildings and quarters and consulting the calendar of events, visitors to Rotterdam can personalize their experience, creating and prefiguring their own itinerary on this large maquette.

Dropping back down to the architectural scale, large museums are updating their way of informing visitors, with new entrance halls dedicated to acquiring the greatest amount of news, and information about the museum, the collections, and temporary or permanent installations. This is how the Louvre inaugurated its Clock Pavilion in July 2016, with a hall completely dedicated to a detailed, interactive physical model of the royal palace and the Tuileries Garden, surrounded by digital displays on which archive documents, films, and works of art could be consulted.

Finally, in the last twenty years, another approach to the model is being seen, which derives from a new means of territorial governance: participatory governance. In an attempt to place common people or disadvantaged classes on a primary plane, the contemporary participatory strategy promotes a bottom-up approach divested of planning practices imposed from above.

In particular, participatory three-dimensional modelling (P3DM) is a process designed to introduce rural communities in the developing world—which live in isolation and depend exclusively on the natural resources in their territory—to technologies that provide geographical information. To create the models, a collective learning process is begun that allows participants to visualize their economic and cultural heritage in the form of three-dimensional maquettes georeferenced in scale, which can be used later for discussions and design proposals. The parts of the model are positioned with the integrated use of traditional maps and georeferenced data obtained from GPS and GIS tools used by the community itself (after appropriate training). Participatory mapping should obtain the greatest possible precision of the final result, the model, so it is possible to produce later maps (in digital format) aimed at the project.

From the results of actions performed with P3DM in countries in Africa, the Caribbean, and the Pacific, both in terms of conflict resolution and interaction with their governments when subdividing the territory, one understands how the capacity of a community to be involved in planning projects can derive from the knowledge and awareness of the physical model (Rambaldi 2010).

4 Conclusion

The reasoning proposed is therefore to reflect on the current applications of physical models to confirm the primary role of physical depiction in understanding the urban and architectural space. This tool assists the design, but is also capable of investigating particular aspects of the buildings and landscapes represented.

As a non-virtual tool, as an apparently traditional object—but in reality "open" to innovation—it can also be realized digitally or proposed as a container of applied technologies. While together with new digital technologies, the physical tool has conserved its effectiveness up to today. Whether it presents colour effects or tailored scenographic effects or not, physical models are preserved as a code that can be easily shared among different subjects of communication, which have always had the privilege of dynamic learning around these objects.

Author Contributions. This work was conceived and designed by Marta Magagnini e Nicolò Sardo. Marta Magagnini has developed and edited the Sect. 3, Nicolò Sardo the Sect. 2.

References

N.B. All direct quotations were translated by the author from the bibliographic sources

Boudon Ph (1991) De l'architecture à l'épistémologie. La question de l'échelle, PUF, Paris
Dolci D (1988) Dal trasmettere al comunicare. Sonda, Torino
Folder (Ferrari M, Pasqual E) (2014a) Italian limes. In: la Biennale di Venezia (ed). Fundamentas. 14. Mostra Internazionale di Architettura. Marsilio, Venezia, pp 440–441
Frampton K, Kolbowski S (eds) (1981) Idea as Model. Institute for Architecture and Urban Studies, New York

Gavinelli C (1993) Storie di modelli esibitivi e critici. Alinea, Firenze

Healy P: The Model and its Architecture. 010 Publisher, Rotterdam (2008)

Levi-Strauss C (1996) Il pensiero selvaggio. Il Saggiatore, Milano

Magnaghi A (2001) Rappresentare i luoghi, metodi e tecniche. Alinea, Firenze

Maldonado T (1987) Questioni di similarità. Rassegna 32:57–61

Maldonado T (1998) Reale e virtuale. Feltrinelli, Milano

Miller M (1987) Il modello di Robert Moses. Rassegna 32:74–75

Moretti L (1952–1953). Strutture e sequenze di spazi. Spazio 7, 9–20, 107–108

Morris M (2006) Models: Architecture and the Miniature. Wiley Academy, Chichester

Porter T, Neale J (2000) Architectural Supermodels. Architectural Press, Oxford

Quaini M (1987) Le forme della Terra. Rassegna 32:63–73

Rambaldi G (2010) Participatory Three-dimensional Modelling: Guiding Principles and Applications, 2010th edn. CTA, Wageningen (the Netherlands)

Rifkin J (2011) The Third Industrial Revolution: How Lateral Power Is Transforming Energy, the Economy, and the World. St. Martin's Press, New York

Sardo N (2004) La figurazione plastica dell'architettura. Edizioni Kappa, Roma

Scolari M (1988) L'idea di modello. Eidos 2:16–39

Scolari M (1984) Elementi per una storia dell'axonometria. Casabella 500:42–49

Serralunga M (1985) Modelli e fantasmi. Stileindustria 1:57–60

Smith AC (2004) Architectural Model as Machine. Architectural Press, Oxford

Zevi B (1964) L'opera architettonica di Michelangelo nel quarto centenario della morte. L'architettura cronache e storia 9:654–712

Online publications

ACF (2016) Cameroon's First Participatory 3D Mapping for Forest Monitoring and Conservation Management. https://africanconservation.org/habitat-news/forest/cameroon-s-first-participat ory-3d-mapping-for-forest-monitoring-and-conservation-management/. Accessed 1 Sept 2018

Di Gessa S (2008) Participatory Mapping as a Tool for Empowerment: Experiences and Lessons Learned from the ILC Network, International Land Coalition. https://web.archive.org/web/ 20081116083144/http://www.landcoalition.org/pdf/08_ILC_Participatory_Mapping_Low. pdf. Accessed 1 Sept 2018

Dumont E (2016) Paris/Le Louvre repense ses accueils et le Pavillon de l'Horloge. C'est raté. http://www.bilan.ch/etienne-dumont/courants-dart/parisle-louvre-repense-accueils-pavillon-de-lhorloge-cest-rate. Accessed 1 Sept 2018

Ferrari M (2014) Italian Lime #3 Confini. http://www.klatmagazine.com/architecture/italian-limes-03-confini-biennale-architettura-2014/14736. Accessed 1 Sept 2018

Folder (2014b) Moving Borders. A cartographic and political enquiry. http://www.italianlimes. net/project.html. Accessed 1 Sept 2018

ICIMOD (2016) A Manual on Participatory Three-Dimensional Modelling (P3DM, International Centre for Integrated Mountain Development: Kathmandu, December 2016. http://www. iapad.org/wp-content/uploads/2016/01/icimod3Dmanual16.pdf. Accessed 1 Sept 2018

Kilgannon C (2007) On the Town, Sized Down, Jazzed Up. https://www.nytimes.com/2007/02/ 02/arts/design/02pano.html. Accessed 1 Sept 2018

Lucarelli F (2014) Moving Boundaries in the Alps: Italian Limes (Venice Architecture Biennale 2014), by Folder and collaborators. http://socks-studio.com/2014/08/28/moving-boundaries-in-the-alps-italian-limes-venice-architecture-biennale-2014-by-folder-and-collaborators/. Accessed 1 Sept 2018

Manaugh G (2014) Where Borders Melt. http://www.bldgblog.com/2014/06/where-borders-melt/. Accessed 1 Sept 2018

Queens Museum (2013) Panorama of the City of New York. https://queensmuseum.org/2013/10/panorama-of-the-city-of-new-york. Accessed 1 Sept 2018

Rnul Interactive (2017) Interactive scale model at Rotterdam.info: http://rnul.nl/projects/. Accessed 1 Sept 2018

Rosenberg Z (2015) Unlocking the Secrets of New York City's Most Famous Model. https://ny.curbed.com/2015/2/27/9986444/unlocking-the-secrets-of-new-york-citys-most-famous-model. Accessed 1 Sept 2018

Carving Time and Space: A Mutual Stimulation of IT and Archaeology to Craft Multidimensional VR Data-Inspection

B. Fanini$^{(\boxtimes)}$ and E. Demetrescu

CNR ITABC, Area della Ricerca di Roma 1, Via Salaria Km 29,
300, 00016 Monterotondo, Rome, Italy
bruno.fanini@itabc.cnr.it

Abstract. Interactive inspection of semantically-enriched Immersive Virtual Environments (IVEs) is designed on top of complex hierarchies combining both semantic and rendering aspects. Within Cultural Heritage, multi-dimensional IVEs represent a common solution in order to understand, query and inspect virtual reconstructions across different time-spans. The contribution presents innovative experiments about how the digital heritage record is organized and represented. Such approaches fit several scientific requirements within the Cultural Heritage domain as the annotation of the sources employed and the reasoning that are behind a reconstructive hypothesis. The methodological implications on the use of IT approaches can improve both the quality of the user fruition and the scientific content, offering, at the same time, formalisms and tools to boost the scientific research with real-time immersive representation of complex CH record. Graph-databases are already employed in such contexts since they represent one of the best solutions to address complex and dynamic relationships in highly connected datasets, also in terms of performance and scalability. A set of formalisms and replicable models for immersive inspection will be presented and discussed, addressing their interplay with a graph-based formalism specifically designed for 3D hypothesis creation and visualization in Cultural Heritage (CH) domain, targeting multitemporal scenarios - namely the Extended Matrix (EM).

Keywords: Graph databases · Real-time visualization · Immersive VR · 3D-UI design · Graph theory

1 Introduction

This article presents a new way of managing and inspecting semantically-enriched immersive virtual environments (IVEs). To explain the approach, we will use the metaphors of the Mayan Veil (Schopenhauer) and the Time Machine. We can describe the reality perceived in the IVEs as "a veil of Maya" represented by the 3D models in the various epochs while the effect of vitality that these virtual worlds transmit to the user passes through some original tools of interaction (which will be discussed in the article). These tools also allow us to have access to what is behind the "Veil of Maya": a Matrix of information organized according to a natural language without fixed

© Springer Nature Switzerland AG 2019
A. Luigini (Ed.): EARTH 2018, AISC 919, pp. 553–565, 2019.
https://doi.org/10.1007/978-3-030-12240-9_58

patterns (node database) and according to a specific formalism: the Extended Matrix (Demetrescu 2015). This language allows to collect and organize information on a timeline and to express also the lifespan of CH actors within the virtual world. The other aspect is the Time Machine: the user's experience is to traverse time-periods in an immersive virtual environment (IVE) thanks to the visual formalisms and inspection tools described in this paper. One complex aspect of IVEs is the maintenance of a stable connection between the scientific information that is the basis of the three-dimensional model (for instance the scientific hypothesis behind a 3D virtual reconstruction) and the virtual experience session. The method can be applied to all those data structures and all those virtual worlds that have behind them data structures organized on a temporal basis as it happens for the simulations, the virtual reconstructions or different 3D surveys made of a site after years. Our contributions focus on:

- A set of reusable formalisms (blueprints) for immersive inspection of multi-temporal IVEs driven by graph databases, specifically the *Extended Matrix*[1].
- Replicable and efficient techniques targeting real-time applications and immersive fruition (through consumer-level HMDs) and its demands
- Multi-temporal scene-graph design to minimize memory footprint and maximize caching within WebVR/XR implementations
- Interaction models and best practices for immersive validation of Extended Matrices
- A prototype inspection tool crafted on top of such blueprints, called *EMviq*[2].

2   Related Work

In the last years there is and increased adoption of graph databases, especially in scenarios where the connections between the information is a valuable aspect. Complex data visualization through graph-based visual structures has been scarcely involved in the field of Cultural Heritage. Apparently in this domain the elements have a better and more compact representation in forms and tables. When it comes to representing strongly interconnected information (linked data), such as in the case of virtual reconstructions, visual graph databases allow for better adherence to the scientific record, better visual appeal, improved effectiveness (for the aesthetic principles for information visualization), and reduced complexity. A graph database (GraphDB) is a database that exploits graph structures for semantic queries with nodes, edges and properties to represent and store data. At the core of the system is the graph directly relating data items: such relationships allow objects to be linked together directly and they are equally as important as the objects themselves. Graph databases are indeed based on graph theory (nodes, edges and properties) directly storing the relationships between records. Such definition presents huge differences compared to relational databases that - through relational database management systems - allow manipulation of the data without imposing implementation aspects like physical record chains.

---

[1] http://osiris.itabc.cnr.it/extendedmatrix/.

[2] http://osiris.itabc.cnr.it/scenebaker/index.php/projects/emviq/.

For instance, links between data are stored in the DB itself at the logical level, and relational operations (e.g. join) can be used to manipulate and return related data in the relevant logical format. Relational queries can be performed through the database management systems at the physical level (e.g. using indexes), allowing to boost performance without modifying the logical structure of the database. Graph databases offer simple and fast retrieval of complex hierarchical structures that can be difficult to model in relational systems. To retrieve data from a GraphDB, a query language other than SQL is required, which was designed for the manipulation of data in a relational system - thus not suitable to handle graph traversals. As of today, no single graph query language has been universally adopted, and most systems are closely tied to specific products. Some efforts to create a standard did lead to multi-vendor query languages like *Gremlin*, *SPARQL* (Harris et al. 2013), and *Cypher* (Batra and Tyagi 2012). Graph drawing tools, and other tools dealing with relational data, must store graphs and related data. Despite the previous attempts to create a standard, there is still lack of a format that is widely accepted and several tools support only a limited number of custom formats typically restricted in their expressibility and specific for a given application field. The Demand for interoperability fueled the research and motivated the definition of an XML-based format. An informal task group was in fact created to propose a modern graph exchange format suitable for data transfer between graph drawing tools and other applications: the GraphML format (Brandes et al. 2013). Interactive inspection of semantically-enriched Virtual Environments (VEs) is designed on top of complex scene hierarchies and combines both semantic and rendering aspects, while maintaining several aspects separated (Tobler 2011). Within Cultural Heritage, multi-dimensional VEs represent a common solution to understand, query and inspect virtual reconstructions across different time-spans. Within such context the Extended Matrix offers a Schema-Less Database Approach. The Extended Matrix is a formal language with which to keep track of virtual reconstruction processes. It is intended to be used by archaeologists and heritage specialists to document in a robust way their scientific hypothesis. It organizes 3D archaeological record so that the 3D modeling steps are smoother, transparent and scientifically complete. The EM offers a standardized workflow and visual tools for analysis, synthesis, data visualization, and publication. Starting from a stratigraphic reading of masonry (Building Archeology), all the sources used in the reconstruction are provided along (and integrated) with the 3D model. In other words, the Extended Matrix is a semantic graph that leads to a schema-less data model: the reconstructed objects and their descriptive elements are heterogeneously fitted into space and time, in a way that better suits the incompleteness of the historical record. The descriptive elements are used as a modular grammar to compose the final description of the reconstruction process (data-driven re-construction). Within immersive virtual environments (IVEs) consumed through common consumer-level HMDs[3] (Oculus Rift, HTC Vive, etc.) additional challenges arise when interactive inspection of Graph databases is performed. First of all, inter-active immersive VR presents several challenges performance-wise: interactive ren-dering of a complex 3D scene (e.g. multi-resolution dataset) has demanding

---

[3] Head-mounted Displays.

requirements due to several factors, including stereoscopic rendering, larger FOVs[4] and display resolution (Kanter 2015). One of the very first ingredients for a smooth experience is in fact to maintain high frame rates (around 90 fps) and low latency using recent HMDs. The second macro-challenge for semantic inspection is at presentational level: how to extract and represent complex relationships at runtime in a suitable manner for immersive VR? What kind of layouts should we use? Past and recent literature (Raja et al. 2004), (Kwon et al. 2015) already investigated information visualization within immersive fruition and best practices using consumer-level HMDs. Furthermore, with the rise of WebVR/XR as a standard (Butcher and Ritsos 2017) already employed by major commercial products such as SketchFab[5], additional challenges arise on data transmission and how to properly handle multiple temporal representations of the scene: what kind of solutions can we adopt to maximize streaming efficiency? What kind of multi-temporal scene-graph design can we exploit?

3 Case Studies

The *EMviq* inspection tool (resulting from the formalisms described in the next section) has been employed on a case study drawn from the Building Archaeology domain: the ancient Roman town Colonia Dacia Sarmizegetusa Ulpia Traiana (a temple and a Bath building built in the Second century AD). These examples show the use of EMviq within two projects of virtual reconstruction of Roman contexts. The hypotheses of virtual reconstruction of the Great Temple and of the Baths (at Sarmizegetusa) have been developed starting from a photogrammetric survey by drone, from a bibliographic study, from an analysis of the architectural elements found in the site and from a comparative study with other similar contexts. Starting from all this information, a virtual reconstruction of the contexts was made. The steps of the reconstruction were annotated using the language of the Extended Matrix and the software tools made available by the EMF (Extended Matrix Framework), namely the EMTools[6], a commercial freeware node editor (yEd[7]) and finally, the *EMviq*.

4 Semantic Inspection for Immersive VR

This section describes and formalize *blueprints* that aim to create a replicable and reusable set of models for different semantic VR inspection contexts. The main goal is to address the interplay of such set with a graph-based formalism - namely the Extended Matrix - specifically designed for 3D hypothesis creation and visualization, specifically targeting multi-temporal scenarios. We define a set of operators also implemented in a VR prototype, called "EMviq" that's also been applied to different

---

[4] Field of View.

[5] https://sketchfab.com.

[6] https://github.com/zalmoxes-laran/EMBlenderTools.

[7] https://www.yworks.com/products/yed.

case studies. At first, we may indeed observe within such framework that we have to deal with multiple 3D representations: an object, a context or a large area during different time periods. This leads to the definition of a collection of scene-graphs, that should be properly mapped into specific temporal spans, given a specific Extended Matrix (EM).

4.1 Extraction Routines at Runtime

In this section we describe routines to be implemented in order to extract runtime data from a single EM (GraphDB). Such procedures have to be designed to create intermediate data structures for fast access by a real-time immersive application. Within XML-based input formats - for instance GraphML - this is achieved by means of fast parsing procedures traversing the file and producing intermediate data structures (runtime graphs). As previously described in a previous research (Demetrescu and Fanini 2017) we define and formalize three different extraction steps applied to Extended Matrix formalism: (1) Timeline extraction; (2) Proxy-Graph extraction and (3) Source-Graph extraction. These computational steps need to be performed only when involved GraphDB is modified: more precisely, it has to be performed only on the modified sub-graphs (localized updates). Within immersive VR contexts, intermediate runtime data generated by such approach has the objective of providing high framerates and low latency during query and inspection.

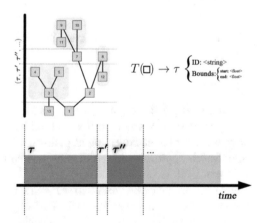

Fig. 1. Timeline extraction from the GraphDB

By EM definition, each node $\square$ in the GraphDB has temporal property, so for timeline extraction (Fig. 1) we define an operator T such as:

$$\mathbf{T}(\square) \rightarrow \tau$$

Where τ is a specific period. We can use T to map to map each node in the GraphDB to a collection of time-periods (τ, τ', τ" ....). Each period has unique ID and < *start, end* > pair, that also defines its duration (centuries, years, days, seconds...). We define also a selector S, such that:

$$S(\tau) \; \rightarrow \; G$$

Where G is a scene-graph associated with input time-period τ. S can be employed at runtime by VR application to switch between different periods, by mean of user input (e.g. VR controller). Using a *naive* approach, we could simply map each time-period τ to a specific scene-graph representation and switching sub-graph during VR session depending on user input (see Fig. 2). Although a given context may present areas or portions having different temporal pacing: for instance, a part of the 3D scene did not evolve during multiple periods. Such approach may indeed result in a waste of resources and poor optimization from a memory footprint perspective.

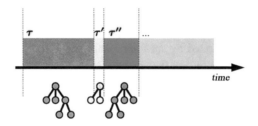

Fig. 2. Mapping time-periods to scene-graphs

4.2   Temporal Instancing

It's a common scenario that a single scene-graph G may include a sub-graph that is shared with another time-period (thus a scene portion re-used by another graph G'). With temporal instancing, we describe the collection as multi-root DAG: each root acts as entry-point for selector S: this approach allows different time-periods to refer to the same scene-graph G or a part of it.

In Fig. 3 a sample temporal instancing between two scene-graphs is shown: note the selector S always returns coherent scene representation with the two graphs sharing a sub-graph that spans across τ and τ'. Such cross-temporal organization allows elegant and compact overall scene design and offers following major advantages due to re-use of scene portions: (1) Compact memory footprint at runtime during VR inspection and (2) Caching for WebVR applications (sub-graphs re-use) thus providing online efficiency.

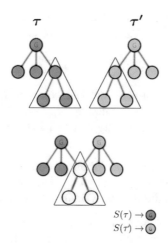

Fig. 3. Sub-graph instancing between two different time-periods

4.3 VR Query Operator

To offer smooth, consistent and efficient 3D queries for immersive VR applications, the application layer must provide routines to extract and automatically build from the GraphDB a hierarchy of semantic 3D descriptors, namely the *Proxy-Graph*.

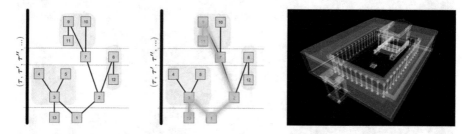

Fig. 4. Proxy-Graph extraction and realization

Similarly to collision routines employed in modern game engines and frameworks, efficient ray-casting procedures are performed on simplified geometries, in this case proxy-nodes. The automated realization of such runtime data structure is defined by the procedure P:

$$\mathbf{P}(G_{db}, f) \rightarrow G_p$$

Where G_{db} is the GraphDB (a single Extended Matrix), f is an optional filtering function to traverse only specific edges of G_{db} and G_p is the realized Proxy-Graph for interactive queries (see Fig. 4). Runtime efficiency in VR is guaranteed by performing 3D queries using common segment intersectors, offered by most modern frameworks and game engines (e.g. *IntersectionVisitor* in OpenSceneGraph[8], *LineTraceByChannel* in Unreal Engine 4[9], etc.). The VR query operator Q can thus be defined as:

$$\mathbf{Q}(s, e) \rightarrow p \quad p \in G_p$$

Where s, $e \in R^3$ represent start and end points of the segment, while p is the returned proxy-node (the 3D semantic descriptor). Notice the definition allows different VR interaction models for semantically enriched IVEs, the following are commonly used:

- s is coincident with current head location in virtual space, and e is defined by current HMD orientation (depending on a given maximum distance - e.g.: 100 m)
- s is attached to a VR controller and e defined by its current orientation

The Q operator allows of course additional interaction models, although the above are generally enough to cover common scenarios (HMD alone and HMD + VR controllers) (Fig. 5).

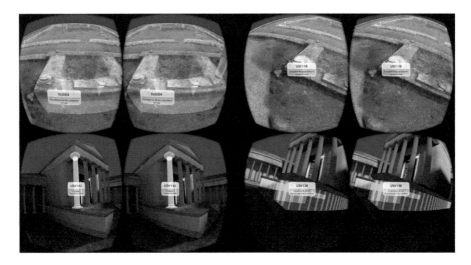

Fig. 5. Query operator during interactive VR inspection

Furthermore, Q operator - together with scene collision geometries (commonly used to simulate physics) - can be employed to implement a proxy-driven locomotion, using common techniques that already proven minimal motion sickness (Boletsis 2017). User input can trigger artificial locomotion on hovered proxy-node to a new computed location depending on surrounding proxy-nodes, physical tracked area of HMD, and physical constraints (scene colliders). Within immersive VR inspection,

---

[8] http://www.openscenegraph.org/.

[9] https://www.unrealengine.com/en-US/what-is-unreal-engine-4.

such approach offers interesting *semantic locomotion* models while inspecting multi-temporal IVE driven by an Extended Matrix.

4.4   Peel Operator

Previous definition for query operator Q still suffers from a common issue that may occur in semantically complex IVEs (complex Proxy-Graphs): occlusion. A proxy-node can be in fact unreachable by ray-based queries (nested proxy-nodes, etc....) thus making the user incapable of inspecting certain spots of the 3D space. The peel operator acts as spherical subtractor given a *center* and a *radius*, thus allowing to *carve* semantic descriptors (and/or visible scene-graphs). The spherical carving can be also localized to specific time-periods or operate on the entire timeline, thus offering great flexibility in terms of VR fruition and experience.

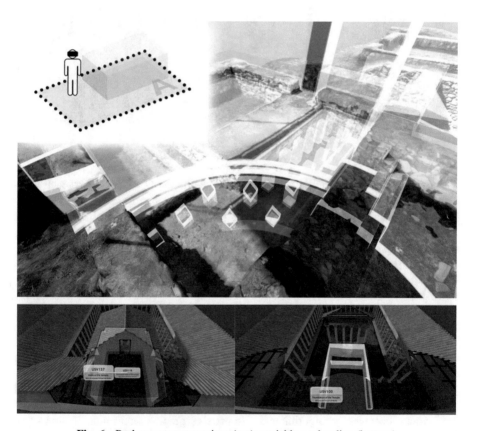

Fig. 6. Peel operator at runtime (top); variable peel radius (bottom)

The peel operator is also particularly useful in combination with positional tracking, including both outside-in (commonly shipped in consumer-level HMDs like Oculus Rift, HTC Vive, etc.) and inside-out tracking approaches. The operator can be in fact attached to user location or VR controllers, also allowing modification of peel radius at runtime. Such interactive approach provides the user with maximum flexibility inside the physical area A (see Fig. 6) for localized inspection during immersive sessions.

4.5   Source-Graphs Presentation

Within the Extended Matrix framework, *source-graphs* represent internal runtime structures of sources relationships (paradata). A single Source-Graph is extracted from a given proxy-node $p \in G_p$, as shown in the example in Fig. 7.

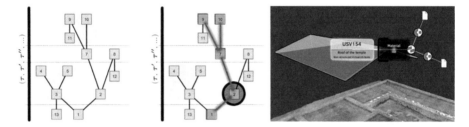

Fig. 7. Source-Graphs Extraction

For a given EM, this leads to a set of Source-Graphs G_u^1, G_u^2, ... G_u^k, each associated with a specific proxy-node. Since the extraction routine from the GraphDB may be computationally expensive in some cases (thus not suitable during VR interaction), the application typically pre-computes all the Source-Graphs and indexes them. Using such approach, the immersive application may safely and quickly access a Source-Graph upon querying a specific proxy-node p. The Source-Graph extraction routine can thus be defined as:

$$U(G_{db}, p, f) \; \rightarrow \; G_u$$

Where f is the usual edge filtering function and G_u is the returned Source-Graph. Once we accessed the graph, how can we present such relationships in VR? In our framework and for the EMviq prototype we adopted a tree analogy by deploying growing 3D layouts. The 3D structure can be spawn in a given location (application point) in the virtual space, typically the queried proxy-node. Runtime generation of such 3D layouts leverages on algorithms for immersive graph visualization (Kwon et al. 2016) exploiting the effectiveness of stereoscopic perception. Furthermore, aesthetic aspects (balance, proportion, etc....) should also be considered for layout generation (Mazumdar et al. 2015), while maintaining robust performances. View-dependent and distance-based techniques may offer good and usable layout presentations considering also past literature and best practices for presentation of information in VR (also including specific fonts for readability). The 3D paraboloid layout here proposed (see Fig. 8) takes inspiration from 2D parent-centered layouts (Pavlo et al. 2006): it allows dynamic growth (including fold/unfold of local branches) of active G_u on application point. Specifically, the 3D layout automatically provides to: (a) Scale the overall graph depending on distance to intersection location and 3D graph extents (bounding box of G_u); (b) Orient the growth axis depending on look direction and (c) "Embrace" the user by using incremental offsets for each graph level (L_1, L_2, etc....).

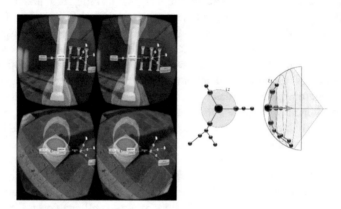

Fig. 8. Presentation of Source-Graph for a proxy-node (column) during VR inspection and 3D paraboloid layout scheme

The paraboloid 3D layout can be pre-computed during extraction routines from current EM and dynamically placed by means of a parent transform. This also allows the Gu (and related interfaces) to be attached on 6-DOF controllers or virtual spots depending on application requirements. Additional amplification techniques (responsive to head orientation) may be employed to boost Source-Graph inspection and - more importantly - support *immersive validation* of current Extended Matrix.

4.6   Cloud-Based Sessions and Workflow

Extraction routines, the graph-based approaches and presented formalizations also allows crafted VR applications to exploit cloud-based scenarios. For instance, the developed EMviq VR prototype (based on OpenSceneGraph framework and own-Cloud) offers inspection of hybrid local/remote scene-graphs and EMs: this allows professionals to design their EM while remote users inspect or validate it without taking off their HMDs, providing a smooth immersive workflow.

5 Conclusions and Current Directions

In this paper we proposed and discussed a set of reusable formalisms (blueprints) for immersive inspection of multi-temporal IVEs driven by graph databases – specifically, Extended Matrices. The work investigated replicable and performance-oriented techniques aiming at real-time, immersive fruition by means of consumer-level HMDs. The routines are also discussed in terms of computational perspective, thus separating those functionalities that require intermediate data structures for efficient access at runtime by the immersive inspection tool. The paper discussed also multi-temporal design for scene-graphs in order to minimize memory footprint and maximize caching within WebVR/XR implementations. Interaction models and resulting best practices for query and inspection were described for different fruition scenarios, including for instance HMD alone and HMD equipped with 6-DOF controllers. A prototype inspection tool (EMviq) was crafted and developed on top of such blueprints, including collaborative perspective by means of cloud-based workflow. This led to novel approaches for Extended Matrices validation through immersive fruition also between remote professionals. Regarding current directions, the development of the EM and its related EMF will result in new versions with the addition of both methodological and technical improvements. The next steps will focus on the support for different, self-excluding reconstruction hypotheses (as a 5th dimension for the EM). In some cases, there are more than one possible reconstructive solution that must be stored and organized accordingly in the EM. A future step within online contexts - already in progress - involves the creation of WebVR/XR component based on described formalisms for the new upcoming version of ATON 2.0[10]. Such process will enable on-line immersive fruition of Extended Matrices on all major browsers without installing any additional plug-in or software, including specific touch interfaces targeting mobile deployment. Described formalisms will also serve to create a plugin component for Unreal Engine 4, thus targeting modern game engines and desktop-based systems.

References

Demetrescu E (2015) Archaeological stratigraphy as a formal language for virtual reconstruction. Theory and practice. J. Archaeol. Sci. 57:42–55

Harris S, Seaborne A, Prud'hommeaux E (2013). SPARQL 1.1 query language. W3C Recommendation 21(10)

Batra S, Tyagi C (2012) Comparative analysis of relational and graph databases. Int J Soft Comput Eng (IJSCE) 2(2):509–512

Brandes U, Eiglsperger M, Lerner J, Pich C (2013) Graph markup language (GraphML), pp 517–541

Tobler RF (2011) Separating semantics from rendering: a scene graph based architecture for graphics applications. Vis Comput 27(6–8):687–695

Kanter D (2015) Graphics processing requirements for enabling immersive vr. AMD White Paper

---

[10] http://osiris.itabc.cnr.it/scenebaker/index.php/projects/aton/.

Raja D, Bowman D, Lucas J, North C (2004 May) Exploring the benefits of immersion in abstract information visualization. In: Proceedings immersive projection technology workshop, pp 61–69

Kwon OH, Muelder C, Lee K, Ma KL (2015 April). Spherical layout and rendering methods for immersive graph visualization. In: 2015 IEEE Pacific Visualization Symposium (PacificVis), pp. 63–67. IEEE

Butcher PW, Ritsos PD (2017 September). Building immersive data visualizations for the web. In: 2017 international conference on cyberworlds (CW), pp. 142–145. IEEE

Demetrescu E, Fanini B (2017) A white-box framework to oversee archaeological virtual reconstructions in space and time: methods and tools. J Archaeol Sci Rep 14:500–514

Boletsis C (2017) The new era of virtual reality locomotion: a systematic literature review of techniques and a proposed typology. Multimodal Technol Interact 1(4):24

Kwon OH, Muelder C, Lee K, Ma KL (2016) A study of layout, rendering, and interaction methods for immersive graph visualization. IEEE Trans. Visual Comput. Graphics 22 (7):1802–1815

Mazumdar S, Petrelli D, Elbedweihy K, Lanfranchi V, Ciravegna F (2015) Affective graphs: the visual appeal of linked data. Semant. Web 6(3):277–312

Pavlo A, Homan C, Schull J (2006) A parent-centered radial layout algorithm for interactive graph visualization and animation. arXiv preprint cs/0606007

An Ongoing Experimentation for VR, AR and MAR of a Design Museum

Cecilia Bolognesi[✉]

Department ABC, Politecnico of Milan, Via Ponzio 31, 20131 Milan, Italy
cecilia.bolognesi@polimi.it

Abstract. This paper traces the experimental path for the virtualization and enrichment with augmented and mixed reality of some modern design objects of the Design Museum of Milan Triennale. The workflow deals with an ongoing experiment with some trainees of Politecnico di Milano and considers to explore strengths and weaknesses of low cost technologies for digital survey in the contemporary design domain, the uses of these technologies for the realization of virtual museums and settings, the relationship that can emerge between storytelling and the creation of virtual museums containing virtual models and the interactions that the latter can have with the user.

Keywords: Low cost technologies · 3d survey · Virtual · Museums · Storytelling

1 Introduction

In Italy no museum appears among the 10 most visited in the world, one in three has less than 1000 visitors a year and 70% of Italians do not visit them (Arnaboldi 2017). The possibilities offered by technological innovation for the digitization of cultural heritage are now indispensable opportunities to support the dissemination of culture, research, teaching, and awareness of our cultural identity. In 2007 the first museum of Italian design was born at the Triennale of Milano. The museum originates from collections and donations from all over the country and includes object of Italian designers starting from 1935 to 2008; it represents a unique example in its kind, a model in our territory while in the meantime our design is famous all over the world. Actually the museum offers one of the exhibitions that took place over the past ten years bringing to light the collections stored in the warehouses; exhibitions are shown in a digitalized web page also. The current digitalization includes forms of digital archiving through static images of the objects and thematic cataloguing forms conveyed by the possibilities offered by the most common social network tools; it works like a digital catalog, without narration, a collection of what you can find in the warehouses. This represents the first showcase of the Italian design museum in the world obviously lacking if related to dissemination of the values of the forms that are linked to a 3D design object (Fig. 1).

The project planned looks at this weakness as an opportunity for development of a new educational and pedagogical path for learning the value of design in the current

© Springer Nature Switzerland AG 2019
A. Luigini (Ed.): EARTH 2018, AISC 919, pp. 566–574, 2019.
https://doi.org/10.1007/978-3-030-12240-9_59

Fig. 1. Four objects from Triennale Design Museum: seat Selene by Vico Magistretti, Heller, 1968; coffeepot by Aldo Rossi, Alessi, 1984; armchair by Cini Boeri, Artflex 1967; table clock, Gino Valle 1966.

museum and for planning a new workflow to fill what is a cultural gap of the representation of modern design objects in the world if related to their historical context (Hess et al. 2017).

2 Methodology and Workflow

2.1 Storytelling

The current page of the museum is set on a selection of objects collected by type, period author. The curatorship established a vision procedure that prefers a list page without any content digressions or narrations for didactic cognitive purposes except simple data sets. Any interaction with the cataloged object is connected with lists of static and two-dimensional images. There is no specific curatorship in cognitive paths, except the exhibitions, nor the possibility of using a narration of simple episodes (Ioannidis et al. 2013). The ongoing experiment wants to use the narration as a tool to learn and explain the objects reality according to a shared logic, linking them to a temporal environment of their own; contextualized representations are proposed in the path and enriched with experiences of augmented reality. The translation of the narrative thought takes place through the virtual reconstructions of the settings of the furnishing or objects or through the assumption of their physical dimension detected with low cost technologies and devices, shared in virtual environments enabling large access to public. In this way the narrative thought organizes the experience allowing the interpretations by those who return the settings, students or museum users (Caspani et al. 2017).

The use of storytelling by users and the need to interface with an audience, obliges the narrator to communicate, through an illustrated story, the memory of the product to control knowledge, and placing of the object in history (Nielsen 2017).

2.2   The Case Studies

The relationship with Triennale Design Museum, referred to the Head of Collections and Archive of Italian Design Museum, led to the selection of different types of objects that represent the variety of the existing collection containing: furnishing elements such as chaise longue, armchair, chair, stool, table lamp, turntable, magazine rack, ice bucket, toilet brush; tableware such as cheese, pots, juicer, jar, ashtray; small work tools such as sewing machine, stapler; objects for the person such as a wristwatch, telephone; small objects such as table clock, radio, fan. Interesting objects for the narration that can light up in the student but also interesting for the different complexity of the survey by size, relief surface, detail to highlight, scale. Il the project the trainee student is invited to tell the story of design in a Storytelling path through the object; the entirety of the objects considered goes from 1935 to 2008 and involves the major production companies such as: Alessi, Arflex, Arteluce, Artemide, Auso Siemens, Balma, Capoduri & C., Brionvega, Enorme Corporation, Flos, Gedy, Kartell, Lorenz, Martinelli Luce, Minerva, O Luce, Produzione Privata, Saporiti, Siemens, Solari, Swatch,Vittorio Necchi, Vortice Elettrosociali, Zani & Zani, Zanotta. The designers of the selected objects also represent a compelling panorama of the history of Italian design by bringing together designers such as Aldo Balma, Mario Bellini, Cini Boeri, Achille Castiglioni, Pier Giacomo Castiglioni, Michele De Lucchi, Design Group Italia, Makio Hasuike, Vico Magistretti, Enzo Mari, Elio Martinelli, Bruno Munari, Marcello Nizzoli, Alberto Rosselli, Aldo Rossi, Richard Sapper, Gino Sarfatti, Ettore Sottsass, Philippe Starck, Giotto Stoppino, Paolo Ulian, Gino Valle, Marco Zanuso.

2.3   Workflow and Methodology

As any real object can be configured as a new digital ecosystem this opportunity has been examined to specify a precise low cost workflow for storytelling linked to the real objects (Lo Turco 2017). The first step of the workflow deals with:

- the modelling of the three-dimensional geometry of the object with simplified photomodelling techniques conveyed by simple software using smrtphone; modeling and texturizing of the same through specific software. included in the app considered looking for a precise virtual image to be used in virtual and augmented reality environments.
- the deepening of the choice of software for modeling virtual environments where specific objects will be embedded. The students have examined the specific literature on the subject trying to verify procedures that are still being tested in the most recent papers dedicated, without any computer programming notions.
- modeling of virtual environments and the insertion of modeled objects for virtual reality use. From here the possibility of inserting the settings in dedicated and usable digital platforms found the basis for a possible digital museum of the samples otherwise stored in the warehouses. The objects are contextualized in specific virtual rooms that differ for the cultural heritage they represent with respect to the years and the authors, to allow a significant variety of choice; different technical choices where adopted to test different surface modeling with different geometric and reflective properties.

- testing Virtual and Augmented reality (William and Gheisari 2014) to be developed in the museum itself.

The project considers to involve a technical partner to be used for providing a network of sensor and technical skills to connect the whole virtual and augmented process starting from fruition of objects in the museum to connect them to virtual models in the web and from the web back to real museum through simple tools and sensors. The possibility of accessing virtual areas through Qcode from the museum itself amplifies the capability offered by the limited nature of any museum.

The possibility to download virtual models allows to make copies of modeled objects from simple 3d printing processes that users can practice from remote.

The whole process is under test processed both by trainees and by students of the master of science of the Polytechnic of Milan coming from different study backgrounds as an experimental flipped class; in the area of a flipped class they can study and test variations within the suggested workflow, offering skills from their field of specific studies and giving the opportunity to develop new tools.

2.4   Technical Tests

To start the experimentation, three design objects were chosen, two of which belonging to the museum collection while one is a furnishing prototype not belonging to the collection. The technical aim is to test with different devices different objects in terms of size, surfaces and detail (from a volume enclosed in a parallelepiped of 15x 10x 3 cm to about 1 m cubic one). The shapes go from the most complex of the precision mechanics of iron to the smooth and slightly reflecting shapes of plastic or leather. The objects presented cavities, convexities, zones of shadows, light and different reflectance (Allegra et al. 2017).

The modeling of the objects takes place through experimentation on smart devices or through low-cost instruments such as that of a student or a large public. The devices tested to create SfM 3D textures through new specific datasets are 3: Sony Xperia XZ1 smartphone and app 3D Creator, Honor 8 with double-focal and 12-megapixel camera with Scan3d app, Samsung Galaxy A3 mono-focal 8-megapixel with Scann 3d. Simultaneously, the capture with traditional photogrammetry was experimented using a Fuji camera fine.

All the chosen devices and connected apps represent the possibility of constructing the models at reduced costs and experimentation for the dissemination of the collections on the web, widening the possibility of use by users, more or less specialized. The features of these applications are ease of use as the image processing is done directly on the device. This reconstruction allows fast processing, such as real-time texturing inside the device, the ability to share the model in a short time, the small size of the model useful for storage in a shared db (Fig. 2).

3D Creator was the app used through Sony Experia Premium camera with a 19megapixel sensor that allows you to take pictures with a resolution of 5056 × 3792 pixels. The app allows different ways of capturing images and independently identifies markers on the object suggesting different capturing paths, depending on the size or morphology; a simple path is used for flat objects. In the case of the stapler, a survey of

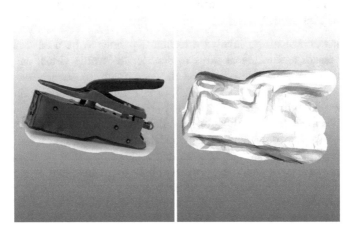

Fig. 2. Stapler, Balma-Capoduri design 1948; virtual model and mesh.

270° was performed around the object with an overlapping of images of 80%, taking care to follow the on-screen indications that allow a transparent overlap between the captures and the real model. It is possible to increase the polygons of the mesh to detail parts that are otherwise not sufficiently defined but the choices of the software are not clarified by the explanation of the app and it is not possible to set the parameters of the captures of the images (Evgenikou and Georgopoulos 2015). The capture phase and the modeling are following steps inside the app process and are carried out quickly within a few minutes. Subsequently it is possible to operate the screen capture of the model or export it with data set of the images in software for modeling.

Scann 3D has been used for 2 different devices: Honor 8 with dual-focal and 12-megapixel camera with resolution images of 4032×3024 pixels and Samsung Galaxy A3 mono-focal 8-megapixel camera. with 3264×2448 resolution images.

The app is compatible for Android and Tablets and it adjusts itself according to the device's camera. There are 3 versions to be evaluated according to the capacity of your smart device. It suggests a capture of the frames as in classical photogrammetry to be developed with an overlap of at least 60% of the image; also the sequence of frames to obtain an optimal result by displaying homologous points in common with two successive images and directing the user to maintain an angle on the vertical of each unchanged, otherwise the images will not overlap (Fig. 3).

The Miss Sissy lamp was surveyed by both phones: in the case of the first one, a textured pattern was generated on a mesh of 26,600 polygons compared to 40 images or 14,000 compared to 30 images. In the second case, meshes of a lower level were obtained with the same number of images. Having to comply with a rapid retopologization, the generated mesh is liable to adjustments, inside it (Lachat et al. 2017).

The model can be saved and in the free version imported in different extention such as. obj. pcd., polygonal mesh., stl. The aberrations due to phenomena related to smooth, reflective or monochromatic surfaces can be avoided by inserting some minute targets affixed to the surface as it was in the Miss Sissi lamp. This app offers a size

Fig. 3. Miss Sissy lamp, Floss, Starck 1990

setting of the frame that hardly supports scans of objects over 1 m also; it sets a variable-size window on the display for capture photographs. Guided instructions suggest a rotation around the object that allows the capture of at least 20 images; less than these it is not possible to build the model (Fig. 4).

Fig. 4. Prototype of an armchair, iron and leather, 1993

To complete the experimentation with the trainees an object of greater dimensions was used with a traditional cameras and methods of photogrammetry.

It is a prototype armchair in colored leather and metal whose large surfaces have been constrained by paper markers derived from the Photoscan software. For this specific objects 120 pictures where captured of the armchair with a Fuji camera fine pix

HS10 con sensore CMOS 1/2.3". The model obtained in a dense cloud had a mesh of about 450.000 polygons. The three objects had common setting of a camera for shooting. For all three it was essential to set up a room with white surfaces to facilitate the processes of identification of the points of congruence. No comparison has been conduct at present in terms of capturing and processing or mesh quality in order to experiment a full pipeline of the experiment.

2.5   First Steps in VR and AR

The workflow considers test of Virtual and Augmented Reality to take advantage of additional information as corollary of the knowledge of the unique object of design (Chua et al. 2014). Of course there is no unique workflow to deal with Virtual and Augmented Reality as technology is continuously progressing, also it deals with different goals of the process (Meža et al. 2014). However, it is possible to define a series of processes where storytelling can be developed in virtual environments. We chose to test Sketchfab platform which allows embedding both point clouds imported in .Las extension from Photoscan software than Sketch up files generated from the software, that we can use for the settings of individual objects. The experiment grows with the development of environments for the placement of 3D models considering thinking of the designers, enriched with semantic contents to be described for individual visualizations. From this point of view, the experiment is open to the contribution of all trainee scholars, to school-work programs, to collaborations with other museums and is finalized to develop digital contents for collections. Generation of Qcode or Bar code is developing to connect real and virtual objects and use them digitally on multiple devices (Fig. 5).

Fig. 5. Simulation of the setting process of the Chiavarina chair

3 Conclusions

This paper links many issues related to heritage education in the digital field; doing so it allows a two-level experimentation: a deepening of the culture of our design and a more specific study on the digitization of the same for inclusion in virtual environments, the realization of augmented reality, the diffusion. This is an ongoing case study whose first conclusions reveal that even in the simplicity of approach technical skills and must be improved in every specific area. For this reason, while the project progresses, we can affirm that: it is necessary to create a connection between humanistic heritage, technical skills and professionalism; relationship between institutions that are most suitable one for the other must be improved (Santagati and Inzerillo 2016); it is the aim of the universities to train skills and professionalism giving training opportunities both to students and professionals (opportunities for work-school turnover); it is always the aim of the universities to keep up new technologies (when not in front of) that are presented to us, favoring phenomena of technological transfer outside and inside the classrooms.

Acknowledgements. The activity presented in the paper is the first phase of a projecy led by the author dedicated to trainees in Politecnico of Milano.

References

Arnaboldi M (2017) Innovazione digitale nei beni ed attività culturali. Osservatorio innovazione digitale nei beni e attività culturali. Press Release 19.01.2017. https://www.osservatori.net/it_it/osservatori/comunicati-stampa/. Accessed 30 Apr 2018

Allegra D, Gallo G, Inzerillo L, Lombardo M, Milotta FLM, Santagati C, Stanco F (2017) Hand held 3D scanning for cultural heritage: experimenting low cost structure sensor scan. In: Handbook of research on emerging technologies for architectural and archaeological heritage, pp 475–499

Caspani S, Brumana R, Oreni D, Previtali M (2017) Virtual museums as digital storytellers for dissemination of built environment. Int Arch Photogramm Remote Sens Spatial Inf Sci XII-2/W5:113–119 XLII-2-W5-113

Chua M, Matthewsa J, Peter ED (2018) Integrating mobile building information modelling and augmented reality systems: an experimental study. Autom Constr 85:305–316

Evgenikou V, Georgopoulos A (2015) Investigating 3D reconstruction methods for small artifacts. Int Arch Photogramm Remote Sens Spat Inf Sci XL-5/W4:101–108

Hess M, Garside D, Nelson T, Robson S, Weyrich T (2017) Object-Based Teaching and learning for a critical assessment of digital technologies in art and cultural heritage. Int. Arch Photogramm Remote Sens Spat Inf Sci XLII-2/W5:349–354

Ioannidis Y, Raheb KE, Toli E, Katifori A, et al (2013) One object many stories: introducing ICT in museums and collections through digital storytelling. In: Digital heritage international congress, pp 421–424

Meža S, Turk S, Dolenc M (2014) Component based engineering of a mobile BIM-based augmented reality system. Autom Constr 42:1–12

Marques L, Tenedório A, Burns M, Româo T et al (2017) Cultural heritage 3D modelling and visualisation within an augmented reality environment, based on geographic information technologies and mobile platforms. ACE: Architect City Environ 11:117–136

Lachat E, Landes T, Grussenmeyer P (2017) Performance investigation of a handheld 3D scanner to define good practices for small artefact 3D modeling. Int Arch Photogramm Remote Sens Spat Inf Sci XLII-2/W5:427–434

Nielsen JK (2017) Museum communication and storytelling: articulating understandings within the museum structure. Mus Manage Curatorship 32(5):440–455

Santagati C, Inzerillo L (2016) Crowdsourcing cultural heritage: from 3D modeling to the engagement of young generations. Digital Heritage. Progress in cultural heritage: documentation, preservation, and protection. Euromed 2016, pp 869–879

Santagati C, Inzerillo L, Di Paola F (2013) Image-based modeling techniques for architectural heritage 3d digitalization limits and potentialities. Int Arch Photogramm Remote Sens Spat Inf Sci XL-5/W2(20):550–560

William G, Gheisari M (2014) BIM2MAR: an efficient BIM translation to mobile augmented reality applications. J Manage Eng 597X/A4014009

Mixed Virtuality in the Communication of Cultural Heritage

Tommaso Empler[✉]

Department of History, Representation and Restoration of Architecture,
Sapienza University of Rome, Piazza Borghese 9, 00186 Rome, Italy
tommaso.empler@uniroma1.it

Abstract. ICTs are today frequently used in the communication of cultural heritage. Among these Mixed Virtuality offers a visualization system on smart devices where, depending on the needs of dissemination, the reconstructions of objects and spaces can be viewed in Virtual Reality or Augmented Reality mode. As a case study, an application is proposed in the archaeological area of the Acropolis of Volterra.

Keywords: 3D modeling · ICT · Augmented Reality · Virtual Reality · Mixed Virtuality

1 Introduction

Today, thanks to ICT, it is possible to return the appearance of objects, spaces or architectures of the past, modifying the perception of cultural heritage by contemporary users. ICTs are a powerful tool to achieve the goal of enhancing cultural heritage: multimedia and interaction have the ability to engage the visitor in a simple and immediate way, offering an innovative and engaging experience.

In this direction, the design of visual and multimedia communication finds an effective field of application associated with ICT. The virtual, considered initially as a simple technique to support new forms of interaction with the public, has, over time, extended its field of action, assuming an autonomous cultural dimension, which, especially in archeology and architecture, finds a field of successful application, as an expression of a vocation inherent in the subject: the tendency towards reconstruction (Borghini and Carlani 2011).

In 3D reconstruction of an archaeological site or of an architecture of the past, two important factors converge in the communication of cultural heritage: the historical object lives again, opening the way to the imagination and to the visitors' interest. With due attention in reporting the scientific and historical data, on which the storytelling must be based, it is possible to grasp in ICT the means that open the way to new perspectives of conservation and research in the archaeological/architectural field, able to create new consciousness and awareness of cultural heritage, as it is able to rethink the condition of fruition and valorisation, through an active vision of what has reached us.

The term "virtual archeology" was born in 1990 when Paul Reilly (Reilly 1990) proposed it in reference to the use of three-dimensional models of monuments and

A. Luigini (Ed.): EARTH 2018, AISC 919, pp. 575–586, 2019.
https://doi.org/10.1007/978-3-030-12240-9_60

objects, configuring it as a discipline through which have a visual access to data difficult to observe. Through the construction of models and simulations it is possible to recreate a cognitive process on the past and to make it accessible to others, through an active presentation system.

Within virtual archeology two components seem to emerge: one strictly related to research and the other to communication. This is a design process that does not end with the simple digital transformation of a cultural asset, but takes as input the results of the research, and then constitutes a channel of visual communication aimed at a broad audience, which, with a due in-depth analysis to an audience of experts. A virtual archeology project is therefore divided into a first phase of data collection and processing and a second phase of dissemination of the message prepared for the general public (Pescarin et al. 2011).

2   Related Works

There are many achievements with which cultural heritage is disseminated through ICT. Some applications, made in recent years in Rome, are taken as related works:

- *Travels in Ancient Rome*, with interest from the Forum of Augustus and the Forum of Caesar;
- *The Ara as it was*, which concerns the divulgation of the Ara Pacis Augustae;
- *Domus Aurea*, with the reconstruction of the appearance it had at the time of Emperor Nero;
- *Caracalla Baths in 3D*, virtual reconstruction of the baths complex in its heyday.

2.1   Travels in Ancient Rome

"Travels in ancient Rome", including the Forum of Augustus and the Forum of Caesar, are exhibitions conceived by Piero Angela and Paco Lanciano in 2014. The story regarding the Forum of Augustus begins with the marbles still visible on site and, through multiprojection, with the use of lights, images, films and animations, focuses on the figure of Augustus, whose gigantic statue, 12 m high, dominated the area adjacent to the temple. In 2015 the opening of the Forum of Caesar reaches an extraordinary success with 140,000 spectators from all over the world and with a very high overall satisfaction. The project "Travels in Ancient Rome" tells the Forum of Augustus and the Forum of Caesar starting from stones, fragments and columns present on site, with the use of cutting-edge technologies. The spectators are accompanied by the voice of Piero Angela and magnificent films and projections that reconstruct those places as they appeared in ancient Rome: an exciting representation and at the same time full of information from the great historical and scientific rigor.

2.2   The Ara as It Was

The exhibition "The Ara as it was" foresees the use of a combination of hardware and software tools for the fruition of a path of discovery and deepening of the *Ara Pacis*

Augustae, based on Augmented Reality and Virtual Reality experiences. At the entrance each visitor receives a VR (Samsung GearVR) viewer, that allow him to live an immersive and interactive experience. Through this tool and thanks to points of interest (POIs) in Virtual Reality, which combine live film shoots, reconstructions in 3D and computer graphics, visitors are immersed in a 360° environment and can admire the Ara Pacis while finding its original colors. The visit begins with a video, designed for a 360° visualization of the environment where the Ara Pacis was located around 14 AD, a green area where Ara Pacis, the Mausoleum of Augustus, the Obelisk of Augustus and the Pantheon were visible; at the end of the introduction video, it is possible to observe particular areas of the monument's surface, come to life and witness a sacrifice, realized with the presence of real actors shot in "green screen" mode. The visit continues through the successive POI, where the original colors of the monument appear and additional information on the stories of the bas-reliefs appear "anchored" to them thanks to Augmented Reality and Virtual Reality.

Samsung Gear VR viewer paired with Samsung S7/8 smartphone, is a solution designed for the use of Virtual Reality, but also for Augmented Reality experiences. At present, this technological solution allows a fusion of real elements and virtual elements.

For the realization of the exhibition, a "3D tracking" system is used for the Augmented Reality experience that uses advanced algorithms in the field of "computer vision". Thanks to this property, the entire proposed AR system is able to recognize the three-dimensionality of the bas-reliefs of sculptural objects and to perform a tracking on them in real time. This recognition system makes the enhanced contents appear as anchored to real objects, contributing to the effectiveness and the immersiveness of the whole experience.

2.3 Domus Aurea: Virtual Journey into Nero's House

Starting from February 2017, the Domus Aurea is visited through a new immersive technology, which allows to see some rooms, especially the "Room from the golden vault", as they were in the times of Nero. Thanks to Virtual Reality, the nymphs and the gods of Olympus, which decorate the vault of the hall at a height of twelve meters, are visible in details. The new technology, usable through twenty-five hi-tech stations equipped with advanced stereoscopic viewers and accompanied by a video-story at the entrance of the monument, allows a multimedia path that revolutionizes the perception of the monument itself.

The effect is a 360-degree time shift that brings the visitor back to the room as it was in the times of Nero and tears off the wall that closes the environment, flooding it with light and bringing to the eyes of the visitor the colonnade and the large garden overlooking the Rome of the first century after Christ. An exhibition that brings to life marbles, frescoes, stuccoes and gilding, commissioned by Nero to his architects, who knew how to measure the light, aiming to erase the palace built above by Trajan to build the baths.

The path, inside the most mysterious monument of ancient Rome, begins with a video story, that welcomes visitors at the entrance of the Domus, reconstructing its history: from the original building to the "damnatio memoriae" desired by Traiano, who buried it, using it as foundations for its baths, up to the time of the second world war, when the galleries were used as refuge for displaced persons. The path continues in the "Room from the golden vault", where the visitor experiences the thrill of immersing himself in Nero's House.

The visit begins with a high-tech biocular viewer (oculus rift), which virtually transforms the environment, today dark and closed from the earth, making it return to its original dimension. Visitors can see the wonders of the Domus Aurea, the walls and the painted vaults, or the famous "grotesques", so called by the Renaissance artists - among which Raphael and Pinturicchio - who discovered, starting from the sixteenth century, these decorations descending into the "cave", through holes.

2.4   Caracalla Baths in 3D

A journey through time, through the fourth dimension: the Baths of Caracalla become the first large Italian archaeological site entirely usable in 3D. Virtual reality allows to see the Baths not just as they are today, but as they were in 216 AD, at the time of their inauguration.

The project, promoted by the Special Superintendence of Rome, offers visitors the opportunity to read and interpret the grand remains of the Baths of the Emperors of the Severi dynasty, in a continuous confrontation between physical and Virtual Reality, between present and past.

The technology is based on a viewer, inside which a smartphone with a specific software is inserted. With simple commands managed by a single button, the device with geo-referencing, reproduces the places where the visitor is located with an immersive perspective, covering all the visual space. The viewers are available at the entrance to the Baths during the normal opening hours of the monument. The visit, articulated in ten steps, of which 6 are with Virtual Reality, is based on philological reconstructions of the Baths, based on the studies of the last thirty years. Inside the digital reconstructions are included real images of some statues and decorations of the thermal plant, coming from various places, including the National Archaeological Museum of Naples.

3   Research

The target of the research is to document how through the use of ICT (Empler 2018), applied to portable devices belonging to visitors, it is possible to obtain a real-time dissemination of the history of an outdoor archaeological in "Mixed Virtuality" mode (MV), understood as a combination of "Virtual Reality" (VR) and "Augmented Reality" (AR). As an application case it is proposed the Acropolis of Volterra, according to the hypothesis of interactive and multimedia dissemination by Anna Montesi[1].

---

[1] Anna Montesi was graduated in the Master's Degree in Design, Visual and Multimedia Communication - Sapienza University of Rome, with a thesis entitled: Velathri. On the traces of a shadow, A.A. 2016-2017. Supervisor: Tommaso Empler; External supervisor: Elena Sorge.

3.1   Mixed Virtuality

In a conventional vision of a Virtual Reality (VR) environment the observer is totally immersed and able to interact with a virtually rebuilt world. The world can imitate the properties of some real-world spaces, existing or fictitious, or it can overcome the limits of physical reality by creating a world where the physical laws that ordinarily rule space, time, mechanics, material properties, etc. do not correspond to what happens in reality. What may be overlooked in this view is that the VR label is often used in association with a variety of other environments, to which total immersion and complete synthesis are not necessarily pertinent, but which fall somewhere along a continuum of virtuality (Milgram et al. 1994).

Augmented Reality (AR) systems aim to increase real-world information by superimposing computer-generated information. Azuma (Azuma 1997) identifies 3 main features in AR systems: (1) combine real and virtual, (2) interact in "real time", (3) record information in 3D.

Applications of AR are mainly addressed to smart instruments, demonstrating how these devices have excellent potential for visualizations based on AR tracking systems, linked to GPS position of the instrument used.

At present, Augmented Reality systems are basically two (Empler 2015):

– Augmented Reality using a mobile device (smartphone or tablet) based on GPS position. System requirements are the equipment of a Global Positioning System (GPS), the magnetometer (compass) and the ability to view a video stream in real time, as well as an internet connection to receive data online. The camera of the device frames the surrounding environment in real time, on which content levels are superimposed, with data referring to geolocalized Points of Interest (PDI) or 3D elements
– Augmented reality on a mobile device with the use of ARTags markers, which, viewed by the camera through a tracking system, are recognized by the application launched on the smart tool, where multimedia contents are superimposed in real time: video, audio, 3D objects. For each ARTag a certain number of information can be hooked up and the application must be able to automatically scan the Tag itself in real time, identifying the characteristic and unique trackpoints for each one.

In this context is proposed the term "Mixed Virtuality" (MV)[2], meaning a display system on smart devices where, according to the dissemination needs, the reconstructions of objects and spaces can be visualized in VR or AR mode. The display on smart instruments can be on the display or in immersive mode, using a low-cost head-mounted device (going from a similiar google card box to a similiar GearVR), with the ability to view the external reality through the camera of the portable device.

Virtual Reality, abbreviated with the initials VR, is able to simulate a reconstructed reality through the complete immersion of the user in a virtual space, created through a

---

[2] The term "mixed reality' is not used because it is mainly recognized as the commercial name that Microsoft has given to its platform that includes VR (the headset MR) and AR (Hololens). It is a framework (integrated with Unity) that allows to develop applications for microsoft devices.

process of 3D modeling and visualized through VR devices, moving inside and inter-acting with the objects present in that specific virtual space, as happens, for example, with the latest generation videogames. The virtual world is an environment suitable for performing artificial life experiments, studying people's social behavior and supporting new forms of communication. Simplifying the concept, the meaning of the virtual experience is given by the relations between two categories: presence and immersion.

"Presence" means the level of psychological realism that a person experiences from the interaction with the virtual world, in the instantaneous relationship with the envi-ronment and in coherence of its evolution with respect to expectations and forecasts. For example, if an object is left on hold, it is expected to fall to the ground and not float in the air; if it is a fragile object, it is expected that, on contact with the ground, it is damaged more or less severely. If this did not happen, the sense of "presence" in the virtual environment would be lost.

The word "immersion" refers, from a perceptual point of view, to the capacity of the virtual environment to directly involve the senses of a person, isolating him from the stimuli of the real environment.

From a psychological point of view, "immersion" is realized with the involvement and use of the cognitive abilities of a person. Taking as an example a body that is dropped, "immersion" is given not only by the tactile sensation of the object that slips away from the hand, by the sound produced from the impact with the ground and by the visual consequences of the action, but by the activation of the automatic processes linked to the attempt to resume it before it touches the ground and it is damaged.

The purpose why this type of technology is chosen is different from the purely play-like end of video games, but retains its immersive characteristic. In the field of cultural heritage, Virtual Reality allows the reconstruction of faithful reproductions of sites belonging to the historical and cultural heritage, which can be published and dissem-inated through various media and platforms (Pimentel and Teixeira 1993).

Archaeological sites are often places where the remains are stratified for millennia and have a state of conservation that does not allow to understand what were the dimensions of the buildings that stood there. This is due to both a stratification of the urban fabric in different eras, and from the construction material of those buildings and from the destruction events of which the archaeological site was victim, which made their perfect preservation until today impossible. It often happens that sites of historical interest can be banned from the public or, because of the passing of years and poor maintenance, it is impossible to interpret them correctly (Pletinckx et al. 2000).

With the help of Mixed Virtuality it is possible to reconstruct replicas of archae-ological sites (caves, natural environments, ancient cities, monuments, sculptures, etc.) facilitating communication and dissemination.

The goal is to be able to reconstruct a journey back in time: to succeed in order it is necessary to "physically" bring the visitor in the period under examination.

As a case study, is taken the Acropolis of Volterra, where are placed 9 points of interest (POI). In two of them is used Virtual Reality: the first, useful to introduce the spectator to the visit, bringing him in the medieval age; the last, useful to internalize what he has learned throughout the journey, since he has the opportunity to perceive in its totality the appearance of the acropolis, when the Etruscan temples still exist, which during the visit had the opportunity to see individually and in thorough way, thanks to the use of Augmented Reality.

From what has been write, can be understand the need to use both Virtual Reality and Augmented Reality: rebuilding what was the atmosphere of certain historical periods is possible only by encouraging total immersion in space, thanks to a special three-dimensional reconstruction of their appearance at the time and the use of an appropriate sound. Mixed Virtuality, applied to such a context, is able to add information to the real scene, through a superimposed process.

3.2 3D Modeling

From the point of view of 3D modeling, two different reconstruction paths are carried out: the reconstruction of the morphology of the Volterra terrain; the reconstruction of buildings present in different historical periods.

3D reconstructions, carried out on surveys and scientific data provided by the Superintendent, see the following models (present in the 9 POIs):

- Etruscan acropolis, II century BC;
- Late archaic temple, V century BC (Fig. 1);
- Temple B of Hellenistic Age, III century BC (Fig. 2);
- The temple of the Goddess Demeter, II century BC;
- Temple A of late Hellenistic age, II century BC (Fig. 3);
- Roman cistern, I century AD (Fig. 4);
- District of "Castello", XIII century AD;
- Towers houses, XII-XIV century AD;
- Sack of Volterra, XV century AD (Fig. 5).

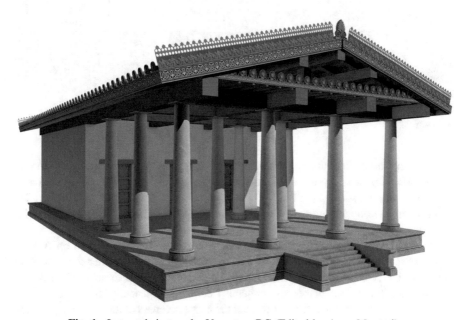

Fig. 1. Late archaic temple, V century BC (Edited by Anna Montesi).

In the realization of the 3D model of the ground morphology of Volterra, is used Rhinoceros Land Design plugin. In the medieval period the morphology of the upper part of the plateau corresponds to that of today, while in the Etruscan period it had a greater extension towards the north-west front, where there were two temples, destroyed with a subsequent landslide of the area. In the reconstruction of the medieval period, Grasshopper was used as a Rhinoceros plugin.

Land Design reproduces the overall dimensions of the buildings present today in Volterra; for an effective historical reconstruction, today's data intersected with the evidence emerging from historical research, aimed at identifying which buildings existed in the fifteenth century. After this phase, the research was directed to identify how the remaining buildings were presented at the time, in order to reconstruct them correctly in 3D. The reconstruction of buildings from the Hellenistic period follows the indications provided by a thorough historical investigation.

Fig. 2. Temple B of Hellenistic Age, III century BC. AR view on the site (Edited by Anna Montesi).

The next modeling phase, which involves texturing, is developed with Maxon Cinema 4D, supported by the CVCam CV plugin, which allows to position cameras capable of capturing images at 360°, thanks to a mesh with radius of 90° display. The path is completed by exporting two movies in stereoscopic format, suitable for viewing in Virtual Reality.

For Augmented Reality is used a 3D real time tracking system, based on ARTag, thanks to which, the whole AR system is able to recognize the three-dimensionality of the archaeological remains present in the site and to perform on them the tracking in real time. This recognition system makes the enhanced contents appear as "anchored" to real objects, contributing to the effectiveness and the immersiveness of the whole experience.

Seven of the nine points of interest within the Archaeological Park are intended for viewing in Augmented Reality through the use of the smartphone placed inside a viewer (such as GearVR) that the visitor uses for the entire time of the visit. In this way, he has the opportunity to dwell on each reconstruction to understand its details, moving from one point of interest to the next, and not perceiving the whole context as a whole, as happens with Virtual Reality.

Fig. 3. Temple A of late Hellenistic age, II century BC (Edited by Anna Montesi).

Also in this case, before proceeding to 3D tracking, we proceed to the three-dimensional reconstruction of the contents that are submitted to this type of visualization, following the indications of historical sources. This reconstruction and texturing operation is carried out by Maxon Cinema 4D.

Once the 3D model and the subsequent texturing phase have been completed, everything is imported onto Unity (in a format capable of maintaining the textures) which, thanks to Vuforia's extension, allows the 3D tracking of the scene, that is to connect in the three-dimensional virtual space, the object reconstructed to the scene to which it must respond, in the position corresponding to the one displayed inside the archaeological site.

In the Mixed Virtuality process there is the need to use a single device for the visitor, both in the reconstructed parts in Virtual Reality, in those submitted to Augmented Reality, and at the different level of immersion: in VR the user must use an instrument that projects him completely into the artificial world, separating him from the real context, hearing and proprioception are under the complete control of the computer; in an AR system, information overlaps with the real world scene.

Fig. 4. Roman cistern, I century AD. AR view on the site (Edited by Anna Montesi).

Fall, therefore, the possibility of using devices that only use Virtual Reality, such as the Oculus Rift, HTC Vive or Playstation VR, and the choice is turned to a VR support for smartphones, where the video component is processed and displayed through the same smartphone, limiting the function of the support to that of support and adjustment of the focus. The advantage of this solution, as well as the costs and the versatility of the support itself (as it can be adapted to any type of smartphone) is to adapt to both types of vision. Another advantage, which allows free use in the archaeological park, is the transportability at every point of the archaeological site, as it does not provide connection to a PC or other external devices, but the multimedia content is contained in the memory of the smartphone itself.

Fig. 5. Sack of Volterra, XV century AD. VR view (Edited by Anna Montesi).

The experience proposes the use of a viewer like Samsung GearVR (2016) compatible with Galaxy S7, S7 edge, Galaxy S6, S6 edge and S6 edge + that provides the ability to use controllers via Bluetooth or micro USB and to activate the camera. It is the most ergonomic and light device with a soft polyurethane strap and padding, equipped with its own sensors such as accelerometer, gyroscope, proximity sensor able to recognize the position of the head and therefore suitable to reproduce the display in Augmented Reality. It has a field of vision that allows 360-degree panoramas and an intuitive touchpad that controls the smartphone placed inside the viewer. It measures 98.6 mm in height, 207.8 mm in width and 122.5 mm in depth with a weight of 345 g and a viewing angle of 101°.

4   Results and Conclusion

The procedure used to document the Acropolis of Volterra demonstrates how ICT is nowadays very useful for disseminating medium and large outdoor archaeological areas.

Using the Mixed Virtuality procedure and devices compatible to the visualization (smart devices + viewer), the visitor can satisfy his personal curiosity needs and completely revive the aspects that the places had in the different historical periods.

Perception is even richer if at least 3 profiles of visitors are considered, each with a different type of need: child or young adolescent, adult with medium knowledge interests and researchers and scholars. A further development of the system should provide the integration of 3D reconstructions with a gamification procedure, making the visitors active during the experience, with a path that allows them to obtain virtual awards, which can be transformed into bonuses or discounts for the visit of other sites or museums or the acquisition of gadgets or souvenirs connected to the Acropolis.

References

Azuma RT (1997) A survey of augmented reality. Presence: Teleoperators and Virtual Environ 6(4): 355–385 (1997)

Borghini S, Carlani R (2011) Virtual rebuilding of ancient architecture as a researching and communication tool for Cultural Heritage: aesthetic research and source management. DisegnareCon, pp 62–70, December 2011

Empler T (2015) APP design con uso della realtà aumentata per la divulgazione dei Beni Culturali. Disegnare, Idee, Immagini, n 50, p 60

Empler T (2018) ICT per il Cultural Heritage. Rappresentare, Comunicare, Divulgare. Dei – Tipografia del Genio Civile

Milgram P, Takemura H, Utsumi A, Kishino F (1994) Augmented reality: a class of displays on the reality-virtuality continuum. SPIE Telemanipulator and Telepresence Technologies 2351 (1994):283

Pescarin S, Fanini B, Lucci Baldassari G, Ferdani D, Calori L (2011) Realism, Interactivity and Performance: a pipeline for large scale Virtual Heritage dataset on line. DisegnareCon, pp 71–78, December 2011

Pimentel K, Teixeira K (1993) Virtual reality. McGraw-Hill, New York

Pletinckx D, Callebaut D, Killebrew A.E, Silberman NA (2000) Virtual-reality heritage presentation at Ename. On-site VR paragraph, in MultiMedia, vol 7, pp 45–48. IEEE

Reilly P (1990) Towards a virtual archaeology. In: Lockyear K, Rahtz S (ed) Computer Applications in Archaeology 1990. Oxford: British Archaeological reports (Int. Series 565), pp 133–139

Advanced Simulation of Frank Lloyd Wright's Fallingwater: Digital Reconstruction and Virtual Reality

Alberto Sdegno[1(✉)], Paola Cochelli[2], Veronica Riavis[2], and Simone Veneziano[2]

[1] Polytechnic Department of Engineering and Architecture (DPIA), University of Udine, Via delle Scienze 206, 33100 Udine, Italy
alberto.sdegno@uniud.it

[2] Department of Engineering and Architecture (DIA), University of Trieste, Piazzale Europa 1, 34127 Trieste, Italy
{paola.cochelli,veronica.riavis}@phd.units.it,
veneziano.simone@gmail.com

Abstract. The aim of the research was the geometric analysis, the digital reconstruction and the real-time simulation of the Fallingwater House designed by Frank Lloyd Wright for Edgar Kaufmann in the forest area of Pennsylvania. The research wants to define a procedure to be used for advanced perception of contemporary architecture designed inside natural contexts using new technologies of Virtual Reality. A detailed study of the spatial configuration of the environment was the main step of the work, considering 3D modeling of terrain morphology and different types of vegetation. Then we used 3D procedural shaders to apply static realistic material effects on surfaces and advanced dynamic shaders for moving materials, such as the water of the river. In this case three different typologies of water were defined, using particle flow procedures, to simulate running water, waterfall and water vapor generated with the collision of water on the rocks. The final step was to use a Virtual Reality System to allow users to explore in real-time the whole exterior and interior space of the scene. Thanks to the advanced restitution we can understand better the close relationship between *natura naturans* and *natura naturata*.

Keywords: Frank Lloyd Wright · Fallingwater House · Digital representation · 3D modeling · Real-time rendering · Virtual Reality

1 Introduction

Frank Lloyd Wright (1867–1959) designed the Fallingwater House (Fig. 1) on behalf of Edgar Kaufmann in the years 1934–37, in the forest area of Pennsylvania, at about 400 m altitude (Riley and Reed 1994). The project is among the best known in the history of architecture and at the same time one of the most difficult to reach, due to its geographical location. Built about 100 km South-East from Pittsburg, in Mill Run, it is surrounded by a mountainous area with dense vegetation, and is crossed by the stream Bear Run, which will become an integral part of the Wright's project.

© Springer Nature Switzerland AG 2019
A. Luigini (Ed.): EARTH 2018, AISC 919, pp. 587–596, 2019.
https://doi.org/10.1007/978-3-030-12240-9_61

Fig. 1. Frank Lloyd Wright, perspective view of the Fallingwater House, 1936 (The Frank Lloyd Wright Foundation).

The aim of the research was to analyze the project inside the context and to reconstruct the natural and architectural scene in order to allow a virtual exploration that could simulate the real conditions of visit. To this end, we decided to proceed by defining an operative protocol that took into account the optimal conditions for a qualitative performance of the experimentation. This protocol concerned first of all the technical-scientific knowledge of the architectural work. Therefore, an investigation has been started on the architect and on the author's theoretical writings, to understand his *modus operandi* above all considering the relationship between *natura naturans* and *natura naturata*.

The close link between the naturalness of the context and architecture, in fact, is essential to understand the particular approach during the design phase. This report is documented in various texts such as Lloyd Wright 1931, 1939, but, above all, an essay which appeared in the journal "Architectural Record" in 1908, entitled *In the Cause of Architecture* (Lloyd Wright 1908), written, as the author claimed, more than ten years earlier. In this paper, the author describes in detail six fundamental principles to which the designer must abide, in order to respect the natural context in which the work should have been carried out. Among them surely the third and fifth principles were carefully evaluated during this work, even if we took into account all the architect's design poetics. The third principle connects topography to architecture, so that the constructed work appears "as if it arose spontaneously from the land on which it is located". A perfect fusion between naturalness and artificiality must be considered by the designer in the concept phase, to allow an ideal fusion between the two subjects. The fifth principle, moreover, is in some ways linked to the previous one, as it is related to the nature of the materials. Each of them – wood, brick, stone, stucco, or other – must appear showing their physical characteristics, such as grain, roughness, smoothness, chromatism, etc. If we take a look of the interior space of the house (Fig. 2) this principle is clearly evident.

If we decline these two principles within the scope of this research, we realize how often they are not taken into consideration in the delicate phase of the simulation of an architecture inserted in its context. Often, in fact, nature is modeled using 3D software in a manner dissimilar to the architectural space, highlighting the formal and chromatic differences in a clear manner. Even the quality of the material performance is almost always underestimated, to rely on the easy application of standard texture files that do not realistically express the formal and chromatic peculiarities of a specific object of investigation.

Further bibliographic references help us to adapt the problems of advanced representation with those relating to the work being studied and above all to the author's design philosophy.

Due to the complexity of the work and to the aims of the research, we decided to define a strict strategy of approach in order to obtain the best result both in terms of simplified procedures and in terms of final outcome. So the relevant steps are: modeling and texturing the architectural space, constructing the morphology for the environment, define the typologies of vegetation, water and chimney's fire and smoke, preparing illumination algorithms, converting all the scene to be explored with a 3D Head-Mounted Display (HMD) used for an immersive real-time navigation of the whole space (Gaiani 2003; Gaiani et al. 2011).

Fig. 2. Photograph of the interior of the living room.

2   Modeling and Texturing Architecture

After the investigation phase, the various aspects related to some specific problems of digital processing have been studied. This second part of the work was subdivided into a series of operative sections, aimed at pointing out the different peculiarities.

The first section concerned the 2D tracing of plans, sections and elevations, in order to obtain the 3D model of the house. In this case all the floors and the walls were constructed using horizontal and vertical linear extrusion, without considering the juts of the stone. The obtained model is a simplified one, used to some preliminary verifications of the correctness of the single parts.

Then we started to analyze every single surface in relation to its material. So if stone slabs are not aligned to the front of a wall, for example, we create a specific model of every jut to render exactly the effect of the material itself. The simple way – normally used – of applying two-dimensional textures on a flat surface (texture mapping), in fact, does not allow to obtain – in this specific case – a significant result, for which it was necessary to work with the hybrid simulation modes described before, that took into account the stereometric yield of the shapes of the materials, on which textures were arranged for each individual element associated, to allow the perfect correspondence between extensions, edges and bound lines.

The materials were also analyzed in detail with regard to the simulation of rocks, both from a morphological point of view and from an environmental verisimilitude (Fig. 3).

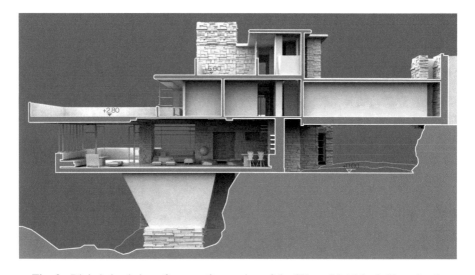

Fig. 3. Digital simulation of perspective section of the 3D model (elab. S. Veneziano).

Another aspect was the way in which the furniture was modeled. To have a final model with a small number of faces – a Low Poly (LP) model – we reduced significantly the number of polygons of every initial object – the High Poly (HP) model –, thinking to work with specific rendering procedures that take into account this solution, as we will present in a further chapter (Fig. 4).

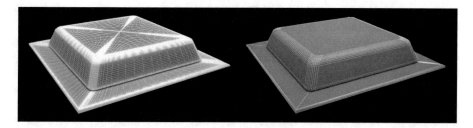

Fig. 4. One of the designer's couch, with different number of polygons: left, the model with 168,514 polygons (HP); right, the model having 1,056 polygons (LP) (elab. S. Veneziano).

3 Sampling Nature

The second relevant aspect was to simulate the natural elements of the scene: the morphology of the terrain with its texture, the vegetation, based on different typologies and positions of trees, the water of the river, the fire and the smoke of the chimney. In this case the simulation modalities have been diversified too, taking into account the 3D topographical lines of the hill, and working with specific procedural shader (Fig. 5a) to interpolate the different configurations of the hill (Fig. 5b).

(a)   **(b)**

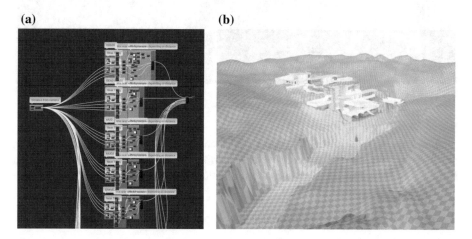

Fig. 5. (a) Procedural shader applied to terrain; (b) Final model of the morphology of the terrain; (elab. S. Veneziano).

Then we passed to consider vegetation. The design of the different types of trees took into account the perception distance from a hypothetical eye of the visitor. To the timely modeling of the essences in the foreground, photographic images of those in the background have been associated, integrating the scene with the control of the physical dynamics, thanks to algorithms that calculate the movement of the foliage if subjected to small and sustained gusts of wind. This strategy allowed us to obtain a good final effect with a model based on a small number of polygons.

The other relevant element was the water – that is the main factor characterizing the whole architectural design. In this case we decided to use three different types of fluid components. On one hand the natural flow of the stream, with a slow horizontal movement; then the vertical waterfall – from top to bottom – and finally the analysis of the collision between the water of the waterfall and the rock below, in order to obtain the visual generation of water vapor, typical of this physical condition. In this case it was necessary to use particle systems prepared ad hoc for every situation, using specific shader procedures (Fig. 6). Single aspects were organized in steps, to calculate in real-time the movement, the density of flow, the collision surfaces, the behavior of the particle model touching the rocks.

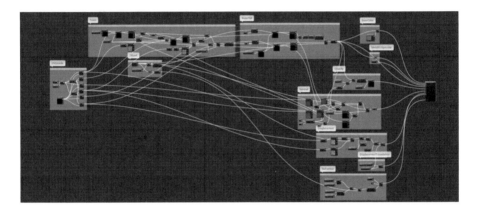

Fig. 6. Procedural shader of the water (elab. S. Veneziano).

Finally, also the fire and the smoke were treated with particle systems, controlling the flame height inside the chimney, the distribution of the fire, the starting of the smoke from there and the direction and diffusion of it outdoors.

4   Global Illumination and Rendering Procedures

The last aspect taken into consideration – before analyzing the type of interface to be used – was the natural lighting of the context, exploiting the potential of Global Illumination (GI) algorithms that allowed the calculation of the direct and diffused light component both inside the house and outside. Often the two specific cases (indoor and outdoor) are simulated differently due to various factors that affect the generation of images and related likely sequences: the reflection of the walls, in fact – as regards the interior – is a value added to the direct component, substantially modifying both the chromatism of the environment (which depends on the color tones of the horizontal and vertical surfaces) and its saturation. In detail two different types of rendering procedures were used: Forward Rendering (FR) and Deferred Rendering (DR). The first one is used to calculate all the elements of the scene, multiplying all the computation of reflecting and diffusing light. The result was very precise but the time of calculation was high, if applied to every object. The second one considers only the surface touched directly from the light source, and so the time of computation is very small, although the final image (or sequence of images in the case of a video animation) has a lower quality than the first one.

So it was necessary to use DR for the great part of objects of the model, assigning FR only to some elements – mainly transparent and specular objects – to reduce the time of computation, and allowing to generate the real-time rendering of the architectural scene (Fig. 7).

Fig. 7. Screenshot of the real-time rendering of the scene (elab. S. Veneziano).

5   Virtual Reality Procedure Applied to Digital Model

The modeling and simulation phase, carried out with a real-time rendering engine based on GPU calculation (Graphic Processor Unit), followed by the use of a virtual simulation interface of HMD interface with datagloves for direct interaction with the model by the user. We must immediately specify that the use of GPU algorithms is based on the different discretization of the model, as we said before (see Sect. 2), in terms of morphological simplification, so to make the dynamism more fluent within the virtual space, with a modeling technique based on low polygons forms (LP modeling).

Also the rendering calculation tools into account the DR (see Sect. 4), which only calculates the shadows of the objects framed in the scene, limiting the computational count to minimum.

A useful additional tool was the planar development of the texture on every surface (Unwrap), which allowed to work on textures in a following phase, to improve the quality of the final yield of the same. To understand the effect of the unwarp procedure we can see Fig. 8, which show a typical chair designed by the architect for this house, with the planar description of every single surfaces. Both textures and shadows can be defined, reducing the time of rendering and allowing real-time navigation.

Fig. 8. Chair designed by Frank Lloyd Wright for the interior of the house: left, 3D model; center, Unwrap texture; right, final GI model (elab. S. Veneziano).

Fig. 9. Real-time navigation of the digital Fallingwater with Head Mounted Display.

The final phase of the work was reserved for implementation the scene into the 3D visualization system, taking advantage of a HMD stereoscopic virtual helmet (Fig. 9) (Sdegno 2018). The modes of movement within the scene have been defined, with collision surfaces and path tracing considering the teleportation system that simulates the discontinuous advancement in a context. This way of behaving inside a space allowed to simulate the progressive approach by a virtual user from the outside of the house, crossing the path on the small pedestrian bridge leading to the house, entering the large furnished living room to pass on the terraced platform that overlooks on the stream. The movement within the space has allowed for each area a 360° visualization in real-time, providing an advanced perception of the architecture, similar – though only visually – to the feeling that a real visitor can have inside of this extraordinary example of contemporary architecture.

6 Conclusion

The results allowed us to define a working protocol, useful for further experimentations to be applied in the scientific field of 3D simulation procedures for architectural contexts (Sdegno et al. 2017). The next step of the research will be dedicated, in fact, to verify the possibility to apply this procedure to some other works by Frank Lloyd Wright we have already considered, such as, for example, the Masier Memorial, designed by the architect for the city of Venice, just in front of the Grand Canal, (Sdegno 2011), or the Imperial Hotel in Tokyo (Sdegno and Masserano 2017), were some pools of water are located in front of the main entrance of the building.

In both cases, as in some other designs by Frank Lloyd Wright, the role of natural landscape is as important as architecture.

References

Gaiani M (2003) Grafica real time. In: Gaiani M (ed) Metodi di prototipazione digitale e visualizzazione per il disegno industriale. Edizioni POLI.design, Milano, pp 307–510

Gaiani M, Ferioli S, Ricci PC (2011) Visualizzazione real-time per l'arredo. Implementazione di sistemi di visualizzazione in real-time per la pre-visualizzazione e la customizzazione di oggetti di arredo d'interni in fase di progetto e di presentazione. In: Docci M, Filippa M, Chiavoni E (eds) Metodologie integrate per il rilievo, il disegno, la modellazione dell'architettura e della città. Gangemi, Roma, pp 144–164

Lloyd Wright F (1908) In the cause of architecture. In: Architectural record, vol XXIII, pp 155–221

Lloyd Wright F (1931) An autobiography. Duell Sloan and Pearce, New York

Lloyd Wright F (1939) An organic architecture. The architecture of democracy. Lund Humphries & Co., London

Riley T, Reed P (eds) (1994) Frank Lloyd Wright architect 1867–1959. The Museum of Modern Art, New York

Sdegno A (2011) The Masieri memorial by Frank L. Wright in Venice. In: Zupancic T, Juvancic M, Jutraz A (eds) Respecting Fragile Places. UNI Ljubljana, Ljubljana, pp 960–966

Sdegno A (2018) Augmented visualization. New technologies for communicating Architecture. In: Rossi M, Buratti G (eds) Computational morphologies: design rules between organic models and responsive architecture. Springer, Cham, pp 197–202

Sdegno A, Masserano S (2017) Reloading the imperial hotel by Frank Lloyd Wright. Graphic analysis and virtual rebuilding. In: Gambardella C (ed) World heritage and disaster. Knowledge, culture and representation. La Scuola di Pitagora editrice, Napoli

Sdegno A, Ranon R, Cabezos Bernal P-M, Masserano S, Cochelli P (2017) Reloading Le Corbusier's architectures with new technologies for advanced visualization of cultural heritage. In: Ceccarelli M, Cigola M, Recinto G (eds) New activities for cultural heritage. Springer, Cham, pp 166–173

Territory and Maps

Representing a Space-Based Digital Archive on Historical Maps: A User-Centered Design Approach

Letizia Bollini[(✉)]

Department of Psychology, University of Milano-Bicocca,
Piazza dell'Ateneo Nuovo 1, 20126 Milan, Italy
letizia.bollini@unimib.it

Abstract. Many of the cultural heritage assets stored in archives are related to past events of whom they are primary or indirect document sources. Furthermore, they are concerned not only with the time evolution, but also with the spatial locations. The richness and complexity of these relationship get often lost when archives are organized and digitized. Portals and websites let access information according to a logical and hierarchical structure: a linear sequence of texts and documents. When displayed on a 2D synchronic space or a map – such as Google Map or OpenGIS – representation is often limited to a distribution of pins. A visual approach to this data could offer a more in-depth and engaging way to understand the facts reported in documents. Moreover, if the cultural heritage can be read along a timeline also representing the environmental evolution along history. The paper presents and discusses how to visualize archival data on historical maps to connect both the document sources – photos, paintings, texts, manuscripts, and so on – and the spatial locations. The design approach, which put people at the center of the process of knowledge sharing, is exemplified by a range of benchmarked best practices and a recent case study.

Keywords: Cultural heritage · Digital archives design ·
Space-based data representation · Historical maps experience ·
Spatial interface design

1 Introduction

Along the year we can identify a sort of evolution in the use of digital technologies applied to cultural heritage and, in specific, to archives and their preservation and communication.

A first phase started in the late 80' based on multimedia cd-rom, databases and other digital repositories and involved the process of mass digitization.

The virtual form of documents offered many benefits both regarding preservation and dissemination. On one hand, the virtualization of fragile and perishable papers, letters, books, fabrics, photos, pictures or other material objects is a way to preserve them from the wear out connected to public exhibit, light, humidity and other deterioration agents. On the other hand, the digital format guarantees much broader and

© Springer Nature Switzerland AG 2019
A. Luigini (Ed.): EARTH 2018, AISC 919, pp. 599–607, 2019.
https://doi.org/10.1007/978-3-030-12240-9_62

easier access to documental sources limited – in the physical world – by the location of collections, libraries of private archives (see Bollini and Borsotti 2016c; Bollini 2013 and Bollini and Borsotti 2009).

Therefore, digitization is the first step to take overpass the limitations for the physical protection of the original documents and the inadequate access service to the collections in the field of historical studies (Camurri 2008).

The Internet and its global pervasiveness – as stated by Rifkind (2000) – has been producing accessibility to remote information, enabling the search of documents outside the actual physical domain, and it has fast become the most relevant medium to share knowledge.

The concept of *access* has to be intended extensively:

- *Accessibility*: data were laid on-line for the dissemination and the sharing of the contents;
- *Availability*: data are findable via the web;
- *Searchability*: actual criteria of the historical domain were set up to search inside the same/distributed systems;
- *Hypertextuality*: correlation of contents through links and references;
- *Intertextuality*: correlation of contents inside different repositories/documents collections;

(For further discussion about information architecture applied to libraries, cultural and knowledge-base see: Morville 2014; Gnoli et al. 2006 and Bollini 2009). If the benefits are multiple, nevertheless they are no more sufficient in a technology-intensive world and a social and mass culture that is even more in search for cultural experiences.

If at the beginning digitizing information and guarantee access to it was enough and a niche activity for scholars and researchers, nowadays people want to experience knowledge to be part of the cultural process. As stated by Rosati (2011), both how we structure information and how we experience it is becoming even more *pervasive*. The way we interact with data is ecosystemic (Bollini 2016a) and we discover meaning in documents about people, places or events comparing, overlapping and connecting them along the time evolution, not just reading them, as well underlined by Nina Simon – Executive Director of the Santa Cruz Museum of Art & History – in her book *The Participatory Museum* (2010).

2 The Pillars of Digital Archives' Experience

Documents preserved and stored in digitized archives mainly focus on three different subjects directly or indirectly related to historical events: (a) protagonists, they can be people, objects, institutions, or any other subject (b) places where events took place, where people are born or lived in and (c) time, both period and specific date.

Sources can have different physical or immaterial nature, such as handwritten letters, manuscripts, books, but also painting, photos, pictures, movies or clips, recorded audio or another multimodal communication supports (Bollini 2004; 2003 and 2001). They can belong to the material culture of a period as well to an ephemeral or lost fragment survived through secondary references. As emerged in a previous experimental study developed inside the "Aspi - Archivio storico della psicologia italiana [Historical Archive of Italian Psychology]" (Bollini et al. 2017) only a few historians and scholars are able to surf across this files.

Experts have a bold cultural background that enable them to read and understand the *big picture*, that means the connections among people and events, the relationships occurred, the catalyst sites, migrations, and other significant phenomena.

But when it comes to people and the mass public, only fews have sufficient cultural skills to see these links and to transform information into real knowledge. Representation and data visualization, in this, case are the enabler of a significant experience. So "the virtual experience could be rich and meaningful if part of the expertise are embedded in a narrative exploration of the documents where the story told by editors and curators is able to present and contextualize the single information in a wider and whole picture in which the scenarios and the connections among elements are shown and made explicit." (Bollini 2016b: 777).

3   Reading Time Through Space

If in historical story-telling, time is one how the narrative driver and the natural one, space is mostly used just to locate information (Fig. 1).

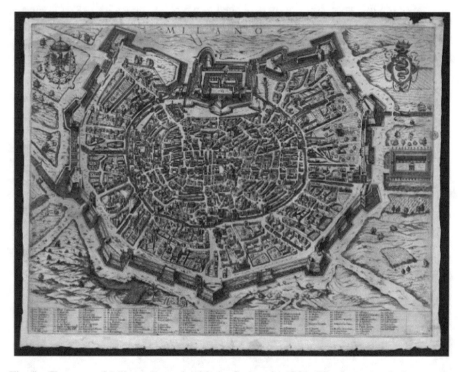

Fig. 1. The map of Milano drawn by Mario Cartaro in 1581. The document is kept at the Biblioteca Nacional de Portugal in Lisbon.

Past documents, people or events are mainly presented on Google Map® – or other georeferencing platforms such as OpenStreetMaps, GIS and OpenGIS – and located according to the nowadays urban morphology, although displayed pins could or could not coincide with a still existing place.

But a spatial and synchronic representation is not neutral. On the one hand, historical maps and pre-geodetic cartography often offer a spatial description according to contemporary knowledge of the world and drawing tools. On the other, they do not propose just a vision, but rather a social interpretation of the period and the undergoing powers. According to significant theoretical and experimental studies in the field – such as the book curated by Bagnara and Misiti Environmental Geography (1978) or the researches conducted by Francescato and Mebane (1973), Proshansky et al. (1983), Buttimer (1978; 1980), Kaplan and Kaplan (1977) – the shared, social and past representation are part of the historical, cultural identity of a place (for a wider understanding of the relationship between physical, digital and social space see: Bollini 2018b; 2012; 2011 Bollini and Cerletti 2009; Bollini and Palma 2004).

Therefore representing historical data on a map should be made according to the urban morphology of the considered period with the same rigorous approach reserved for the timeline sequence.

Many new digital applications and online websites are exploring the possibility to use historical maps to overlap to the nowadays display to offer a philological vision of the data location.

During the five years-long study dedicated to a mobile application – *The Bethroted 3.0* (see: Bollini and Begotti 2017; Bollini et al. 2014; Bollini et al. 2013; Bollini and Falcone 2012) – the field has been mapped and critically analyzed to create a taxonomy of archives using geo-based data on historical cartography, as shown in Fig. 2.

A GEO-BASED ARCHIVE TAXONOMY

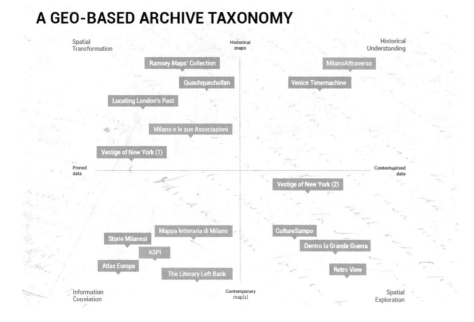

Fig. 2. A geo-based archives' taxonomy developed between 2013 and 20

In particular, the research has focused on the type of dataset presented, the solutions adopted to manage pre-geodetic cartography and the kind of interaction and experience offered to people. Exploration of the spatial representation, the dynamics of urban and environmental transformations and a deeper understanding of history through spatial visualization where some of the analysis criteria adopted.

Furthermore, the research has explored the relationship between time and space according to space-based digital storytelling of historical events and protagonists (Bollini et al. 2015).

4   *MilanoAttraverso* a Case Study

According to the below mentioned on-going phenomena in the field of cultural heritage, ICT applied to spatial, situated and time interactions, and the social construction of the space identity, both physical and symbolic, the paper proposes a research experience in which these aspects have been investigated, projected and tested to define a conceptual and design framework in the field.

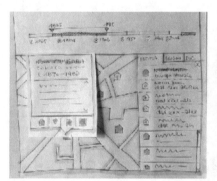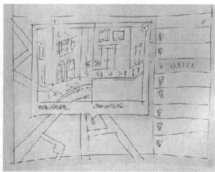

Fig. 3. Co-design and visual facilitation activities.

MilanoAttraverso. People and places that transform the city is a research project promoted by the municipality of Milan, the Golgi-Redaelli welfare Institution and financed by the Cariplo Foundation started in 2018.

The aim of the project is to let known to today's citizens the worth of past experiences of Milan's solidarity, to be interpreted also as cues to read the present differently. The project is based on a dynamic research and enhancing the sources with the intent of involving the public trying to activate processes of critical awareness.

The project goals are:

- Give a common platform to the subjects of the network, entities with strong territorial roots and historical archives
- Telling the history of the territory, of people and of the communities from the 800 to the contemporaneity
- Valorize and make sources accessible also to non-specialized publics
- To present the historical evolution of the territory through the use of archive sources

604   L. Bollini

(a)

(b)

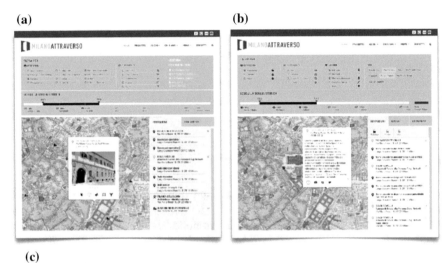

(c)

Fig. 4. First (a) and second version (b) of the historical maps section. The historical maps section: online version (c).

To create both the digital archive – a custom platform integrated with Wordpress Content Management System – and the historical cartography tool a human-centered approach has been adopted (See Fig. 2). User testing task-based method have been used both in the analysis and the assessment phase to improve the ongoing result.

In particular, in the first phase a target group of scholars, archivists, historians, fine arts/art history students, architect and pros age 18–54 have been involved. The 24 participants have been divided in 2 groups and asked to navigate the first release of the project surfing into archives and maps according two different modalities: logical/texts + visual/maps (see Fig. 3). Three tasks have been proposed:

(1) locate information (2) find extended card description (3) contextualize info in time and space. Results have been evaluated according to the criteria:

(1) efficiency: execution time; (2) efficacy: errors/completed tasks; (3) satisfaction: a final interview.

User tests highlight have been organized according to Norman's guide line: (a) visibility (b) feedback (c) constraints (d) mapping (e) consistency (f) affordance. Frequency and priority are the other two criteria adopted to rank the results and the feed-back to be implemented in the second iterative design cycle (Fig. 4).

5 Conclusions

The project was presented and published n line on September 25th, and some further improvements have been already planned for the next few months. At the moment gathering feedback from the public, the participants, from users who have started using it is an ongoing and daily activity.

Nevertheless, some issues are still open. A final user-test session is going to take place in a short time: the aim is to have further evaluation and assessment on the published version.

Among the possible development, two options have been proposed.

In the first case, the possibility to pin and filter information on the maps would also be applied to whole communities and single people, protagonists or witness of the migration history. This solution would display the dynamic transformations and the movement across the urban space. On the other hand it would also make visible the social clusters and their relationship with the territories occupied.

Finally, in a cooperative and participatory evolution of the project, a way to publish user-generated content would be given to people to share their personal and familiar documents – such as photos and stories – to be pinned and included in the online database.

Acknowledgements. The activity presented in the paper is part of the research project promoted by the Azienda di Servizi alla Persona "Golgi Redaelli". Special thanks to Marco Bescapè and Lucia Aiello, leaders and coordinators of the project and the partner associations network. Thank you to Sara Radice, Fabio Sturaro and Michele Zonca with whom we designed and developed both the archive and the historical maps section; thanks to all the archivists and users who helped us to test, assess and improve the project: www.milanoattraverso.it.

References

Bagnara S, Misiti R (eds) (1978) Psicologia Ambientale. Il Mulino, Bologna
Bollini L (2018b) The urban landscape and its social representation. A cognitive research approach to rethinking historical cultural identities. In: Amoruso G (ed) Putting tradition into practice: heritage, place and design, INTBAU 2017. Lecture notes in civil engineering, vol 3. Springer, Cham, pp 834–842
Bollini L, Begotti D (2017) The time machine. Cultural heritage and the geo-referenced storytelling of urban historical metamorphose. In: Murgante B (eds) ICCSA 2017, Part III, LNCS 10406. Springer, Heidelberg, pp 239–251
Bollini L (2016a) Large, small, medium. Maggioli Editore, Rimini
Bollini L, De Santis D, Radice S, Zocchi P (2016b) Le trame invisibili. Nuove modalità di esplorazione online dell'Archivio storico della psicologia italiana. Umanistica Digitale 1 (1):59–84
Bollini L, Borsotti M (2016c) Strategies of commutation in exhibition design. Int J Architectonic Spat Env Des 10(1):13–21
Bollini L (2016d) The open heritage of digital archives. Preservation, sustainability and accessibility of historical documentation to map the field of Italian Mind Science. In: Amoêda, R, Lira S, Pinheiro C (eds) HERITAGE 2016 - 5th international conference on heritage and sustainable development. Green Lines Institute, Lisbona, pp 773–782
Bollini L, Busdon G, Mazzola A (2015) GeoLapse. A digital space-based and memory-related time-capsule app. In: Gervasi O, et al (eds) Computational science and its applications – ICCSA 2015, Part II, LNCS 9156. Springer, Heidelberg, pp 675–685
Bollini L, De Palma R, Nota R, Pietra, R (2014) User experience & usability for mobile geo-referenced apps. A case study applied to cultural heritage field. In: Murgante B, et al (eds) Computational science computational science and its applications – ICCSA 2014, Part II, LNCS 8580. Springer, Heidelberg, pp 652–662
Bollini L, De Palma R, Nota R (2013) Walking into the past: design mobile app for the geo-referred and the multimodal user experience in the context of cultural heritage. In: Murgante B, Gervasi O, Misra S, Nedjah N, Rocha AMAC, Taniar D, Apduhan BO (eds) Computational science computational science and its applications – ICCSA 2013, vol 3. Springer, Heidelberg, pp 481–492
Bollini L (2013) Lo spazio digitale del sapere: dalla forma archivio alle knowledge-base culturali. Aggregazioni, narrazioni e migrazioni. In: Trocchianesi R, Lupo E (eds) Progetto e memoria del temporaneo, vol 3. Electa, Milano, pp 53–67
Bollini L, Falcone R (2012) Geolocalization as wayfinding and user experience support in cultural heritage locations. In: Murgante B, Gervasi O, Misra S, Nedjah N, Rocha AMAC, Taniar D, Apduhan BO (eds) Computational science computational science and its applications – ICCSA 2012, vol 7334-II. Springer, Heidelberg, pp 508–516
Bollini L (2012) Comunicare con il colore spazi e percorsi: Aspetti metodologici, ergonomici e user-centered. Campus Bicocca: Un caso studio. In: Rossi M, Siniscalco A (eds) Colore e colorimetria. Contributi multidisciplinari, vol VIII. Maggioli Editore, Rimini, pp 431–438
Bollini L (2011) Territories of digital communities. Representing the social landscape of web relationships. In: Murgante B, Gervasi O, Iglesias A, Taniar D, Apduhan BO (eds) Lecture notes in computer science - ICCSA 2011 - ICCSA 2011, vol 6782. Springer, Heidelberg, pp 501–511
Bollini L, Borsotti M (2009) Reshaping exhibition & museum design through digital technologies: a multimodal approach. Int J Virtual Reality 8(3):25–31

Bollini L (2009) From paper to bytes: digital knowledge sharing. A multi-level approach to document digitalization. A case history in Italian historical studies. In: Filipe J, Cordeiro J (eds) Proceedings of the fifth international conference on web information systems and technologies, Lisbona, pp 567–571

Bollini L, Cerletti V (2009) Knowledge sharing and management for local community: logical and visual georeferenced information access. In: Granville B, Majkic Z, Chunping L (eds) International conference on enterprise information systems and web technologies (EISWT-09) conference proceedings. IRST, Orlando, pp 92–99

Bollini L (2004) Registica multimodale: Il design dei new media. CLUP, Milano

Bollini L, Palma G (2004) Cognitive maps: new paradigms in information architecture and interface design for the web. The Opsis identifier descriptive model for web information architecture based on cognitive maps: designing-x a case study. In: Canas AJ, Novak JD, Gonzalez FM (eds) Concept maps: theory, methodology, technology (2). Nova Text, Navarra, pp 95–98

Bollini L (2003) MUI: design of the HC interfaces as a directing of communications modes targeted on human senses. In: Callaos M (ed) Senses and sensibility in technology. IADE, Lisbona, pp 182–186

Bollini L (2001) Multimodalità vs. Multimedialità. Il Verri 16:144–148

Buttimer A (1978) Home reach and the sense of place. In: Symposium UNIV UPS, Svezia

Buttimer A (1980) Social space and the planning of residential areas. In: Buttimer A, Seamon D (eds) The human experience of space and place. Croom Helm, London

Camurri D (2008) Il progetto "Una città per gli archivi". Storia e futuro. Rivista di Storia e Storiografia, 17. Ibc, Bologna

Francescato D, Mebane W (1973) How citizens view two great cities: Milano and Rome. In: Downs RM, Stea D (eds) Image and environment. Cognitive mapping and spatial behaviors. Aldine Publishing Company, Chicago, pp 131–147

Gnoli C, Marino M, Rosati L (2006) Organizzare la conoscenza. Dalle biblioteche all'architettura dell'informazione per il Web. Tecniche Nuove, Milano

Kaplan R, Kaplan S (1977) Humanscape: environments for people. Ulrich's Books, Ann Arbor

Morville P (2014) Intertwingled: information changes everything. Semantic Studios, Ann Arbor

Proshansky HM, Fabian AK, Kaminoff R (1983) Place-identity: physical world socialization of the self. J Environ Psychol 3(1):57–83

Rifkin J (2000) The age of access. Putnam Publishing Group, New York

Rosati L (2011) Cross-channel, cross-media, multi-channel: where's the difference. Pervasive information architecture. http://pervasiveia.com/blog/cross-channel-definition

Simon N (2010) The participatory museum. http://www.participatorymuseum.org/read/

A Digital Map as a Representational Tool Implications for the Instructional Design Process

Laura Fedeli[✉], Valentina Pennazio, and Maila Pentucci

Dipartimento di Scienze della Formazione, Beni Culturali e Turismo,
Università degli Studi di Macerata, piazzale Bertelli 1, 62100 Macerata, Italy
{laura.fedeli,valentina.pennazio,
maila.pentucci}@unimc.it

Abstract. The dimension of designing is one of the essential skills included in the professional teacher's profile. Nowadays the complexity of the classrooms requires a specific competence in the design of learning disciplinary paths that take into account the different students' needs. The article describes a prototype of a graphic organizer designed within the European DEPIT project, to support teachers and the need of an inclusive approach in the design process and students who can take advantage of a full visualization of the whole learning path.

Keywords: Design · Inclusion · App · Graphical organizer · Primary school

1 Introduction: Making Visible the Learning Design

The dimension of designing is one of the essential skills included in the professional teacher's profile: it matches, on one side, with the intelligence of the situations, which enables the teacher to grasp the essence in the contexts where he/she acts, reifying them in representations of the action that could lead to results in terms of learning; on the other side, with the necessary expertise of anticipation and prevision (Rivoltella 2014), which are the assumptions for the organisation of design patterns placed according to the needs and the potentiality of the class.

Designing means first of all planning macro structures that are the backbone of the organisation and the concepts of the learning path and that account for the epistemological, pedagogical and didactic lines followed by the teacher. At the same time, the designing also concerns the micro dimension, that is to say that whole of Learning Activities (LA), linearized in sequences of teaching-learning (Rossi 2017) and represented by the designer teacher in different and mixed shapes, depending on one's didactics habitus, as well as on the content of which one is activating the mediation process and the reference context. The teacher produces some mediation artefacts (Conole and Wills 2013), through which he/she codifies and represents both his/her

---

The article is the result of a common vision among the authors with the following responsibilities: Laura Fedeli is the author of paragraphs 5 and 6; Valentina Pennazio is author of paragraphs 2, 4, and 7; Maila Pentucci is author of the paragraphs 1, 3 and Conclusion.

© Springer Nature Switzerland AG 2019
A. Luigini (Ed.): EARTH 2018, AISC 919, pp. 608–617, 2019.
https://doi.org/10.1007/978-3-030-12240-9_63

choices and intentions, illustrating the intrinsic meaning of the planned activity. Those artefacts can be of a narrative, iconic, taxonomic, modular type (Falconer and Little-john 2008) and refer to the material and semiotic tools through which, according to Vygotskij (1990), the subject exercises a control and governs the changing processes he/she wants to activate to produce the cognitive development.

The designer teacher needs to be supported when making some informed decisions in the moment when he/she realises the planning sequences, an operation that is codified in the Learning Design (LD), that is to say in the practice of conceiving effective learning experiences, aimed at reaching educational goals defined in a given context (Mor et al. 2015). The LD helps in fact to document, create a pattern and share the didactic practice thought and activated, keeping the process of planning and its product, meant as an artefact, as a formal representation of the didactic path integrated in the foreseen learning environment together. Such a process is a generative one, as it re-codifies the product in time and it does not have since the beginning a complete idea of what one wants to realise (Goodyear and Yang 2008): the LD is not exactly a method, but it can be considered a way of being inside a system, the teaching learning one, which considers the planning as a central and essential element, a connector among the actors populating it (teacher, student, cultural item, according to the vision by Houssayé 1988).

The basics characterising the design for learning are basically two, both linked to the result alignment, meant as recursive repositioning between two subjects (or between a subject and an item) in order to shorten the distances, both at the conceptualisation level and at the practice one. On one side the LD presupposes the teacher's taking on the student's agency. The student shares with the teacher the didactic path, through the planning representation and can act in a transformative sense on it (alignment student teacher).

On the other side, through the planning there is the recomposing of different levels of granularity, which enable the recursive passage from macro to micro, the under-taking of a different perspective at variable focusing levels, without losing sight with the coherence elements inside the process and the relationship (or better, the alignment) between learning outcomes, TLA and evaluation (Laurillard 2012).

2 Visible Learning Design for Inclusion

Both macro and micro design studies and the concepts of alignment and transposed curriculum (Joannert 2011) as well as the concept of visible design, become particu-larly useful in relation to the need of inclusion within the classroom and to a more general inclusive culture of the whole school institute. As stated by Dovigo (2008), it is recommendable not to aim exclusively at the design of special programs to foster inclusive processes, but to widen and diversify the "common curriculum" by making it more suitable to the needs of everybody. Such presupposition implies a shift of the focus on the design dimension. Nowadays the complexity of the classrooms in Italy (presence of students with disabilities, with specific learning disorders, or immigrant students) requires a specific competence in the design of learning disciplinary paths that take into account in a deep way the different students' needs. Starting from Law 170/2010 and the following norms the teacher is expected to set not only different kind of design documents (the Individualized Educational Plan for students with disabilities and the Personalized Educational Plan for students with specific learning disorders) but in order to make them embrace the inclusive approach the teacher needs to connect them to the design process within the school. In such perspective, the methodologies to design the teacher activates should let all students, independently from their functioning (according to the ICF rationale), to access the different disciplinary content and the related learning processes.

An investigation run with Italian teachers (Giaconi 2013) has highlighted, among the different obstacles, the difficulty in setting a dialogue, a connection between the individualized/personalized paths and the common class curriculum. The main issue is to combine different paths in the design of every lesson (Giaconi 2016).

The concept of alignment (Laurillard 2012, Rossi 2017, Giaconi 2015) become of primary importance to design with an inclusive perspective since, as stated by Rossi and Giaconi (2016), it includes different level of actions. The alignment is set between macro and micro design, between class paths and personalized/individualized paths, between disciplinary objective, quality of life domains and identification of actions in an inclusive approach (Giaconi 2015, p. 87). The management and the integration of different levels in the design process can be handled with the key notion of visible design described in the previous paragraph.

3   The Starting Idea: The PROPIT Project

From these premises the idea of the PROPIT (Planning the personalisation and the inclusion through technologies) project was born, an experimentation led by the Department of Educational Science of the University of Macerata starting from 2012 on over 40 classes of primary and secondary school in different regions all over Italy.

The project required to the involved teachers to make the topologic representation of the didactic transposition through graphic organisers that could convey the TLA, to share them among teachers and students and make them deep, that is to say enriched by all the materials necessary for the mediation, made available in digital format.

In order to produce such a project artefact what Conole (2013) calls «ungeneric tool for visualising learning» was used, specifically a map generator (VUE) that can be used both online and offline, able to realise aggregators in the form of a map that could represent either the whole path of the individual subject, and the modules or units where it was scanned by the teacher, or finally the single activities to which it was possible to incorporate digital materials to be used with the students. The hypermedia dimension of the map enabled to go from a level to another through a single click, from the macro to the micro and vice versa, as well as to either enrich or modify the product directly along the didactic action, uploading other materials, adding or removing knots, moving the order of the realised items (Rossi 2014).

Experimenting the designing through the PROPIT system has enabled to try to exploit the potentialities characterising the Graphic Organizer as a logical – cognitive structure, able to support the abstract thinking (Starling 2017) through the visualisation of the connections and the articulations of the paths, both linear and reticular.

In particular, the elements brought to the attention after the first phase were two: the first one concerned the possibility of using the map not only as a designing and aggregating tool, but also and most of all as a sharing and representation in class of the paths, of the activities and the contents, with the added value of the change in action, of the shared re-planning, implementing the alignment between student and teacher (Rossi 2016).

Secondly, collecting the teachers' observations, we highlighted that the spatialization in the map of the teaching – learning process, has activated positive effects concerning the awareness of the path realised and to be realised, strengthening the attitude to prevision, to the anticipation, to the organisation of time in class.

4 The PROPIT Project for Inclusion

The PROPIT project underlined several advantages in terms of inclusion. In order to clarify them we will then report some observations by Giaconi (2016) that can be summarized with the following key words: technology, visual organizer, anticipation, diverse mediators and paths.

PROPIT highlighted how technology and, specifically, the smartboard used to collective visualize the maps which represented the design of the lesson or the design of a single unit has helped guiding, in an intuitive way, the students who can discover that different paths can be used to access the same assignment and can have the chance to act on the assignment by contributing with a personal input.

A visual organizer, like a map, that makes it clear the sequence of the proposed activities in class can offer a vision of the whole learning path and results very useful for students with learning and attention difficulties since the organizer let them orientate in a better way during the class development and follow the teacher's explanation when the attention problems can occur. The literature is rich in terms of studies about the effectiveness of the use of maps and graphical organizers for the learning/elaboration processes of information and in the acquisition of a method of study by students with specific learning disorders (Dexter 2010; Dexter and Hughes 2011; Kim et al. 2004; Bos and Vaughn 2002; Rivera and Smith 1997) or with Autism Spectrum Disorder (Connelly 2016; Zakas et al. 2013; Keri et al. 2013).

The visual organizer has also an anticipatory function that let teachers structure the timetable by making it more suitable to students' needs.

Finally, thanks to a lesson-map the teacher has the opportunity to design different personalized/individualized activities and paths. In the first case the teacher can keep the common path and suggest several ways to access with the use of mediators chosen for specific students with difficulties. In the second case the teacher creates connection points with the activities proposed for the whole class and provides different modalities to access the content and assignments for students with disabilities.

5   The DEPIT Project

In late 2017 the European DEPIT project (designing for personalization and inclusion with technologies) was activated within the Erasmus + framework. The three year proposal (1-9-2017/31-8-2020) was promoted by the University of Macerata (Italy) as lead partner with the joint effort of different partners among university institutions like the University College London (UK), the Catholic University of the Sacred Heart (Milan, Italy) and the Universidad de Sevilla (Spain), net of schools in Italy and Spain (Friuli Venezia Giulia region and Marche region in Italy and Centro del professorado Sevilla in Spain), teachers associations (AEDE European Teacher Association and with the associated partner ATEE, Association for teacher education in Europe) and finally one society expert in digital solutions and web design (Infofactory, Italy).

The chosen members in the partnership clearly show the different levels of involvement needed to carry on a project whose main objectives are to:

- Create a prototype, a graphic organizer following usability and accessibility standards and taking care of the primary need for an inclusive teaching/learning process: the creation of the technological infrastructure (a digital map software) needed the expertise of different profiles from the pedagogical area as well as from the technical one;
- Draw a synergic connection in terms of collaboration and shared visions between the university context and the school context: researchers and school teachers work together to design and test an app to be used as (1) a planning tool for any discipline at primary school, (2) a pedagogical scaffold for the multiliteracies in which students are today immersed; (3) a reflective tool for teachers and their professional awareness;
- Analyse the teachers' need at European level, test it broadly at school and disseminate the results and the artefact (the software itself): teachers' associations will play e relevant role in this step since the validation of the whole process lies also in the project capacity of reaching a diverse audience in terms of schools and student population.

The theoretical framework that oriented the creation of the app was based on different inputs coming from instructional design (Laurillard 2012), research on digital and media literacy and multimodality (Cope and Kalantzis 2009; Kress 2015; Mayer 2014) and the concepts of didactical mediation (Damiano 2013).

The digital infrastructure of the app is aimed at:

- Playing a generative role and be an aggregator of different autonomous inputs and different materials (textual, visual, symbolic); that is, it should aggregate pedagogical indicators, the mediators used by the teacher and inputs coming from students;
- Connect different levels of granularity (with a graph of intersected cards representing course curriculum with modules; modules with lessons, and lessons with activities);
- Foster inclusion and personalization with a proper use of available formatting options (colors, shapes, size, etc.) and suitable content.

6   The DEPIT App

The prototype of the app is currently being tested by nets of schools in Italy and Spain through training seminars for teachers involved in the project. Graphic organizers have been widely researched for their effectiveness in improving learning (Alshatti et al. 2011) also with students with disabilities (Ellis and Howard 2005) and with the opportunities provided by the web 2.0 freeware and collaborative applications teachers began using more and more frequently digital tools that could improve their needs both in the organization of their teaching process in terms of design and in its sharing among colleagues (Laurillard 2012).

The graphic organizers can come in many types (the connections can be temporal, spatial, sequential, hierarchical) and in this case the app allows a multimodal content organization with a three level hierarchical structure (Module, Lesson, Activity).

The DEPIT prototype offers teachers the opportunity to design their teaching process using an intuitive graphical interface that is based on the concept of "card" (Fig. 1): Module and Lesson cards have the same format (title, duration, Information area) and an "open" area that, when clicked, brings to sub-cards (Lesson, Activity); Activity card is differently structured since it allows to attach students' works and teacher's files. Every card can be locked/unlocked by the teacher according to the set timetable and course organization.

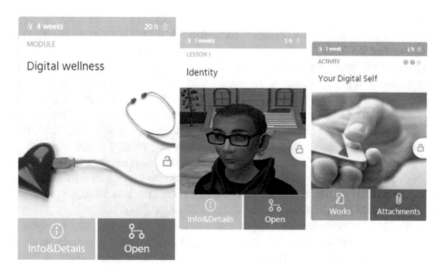

Fig. 1. The three-level cards: module-lesson-activity.

Beside the creation of cards the app working area consists of the following options: uploading file, linking web resources (e.g. videos), including shapes, drawing connections (Fig. 2). All those features let the teacher create meaningful and clear connections among the various elements and provide different kind of resources (textual, audio, video, symbolic) that can be personalized/enriched also by students' suggestions.

Fig. 2. Overview of the editing mode of a single module on digital wellbeing with three lessons.

Students can visualize the organizer either from their own device (e.g. a tablet since the app is mobile friendly) or collectively from a smartboard. Being able to have an overview of the teaching/learning process through a dynamic visual makes students actively involved in the design as main actors. Moreover the digital design through a visual structure allows students to integrate it with their inputs using different languages/codes, what Gee (2008) calls "social languages", that is, the way students use to communicate in informal settings and that can be easily integrated in the "school-like" language, the one related to discipline and present in books.

Thanks to the graphical organizer students can also develop their visual literacy:

"Visuals continue to grow exponentially as an important part of contemporary society, expedited by the popularity and ease of the creation and sharing of images via social media and mobile technologies" (Mayer 2014, p. 277).

Since cards are enriched by images teachers can, for example, take advantage of this feature to reflect and discuss with the students about digital copyright issues and involve them in the search of freely downloadable and modifiable images in the web databases.

7   The App and Its Inclusive Features

From the perspective of the inclusion promotion the app shows different advantages, some tied to the rationale of the app itself and others more connected to the graphical interface.

The app offers the chance to use different learning resources such as videos and images and, in this way, clearly satisfies the adaptation needs (privileged strategy in the inclusive didactics) that are essential to create personalized paths and create contact points between the design for the whole class group and the one for students with difficulties. The adaptation process requires to act on the initial input of an activity or on the related output (elaboration-comprehension-reply) by simplifying, facilitating, replacing, dividing them in core contents. In such perspective the app, for example, can at the same time provide the initial input of an activity using a text, an image, or a video and the students have the chance to choose the preferred way.

The visual structure of the graphical organizer, privileged feature of the app, is consistent with the Dual Coding Theory (Paivio 2006, 1991, 1986; Clark and Paivio 1991) that assigns the same value to the verbal learning process and non verbal one and explains the behaviour and the experience in terms of "dynamic associative processes that operate within a network of multimodal verbal and non verbal representations".

The association of verbal and non verbal plays a primary role in the knowledge representation, in memory, in the effective didactical strategies, in the comprehension of the individual learning differences, in the motivation and in the execution anxiety, all those aspects acquire importance for all students but specifically for the ones who have a special need (Hyerle 1996; Lyons 2003).

Finally, the teacher can rely on the availability of the visualization of the teaching-learning process and can avoid an overload of text/speech that could let students with difficulties to keep the attention on the general process and restructure in an easier way the content but also to become aware of the connections and relationships among ideas and information and to gradually experiment a major autonomy in the learning processes (Hyerle 1996; Lyons 2003).

8   Conclusion: The Experimentation in Schools' Network

The DEPIT app in its beta version will be issued to a group of teachers selected among those being part of the networks of schools related to the European project. At the beginning of the school year 2018–2019 they are asked to realise their didactic designing through the graphic and aggregation possibilities provided by the tool, sharing the artefacts with the students in class.

The hypothesis for the second part of the research that will investigate the action of the experimenter teachers and to analyse their thought concerning the experimentation activated, will focus on two fundamental aspects: the transformative potentiality both on the teachers' practices and on the students' learnings and the implementation of the reflective posture of the teachers, thanks to the visual evidence that the produced GO grants to the teaching-learning path. The open questions, to which we will try to give an answer through the data collected are the following ones:

- How and at which level can the complexity in the app be transformative for the transposition process of the teachers?
- Does the teacher adjust the app to his/her mental patterns or does it lead to modify those models of the artefact?

– In the use: how much will the function of aggregating item prevail and how the one of an organising one?
– When could the app also become a tool for the recalling and for the post-action reflection?

Acknowledgements. The app prototype presented in the paper is framed in the research developed within the Erasmus + project DEPIT (Designing for Personalization and Inclusion with Technologies - 2017-1-IT02-KA201-036605).

References

Alshatti S, Watters J, Kidman G (2011) Enhancing the teaching of family and consumer sciences: the role of graphic organizers. J Fam Consum Sci Educ 28(2):14–35. http://eprints.qut.edu.au/41227/
Bos CS, Vaughn S (2002) Strategies for teaching students with learning and behavior problems, 5th edn. Allyn & Bacon, Boston
Clark JM, Paivio A (1991) Dual coding theory and education. Educ Psychol Rev 3(3):149–170
Connelly J (2016) Effect of Wh-question graphic organizer on reading comprehension in students with autism spectrum disorders. Marshall University, Marshall Digital Scholar
Conole G, Wills S (2013) Representing learning designs – making design explicit and shareable. Educ Med Int 50(1):24–38
Conole G (2013) Designing for learning in an open world. Springer, New York
Cope B, Kalantzis M (2009) "Multiliteracies": new literacies, new learning. Pedagogies Int J 4(3):164–195
Damiano E (2013) La mediazione didattica. FrancoAngeli, Milano
Dexter DD (2010) Graphic organizers and their effectiveness for students with learning disabilities. Thalamus 26:51–67
Dexter DD, Hughes CA (2011) Graphic organizers and students with learning disabilities: a meta-analysis. Learn Disabil Q 34:51–72
Dovigo F (2008) L'Index per l'inclusione. Promuovere l'apprendimento e la partecipazione nella scuola. Erickson, Trento
Ellis E, Howard P (2005) Graphic organizers: power tools for teaching students with learning disabilities. Graph Organizers Learn Disabil 1:1–5
Falconer I, Littlejohn A (2008) Representing models of practice. In: Lockyer L, Bennett S, Agostinho S, Harper B (eds) Handbook of research on learning design and learning objects: issues, applications and technologies, pp 20–40. IGI Global, Hershey, New York
Gee JP (2008) Social linguistics and literacies: ideology in discourses, 3rd edn. Taylor and Francis, London
Giaconi C (2013) Elementos de didática inclusiva em classes com alunos com Dislexia. In: Capellini SA (ed) Dislexia, pp 400–419. WAK EDITORA, Brazil
Giaconi C (2015) Qualità della vita e adulti con disabilità. Franco Angeli, Milano
Giaconi C (2016) Una via per l'inclusione: il Progetto PROPIT tra allineamento e sostenibilità. In: Rossi PG, Giaconi C (eds) Micro-progettazione: pratiche a confronto. Propit, Eas, Flipped Classroom, pp 39–49. Franco Angeli, Milano
Goodyear P, Yang DF (2008) Patterns and pattern languages in educational design. In: Lockyer L, Bennett S, Agostinho S, Harper B (eds) Handbook of research on learning design and learning objects: issues, applications and technologies, pp 167–187. IGI Global, Hershey, New York

Houssayé J (1988) Théorie et pratiques de l'éducation. Peter Lang, Berne

Hyerle D (1996) Visual tools for constructing knowledge. Association for Curriculum and Development, Alexandria

Joannert P (2011) Curriculum, entre modèle rationnel et irrationalité des sociétés. Revue internationale d'éducation - Sèvres 56:135–145

Keri S, Bethune C, Wood L (2013) Effects of Wh-question graphic organizers on reading comprehension skills of students with autism spectrum disorders. Educ Train Autism Dev Disabil 48(2):236–244

Kim AH, Vaughn S, Wanzek J, Wei S (2004) Graphic organizers and their effects on the reading comprehension of students with LD: a synthesis of research. J Learn Disabil 37(2):105–118

Kress G (2015) Multimodalità. Progedid, Bari

Laurillard D (2012) Teaching as a design science: building pedagogical patterns for learning and technology. Routledge, New York, London

Lyons CA (2003) Teaching struggling readers: how to use brain-based research to maximize learning. Heinemann, Portsmouth

Mayer J (2014) Visual literacy across the disciplines. In: Keeran P, Levine-Clark M (eds) Research within the disciplines, 2nd edn. Rowman & Littlefield, Lanham, pp 277–299

Mor Y, Ferguson R, Wasson B (2015) Learning design, teacher inquiry into student learning and learning analytics: a call for action. Br J Educ Technol 46(2):221–229

Paivio A (2006) Dual coding theory and education. University of Western Ontario, London

Paivio A (1991) Dual coding theory: retrospect and current status. Can J Psychol 45(3):255–287

Paivio A (1986) Mental representations: a dual-coding approach. Oxford University Press, New York

Rivera DP, Smith D (1997) Teaching students with learning and behavior problems, 3rd edn. Allyn & Bacon, Boston

Rivoltella PC (2014) La previsione. Neuroscienze, apprendimento, didattica. La Scuola, Brescia

Rossi PG (2014) Le tecnologie digitali per la progettazione didattica. ECPS J 10:113–134

Rossi PG (2016) Progettazione didattica e professionalità docente. PROPIT: l'artefatto progettuale come mediatore didattico. In: Rossi PG, Giaconi C (eds) Micro-progettazione: pratiche a confronto. PROPIT, EAS, Flipped Classroom, pp 13–38. Franco Angeli, Milano

Rossi PG (2017) Visible design. Revista Fuentes 19(2):23–38

Rossi PG, Giaconi C (eds) (2016) Micro-progettazione: pratiche a confronto. Propit, Eas, Flipped Classroom. Franco Angeli, Milano

Starling JM (2017) The effects of graphic organizers on the comprehension of expository text: examining individual differences for the multimedia principle based on visuospatial abilities. Ball State University, Muncie

Vygotskij LS (1990) Pensiero e linguaggio. Ricerche psicologiche. Laterza, Bari

Zakas TL, Browder DM, Ahlgrim-Delzell LA, Heafner TL (2013) Teaching social studies content to students with autism using a graphic organizer intervention. Res Autism Spectr Disord 7(9):1075–1086

Territorial Diagrams Planning Cycle Routes with Digital Tools Oriented to the Knowledge of the Territory

Andrea Alberto Dutto[(✉)] and Stefano Dighero

Department of Architecture and Design (DAD), Politecnico di Torino,
Viale Pier Andrea Mattioli 39, 10125 Turin, Italy
{andrea_dutto, stefano.dighero}@polito.it

Abstract. Scientific research on cycle-routes planning opens up an innovative field of experimentation on drawing techniques based on geo-territorial datasets. Unlike infrastructural networks dedicated to automotive flows, EuroVelo International Cycle route networks promotes a slow mobility model, compatible with the shape of sites, variations of geography and valorization of places characterized by the presence of historical and landscape values. Cycling itineraries are conceived as museum itineraries on the territorial scale; sport activities combine themselves with knowledge of the heritage. Computer-based algorithms introduce the possibility to translate topographic surveys into topological maps which portray a source for planning 'slow mobility networks' that aim at turning the journey into a cultural experience. The choice of the instrument of representation plays a decisive role and, in particular, the Geographic Information System (GIS) offers a crucial support to the research. With this kind of digital representation, the image of the territory is subdivided into a series of thematic layers made of 'linear' patterns that highlight the hybrid textures of the territory. Moreover, this kind of topological translation acts as an interface for dialogue with administrators and social actors involved in the promotion and administration of cycle routes.

Keywords: Diagrams · Cycle routes · Territory · GIS · Geography

1 The Territory as Museum

The extension of the concept of 'heritage' to the whole territory is widely accomplished nowadays. In order to clarify what is intended with such concept, in the domain of this article, it can be assumed as starting hypothesis Andrè Corboz's essay "The territory as a palimpsest" (1983), where territory is conceived as a hybrid entity, both natural and cultural at once. According to Corboz, 'palimpsest' stands for the continuous process of re-writing the territory; a process that is supposed to be, at least, twofold. On the one side, it is spontaneous, thus caused by natural agents, and, on the other side, it is artificial, or rather transformed by human beings for productive and cultural needs.

In order to express this duplicity of the territory, our research focuses on slow mobility networks as an opportunity to rethink design-oriented techniques of representation of the territory itself. Unlike the vehicular and railway mobility networks,

A. Luigini (Ed.): EARTH 2018, AISC 919, pp. 618–626, 2019.
https://doi.org/10.1007/978-3-030-12240-9_64

which display marked artificiality and overall indifference towards the contexts, slow mobility networks are infrastructures that look for a dialogue with places: they introject the shape of the place in order to outline the mobility.

In particular, the project of the EuroVelo International Cycle route networks conceived by the European Cyclist Federation focuses precisely on this hybrid natural-cultural value of the territory. Unlike the infrastructural networks dedicated to automotive flows, EuroVelo promotes a slow mobility model, compatible with the shape of sites, variations of geography and valorization of places characterized by the presence of historical and landscape values. Cycling itineraries are conceived as museum itineraries on territorial scale, along which sport activities combine themselves with knowledge of the heritage. In this sense, the concept of tourism appears to be reformulated as a paradigmatic form of mobility that establishes the primacy of journey over destination (Clancy 2018).

In this way, this emerging form of 'slow mobility' highlights an innovative scientific aim, where cycling holds an instrumental role in the domain of site-specific way to portray education. At the same time, it promotes the rethought of territorial facts (i.e. disused routes and railways) which, precisely because of cycling re-use, find a reason to be further valorized in terms of architectural and landscape design (Occelli et al. 2012).

For this purpose, the research focused on the possibility of cartography as a tool aimed at reconciling the representation of places and that of slow mobility networks. The map translates the place into a set of lines that describe the geographic characters of settlements made of layers that overlap (Motta and Pizzigoni 2016). Such lines are diagrammatic, namely "set of lines, spots, traits that for themselves can only be 'unrepresentative' but, however, introduce effective possibilities" (Pizzigoni 2011). Indeed, as strategic policies would be inevitably related to these lines, and the way such lines could be experienced and administered, the research we undertook concerned the possibility to evaluate these lines in terms of new uses such as that of cycling.

2 Rendering Territorial Textures Through GIS

The choice of the instrument of representation plays a decisive role and, in particular, the Geographic Information System (GIS) offers a crucial support to the research. With this kind of digital representation, the territorial image is subdivided into a series of thematic layers made of 'linear' patterns that highlight the hybrid textures of the territory (i.e. cadastral plots, paths, rivers) (Bolstad 2012).

The goal of the GIS elaboration is to produce thematic maps able to highlight the link between geographic lines and cycle routes. By isolating lines from the whole of the territory, it emerges the possibility to enhance forgotten historical routes, and, at the same time safeguard the territory with interventions aimed at consolidating critical facts threatened by environmental and hydrogeological risks. Hence, the territory is represented through a series of maps related to different techniques of representation, emphasizing separately the character of each of the components that make up a place.

Basic data of the GIS elaboration is the Digital Elevation Model (DEM) that is a raster-type digital file, which pixels are associated to the absolute altitude of a landform, including vegetation, buildings and other artefacts (Ackermann 1994). The DEM is easily available at various image resolutions on numerous Open Data platforms available thanks to the INSPIRE directive (Hirt 2016) and it is paired to the GIS that allows the separation of territorial layers and resources like: water, vegetation, settlements, infrastructural networks among the many.

In particular, for the purposes of the research, this type of DEM altimetric data processing, is aimed at identifying those territorial lines able to improve planning choices related to both the territorial development of the cycle route path and the infrastructures that serve the route, like buildings and devices. To this extent, the GIS processing led to the identification of territorial textures that combine the forms of the route with smaller artifacts that allow its continuity throughout the territory, like bridges, walkways and other equipment. This link between architectural and territorial facts, operated through the GIS, is an example of the type of design achievable through this digital technology. At stake is a design-oriented approach that links strategic choices on the large scale (i.e. the EuroVelo cycle pathways) with the economies and administrative choices of small towns, scattered throughout the territory, that are in the need to enhance their architectural and landscape assets through innovative systems of integrated mobility capable of combining local and international scale (Di Marcello 2016).

In order to demonstrate this hypothesis, we propose a case study concerning the stretch of Eurovelo8 route developing along the hillside of Turin, along the river Po, at the foot of Superga hill (Fig. 2a). Here, the geographical shape of the hill has been identified as a geographic support for a project of cycle walkway overcoming the highway that abruptly splits the Meisino park in two independent sides.

The purpose of this project is to design a strategic site for the enhancement of the Turin hillside as well as the integration and safety of an area threated by hydrogeological risk. Therefore, a geometrical representation of the landform was developed in order to design the walkway and its basement working as a defense infrastructure from the flooding of the river Po.

How was this geometric translation implemented? Starting from the GIS database the ground image was simplified into a grid of points that were subsequently used to produce a TIN (Triangulated Irregular Network) surface. In this way the contour lines were transformed into polylines which were then used as formal references for the design of infrastructures like retaining walls and embankments. More specifically, this procedure implied three steps. At first the grid was generated following the geometry of the equilateral triangle with its barycenter placed at 50 m from each vertex (Fig. 2b). Secondly, the DEM provided the specific altitude related to each node of the grid; for this purpose, it was necessary to sample the DEM values in the table that composes the shapefile and to assign such values to the corresponding nodes of the grid (Fig. 1). Finally, it was generated a TIN surface through the interpolation of the points previously elaborated; this elaboration implied the use of the Kriging method, a regression method used in the Geostatistics that allows to auto-determine the altitude in the nodes for which no specific measurement data could be provided.

This mesh provided the structure for the thematic map oriented to the design of the cycle route and the walkway. In particular, the 'Map of the flooded ground', shows the relationship between the profile of the embankment that defends the project site on the side facing the river Po and the grid. Moreover, this embarkment line defines the plane

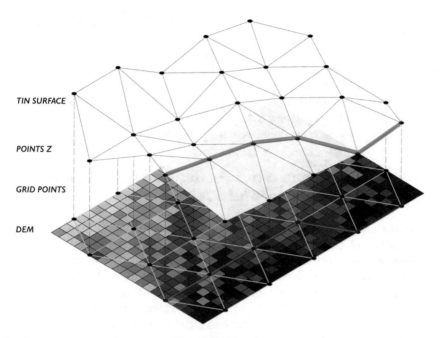

Fig. 1. Scheme of translation of a DEM into a TIN surface; marked in red is the cycle path.

that supports the walkway structure (Fig. 2c). In addition, other project-oriented maps were developed through the use of GIS tools, such as the 'Map of the built environment', which displays the typological relationship between the wall that supports the walkway and other walls spread in the settlement near the project site.

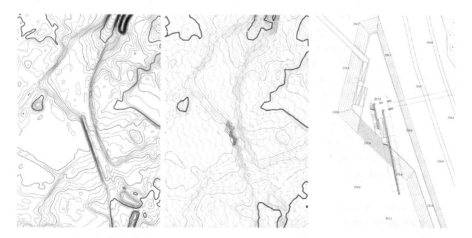

Fig. 2. Map of the Meisino Park and its surrounding represented through contour lines (a). Definition of the territorial texture based on triangular grid of 50 m of side (b); at the center, in red, the project site. Definition of the embankment boundary against the flooding of river Po (c).

Therefore, as exemplified by these case study, the GIS representation establishes a continuity between the shape of the territory and its design. The analysis of the digital layers of the territory leads to the identification of those territorial patterns that can represent a support for real infrastructures for the new mobility project. The opportunity to restore this continuity through the project of cycling networks appears as an opportunity to overcome the idea of the architectural project as an isolated expression of an intention and to reach a new form of project in which the choices are evaluated in relation to pre-existences, economic resources and landforms.

3   Territorial Diagrams. From the Geographical Characters of Sites to the Forms of Their Use

As we have seen so far, the GIS allows a kind of continuity between the shape of places and the shape of paths that cross these places. In this section, we focus on how techniques of representation can render this continuity in the specific case scenario of cycle route design. More precisely, the hypothesis is that the cycle route can be conceived and perceived as on among the possible expressions of territorial geomorphology; thus, they are intended as geographical architectures (Palma 2015). In this way, the cycle route avoids being simply an itinerary though environmental beauties and turns itself into a device that highlights the variety of geographical landforms and the way the cycling travel allows the user to perceive geomorphological variations of places. In particular, the experimental side of the research conducted on the GIS tool, concerns the possibility of translating the Digital Terrain Model (DTM) into a diagram, or, more precisely, into a territorial diagram. This procedure implies a shift from topographical to topological space, thus a translation of the DTM into a three-dimensional low-poly model.

Unlike the experimentation described in the previous paragraph, which aimed at manipulating landform within the domain of Cartesian space, this time the goal is to elaborate a model, of the place, that has no topographic relationship with it. Thus, in order to carry out this operation, geographical features are translated into a series of symbolic elements: the map is turned into a diagram. Aim of this procedure is to describe how the territory is made, namely the specificity of the geographical structure crossed by the cycle route. In this way, for instance, when the cycle route crosses the plain the path itself is supposed to highlight the orthogonal layout of cultivated fields that provides the plain with a specific geographical shape; similarly, along the riverbanks the path will follow the embankment lines, and so on. This kind of topological simplification identifies the variety of geographical characters included within a territory. In the next paragraphs, we show several examples that better exemplify this approach.

In particular, we assumed two case studies placed on two different areas of Piedmont crossed by the Eurovelo8 cycle route. The difference among geographical characters of these two places helps us to exemplify two different modes of diagrammatic representation oriented to cycle route design. Nevertheless, it is important to state that the outcome we intended to achieve concerns the logical relationship between cycle route and landform which is alternative to other more diffused tendencies of cycle route design that simply look for the connection between points of interest. Therefore, the two case studies we worked on portray the possibility to apply our specific kind of geographical-oriented methodology to different kind of territories.

The first case study is situated in the north-western area of the Turin Metropolitan Area, known as Zone 10, between the municipalities of Chivasso in the south, the municipality of Mazzè in the north, the river Orco in the west, and the river Dora Baltea in the east (Fig. 3a). This area is directly affected by the route of the EuroVelo 8, which runs along the Po river line and is also supported by the cycle route along the Canale Cavour, that allows a direct cycle connection between Turin and Milan. This area plays a strategic role in the development of a branch of EuroVelo8 towards France and Switzerland. Moreover, this metropolitan area displays a variety of geographical contexts that includes, from south to north: the river bank of the Po, a large plain area between Chivasso and Mazzé and finally, the Moraine Amphitheater of Ivrea.

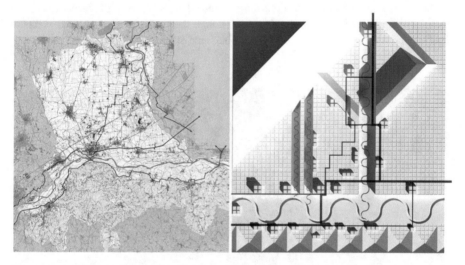

Fig. 3. Map of the Zone 10 of the Turin Metropolitan Area; marked in red are the cycle routes designed through the research (a). Territorial diagram (b).

Therefore, we attempted to stage the variety of geographical contexts of this area, simplifying the landform with a diagram expressing the relationship between the shape of the cycle route and the shape of geomorphological elements (Fig. 3b). For this purpose, four geographical characters, were identified, namely: the river, the plain, the settlement, and the hill. The river is represented by a sinuous line that cuts the plain and digs the river valley of both the Po river (the larger one to the south) and the Dora Baltea river, to the east. Secondly, the plain is represented by an orthogonal grid that refers to the geometric plot of agricultural fields that stands for the legacy of Roman centuriation. Thirdly, the inhabited center is represented by parallelepipeds arranged in the form of a 'castrum' and juxtaposed in variable configurations according to the size and layout of settlements. Finally, the hill is represented by a triangular prism that indicates the layout of the main and secondary ridges as well as the enclosure represented by the Moraine

Amphitheater of Ivrea. In this way, the site is transformed into a territorial diagram representing the relationship between such geographical characters and the cycle route configuration. In order to do so, the cycle route follows the shape of the geographical characters with the aim of unifying them into a continuous path; therefore, starting from south toward the north, the path marks the orthogonal layout of agrarian crops; next, it bends over the hill to reach once more the plain within the Moraine Amphitheater of Ivrea. Therefore, by lying on the outlines of geographical characters, the cycle route describes the places it crosses throughout its itinerary.

The second case study concerns the EuroVelo 8 in the area that extends between the municipality of Carignano (north) to that of Casalgrasso (south). Unlike the previous case study, this area, is predominantly characterized by plain and the cycle route is set to develop along the banks of the river Po that diagonally crosses the plain. In correspondence with the bridge crossing the river Po, a series of possible branches towards the southern area of Piedmont were considered. In view of this strategic choice, the diagram was crucial in order to define the range of possible configurations the Euro-Velo8 could portray in this node. However, unlike the previous case study, a series of possible variations of a single geographic character, namely the river, were evaluated.

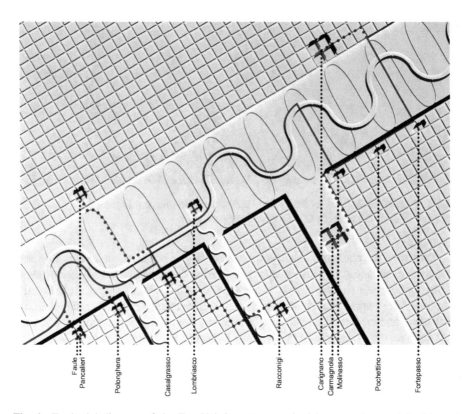

Fig. 4. Territorial diagram of the EuroVelo8 route comprised between the municipalities of Carignano and Casalgrasso.

The analysis of the river, the shape of the riverbed, the fluvial terraces and the traces of the palaeoriver revealed a landscape of lines nested into this single geographical element. In particular, four types of lines were identified; the first category consists of the 'terrace lines', defined by edges of the fluvial terraces engraved in the alluvial plain; the second category consists of 'embankment lines', namely lines that follow from a distance the shape of the riverbed; the third category refers to the 'bank lines' formed by the course of the river and its edges; finally, the fourth category is represented by the 'palaeoriver lines' left by the stretches of riverbed abandoned over time. Following this classification, the cycle route was conceived as continuous line throughout these lines in order to describe the shape of the river (Fig. 4).

Therefore, the territorial diagram appears as a crucial device that is able to combine the form of the cycle route and that of the geomorphological layout of the territory. In this sense, the territory is no longer understood as a set of landscape views, but rather as a basin of possible ways of traveling: moving in a zig-zag, climbing along a ridge, cycling along the lines described by the flow of the river. Thus, the territorial diagram appears as a strategic planning tool through which it is possible to establish a hierarchy between main and secondary routes, so that not only the artefacts, but also the physical form of the places and paths can itself become a feature worth to be experienced.

4   Concluding Notes

The research on cycle routes opens up several experimental sides in the domain of the representation of the territory.

The first experimentation side concerns the tools available to designers, thus the use of cartography as an effective support for design choices. Mainly, the research (briefly outlined in this essay) developed in this direction with innovative techniques of representation related to a combination between GIS and 3D modelling tools.

The second side of experimentation concerns the relationship between users, namely cyclists, and cycle routes, thus the possibility of conferring to the path a specific awareness of the place crossed throughout the itinerary. This observation also introduces a further step of the research that will look for technological devices for cyclists that will allow a virtual navigation of the itinerary by means of digital update of physical information plaques. In this sense, the research is going to integrate a wider field of research related to the domain of multisensory approach applied to the built environment (Piga and Salerno 2017).

Finally, the third side of experimentation concerns the local administrators involved in the strategic choices on mobility, in the need for models of representation and interface devices, that can clarify decision-making processes regarding the relationship between local and international mobility networks. The territorial diagram appears as a strategic tool aimed at improving the dialogue between administrators and social actors involved in the promotion of slow mobility networks.

Acknowledgements. The activity presented in the paper is part of the research grant "Geography and historical infrastructures in the architecture of cycle routes of MAB Unesco CollinaPo", coordinated by prof. Riccardo Palma, at the Department of Architecture and Design (DAD) of the Polytechnic University of Turin. The case study described in paragraph 2 is related to the master thesis written by Stefano Dighero, entitled "Uso sperimentale di strumenti GIS per lo studio e la produzione di carte orientate al progetto: architetture per la ciclabilità nel Parco del Meisino a Torino", tutored by Antonia Teresa Spanò and Riccardo Palma and defended on the 22/12/2013 at the Polytechnic of Turin for the master degree course of 'Architettura e sostenibilità'. The first and the third paragraph of this paper is conceived and written by Andrea Alberto Dutto. The second paragraph of this paper is conceived and written by Stefano Dighero.

References

Ackermann F (1994) Digital elevation models - techniques and application, quality standards, development. Int Arch Photogrammetry Remote Sens. 30:421–432

Bolstad P (2012) GIS fundamentals. Eider Press, White Bear Lake (Minn.)

Clancy M (ed) (2018) Slow tourism, food and cities: pace and the search for the good life. Routledge, London

Di Marcello R (2016) I turismi in bicicletta come strumenti di sviluppo del territorio. Analisi e prospettive in Europa e in Italia. Homeless Book, Faenza

Hirt C (2016) Digital Terrain Models. In: Grafarend E (ed) Encyclopedia of geodesy. Springer, Cham

Occelli C, Palma R, Sassone M (2012) La ciclostrada del Canale Cavour: una via a bassa velocità tra Torino e Milano. Araba Fenice, Boves

Motta G, Pizzigoni A (2016) Tracciare piani, disegnare carte. Spazi e linee della cartografia nel progetto di architettura. In: Dutto A, Palma R (eds) Tracciare piani, disegnare carte: architettura, cartografia e macchine di progetto | Sketching plans, drawing maps: architecture, cartography and architectural design machines. Accademia University Press, Torino, pp 3–44

Palma R (2015) Forma orbis. Il campo di fondazione dell'architettura. FAmagazine 32:12–22

Piga BEA, Salerno R (eds) (2017) Urban design and representation. A multidisciplinary and multisensory approach. Springer International Publishing, Cham

Pizzigoni A (2011) Il luogo: spazio cartografico e dispositivi del progetto. In: Motta G, Pizzigoni A, Palma R (eds) La nuova griglia politecnica: architettura e macchina di progetto. Franco Angeli, Milano, pp 223–265

3D Image Based Modelling Using Google Earth Imagery for 3D Landscape Modelling

Laura Inzerillo[1]([⊠]) and Ronald Roberts[2]

[1] DARCH - Department of Architecture, University of Palermo,
Viale delle Scienze ed. 8, 90128 Palermo, Italy
laura.inzerillo@unipa.it
[2] DICAM - Department of Civil, Environmental, Aerospace,
Materials Engineering, University of Palermo, Viale delle Scienze ed. 8,
90128 Palermo, Italy

Abstract. In recent years SfM technique experiments have been innumerable and increasingly refined under metric profiles. The techniques rely on photographic datasets of the objects or landscapes which can require in most cases time consuming and expensive surveys. Recently however there have been increases in the available 3D data of sites worldwide on the Google Earth (GE) platform. This paper presents a unique experimentation that considers integrating readily available datasets from GE and images taken during surveys on ground level for 3D replication without the use of expensive aerial surveys. This will enable practitioners the ability to more easily create 3D models of cultural heritage significance. This paper utilizes the methodology using a church with cultural and architectural significance to the city of Palermo: Santa Caterina D'Alessandria d'Egitto. It aims at verifying the process' reliability using three chunks of data on the same object; 2 from Ground level cameras and one from GE.

Keywords: SfM · Photogrammetry · Google Earth · Landscape modelling · 3D models

1 Introduction

Structure from Motion (SfM) is a technique that has empowered users with the ability to create 3D Models simply from photo data sets (Verhoeven 2010; Inzerillo and Santagati 2016). To date, this technique has been applied to various applications in cultural heritage, architecture and archaeology (Barsanti et al. 2012; Menna et al. 2016). One of the issues with these reconstructions however is the verification of the accuracy of the rendered models.

Typically, imagery obtained from Unmanned Aerial Vehicles (UAVs) have been utilized for creating 3D models of vast landscapes and for environmental purposes, using photogrammetric techniques (Lausch et al. 2015; Gillan et al. 2017; Nikolakopoulos et al. 2017; Remondino et al. 2017). However, UAVS have limitations and are plagued by issues including their rental costs and cumbersome government regulations surrounding their use (Inzerillo 2017). Recent advancements in GE imagery has led to researchers

© Springer Nature Switzerland AG 2019
A. Luigini (Ed.): EARTH 2018, AISC 919, pp. 627–634, 2019.
https://doi.org/10.1007/978-3-030-12240-9_65

considering the use of these online datasets for 3D model replication (Chen and Clarke 2016; Inzerillo 2017; Lubis et al. 2017; Liu et al. 2018) as they offer a cheap and readily available alternative without the need to do additional onsite surveys.

This paper presents a case study of a church in Palermo, Italy: Santa Caterina D'Alessandria d'Egitto (Fig. 1), using two datasets for the 3D modelling: A GE dataset and a combined dataset from a camera at ground floor level. The GE dataset was created using simulated flights in GE to observe various oblique grades and levels of the ground for modelling purposes. This data set was then integrated with one captured using a Nikon D5200 camera with a 24 Megapixel resolution with images taken at ground level. The camera dataset further comprised of two individual datasets. The first of the two camera datasets focuses on the general façade of the building and the second focuses on the steps at the centre of the building. Each dataset offering the ability to have more clearly defined features of these sections of the building.

Fig. 1. Building used for 3D model - Santa Caterina D'Alessandria d'Egitto

2   Methodology

Santa Caterina D'Alessandria d'Egitto, which was chosen for the case study is a church within the city centre of Palermo in the midst of the tourist attractions and holds significant cultural architectural significance to the city and it is within the vicinity of the notable Fountain of Pretoria. Building on the workflow proposed by Inzerillo 2017, the methodology utilizes two dataset chunks to produce a final 3D Model in the SfM software, Agisoft Photoscan.

The two dataset chunks were used with the Photoscan software to go through the SfM workflow including the photo alignment and then dense cloud building. Markers were used on the two datasets to allow for one integrated model to be created by merging the two chunks. The dataset obtained from the camera was obtained through two separate datasets of surveys on the façade and the steps of the building so as to pick up more details of these sections of the building. (Illustrated in Fig. 2a and b below).

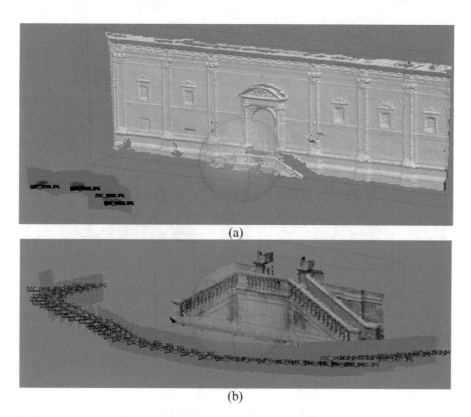

(a)

(b)

Fig. 2. Facade (a) and Step (b) Dense clouds obtained from camera datasets from ground level

These two camera datasets are combined before being combined with the dataset from GE. This is illustrated in the workflow in Fig. 3.

The above workflow can also be amended for more sub processes wherein multiple sections can be combined under the camera dataset section of the workflow. This can be done as is required by the specific sections of a model where intricate and detailed features are required as the GE model will produce a general overview of the object without the details. This is possible once markers are made on all the subsets used for the final combined 3D model.

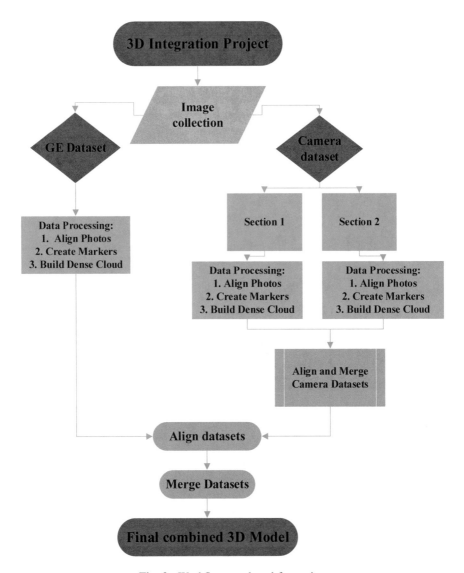

Fig. 3. Workflow employed for project

2.1   GE Dataset

To build the dataset from GE, typical photogrammetric rules were followed (Mikhail et al. 2001). Screenshots were taken from moving around GE images at different viewing angles and altitudes. These screenshots were then optimized utilizing the Microsoft 4 Screen Capture Software on a NVIDIA Quadro K1100M (2560 × 1440 pixel) monitor. This produced the images at an effective 3.2 Megapixel (MP) resolution

(2464 × 1312 pixel). The dataset is illustrated in Fig. 4. This resolution was created after some preprocessing, involving the removal of elements that were not representative of the object in question including borders and toolbars from the Google platform.

Fig. 4. GE dataset for 3D model

2.2   Camera Dataset

For the second chunk, a Nikon D5200 camera, 18/55 mm was used and **2 separate datasets taken for the façade (51 images) and the steps (44 images) each** with 6000 × 4000 image pixel size were used. A similar approach was applied as with the GE model to carry out this model with the photos taken at ground level. For this dataset, the focus of the model was placed on the center of the church where the entrance to the church lies. This was done so as to clearly identify features of this section of the church which contained more intricate features around the door and steps. Images were taken in various distances from the church with an average overlap of 80% between images to ensure features were captured. The dataset produced dense clouds as shown in Fig. 2a and b.

Markers were then detected on the two chunks so that a combined model could be created. These markers were based on measurements taken during the survey of specific points on the steps of the church and the columns of the portico so that there could be overlap of the chunks.

3   Results and Discussion

After detecting the markers, the chunks were aligned and the process completed with the model being scaled within the software. Details of the models produced by each dataset are shown in Table 1.

Table 1. Characteristics of SfM models

	N-SfM		GE-SfM
Device	Nikon D5200		Google Earth
Camera resolution	24		3.2
Object captured	Facade	Steps	Entire building
Distance from object (m)	≈39 m	≈15 m	
Number of photos	51	44	94
Mesh faces	372,389	38,861	118,992
Processing time	2 h 6 min	2 h 45 min	33 min
Ground sampling distance (mm/pixel)	4.76	1.41	–

The model produced from ground level utilized significantly more pictures to capture more details at a particular point of the church and thus had a long processing time. On the other hand, the model produced by the GE dataset was done relatively quickly and was able to give an overview of the building as shown in Fig. 5.

Fig. 5. 3D model produced by GE dataset

This overview however is not detailed across the façade but it does provide a solid overview of the building and captures the roof which would be impossible to replicate from a ground level survey. In Fig. 6, the rendered model from the combined dataset is shown.

Within this model the features of the façade are more clearly defined providing a more complete overall model. However, the calculation of the GSD was not possible given the fact that the dataset was done at various heights and utilizing screenshots from GE. This is therefore a limitation of the methodology.

The model produced by the camera at street level can be used over points where a higher resolution is needed and the combination of the two models would yield a replication of a large landscape with a higher resolution captured at particular points of interest. It should also be noted that the model produced at street level could not incorporate the features of the church at the higher points and on the roof. The dataset provided by GE therefore allows these features to be included in one complete model.

Fig. 6. Combined 3D model produced

The final model shows a complete replication of the Church with the use of low cost techniques and a readily available dataset provided by GE. This can be key in augmented and virtual reality applications (Inzerillo 2013) where landscape creation is needed. There are drawbacks associated with this workflow with no quality standardization and the dependence on updates provided by the GE platform.

4   Conclusions

The results obtained within the paper show that the workflow can be utilized for the modelling of buildings and outdoor landscapes. There are limitations to the workflow with respect to numerical quality parameters. However, if you need to create a 3D Model of a large outdoor area, you can use this combined methodology to carry out a model that reproduces the reality of the area (using GE dataset) and that gives you the metric information in a specific area where you require a higher resolution (dataset at ground floor level).

Acknowledgements. The research presented in this paper was carried out as part of the H2020-MSCA-ETN-2016. This project has received funding from the European Union's H2020 Programme for research, technological development and demonstration under grant agreement number 721493.

References

Barsanti SG, Remondino F, Visintini D (2012) Photogrammetry and laser scanning for archaeological site 3D modeling-some critical issues. In: Roberto V, Fozzati L (eds) Proceedings of the 2nd workshop on 'the new technologies for aquileia', pp 1–10. http://ceur-ws.org/Vol-948/paper2.pdf

Chen J, Clarke KC (2016) Rapid 3D modeling using photogrammetry applied to Google Earth. In: Proceedings, AutoCarto2016, The 19th international research symposium on computer-based cartography Albuquerque, New Mexico, USA, September 14–16, 2016. Edited by S.M. Freundschuh. Online Proceedings published by the Cartography and Geographic Information Society

Gillan JK et al (2017) Fine-resolution repeat topographic surveying of dryland landscapes using UAS-based structure-from-motion photogrammetry: assessing accuracy and precision against traditional ground-based erosion measurements. Remote Sens 9(5):1–24. https://doi.org/10.3390/rs9050437

Inzerillo L (2013) Augmented reality: past, present, future. In: Proceedings of SPIE- The international society for optical engineering, 8649, 86490 E

Inzerillo L, Santagati C (2016) Crowdsourcing cultural heritage: from 3D modeling to the engagement of young generations. Lecture Notes in Computer Science (including subseries Lecture Notes in Artificial Intelligence and Lecture Notes in Bioinformatics), LNCS, vol 10058, pp 869–879. https://doi.org/10.1007/978-3-319-48496-9_70

Inzerillo L (2017) Integrated SfM techniques using data set from Google Earth 3D model and from street level. ISPRS Int Arch Photogrammetry Remote Sens Spatial Inf Sci XLII-2/W5:361–367. https://doi.org/10.5194/isprs-archives-xlii-2-w5-361-2017

Lausch A et al (2015) Understanding and quantifying landscape structure - a review on relevant process characteristics, data models and landscape metrics. Ecol Model 295:31–41. https://doi.org/10.1016/j.ecolmodel.2014.08.018

Liu K et al (2018) Large-scale mapping of gully-affected areas: an approach integrating Google Earth images and terrain skeleton information. Geomorphology 314(2):13–26. https://doi.org/10.1016/j.geomorph.2018.04.011

Lubis MZ et al (2017) Interactive modelling of buildings in Google Earth and GIS: a 3D tool for urban planning (Tunjuk Island, Indonesia). J Appl Geospatial Inf 1(2):44–48

Mikhail EM, Bethel JS, Mcglone JC (2001) Introduction to modern photogrammetry. Wiley, New York

Menna F et al (2016) 3D digitization of an heritage masterpiece - a critical analysis on quality assessment. Int Arch Photogrammetry Remote Sens Spatial Inf Sci ISPRS Arch 41:675–683. https://doi.org/10.5194/isprsarchives-xli-b5-675-2016

Nikolakopoulos KG et al (2017) UAV vs classical aerial photogrammetry for archaeological studies. J Archaeol Sci Rep 14:758–773. https://doi.org/10.1016/j.jasrep.2016.09.004

Remondino F et al (2017) A critical review of automated photogrammetric processing of large datasets. ISPRS Int Arch Photogrammetry Remote Sens Spatial Inf Sci XLII-2/W5:591–599. https://doi.org/10.5194/isprs-archives-xlii-2-w5-591-2017

Verhoeven G (2010) Taking computer vision aloft-archaeological three-dimensional reconstructions from aerial photographs with photoscan. Archaeol Prospection 62:61–62. https://doi.org/10.1002/arp

Memory in Names. Toponyms in Historical Cadastres for the Analysis of the Religious Presence in the Walled City

Donatella Bontempi[✉]

Department of Engineering and Architecture (DIA), University of Parma,
Parco Area delle Scienze 181/A, 43124 Parma, Italy
donatella.bontempi@unipr.it

Abstract. The study of historical toponyms can be considered a field of research limited to historiography. However, if transposed as an iconographic layer on the representation of the current city by the means of interactive digital navigation, it can return interesting results for both historical knowledge, and cultural and tourist disclosure. The paper presents as case study a research about the analysis of the present and past existence of churches, convents and religious buildings in the historic centre of the city of Parma. The georeferenced planimetry drawn on the basis of historical cadastre has been imported into an online geolocated app, to be explored in real time to discover hidden aspects as a touristic serious game, but also for the scientific study of city transformation over time.

Keywords: Graphical analysis · Toponymy · Interactive map · Geolocation · Point of interest

1 Toponyms, Why? Disciplinary Area and Purpose

A project on historical toponymy can become innovative, when the digital graphic medium is used to bring the memory of the places, lost in urban transformations, into the actuality and distracted causality of daily journeys. The disciplinary field of Drawing, applied on an urban scale, can ensure the proper application of technical means, at the same time playing with the graphics and the potential of digital, to improve the comprehensibility of the theme for a wider audience. The key of the names of the streets opens up the knowledge of a chapter of urban history that can be useful for the purpose of scientific study and cultural dissemination.

The Drawing group in the Department DIA of the University of Parma, has always dealt with surveying on both an architectural and urban scale (Giandebiaggi and Vernizzi 2011; Vernizzi and Bontempi 2015). They provided both the database from which to draw, and a term of comparison on the results achieved to evaluate aspects such as accessibility, sharing, updatability, user-friendliness, in general the possibility of understanding and disclosure also to an audience of non-technical and the sharing of knowledge (Brusaporci 2010; De Carlo 2015; Cennamo 2016).

© Springer Nature Switzerland AG 2019
A. Luigini (Ed.): EARTH 2018, AISC 919, pp. 635–646, 2019.
https://doi.org/10.1007/978-3-030-12240-9_66

This specific study started as a side application of a research topic that engaged for many years the group, with regard to the permanence and transformation of religious buildings in the historic centre of the city, of which a large volume is upcoming (Giandebiaggi et al. 2001; Giandebiaggi and Vernizzi 2012).

The survey of all the remaining monasteries and convents inside the circle of walls has been enriched by historical research, cataloguing and mapping of all the historical buildings that no longer exist. The sources of data varied from the comparison of all the historical urban cartography (Fig. 1) to the researches by the various scholars who contributed with their thematic essays. The large part of the analysis on an urban scale concerned the physical and functional transformation of the buildings, supplemented by reasoning concerning the roads, the vegetation, the construction techniques, the symbology etc. Updating the search in the last year allowed to integrate new information, such an in-depth study on confraternity speakers and minor religious houses.

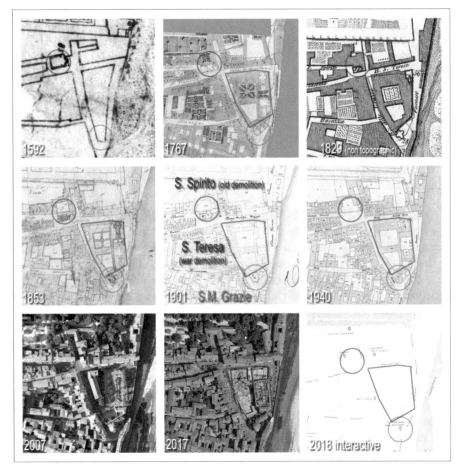

Fig. 1. Chronology of the principal cartography used to map the borders of lost religious structures and check the today situation (by D. Bontempi).

The use of the latest software brought further improvements: the digitalization of historical maps was carried out in collaboration with the Topography and History groups during another recent research, which involved the high resolution scanning, georeferencing and mosaicking of the of the original historical maps for the implementation of an hGIS of the city's historical cadastres (Bruno 2013; Zerbi et al. 2013; Bianchi 2015; Bruno et al. 2015; Zerbi and Bianchi 2015 and Fig. 3).

Continuous provocations come from outside the academic world and everything suddenly seems to move very fast: the weight and power of images cannot be ignored. However, it can be exploited to the advantage of scientific discipline. In bibliography, there are wide references as regards the representation and analysis of the city (Cundari 2005: Coppo and Boido 2010; Marotta and Novello 2015; Capano et al. 2016), while for the augmented reality projects, some experiments were conducted on different available software to implement app of specific case study, but the scientific literature is still poor, especially in the disciplinary field ICAR/17.

2 Surviving and Lost Religious Buildings in Parma Historic Centre: Case Study

The work of catalogue, mapping and urban and architectural survey conducted by the researchers over the years has mainly concerned the restitution drawing of the monastic and conventual religious complex still existing in the old city. To have a complete picture of the chronological evolution and of the overall consistency of the religious presence, it was also necessary to reconstruct the events of demolished or heavily transformed monasteries, which shaped the urban development with their volumetrically relevant presence, even if they have been replaced by other buildings in more or less recent times.

The minor entities complete the mapping (Fig. 2): 28 buildings with church or oratory, which, due to their size or permanence over time, did not have impact on urban scale, but whose localization and extension has been reconstructed from historical cartography. For the structures extinct before the 1600s, there were not enough descriptive data to consider them. The list includes temporary used convents and with little architectural importance, several "Conservatories" (housing for poor, beggars, orphans and unmarried), religious schools and a big group of hospices/hospitals/xenodochs (for sick, convalescent, poor or pilgrims).

A category of religious organizations often architecturally modest, but capillary present in the city, is the one of the lay Confraternities. A complex phenomenon of ancient origin, which flowed into the Municipal Congregation of Charity and for the most part is extinct (in Parma survives one Opera Pia). If they built or modified an oratory for their headquarters, they have been mapped in 32 cases of which 17 are lost, others transformed and 14 still visible. Finally, there are 24 churches and oratories without annexes, both existing and demolished, almost all present in the Sardi Atlas of 1767. A series of churches and small orators of ancient foundation or short existence, weren't considered because they were already disappeared in the first topographic maps and it was impossible to find their exact location.

Throughout this work, the cross reading of the street odonomancy in its chronological transformation helped the localisation of the oldest structures of which today

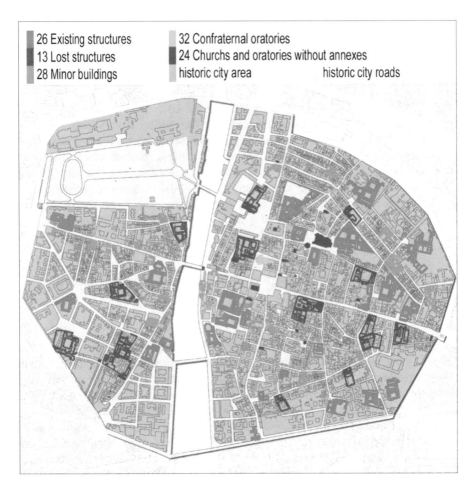

Fig. 2. Mapping of the religious presence in history (by M.E. Melley and D. Bontempi).

every architectural trace is lost. Often, only the name of the streets preserve the memory. It is remarkable to read as in the seventeenth and eighteenth centuries almost all the urban streets were dedicated to saints whose churches stood nearby.

3   From the Iconographic Historical Research to the Interactive Navigation: Methods and Tools

The qualitative and quantitative data graphically displayed in the digital maps to be experienced in real time navigation, are drawn from many historical graphic sources, by comparing cartographies and urban iconography. They were used both modern zenithal results of topographical surveys, and ancient urban iconography in which the religious presence was represented (frequently with dedicated legends). All the information about localization, properties and chronology were validated by the texts of local history (Sitti 1929; Da Mareto 1978; Miani Uluhogian 1984; Marcheselli 1988).

The historical cadastres had the maximum metric accuracy on the urban representation, together with the first known topographic survey of S. Smeraldi in 1592 and the map of E. Azzi, dated 1829, not very accurate from the dimensional point of view but very important because documenting the suppressions. In particular in Sardi's Atlas, the religious presence is documented at its best, since all constructions have been practically concluded and not yet perpetrated the numerous transformations of use, tampering and demolitions, carried out largely following the Napoleonic suppressions.

The work made on the land registries consisted in the redesign of all the graphic entities and the constitution of a database that contained all the information of the owner registers. In the 2D GIS environment, the geometric/spatial and textual/thematic data were linked in order to be able to query and obtain statistical reports and thematic maps. The model is very accurate and has profound implications in the analysis of the state of the city at that time, but remains confined to a specialized technical software: the creation and management of interactive real-time navigation and augmented reality requires more friendly interfaces.

Various examples, applications and software have been compared by evaluating their potentialities, criticalities and possibilities of use, to choose the optimal solution in which to implement the specific project. The priority features required were low cost, low technical IT competence of the operator and user (even with a great technological complexity behind it) and friendly interface.

4   Urban Data Mapping and Visualization: State of the Art

Infographics, information mapping, information design and visual storytelling are very interesting and objectively captivating sectors of image production (it is said: "information is beautiful" cfr. McCandless 2009). Thanks to the immersion in the "society of images", the vocation of the drawer to try to transmit information through the graphic medium seems to have greater consent. At the same time, other sectors can provide examples of truly effective and immediate communication through the eye.

The same phenomenon is found from the point of view of mapping ("It's Map Time"), or information georeferenced in the territory expressed through a mixture of graphic symbols and text. Today personalization and user generated content are encouraged, sometimes to the detriment of the accuracy of the data to which, fortunately, scientists pay special attention.

This is not a new theme: at the origins of cartographic science, representations were very rich in various kind of information. Over time, the graphics have become more meticulously accurate and standard, but losing many of the qualitative information.

Partially, they can be retrieved through the superimposition of informative levels that are graphical or textual, numeric and of another nature. The so-called "vestments" or "themes". Today, the scope of representation on an urban and territorial scale has been extended to include, in addition to data collected with different tools, also photographic and graphical sources. The skills are increasingly multidisciplinary and transversal, and the variables to be monitored grow exponentially.

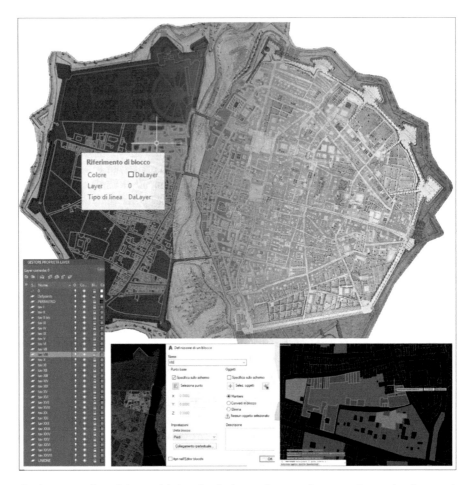

Fig. 3. Preparation of the spatial data for the interactive mapping: georeferenced ortho-mosaic of Sardi 1767 cadastre, CAD redrawing (by N. Bruno), creation of blocks and textures for the export (by D. Bontempi).

Geolocalisation (active, passive and geofencing) can be included in the Augmented Reality devices. A tool that we are used to, but which actually is a recent achievement that allows to monitor in real time the position of user with respect to a system of GPS coordinates. It is usual to have a current map, but it is possible to tap into information and drawing of any time. The technological development promises, in a near future, the possibility of immersive visualization (Pierattini 2016; Massidda 2016; Fingas 2017; Yeeply 2017).

Fig. 4. Problems of interoperability between software and synchronization between different geographic coordinate systems (by D. Bontempi).

5   Tests on Data and Software

The app Google My Maps has been chosen for this first test because of the widespread use of Google Earth/Maps and of its complete compatibility on all the currently used devices for GPS positioning and geo-data formats. The map can be processed within a CAD drawing in which the geo-referencing data are embedded, and loaded as a customized information layer on the common basis of the viewer that everyone knows, then shared. When the GPS navigation is activated in real-time, the track will move over the map that indicate the points of interest with description and the highlighted streets.

This system was chosen because the procedures are tested and simple, although it is a step away from Augmented Reality, as there is no data display overlaid to the reality framed by the camera. This technology is still immature and in testing for road navigation (AR City app for iOS, 2017), but rapid development is guessable, which will allow to get a more engaging immersive visualization.

Fig. 5. Layers of information in CAD and transposed on real-time map: categories of edifices with related photo and description, and old religious names of the roads (by D. Bontempi).

There are numerous examples of shared maps, but rarely for study or scientific dissemination purposes. Representative is the case of the historical Land registry of Bologna city centre (Origine di Bologna 2018).

The app allows to import lines or shapes in the formats .csv .xlsx .kml .gpx, insert geolocated images, create placeholders and paths. It can have a maximum of 10 levels, each with up to 2000 items, for a total of up to 10,000 total entities.

For this reason, the cad file must be previously optimized for the .kml format from . dwg through .dxf (Fig. 4) with the choice of the appropriate format of geographic coordinates with or without GPS converter, creation of blocks (to reduce the number of entities) and of patterns (to maintain the areas of coloured texture). Both Autodesk AutoCad 2019 and Autocad Map 3D 2019 were used in parallel to preserve the largest quality of features.

Figure 5 shows a part of the real visualization in the exploration of the map, on the left the layer of existing and disappeared buildings and on the right the streets with existing religious names or renamed. It is possible to walk having in our hands the support of the historical map, metrically rigorous, from which to recall the data.

6   Conclusion

Reading the history of the city in the permanence or transformation of urban blocks and in the name of its streets is a piece of global understanding of the phenomenon of city evolution. Graphically displayed at 1:1 scale on the geographical extension, it is both captivating and compelling as a path of exploration and cultural discovery, and indeed useful to "connect the dots", from infrastructures to blocks and buildings, from floor plans to volumes and facades (Fig. 6).

The application case of the religious presence in the historical walled centre of the city of Parma, which has deeply permeated and conditioned buildings and open spaces, was a test on the operational tools and challenges encountered when we want to reconcile the two worlds, that is to valorise the results of scientific research through a dissemination that knows how to dialogue with the current demands of society. It wants to be a starting point and a stimulus to start thinking in a different and more organic way about data sharing.

This can be replicated in the field of production, commerce, politics, health and every environment of civic life, to provide an alternative and "portable" in-situ study tool that can also have a touristic interest, as a further element of enhancement to "catch" the attention of those who move in the city in search of culture and heritage to be enjoyed.

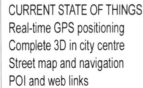

CURRENT STATE OF THINGS
Real-time GPS positioning
Complete 3D in city centre
Street map and navigation
POI and web links

PROJECT
Historical map layer
and personalised POI
powered by Google My Maps
2D Real-time navigation
through Google Map app

NEXT FUTURE
Augmented Reality
3D Real-time navigation
and access to informations
though the display camera

Fig. 6. Concept of the project (by D. Bontempi).

Acknowledgements. The activity presented in the paper is a personal research of the author, spin-off of a decennial research called "Churches and Convents" of the Representation Group (ICAR/17) of the DIA Department in Parma University, of which a book is in the process of being printed.

References

Bianchi G (2015) Gli Historical Geographic Information Systems su base catastale per la conoscenza e la rappresentazione della città. Una prima applicazione su Parma (secc. XVIII–XX) PhD thesis, Università di Parma

Bruno N (2013) L'Atlante Sardi informatizzato. Un GIS storico per l'analisi di Parma nel Settecento. Master thesis, Università di Parma

Bruno N, Bianchi G, Zerbi A, Roncella R (2015) An open-HGIS project for the city of Parma: database structure and map registration. In: Geomatics workbooks, vol. 12. Free and Open Source Software for Geospatial Open Innovation for Europe. Laboratorio di Geomatica Politecnico di Milano Polo Territoriale di Como, Como, pp 189–203

Brusaporci S (ed) (2010) Sistemi informativi integrati per la tutela la conservazione e la valorizzazione del patrimonio architettonico e urbano. Gangemi, Roma

Capano F, Pascariello MI, Visone M (eds) (2016) Delli aspetti de Paesi. Cirice, Napoli

Cennamo GM (ed) (2016) Processi di analisi per strategie di valorizzazione dei paesaggi urbani. Ermes, Roma

Coppo S, Boido C (eds) (2010) Rilievo urbano. Conoscenza e rappresentazione della città consolidata. Alinea, Firenze

Cundari C (ed) (2005) Il rilievo urbano per sistemi complessi: Un nuovo protocollo per un sistema informativo di documentazione e gestione della citta: Materiali dalla ricerca co-finanziata dal MIUR nel 2002. Kappa, Roma

Da Mareto F (ed) (1978) Chiese e conventi di Parma. Deputazione Storia Patria, Parma

De Carlo L (ed) (2015) Metamorfosi dell'immagine urbana. Gangemi, Roma

Fingas J (2017) AR navigation app promises better accuracy than GPS alone. Walk the streets as if you had a local by your side. www.engadget.com/2017/11/07/blippar-ar-city-navigation-app/. Accessed Sept 2018

Giandebiaggi P, Vernizzi C (2011) Rilevare le città/rappresentare la conoscenza con i sistemi informativi. In: Gambardella C (ed) Le Vie dei Mercanti. Rappresentare la conoscenza: Atti del 7° Forum internazionale di Studi, Capri. La scuola di Pitagora, Napoli. 6 p

Giandebiaggi P, Vernizzi C (2012) Conventi e Monasteri a parma: relazioni e ricadute sul tessuto storico della città della costruzione di organismi religiosi. Lettura e analisi dall'iconografia storica al rilievo urbano. In: Bertocci S, Parrinello S (eds) Architettura eremitica: sistemi progettuali e paesaggi culturali: Atti del 3° Convegno internazionale di studi, Camaldoli 2012. Edifir, Firenze, pp 156–163

Giandebiaggi P, Vernizzi C, Zerbi A, Melley ME, Fioretti I, Paltrinieri D (2001) Sistemi informativi per il rilievo: chiese e conventi in Parma. In: AA.VV. Trenta anni di Disegno nelle Facoltà di Architettura e di Ingegneria. Kappa, Roma, pp 221–222

Marcheselli T (1988) Le strade di Parma, vol 1–3. Benedettina, Parma

Marotta A, Novello G (eds) (2015) Disegno, & città: Cultura, arte, scienza, informazione: Atti del 37° Convegno internazionale dei docenti della rappresentazione, Torino. Gangemi, Roma

Massidda M (2016) Il turismo e la realtà aumentata. www.madeinpuglia.com/journal/il-turismo-e-la-realta-aumentata/. Accessed Sept 2018

McCandless D (2009) Information is beautiful. Collins, London. https://informationisbeautiful.net/. Accessed Sept 2018

Miani Uluhogian F (1984) Le immagini di una città: Parma (secoli XV–XIX): Dalla figurazione simbolica alla rappresentazione topografica. Casanova, Parma

Pierattini L (2016) WELC Map, la mappa cartacea di Milano in realtà aumentata. www.gqitalia.it/gadget/hi-tech/2016/08/04/welc-map-la-mappa-cartacea-di-milano-in-realta-aumentata/. Accessed Sept 2018

Sitti G (1929) Parma nel nome delle sue strade. Fresching, Parma

Vernizzi C, Bontempi D (2015) La rappresentazione della città per lo studio dei fenomeni urbani. Evoluzione metodologica attraverso casi studio. In: Marotta A, Novello G (eds) Disegno, & città: Cultura, arte, scienza, informazione: Atti del 37° Convegno internazionale dei docenti della rappresentazione, Torino. Gangemi, Roma, pp 871–878

Zerbi A, Bianchi G (2015) Un HGIS per lo studio dei catasti storici della città di Parma. In: Cerasoli M (ed) Città Memoria Gente: Atti del 9° Congresso "Città e Territorio Virtuale, Roma 2013. Roma Tre-Press, Roma, pp 810–816

Zerbi A, Bianchi G, Roncella R (2013) Ricomposizione georeferenziata dell'Atlante Sardi. In: Fiaccadori G, Malinverni A, Mambriani C (eds) Guglielmo Du Tillot regista delle arti nell'età dei Lumi: Catalogo della mostra, Parma 2013. Fondazione Cariparma, Parma, pp 92–94

Yeeply (2017) La geolocalizzazione nello sviluppo delle applicazioni. https://it.yeeply.com/blog/geolocalizzazione-sviluppo-applicazioni/. Accessed Sept 2018

#maptime! http://maptime.io/. Accessed Sept 2018

Field Trip. www.fieldtripper.com/. Accessed Sept 2018

Google My Maps. www.google.com/intl/it/maps/about/mymaps/. Accessed Sept 2018

WELCmap. http://welcmap.com/. Accessed Sept 2018

Origine di Bologna – Mappa. www.originebologna.com/. Accessed Sept 2018

The Mediated Landscape. Methods and Media for the Re-knowledge of the Torbiere del Sebino

Ivana Passamani[(✉)] and Olivia Longo

Department of Civil, Environmental, Architectural Engineering and Mathematics
(D.I.C.A.T.A.M), Università degli Studi di Brescia, Via Branze 43,
25123 Brescia, Italy
ivana.passamani@unibs.it

Abstract. The "Torbiere del Sebino" is a natural reserve declared a wetland of international importance under the Ramsar Convention (Ramsar, Iran, 1971). Due to its social-economical history and to the variety of species and habitats it's considered a priority area for biodiversity in the Po Valley.

That's why we consider this area an optimal training ground in which it is possible to experiment a multisensory approach to sense the atmosphere that "is" the site itself.

An educational path about landscape and environment starts from the photographic media and develops into a preconstructed graphic/textual tool. The photographic tool acts as a filter between the individual and the outside world when is required to discriminate and interpret the characteristics of the area; another tool, the dynamic diary, helps the researchers to search for "genius loci", following a preordinated index.

After this preliminary activity, it would be possible to face the design of the microarchitectural structures, useful for enhancing and highlighting the peculiarities of the itineraries of the visit.

The final outcome can be considered a "mediated landscape". The mediation process works through some steps:

- the survey and study of the Torbiere landscape with a focus on the outcomes from the 5 senses
- the selective attention to the outcomes of a single sense and the consequent project proposals for the enhancement of this site, focused only on one sense.

Keywords: Heritage education · Knowledge · Torbiere · Digital photography · Dynamic diary · Microarchitectures

© Springer Nature Switzerland AG 2019
A. Luigini (Ed.): EARTH 2018, AISC 919, pp. 647–655, 2019.
https://doi.org/10.1007/978-3-030-12240-9_67

1   Introduction

The experience presented concerns a re-reading of a particular landscape site, the Nature Reserve of Torbiere del Sebino, set up and conducted by the Authors as part of a collaboration between the University of Brescia and the Ente Torbiere; it's included in the broader project "I like Torbiere" financed by Bandi Cariplo.

As it is showed in Fig. 1, this landscape is very complex because of its size (it is an area of about 360 ha), its location (it belongs to the morainic amphitheatre of Franciacorta and Sebino), its beautiful natural scenery and its colours and sounds, that change in relation to the seasons. Furthermore, visual and perceptive relationships must not be overlooked with what there is in the neighbourhood, which is rich of historical and artistic buildings, like for example the Monastery of Saint Peter in Lamosa, which is also reflected on the clear water of the basin. All these peculiarities make this area an optimal training ground in which to experiment a multisensory approach to sense the atmosphere that "is" the site itself.

Fig. 1.   Torbiere del Sebino, Iseo (Brescia). An anthropic and natural landscape to be re-known (Photo IPassamani)

The project "I like Torbiere" had the macro-objective of promoting the growth and the active inclusion of the local community (citizen, aspiring tourist guides, naturalists), strengthening the relationship with the Reserve through innovative models of education and awareness of the protection of the landscape heritage.

According to this broader project, the main aims of our training and cultural activity "Re-knowing the landscape of the Torbiere" are:

– to integrate the environmental planning of the area with the protection and culture of the territory
– to strength the relationship between citizens and the area
– to propose multi-sensory points of view to re-learn the landscape of the Torbiere, to perceive and inhabit it with the awareness of the direct relationship between the body, the 5 senses and the specificities of the nature and the landscape.

In conclusion, reach a new awareness of the landscape in an open-mind way: discover this unique area through signs and peculiarities to know it in a new way, with a new point of view.

This aim can be pursued through the activation of the social, cultural and political realities that already operate in the territory, to promote shared and enriching experiences.

It is therefore essential to find new models of education, supported by digital languages and tools, to spread a responsible approach to the protection of the natural heritage and its transmission to future generations.

Moreover it is important to highlight that one of the main strengths of this project is the active involvement of the local populations. The citizens need to be instructed, trained and guided (for instance with workshops and working groups) in the process of acquiring the awareness that their territory has a valuable landscape and a propulsive force with all the markings for a future development.

The coherence between this project and the previsions of the European Landscape Convention and the Italian "Codice Urbani" is evident: that's why it is very important to know perfectly the cultural and legislative contents of these laws about landscape.

2 References

It is fundamental to highlight the role of Photography as a medium of knowledge; Drawing has the same role, it's a powerful tool to transfer knowledge. The participants should be aware of it, to use these tools correctly.

The request to take photographs according to preordained reading keys was in fact preparatory to the first check organized using – all together - a large map of the Torbiere.

We were inspired by a very effective and incisive tool, widely used in Great Britain since the Eighties: the "parish maps", that are called in Italy "community maps".

They integrate the basic cartographic representations with photographical, graphical and alphanumerical data.

The local communities, as long as they daily live a definite territorial context, are invited to self-represent their heritage, their memories, the auto-perceived landscape, the knowledge in which they recognize themselves and what they intend to transmit to the new generations. In all those expressions of "spontaneous dynamic drawings" values and disvalues are found, as well as some references to the intangible heritage: after all its key role is confirmed by UNESCO's attention, which now includes intangible assets in the values to be protected.

If we browse the Web-sites looking for Parish maps examples, we can find many representations which testify the efficacy of this tool to visualize, in the various graphic forms (iconic, iconographic, diagrammatic), the peculiarities, the values and the critical aspects of a place.

The expressiveness of these works is really remarkable: sometimes, in their spontaneity, translate themselves into autonomous artistic forms, as in the example proposed in Fig. 2.

In our experience and how it will be more explicitly explained in the next paragraph, the map of the Torbiere has been covered with post-it of three different colors, representative of different interpretations on how to approach the site.

Fig. 2. A "Parish map" example (from https://www.commonground.org.uk/parish-maps-gallery/)

The action of "grip the posts", which each one has performed three times after waiting his/her own round, represented the first concrete action of participation and critical and conscious appropriation of the site.

Like a perish map, this document is an outcome of a community and testifies the peculiarities, the values and the critical aspects of the place Torbiere.

3   Methodologies Adopted

3.1   Think About the Essentials

The pre-investigation phase was the fundamental precondition for the success of the laboratory activity: it was carried out by each member individually, before the beginning of the course. Indeed each participant was asked to use the photographic medium as an opportunity to reflect on his/her subjective link with the Torbiere, and to represent it taking three photographs following precise requests (Fig. 3).

The pictures had to show an emotional sensation, an unmissable landscape view, a problem/criticality related to the current use.

These documents constituted the starting point of the community map-activity.

EMOTIONAL SENSATION	UNMISSABLE LANDSCAPE VIEW	PROBLEM / CRITICALITY
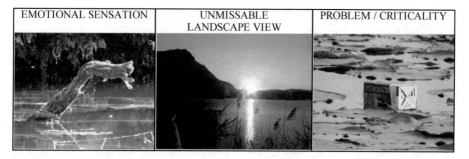		

Fig. 3. Pre-investigation activity: the photos as a medium (Photos of Gianluigi Lazzari).

3.2 Orient Yourself into the Space: From the Map to the "community map"

On the beginning of the Laboratory activity the three photos previously taken by each participant were associated with post-it in different colors (Fig. 4):

- light blue for an emotional sensation
- light green for a visual landscape that cannot be renounced
- fuchsia for a critical issue related to the present use.

Fig. 4. Orienting into the space: the post-it sticking activity to commute the map into a "community map"

The various post-it were subsequently placed on the large map of the Torbiere, in the corresponding visual points of the photographic shoots. Each participant, standing in front of the map, searched the right position of each point of view and sticked his three post-it.

It was a situation developed in a relatively short but very significant time, necessary to compare sensations, considerations and judgments of the other participants.

Step by step, post-it after post-it the personal interpretations of places have taken on consistency.

The simultaneous visualization on the map allows to highlight the focal points, such as the central walkway or the path up to the little wood observation tower, and at the same time describes the critical areas, providing useful informations to the managers of the Park Authority.

3.3 Employ the Dynamic Diary

The diary is widely used by many designers to write down everything they observe in their surveys. We would like the participants to become designers and to go through a new way to understand and explain this special site.

The dynamic diary it's an innovative tool, designed for this specific training and this cultural experience. In our idea, it represents the tool for exploring the landscape of the Torbiere in a multi-sensorial way, feeling by the body and paying attention to the feedback of the five senses while they sense the Torbiere del Sebino. It contains graphic exercises, organized according to a logical sequence, which stimulates both the drawing based on memory and that done on open air (Fig. 5).

Fig. 5. The dynamic diary helps to think about the landscape and its characters. The examples concern: the plan by memory (R. Denti), skyline and section (C. Piantoni), signs of infrastructures and work activities (S. Dalena).

The diary thus becomes a revealing mirror of the emotional contents of the participants' physical experience; it contains a graphical expression of their sensorial involvement, which is activated by the specificity of the site.

The dynamic diary acts as a bridge towards the drawings containing the planning proposals, that are the second step of the following activity: the project.

In both activities, drawing is the most suitable channel of expression to search for clues and signs, like natural signs of plants and animals or anthropic proofs. These anthropic proofs concerns human inhabits, religiosity buildings, infrastructures, work buildings.

Drawing allows to capture peculiarities and characteristics of places, which is called *genius loci*.

4 Towards the Project Idea

4.1 Genius Loci and the Inhabit Idea

Each place is characterized by a "guardian spirit", the *genius loci*: we can associate it with a creative force capable, over time, of re-elaborating conditions and relational potentials. Every place is in fact conditioned by the work of man and its identity is always the result of the dialogue of many different things.

In this peculiar area, human beings and their activities can be considered in stark contrast with nature, which here takes on a dominant role: the nature preserves a wild and uncontrollable identity.

Our working method aims to bring the participants closer to these prerogatives by using several media tools. Some contemporary technologies (such as photography and digital video) are mixed with natural media: the five senses, that separate the human emotional sphere from the outside world.

According to the methodological idea, the visitor of the natural park is considered just as a natural element, so the digital representation of reality helps and integrates the sensorial experience: images, visual sequences and sounds capture the emotional effects, stimulating *ex post* the memory of smells, flavors and tactile sensations.

The ancients conceived their environment as constituted of defined characters and recognized the importance of coming to terms with the *genius loci* of the site in which they would like to live. They were aware that their survival depended on a good relationship with the place, both physically and mentally.

Nowadays men believe that science and technology had freed them from a site-dependence. This is an illusion: the pollution and the caos of the environment remind us that we need to reassess the key-role of the *genius loci*.

4.2 Sustainable Tourism

During the second class we introduced and spoke about a type of tourism congruent with the sites, respectful of the environment and of its cultural resources, according to the contents of the European Charter for Sustainable Tourism.

The project proposals of the participants are inspired by these principles, having to deal with a geographical area of high landscape and environmental value.

4.3 Multi-sensory Paths and Micro-architectures

We also presented and talked about the possibility of creating various multi-sensory thematic paths, aiming to attract lots of visitors, coming from every cultural background.

The paths could connect different observation points (Fig. 6).

Fig. 6. Drawings examples containing the planning proposal about sense of smell (R. Denti) and of hearing (L. Peroni).

The participants were organized in five working groups (one for each sense) to discuss and to draw, individually, same proposals such as pedestrian paths or equipments or micro-architectures, depending on the specific working group focus.

The equipments and the microarchitectures should be able to support the visitors and, in the same time, to become almost invisible, both because of their formal relationship with the landscape and thanks to the materials used.

5   Conclusions

Our daily existence is made up of concrete *phenomena*: people, animals, flowers, stones, earth, wood, water, cities, streets, sun, moon, clouds, night, day, seasons… but it is also made up of intangible *phenomena* like emotions.

We highlighted the importance of the senses and of the emotions in this experience, knowing that it could be a great way to better understand, live and respect the landscape of the Torbiere.

The exhibition of the results of the Laboratory, where both diaries and drawings will be shown, will give many outcomes to talk about.

Acknowledgements. The experimental activity about the Torbiere del Sebino is part of a large-scale research about the landscape of the north-east Lombard district. Despite having shared approach, objectives, methodologies, activities and results of the research, we declare that Ivana Passamani is the author of sections 1, 2, 3 and Olivia Longo of sections 4 and 5.

References

Barthes R (1980) La chambre claire. Note sur la photographie, Seuil; trad. it.: Guidieri R a cura di (2003) La camera chiara. Nota sulla fotografia, Giulio Einaudi editore, Torino

Calcagno Maniglio A (2015) Per un paesaggio di qualità. Dialogo su inadempienze e ritardi nell'attuazione della Convenzione Europea. Franco Angeli, Milano

Codice dei beni culturali e del paesaggio (2004)

Convenzione Europea del Paesaggio (2000)

Ejzenštejn SM (1958) Na urokach rezissury, Moskva; trad. it.: Gobetti, P., a cura di (2000) Lezioni di regia. Giulio Einaudi editore, Torino

Norberg-Schulz C (1979) Genius Loci. Electa, Milano

Perec G (1989) Specie di spazi. Bollati Boringhieri, Torino

Turri E (1998) Il paesaggio come teatro. Dal territorio vissuto al territorio rappresentato. Marsilio, Venezia

Zagari F (2006) Questo è paesaggio. Mancosu Editore, Roma

Archeology

Real Scale Augmented Reality. A Novel Paradigm for Archaeological Heritage Fruition

Aldo F. Dragoni[1], Ramona Quattrini[2(✉)], Paolo Sernani[1], and Ludovico Ruggeri[2]

[1] Department of Information Engineering (DII), Università Politecnica delle Marche, Via Brecce Bianche, 60131 Ancona, Italy
{a.f.dragoni,p.sernani}@univpm.it
[2] Department of Construction, Civil Engineering and Architecture (DICEA), Università Politecnica delle Marche, Via Brecce Bianche, 60131 Ancona, Italy
r.quattrini@univpm.it, l.ruggeri@pm.univpm.it

Abstract. 3D contents have great potential in improving the communication and fruition of Cultural Heritage (CH). The visiting experience on an archaeological site or historical building can be improved by digital contents that help visitors to discover and learn how they once appeared. Augmented Reality (AR) is one of the technologies nowadays used for CH exploitation and it has the great quality of superimposing digital contents on elements of the reality. This paper shows a new interactive application on the archaeological site of Forum Sempronii: thanks to SLAM technology it allows the visitors to see several virtual reconstructions superimposed on the ruins walking around the site, so that they can see how anciently the roman city was. Great attention has been given to the creation of 3D contents: after the creation of high poly models they have been decimated and optimized in terms of number of polygons and textures in order to be fluently managed on mobile devices. The fruition of real scale contents on the real context increases immersive users' experiences.

Keywords: Virtual anastylosis · AR · Cyberarchaeology · Immersive augmented reality · SLAM

1 Introduction

In last decades, advances in data capturing and digital modeling tools allowed to handle several interactions with 3D contents. Cultural Heritage domain, above all Archaeological Heritage (AH) significantly benefits from the introduction of digital 3D models, which represents a powerful means of communication and dissemination. 3D reality-based contents and virtual anastylosis have great potential to improve the visiting experience of the archaeological heritage, giving more communicative and satisfying results with particular reference to outdoor archaeological excavations. In fact the majority of this kind of sites are hard to perceive and comprehend during the visit, due to the fragmented evidences and conservation needs.

© Springer Nature Switzerland AG 2019
A. Luigini (Ed.): EARTH 2018, AISC 919, pp. 659–670, 2019.
https://doi.org/10.1007/978-3-030-12240-9_68

In order to overcome this issue, a portable and promising technology is certainly the Augmented Reality (AR), based on mobile devices. It generates minimal management costs, especially if compared to the quality and effectiveness of outputs and possible applications when it manages 3D contents with photorealistic textures, being an opportunity to increase the competitiveness of Cultural Heritage applications (Tscheu and Buhalis 2016).

Efficient and quite novel techniques of representation are often applied to explore the potential communicative of various kind of 3D models (reality-based, 3d printed, knowledge-based reconstruction etc.) and to create Spatial Augmented Reality (SAR) dissemination strategies (Cirafici et al. 2015), Augmented Reality (AR) app (Bontempi and Ratotti 2017) or Mixed Reality experiences (Meschini et al. 2017), extremely safe and precise methods also borrowed from medical and surgical domains (De Paolis et al. 2011). The workflows, from the contents generation to the processing and the realization of the final application, have to face several difficulties. The improvement and assessment of dedicated workflows (Clini et al. 2017) is even now an open point, notwithstanding the availability of proprietary or open source platforms for AR/VR and so on. The present work might contribute to develop new interactions at real scale and to increase immersive experiences. In fact, a major achievement from the presented application lies in the chance for users to move and browse the model in coherence with their point of view.

The work also investigates how specialist knowledge, such as archaeological analysis and reconstructions, could enter into a relationship to collective intelligences and if it is possible to build new experiences with heritage towards increasing awareness of the past expressions of civilizations and connected intangible heritage.

2   A State of Art Towards the Real Scale AR

Applications devoted to the use of AR to empower the visit of a museum or an archaeological site are emerging in the scientific literature. One possible use case is during the visit, where the visitors are usually "overwhelmed" by a lot of interesting information, but hard to assimilate. Information such as the biography of a painter or the details about the shown artifacts are essential in understanding and enjoying the visit. However, such information might also cause the visitors, especially the youngest, to lose focus, even when summarized by a human guide. In such use case AR is often used to implement gamified visits, exploiting the game elements to encourage visitors in moving towards specific points of interest or providing additional content, as in, for example, Mortara et al. 2014 and Hammady et al. 2016. Nevertheless, AR also allows visitors to visualize the ancient shape of an archaeological site, by using the screen of a mobile device to superimpose 3D models over the ruins framed by the camera. In fact, some case studies exploited low cost technologies (mobile devices such as smartphones and tablets) to share and visualize through AR the reconstructions of the archeological sites (Canciani et al. 2016; Empler 2015). Nevertheless, the tracking of 3D models in real scale through AR and the mapping of reconstruction on original evidences is an innovative scenario, not already tested.

3   How to Improve the Archaeological Visit Experience: The Forum Sempronii AR App

The present paper shows a quite novel workflow with the purpose of reconstructing the scenario of the Forum Sempronii (modern Fossombrone), using AR and 3D models in a mobile app. As explained in the next sections, the challenge is to provide a stable visualization of the 3D models over the existing ruins framed by the camera, implementing real-scale AR.

We have tried to select the contents available on the case study in order to manage different types of contents typical of archaeological databases, in fact the app shows two kind of 3D contents: reality-based models of artifacts now preserved in the civic museum and 3D models of virtual reconstructions of lost or damaged architectures. The reality-based model is obtained with digital photogrammetry and Structure from Motion (SfM) technique. The result of the SfM process is a textured high poly model (Fig. 1). For the virtual reconstructions, starting from a survey of the archaeological area, several roman architectures were virtually reconstructed and modelled according to the remains and the treaty (Fig. 2).

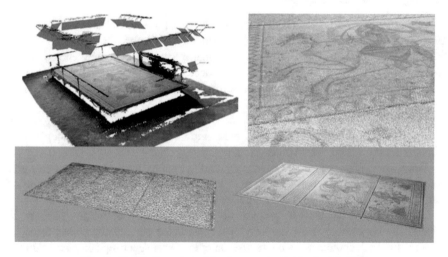

Fig. 1. Reality-based model of a mosaic digitized with SfM

Dealing with virtual reconstructions another mandatory issue to manage is the LoR (Level of Reliability), in fact archaeological reconstructions must comply with the principles of the Seville Charter (Lopez-Menchero and Grande 2011) about the identification of the interpretive phases and have to return the philological correctness of digital reconstruction.

Fig. 2. Virtual reconstruction of the "Botteghe", according to the remains and the treaty

3.1   Application Development

The Forum Sempronii AR app has been developed for Android and iOS, using the Unity (version 2017.3.1) development platform and the Vuforia library (version 7) for the real scale AR. The app consists of a main scene, a top view picture of the archaeological area, from which the user can access to the pages dedicated to the four point of interests (POIs) of the Forum Sempronii, where the user can switch to AR mode, activating the real scale AR.

In the main scene, the user can tap over one of the four POIs, according to her/his current position in the archeological area: the "Decumano", the "Botteghe", the "Domus Europa", and the "Anfiteatro" (Fig. 3).

Once the user selects one POI, the app displays some images and a text that gives historic information about it as well as a button to activate the AR. Before the AR starts, some instructions explain to the user how to use the application.

The four POIs are used to perform the three typologies of fruition (Fig. 4): the "Decumano" is used to show the LoR of reconstructed parts of the roman town; the "Domus Europa" demonstrates the reposition of artifacts, superimposing a mosaic now conserved in a civic museum on the floor of the house which decorated in ancient age; finally, the "Botteghe" and the "Anfiteatro" use AR to provide the users the virtual reconstructions of lost architectures.

In all the scenes linked to the four POIs, 3D Models are superimposed on the ruins available in the POI. To obtain a stable real-scale AR, the features offered by the Vuforia library have been mixed: both image-based target recognition and Simultaneous Localization and Mapping (SLAM) have been used.

In general, the image-based target recognition is used in the marker-based AR: the image is a reference for computer graphics (2D and/or 3D) to be overlaid (Amin and Govilkar 2015). However, the image-based target recognition is used in a slightly different way in the Forum Sempronii app: it uses the image target to understand in

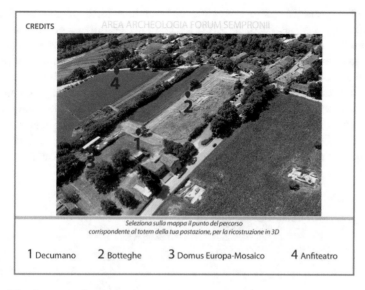

Fig. 3. The main scene of the app with the aerial view and the four POIs

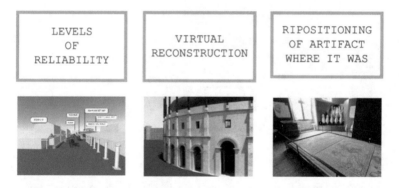

Fig. 4. The typologies of fruition conceived for the App

which POI the user finds her/himself. Hence, the image-based target recognition is applied once the user switches to AR mode in the scene of a POI: she/he is asked to frame a plate with an image (the number which identifies the POI) from a specific position, in order to generate and place the 3D models of the targets. At this point, SLAM is applied in the Forum Sempronii app.

SLAM is a mapping technique used in robotics to build a map of an unknown environment where a mobile robot should localize itself and operate autonomously (Durrant-Whyte and Bailey 2006; Bailey and Durrant-Whyte 2006). However, in addition to be applied in autonomous robotics (in fields such as embedded robotics, unmanned aerial vehicles, and self-driving cars), it has been recently applied to AR to improve the tracking of objects (Gao et al. 2017).

One of the innovations of this work is to combine image targets and SLAM, in order to achieve a stable real-scale AR (Fig. 5). In the Forum Sempronii app, when the image target is acquired, i.e. the POI is recognized, the app automatically switches to SLAM mode to perform instant tracking, decoupling the 3D models from the image target and assigning them to a virtual ground plane. This means that the user can move around the virtual reconstructions offered by the 3D models as well as going towards them to be able to visualize some specific characteristics. Therefore, using an image target to recognize the POI and the SLAM to perform the object tracking leads to the achievement of a real-scale AR to provide a reliable immersive user-experience while the 3D models are superimposed to the objects of an archeological area.

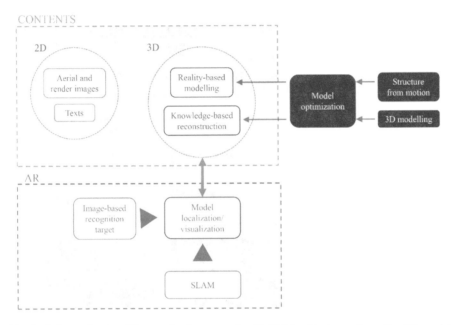

Fig. 5. Scheme for the AR app development: the SLAM is able to perform the 3D model tracking

3.2 Model Optimization

The main issue using VR and AR applications on mobile devices such as smartphones and tablets is the creation and management of contents, especially 3D models (Fernàndez-Palacios et al. 2013). In fact, real-time visualization and rendering of 3D contents require very high performances for the used hardware. It is necessary, for this reason, to make models with a low number of polygons, a so-called *low poly model*, trying to preserve a realistic visualization (Cipriani et al. 2014).

The process to obtain a photorealistic low poly model is similar to the production concept of the videogame 3D scene and consists in three main steps: (a) the high definition and high poly modelling, (b) the decimation and faces reduction and finally (c) the projection of the geometric characteristics from the high poly to the low poly one (Pecchioli et al. 2012).

After the high poly modelling it is necessary to decimate the number of the polygons of the model in order to make a lighter file and to let the application running on low performance systems as mobile devices (Fig. 6). The geometric optimization process (in 3ds Max) allows to reduce the geometric resolution, without great damages to the model corners and edges. However, we must pay attention during this process because if the 3D model' geometry is reduced to the limit, it starts to look sharp and edgier, with too big polygons and a loss of details. The result of this process is a huge decimation of the four 3D models used for the application (Table 1).

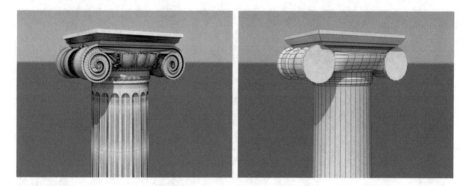

Fig. 6. Decimation of an ionic column from a high poly (147 k faces) to a low poly (1.1 k faces)

Table 1. Number of polygons and file size of the models before and after the optimization

	"Decumano minore"	"Botteghe"	"Domus" mosaic	"Anfiteatro"
Num. of polygons	7 Mln	4 Mln	100 k	7 Mln
Size of the original 3D model	114 MB	551 MB	12 MB	933 MB
Num. of polygons of the reduced model	66 k	46 k	12	30 k
Size of the optimized 3D model (FBX file)	40 MB	35 MB	6,7 MB	49 MB

The last step of the optimization process is the projection of the geometric characteristics from the high poly to the low poly one just obtained. While the previous process make the 3D model lighter, this step is fundamental to reacquire the visual realism lost in the previous step. This is possible thanks to the use of a normal map, a UV map that permits to reproduce high resolution geometry details when it's mapped onto a low resolution 3D model. Each pixel of the normal map stores a normal, a vector that describes the surface slope of the original high resolution 3D model at that point. The creation of the normal map consists in 4 main steps: the unwrapping of the 3D mesh into a UV map (Fig. 7a); the projection of the high poly model on the low poly one (Fig. 7b); the baking (with "render to texture" tool) process, utilized for the production of normal maps from the high-poly model to the low poly one (Fig. 7c); the application of the baked map on the low poly model (Fig. 7d).

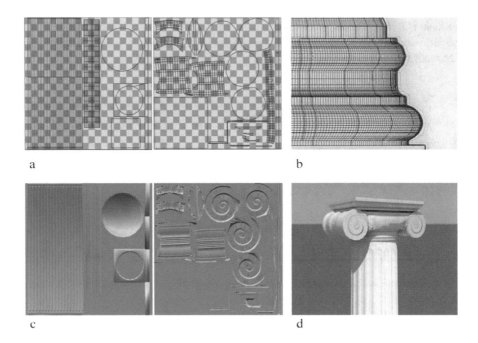

a   b

c   d

Fig. 7. The procedure for the creation of the normal map

With the baking procedure it's possible to obtain also other kind of maps as Ambient Occlusion (AO) map and displacement map to enrich the final texture of realist particulars.

Following this workflow, in our case study we created four models according to three different typology of fruition: virtual reconstruction of lost or damaged architectures, reposition in the real place of a scattered artefact and the Levels of Reliability (LoR) of the reconstructions, according to the virtual archaeology guidelines.

4   Conclusions

The proposed study, already tested on the field with the AR app, shows how it is possible to develop high quality 3D models referring to Virtual Archaeology (VA) principles and to interact with them during the visit of an archaeological site. The models are connected to geometrical survey of evidences and show validated and affordable reconstructions (Figs. 8e and 9).

Fig. 8. Visualization of the digitized mosaic on the floor where once it was.

Fig. 9. Screenshot of the app during the superimposition of the 3D reconstruction of the Botteghe on the remains

The present stage constitutes a first tangible achievement although some implementations will make the application and the project more complete: a totem for each POI will guide the visitors across the archaeological park and will work also as image target for the AR so that the user will not see the target on the floor. The totems and the AR app will have a corporate image coherent with the Flaminia Nextone project one.

After several tests on the field, it is possible to conclude that ambient lighting and user confidence with other AR applications highly influence the results in order to achieve matching between existing evidences and 3D reconstructions. For this and other reasons such as the lack of a wireless connection in the park, the application can not be downloaded but it is installed on a tablet and a guide will help the user during the use of the app.

SLAM is a heavy technology that stresses the devices on a computation point of view. It recognises and collects points of the real world with the camera so if the user uses it for a long time, for example on the Decumano where he can walk for dozen meters, the tablet starts to overheat. This kind of problem will surely overcome with more powerful devices or improved algorithms of SLAM technology.

Future works concern the improvement of the quality and the number of the information on the LoR and the addition of interactive elements that will help the user to learn and know better the archaeological park. In addition it is necessary to conduct user test in order to evaluate the clarity and the comprehension of the contents and the usability of the application.

The workflow explained in the present paper allows us to build a new kind of AR app mixing several sources and using different mapping technologies for the visualization of high quality models superimposed on archaeological evidences: the challenge is to validate the method for carrying out real scale 3D modelling perception experiences.

Acknowledgements. App "Forum Sempronii AR" is a pilot of DCE Flaminia Nextone project (Funging POR_FESR Marche region). Scientific responsible Paolo Clini, Università Politecnica delle Marche - DICEA. The app has been developed with the supervision of Paolo Clini and the advising of Oscar Mei for archaeological contents. Virtual reconstructions: Laura Invernizzi, Laura Cocon, Anna Marconi. 3D modelling: Ludovico Ruggeri, Floriano Capponi. APP development: Elia Alesiani, Luca Quercetti, Angelo Serafini. Layout: Anna Paola Pugnaloni. Other contents: Romina Nespeca, Gianluca Gagliardini, Luigi Sagone. The research presented here is also framed in the Univpm project CIVITAS (ChaIn for excellence of reflective societies to exploit dIgital cultural heritage and museumS).

References

Amin D, Govilkar S (2015) Comparative study of augmented reality Sdk's. Int J Comput Sci Appl 5(1):11–26. https://doi.org/10.5121/ijcsa.2015.5102
Bailey T, Durrant-Whyte H (2006) Simultaneous localization and mapping (SLAM): Part II. IEEE Robot Autom Mag 13(3):108–117. https://doi.org/10.1109/MRA.2006.1678144
Bontempi D, Ratotti A (2017) The Sandcastle by the Sea. IT and AR for Survey, Graphical Analysis and Representation of the "Skyscraper" by R. Bibbiani in La Spezia. Proceedings 1 (9):896. https://doi.org/10.3390/proceedings1090896

Canciani M, Conigliaro E, Del Grasso M, Papalini P, Saccone M (2016) 3D Survey and augmented reality for cultural heritage. The case study of Aurelian wall at Castra Praetoria in Rome. In: International archives of the photogrammetry, remote sensing and spatial information sciences - ISPRS archives. https://doi.org/10.5194/isprsarchives-xli-b5-931-2016

Cipriani L, Fantini F, Bertacchi S (2014) 3D models mapping optimization through an integrated parameterization approach: cases studies from Ravenna. In: International archives of the photogrammetry, remote sensing and spatial information sciences - ISPRS archives, vol 40, pp 173–180. https://doi.org/10.5194/isprsarchives-xl-5-173-2014

Cirafici A, Maniello D, Amoretti V (2015) The magnificent adventure of a "fragment". Block NXLVI Parthenon north frieze in augmented reality. SCIentific RESearch and Information Technology Ricerca Scientifica e Tecnologie Dell'Informazione 5(2):129–142. https://doi.org/10.2423/i22394303v5n2p129

Clini P, Quattrini R, Frontoni E, Pierdicca R, Nespeca R (2017) Real/Not real: pseudo-holography and augmented reality applications for cultural heritage Paolo. In: Handbook of research on emerging technologies for digital preservation and information modeling. https://doi.org/10.4018/978-1-5225-0680-5.ch009

De Paolis L, Ricciardi F, Dragoni AF, Aloisio G, De Paolis LT (2011) An augmented reality application for the radio frequency ablation of the liver tumors. In: Computational science and its applications (ICCSA 2011), vol 6785, pp 572–581. http://dx.doi.org/10.1007/978-3-642-21898-9_47

Durrant-Whyte H, Bailey T (2006) Simultaneous Localization And Mapping (SLAM): Part I. IEEE Robot Autom Mag 13(2):99–110. https://doi.org/10.1109/MRA.2006.1638022

Empler T (2015) Cultural heritage: displaying the forum of Nerva with new technologies. In: Digital heritage international congress (Digital Heritage 2015), pp 581–586. https://doi.org/10.1109/DigitalHeritage.2015.7419576

Fernàndez-Palacios BJ, Remondino F, Stefani C, Lombardo J, De Luca L (2013) Web visualization of complex reality-based 3D models with NUBES. In: Proceedings of the digital heritage 2013 - federating the 19th Int'l VSMM, 10th Eurographics GCH, and 2nd UNESCO memory of the world conferences, plus special sessions from CAA, Arqueologica 2.0 et al., vol 1, pp 701–704. https://doi.org/10.1109/DigitalHeritage.2013.6743821

Gao QH, Wan TR, Tang W, Chen L (2017) A stable and accurate marker-less augmented reality registration method. In: Proceedings of 2017 international conference on Cyberworlds, CW 2017 - in cooperation with: Eurographics association international federation for information processing ACM SIGGRAPH, January 2017, pp 41–47. https://doi.org/10.1109/CW.2017.44

Hammady R, Ma M, Temple N (2016) Augmented reality and gamification in heritage museums. In: Lecture notes in computer science (including subseries lecture notes in artificial intelligence and lecture notes in bioinformatics). https://doi.org/10.1007/978-3-319-45841-0_17

Lopez-Menchero VM, Grande A (2011) The principles of the Seville Charter. In: Proceedings XXIIIrd international CIPA symposium, pp 12–16

Meschini A, Rossi D, Petrucci E, Sicuranza F (2017) Expanded cultural heritage representation: digital applications for mixed-reality experiences. In: Handbook of research on emerging technologies for digital preservation and information modeling. IGI Global, pp 256–287. https://doi.org/10.4018/978-1-5225-0680-5.ch011

Mortara M, Catalano CE, Bellotti F, Fiucci G, Houry-Panchetti M, Petridis P (2014) Learning cultural heritage by serious games. J Cult Heritage. https://doi.org/10.1016/j.culher.2013.04.004

Pecchioli L, Pucci M, Mohamed F, Mazzei B (2012) Browsing in the virtual museum of the sarcophagi in the Basilica of St. Silvestro at the Catacombs of Priscilla in Rome. In: Proceedings of the 2012 18th international conference on virtual systems and multimedia, VSMM 2012. Virtual Systems in the Information Society, pp 413–420. https://doi.org/10.1109/VSMM.2012.6365953

Tscheu F, Buhalis D (2016) Augmented reality at cultural heritage sites. In: Information and communication technologies in tourism 2016, pp 607–619. https://doi.org/10.1007/978-3-319-28231-2_44

Digital Technologies for the Fruition of Archaeological Heritage. The Visualisation of the Temple C Metopes Polychrome in Selinunte

Vincenza Garofalo[✉]

Department of Architecture (DARCH), Università degli Studi di Palermo,
Viale delle Scienze edificio 14, 90138 Palermo, Italy
vincenza.garofalo@unipa.it

Abstract. Through the tools of the representation this paper investigates a hypothetical virtual re-presentation of the metopes original polychromies. The reconstructive interpretative process was carried out through a critical reading of historical and iconographic sources. Starting from the reading of drawings made by Angell and Harris at the time of the archaeological finds, of Hittorff's studies and watercolors, and of some coloured fragments still observable in the original metopes, the graphic elaborations that simulate the original polychromes have been prepared.

The purpose of this study and of the analysis here described is the experimentation of an interactive visualisation application (augmented reality) designed for the "Antonino Salinas" Regional Archaeological Museum of Palermo. The study is part of the repertoire of virtual reconstructions, through the use of light, of lost colour configurations. The project aims to propose a new modality for the use of archaeological finds, thanks to an inedited teaching and immersive experience of the metopes and to the experimentation of a new visual environment that overlaps the real one leading to rethink the relationship between reality and its representation.

Keywords: Augmented reality · SfM survey · 3D model · Video mapping

1 Introduction

In March 1823, William Harris and Samuel Angell, architects of the Royal Academy of Arts in London, during an excavation campaign in Selinunte, found in very small fragments, three metopes that were part of the oriental frieze of the temple C, located in the Acropolis, made probably after the middle of the sixth century BC and dedicated to Heracles or Apollo. Immediately restored by Pietro Pisani, an officer of the Ministry for International Affairs in Palermo, the metopes were exhibited at the University of Palermo Museum, today the "Antonino Salinas" Regional Archaeological Museum.

© Springer Nature Switzerland AG 2019
A. Luigini (Ed.): EARTH 2018, AISC 919, pp. 671–680, 2019.
https://doi.org/10.1007/978-3-030-12240-9_69

They represent Apollo on a chariot flanked by Leto and Artemis, Herakles and the Kerkopes, Perseus beheading Medusa in the presence of Athena and the birth of Pegasos[1].

Angell and Harris found the eastern frieze complete with metopes interspersed with strongly protruding triglyphs, where they fell. Therefore the direct testimonies of the two architects provide information on the location of the metopes in the temple and on the traces of color that were still visible[2]. Drawings and surveys of Angell and Harris were published in 1826 by Angell and Evans[3] (Fig. 1).

Fig. 1. The metopes represented by Angell and Evans (1826)

In 1823 Jakob Ignaz Hittorff[4], Royal architect in Paris, arrived in Sicily together with the architect and pupil Karl Ludwig Wilhelm Zanth to "survey the ancient monuments of Sicily in all their details, (…) give a faithful image of their current state, and an idea as complete as possible of their original state"[5]. And indeed, their drawings "are so precisely finished that they are often correct down to the millimeter. As such, these drawings offer clear documentation of the actual state of the buildings, and serve as an accurate base for their reconstructions"[6].

Immediately became aware of the discovery of the metopes, Hittorff went to visit the museum of the University to meet Angell and to see and draw the reliefs from life.

---

[1] For a complete description of the metopes see Angell and Evans (1826), 44–54 and Marconi (2007), 234–239.

[2] The quadriga occupied the central part of the frieze. It is a relief that testifies the expertise and the level of knowledge of the perspective of that time.

[3] Evans replaced Harris died in Selinunte of malaria where he remained to study the topography of the site. Marconi (2007), 133. Angell and Evans (1826).

[4] J.I. Hittorff trained at the Paris school of architecture and was a pupil of Léon Dufourny and Quatremère de Quincy.

[5] Hittorff (1870), XX.

[6] Kiene et al. (2016), 25.

However, his drawings differ by the engravings of Angell and Harris because Hittorff and Zanth "were able to see the metopes only in the museum in the presence of guards. Additionally, they were not allowed to draw in front of the originals, because Angell and Harris had been granted the exclusive right to reproduce them for one year. Hittorff and his team thus drew from memory"[7].

The drawings of Hittorff and Zanth received many appreciations compared to those made by Pisani, who were judged by Thiersch "of lesser quality and do not reveal the style of these metopes"[8] (Fig. 2).

Fig. 2. The metopes represented by Hittorff and Zanth

The corpus of drawings by Hittorff includes minutes, finished drawings (generally drawn with graphite and black ink), engravings and watercolors used for exhibitions and scientific discussions. Sometimes the sketches and published illustrations show significant differences, as in the case of the fragments breaks' representation forming the metope of Perseus and Medusa (Fig. 3).

Fig. 3. The metopes. Sketches by Hittorff (pen and graphite)

---

[7] Kiene et al. (2016), 75.

[8] Kiene et al. (2016), 43.

Drawings and studies of Hittorff became well known soon, so much that the Duke of Serradifalco, in his *Antichità della Sicilia* (Serradifalco 1834) used "the model for the measuring and drawing of the monuments of ancient architecture[9]" of *Architecture antique de la Sicile* receiving an accusation of plagiarism by Hittorff (Fig. 4).

Fig. 4. The metopes reproduced by Serradifalco (1834-1842)

2   Hittorff and the Classical Polychrome

The metopes of Temple C have been of great importance in the archaeological field and for studies on classical polychrome. Hittorff was the first to study the coloured traces on the sculptural and architectural fragments found in Selinunte. Starting from the drawings of Agrigento by Hittorff, "which will follow those of Selinunte a few days later, the plots of the most intense nineteenth-century architectural debate will develop, the one on the polychrome, whose theoretical foundations were already thrown into countless essays, but whose architectural evidence had to wait for the fascinating plates and watercolors of Hittorff and Zanth because a new and original vision of Greekness evolved from the neoclassical imaginary"[10].

Before reaching Selinunte, Hittorff visited Agrigento and, among the findings during the excavations, he also found architectural and sculptural fragments with traces of coloured stuccos, from which he elaborated his theory on the classical polychrome that was destined to undermine the convictions of Winckelmann.

His studies were published, together with a collection of plates and watercolors, made together with his pupil, Karl Ludwig Zanth, in *Architecture antique de la Sicile* and became the basis for subsequent hypotheses[11].

---

[9] Kiene et al. (2016), 21.

[10] Cometa (1993), 22–23.

[11] The work was published in its first edition in 1827 (Hittorff 1827) and was later expanded and published after Hittorff's death by his son Charles in 1870 (Hittorff 1870).

In a letter to Schorn, Hittorff reported that he had seen that parts of temples of Selinunte were still covered in red, blue, yellow, and green stucco[12] (Fig. 5). Therefore, he also extended to the architecture of the temples the intuitions of Quatrèmere de Quincy on the polychrome of the sculpture of the Greeks[13]. From book 4 of *De Architectura* by Vitruvius he drew that, in the early buildings, the wooden triglyphs were covered in blue wax[14]. On the occasion of an essay presented at the Académies des Inscritions et Belles-Lettres et des Beaux-Arts de Paris, Hittorff noted that the slight traces of blue and yellow on the background of the metopes and the red, green and blue on the architrave of the Temple of Empedocles in Selinunte, suggested that the pediment was originally entirely coloured[15]. This thesis would also be supported by the similarity of the pottery's coloured ornaments to the elements of the Doric frieze. From Alexis Paccard's studies on the Parthenon, he derived the use of blue tones for triglyphs and mutules, of red for guttae and for the backgrounds of metopes[16]. Encouraged by the discovery of other coloured fragments in Athens, Syracuse, Agrigento, he

Fig. 5. Polycrome details by Hittorff

---

[12] Cometa (1993), 68.

[13] See Quatrèmere de Quincy (1815) *Le Jupiter olympien, ou l'Art de la sculpture antique considéré sous un nouveau point de vue, ouvrage qui comprend un essai sur le goût de la sculpture polychrome, l'analyse explicative de la toreutique et l'histoire de la statuaire en or et en ivoire, chez les Grecs et les Romains.* De Bure frères.

[14] Hittorff (1851), 13, 444.

[15] Hittorff (1993), 76.

[16] Hittorff (1851), 420.

hypothesized the restoration of the colours of the Temple of Empedocles (Temple B) in Selinunte[17]. Observing the drawings of Hittorff and Zanth on the temples of Selinunte, it is clear that the red colour was used mainly for the backgrounds, the meanders, the belts, yellow for weapons and accessories, blue for the triglyphs, the guttae and the cornice. In the hypothesis of reconstruction of Temple B (Temple of Empedocles), Hittorff also assigned the yellow colour to the columns, the façade, and the stylobate.

3   The Analysis of the Metopes

Through the tools of representation the paper investigates a hypothetical virtual representation of the original polychromies of the metopes (Fig. 6). The reconstructive interpretative process was carried out through a critical reading of historical and iconographic sources. Starting from the reading of drawings made by Angell and Harris at the time of the archaeological finds, of Hittorff's studies, and watercolors and of some coloured fragments still observable in the original metopes, the graphic elaborations that simulate the original polychromes have been prepared.

Fig. 6. Hypothesis of colour reconstruction for the processing of video mapping (Giorgia Biancorosso)

The quadriga has red traces that have been found on background, breast straps, draft pole and dress of Apollo and right figure[18].

The metope with Perseus and Medusa has red traces on background, eyes of Medusa, meander and low neckline on the dress of Athena, cap and belt of Perseus. Eyes and eyebrows have a dark color, as the interior decoration of the belt of Perseus[19]. A red meander band, of which remains a small fragment, decorated the metope at the top.

The metope with Herakles and the Kerkopes has red traces on background, details of dresses of the three figures, cross belt and scabbards of Herakles, ropes of Kerkopes. This metope is crowned at the top by a red meander and stars band, too[20].

---

[17] Hittorff (1851), 446.

[18] Marconi (2007), 234.

[19] Marconi (2007), 237.

[20] Marconi (2007), 238.

4   Experimentation for the Visualisation of Polychromies

The purpose of this study and of the analyses described above is the experimentation of an interactive visualisation application (augmented reality) designed for the "Antonino Salinas" Regional Archaeological Museum of Palermo (Biancorosso 2016). The study is part of the repertoire of virtual reconstructions, through the use of light, of lost colour configurations[21] (Fig. 7). Augmented reality allows adding to an object, an architecture, a real context, information, elaborated and conveyed through digital tools, which otherwise would not be perceptible Bertuglia et al. (1999), 42–47.

Fig. 7. a. "I colori dell'Ara Pacis" video mapping. b. "Santa Maria Antiqua" video mapping

The ability to simulate reality, through the use of video projections (video mapping), allows to visualize the imagined missing original chromatic aspects on the real element and to evaluate the impact as if it were a digital restoration operation. Video mapping is a projection technology that turns any surface into a dynamic screen on which to project images through one or more video projectors[22].

Given the complexity of the metopes, characterised by the presence of shaded areas, the first phase of the experimentation required the elaboration of an accurate digital three-dimensional model of the same. This model was developed thanks to a photogrammetric survey, carried out with SfM (Structure from Motion) techniques, which produced a three-dimensional point cloud (Fig. 8). The geometry of the object was generated virtually by converting the point cloud into a polygon mesh from which the 3D model was then processed. This virtual model formed the basis for digitally replicating the exact shapes and dimensions of the metopes and ensuring perfect overlapping of the digital projections to the real artifact.

Several steps were necessary for the creation of the video. Using a vector graphics software, the metopes have been redrawn, subdividing the elements of the drawing into different levels, prepared and ordered for the following animations (Fig. 9a). The vector organised drawing was imported into a graphics animation and compositing software that allowed the realisation of all animations - animated drawing of metopes, geometric

---

[21] Effective experiments were conducted, among others, at the Rocca di Vignola, and in Rome at the Ara Pacis, at the Domus Aurea and at Santa Maria Antiqua.

[22] In the Anglo-Saxon world, video mapping is also often called *spatial augmented reality*.

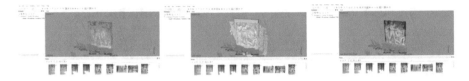

Fig. 8. Phases of the SfM survey (Giorgia Biancorosso)

constructions, and insertion of colour (Fig. 9b). The last phase achieved with the use of video editing software, allowed to carry out the editing aimed at the final export, also synchronizing the video with the narration's audio track that explains in detail the histories represented in the metopes and the colour virtual reconstruction (Fig. 9c).

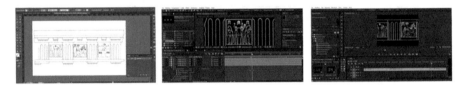

Fig. 9. The video phases; a. the vector drawing; b. the realisation of all animations; c. the final editing (Giorgia Biancorosso)

The image to be projected was calibrated and adjusted through the use of digital masks to coincide with the shape of the target object. In order to control, in the design phase, the correctly superimposition of the final elaboration to the metope's real complex surfaces, it was decided to make a 1:5 scale model, by 3D printing, as simulation support and verification of the final projection (Figs. 10 and 11).

Fig. 10. 3D printing of the 1:5 scale model (Giorgia Biancorosso)

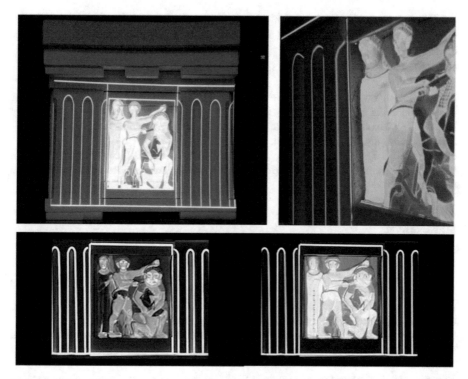

Fig. 11. The calibration of the image and the verification of the final projection (Giorgia Biancorosso)

In the final elaboration, still to experiment, the real surfaces of the metopes will become the support on which to project the previously elaborated images. If on the one hand video technology will be introduced into the real environment, on the other hand, it will take possession of it virtually including it within the video itself.

5   Conclusions

For a few years now, in the context of communication, use, and enhancement of cultural heritage, more and more importance is given to the emotional involvement of the user who is often called upon to live "immersive", multisensory and interactive experiences. The user is guided towards new levels of knowledge through multimedia performance.

Digital technology has assumed a fundamental role in the management, understanding, enhancement, and dissemination of cultural heritage. The video projections here presented are configured as virtual copies of lost elements, on-site real-scale reproductions, which show all their communicative potential. The project aims to propose a new modality for the use of archaeological finds, thanks to an inedited teaching and immersive experience of the metopes and to the experimentation of a new visual environment that overlaps the real one leading to rethink the relationship between reality and its representation.

Through the real-time projection of the 3D model on the same area of the real site, it will be possible to view different aspects of the surfaces without intervening directly on the artefact. The real elements will be transformed through virtual animations, providing an original and unusual sensorial experience.

Acknowledgements. Survey and video mapping experiment presented in this essay are part of the graduation thesis *L'immagine del Passato. Progetto di Video Mapping per le Metope del Tempio C di Selinunte*, Supervisor Prof. Vincenza Garofalo, graduation student Giorgia Biancorosso, University of Palermo, Academic Year 2015–2016. (NB this specification is very important and for a mistake it was not introduced in the paper). The author wishes to thank Dr. Francesca Spatafora, Director of the Salinas Museum, for having given permission to survey the metopes.

References

Angell S, Evans T (1826) Sculptured metopes, discovered amongst the ruins of the temples of the ancient city of Selinus in Sicily by William Harris and Samuel Angell in the year 1823, described by Samuel Angell and Thomas Evans. Priestley and Weale

Bertuglia CS, Bertuglia F, Magnaghi A (1999) Il museo tra reale e virtuale. Editori Riuniti, Roma

Cometa M (ed) (1993) Jakob Ignaz Hittorff. Viaggio in Sicilia. Sicania

Biancorosso G (2016) L'immagine del Passato. Progetto di Video Mapping per le Metope del Tempio C di Selinunte. Graduation Thesis, Supervisor Vincenza Garofalo, University of Palermo

Hittorff JI (1827) Architecture antique de la Sicile, ou Recueil des plus intéressants monuments d'architecture des villes et des lieux les plus remarquables de la Sicile ancienne mesurés et dessinés par JI Hittorff, J Renouard

Hittorff JI (1851) Restitution du temple d'Empédocle à Sélinonte, ou L'architecture polychrome chez les Grecs/par J-J Hittorff Librairie de Firmin Didor Frères

Hittorff JI, Zanth KL (1870) Architecture antique de la Sicile, ou Recueil des monuments de Ségeste et de Sélinonte. E. Donnaud

Hittorff JI (1993) De l'Architecture Polychrome chez les Grecs, ou Restitution Complète du Temple d'Empédocle, dans l'Acropolis de Sélinunte. In: Cometa M (ed) Jakob Ignaz Hittorff. Viaggio in Sicilia, Sicania, pp 70–101

Kiene M, Lazzarini L, Marconi C (2016) "Sicile Ancienne": Hittorff and the architecture of classical Sicily. Universitäts- und Stadtbibliothek Köln

Marconi C (2007) Temple decoration and cultural identity in the archaic Greek world. The metopes of Selinus. Cambridge University Press, Cambridge

Serradifalco D (1834) Le antichità della Sicilia. Tipografia del giornale letterario

Communicating Archaeology at Poggio del Molino. 3D Virtualization and the Visitor Experience On and Off Site

Carlo Baione[1(✉)], Tyler D. Johnson[2], and Carolina Megale[1]

[1] Archeodig Project, University of Florence, Florence, Italy
`carlo.baione@gmail.com`, `info@archeodig.net`
[2] Interdepartmental Program in Classical Art and Archaeology (IPCAA),
University of Michigan, Ann Arbor, MI, USA
`tylerdjo@umich.edu`

Abstract. Although the digital data which archaeologists collect in the field are generally valued for their ability to enhance the scientific, research-oriented goals of field projects, they also promise great potential at a level of communication with the public. The 3D digital documentation produced by the *Archeodig* project at Poggio del Molino (Populonia, IT) is a valuable tool for communicating an engaging and thorough understanding of the multi-layered archaeological site. Publishing the 3D models of structures and artifacts on the online platform Sketchfab, as well as the creation of virtual environments and reconstructions with Unity3D, archaeologists at Poggio del Molino are experimenting with new ways to supply more detailed scientific information about their discoveries and convey these findings to a broad audience. This open virtual communication of the excavation is in line with *Archeodig's* guiding principles, namely of seeking meaningful forms of engagement with the public community which supports it. *Archeodig's* 3D approach serves as a powerful example of how modern archaeology can harness the benefit of digital technologies to strengthen its bond with the public community.

Keywords: Digital outreach · 3D visualization · Public archaeology ·
Virtual environment · 3D modeling

1 Introduction

Archaeology seeks to understand the past via the study of material culture. As a result, archaeologists spend much time analysing the structures, artefacts, and physical remains of ancient cultures in an attempt to answer a wide variety of questions about them. Often the questions archaeologists ask of material culture are complex, addressing matters of political organization, religion, economy, and other categories which define communities at a social level. For all that they might ask such complicated questions, however, archaeologists always remain separated from the cultures they study by time (archaeology, by definition, involves the study of societies which no longer exist). It is the material culture of such societies, then, which guides the archaeologist's interpretation. Every detail of an object or structure – such as its material composition, form, adornment, or

© Springer Nature Switzerland AG 2019
A. Luigini (Ed.): EARTH 2018, AISC 919, pp. 681–690, 2019.
https://doi.org/10.1007/978-3-030-12240-9_70

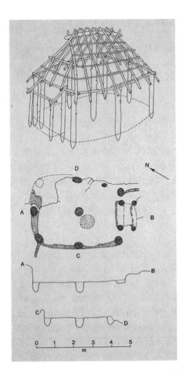

Fig. 1. Hut foundations from the Palatine Hill of Rome, c. 9th–8th centuries BCE. Conventional archaeological illustrations of this sort are a standard way for archaeologists to share information with one another, but are not always well suited to public-facing communication.

evidence of wear and tear – represents an opportunity for archaeologists to understand something of the people who produced or used it (Fig. 1).

Archaeology's constant emphasis on visual and haptic interaction with artefacts and structures has an influence on how the field's researchers communicate with one another and with the public. Traditionally, archaeology has developed a highly standardized visual language for representing material culture in print publications (Adkins and Adkins 1989). Standard practices for how an artefact is drawn or photographed, for instance, are intended to facilitate an understanding of the object for researchers who cannot analyze it in person but are familiar with the conventions used to represent it. While such conventions have undoubtedly been successful in facilitating archaeological research, their potential for communicating with the public is more limited. Because archaeological illustration is highly conventional, it is not always intuitive to non-specialists (nor was it ever intended to be so).

Nevertheless, archaeology's value as a public asset is only as strong as its ability to maintain a communicative relationship with the community which supports it. In recent years, many archaeological projects have begun to harness the capabilities of digital communication – via social media or web-based content – to communicate their discoveries, transforming the remains of ancient cultures into visual and narrative media for the presentation of history[1]. As part of this movement, archaeologists at Poggio del Molino, a Roman archaeological site in the territory of Populonia, Italy, have sought to open the excavation to the public via the use of digital technologies. 3D content, in particular, serves as a platform at Poggio del Molino for creating meaningful, impactful forms of interaction between the archaeological site and interested members of the public community.

2 The *Archeodig* Project at Poggio del Molino

Poggio del Molino was a Roman settlement occupied from the 2nd century BCE to the 5th century CE and located on a large promontory on the north side of the Gulf of Baratti (Tuscany, Italy). The Romans valued Poggio del Molino from an early period for its strategic defensive location, but later it was used as a production site for fish-sauce (an important commodity in the ancient Roman world). Later still, the area was converted into a maritime villa, only to be abandoned and sparsely occupied until the 5th century CE. In general, the site of Poggio del Molino forms a key piece of evidence in understanding the archaeological development of the territory of the Etruscan settlement of Populonia.

The archaeological excavation of Poggio del Molino started in the 1980s and was carried out by the University of Florence for four years, only to be interrupted due to lack of funds. The cultural association *Past in Progress*[2] resumed excavations in 2008, forming a new archaeological field project at Poggio del Molino, *Archeodig*[3], which united the work of professional archaeologists and restoration specialists with international students and volunteers. The excavations are conducted in collaboration with the Superintendence of Archaeological Heritage of Tuscany, the international Earth-Watch Institute and with Italian and foreign universities, including the University of Florence, The International Studies Institute at Palazzo Rucellai, and the University of Arizona.

In addition to its scientific aims, a major emphasis of the *Archeodig* project has been interaction with and support of the public. Public events and lectures, guided tours, and local conferences have been a mainstay of the project's activities over the past ten years, especially as the excavation of Poggio del Molino occurs in close conjunction with the local Museo etrusco di Populonia Collezione Gasparri. Volunteers, many of whom are affiliated with the institutions mentioned above, regularly participate in the excavation and interpretation of the site. Students, be they from international universities or local primary/secondary institutions, lend excitement to field operations and make Poggio del Molino a site of instruction as well as research.

---

[1] See for example the digital projects at Gabii, Italy (https://gabii.cast.uark.edu/gabiigoesdigital/, University of Michigan), at Karnak, Egypt (http://wayback.archive-it.org/7877/20160919152116/http://dlib.etc.ucla.edu/projects/Karnak//), and the Pompeii project of the Swedish Institute (http://www.pompejiprojektet.se/).

[2] http://www.pastinprogress.net/.

[3] http://www.sitetech.com.au/archeodig.com/index.html.

Financially, *Archeodig* is closely tied to private sources of funding (but also public funds such as the Art Bonus[4] or the 2×1000) and the networks of support established by its parent organization, the *Past in Progress* cultural association. As a beneficiary of these various resources and networks, *Archeodig* consistently seeks to return the goodwill of its support by making its operations open and accessible to the interests of the community.

In this spirit, in 2016, the *Archeodig* project began taking steps to develop a viable infrastructure for supporting visitors onsite, deeming the area of Poggio del Molino a "shared archaeology park", or PArCo (Parco di Archeologia Condivisa)[5]. The PArCo designation has allowed the *Archeodig* project to begin formalizing and realizing plans to make the site more accessible to the public. Physical accessibility is being approached through the creation of new common spaces for archaeologists and the community, guided paths and integration into the existing Parchi Val di Cornia[6] which encompasses the archaeological site. Accessibility in terms of learning and information is being addressed through a variety of strategies, including close coordination with local museums and high schools. In the process of these developments, *Archeodig* hopes to make Poggio del Molino a site which dismantles the barriers between archaeologists and citizens, an open excavation where all of the aspects of the research will be continuously shared with visitors on and off the site.

3   3D Documentation at Poggio del Molino

After ten years of regular field activity with the *Archeodig* project, the site of Poggio del Molino is now widely excavated and many structures, belonging to different phases of the site, have been cleared of the soil that preserved them from the ancient period until today. Rooms with mosaic floors occupy the south-west corner of the villa, while a grand bath complex, partially collapsed into the sea, is still visible in the northernmost area. Many of the structures around the area have been built, destroyed, used and repurposed throughout the centuries, thus complicating an interpretation of the site's development and chronology. Thorough documentation of the walls, pavements and other features of the site are thus indispensable for understanding the story of the Roman settlement and, ultimately, communicating it with the public.

In 2015, the *Archeodig* project began exploring the potentials of structure-from-motion photogrammetry (SFM) - a cost-efficient technique for generating 3D models from sequences of 2D images - to create detailed 3D records of the structures being excavated at Poggio del Molino. The decision to adapt SFM as a field documentation technique had more than one motivation. Operating under a relatively accessible workflow, SFM requires no more than a standard digital camera (or smartphone) and a total station to survey the remains topographically (both of which items were already

---

[4] http://artbonus.gov.it/area-archeologica-di-poggio-del-molino-populonia.html.

[5] For more information about the PArCo see for example https://www.ilfattoquotidiano.it/2017/11/13/toscana-il-primo-parco-di-archeologia-condivisa-in-italia-la-nostra-missione-restituire-il-passato-ai-cittadini/3932633/ and https://www.rivistasitiunesco.it/un-parco-di-archeologia-condivisa-a/.

[6] http://www.parchivaldicornia.it/en/.

being used in the field at Poggio del Molino for other purposes). The 3D models produced by SFM are highly accurate and render both the geometry and color of archaeological remains in exceptional detail (Fig. 2).

Fig. 2. Balneum complex: *laconicum*. Detail of an orthophoto from 3D model.

The process is non-labor intensive and, compared to traditional approaches of hand drawn in archaeology, extremely time efficient. Furthermore, 3D models are also a great asset for the kind of analysis and interpretation of archaeological sites that occurs outside of the field, when archaeologists may be far away from the materials they are studying and have need of data and representations that are accurate and detailed as possible. For the *Archeodig* project, the adoption of SFM has certainly had an impact on the way archaeologists understand the site's overlaying structures and the sequence of actions that shaped them. Furthermore, as we shall see, it has also played an important role in providing informative experiences to members of the public and visitors to the site.

4   Archaeology and Communication at Poggio del Molino

As noted above, the *Archeodig* project has emphasized efforts to communicate its findings to the public community, both at a local level and beyond, from its very inception. The assistance of public volunteers and students during onsite operations has been particularly indispensable and has encouraged professionals with the project to think carefully about how archaeology is communicated to non-specialists. Most students and volunteers arrive with limited or no archaeological experience. Their success in the field has depended on the project's ability to effectively explain the complexities of the site and involve assistants in the process of its documentation and interpretation. Meanwhile, related to *Archeodig*'s goal of establishing a "shared archaeological park" at Poggio del Molino, the excavation area is open free of charge to any member of the public who wishes to visit and/or participate in operations. As a result, tourists and members of the local community visit the site regularly, further motivating the project's interest in how the site can be communicated to a public audience.

Two obstacles in communicating the complexities of Poggio del Molino are immediately apparent. First, scientific research at Poggio del Molino is driven by a constant physical interaction with the ancient remains through which archaeologists read and the interpret of the history of the site. However, the details of physical remains which an archaeologist might find information-rich and essential can perhaps be less obvious to non-specialists. As a result, the team seeks to emphasize the *narrative* element of the site to visitors while still maintaining a close focus on how archaeologists gleam this narrative from the physical remains themselves. Secondly, *Archeodig* recognizes that many of the individuals who might be interested in the materials at Poggio del Molino will be unable to physically visit the site, and thus wishes to develop a strong presence on the web in order to disseminate its findings as widely as possible to the global community.

Given Poggio del Molino's commitment to 3D documentation, virtual environments represent a path forward for addressing both of these challenges. Photorealistic models such as those produced onsite are capable of being packaged into a user-friendly digital interface which functions as a communicative medium between members of the public and archaeological remains. Moreover, by viewing and interacting with the highly detailed and accurate 3D models produced onsite at Poggio del Molino, visitors come as close as possible to the type of visual and haptic interaction with artefacts and structures experienced by archaeologists in their daily work.

5   Sketchfab and Unity3D: Challenges and an Unfolding Strategy

Archaeologists with *Archeodig* seek to benefit from the adoption of SFM by sharing their 3D models with the public community via two methods: the online platform Sketchfab and interactive content created "in house" using Unity3D. These two platforms can potentially serve as more than simple, but engaging, tools for updating the public on new discoveries and goings-on in the field. They can also allow the *Archeodig* team to craft new forms of experiences between the public and archaeological materials, encouraging exploration, critical examination and enjoyment.

At the same time, 3D models in archaeology cannot be applied uncritically. Despite their promise and vast appeal, archaeological research has also remained critical of 3D approaches at a theoretical level. Criticism of 3D modelling is frequently oriented around questions of fidelity, representation, and user experience[7]. Furthermore, any archaeological project which wishes to invest in digital communication must confront a variety of technical decisions and challenges. *Archeodig* seeks to maintain a balanced approach to these various concerns and has created a 3D strategy that is both technically feasible, beneficial to members of the public community, and responsive to the theoretical concerns raised by academic archaeology.

Archaeology's concern with accuracy and fidelity is partially responsible for the field's adoption of increasingly powerful tools for gathering 3D data, including SFM photogrammetry. Despite this, the field has yet to produce a standard method for gauging the accuracy of 3D models or best practices for disseminating them via virtual interfaces.[8] Archaeologists at Poggio del Molino seek to remain cognizant that 3D models are crafted items which depend on the quality of source data and their post-processing, "including decimation, trimming and other modifications to the actual models that are produced" (Molloy and Milić 2018). Nonetheless, recent advances in SFM mean that the software and tools used by *Archeodig* specialists result in 3D models of undeniably high fidelity (Fregonese et al. 2016). Possible minor margins of error may occur but tend to fall in the range of a few centimetres, at most. Such a degree of fidelity, especially for big areas, is much higher than can be expected in traditional hand drawn archaeological illustration and, at any rate, offers a vast communicative potential that offsets any minor margins of error.

Once the *Archeodig* project developed a 3D workflow that produced models of sufficient fidelity and communicative potential, there still remained questions of representation (how to present 3D content in order to communicate with a broad audience, which platforms to use, how to present 3D models alongside information-rich annotations and reconstructions) and user experience (the so-called the "immersive imperatives" of 3D representation, including embodiment, space and place, vision, sound, and touch) (Fredrick 2014). In response, *Archeodig* sought a strategy which would faithfully represent 3D content in its rich detail but also be capable of actively engaging members of the community. *Archeodig*'s strategy also needed to weigh financial and time commitments. "Homegrown" approaches wherein archaeologists themselves develop communication strategies are lower cost and more flexible but labor intensive. "Outsourcing" approaches wherein archaeologists seek the help of designers and technical specialists are less labor intensive for archaeologists themselves but more expensive and less flexible (Fig. 3).

Ultimately, archaeologists with *Archeodig* took a dual approach to overcoming the technical demands of disseminating 3D content to the public, sharing models with both the ready-made, free online platform Sketchfab and a custom-made, "homegrown" 3D interface developed with the game engine Unity3D. The use of Sketchfab[9] guarantees low technical demands out of the archaeologist and provides immediate visible results

---

[7] For an overview and discussion of some of these and other concerns, see Olson and Caraher 2015.

[8] Documents such as the "London Charter" (Beacham et al. 2006) which seek to establish best practices for the creation of 3D models in archaeology have experienced limited acceptance. See Fredrick 2014 for a discussion on the challenges of reaching a unanimous consensus on approaches to 3D in cultural heritage.

[9] https://sketchfab.com/PArCo-poggiodelmolino

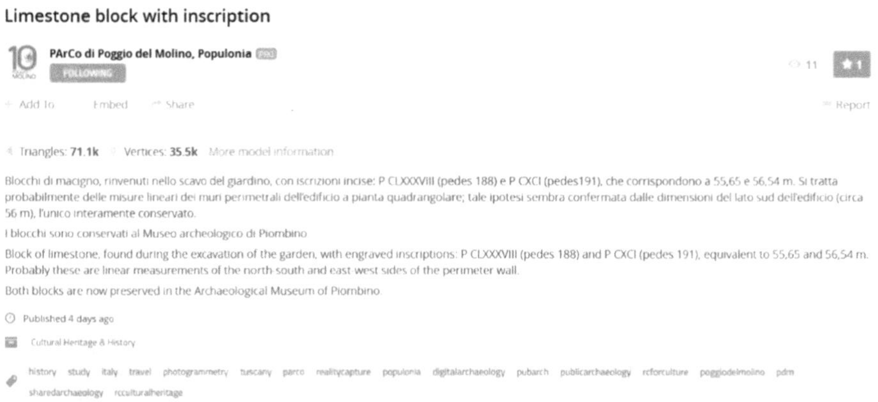

Fig. 3. Sketchfab page of Poggio del Molino archaeological area, 3D model caption example. https://skfb.ly/6yXxu.

which can be easily enjoyed through the ready-made accessible user interface. Sketchfab is a free and accessible online tool for discovering and sharing 3D models of any kind. 3D models can be visualized and navigated using an intuitive user interface similar to what Youtube offers for videos. Sketchfab allows interaction with 3D content on any mobile device or computer browser with no need of installing applications or software of any kind. 3D models from Poggio del Molino can be explored in detail, orbiting around a preset centre which can be changed at will. Contextual information is provided by captions in both Italian and English, including dynamic annotations on the surface of models themselves.

Sketchfab is an extremely efficient and beneficial tool to the *Archeodig* project, but is nonetheless limited in terms of flexibility. While individual models can be hosted and annotated, it does not offer other features useful for realizing *Archeodig's* communication strategy, such as interactive animations, site-level views of multiple models, or immersive lighting and movement. In order to explore the benefits of such 3D design elements, *Archeodig* has recently initiated a plan for designing a custom-made visualization of the excavation area using the game engine Unity3D. This second element of the project's approach ensures more formatting flexibility and immersive forms of navigation and exploration of virtual environments. On the other hand the use of a game engine requires higher technical skills and longer development timelines. The results are not immediate like the publication of 3D models via Sketchfab, but a game engine-based approach promises several profound communicative advantages.

As a first pass at developing content with Unity3D, the team has begun developing a series of reconstructions of the various sectors of Poggio del Molino and hopes to publish visualizations of this content before the 2019 field season. The interface is being designed with the aim of providing an intuitive, engaging, information rich virtual experience with the site, both as excavated and as reconstructed through the attentive fieldwork and interpretive work of the project's professionals. *Archeodig* envisions its Unity3D content as a platform for generating interest in Poggio del

Molino, sharing its discoveries with the public, and seeking out the public's commentary and feedback on the project's scientific direction.

Having been committed to communication with the public from the beginning, *Archeodig* has embraced Sketchfab and Unity3D in order to continue a strategy which has long been a core of its operational strategies. On the other hand, the adoption of such technologies are sure to themselves have an influence on the operations and concerns of the project. In a period when many archaeological excavations are weighing the communicative potential offered by various 3D workflows and platforms, the professionals with *Archeodig* are optimistic about the strategies they have adopted and look forward to reporting their progress over the next years as developments occur.

6 Conclusions

Archaeology is frequently called a "destructive science" because once the soil which preserves the archaeological record is removed, it can never be replaced. This destruction must be compensated by thorough and accurate documentation of excavated sites as well as their effective communication to both an academic and public audience (Manacorda 2007; Roosevelt et al. 2015). Communication is a tool to transmit culture and information at every level (Antinucci 2014; De Kerckhove's 1999), and archaeology's value to the people and communities it ultimately serves can only be as robust as its ability to make itself open, available, and enjoyable. Often, this is not only a question of making archaeological remains visible and physically accessible, but also of telling a story and sharing a narrative that is socially meaningful. Scientific analyses, qualitative observations, and physical labor are part of every archaeologist's work, but the role of the archaeologist ultimately consists of deciphering the "stories" that the earth can tell and communicating those stories to a global community (Manacorda 2007).

In fact, the basis of *Archeodig's* project of shared archaeology, both physical and digital, is the awareness that cultural heritage does not represent a value in itself, but embodies a relational value[10]. An archaeological site can only lay claim to the value that civil society and the community of reference give to it, and is therefore crucial to involve citizens in the process of defining and managing our cultural heritage. The digital tools discussed in this paper, because they place public interaction and communication at the forefront, are a means of facilitating an ongoing and rewarding relationship between the *Archeodig* project and the community who supports it.

References

Adkins L, Adkins R (1989) Archaeological illustration. Cambridge University Press
Antinucci F (2014) Comunicare nel museo, Laterza
Barrettara M (2013) New methods for sharing and exhibiting 3D archaeology. Post Hole 31:8–13

---

[10] As states the Convention on the Value of Cultural Heritage for Society (Faro Convention, 2005), https://www.coe.int/en/web/conventions/full-list/-/conventions/treaty/199.

Beacham R, Denard H, Niccolucci F (2006) An introduction to the London charter. In: Joint event CIPA/VAST/EG/EuroMed

De Kerckhove D (1999) L'intelligenza connettiva, De Laurentiis Editore

Fredrick D (2014) Time.deltaTime: the vicissitudes of presence in visualizing Roman houses with game engine technology. AI Soc 29(4):461–472

Fregonese L et al (2016) 3D survey technologies: investigations on accuracy and usability in archaeology. The case study of the new "Municipio" underground station in Naples. ACTA IMEKO 5:55–63

Manacorda D (2007) Il sito archeologico: fra ricerca e valorizzazione, Carocci

Molloy B, Milić M (2018) Wonderful things? A consideration of 3D modelling of objects in material culture research. Open Archaeol 4(1):97–113 https://doi.org/10.1515/opar-2018-0006

Olson B, Caraher W (2015) Visions of substance: 3D imaging in mediterranean archaeology. The Digital Press at The University of North Dakota

Roosevelt CH et al (2015) Excavation is destruction digitization: advances in archaeological practice. J Field Archaeol 40(3):325–346

The Cortona Heritage Project: Digital Applications in Education to Architectural and Archaeological Heritage

Paola Puma[(✉)]

Department of Architecture (DiDA), Università degli Studi di Firenze,
Piazza Ghiberti, 27, 50121 Florence, Italy
paola.puma@unifi.it

Abstract. The paper presents the first results of the Cortona Heritage Project, which takes the opportunity to use the techniques of Virtual heritage to implementing concrete and innovative modes making the very rich cultural heritage of ancient Tuscan cities accessible for more people and engaging new publics by promoting its knowledge among young generations.

The project includes some digital applications aimed at valorisation conceived for the adoption of smart forms of complementry education to the architectural and archaeological heritage of Cortona, made of architecture, archaeology, art; despite Cortona is already a city characterized by a very tourism developed in quantitative terms then to improve more in terms of quality of the visit. *Cortona Heritage* is therefore set on three following axes. Enhancing the cultural heritage of the city by favouring a simultaneously deeper and smart knowledge, promoting slow mode of visit to already too much abundant streams of tourists streams, overcoming the concentration of people only in the historical centre enlarging the area of interest to the newly established archaeological park. The project was founded in 2017 in the context of the collaboration between the Department of Architecture of the University of Florence and the Municipality of Cortona (Tuscany, Italy) and foresees three years of didactics and research activities.

Keywords: Cortona · Maec · Digital survey · SFM · Virtual heritage

1 Introduction

The Cultural heritage is in principle associated with positive values of strengthening identity, social cohesion and economic development, especially for the close relationship between cultural heritage and tourism, one of the sectors that in special extent reap the benefits of cultural heritage, so that the 2018 European Year of Cultural Heritage focuses particularly on promoting the connections between tourism and cultural heritage[1].

---

[1] "Cultural heritage: for a more sustainable future in Europe", Opening of the Conference, Plovdiv, 26/3/2018, (https://ec.europa.eu/commission/commissioners/2014-2019/navracsics/announcements/opening-statement-eu-presidency-conference-cultural-heritage-more-sustainable-future-europe_en).

© Springer Nature Switzerland AG 2019
A. Luigini (Ed.): EARTH 2018, AISC 919, pp. 691–699, 2019.
https://doi.org/10.1007/978-3-030-12240-9_71

But the relationship between Cultural heritage and tourism can take on characters of particular delicacy in contexts of ancient history and a special attention needs to be focused on the sustainability of tourism, in order not to take risk due to material or immaterial damages to the places which attract so many people and promoting any development taking into account the needs of the inhabitants.

One of the approaches that can help mitigate the problem of mass tourism is the use of ICT technologies.

"Cultural heritage breathes a new life with digital technologies and the internet. The citizens have now unprecedented opportunities to access cultural material, while the institutions can reach out to broader audiences, engage new users and develop creative and accessible content for leisure and education. New technologies bring cultural heritage sites back to life"[2]: in this expression, although in a general tone, the virtuous link that can be established between the cultural heritage and the use of technologies or internet is recognized on the level of the European Commission (Directorate General for Communications Networks, Content & Technology).

The current potential of ICT systems for Virtual Heritage, in particular, whether is declined as tools for the production of contents elaborated through methodologies of significant and highly digitized representation or as tools of immersive exploration of the contexts, they are in fact a field of research and technological transfer, in particular in the discipline of Drawing, today in fast transformation: for the development which is taking among the specialists, for the rapid expansion of its use by people that frequents more and more museums, exhibitions, sites and archaeological areas, for the growing interest and expectations of museum administrators and curators (Brusaporci 2015; Pescarin 2016).

The scientific research in the field of surveying and digital representation has well established methodologies that have seen an ever-increasing hybridization with new languages: a more advanced use of 3D visualizations to describe the environment has forced us to look more closely at those experiences of digital visual storytelling and multimedia languages, e.g. movies and videogames.

At the same time, the massive diffusion of mobile devices as well as their technological development, gave us the opportunity of reaching an increasing number of users who approach the newest ICT technologies.

Therefore, the virtual reconstructions based on the data collected during the surveying campaigns offers the possibility to make interactive simulations and interpretations of a context and to display complex information in visual way using a communication tuned on a wide and diversified audience of users (Forum Internacional de Arqueologia virtual 2011).

Finally, this kind of promotion of CH in all categories of citizens, together with the renewal of approaches and languages, is the crucial key to attaining cognitive and emotional knowledge through active educational activities.

Basing on these critical premises in 2016 the project Cortona Heritage has been established, held by the University of Florence-Department of Architecture and which takes place in the framework of the collaboration with the Municipality of Cortona.

---

[2] https://ec.europa.eu/digital-single-market/en/digital-cultural-heritage.

2   Goals of the Research

Cortona Heritage was conceived with the general aim of strengthening the unitary perception of the various material expressions that make Cortona a very popular and turistically appreciated city, but also characterized by a considerable imbalance in the flows of visit between the historical centre, the renewed "Museum of the Etruscan Academy and the city of Cortona-MAEC" and the recently opened archaeological Park of Cortona; Cortona Heritage was therefore in wider terms conceived to simulate a digital information environment of education to the whole Cortona cultural heritage - and not only aiming to the tourist promotion, indeed already present with high intensity flows- with technologically advanced spreading modalities.

The project is based on a few and clear strategic axes centered on multidimensional objectives: the general one, wide-spectrum dissemination of the city's cultural heritage (in its meanings of urban environment, architecture, archaeological and artistic heritage), and a specific topic related to the promotion and the support through smart fruition to the visit of the new Archaeological Park of Cortona (Bertocci and Arrighetti 2015) (Fig. 1).

3   Innovative Patterns

According to the definition already present since 2004 in the Italian "Code of Cultural heritage and landscape", the cultural heritage includes cultural and landscape heritage to be protected and exploited to preserve the memory of the community and the territory and to promote its development: besides the many other general and constitutive presumptions, the cultural legacy is therefore defined also by the characteristic of being constantly changing, following the transformations of the social environment of which it is simultaneously memory and development trigger; in this key is to be read the effort of the most recent lines of cultural policy that explicitly challenge the engagement of new publics as one of the most important fields of action of the actual museography (Luigini and Panciroli 2018).

Cortona Heritage works on this track following the guidelines already developed in the program Digitch (Puma 2018), implementing it in spite of previous experiences through the experimentation of context responsive thematic applications, which are coinceived by a same linguistic and technical functionality but they change following the present context (city, museum, archaeological area) automatically adapting itself to the visited place. *Cortona Heritage* is designed to implement instruments that promote as much as possible a personal, autonomous and constantly updated interpretation of the Cortona material traces, both by its inhabitants and tourists visiting the city.

By assisting the visitor in a deep knowledge of the environment -supporting him in reading the physical structure and its history, and above all making visible the evolution of time (The Charter for interpretation 2008)- is possible to achieve a form of "Significant learning" and discourage consumerist approaches to "selfie tourism" (D'Eramo 2017).

This concept of valorisation is based on these principle which involves two spaces of action for dissemination and education.

Cortona Heritage/project chart

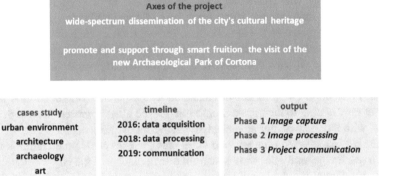

Fig. 1. The strategy of *Cortona Heritage*

The first one acts with interventions towards both to public in presence and on-line, in order to foster a conscious and mature general attractiveness of the territory.

The second axis acts only in the material dimension and targets mainly to enlarge the range of visit outside the old city-center, "doubling" it with a second center of interest centered on the archaeological park.

4   The Context of the Case Study

Cortona is an ancient Tuscan town located on a hill and placed in a dominant position towards the west and south on the Valdichiana valley and protected to the north and east by the mountains that overlook the Fortress of Girifalco (Fig. 2).

The city assumed significant importance in Etruscan age, becoming important lucoumonia and establishing in this period the next predominance on the wide valley of the Chiana, to become a border town subdued by Florence at the end of the period of passage from "Free Commune" to the lordship of the Casali family.

Between the XV and the XIX century Cortona was interested only in successive events that overrun the local history. The power of Cortona in the Etruscan period is testified by the wide city walls whose whole perimeter is about 3 km, by other buildings preserved in the city and especially by the important necropolis of Sodo, located in the countryside below.

Here, a few meters from the great Tumulus II, between 2005 and 2012 have been found two groups of burials delimited by circle, now covered again, dating between the second half of the VII and the beginning of the sixth century. BC and probably referable to the same family group that already had built the Sodo's monumental burial starting from the end of the century VII until IV-III B. C. (Bruschetti et al. 2014; Fortunelli 2005).

Come from here rich and abundant furnishings preserved in the MAEC museum: large ollas in impasto ware, vases with lids containing ashes of the deceased and

Cortona Heritage/the context

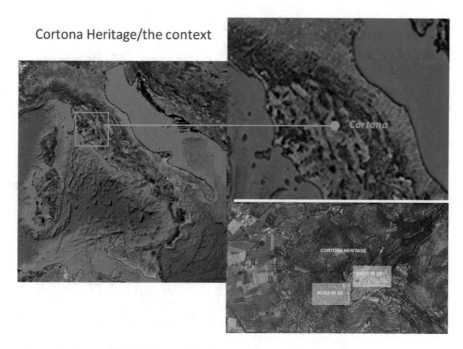

Fig. 2. Geographic framework and two study cases

objects of personal ornaments. From urban context has been extrapolated the first case study of Cortona Heritage related to the architectural topic and concerning the documentation of the part of city walls between the Porta S. Agostino and the Porta Bifora.

The second case study has been choosen from the Sodo archaeological area and is focusing on the documentation of grave goods to be linked in Cortona Heritage in a unified storytelling exhibition that highlights the common nature of the historical and cultural context of the two studies.

Cortona Heritage/project output

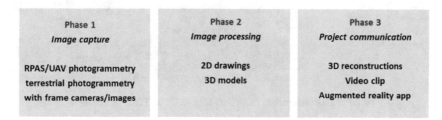

Phase 1	Phase 2	Phase 3
Image capture	*Image processing*	*Project communication*
RPAS/UAV photogrammetry	2D drawings	3D reconstructions
terrestrial photogrammetry	3D models	Video clip
with frame cameras/images		Augmented reality app

Fig. 3. Chart of the project output

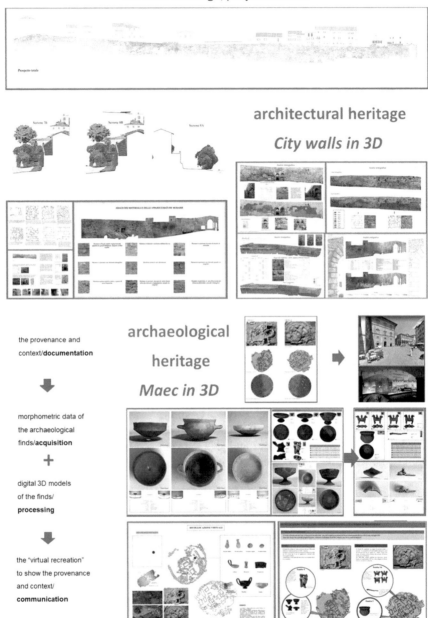

Fig. 4. Some results concerning "Cortona city walls in 3D" and "MAEC in 3D"

Cortona Heritage/project results

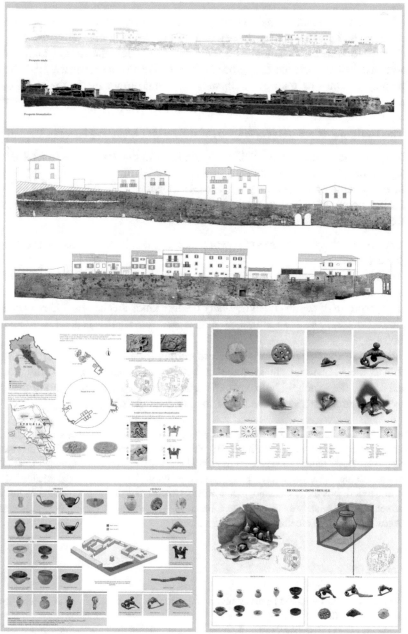

Fig. 5. Some results concerning "Cortona city walls in 3D" and "MAEC in 3D"

5 Methodology and Some Results of the Project

The disciplinary domain of main work governing the workflow is represented by the architectural and archaeological Survey and by the Drawing discipline.

Architectural and archaeological Survey makes possible the documentation of the investigated artifacts and the data processing in metadata congruent with the purposes of the project; Drawing realizes the themes communication suitable for an immersive fruition of the slow approach, in line with the type of tourism that interests the city of Cortona.

The workflow of the project (Fig. 3) is articulated in three phases:

- Image capture: realized by RPAS/UAV photogrammetry and by terrestrial photogrammetry with frame cameras/images;
- Image processing by 2D drawings and 3D models;
- Project communication: realized by 3D reconstructions, video clip, Augmented Reality app.

Cortona Heritage is a three-year work program and is now in its central phase of implementation.

The results we present here are therefore related to the first initial outputs deriving from the documentation and surveys of both sample cases (Figs. 4 and 5).

The spectrum of actions includes many flexible kinds that can be differentiated time by time according to the cultural strategies as well as the general and logistical variables.

The timing of the program is therefore defined in a scalar way over 3 years and articulates the immaterial enhancement in actions to increasing complexity from the virtual tour to the handheld hologram, to the interactive environment and to the virtual scene (Remondino and Campana 2014; Ioannides et al. 2018).

Acknowledgements. Cortona Heritage is an educational and research project of the University of Florence-Department of Architecture; BA degree Scienze dell'Architettura, Laboratory of Survey, Prof. Paola Puma; coordinators: dott. Stefano Rossi-Maec, arch. Lorenzo Cantini, Phd student Giuseppe Nicastro; tutors: Elena Leonardi Vugi, Elena Migliorati, Matteo Morana, Roberto Olivieri, Noemi Policicchio, Adele Rossi, Cristina Scicchitano, Valentina Usignoli.

Partnership: University of Florence-Department of Architecture, Comune di Cortona, Museo dell'Accademia etrusca e della città di Cortona.

References

Bertocci S, Arrighetti A (2015) Survey and documentation for archaeology. A special issue of Scires-it, vol 5(2)

Brusaporci S (2015) Handbook of research on emerging digital tools for architectural surveying, modeling, and representation. IGI Global, Hershey

Bruschetti P, Cecchi F, Giulierini P, Pallecchi P (2014) Cortona, l'alba dei principi etruschi. Thiphys

D'eramo M (2017) Il selfie del mondo. Feltrinelli, Milano

Ioannides M, Fink E, Brumana R, Patias P, Doulamis A, Martins J, Wallace M (eds) (2018) Digital heritage progress in cultural heritage: documentation, preservation, and protection, proceedings, Part I & II of 7th international conference, EuroMed 2018, Nicosia, Cyprus. Springer International Publishing, Heidelberg

Fortunelli S (2005) Il Museo della città etrusca e romana di Cortona: catalogo delle collezioni. Polistampa

Forum Internacional de Arqueología Virtual/International Forum of Virtual Archaeology (2011) Principles of Seville, International principle of Virtual Archaeology

Luigini A, Panciroli C (eds) (2018) Ambienti digitali per l'educazione all'arte e al patrimonio. FrancoAngeli, Milano

Pescarin S (2016) Digital Heritage into Practice. Scires-it **6**(1), 1–4

Puma P (2018) Sperimentazioni di didattica museale per l'attivazione di processi educativi evoluti nel programma Digital Cultural Heritage- DigitCH. In: Luigini A, Panciroli C (eds) Ambienti digitali per l'educazione all'arte e al patrimonio. FrancoAngeli, Milano

Remondino F, Campana S (2014) 3D Recording and Modeling in Archaeology and Cultural Heritage. Theory and best practices, BAR International Series 2598. Archaeopress, Oxford

The charter for the interpretation and presentation of cultural heritage sites (2008) 16th ICOMOS General Assembly

Museum Life

The New Muses and Their House

Some Comments About Museographic and Digital Contaminations

Santi Centineo[✉]

Department of Civil Engineering Sciences and Architecture (DICAR),
Politecnico di Bari, Via Orabona 4, 70125 Bari, Italy
santi.centineo@poliba.it

Abstract. When in 18th Century, the modern museum was born, the enlightenment imprinting was consecrating the intersubjective connection of the society with its own memory. Not by chance, the metaphoric inhabitants of this building, the Muses, are daughters of Zeus and the Memory.

The phenomenon of collecting (born some centuries before of the modern museum) asked to settle the accumulation of the objects according to thematic arrangements, that allowed a transversal possibility for artworks to be read according to cross-reading possibilities.

Today these formalities are progressively changed, thanks to the role of the digital technologies that implicate the redistribution of the task of the support, of the medium and of the device in the aesthetical fruition.

From the scientific point of view, both cataloguing and maintenance surely benefit so much of this process. The digitization allows moreover the virtual diffusion of the museum, overcoming the geographical barriers.

Currently it is therefore necessary:

(1) to define a new aesthetics scenario for the artistic image, from the moment in which the application of the digital technology to the museum interior takes hold.
(2) to verify if it is possible to compare the aesthetical dialectics between spectator and past artwork with the contemporary (and possibly future) one.
(3) to show a reasonable scenery for the museography, not only upgrading some scientific definitions, but also redefining the notion of masterwork.

Keywords: White cube · Black box · Digital art · Dynamic picture · Contemporary museography

1 Introduction

In the genetic code of the museum's functional typology, some clear phylogenetic aspects are engraved: (1) the imprinting of the classical culture; (2) the Renaissance practice of collecting; (3) finally, the predominant cognitive model, that presents a prominently textual nature.

© Springer Nature Switzerland AG 2019
A. Luigini (Ed.): EARTH 2018, AISC 919, pp. 703–715, 2019.
https://doi.org/10.1007/978-3-030-12240-9_72

These three genomes are not only indissolubly tied among them, but also to social, artistic, cultural and political phenomena of great significance.

1.1 The Classic Culture

From different points of view, the museum phenomenon is undoubtedly based on the classical culture. The etymology itself is already connected to the Muses, patron goddesses of the arts. However, it does not concern the modern meaning of the Arts.

Being initially born from the musical, melodious and choreographic practices, in the more divulged tradition (the Homeric and then the Hesiod's one) the Muses protect those that were considered arts by the Greeks (the epic poetry, lyric, the comedy, the tragedy, the history, etc.), that were textually expressible, as they were originated from the memory.

Painting, sculpture and other forms of figurative arts were excluded from the group, mainly for the strong imprint of the platonic thought, being them not evocation or memory of the reality, but one defective (and therefore deceptive) imitation of it.

Nevertheless, the man has learned to draw, a lot before learning to write.

However for being the letters more peculiar signs than others, and above all, as the sequence of these particular images produces ideas and concepts that would not be produced from the single letters (otherwise we would speak of 'ideograms'), it is quite rightly possible to affirm that with the birth of the writing, and therefore of the history, the man starts a process organizer of sense, attributing to the attractive images another role, justly defined for his epoch by Plato as "deceptive" (Flusser 2004: 8–12).

During the Middle Ages, in which the classical thought continually melts itself with the Christian one, the two aspects, textual and figurative, will live together.

Guilds of works protect the pragmatic aspects of the images, covering the walls with dreamlike or nightmarish explanatory sculptures, transfiguring the light through colored descriptive glasses, creating marvelous capital letters, in which a single element (that, if alone, it would be deprived of sense) represents a cosmogonic image, from which the whole text seems to flow.

Leaving aside how the group of the Arts was entered by figurative ones (Hauser 1964), a second element that engraves the classical matrix in the modern museum is the kind of relationship that the man has always had with very ancient objects, according to a logic that, overlapping *ethos* and *aisthesis*, assigns as greater value to the objects, the more ancient they are: if ancient, it is (automatically) beautiful and therefore correct, ethically valid.

The Italian Renaissance is submitted to this principle, when it begins to invest the ancient world of a guide-role, also at the cost of reinventing a classicism not well supported by scientific evidence: it is the satisfying attempt to recompose a lost visual universe, whose symbolic case is the attempt to reconstruct the Vitruvius' text iconography (Kruft 1994).

Although basing this theory on the studies of lettered humanists, that memorize whole tomes of the Greek and Latin writers, the whole Renaissance would like to retrieve an image of the ancient world that gradually from imitative ends up being emulative.

Thanks to this conviction ('mistake' would be a final judgment), the final phases of the Renaissance progressively disconnect from the classical culture, although they actually will continue carrying strong and evident signs of it.

1.2   Collecting

The collecting trend starts to develop in the Renaissance, but it was born earlier, connecting the objects to a mythical-magic meaning.

The collection of religious relics, also subject of a funny Boccaccio's tale[1], confirms Vilém Flusser's analysis (2004), when he separates the hidden cults, connected to the images and practiced by the poorest (or most illiterate) social classes, from the affection to the written text, connected to a linear interpretation and reserved to the most elevated classes.

With the birth of the collecting two phenomena are produced. From one side the collections of objects becomes more and more secularized: not only (presumed) sacred objects anymore, but also the collector is no more a cleric: it is a gentleman, a noble or a rich, whose collections integrate the meanings of that classical philology whose he is a great researcher and expert.

These objects are an explanatory device to support his textual doctrines, and if each object implies a textual apparatus, from the interaction of them it could derive the possibility to implicitly connect the subtended texts in a sort of meta-text that carries the sign of a common and shared action.

If "to write" (*graphein*, in Greek) also means "to trace", "to plough", instead "to read" (*leghein*) wants also to say "to pick up". If the primary etymon of "to collect" it is recognizable in "to pick up together", semiotics also show the possibility of "reading together" the different objects.

From a semiotic point of view, it is absolutely true, in the sense that the value of a collection increases with the number of objects, as they represent an enrichment of meaning (Fontanille 2003: 78–82).

1.3   The Linear Text

With Neoclassicism, a new possibility of reading the classical world incomes. Beginning from the technological, economic and social renewal, a change is introduced in the human conscience, that opens new possibilities of approach to knowledge. Disciplines as the aesthetics, the pedagogy, the historiography, the archaeology and the sociology are born (Frampton 1980: 2–3).

They are all disciplines that actually read other disciplines and above all offer a complex and articulated interpretative key of the textual linearity of their corresponding constitutive axioms.

Inevitably the neoclassic clarity immediately leads these disciplines to a materialization. Particularly in the new schools of architecture, new ideas and, with them, new libraries, new theaters and new museums, come to life.

---

[1] Giovanni Boccaccio, *Decameron*, tale 10, day 6°, "Monk Cipolla and Archangel Gabriel's feather".

2 Analogic Pictures and Modern Museums

Postponing the treatment of the genesis and the configuration of the modern museum of the XVIII Century, and entrusting this task to other researchers (Basso Peressut 2005), in this reflection it is important to draw some data, especially on the existing relationship in these buildings among architecture, exhibition, image and public.

First of all, in the modern museum it is evident that the type of artwork exposed is autographic: a unique piece that brings, directly or indirectly, the author's signature, in every case the trace of his/her hand.

It is not only the image of the work to be exposed therefore, but also its physical support, and with it, the creative procedure. All these elements are exposed in their uniqueness.

This unbreakable bond starts to be shattered by the advent of photography before and subsequently by the advent of the industrial design and of the fashion, with all their market meanings (Settembrini 2006: 88–90).

But the 'allographic' arts have already been preceded by the music, from the theater and from the reproductions of images in series, when the "text" of an author can live only thanks to the interpretative process by a performer.

As it will be more evident in the conclusions, today it is not casual that the museum is more and more becoming a performative space. The substantial difference is that today this reproduction is made possible thanks to the technique (Benjamin 1936: 20).

The uniqueness of the autographic artwork is coherently underlined instead by its "frame", intended clearly not in the meaning of decorative contour of the object (it would only be a redundant semantic overlapping), but rather in its intent of 'offering' the object and of its value's reinforcing.

From one side in fact the frame underlines the uniqueness and the value of the image: if an image is framed it is not to exclusively considered from the eidetic point of view, but also evocative and symbolic.

From a different point of view, being an artwork generally exposed inside a building that is also a piece of art, the frame underlines the separation, the line of border between two entities of value. For this reason, most of the time it is also an object of great value.

The Enlightenment museum brings some order to this bundle of signs, by optimizing the architectural container, that, in comparison to the "quadreria" of the private buildings, seems 'to contract', at least in its decorative aspects, to let the artwork and its frame stand out. Expressly this building is formally inspired to the linearity of the classical temple: it is the house of the Muses.

In the contemporary museums, this process is more complex: if the frame still has a reason for being, the building tends to be 'silent': Carlo Scarpa's museums (Fig. 1) are a clear example of it (Albertini and Bagnoli 1992; Dalai Emiliani 2008).

But, when in front of the digital image, especially when this one rises to the role of artwork, how do the frame and the building behave (Glusberg 1983)?

Let's leave an even more anxious question to the sociologists of the art: how does the user behave (Hauser 1964)?

Fig. 1. Carlo Scarpa's Castelvecchio Museum (interior).

3   Digital Pictures and Contemporary Museums

The advent of the digital images and their introduction in the museum interior substantially produces three types of effect:

(1) on the methods of cataloguing, preservation and scientific dissemination. It is in fact undeniable that these methods are increased by the introduction of the digital image.

   The incredible potential is evident: the cataloguing is not only made thanks to images, allowing therefore to fix the state of maintenance or the historical sequence of artefact, but it also can be shared online facilitating the task of researchers and scholars.

   Leaving the explosive potentiality of the matter in the hands of museology, this aspect introduces the second point;

(2) as an immediate result, the progressive separation of the user (studious, researcher or audience) from the artwork can be observed.

   The digital cataloguing not only exonerates the scientist from the direct contact with the artwork, but also for the people a new possibility of fruition of art can be hypothesized, in which digital technology will progressively complement the artwork, then overlapping to it, up to replace it definitely (Gunthert 2015).

   It is what happens in the so-called "white cube", prophesied by Le Corbusier with the project of *La boîte à miracle* for Tokyo[2]: a white container (Fig. 2), able to take the form and to perfectly conform to its content, according to the most exact spirit of the globalization (McLuhan 1967).

---

[2] Le Corbusier designed a whole service area in Tokyo in the post-war years, including a museum, a park and the open-air theatre. This "white cube" theatre had been already designed in 1949. The only building that has been realized is the Museum of Western Art, Ueno Park, 1955-59.

Fig. 2. Le Corbusier's *boîte à miracle*, Tokyo, 50s years.

From an emotional and sensorial point of view in this trial there is an attractive potential, certainly not entirely explored.

On the one side this process allows to host in the museums an impressive number of artworks that before would have been unthinkable to circulate; on the other hand, their fruition can take place with a deformation of the sensorial scale (enlargements, details, trips through and inside the three-dimensional artwork).

It is an evidence the recent show *The Universal Judgment*[3], in which the spectator travels through and inside Michelangelo's masterwork, or the recent virtual exhibition "French Impressionists"[4], in which Impressionist pictures can be entered by the visitor (Fig. 3). And, as it happens "virtually", it can happen everywhere. With that shows, everywhere pictures can be 'visited', or any place can be transformed for the time of the vision into the Sistine Chapel.

The adjective "virtual" recovers so its etymological meaning, that of a potential future existence: immersive environments and synesthesias that produce new catharsis; the device's 'aura' replaces the artist's mastery; the possibility of reset the place of the exhibition, but also to confuse preparation, artwork and architecture in an unity capable of remarkable theoretical implications, but, at the same time, to separate museographic design and museological project, generally with the prevalence of the first one on the second.

---

[3] "Giudizio Universale – Michelangelo and the secrets of the Sistine Chapel", by Marco Balich, with scientific expertise of Vatican Museums, main theme song by Sting, video designer Luke Halls, produced by Artainment Worldwide Show, 2018.

[4] "Impressionisti francesi", by Giancarlo Bonomo, Palazzo degli Esami, Rome, october 2018.

Fig. 3. A room at the exhibition *Impressionisti francesi*, Rome, October 2018

From the experimentations by Studio Azzurro, to the contemporary thematic museums "*in absentia phoenomeni*", the so-called "immersive environments" join together performative aspects with a dynamism (not to say 'continuous transformation'), in which the exhibition design is no more the preparation to the exploitation of the artwork, but on the contrary it writes a new (sometimes even dominant) text.

(3) on the exhibition and therefore progressively on the architecture of the museum. It is evident that nowadays the role of the exhibition design is more and more prominent in the space of the man.

The alternation of different exhibitions always in narrow times expresses the transience of the human life, but the type of reversing process that it embodies, is not equally able to express the reversibility of the time, that inexorably continues to flow.

Furthermore, the multimedia artwork (especially if interactive) replaces a type of collective catharsis (that one of the Greek theatre or of the classical museum, in which the presence of the public and the sharing of the aesthetical experience is fundamental), with another individual and hypnotic one.

The new media address the single subjects, they enter intravenously through portable devices, they deceive the spectator on a precise point: they induce to the conviction that the artwork is exclusively addressed to which owns the privilege to share it with a global tribe that however as a fact is not all around, but somewhere else.

This datum is fundamental to understand the passage, already started by recent architectural experiences, from 'white cube' to 'black box'.

The logic and the potentialities of the white cube in fact have brought the museum building to some limits, not to say contradictions.

Immersive environments, in which sound and visual message quickly are sent, not only remove the user far from a scientific perception of the represented object, but also, from the point of view of the perception, they dilate the objective perception of the reality, creating as a fact an extremely seductive magic box, capable to distort the exact perception of the time and the space (Vitta 1999).

An augmented reality, an augmented space, a dilated time, a hypnotic perception: seductive elements on one side (and surely they contain aspects worthy of consideration and interest), but that actually impose a reflection on the essence of the new museum building.

The building and the museum exhibition assume so an unprecedented power, aligned to the recent trend of the contemporary art:

The object of the representation rises to the role of artwork, just for being contained inside them, but this aura appears even in front of an object that the most of times has lost its physical feature and has become virtual.

What physically remains (and in fact aim at prevailing) is the highly technological device, that is physically the unique present object (Gehlen 1957).

The aesthetical phenomenon continues existing (and it is also interesting), but it aims at resembling mostly to a show, that, as it will be seen in the conclusions, causes theatres and museums today to be considered as a unique typology.

In Gehry's Biomuseo[5], thanks to digital technologies, the exhibition reproduces an immersive ecological environment, very improbable to be visited.

Comparing this experience with Youki Hirakawa's video-installation[6], it is evident that the borders are increasingly thin (Fig. 4).

(4)   once this awareness has been verified, some recent architectural experiences, giving expression to the concept of black box, try to express the necessity to freeze in the time the frontal experience with the digital artwork.

In what does the black box differ from the white cube? Apparently in the black box both the architectural container and the exhibition cancel each other out.

They not only actually keep on existing, but, through some design qualities, conduct the user toward a "decreased" atmosphere that allows a frontal reading, closer and direct with the artwork that can very often be a multimedia product.

It is given the possibility of distinguishing exposed work from exhibition and architecture. Through a "frame", that is not only the physical frame of a picture, but it is something that metaphorically lead the same way, the artwork recovers its frontal dialogue with the people, that in this way can be users of an aesthetical rule-based process.

4   Conclusions

In another research (Centineo 2005) it has been possible to demonstrate how another building born to "exhibit" something else, the theatre building, during these last decades has been subjected to a double semantic rotation.

---

[5] Frank Gehry, Biomuseo, Amador Causeway, Panama City, 1999-2014.

[6] Youki Hirakawa, *Vanished Tree – Barn*, video installation, Akademie Schloss Solitude, Stuttgart, 2013.

Fig. 4. A room at Gehry's *Biomuseo*, Panama and Hirakawa's *Vanished tree.*

This means that the literary text, or the building, or the way of the *mise en espace*, that in Italian we commonly call "theater", they have switched their spheres of pertinence, from text, to context and pretext[7].

An analogous phenomenon is happening with the museum. Artwork, building and exhibition are switching their places: the artwork, that was the text, is becoming a pretext and aims at becoming a context; the building from context has become text (the Guggenheim of Bilbao is a clear example) and it aims at becoming pretext; and finally, conclusive element, the exhibition from pretext (when the museology prevailed on the museography) has become context and then, after having crushed or invaded the task of the museum building, aims to become (or has already become) text, fading a lot of times with the artwork, whose boundaries often disappears and, on the base of the modern technologies, result in the exhibition itself.

It is possible to conclude with three final considerations.

4.1   Thorough the Black-Box

From a side the museum building, as it is happening for the theatre, aims to become a black box. This is the most effective and linear way to isolate the exhibition and to understand if museum still has something to say.

In the black box the artwork is framed by its same boundaries and the catharsis produced between user and artwork does not require the demolition of the so-called 'fourth wall'.

During the 20th Century the fourth wall has continually been put in discussion by numerous writers of theatre or *metteur en scenes*, originating an idea of building in which it is not to be demolished anymore, as it does not exist anymore. Likewise, in the

---

[7] Extraordinary ambiguity is mostly present in the Italian language, where the word 'theater' can indifferently make reference to the building (es: the Globe Theatre), to the literary text (es: Shakespeare's theater), to the *mise en scene* (es: Bob's Wilson theater). In English, according to the context, words like ``theatre', ``drama' or ``performance' are preferred.

case of the museum, the frame of the artwork (or the pedestals of the sculptures) have decidedly been overcome by an abstraction of the artwork that pervades exhibition and architecture (Forino 2008: 51).

Meanwhile it is often the artwork itself, especially in the case of the digital technologies, to invade the exhibition walls, confusing medium and device of the representation (Pinotti and Somaini 2016: 137; Fagone 1990). The black box contours the artwork, forcing it to talk face to face to the user (if it is able to do it).

For instance, in Arquipélago Museum[8], the dark rooms of an old tobacco factory are converted into exhibition spaces expressly thought for video-projections or installations (Fig. 5).

On the other side, it returns to the artwork its mystical aura, that had been put in discussion by the precedent passage, the one of the white cube (O'Doherty 1976), and that had previously been analysed by Benjamin (1936, 2012) and strongly defended by Adorno (1975).

In such a sense, it is particularly significant a work by César Paternosto, *La inflación de la semiótica*[9], in which a white canvas is entirely painted on the side edges. The sense of the work is clear: not only a white work on a white background produces an inflation of its possibilities of reading, but above all it realizes how today the most actual considerations must be conducted in direction of the frame, the separation of artwork from the building that contains it. Re-establishing the boundaries of the artwork will be one of the tasks of today's society.

4.2   The Need of a Non-linear Text

If Flusser's analysis is correct (a surprisingly prophetic analysis unfortunately concluded for the death of the author, just when the phenomenon was becoming explosive), a moment will soon come in which the new figurativeness, the digital one, will overlap, encounter, gobble up, and surely correlate to a textual apparatus.

But if the static image previously allowed to follow with the correct rhythm the linear text that accompanied it and what joined together text and image it was a structuralist vision (Flusser 1985, 2004), now the dynamic image, the digital one, aims to overhang the value of any text (Eco 1968). The evidence is the difficulty in quoting one of these images, that are completely different from their physical support (a CD-ROM), and need a performance to exist.

It is not casual that in a show held at the Foundation Cartier in Paris, Andrea Branzi, acute as always, chooses a particular text to support of the visual part of the show: an audio signed by Patti Smith, also author of the exhibited photos, in which a sonorous carpet and the recorded voice of the singer/performer lead the spectator to an unprecedented synesthesia (Fig. 6).

---

[8] Menos é Mais Arquitectos, João Mendes Ribeiro, Arquipélago, Ribeira Grande, San Miguel, Azoras (PT), 2014.

[9] César Paternosto, *Inflación de la semiótica*, acrylic painting on canvas, Galería Guillermo de Osma, Madrid, 1971-1996.

Fig. 5. Menos é Mais Arquitectos and João Mendes Ribeiro, *Arquipélago*, Azoras (PT).

Fig. 6. Andrea Branzi's Open Enclosures, Fondation Cartier, music by Patti Smith, 2008.

In a writing like this, for instance, we can quote a frame of a digital movie, but nor the whole sequence of frames can be brought here, neither so much the kind of dynamism that connects them, much less the audio of accompaniment.

And then paradoxically, considering that the digital image is also involving the publishing world, from e-books to the open-access magazines, this potentiality should be exploited joining a meta-text (nowadays a very common concept) to a dynamic image (nowadays even more common).

From this union, something not only unprecedented, but also revolutionary, could be born, as it would condition even the way to transmit knowledges in the centres of education, requiring a new type of school and teacher.

4.3   A House for the New Muses

It is evident that the one of the new museum won't be a linear reading, like in the past, a reading based on the evocation of the Memory.

The museum, as a place of scientific accumulation and preservation will continue to exist, rather this aspect will surely be implemented, thanks to the potentialities of the digital image, but this function will be even more hidden, exclusive prerogative of the researchers.

The new type of reading, that one destined to the user, will be a kind of meta-textual reading, done by knots of information or links.

Nevertheless, it will allow to establish, time by time, the rules of a new possibility of reading the artwork, without dealing here (the matter mostly concerns the art and contemporary aesthetics researchers) with giving a complete definition of what today the artwork could be.

This kind of subdivision in the functional program of the contemporary museum produces an ideal and formal hiatus between a "backstage", where researchers, scholars and scientists will keep on writing the rules of the new arts and where they will almost secretly be voted to the cult of the New Muses, and an ideal "stage", where the new art can be exhibited.

This separation recalls once more a comparison with the theatre building.

where new forms of performative arts and of contaminated genres ask for a complex and articulated functional program.

At the end of the 50s and the beginnings of the 60s Maurizio Sacripanti plans a building, not realized, completely changing, that from theatre can nimbly change in museum, in the exhibition gallery, in sporting stadium or in stage for fashion shows, events and so on (Centineo 2018).

It was the prophetic vision of a sensitive interpreter of the social upsetting that the revolution of the images was already outlining: nowadays it is common to have concerts in the stadiums, défilé in the theaters and theater in the industrial sheds. Why cannot the architecture make interpreter of this necessity then?

With the explosion of the digital images and with the experience of the black box the boundaries between theatre and museum definitely fade out, not only because the society asks a building where can be revealed the contemporary visual complexity, but also because the functional program, the interior of the building, is becoming even more complex and particularly the images, assuming a new value of ideogram (once again they are becoming image-text), they address the new temple of the Muses toward a neo-tribal conception.

The New Muses (those ones of the cinema, of the photo, of the television, of the publicity, of the graphics, of the images on the socials network, of the video-mapping, of the augmented reality and of the interactive image), those that will live in these new houses, are not the daughters of the Memory anymore, but of the Image, of the Light and of the Time.

References

Adorno T (1975). Teoria estetica. Einaudi

Albertini B, Bagnoli S (1992) Scarpa: i musei e le esposizioni. Jaca Book

Basso Peressut L (2005) Il museo moderno: architettura e museografia da Auguste Perret a Louis I. Kahn, Lybra Immagine

Benjamin W (1936) Das Kunstwerk im Zeitalter seiner technischen Reproduzierbarkeit. Zeitschrift für Sozialforschung

Benjamin W (2012) Aura e choc: saggi sulla teoria dei media. Einaudi

Centineo S (2005) Representamen. Il ruolo dell'architettura degli interni nel ripensamento del rapporto arhitettura/musica/società. PhD tesis in Interior and Exhibit Design, XX Cicle, tutor: Andrea Branzi, Politecnico di Milano

Centineo S (2018) Like a machine in motion. The modernity of the Cagliari Opera House and of the Osaka Expo Pavilion by Maurizio Sacripanti. In: Monteiro M, Kong MSM (Chief-Editors), Maria João Pereira Neto (Co-Editor). Progress(es) – theories and practices, proceedings of the 4th international multidisciplinary congress (phi 2018 – Progress(es) – Theories and Practices), Ponta Delgada - S. Miguel (Azores, PT), 3–6 October 2017. CRC Press, Taylor & Francis Group

Dalai Emiliani M (2008) Per una critica della museografia del Novecento in Italia. Il "saper mostrare" di Carlo Scarpa. Marsilio

Eco U (1968) La struttura assente. Bompiani

Fagone V (1990) L' immagine video. Feltrinelli, Arti visuali e nuovi media elettronici

Flusser V (1985) Ins Universum der technischen Bilder. European photography

Flusser V (2004) La cultura dei media. Bruno Mondadori

Fontanille J (2003) La patina e la connivenza. In: Marrone G, Landowski E, (eds) La società degli oggetti. Problemi di interoggettività, Meltemi

Forino I (2008) Dalla merce all'idea di abitare. In: Bossi A (ed) Allestire, problematiche disciplinari. Vpoint

Frampton K (1980) Modern Architecture: a critical History. Thames and Hudson

Gehlen A (1957) Die Seele im technischen Zeitalter: Sozialpsychologische Probleme in Der Industriellen Gesellschaft. Rowohlt

Glusberg J (1983) L'ultimo museo: musei freddi e caldi, vecchi e nuovi, immaginari, integrati. Sellerio

Gunthert A (2015) L'image partegée. La photographie numerique, Éditions Textuel

Hauser A (1964) Storia sociale dell'arte. Einaudi

Kruft HW (1994) A history of architectural theory: from Vitruvius to the present. Zwemmer

McLuhan D (1967) Il medium è il messaggio. Einaudi

O'Doherty B (1976) Inside the white cube: the ideology of the gallery space. The Lapis Press, Santa Monica

Pinotti A, Somaini A (2016) Cultura visuale: immagini, sguardi, media, dispositivi. Einaudi

Settembrini L (2006) L'arte e l'informazione contemporanee come leve del city marketing. In: Lazzaroni L, Molinari L (eds.) The Art of Display. L'arte di mettere in mostra. Skira

Vitta M (1999) Il sistema delle immagini. Liguori

Communication Design for the Dissemination of Scientific Knowledge. Languages, Tools, Technologies, Collaborative Processes for Museum Education

V. M. Viviana Trapani[✉]

Dipartimento di Architettura, Università degli Studi di Palermo,
Viale delle Scienze, Ed. 14, Palermo, Italy
viviana.trapani@unipa.it

Abstract. This paper sets out to report an articulated research-action process, which started with some educational-scientific experiments carried out in a collaborative effort between the disciplines of design, multimedia representation and botanical sciences at the University of Palermo. The project in question focused on scientific communication and the development of communication products for the museum and institutional education of the Botanical Garden of Palermo. Within this initiative, design tools, technologies and methods of expression were experimented and later re-proposed in a territorial development project which led to the creation of the "Intangible Heritage Micro Museum of Wheat and Bread. Memory, knowledge, interaction" of Borgo S. Rita (CL). Today the micro-museum of Borgo S. Rita offers visitors an articulate narrative path with interactive elements; combining the educational-scientific dimension of learning with the historical-anthropological dimension of the small community memory, linked by the sharing of knowledge gathered over time as regards wheat production and bread-making. Moreover, the use of specific methods, techniques and technologies of communication and representation has helped to explore an "open" and collaborative design dimension, which can facilitate new co-design practices for social and cultural innovation within territorial development processes.

Keywords: Communication and information design ·
Museum education and technologies · Education through digital media ·
Multimedia representation

© Springer Nature Switzerland AG 2019
A. Luigini (Ed.): EARTH 2018, AISC 919, pp. 716–725, 2019.
https://doi.org/10.1007/978-3-030-12240-9_73

1 An Interdisciplinary Experimentation to Communicate the Specificity of the Botanical Garden of Palermo

The paper outlines an articulated research-action[1] process, launched within the degree course of Industrial Design at the University of Palermo and developed through the contribution of various disciplinary skills; an experience started within an essentially educational process which developed design tools, techniques and methods of expression, all of which were then applied concretely in a territorial development project oriented towards social and cultural innovation (Fig. 1).

The initial project idea, developed as part of two bachelor degree theses[2], was in fact born from an interdisciplinary collaboration between design, representation and visual communication, botany and plant ecology, in an effort to seriously revise and update the way of communicating the mission message and scientific activities of the Botanical Garden[3] of Palermo, the largest of its kind in Italy, and part of the Department of Agricultural, Food and Forest Sciences at the University of Palermo.

New communication tools and languages were tested to activate a greater degree of involvement and awareness among citizens and visitors regarding the important scientific and urban role of the Botanical Garden; an institution that today, alongside its historic urban function as a "scientific garden", also plays an important role of territorial safeguarding of plant biodiversity and environmental education (Pantina 2013).

In fact, as now occurs in all leading contemporary museum institutions, in addition to its mission of preserving and exhibiting a wide range of botanical species, the Botanical Garden has also undertaken its own socio-cultural project which is committed to the dissemination of scientific culture even further afield (Irace 2013). Widespread knowledge processes have therefore been activated, also concerning complex scientific and environmental issues, through increasing numbers of initiatives and events open to the city, all of which have developed new uses and connections between urban and natural spaces. The work carried out within the University instead focused primarily on communication via internet, producing specific multimedia and multimodal products: hypertextual and authorial narratives, which are based on directorial control and proposed as communicative artefacts able to activate complex and significant cultural learning processes.

In fact, it is necessary to note how internet surfing is considered today as a real form of learning, in that there is a continuous flow of information and ideas:

---

[1] The research-action, peculiar to the discipline of design for the territory, expresses a qualitative nature, which is defined during the analysis of the research context, not operating through precise analysis and data, nor through prescriptive and normative indications, but constantly negotiating its own reasons and adhering in a targeted way to situations and context.

[2] "Design for scientific communication. Reproduction of vascular plants", degree theses of Giovanni Dioretico; "Design for scientific communication. Ancient Sicilian fruit trees", degree theses of Sara Farruggia. Supervisors proff. V. Trapani, G. Bazan, Degree course of Industrial Design, University of Palermo, A.Y. 2015-16.

[3] For more complete information, consult the institutional website www.ortobotanico.unipa.it.

Fig. 1. Diagram of the institutional activities of the Palermo Botanical Garden

"This cultural change has closely affected the knowledge acquisition system itself: the learning of the new generations, in fact, is increasingly being implemented alongside the traditional systems provided with a digital system that prefers, where possible, direct experience or simulation which leads to a faster understanding and assimilation of the contents" (Patti 2018).

Based on an approach already successfully tested by the main botanical gardens in the world - such as Kew Gardens in London and Le Jardin des Plantes in Paris - it was decided to develop the communication of teaching activities and applied research carried out by the Botanical Garden through internet, focusing on audiovisual processing as the most effective and immediate tool to communicate the importance of biodiversity and the themes directly linked to it towards an extended audience.

The project revolves around three main objectives: experimentation with languages and methods of scientific communication; a dynamic representation of biodiversity processes through the methodological approach typical of information design; the transfer of applied research activities by the Botanical Garden in its educational displays and programmes.

In particular, two audiovisual products have been developed: these intertwine the languages of motion graphics, filmic representation and the various facets of information design, displaying complex issues and data in an immediate and direct communicative form while respecting strictly scientific parameters.

2   "Designing the Understanding" for Territorial Biodiversity

"Ancient Sicilian fruit trees" proposes the themes of safeguarding the environment and traditional Sicilian agriculture through the narration and representation of the progressive territorial impoverishment and attempted revitalization of Sicilian fruiting biodiversity.

The work was also included among the activities of the "MEMOLA FP7 project - MEditerranean MOuntainous LAndscape, an historical approach to cultural heritage based on traditional agrosystems", a project funded by the European Community for the understanding of formation processes of historical landscapes, with the aim of designing strategies for conservation, dissemination and enhancement of cultural heritage (both tangible and intangible) and the environment.

In Sicily there is still a very rich heritage of natural biodiversity, which is however likely to be lost in the future. During its history the island has been enriched with many botanical species which originated in different parts of the world before being imported through a succession of different cultures and commercial trading in the Mediterranean. In particular, this phenomenon happened in the fruit growing industry, where produce was intended for family consumption whilst surplus quantities were sold in local markets; to support their families and ensure sufficient supply throughout the year, farmers began to select the tree species, cultivating a vast heritage of varieties: very early, precocious, late and very late flowering species.

But since the 1960s, as a result of the agricultural crisis, mixed crops and their specialization have been abandoned in order to increase intensive monocultures aimed exclusively at increasing productivity. Thus, a progressive industrialization of crops and consumption has taken place, inevitably provoking the impoverishment of a rich botanical heritage created by natural selection and dedicated human efforts over the ages.

The Botanical Garden of Palermo and the Regional Forests Company (ARFD) conducted a research project between 2005 and 2008 which was funded by the European Union and aimed at the conservation of the Plant Genetic Resources of Sicily (RGV) through research and detailed documentation of ancient varieties and identification of the greatest distribution sites. The germplasm of rare tree species was collected and set within the Garden to initiate reproduction processes and then launch several experimental production fields on the island.

The video-infographic project about "Ancient Sicilian fruit trees" sets out to "design the understanding"[4] of these important aspects of territorial culture and the complex process of biodiversity recovery and protection implemented through research and scientific experimentation, addressing the many potential users who access the Botanical Garden online or visit its educational installations.

The project evolves through a video that begins by showing - using the synthetic and dynamic mode of motion graphics - the history and local diffusion of the Sicilian fruit tree heritage; from the social and anthropological processes to the activities that allow it to be restored, decrying the cultural loss that its disappearance could determine.

In the central section of the video - through effective film footage - the consequences of the industrialization processes of agriculture are shown from environmental, cultural, social, economic and anthropological points of view.

In the final section, video-infographics illustrate the role of the Botanical Garden, with its activities of research and cataloguing of endangered species and varieties, of their restoration and repopulation. This last part of the video is divided into:

- identification of the specimens, in which the indigenous varieties are presented;
- collection of plant material for reproduction;
- agamic multiplication, by grafting and cutting.

---

[4] According to an expression by the Italian information designer Angela Morelli, who is particularly committed to the communication of environmental issues around water resources. She is also co-founder of InfoDesignlab.

The filming took place in the Municipality of Pollina (ME), specifically in the Madonie, an area characterized by the presence of traditional crops which have been generally abandoned elsewhere; in the region of Petralia Soprana (PA), where the "Petraviva Madonie" Cooperative preserves and reproduces ancient Sicilian varieties; and in the region of Gela (CL), where the spread of greenhouse cultivation has profoundly changed the original landscape (Fig. 2).

3   Representing Knowledge: Biodiversity and Evolution

"Reproduction of vascular plants" deals with the principles of bio-diversity in plants: evolution, adaptation of reproductive systems in plant systems and the exchange of genetic information.

According to the principle on which this project is based, in order to preserve biodiversity, it is not enough simply to safeguard endangered species. Instead, it is necessary to keep the whole eco-system alive, a system which we can envisage as a long chain where each ring corresponds to a species or a habitat. Many of these "rings" have already disappeared, so it becomes essential to preserve what still exists today and also try to reintegrate the connecting elements of the system.

The design concept of "Reproduction of vascular plants" focuses particularly on the primary goal of communication design: to make even very complex and multifaceted topics easily comprehensible, not summarizing or simplifying but instead selecting the concepts and re-elaborating them through an original "sensorial message".

The result is a video in which, by alternating still shots with infographic elements and animations, the complex evolution history of the reproductive systems of vascular plants[5] is explained: from their original dependence on random elements such as water and wind, until - about 200 million years ago - the plants evolved into individuals able to dialogue with other living species in order to gain mutual benefit, colonizing all environments on Earth.

The video opens with an image of the Earth, gray and devoid of life forms; then a dynamic timeline with detailed information shows the appearance of life on Earth and the steps that led to the appearance of primordial plants. It then describes the advent of the pteridophytes (ferns and fern allies), which are introduced by a short film with overlapping infographics; later an animated section illustrates the process of reproduction by spores. To conclude, the timeline re-appears, this time continuing up to the appearance of gymnosperms (arboreal plants without flowers and fruits). Again, a short clip explains the reproductive system, showing the process of pollination and genetic exchange between the gametes and ending by revealing the various fruit shapes that have characterized the adaptation of angiosperms to different environments. The video

---

[5] These are plants that have a system of vessels for conducting water, practically all plants with the exception of algae, mosses and liverworts.

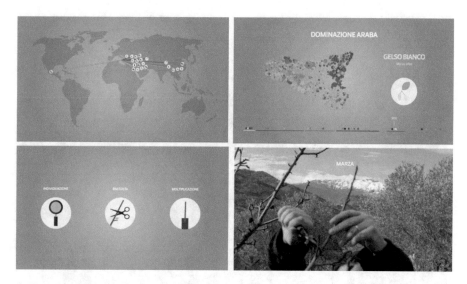

Fig. 2. Frames from "Ancient Sicilian fruit trees": animated infographics and film footage representing the diffusion of tree species and reproduction systems by grafting

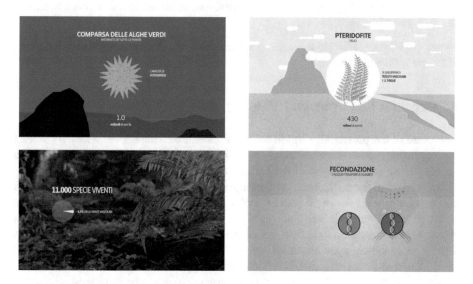

Fig. 3. Frames from "Reproduction of vascular plants": animated infographics and film footage representing the evolutionary processes of plants

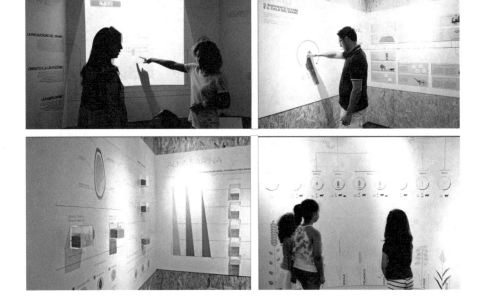

Fig. 4. Educational spaces of the Micro Museum of Wheat and Bread of Borgo S. Rita

adopts photographic techniques, infographics, motion graphics, motion tracking and 3D camera tracking (Fig. 3).[6]

4   Creation of Contextual Value

The value of the project also lies in the development of a design methodology and an essential linguistic and technical syntax, which has been exported and shared also outside the scientific context of the University.

In particular, the project has merged into the design of communication and fruition processes regarding the implicit skills and knowledge which is widespread within the territory; real intangible cultural assets that are today at the centre of territorial development strategies. In fact, some of the most innovative readings on post-crisis social and economic dynamics highlight and hope for the emergence of a cultural and ideal dimension (Trapani 2016), which must support and revitalize the technical-productive dimension; a trend reversal is proposed, which can be developed around the concept of "contextual value" or shared value, as a premise to reconnect the economy and society once again.

---

[6] Motion tracking allows tracking the movement of a contrast point in the video; 3D camera tracking is a reverse engineering of the movement performed by the camera while analysing the video frames; filming becomes a virtual environment where it is possible to insert three-dimensional objects that move together with the camera movements.

«The basic idea is that the creation of economic value, in the opening phase of capitalism, is linked to the relationship between individuals and between them and the surrounding environment, therefore the enhancement of the context in which we live (…). The contextual value translates very concretely into the production of those goods that we define contextual, as they improve the quality of the context in which we carry out our activities as individuals and citizens» (Magatti and Gherardi 2014)

5   A "Micro Museum" for Territorial Development: Narration and Interaction

The chance to verify these theoretical knowledges and practical experiments arrived with the design and implementation in 2016 of the "Intangible Micro Museum of Wheat and Bread. Memory, knowledge, interaction" of Borgo S. Rita (CL), elaborated by a team of teachers and some young graduates[7] of the Palermo School of Design, who had already participated in the design research about the scientific communication of the Botanical Garden.

The initiative of the Borgo San Rita Micro Museum started in 2013, when the Santa Rita Cultural Association was founded by women united by the common goal of redeveloping the ancient village of Santa Rita, preserving its historical, religious, cultural and gastronomic identity in order to reactivate the economy of the village and make it a destination of quality slow tourism.

The original idea was transformed into a real project thanks to a loan obtained by the GAL "Terre del Nisseno" within the PSR (Rural Development Program) Sicilia 2007/2013, which was intended to redevelop, and make accessible, the building heritage, culture and traditional activities of small rural villages within the Sicilian territory, thus encouraging rural tourism. The variety of skills and interests that generated the project idea - almost in a co-design[8] mode - produced an original design "laboratory" characterized by an intense dialogue with the community of S. Rita. This was aimed at the museum's communication and education strategies, in particular as a resource and service for educational institutions.

Today the micro-museum of Borgo S. Rita offers visitors an essentially narrative path (Trocchianesi 2014), also equipped with some basic interactive devices; it proposes an experience that combines a scientific-educational dimension with the historical-anthropological dimension of the small community memory, linked by the sharing of knowledge gathered over time regarding wheat production and the skill of bread-making as practiced in the village.

---

[7] F. Monterosso, concept, set-up, direction and scientific coordination; D. Emanuele and M. Di Piazza, direction and screenplay of anthropological documentaries; G.Dioretico and S.Farruggia, direction and screenplay of educational documentaries; L. Di Martino, graphics and communication; M. Schifano and M. P. Erice, Arduino and processing; U. Di Piazza, sound design.

[8] The term indicates the design methodologies and tools for designing with the user's active involvement.

The nineteenth-century baronial building, only recently restored, is equipped with:

– a series of infographics (static and animated) illustrating the cultivation processes of wheat, its traditional processing as opposed to industrial methods; then the bread-making process, together with a description of the chemical-physical and organoleptic characteristics that determine its particular qualities;
– some documentaries that retrace the narrative path, bringing the visitor back from an abstract representation to the real context of production and environments as well as real-life accounts from local residents;
– a series of illustrations related to small interactive sensorial installations that foster involvement and quality of the museum visit experience, especially for young visitors (Fig. 4).

Visitors receive different channels of information "staged" with different techniques (audiovisuals, installations, documentaries, infographics, animations) together with low-cost and open digital technologies (Monterosso 2013), such as the Arduino hardware platform related to the Processing programming language.

6   Conclusions

The project of the Borgo S. Rita Micro Museum integrates and develops also in a professional context - of a collaborative and inclusive nature for all those involved - the experience acquired from scientific and educational experimentation carried out within the university framework: in fact, the project elaborates further and proposes a range of languages, tools and technologies for a communication design with expertise and scientific characters in content management. At the same time, the use of specific methods, techniques and technologies of communication and representation has led to the exploration of an "open" and collaborative project dimension (Rizzo 2009), characterized by a predisposition to share, and an ability to contribute in local territory processes to the introduction of tools and methods suitable for activation of co-design practices for social and cultural innovation.

References

Magatti M, Gherardi L (2014) Una nuova prosperità. Quattro vie per una crescita integrale, Feltrinelli, Milano
Irace F (a cura di) (2013) Immateriale, virtuale, interattivo. Intagible, virtual, interactive, Electa, Milano
Monterosso F (2013) Open Design. Pratiche di progetto e processi di conoscenza. LetteraVentidue, Siracusa
Pantina A (2013) I musei naturalistici come presidi ambientali e culturali. L'Orto Botanico di Palermo. In: Trapani V, Daverio P (a cura di). Il design dei Beni Culturali. Crisi territorio, identità/ Cultural Heritage Design. Crisis, territory, identity, Rizzoli, Milano
Patti I (2018) (Video)giocare con il Design. Un'esperienza estetica significativa nel gioco di simulazione applicata. In: Chimez L, Fagnoni R, Spadolini MB (a cura di), Design su misura, Società Italiana di Design, Genova

Rizzo F (2009) Strategie di co-design. Teorie, metodi strumenti per progettare con gli utenti, Franco Angeli

Trapani V (2016) Design e cultura. Osservazioni e connessioni per un nuovo paradigma culturale, LetteraVentidue, Siracusa

Trocchianesi R (2014) Design e narrazioni per il patrimonio culturale, Maggioli, Sant' Arcangelo di Romagna

The Virtual Museum of the Upper Calore Valley

A Cross-typological Application for Local Cultural Heritage

Bruno Fanini, Alfonsina Pagano, and Augusto Palombini[✉]

CNR - Istituto per le Tecnologie Applicate ai Beni Culturali, Montelibretti, Italy
{bruno.fanini,alfonsina.pagano}@itabc.cnr.it,
augusto.palombini@cnr.it

Abstract. Despite the term "Virtual Museum" (VM) is currently used with several meanings, two branches can be identified, not usually intersecting each other: applications (interactive or not) oriented towards a "visual database" approach, in which historical/art informations are given to the user by mean of the application dynamic; and "dramatized" or "narrative" applications, consisting in digital storytelling structures which focus their attention on emotion, sensorial involvement and physical-virtual inclusion. The Virtual Museum of the upper Calore Valley (http://osiris.itabc.cnr.it/vallecalore/), is an attempt to make converging these two applicative fields. Based on ATON, an open-source front-end developed by CNR ITABC, this web gis application allows users to discover old stories, characters and traditions of the Avellino countryside, in the south of Italy, while navigating the territory lively and dynamically.

Keywords: Virtual Museums · Web GIS application · Digital storytelling · Technology

1 State of the Art: Technology vs. Content

Technology has changed the way we conceive today information, communication and relations. Technology has revolutionized the way we think of content. Both inarguably go hand in hand, but what comes first? Does technology inspire the formation of the units of content, or does our need to tell stories, to shape up innovative and personal content, drive us to conceptualize new technologies that can best fit our necessities?

It is commonly believed that content drives technology. Human curiosity usually does not want to face technical issues like usability constraints or unreadable interfaces: it means that we're usually creating technology to address a certain need, to answer specific learning questions. Why develop a piece of software or hardware if it's not meant to play a certain role in changing or facilitating the way we do understand the world around us?

Whichever may best grab our feeling cannot be activated only by hands, when interacting with technology. All our senses need to be stimulated in order to reach a powerful experience of our lives. That's why the successful marriage between content

© Springer Nature Switzerland AG 2019
A. Luigini (Ed.): EARTH 2018, AISC 919, pp. 726–736, 2019.
https://doi.org/10.1007/978-3-030-12240-9_74

and technology (and between information and operations) has the advantage to solicit us in a way that written communication can't compete with. Thanks to digital media, the cultural message has infinite possibilities of expression and it survives in alternative scenarios of life - "real" or virtual. Combining contents such as sounds, images, texts, voices, and videos and still viewpoints, languages, duration, types of interaction and uses, one-dimensional stories give birth to manifold and various plots and meanings. Thus the expressive capabilities of digital technology offer an extensive base to be integrated. They enhance the experience of people and allow greater interactivity. In such a way, Digital turns to be significant as a mean through which delivering narratives that reflect society's best values and understandings.

Sure enough, our perception of the world is formed in our childhood, through experiences primary done within the family and then within the surrounding community (Gianoutsos 2006). The stories we hear, watch, and read as children play a substantial role in helping us become members of our society and understanding its values. Our culture is indeed composed by symbols, ideas and beliefs acquired throughout our life. It moves from one person to another mainly in the form of behaviors, spoken words, physical gestures, written texts and attitudes, as well as in the generation of visual representations and sounds. The social context in which each of us is embedded provides the symbols needed for the recognition of the world and the development of communication forms. When it comes to technology, however, the latter highly influences the social context in which we live in; so every gesture, every action and every behaviour that a person performs, are influenced too and they are shaped according to the medium used for that specific communication. Gestures, actions and behaviors acquire thus a "new" value that is digitally-mediated.

Summing up, content is the origin a person derives value from. Such content can vary according to (a) the type of information provided by the medium, (b) the way in which the information is presented by the medium, as well as (c) the added features included in the medium through which that information is delivered. The philosopher Marshall McLuhan coined the phrase "The medium is the message" (McLuhan 1964) expressing his convincement about the fact that, in the case of content, the channel through which information is delivered, the "medium", inherently affects how the end user perceives the content - the real "message" of every communication process.

In the last decade, media production and delivery technology massively enhanced the domain of content development and digital storytelling, combining together original sources and technical expedients for new audiences within new contexts of fruition.

Storytelling, in its original form, is characterized by words and actions, verbalization and gesture, which give shape at the inner fictional world of listeners by using a detailed and colored description of facts. They allow the *mise en scène* of deep feelings, emotions and values, which favorably shake the listener's mental models and points of reference, while the storyteller is interacting with him in a continuous cycle of crosstalk. A central focus of storytelling is thus its reliance on the audience to develop specific visual imagery and complete – co-create with the speaker – the story with personal details.

Nowadays, this mechanism of "co-creation" is much more empowered by the use of Digital (and Virtual) devices, so that listeners can easily figure out what the narration is about, and start living within the story immediately and intensively (Miller 2004). The same definition of storytelling has moved forward, incorporating the latest trends in the field of digital technologies. So doing, the art of narration has become a new technique of communication. As the expert of Communication and Media, Janet Murray predicted, digital storytelling "promise[s] to reshape the spectrum of narrative expression, not by replacing the novel or the movie but by continuing their timeless bardic work within another framework" (Murray 1998). This new "framework" is the domain of Virtual Reality and, specifically, of Virtual Museums (VMs) (Pescarin et al. 2014).

VMs are digital products which draw their characteristics starting from real museums, but with the aim of complementing, enhancing, or augmenting the interested Cultural Heritage through personalization, interactivity, diversified user experiences and richness of content (https://www.vi-mm.eu/2018/01/10/the-vimm-definition-of-a-virtual-museum/). More deeply with the subject, the final goal of VMs is the sensorial and communicative enhancement of cultural artifacts and heritage contexts which can be translated into a fruitful exchange between the environment (physical and mental) and the visitors (Pescarin et al. 2014; Pescarin et al. 2015). VMs support indeed the comprehension of the Cultural Heritage artifacts, their relations and connections with the original context of fruition, their function and their symbolic values (Antinucci 2014). Telling such values, in a digital manner, is the real focus of communication. Digital Storytelling is the technique through which it is possible to activate this "preferable channel" for delivering information and cultural notions to people.

Having the chance to direct perceive what is being told, a person does not have to hardly re-create and remember the visual images of a story by himself; thus the medium turns to be the "direct" transposition of the listener's imagery. In another way, digital medium anticipates the listener's process of events' construction, giving more "time" to the meaning-making moment. Somehow, the possibility to quickly see what happens lets the audience immediately realize and understand what it is happening in front of them. By directly experiencing, we shape more easily our memorization and learning. In this scenario, interactivity plays the major role: through the use of the whole human senses, audience can live a story not only in its mind but also for real, that is even more important if we are attending at a prehistoric or a medieval narration, for example: in both cases, digital medium helps us to transpose ourselves in another environment, far from our daily life, probably unimaginable. Finally, what digital technology and VMs introduce, is the possibility to share stories and being connected with the others. In "Mediated Memories in the Digital Age", José Van Dijck states that media "invariably and inherently shape our personal memories, warranting the term mediation" (Van Dijck 2007). The ability of digital medium to extent beyond our immediate circles is what makes digital storytelling so exciting, compelling, completely changing the framework of how we experience and remember events.

In this paper, the term "digital storytelling" will be used with a broader definition: the *digital* here is more related to the communicative opportunities offered by a new advanced tool developed by CNR ITABC, the ATON platform, rather than the technology itself. The accent will be indeed put on the community's benefits arising from the project developed - "The Virtual Museum of the upper Calore Valley" - which are: sharing, connectivity, immersion, and interactivity.

The following chapters will present the role of digital storytelling in the development of a valorization strategy for a rural and peripheral cultural context like the province of Avellino; the technological approach used by the CNR ITABC in this process of enhancement of local cultural heritage; the description of the pipeline of work which gave birth to the prototype of the "The Virtual Museum of the upper Calore Valley"; finally, the potential of such research and the study of how audience's enculturation changes according to use of digital solutions.

2   The Role of Digital Storytelling in Local Cultural Heritage

Digital technology has burst into the cultural domain radically changing the way to deliver education and amusement to people. The added value of this communication strategy resides into:

- The possibility of digital narratives to guarantee a "space" where making new and unpredictable experiences and discovering personal and intimate reactions and abilities. Following an always-changing storyline, people are immersed in a fixed and finished environment that simulates physical presence and social interactions.
- The immediacy of Digital to make things happen. This technology allows listeners to quickly watch what they were only imagining before, accelerating the primary process of events' cognition and contextualization, and directly developing both understanding and interpretation moments.
- The hypertextuality of digital narratives. It stands in not-closed endings, great network of interconnections, immediate contents accessibility, dynamic sequences of events and plurality of these sequences. Not certainly every product of digital storytelling has such features, but the same use of multimedia devices and set of tools give stories a new lively style.

What thus makes storytelling a fertile ground for people's enculturation and social growth is its new digital dress, which provide the (a) available space for (b) users' responses at events to be performed in (c) interactive e dynamic way, creating connections and sharing experiences. That is what connotes the being participatory of digital storytelling.

The power of storytelling strategies in Cultural Heritage domain has been deeply discussed by researchers and academics. Traditional communication lets the public directly face historical informations, which are hard to be read, elaborated, understood and connected each other unless the visitor is already expert of the matter. Traditional communicative effectiveness is so proportional to people individual culture. As a result, if the (unwritten) rules of cultural communication assume user's expertise, then the effectiveness of communication will be proportional to the knowledge the user already has, and the message will be less effective to who would need it more (Palombini 2017).

The concept behind VMs has been theoretically shaped according to a storytelling-oriented vision (Pescarin et al. 2015). From this point of view, two types of VMs can be distinguished: information-based applications based on technological aspect and interaction; (b) dramatized or narrative-based applications, consisting in digital storytelling structures which focus their attention on emotion, sensorial involvement and physical-virtual inclusion. Information-based VMs are shaped as a sort of database tagged and indexed to objects thanks to a taxonomical or geographical criteria (e.g. GIS applications, or virtual "rooms" giving access to digital data): users are called for a critical and active role in finding the answers to their curiosity. Narrative-based VMs, instead, are focused on the storyline, which draws them into the timing and the events of the story; here, they do not need a great interaction because the units of information are provided to them progressively and following the author's streamline.

Both approaches are promising but in the case of "The Virtual Museum of the upper Calore Valley" we followed a narrative-based strategy in order to enhance the real impact of the community belonging to the territory: the province of Avellino. It is a project about people, places, traditions and belief; everything is told in an always-changing but plausible historical framework, where fiction is mixed with real facts, cultural legacy is fostered by word-of-mouth and characters reflect the society of a small territory in the south of Italy.

Places walked thousands of years ago often have cultural heritage stories connected to them, but many of them remain unknown and many get lost (Floch and Shanshan 2015). Telling unofficial histories to support local heritage dissemination is considered educative by a growing literature (Purkis 2017).

Unofficial stories contribute new perspectives on the heritage identity of a region. The digital environment provided in this VM and the scenarios opened to some historically-based characters allow a virtual contact zone to take place, merging unofficial and personal narratives together (Davis et al. 2010).

Fig. 1. Location of the upper Calore Valley (Alta Valle del Calore), in Southern Italy.

3   The Project: Virtual Museum of the Upper Calore Valley

The "Virtual Museum of the upper Calore Valley" is an attempt to overcome the distinction between informative-based and narrative-based VMs, through the creation of an ideal online environment, with a 3D web gis approach. Here users can autonomously look for different units of information (tagged within the geographical dimension) as well as fictional videos thanks to a movie-storytelling approach which provides users with a narrative overview of the historical facts.

The "Virtual Museum of the upper Calore Valley" (http://osiris.itabc.cnr.it/vallecalore/) is a CNR-ITABC project, funded by the province di Avellino (Administration of Avellino's County); it has been conceived as a way to easily tell and explain the Cultural Heritage and history of a specific geographical region in Irpinia area, along the northern path of the Calore River (Fig. 1). The typology of VM, in this case, refers to the merely digital application, as it is not associated to a specific physical museum. Nevertheless, a place which can be considered crucial in this context (involving a museum and a church) is the Conventual Complex of San Francesco a Folloni (Strazzullo 2000), whose community actively collaborated to the project.

The application is website based on the ATON framework (see below), which allows users to browse the territory, and accessing information tagged on the areas at different levels of visualization as:

- Simple terrain topographic marks, for user's orientation;
- Information sheets concerning monuments and towns;
- Information cards concerning food and wine's traditional products;
- Six short videos based on the storytelling of specific historical timespan of local history.

Specifically about this level of information, the use of movies for Cultural Heritage storytelling represents a specific field of study in the current approach to VMs (Demetrescu et al. 2016).

3.1   Characters, Lives and History

The "Virtual Museum of the upper Calore Valley" videos are conceived to allow in short time a brief summary of local history of Irpinia region, focusing some episodes in crucial historical situations.

Characters belong to a particular period in time and to a particular location:

(1) *Epiphania.* VI cent. A.D.: a man is preparing the tomb for his young wife, just dead. He can hear her voice foretelling the fall of Roman Empire and the forthcoming Longobards[1].
(2) *Rudolf.* XI cent. A.D.: A norman soldier tells his arrive in this land from the far french country, and his discovering of local treasures.

---

[1] Epiphania gravestone survived to our time and was re-used for the grave monument of Diego Cavaniglia (Schiavone 2010).

(3) *Angiolo.* Year 1324: two friars, travelling from Folloni Convent southward, talk
     about the murder of Guglielmo Scarrerius, just occurred in the convent. They
     hypothesize the killing is connected to the Angevin-Aragonese political conflicts[2].
     A possible identification of him with the bone remains found near the Convent has
     been proposed by A. Stoa (Stoa, pers. comm.).
(4) *Margherita.* Year 1487: Margherita Orsini, the wife of Count Diego Cavaniglia
     come to the atelier of Jacopo Della Pila, a sculptor, to ask for his husband's grave
     monument. Jacopo, touched by her sorrow, promises to create the best monument
     of the Reign[3] (Fig. 2).
(5) *Raimondo.* Year 1510: two members of a Brotherhood met and discuss about
     Pope Leone X, Diego Cavaniglia nephew, who granted new power to local
     communities[4].

Fig. 2. The funeral monument of Count Diego Cavaniglia, created by Jacopo della Pila, in the
Folloni Convent (photo by B. Trabassi CNR-ITABC).

---

[2] Guglielmo Scarrerius was an eminent character at Angevine's court, murdered in 1324 (Scandone
     1916:160–162).

[3] The grave monument of Diego Cavaniglia, in the Folloni's Convent is known as one of the best
     sculpture of the 15th century in this area (Negri Arnoldi 2010).

[4] Brotherhoods had a crucial role in 16th century social organization and the affinity between Troiano
     Cavaniglia and Pope Leone X crucially influenced the local institutions in the early 16th century
     (Donati 2010).

(6) *Cristina*. Year 1866: Cristina, a young school teacher coming from northern Italy after the unification, tries to write to the King of Italy and describe the bad conditions of the country and the arrogance of the new rulers[5].

3.2   The Technology Behind: ATON

The "Virtual Museum of the upper Calore Valley" leverages on ATON[6] platform. ATON is a flexible Front-End to publish and interactively explore multi-resolution 3D assets and scenes online through modern browsers. The HTML5/WebGL component is developed on top of open-source library osgjs[7], also at the core of SketchFab platform[8]. Since its initial release (v 1.0) born within the european project ARIADNE (Meghini et al. 2017) and the "Landscape Services"[9] developed by CNR ITABC, ATON was conceived to interact with complex and multi-resolution 3D landscapes and virtual objects, while maintaining high performance on both mobile and desktop devices. At the very core of the project in fact, the state-of-the-art scene organization (through the use of scene-graphs) and paging techniques allow optimal resource management and scalability from desktop to mobile browsers.

Since the beginning the project focused on specific features, specifically:

1. Rendering quality, by employing modern approaches like PBR[10]
2. Multimedia annotation, using rich HTML5 mixed content (audio, video, formatted text, embedded web components)
3. Multi-touch interaction
4. WebVR presentation for modern HMDs[11]

Within 3D landscapes and content spatialization, advanced effects can be used to simulate fog while PBR capabilities can be employed for instance to craft multi-resolution, multi-layered terrain datasets to simulate lakes reflections (exploiting for instance roughness channel) or more advanced materials (Fig. 3). Built-in annotation system offered by ATON can be employed to spatially enrich 3D hotspots with complex HTML5 content. Using a WYSIWYG[12] interface, it is possible to easily add, edit and format annotation content in a specific 3D location (e.g. brief text description and embedded video).

---

[5] The problem of Southern Italy occupation, neglected by the historians up to some decades ago, represents an open debate in Italian historiography (e.g. Del Boca 2004).

[6] http://osiris.itabc.cnr.it/scenebaker/index.php/projects/aton/.

[7] http://osgjs.org/.

[8] https://sketchfab.com.

[9] http://landscape.ariadne-infrastructure.eu/.

[10] Physically-based Rendering.

[11] Head-mounted Displays.

[12] Acronym for: What You See Is What You Get.

Fig. 3. The PBR terrain dataset generated for the project and input roughness layer used for the sea.

4   Conclusion: Future Perspectives of Narrative-Oriented VMs

Digital Worlds (DWs) are evolving for educational and entertainment purposes: this fact led the storytelling practice through cycles of technological change. The virtualization of the oral tradition began long ago with the technologization of the word and, up to now, it deals with natural interaction's interfaces and three-dimensional environments.

A well-told story can be the key element in the survival of single individuals or groups: a phenomenon which started in form of myth, soaked of emotional stimuli and precise and practical references, and arrives today to provoke the total embodiment of the listener into the story. So far, storytelling can be considered as the big-reflexed mirror of knowledge (De Jong 2012). It allows social groups to have common fixed points of reference around a shared fact or object, so generating several forms of culture and enabling the use of different media to foster their knowledge.

When designing a VM we need to have clearly in mind how a user gets in contact with it, which are the receptive canals that he activates in his mind, how the interaction takes place, and what are the benefits derived from such interaction in terms of satisfaction, sensory and emotional involvement and learning in the proposed virtual world.

The entry of cultural resources in the Digital Era has rapidly imposed some crucial epistemological concepts to take into account, since Cultural Heritage is even more changing in Digital (and Virtual) Heritage. This last tendency is born from the necessity of cultural institutions and entities to take objects away from the free circulation, protect them from extinction, grant the public fruition and fostering the knowledge of the Past. How to accomplish these important tasks in this new Era? It has been possible through the digital and virtual technologies at disposal, which extend the field of action of both exposition criteria and learning mechanisms. In this sense, museums, real or virtual, absolve the role of "catalysts" of cultural information that communicate and share knowledge with the surrounding collectivity focusing the attention on the surrounding communities. Specifically about the concept of "catalyzer", it embraces both the principles of communication and interpretation:

- through storytelling techniques, cultural places promote potential educational paths and activities related to the Past while enabling an effective communication between people and artifacts (or venues);
- with respect to digital technology, museums also interpret and simulate potential cultural scenarios, stimulating in the audience's imagination and abstraction.

The former helps to re-contextualize artifacts providing a sense of belonging with the recreated specific environment; the latter, instead, is the will of "physically" fix something we have in mind in order to "see" it better and fully experience it. Combined in a digital storytelling-enhanced strategy, imagination and abstraction can thus generate an altered world(s) in which people can immerse and engage themselves.

In "The Virtual Museum of the upper Calore Valley", here presented, it becomes also important the definition of the museum's function, intended as public mission and not as physical site. Curators and museum professionals are recently shifting their attention from objects to subjects, that is to say, highlighting the background stories of artifacts and places rather than merely exhibit them. It is indeed important to create mental connections between items and the contextual environment, even if the real places cannot be visited anymore. This certainty helps tangible and intangible cultural remains to be seen and understood in a more enriching way, no more deprived of their original atmosphere. Hence museums - as places devoted to the cultural fostering - are changing their status: from the idea of monumental and silent halls, storages of knowledge, till becoming virtual places, virtual minds, "meta-territories". This last definition recalls the attention on maps and territories (Floch and Shanshan 2015). The former is an imaginary situation, an artificial place, a virtual environment; the latter, instead, is the physical space, the reality, the tangible environment. So "the museum or the musealized areas are meta-territories because they de-territorialize cultural finds or objects from the original contexts for creating new grammars; so they are not completely territories and not completely maps" (Forte 2002). When speaking about "de-territorialize", it is intended the possibility to elevate artifacts and archaeological areas from their static narrative dimension to other multiple and overlapped levels of communication, in order to give birth at new interpretations, cultural paths and stories - and that is possible thanks to digital technology. In definitive, museums and VMs have to become organic, alive entities, "autopoietic institutions" (Maturana and Varela 1980) able to reflect on themselves and to generate additional reticular information for the community's benefits.

Acknowledgments. This project has been funded by the province of Avellino, Irpinia region, Italy. Special thanks go to the Franciscan Community of the Folloni Convent for their contribution to the stories and settings. A special thank is due to Brothers Agnello Stoia, Simone Schiavone, Cirillo Kpalafio; to Immacolata Gatto, and to the orchestra of the Cantori Francescani, directed by Brother Gennaro Maria Becchimanzi, who granted the use of their performances as soundtrack for the videos.

References

Antinucci F (2014) Immagine e parola, storia di due tecnologie. Laterza, Roma
Crooke E (2007) Museums and communities. Routledge, Oxon
Davis P, Han-Yin H, Wan-Chen L (2010) Heritage, local communities and the safeguarding of 'Spirit of Place' in Taiwan. Mus Soc 8(2):80–89
De Jong S (2012) Who is history? the use of autobiographical accounts in history museums. In: Hill K (ed) Museums and biographies: stories, objects, identities. The Boydell Press, Newcastle, pp 295–308
Del Boca L (2004) Indietro Savoia!. Piemme, Casale Monferrato
Demetrescu E, Palombini A, Pietroni E, Forlani M, Rufa C (2016) Making movies: nuove frontiere per la comunicazione audiovisiva del passato. In: Basso P, Caravale A, Grossi P (eds) Archeofoss: atti del IX workshop (Verona 19–20 giugno 2014) Archeologia e Calcolatori, Suppl 8, pp 203–210
Donati MP (2010) Leone X e Troiano Cavaniglia. In: Stoa A (ed) Diego Cavaniglia, la rinascita di un conte, CEFRASM, pp 161–166
Floch J, Shanshan J (2015) One place, many stories digital storytelling for cultural heritage discovery in the landscape. https://doi.org/10.1109/DigitalHeritage.2015.7419566
Forte M (2002) Communicating the virtual. Research paper, Merced, USA
Gianoutsos J (2006) Locke and Rousseau: early childhood education. Pulse 4(1):1–23
Maturana H, Varela F (1980) Autopoiesis and cognition: the realization of the living. In: Cohen RS, Wartofsky MW (eds) Boston studies in "the Philosophy of Science", vol 42, Dordrecht, Holland
Mcluhan M (1964) Understanding media: the extensions of man. MIT Press, Cambridge
Meghini C, Scopigno R, Fanini B et al (2017) ARIADNE: a research infrastructure for archaeology. J Comput Cult Herit (JOCCH) 10(3):18
Miller CH (2004) Digital storytelling: a creator's guide to interactive entertainment, 2nd edn. Focal Press, Burlington
Murray J (1998) Hamlet on the holodeck: the future of narrative in cyberspace. The MIT Press, Cambridge
Negri Arnoldi F. (2010) Il sepolcro marmoreo del cavaliere Diego Cavaniglia. In: Stoa A (ed) Diego Cavaniglia, la rinascita di un conte, CEFRASM, pp 69–74
Palombini A (2017) Storytelling and telling history. Towards a grammar of narratives for Cultural Heritage dissemination in the Digital Era. J Cult Herit 24:134–139
Pescarin S, et al (2014) Keys to Rome. Roman culture, virtual museums. CNR ITABC, Rome
Pescarin S, et al (2015) Del. 7.1 virtual museum quality labels. In: V-Must.net deliverables' collection, Rome
Purkis H (2017) Making digital heritage about people's life stories. Int J Herit Stud 23(5):434–444. https://doi.org/10.1080/13527258.2016.1190392
Scandone F (1916) L'Alta Valle del Calore. Trimarchi, Palermo
Schiavone S (2010) Due lastre marmoree con iscrizione funeraria reimpiegate nel monumento rinascimentale di Diego Cavaniglia. In: Stoa A (ed) Diego Cavaniglia, la rinascita di un conte, CEFRASM, pp 167–185
Strazzullo F (2000) Il Complesso monumentale di S. Francesco a Folloni a Montella. Biblioteca S. Francesco
van Dijck J (2007) Mediated memories in the digital age. Stanford University Press, Stanford

Reshaping the Identity of University Museums: The Museo della Rappresentazione in Catania as Digital Innovation Hub for the Engagement of New Generations and the Development of the Territory

Cettina Santagati[1(✉)], Mariateresa Galizia[1], Alessandro Basso[2], and Federico Mario La Russa[1]

[1] Department of Civil Engineering and Architecture (DICAR), Università degli Studi di Catania, Via Santa Sofia n. 64, 95125 Catania, Italy
cettina.santagati@dau.unict.it
[2] Department of Architecture (DDA), Università degli studi G.D'Annunzio Chieti Pescara, Viale Pindaro, 65127 Pescara, Italy

Abstract. The contribution deepens the results of the innovative experiments carried out at the Museum of Representation pertaining to the Department of Civil Engineering and Architecture of the University of Catania, aimed at the preparation of the section on digital representation for the communication and enhancement of cultural heritage. The design took place according to a bottom-up participatory process that involved millenials and potential museum users - a sample of students from the Building Engineering-Architecture courses – who acted as protagonists of the process, investigated the concepts of "virtual museum", "citizen science 2.0" and "open science" reinterpreting them according to a sustainable logic of reuse and optimization of digital assets linked to the so-called orange economy according to a continuous exchange of ideas and visions for the future. They were asked design the setting-up, to envision new contents/ways of communication even low cost solutions and easily accessible from the web for augmenting audience's experience (in terms of immersivity and interactivity).

Keywords: Digital cultural heritage · Participatory process · Open science · Digital representation · Retopology · Virtual reality

1 Introduction

University museums, testimonies of the path and evolution of science and knowledge, are one of the fundamental institutions for the relaunch of the country's scientific and technological activities. They play a fundamental active role towards the civil society awareness linking the cultural function of the collections, the tools and the results of research, teaching and the dissemination of knowledge to the territory. The combination of a vibrant environment of research and experimentation with the use of current

© Springer Nature Switzerland AG 2019
A. Luigini (Ed.): EARTH 2018, AISC 919, pp. 737–746, 2019.
https://doi.org/10.1007/978-3-030-12240-9_75

IT tools brings towards novel approaches in terms of digital innovation for Cultural Heritage enhancement and communication as well as novel ways of curation and visitor engagement.

The paper deepens the results of the innovative experiments carried out at the Museum of Representation, pertaining to the Department of Civil Engineering and Architecture of the University of Catania, aimed at the setting up of the digital representation exhibition related to the research and didactic activity in the field of cultural heritage documentation, communication and enhancement.

The design took place according to a bottom-up participatory process that involved millenials and potential museum users - a sample of students from the Building Engineering-Architecture courses – who acted as protagonists of the process.

Furthermore, it has been experimented a workflow aimed at optimizing 3D textured mesh models (obtained via digital photogrammetry or laser scanning acquisition) by means of re-topology algorithms for 3D Sculpting and Virtual Reality assets, that allows to obtain low poly high quality models easily and quickly seen from the web.

2   The Museo della Rappresentazione (MuRa) at the University of Catania Museum System

The *Museo della Rappresentazione* was originally established in 1996 thanks to Catania-Lecce Coordinated Project. The project was aimed at the preservation, conservation and use of the tangible and intangible heritage of the University through several initiatives. Indeed, the initiative number 15 assigned Villa Zingali Tetto (a liberty palace built in 1930 and owned by University of Catania) to the Department of Architecture and Town Planning (DAU) to institute the *Laboratorio e Museo della Rappresentazione* (Laboratory and Museum of Representation). The museum would keep, preserve and exhibit the graphical historical archives and collections possessed by DAU (Francesco Fichera, Giovan Battista Piranesi and others), the project foresaw an intervention of restoration and re-functionalisation of the villa to be used as a museum (Fig. 1).

Initially, the head of the structure, Prof. Piera Busacca, identified as main mission of the museum its role as catalyst for 'shared participation' in town planning choices for the city and the territory. Much so, it became known as *Casa della Città* (House of the City) and lasted till 2006, when it has been regained by the University of Catania. Then, in 2016 the noble floor of Villa Zingali Tetto has been returned to the Department of Civil Engineering and Architecture (DICAr) to restart the *Museo della Rappresentazione* (MuRa) activities. This action can be seen as the result of the renewed interest of the university on the role that university museums can play as an active part of the cultural system of the territory, promoting the spread of culture.

Indeed, in 2015 the Museum System of University has been established with the scope to systematize the 22 potential museums belonging to the several departments and the aim to preserve, protect, enhance and make available to the scientific community and the wider community, those assets, tools and results acquired by the centuries-old research, education and dissemination of knowledge. The operation currently underway therefore sees the approach of 'Knowledge' to the territory,

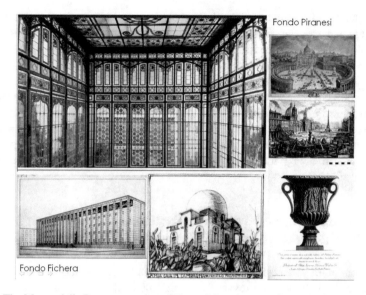

Fondo Piranesi

Fondo Fichera

Fig. 1. The Museo della Rappresentazione. View of the winter garden and of some engravings (Piranesi collection) and drawings (Fichera collection)

through the organization of cultural meetings in which not only the material heritage is shown, exhibiting its own collections, but above all the intangible heritage whose greatest asset is the Knowledge gained through research.

Faced with this new attitude, the mission of MuRa is to pursue the promotion, knowledge and understanding of cultural heritage for a wider audience, improving the conditions of use and public fruition of cultural heritage, promoting innovative communication ways, which aims to reach the widest possible range of users in order to increase the degree of usability of museums and cultural sites by putting the needs of visitors first, developing a culture of hospitality, understanding and participation shared by citizens and institutions (Antinucci 2014; Luigini and Panciroli 2018).

In line with the objective of the third mission set by the universities, in order to get in direct contact with subjects and social groups further than those established (students and research institutions) through modes of interaction with variable content and form and depending on the context, the MuRa is not only a container of historical and cultural heritage but also a 'container of innovative content' aimed at improving the overall experience of communication of cultural heritage through a co-creation of content according a bottom up approach.

With this in mind, two laboratories have been set up within the museum to support teaching and research – Digital Representation Surveying Reconstruction Laboratory and Tools for the project of Architecture Laboratory - which carry out their actions in the field of architectural and cultural heritage, for its conservation, enhancement, communication and fruition.

The path taken aims to transform the data acquired into information, information into knowledge and knowledge into action, experimenting and testing innovative ways of communication and use of cultural heritage to be used as a guide for some interventions to improve the quality of dissemination of cultural contents. The innovation lies in the fact that MuRa is the place where there is a fully osmosis of experiences between students and teachers/experts: students can experiment new approaches to acquisition and communication, guided by the experience of teachers, who vice versa take advantage of a different gaze given by new eyes and minds of contemporary generations. Achieving this goal implies, on the basis of what is indicated by **ICOM**, the performance of a variety of activities, involving the acquisition, preservation, research, communication and exhibition of content.

3   Engaging New Generation: A Participatory Approach to the Design of the Digital Exhibition

The design of the exhibition linked to the Digital Representation, Surveying and Reconstruction Laboratory foresaw the participation of the interns (students of the Building Engineering-Architecture courses) as active protagonists of the process, playing a dual role as future curators/designers and future visitors of the museum. The contents to be exhibited deal with the research and the didactic activity (Fig. 2) carried out in the field of cultural heritage documentation, communication and enhancement by means of integrated 3D acquisition technologies (Bonacini et al. 2018).

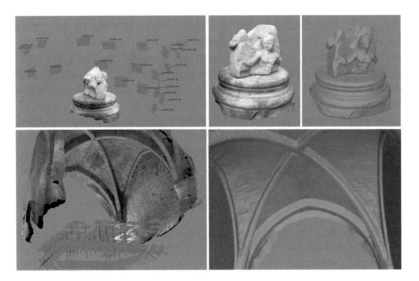

Fig. 2. 3D models of Museo Civico Castello Ursino collections and rooms created during the didactic activity #invasionigitali3D

The students – millenials and potential museum visitors – have been questioning on the concepts of "virtual museums", "citizen science 2.0" and "open science" reinterpreting them according to a sustainable logic of reuse and optimization of digital assets linked to the so-called orange economy according to a continuous exchange of ideas and visions for the future (Levy 2001; Godbersen 2008; Candy and Ferguson 2014).

With regard to the web accessibility of the models produced, various solutions were examined, including the use of Sketchfab, Europeana, and 3DHop. Europeana allows you to upload 3D PDFs of objects, while 3DHOP (3D Heritage Online Presenter), an open-source software package for the creation of interactive web presentations of high-resolution 3D models, is customisable but requires at least the minimum level of knowledge in programming web pages.

The online platform Sketchfab was chosen as it is the most widespread that was used for years by various museums (British Museum, Musée d'Archeologie Nationale and others), for the ease of embed 3D content on websites and platforms and for the possibility of direct access to social networks or the connection to guided tour apps (GuidiGO).

Fig. 3. View of one of the exhibition board layout and user experience

In particular, the potentialities envisioned in the use of Sketchfab platform as a of low cost and easily accessible tool, has given the catalyst towards new contents/ways of communication for augmenting audience's experience (in terms of immersivity and interactivity).

Through the eyes of the students, in a continuous experimentation process, the digital exhibition has taken shape unlocking the hidden potential of creativity and developing novel digital skills for the future (Anderson et al. 2010; Sensi 2010; Basso 2017; Hossaini and Blankenberg 2017).

Indeed, they envisioned and tested a workflow through which a visitor entering the room of the temporary exhibition would first be confronted with the graphic content of the exhibition board and then, through a QRCode placed near each object, would have access to the digital dimension of the model itself (Fig. 3). In fact, by scanning these

QRCodes, the smartphone is redirected to the Sketchfab platform that allows you to explore the three dimensions of the models loaded. The digital models not only faithfully represent the geometries of the real models, thanks to the application of textures on the meshes obtained by photogrammetric techniques (SFM: Structure from Motion) also allowed a critical reading of the same especially if in the presence of frescoes and similar painted surface.

In addition, the models can be enriched with text annotations and audio content, and be explored in VR/AR allowing a more engaging use of the collections on exhibit, through a dynamic exploration, that is multisensory and particularly effective from the communicative point of view (Fig. 4). So, after this exploration phase it is also possible to allow an immersive navigation of the models in virtual reality by means of user's smartphone with Google Cardboards. According to this workflow, the user experience in terms of interactivity and immersivity with the graphical representations of the exhibition is gradually growing and can be even improved.

Till now, the visitors feedback from these activities have been very positive, they really liked the possibility to interact and visualize the 3D models of the exhibited boards easily and directly on their mobile and to get immerse in the 3D reconstructed environment through the use of cardboards. Furthermore, in most cases they did not have too many difficulties in interacting with these technologies.

Fig. 4. Setting up of the virtual scene in Sketchfab

However, the workflow is still under testing, several expedients have been taken for augmenting audience's experience. One of the main problems is the optimization of the models in terms of number of polygons, because it affects the loading times and the fluidness of the navigation (then of the immersive experience). Another critical aspect of this mode is the quality of the mobile data connection to which the device that uses the user must access in order to view and explore the models. In the next section a fluid workflow for virtual transfer on interactive platforms that has been developed is shown.

4 3D Optimization by Fluid Workflow for Interactive Platforms

3D scanning and automated photogrammetric modeling techniques play a fundamental role in projects aimed at recreating existing objects in virtual worlds or aimed at virtual fruition of existing cultural heritage objects and sites. However, the digital features of 3D models (very detailed triangular mesh), not often make them suitable for inclusion in virtual spaces for real time exploration. In this regard, it is fundamental to set up specific workflows to optimize the 3D assets to make it light in terms of digital weight, remaining at the same time in non-simplified form (Palestini and Basso 2017).

The self-optimization procedures often present in 3D photogrammetry programs are an interesting resource but they often modify the original topology of the surface, that can lose the plastic detail and generates several problems related to sparse triangulation. Furthermore, the meshes obtained by the automated procedure have an excessive polygonal triangulation and problems caused by UV maps not correctly distributed on the surfaces. The proposed pipeline therefore includes a series of procedures that bring this particular methodology closer to that used in the editing of the new generation videogames, where the graphics and lightness are essential to make 3D assets exploitable on interactive platforms such as Unreal Engine, born as a platform for the creation of videogames, and now used in projects that span from museum dissemination to architectural design (Thomas and Donikian 2000; Unali 2014; Basso and Palestini 2016). The workflow is based on the semantic decomposition of elements, on the polygonal retopology of closed meshes and on the generation of multiple texture maps capable of containing not only information regarding the chromatic-material components of the models but above all data relative to complex geometric detail, simulating a "high definition" on a low-poly model.

The procedure is quite simple and allows you to follow a series of steps smoothly: the digitized models are first imported in Maxon's Cinema 4D, which offers numerous tools for editing and correcting the meshes. It is important not to modify the setting of the spatial coordinates of the model in order not to affect the possibility of importing the optimized model in the original photogrammetric survey software for texture re-projection. The initial polygon topology, the hidden geometry generated by the TIN self-construction algorithms of the newly exported 3D assets, is extremely triangulated. In addition, triangulation without topological criteria can generate multiple visual artifacts up to exceeding the limits allowed by the RTR (Real Time Rendering) platforms in terms of file size. After a phase of verification and an appropriate intervention to identify and close any gaps, we proceed to a segmentation into sub-objects with particular emphasis on decorative parts which need a more full-bodied density of detail in the following retopology step.

Retopology has been carried out by using ZBrush, a 3D Sculping software capable of managing millions of polygons at once, and able to the manage Voxel algorithms and polygonal subdivision, as well as interesting automatic (Z-remesher) and semi-automatic (topology Brush) retopology tools. In addition, interesting plugins allow a balanced optimization of 3D assets and the creation of new UV Map. Any three-dimensional polygonal model can therefore be easily managed by the software in question while also maintaining a high polygonal density and therefore a level of HD detail. The passage from Cinema4D to ZBrush is done by means of GoZ, which allows to maintain the object segmentation. The objective of this phase of the workflow is to add detail manually and reorganize into subtool the imported model, generate new UV maps and create other texturing maps, which reproduce the detail of the original model in high resolution.

Once imported, the model is duplicated in two identical versions, the first is the target object (triangular mesh) that will give the details to the retopologized model, the second model will be retopologized, in order to obtain a new 4 vertex (quad) mesh which will respect in its distribution the actual geometric shape and correct topology of the model (Fig. 5).

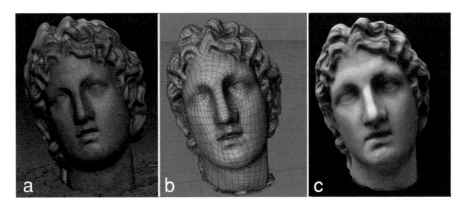

Fig. 5. Workflow test on Alexander the Great head: (a) triangulated model, (b) retopologized model, (c) rendered model

In order to clone the level of detail from the first target object to the second retopologyzed object, a polygonal geometric detail projection tool (Project All) will be used. This operation makes it easy to exploit the voxel subdivision to make the new generated asset denser at the polygonal level in compliance with the correct topological morphology, and therefore to be able to accept the detail of the original model with the wrong configuration. Increasing subdivision levels allows lower polygonal levels to be maintained. This feature will allow us to generate maps, from the Normal Map to the Bump Map, the Displacement Map and Vector Displacement map, which in fact will be a trick to simulate a hd detail on a low-density polygonal model.

Once all the texture channels have been obtained, including the colour texture, which can be retrieved using a clone digital painting methodology from the original model, previously imported and already provided with photographic textures, the model in question is then brought back to the Cinema 4D platform at its lowest polygonal density, consisting of the first subdivision level defined in Zbrush and then imported in Cinema4D to check the direction of the normals on the polygons of the mesh whose flipping may cause problems in RTR rendering or incorrect lighting on objects. Once verified the model can be exported into. OBJ or FBX format, able to preserve all the materials and textures previously assigned and be uploaded on Sketchfab or imported in game engine software such as Unreal for creating virtual environments to explore.

5 Conclusions

MuRa today is strongly committed to the communication and visualization of infor-mation in order to constantly initiate information flows inside and outside the museum, allowing it to become a system of the heritage of knowledge that it holds and that allows it to pursue the educational, pedagogical and cognitive purposes from which it derives its collective legitimacy.

MuRa is also actively engaged in the construction of tools for dialogue and loyalty, as a way to bring the public of young people and citizens, through innovative ways of digital communication based on social networks and in providing more information through the use of new information technologies (smartphones, tablets, etc.) in order to better communicate with new generations.

The results of this experimentation are promising both in terms of visitor's response and in terms of stimulation for the new generations. Visitors are enthusiasts of seeing the tangible results of digital technologies innovations getting aware of the role that university plays in terms of developing new skills for the territory and of experimenting novel immersive and interactive ways for cultural heritage communication and fruition (both on line and on site). From the other side the students have developed a strong sense of belonging to the museum and the research and teaching laboratories, becoming aware of the importance of the active role that they can play in the study and enhancement of cultural heritage.

The passionate environment of research and experimentation with the use of current IT tools leads to new approaches in terms of digital innovation for the improvement and exposure of cultural heritage, as well as new ways of engaging and engaging visitors.

References

Anderson EF, McLoughlin L, Liarokapis F, Peters C, Petridis P, De Freitas S (2010) Developing serious games for cultural heritage: a state-of-the-art review. Virtual Reality 14(4):255–275

Antinucci F (2014) Comunicare nel museo. Edizioni Laterza, Roma-Bari

Basso A (2017) La realtà virtuale come metodologia di sviluppo di nuove figure professionali. In: UID NAPOLI 2017, 39° convegno internazionale dei docenti e delle discipline della Rappresentazione; territori e frontiere della Rappresentazione, Gangemi, pp 1617–1624

Basso A, Palestini C (2016) Gli Ossimori del museo virtuale, sperimentazioni attraverso la rappresentazione. Disegnarecon 9(17):6.1–6.15

Bonacini E, Marcucci M, Santagati C (2018) #InvasioniDigitali: co-creazione di valore culturale attraverso la partecipazione attiva dei pubblici alla narrazione archeologica. In: D'Eredità A, Falcone, A (eds) ARCHEOSOCIAL, L'archeologia riscrive il web: esperienze, strategie e buone pratiche (TourismA, Firenze - 17 febbraio 2017). Dielle editore, Mozzecane (VR), pp 169–187

Candy L, Ferguson S (eds) (2014) Interactive experience in the digital age. Springer, New York

Godbersen H (2008) Virtual environments for anyone. IEEE Multimedia 15(3):90–95

Hossaini A, Blankenberg N (eds) (2017) Manual of digital museum. Planning Rowman & Littlefield Publishers, Lanham

Levy P (2001) Cybercultura. Gli usi sociali delle nuove tecnologie. Feltrinelli, Milano

Luigini A, Panciroli C (eds) (2018) Ambienti digitali per l'educazione all'arte e al patrimonio. Franco Angeli, Milano

Palestini C, Basso A (2017) The photogrammetric survey methodologies applied to low cost 3d virtual exploration in multidisciplinary field. In: International archives of the photogrammetry, remote sensing and spatial information sciences, vol XLII-2/W8, pp 195–202

Rete dei Musei Universitari Italiani. http://www.retemuseiuniversitari.unimore.it/site/home.html. Accessed 19 May 2018

Sensi N (2010) Musei virtuali e musei online: learning objects per scienza e arte. Scriptaweb, Napoli

Thomas G, Donikian S (2000) Virtual humans animation in informed urban environments. In: Computer animation, pp 112–119

Unali M (2014) Atlante dell'Abitare Virtuale, il disegno della città virtuale fra ricerca e didattica. Gangemi Ed., Roma

Sistina Experience
The *Giudizio Universale* in the Age
of "Artertainment"

Paolo Belardi[1(⊠)] and Simone Bori[2]

[1] Department of Civil and Environmental Engineering (DICA),
University of Perugia, via Duranti 93, 06125 Perugia, Italy
studiolo@abaperugia.org
[2] Academy of Fine Arts "Pietro Vannucci" of Perugia (ABAPG),
piazza san Francesco al Prato 5, 06123 Perugia, Italy

Abstract. The replication of the art locations in which the values of tradition are reinterpreted in a contemporary key triggering a synergistic union between art and technology is a very current research topic that breathes new life into the commonly understood museum space. In this field of experimentation, following a sophisticated laser scanner and photogrammetric survey campaign, the idea was born for the *Sistina Experience* that is, the concept of itinerant multifunctional, multimedia replication of the Sistine Chapel: an architectural idea aimed at experimenting with new ways of enjoying, enhancing and gaining knowledge of the historical-artistic heritage. *Sistina Experience* it is a traveling architecture aimed at expanding and diversifying the museum experience both in terms of art perception and art education: an immersive exploration of a place of art that promotes innovative digital ways to educate in the knowledge of heritage in the age of "artertainment".

Keywords: Replica · Art · Digital · Multimedia · Itinerant

1 Introduction

"You can travel around the world without seeing anything. To reach understanding, it is not necessary to see much, but to look carefully at what one sees" Giorgio Morandi.

While raising strong criticism for their alleged "Disneyland style", the precise replicas of the Lascaux caves (Fig. 1) and the tomb of Tutankhamun created in recent years for the general public, as well as for study purposes, represent two pioneering initiatives. Not so much because they helped to protect the originals (the sculptural group of *I Cavalli* that seal the portal of the Basilica of San Marco in Venice are replicas as is the *David* by Michelangelo that stands in the Piazza della Signoria in Florence), but because, thanks to the wise combination of art and technology (just think of the enlargements displayed in the *Magister Giotto* and *Van Gogh tra il grano e il cielo* exhibitions) they have proved to be precious instruments for expanding and diversifying the specific museum experience both in terms of the perception of art and art education. Enough to create a bunch of questions concerning the actual usefulness (or not) of replicating and cloning the masterpieces of the past (Benjamin 1966; Casarin 2015).

© Springer Nature Switzerland AG 2019
A. Luigini (Ed.): EARTH 2018, AISC 919, pp. 747–754, 2019.
https://doi.org/10.1007/978-3-030-12240-9_76

Fig. 1. *Lascaux IV*, view of one of the halls of the museum in which parts of the Lascaux caves have been replicated.

2   Replication of Art Locations

Certainly the monuments faithfully replicated with advanced technologies (laser scanners, 3D printers etc.) may be valuable in many respects, for example, to reconstruct the setting of stolen works (as was the case in the Oratory of San Lorenzo di Palermo with the replica of the *Natività* by Caravaggio) or forgotten works (as was the case in the National Archaeological Museum of Reggio Calabria with the replica of the *Auriga di Delfi*), but more importantly to increase physical accessibility (as was the case in the Cathedral of Milan with replica of the *Madonnina*) and sensory accessibility (as was the case in the Uffizi Galleries with the scale replica of the *La Nascita di Venere* by Sandro Botticelli) and expand the spectrum of possible users (Bolognini 2008; Barbanera 2011). Nevertheless, it could be useful to adopt advanced multimedia technologies such as augmented reality applications developed by Samsung for the Gallerie dell'Accademia in Venice and by Epson for the Santa Giulia Museum in Brescia. But above all, considering the vastness and heterogeneity of Italian artistic heritage, the replicas of the works of art, if designed as itinerant, could constitute real cultural ambassadors, aimed at attracting less superficial and distracted tourists to our cities of art, because they would be more prepared and, therefore, more interested and involved (Roscelli 2011). Just think of the Cité *de l'*architecture *et du patrimoine* in Paris, where, thanks to multimedia support and full-scale plastic reproductions, visitors can embark on a perfect journey through French architecture of every time and place, passing under the portal of the Moissac abbey, caressing the wings of the smiling angel of the cathedral of Reims and staying in a flat of the housing unit built by Le Corbusier in Marseille.

3   The Vatican Museums Architectural Survey

And it is precisely in the deepest sense of the Parisian museum, moreover, among those most frequented by the French themselves, that the idea of the *Sistina Experience* developed: a multimedia and itinerant replica of the Sistine Chapel that has as its basis a sophisticated laser scanner and photogrammetric architectural survey campaign of all the exhibition spaces of the museum complex of the Vatican Museums (the Gregorian Etruscan Museum, the Chiaramonti Museum, the Braccio Nuovo, the Pio Clementino Museum, the Stanze di Raffaello, the Nicolina Chapel, the Torre dei Borgia, the Pinacoteca, the Cortile della Pigna, the Scala del Bramante and the Sistine Chapel), performed by Archimede srl (Fig. 2). The results of the architectural surveys at the highest level of detail (less than a millimetre pixel) were immediately used in the fascinating 360° virtual tours of the Vatican Museums that allow visitors to admire even the smallest details of frescoes, marbles, decorations and many other precious works, thus benefit from the artistic heritage in all its splendour. At the same time the georeferenced architectural surveys generated point clouds and 3D representation that are used by the staff of the Vatican Museums in the indispensable activities of cataloguing, managing and restoring the works therein.

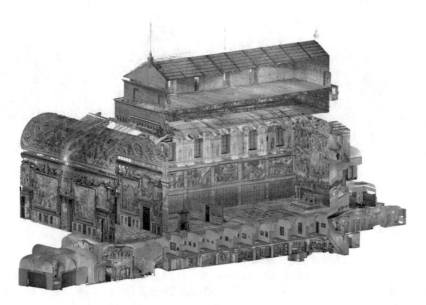

Fig. 2. Texturised point cloud of the Sistine Chapel and some adjacent spaces within the complex of the Vatican Museums.

4 The Idea

An important campaign like the one just described for the Vatican Museums could not but also inspire some form of improvement. Hence the reasons why Archimede srl is relying on a structured interdisciplinary team (Department of Civil and Environmental Engineering of the University of Perugia, Academy of Fine Arts "Pietro Vannucci" of Perugia, Tecla srl of Gubbio) to advance the proposal of a concept for an itinerant multimedia replication of the Sistine Chapel (that can be dismantled and freely re-assembled in every part of the world, from Beijing to Moscow and Rio de Janeiro) (Figs. 3 and 8). A concept that, moreover, as the slogan *Sistina Experience* makes clear, embodies an idea that is only apparently unusual, but in reality is absolutely coherent with the most advanced contemporary exhibition trends, because, by virtue of a high profile director dedicated to communicative and methodological-didactic aspects, it provides the chance of experiencing one of the most famous artistic places in the world (Paolucci 2016) in a multi-sensory and multi-functional way (it can in fact also host exhibition displays or can be transformed into a hall for conventions, concerts, shown in Fig. 7, or workshops).

Fig. 3. *Sistina Experience*, concept, infographic simulation of a photo insertion in the square of the China Central Television in Beijing that describes the itinerant character of the structure.

5 Sistina Experience

On the outside *Sistina Experience* presents itself as a candid elementary volume (Fig. 4), marked by a rhythmic succession of lamellar wood frames measuring a volume that is the actual size (Fig. 5) of the Sistine Chapel (15 m wide, 42 m long and 33 m high outside) that protects the replication of the works of art inside, created by a mix of traditional and innovative technologies aimed at guaranteeing the multimedia

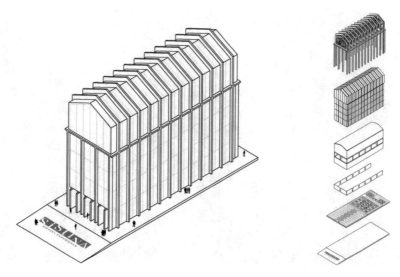

Fig. 4. *Sistina Experience*, concept, overall axonometry and axonometric explosion of the main constituent elements.

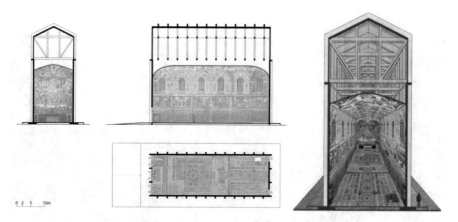

Fig. 5. *Sistina Experience*, concept, plan, sections and perspective section.

character. In fact, a series of led panel videowalls is combined in a series of UV ray direct print reproductions, presenting values of content to content pitch and visibility designed to maximise vision performance to replicate "the 15th century cycle", while architectural videomapping techniques (that take advantage of high brightness and high resolution projectors) allow the vault to be reproduced using a projection system (using lenses with a low throw ratio value for projecting large images at short distance) and the wall of the *Giudizio Universale* is expected to be reproduced using direct projection. Of course, these techniques will also allow the organization of real experiential visual paths, which will magnify the details of the frescoes to occupy entire walls,

Fig. 6. *Sistina Experience*, concept, infographic simulation of a possible internal setting obtained thanks to the application of different multimedia techniques (videowall and videomapping direct and rear-projection).

Fig. 7. *Sistina Experience*, concept, infographic simulation of a possible internal setting in the concert hall version.

Fig. 8. *Sistina Experience*, concept, infographic simulations of photo insertions (clockwise from above) inside the Maracaña stadium in Rio de Janeiro, near the Red Square in Moscow, on the Yale University campus in the United States and in a village in Burkina Faso in Africa describing the itinerant character of the structure.

allowing otherwise imperceptible details to be appreciated or allowing the visitor to experience the perceptive experience of the Sistine Chapel with the starry sky painted by Piermatteo d'Amelia before the intervention of Michelangelo (Fig. 6) or with the tapestries made by Raphael for the lower register.

It is also possible to touch reproductions of frescoes made with innovative techniques that enhance the material component of the painting. The concept provides a lamellar wood structure with interlocking systems that can be easily assembled/disassembled as well as easily transportable (Roke 2017). The wooden frames are embedded on a base that makes the entire volume self-supporting and allows the passage of the technical systems necessary for the functioning of all the applied technologies and the regulation and control systems of the internal micro-climate.

6   Concluding Comments

The result is an extremely sustainable and above all easily accessible soft-tech concept. In this sense, as Tomaso Montanari pointed out on "il Venerdì di Repubblica", addressing the issue of the relationship between technology and art, "a reproduction of the Sistine Chapel to actual scale [...] could make sense. As does every attempt to increase the awareness and experience of art". Absolutely consistent with the conceptual spirit of the architectural concept of *Sistina Experience*: an immersive exploration of an art location that promotes innovative digital ways to educate people about heritage in the age of "artertainment".

References

Benjamin W (1966) L'opera d'arte nell'epoca della sua riproducibilità tecnica. Giulio Einaudi Editore, Torino

Bolognini M (2008) Postdigitale. Conversazioni sull'arte e le nuove tecnologie. Carocci Editore, Roma

Barbanera M (2011) Originale e copia nell'arte antica. Origine, sviluppo e prospettive di un paradigma interpretativo. Tre lune, Mantova

Roscelli E (2011) La riproducibilità digitale dell'opera d'arte. Nuovi strumenti di fruizione, valorizzazione e conoscenza del patrimonio culturale. Politecnico di Torino, Torino

Casarin C (2015) L'autenticità nell'arte contemporanea. ZeL Edizioni, Treviso

Paolucci A (2016) La Cappella Sistina. Scripta Maneant, Bologna

Roke R (2017) Mobitecture. Architecture on the Move. Phaidon, London

Correction to: Proceedings of the 1st International and Interdisciplinary Conference on Digital Environments for Education, Arts and Heritage

Alessandro Luigini

Correction to:
A. Luigini (Ed.):
Proceedings of the 1st International and Interdisciplinary
Conference on Digital Environments for Education,
Arts and Heritage, **AISC 919,**
https://doi.org/10.1007/978-3-030-12240-9

In the original version of the book, editor provided belated correction has been incorporated in the frontmatter. The correction book has been updated with the change.

The updated version of the book can be found at
https://doi.org/10.1007/978-3-030-12240-9

A. Luigini (Ed.): EARTH 2018, AISC 919, p. C1, 2019.
https://doi.org/10.1007/978-3-030-12240-9_77

Author Index

© Springer Nature Switzerland AG 2019
A. Luigini (Ed.): EARTH 2018, AISC 919, pp. 755–757, 2019.
https://doi.org/10.1007/978-3-030-12240-9